W9-BCE-441

TUG OF WAR

CARLETON LIBRARY SERIES

The Carleton Library Series publishes books about Canadian economics, geography, history, politics, public policy, society and culture, and related topics, in the form of leading new scholarship and reprints of classics in these fields. The series is funded by Carleton University, published by McGill-Queen's University Press, and is under the guidance of the Carleton Library Series Editorial Board, which consists of faculty members of Carleton University. Suggestions and proposals for manuscripts and new editions of classic works are welcome and may be directed to the Carleton Library Series Editorial Board c/o the Library, Carleton University, Ottawa K1S 5B6, at cls@carleton.ca, or on the web at www.carleton.ca/cls.

TUG OF WAR

Surveillance Capitalism, Military Contracting, and the Rise of the Security State

JOCELYN WILLS

Carleton Library Series 242

McGill-Queen's University Press
Montreal & Kingston · London · Chicago

© McGill-Queen's University Press 2017
ISBN 978-0-7735-5047-6 (cloth)
ISBN 978-0-7735-5048-3 (ePDF)
ISBN 978-0-7735-5049-0 (ePUB)

Legal deposit third quarter 2017
Bibliothèque nationale du Québec

Printed in Canada on acid-free paper that is 100% ancient forest
free (100% post-consumer recycled), processed chlorine free.

McGill-Queen's University Press acknowledges the support of
the Canada Council for the Arts for our publishing program.
We also acknowledge the financial support of the Government
of Canada through the Canada Book Fund for our publishing
activities.

Library and Archives Canada Cataloguing in Publication

Wills, Jocelyn, 1960–, author
    Tug of war : surveillance capitalism, military contracting, and the
rise of the security state / Jocelyn Wills.

(Carleton library series ; 242)
Includes bibliographical references and index.
Issued in print and electronic formats.
ISBN 978-0-7735-5047-6 (cloth). – ISBN 978-0-7735-5048-3 (ePDF). –
ISBN 978-0-7735-5049-0 (ePUB)

    1. Security, International. 2. Space security. 3. Defense contracts.
4. Electronic surveillance. 5. Capitalism. I. Title. II. Series: Carleton
library series ; 242

JZ5588.W55 2017   355'.033   C2017-902183-4
                                             C2017-902184-2

This book was typeset by True to Type in 10.5/13 Sabon.

For Tom

Contents

PART THREE   THE SYSTEMS INTEGRATORS

Acknowledgments

This book has been long in the making, and I have many people and institutions to thank. First and foremost, I am deeply grateful to those I interviewed during the early 1990s, most I had never met before, but all graciously hosting me in homes and offices to share their stories about and experiences with MacDonald, Dettwiler and Associates during the firm's first quarter century. Some are cited here; others are not, but together, they provided critical information for the chronology on which this book is built. More than twenty years later, I can still recall my time with most of them, but several continue to occupy a special place in my memories of those years. On a clear, crisp day in January 1993, Colin and Pat Lennox welcomed me into their home in Victoria, British Columbia, where Colin sat for an interview that began early and ended late. Pat joined us for most of the ten-hour session, jogging and sharing memories, then disappearing periodically to search for photographs and documents, always returning with food and drink to reinvigorate an already lively rendering of MDA's early years. During the late afternoon, another former employee – Jan Price – arrived to join the conversation, where she also generously provided insights that carried us through the early evening. The firm's principle founders, John MacDonald and Vern Dettwiler, also sat for long, multiple interviews, generously receiving me into their world, providing moving recollections of times both exhilarating and painful, and imparting lessons learned as well as future hopes. John MacDonald, Dave Caddey, Dan Gelbart, Ray Maxwell, Dave Sloan, and Neil Thompson made me laugh and tear up during interviews. Harry Dollard and Doug Seymour shared their experiences as well as graduate work, both supplying careful analyses of MDA's trajectory at critical moments in the company's history. And John Pitts assisted me more than he could ever have known by providing support for the oral history project, crucial insights, and an initial interview list.

While I was in Vancouver, many people went out of their way to ensure my interview/research trips were comfortable and successful. Joy Birck, Johannes Halbertsma, Geri Jones, Heather Meehan, Rhonda Schultz and Rory Dafoe, and especially Iain Bruce and Peri Mehling opened their homes to me, providing the warmth, hospitality, and love I still cherish as I recall the days, then weeks and months they housed and fed me. I remain grateful that they continue to invite me back. My sister, Rhonda, and mother Beth McMurchie indulged my need to transcribe interviews while on our road trips together during the summer of 1993. And Harold Livesay and David Lux trained me in business history and the innovation process, read early drafts of the work I produced from the transcripts, and in later years continued to encourage my work on the larger project that has become this book.

When I began to revisit the transcripts and undertake research into surveillance capitalism after 2003, others continued to nurture this book project. Michael Bernstein, Phil Scranton, and Mark Wilson encouraged me to write an article, and together with anonymous readers, they provided superb editorial advice. Their suggestions have allowed me to acknowledge my gratitude to Oxford University Press for the rights to reuse sections from "Innovation in a Cold [War] Climate: Engineering Peace with the Military-Industrial Complex," *Enterprise and Society* 12, no. 1 (2011): 120–74. From that first article, Peter Dickens and James Ormrod invited me to craft a chapter for their edited volume on the social production of outer space, carefully reviewed my work, and offered insightful critiques. Thanks to their efforts, I am also indebted to Palgrave MacMillan for permission to sprinkle this book with passages from "Satellite Surveillance and Outer Space Capitalism: The Case of MacDonald, Dettwiler and Associates," in *The Palgrave Handbook of Society, Culture and Outer Space*, ed. Dickens and Ormrod, 94–122 (Palgrave MacMillan, 2016).

At McGill-Queen's University Press, my acquisitions editor Kyla Madden also championed the book project from the beginning, and shepherded it through a process that included critical advice from several external evaluators, with the most significant reader report suggesting additional research into the wealth of materials contained at Library and Archives Canada (LAC) in Ottawa. During several rewarding visits to the LAC, I found crucial sources to complete this book, thanks in no small measure to the many wonderful research librarians and archival staff who guided me to several special collections, including those of the Ministry of State for Science and Technology. Their kindnesses and assistance with my freedom of information requests daily confirmed that the LAC remains an exceptional research institution. Alana Gralen and Don Schultz graciously hosted me in their home in Ottawa, where they cared for my every need and sparked the stimulating conversations that helped me to incorporate changes MQUP's external reviewers had recommended. As a bonus, my nieces Eva and Delia Schultz offered to keep me company as I travelled back to New York after my last Canadian-based research trip. I will always treasure our meandering road trip together, and the patience and wit they put on display. As MQUP's senior editor, Kyla Madden then ensured that I reached the finish line, a feat I could not have accomplished without her commitment and the assistance I received from MQUP's executive director Philip Cercone, as well as its managing editor Ryan Van Huijstee, associate managing editor Kathleen Fraser, and their wonderful marketing and production staff, including my meticulous and good-humoured copy editor Ian MacKenzie.

At my academic home since 1999 – Brooklyn College, City University of New York – I have had the good fortune to receive plentiful financial and intellectual support. The Ethyle R. Wolfe Institute provided a year-long fellowship that freed me from teaching and service so I could concentrate on research. My union, the PSC-CUNY, bestowed additional research grants that shaped my work. While serving as the History Department chair, David Troyansky championed the project and my application for another year-long leave from Brooklyn College so I could write without interruption. That assistance paved the way for the continued encouragement I have received from the department chairs who followed – Chris Ebert and now Gunja SenGupta – the two best officemates and among the most generous colleagues I have ever known. Both read multiple versions of book chapters over many years, and Gunja supported my application for the CUNY Book Completion Award I am grateful to have received. I trust Chris and Gunja know how much I esteem them as scholars and friends.

Space limitations make it impossible to thank the many anonymous evaluators, colleagues, and friends who deserve recognition, but I would be remiss if I did not mention the following people whose solidarity and critiques mattered in ways both large and small: Jennifer Adams, Alan Aja, Bonnie Anderson, Swapna Banerjee, Carolina Bank-Muñoz, Becky Boger, Cynthia Bouton, Barbara Bowen, Naomi Braine, Prudence Cumberbatch, James Davis, Joseph Entin, Ken Estey, Mike Fabricant, Melissa Fisher, Verna Gillis, Jean Grassman, Lorraine Greenfield, Mobina Hashmi, Richard John,

Angel Kwolek-Folland, Pam Laird, Lauren Mancia, Marisol Marin, Mike Menser, Manny Ness, Carol Noblitt, Brigid O'Keeffe, Corey Robin, Janet Rose, Vicky Rosenwald, Therese Schechter, Bambi Schieffelin, Rich Schultz, Tim Shortell, Irene Sosa, Jeanne Theoharis, Alex Vitale, Craig Steven Wilder, Barbara Winslow, Mary Yeager, and Susan Yohn. And several standout students – Afrah Ahmed, Jesse Bayker, Philip Coard, Ina Johnson, Veronica Ordaz, Les Robinson, Heather Squire, Jasmine Toledo, and Jahongir Usmanov – have enriched my work and life beyond measure.

Finally, I owe my greatest debt to Tom Predhome, the writer who swept me off my feet and continues to make all things possible. He has read every draft of this book, offered sagacious editorial advice, and shared his politics, sense of humour, travel itineraries, and life with me for eighteen years. I cannot imagine having taken this journey without him. For his love, patience, and reality checks, I dedicate this book to him.

Abbreviations

ASAT anti-satellite weapon

ATK Alliant Techsystems, an American weapons manufacturer that merged with Orbital Sciences Corporation during 2014. ATK attempted to acquire MDA in 2008, launching a political firestorm that resulted in the decision, for the first time in the twenty-three-year history of the Investment Canada Act, that the sale of a Canadian firm to a foreign entity was "not in the national interest."

AWDS Automated Weather Distribution System, MDA's first technology developed directly for the US military.

CAATS Canadian Automated Air Traffic System

CCRS Canada Centre for Remote Sensing, located within the Canadian Department of Energy, Mines, and Resources, headquartered in Ottawa, and established in February 1971 to promote private-sector research and development in Earth observation systems.

CRC Communications Research Centre Canada, established in 1969 as an arm of Canada's Department of National Defence and charged with improving indigenous expertise in satellite-based communications.

CSA Canadian Space Agency, established in 1989.

DARPA Defense Advanced Research Projects Agency (US), established in 1958 in response to the Soviet launch of *Sputnik*.

DDP Department of Defence Production, created in 1951 to oversee government procurement as well as the organization, mobilization, and conservation of Canada's resources to meet current and prospective commitments to continental defence.

DDSA Canada-US Defence Development Sharing Agreement, signed in 1963 as an agreement to fund joint research and development for continental defence.

DIPP   Defence Industry Productivity Program, created in 1959 to
        support and improve the competitiveness of Canadian compa-
        nies producing military goods, particularly for the US armed
        services.
DND   Department of National Defence (Canada)
DOD   Department of Defense (US)
DPSA   Canada-US Defence Production Sharing Agreement, signed in
        1956, established a common market in military production
        between the two countries, particularly in the aerospace indus-
        try. The agreement established that Canada would buy most of
        its military equipment from the United States and produce
        components and subsystems for US industry.
DPSP   Canada-US Defence Production Sharing Program, established in
        1958 as part of the North American Aerospace Defense Com-
        mand (NORAD) for continental defence.
DRTE   Defence Research Telecommunications Establishment, created
        in 1951, launched *Aloutte-1* in 1962, and superceded by the
        Communications Research Centre (CRC, 1969) when Canada
        established the Department of Communications.
DSS   Department of Supply and Services (Canada), established in
        1969 as the accounting and purchasing arm of the federal gov-
        ernment, and absorbed into the Department of Public Works
        and Services (established in 1993).
EDC   Export Development Canada, established in 1969 to develop
        Canada's export trade, make loans to foreign buyers of Canadi-
        an capital equipment and services on terms and conditions
        competitive with those of other major trading nations, insure
        Canadian firms against non-payment on products and services
        sold abroad, and guarantee financial institutions against invest-
        ment losses.
EMR   Department of Energy, Mines, and Resources, established in
        1966 and absorbed into Natural Resources Canada in 1995.
ESA   European Space Agency, established in 1975 and headquartered
        in Paris, as the world's only intergovernmental organization
        dedicated to space exploration, with twenty-two member states
        (including Canada as an associate member since 1979).
FIRA   Foreign Investment Review Agency, created in 1975 to screen all
        proposed takeovers and ensure that the foreign acquisition and
        establishment of businesses in Canada would serve Canadian
        interests and bring "significant benefits" to Canada.

FIRE Film Image Recorder, MDA's most significant product adventure during the 1980s.

FOCUS Flight Operations Computer System, MDA's first airline industry product during the 1970s.

GICS Geocoded Image Correction System, MDA's first generic product during the 1990s.

ICA Investment Canada Act (1985) empowered the federal government "to forbid foreign investments" of "significant" size only if they did not present a "net benefit" to Canada.

IMF International Monetary Fund

IRIS Integrated Radar Imaging System, a product MDA developed during the early 1980s as a real-time, all-weather, high-resolution radar surveillance system for use on small aircraft.

ISS International Space Station

MOSST Ministry of State for Science and Technology, created in 1971 to coordinate Canada's scientific and industrial efforts, and absorbed into the Industry, Science and Technology portfolio during 1990.

NRC National Research Council (Canada), established in 1918 to advise the federal government on science and industrial research during World War I, became Canada's military science and weapons research organization during World War II.

PERGS Portable Earth Receiving Ground Station, MDA's first major milestone in the Canadian remote sensing industry during the early 1970s.

SAR Synthetic Aperture Radar, a high-resolution device installed on Earth observation (remote sensing) satellites to provide surface mapping no matter the weather conditions, cloud cover, or levels of darkness.

UPP Unsolicited Proposal Program, established in 1974 by Canada's Ministry of State for Science and Technology to provide bridge financing for projects suggested to federal government departments and agencies by underdeveloped private companies.

WTO World Trade Organization

TUG OF WAR

Satellites and Surveillance Capitalism

On 4 October 1957, the Union of Soviet Socialist Republics launched *Sputnik*, the world's first artificial satellite. Humiliated by the Soviet feat, the United States quickly countered, launching its *Explorer* satellite on 31 January 1958. On 29 July 1958, the US Congress then passed the National Aeronautics Space Act, declaring that "activities in space should be devoted to peaceful purposes for the benefit of humankind."[1] Signed into law by US President Dwight D. Eisenhower, the Act established the National Aeronautics and Space Administration (NASA) to conduct all non-military activity in outer space while also incorporating elements of the US Army Ballistic Missile Agency and Naval Research Laboratory. NASA began its official operations on 1 October 1958, with a mission to create a space program based on non-military and commercially promising satellites for scientific research, communications, terrain mapping, meteorological and environmental monitoring, and other Earth resource applications. Knowing that NASA's satellites would collect images from countries other than the United States, the agency's representatives also entered into cooperative agreements with US allies, assuring other countries' representatives that NASA had peaceful intentions.[2]

Sputnik-1, *Explorer-1*, the creation of NASA, and a quick succession of additional satellite launches by the United States and the USSR captured the imagination of technological enthusiasts around the world. As conspicuous political acts performed on the world stage during the Cold War, those launches also inaugurated a global space race, accelerated the arms race, and encouraged other nations to compete for the military and commercial spoils of satellite surveillance.[3] In an agreement with the

United States, the United Kingdom soon entered the space race, sending its *Ariel* satellite into orbit on 26 April 1962. Constructed by NASA at the Goddard Space Flight Center in Maryland, and launched aboard an American rocket from Cape Canaveral Air Force Station in Florida, *Ariel* distinguished the United Kingdom as the third nation to send a satellite into orbit. Damaged by an American high-altitude nuclear test, *Ariel* never lived up to its promise. Nevertheless, the launch signalled the United Kingdom's commitment to the development of a space program, including a pledge to devote its efforts to peaceful scientific research and commercial applications.[4]

On 29 September 1962, Canada followed the United Kingdom into outer space, sending its *Alouette* satellite into orbit aboard an American rocket launched from the Pacific Missile Range at California's Vandenberg Air Force Base. Built by the Special Products Applied Research (SPAR) division of de Havilland Aircraft of Canada, and assembled by the Electronics Division of Canada's Defence Research Telecommunications Establishment (DRTE), *Alouette* distinguished Canada as the fourth country to launch and the third one to build a satellite. Although several more years passed before satellite technologies reached beyond military, government, and scientific communities, Canada announced its stake in peaceful Earth observation, including its intention to develop remote sensing technologies (to acquire information via aerial photographs, satellite images, and other observation systems, and to detect and classify objects and phenomena without making physical contact with them). The country's policymakers also tied Canadians to American developments, both signing continental trade and defence sharing agreements as well as vigorously promoting space exploration, scientific research, and the engineering disciplines as vital for protecting both national and continental interests.[5]

As other nations joined the space race over the next thirty years, developments in computing, digitization, and satellite reconnaissance, imaging, and communications pushed the boundaries of surveillance capitalism. Following the formal dissolution of the USSR on 26 December 1991, Americans then moved swiftly to commercialize the Internet, deregulate communications and financial industries, and assist in the further liberalization of the global economy and the evolving space industry. By the end of 2012, NASA's National Space Science Data Center confirmed that more than 6,600 satellites had launched into orbit since *Sputnik*, with the vast majority of them reaching outer space after 1993.[6]

By 2012, *Space Security Index* (SSI) reported that artificial orbiting objects had reached approximately 8,300. The United States owned about half of all active satellites, with fifty other countries and several international consortia and nongovernmental organizations (NGOs) owning the others. Although satellites have declined in price, launching them remains expensive. As a result, by the end of 2012, only nine countries and one intergovernmental organization (the European Space Agency) had launching capabilities, with the United States dominant. In 2011 alone, global actors had embarked upon eighty space launches that placed 126 new satellites into orbit, with participating nations contributing billions of dollars to the effort. *SSI* further revealed that the International Space Station (ISS) had already cost US$100 billion, with most of it paid for by the taxpayers who helped to fund billions of dollars' worth of other space initiatives. "Advanced and developing economies alike depend on these space-based systems," *SSI* observed, with commercial space revenues "steadily" increasing "since the mid-1990s. From satellite manufacturing and launch services to advanced navigation products and the provision of satellite-based communications," *SSI* declared, "the global commercial space industry is thriving, with estimated annual revenues in excess of $200 billion."[7]

SSI also disclosed that operational satellites accounted for fewer than 5 per cent of the objects orbiting the Earth during 2012, while the remaining 95 per cent represented orbital debris due to anti-missile testing, accidents, and dead batteries.[8] One of China's older weather satellites is among that debris, blown out of the sky in January 2007 when the Chinese conducted their first test of an anti-satellite weapon (ASAT) and, according to one commercial space writer, put "other nations on notice that their commercial and military space assets were vulnerable to attack."[9] As part of an article on *Sapphire*, Canada's first military satellite, the commercial space writer mentioned neither the fifty-year history of US and USSR anti-missile testing nor the more recent space-based collisions and accidents cited by *Space Security Index* as central to the creation of orbital debris. Regardless, the article reflected a trend among business-friendly space writers employing national security concerns to justify increased budgets and private-public initiatives for ASAT detection, "collision avoidance maneuvers," and "debris mitigation efforts."[10]

All of these initiatives now promise to become as significant as satellite launches and what their information-gathering capabilities have revealed about the Earth and its people, with "rapidly increasing revenues associated with satellite services" and the protection of commercial space systems linked to the government contractors who manufacture and maintain the satellites, ground receiving stations, advanced navigational products, and security systems that receive data for both civilian and military users.[11]

This book weaves the history of one of those government contractors – Canada's MacDonald, Dettwiler and Associates (MDA) – into a larger narrative about the ways in which the forces of surveillance capitalism integrated Canada into regional, industrial, academic, and military alliances, particularly but not exclusively with the United States. Founded in Vancouver, British Columbia, during 1969, MDA evolved from a four-person software consultancy into a multinational supplier of space-based systems. A significant provider of the world's ground stations that receive, process, archive, and exploit satellite data, MDA received global recognition in the 1970s for its pioneering work in the commercial applications of remote sensing and synthetic aperture radar (SAR, a high-resolution device that provides surface mapping no matter the weather conditions, cloud cover, or levels of darkness). MDA also became the prime contractor for Canada's powerful *Radarsat-2* Earth observation satellite and the official data distributor for *Radarsat* images worldwide. Other notable feats include MDA's global delivery of the navigational systems that support aircraft and unmanned aerial vehicles (UAVs, commonly known as drones), as well as its role as primary builder of *Sapphire*, and central contributor to *Canadarm-2* (the remote manipulator component of the robotic, mobile servicing system that moves equipment and supplies around the International Space Station and supports astronauts working in space). MDA has additionally received credit as the incubator for Vancouver's high-technology corridor, with many of the firm's former employees launching some of British Columbia's most successful technology ventures. Of the surviving firms, most work as important surveillance-related government contractors in their own right.[12]

As Canadians celebrated the fifty-year anniversary of *Alouette-1*, and the Canadian Space Agency (CSA) readied the nation for the launch of *Sapphire* at the end of 2012, MDA's strategies culminated in the acquisition of the US Space Systems/Loral (SS/L), a global provider of communications satellites and subsystems. According to industry analysts, the SS/L acquisition furnished MDA with a "critical mass in the commercial satellite manufacturing industry."[13] When the deal closed on 2 November 2012, MDA had also created one of the world's most significant communications and information systems integrators, an achievement that promised "to boost estimated earnings" and provide "a platform to win upcoming space contracts" and more "defence and intelligence work" from the US government. The US government soon fulfilled that promise, in multiple contracts that gave MDA the market value and visibility its executives and shareholders had long craved as "the top technology stock in Canada over the past year."[14] Although financial news reports finally acknowledged MDA's significance to Canada's place within the global surveillance power core, the firm still remains largely invisible in the historical record and to the general public. According to David Ebner of the *Globe and Mail*, MDA's obscurity has much to do with the ephemeral nature of systems engineering. Whereas one can touch and see products, MDA's "technology isn't widely recognized by most people because" the firm "generally operates unseen, in the background," Ebner argued. As a result, "when MDA's *Radarsat* satellites monitor Canada – the surveillance can spotlight down to a single metre – there isn't any obvious MDA or Made in Canada stamp that people can see or cheer."[15]

Operating "unseen, in the background," MDA has played a critical role in the long-term development of the information systems and products that proliferate in global positioning devices, flight navigation systems, drones, mobile satellites, Command, Control, Communications, Computers, Intelligence, Surveillance and Reconnaissance (C4ISR, also known as "Battle Command"), and a host of other networks that dominate various industries, from communications and financial services to environmental monitoring and resource extraction. Although they did not initially work on surveillance technologies for overtly political reasons, MDA's scientists and engineers also played a part in turning satellites into a multi-billion-dollar commodity and outer space into a competitive, militarized zone. Along with other technological enthusiasts, they embraced satellites, the commercialization of space, and a notion of the "end of ideology." In practice, however, their work has contributed to the expansion of the neoliberal project of privatization, fiscal austerity, deregulation, free trade, and reduced social spending, as well as the use of more efficient data mining systems, precision surveillance, first-strike capabilities, and the use of robotics for commerce as well as war. Engineering systems such as the ones they developed have also helped to remove the last barriers to routine aerial surveillance and the monitoring of everyday life.

It would be a mistake, however, to see MDA's founders, executives, scientists, and engineers as principal architects of this change; recent scholarship on the importance of social capital networks as well as ongoing revelations about surveillance and military-industrial adventurism have exploded the myths that a bright line divides business from government and the "great" man or woman from the socially constructed universe in which they operate. That MDA existed at all made it an entrepreneurial enterprise: the first of its kind in Vancouver, the firm helped to establish a high-technology presence in BC's Lower Mainland. But MDA's history also reveals that business enterprises succeed or fail not simply on technological innovation, the personal qualities of those who lead them, the first-mover advantages that early entrants enjoy, or the "visible hand" of executives and managers who develop strategies and structures for continued expansion. Indeed, business survival always reflects the contingencies of larger social structures and cultural tropes, government priorities and changing educational, legal, and political policies, and unanticipated events and exogenous shocks beyond the control of any inventor, business founder, investor, executive, worker, government bureaucrat, or policymaking body. No different, MDA depended on these phenomena as well as the taxpayers who supported government spending on surveillance and those who hoped to profit from enhanced information-gathering techniques. "Without the benevolence" of the Canadian government, one long-time employee suggested, "MDA would never have grown beyond the size of a very, very small company."[16] MDA's history therefore reminds us that corporations are juridical constructs and entrepreneurs instruments of state power, with both providing ways for governments to spread risk and for gatekeepers to favour certain individuals and businesses over others.

By placing surveillance capitalism at the centre of Canada's political economy, this book argues that MDA matters to our understanding of policymaking and business-government relations during the Cold War and into the twenty-first century. Reflecting the assumptions of capitalism's culture of individual striving, people at MDA hoped to profit from living and working in a society where government officials promised to nurture their technical skills, reward their surveillance-based work, and bail them out when they stumbled. No matter their technical, business, or political skills, some realized their ambitions while others did not. Some had the ability to sell their ideas and motivate others, but lacked the skills to make the firm a profitable one. Others had excellent negotiating, managerial, and marketing skills, but still failed to realize returns from the "best practices" they had learned from management literature and the experiences of others in similar circumstances. Always, they engaged in complex negotiations with the capitalist system and government policies that provided incentive for some activities and discouraged others. MDA survived because members of the firm's evolving executive team ultimately embraced MDA's role as a systems integrator and procurement contractor for governments worldwide. Over time, they also understood that power resided not in the technologies they developed but rather in Ottawa and Washington, DC. Once done, they learned how to lobby the government to keep Canada's space program on the budgetary agenda. In turn, the federal government encouraged MDA's surveillance-based work because it promised to expand Canada's influence as a significant, albeit junior member of the international power club. Canadian policymakers also appreciated that "countries which have less competitive industrial strengths in the areas of information technology face an increasing risk of losing trade, influence and economic power both within the community of developed nations and in the broader context of trade with developing countries."[17]

MDA therefore provides more than a case study about how one particular firm managed to survive in the competitive space industry; it serves as a window into a corporate world girded by potent forces at the nexus of state, capital, and geopolitical power games. That nexus has included myths about space exploration's peaceful purposes as well as competitive posturing for the spoils of surveillance-based commerce. Largely well-intentioned and with little interest in war, people at MDA nevertheless got caught up in the excitement of technological development, capitalist ambitions, and state incentives for both. Their eventual move into military work also reflects the unique security but problematic cultural relationship that integrated Canada into a continental defence economy with the United States while members of each country struggled to define their national identities and the imperial role each would play during the Cold War and beyond. As that relationship played out, Canadians consistently feared the overwhelming influence of their more powerful southern neighbours. Whether Conservative or Liberal, policymakers thus attempted to protect Canadian sovereignty and an autonomous international identity while simultaneously enjoying the benefits of their geographical proximity to as well as trading relationship with the United States. They also concerned themselves with foreign investment in the Canadian economy and the brain drain of technical talent that such investments might engender. Hoping to realize a "fair share" of the bounty promised by participation in world trade organizations and international governing bodies, they additionally wrestled with balancing desires to project Canada's peacekeeping role and the realities of the country's place within the American military-industrial complex. Satellites played a prominent role in that struggle.

THE SIGNIFICANCE OF SATELLITES, SOVEREIGNTY, AND SURVEILLANCE STUDIES

Artificial satellites, those ubiquitous "eyes in the sky," twinkle as stars in various orbits. Some stand alone; others work in constellations. All contain powerful computers and subsystems, including those for propulsion, power, and communications. They vary in size and purpose, but ultimately they all gather information, with each of them launched to perform particular jobs for military and commercial purposes, often both. Whether for reconnaissance, remote sensing, or communications, satellites track assets, map resources, and communicate information to users on Earth and in outer space. In constant competition, those who own satellites seek to create more powerful features and capture more information for their own uses and profit, for "without a comparable capability," one Canadian task force on satellite surveillance stressed, "we may never learn what other nations know about us, which must be viewed as a serious non-military threat."[18]

Governments and their private contractors use reconnaissance (or spy) satellites to gather intelligence on military and other activities in outer space and on Earth. Launched into polar orbit, the most powerful among them can cover the entire globe every fourteen days. They come in four basic varieties and interact with each other. Optical-imaging satellites use light sensors to detect missile launches and weapons on the ground. Radar satellites use synthetic aperture radar to see through clouds and darkness. Signals-intelligence satellites employ powerful receivers to capture radio and microwave transmissions from every foe and friend. Relay satellites quickly move data from spy satellites to military bases on Earth, thereby speeding up the communications process for engagement. As surveillance studies scholars remind us, reconnaissance satellites are very useful tools for militaries and the police-security state.[19]

Remote sensing (also known as Earth observation) satellites measure and photograph the surface of the Earth and oceans as well as the atmosphere. Like most non-military satellites, Earth observation satellites typically launch into geostationary orbit over the equator. They use sensor technologies to detect objects and other phenomena via electromagnetic radiation signals from aircraft, satellites, and other systems, taking pictures of and classifying those objects without having to make physical contact with them. With SAR onboard, remote sensing satellites can map the entire surface of the Earth in the same ways that sonar technologies map the oceans, day or night, in all weather. Google Earth provides just one example of their power. Because they are very expensive to launch, Earth observation satellites are funded and used mainly by governments, to detect mineral and oil deposits, changes in agricultural activities and forests, weather damage, military bases, submarine wakes in the ocean, and other assets. MDA's *Radarsat-2*, launched into the sun-synchronous polar orbit during 2007, can cover the Arctic daily, Canada every seventy-two hours, and the entire Earth every twenty-four days. The Canadian government has given MDA the right to sell *Radarsat* images to others around the world, as an export for economic development. MDA can downlink images to multiple ground stations in real time, or store them in the satellite's computer until within range of a ground station. Once other countries, companies, and individuals have those images, they too can see resources, thereafter exploiting them for various applications, including city and regional planning, resource extraction, market segmentation, intelligence work, warfare, and a host of other reputable and nefarious activities.[20]

Most communications satellites also launch into geostationary orbit so they can circle the Earth within the same time that the Earth rotates just once. With their powerful antennas, these satellites send radio, television, and telephone transmissions, so that the Earth-bound can receive live broadcasts, use cellular telephones, and communicate by e-mail, among other activities. All of these devices record activities, making it easier for their owners to share information with each other.[21] There are many other satellites, including those used for astronomy, meteorology, navigation, search and rescue, space exploration, and other scientific applications.

Working interactively with the space stations that make living in outer space possible, as well as with aircraft (including drones), ground-based computers, multimedia platforms, geographical positioning systems (GPS), and other technologies, satellites have created the panoptical architecture for the global surveillance state we experience and serve, all the while increasing the power of the elite who own and control the technologies and firms that produce them. As Michel Foucault observed, surveillance networks make us self-policing subjects. We daily use technologies we can no longer seem to do without, whether on the job, through the cash register, or at the ballot box. We "check in" with authority figures, even perform for them. We congregate with online communities because we have few public spaces left to meet. We trade civil liberties for protection because we receive daily reminders that we live in a dangerous world. We consign our control to the awesome power of the networks and inanimate objects created to extend shareholder value and the power of the elite. Ultimately, we even connect our identities to machines, watching, touching, and speaking into them, inviting them to become one with us.[22] Investigative journalist Christian Parenti has argued that we do all of these things because surveillance techniques developed in earlier eras have gone global, become ubiquitous, "mundane, decentralized, and even convenient."[23]

The conveniences of surveillance technologies come at a price, just as earlier conveniences came at a price to those enthralled by railroads and

telegraphs, automobiles and radios, and airplanes and televisions. Technological revolutions have created great wealth, but they have not necessarily effected a greater distribution of that wealth or a more peaceful and
inclusive world. "If the twentieth century has shown us anything," Joel
Mokyr concluded in his intellectual history of technology and the "useful" knowledge economy, "it is that the capacity of humans for intoler-
ance, stupidity, and selfishness has not declined as their technological
power has increased." He also conceded, "The institutional setup of the
world is such that holdouts that reject modern technology or cannot
adopt it will eventually have to change their minds." Canadian policymakers therefore embraced space exploration and surveillance technologies as a way to maintain Canada's sovereignty and relevance, marketing
both on their abilities to create a "new" world order of economic and
social opportunities without end.[24] Sociologist Vincent Mosco captured
the force of such strategies a decade ago while tracing the dot-com bust of
the late 1990s to the seductive power of the Internet. With Internet enthusiasts demonstrating "a remarkable, almost willful, historical amnesia,"
Mosco observed that each generation "has renewed the belief that, whatever was said about earlier technologies, the latest one will fulfill a radical
and revolutionary promise." As a result, when the dot-com bubble burst,
many Internet enthusiasts were shocked to learn that the power structures
they thought they had overthrown remained remarkably resilient.[25]
MDA's history resonates with these findings.

Thanks to the mythological power of space exploration, MDA's engineers and scientists thought they were different from previous generations, that their technical expertise could insulate them from past imbroglios. After all, they reasoned, they were well-educated, scientifically
adept, computer-literate professionals, the vanguard of a new economy.[26]
People from all walks of life rationalize their decisions and choose selective memories to make sense of their current circumstances and imagine
themselves as active agents of the systems they develop and the structures
they support. But as social anthropologist Hylton White recently observed, in an environment structured for competition and unending
expansion, capitalism inevitably turns each new wave of technological
enthusiasm, every gadget and new profession from an exotic first to a
ubiquitous necessity.[27] This is just one of the consequences of the willful
innocence people at MDA and elsewhere possess. In her study of engineering and the legitimacy of state power, sociologist Chandra Mukerji
has argued that "the intelligence of engineering is not just pragmatic, but
also deeply invested in social, legal, and moral conceptions of power" that

privilege efficiencies over ecological awareness and quality-of-life issues as well as "produce an engineered world that shapes our lives – in ways we systematically ignore."[28] Surveillance studies scholars concur, including David Lyon, whose work continues to stress that surveillance is a "morally and politically loaded activity," with what "we disclose to whom, and under what conditions" a highly significant act of state power.[29]

Sociologists and surveillance studies scholars have contributed a great deal to our understanding about the synergies between capitalism, state power, military aims, academic research, and technological change, particularly in the Internet era. With few exceptions, however, most tend to focus on the United States, the United Kingdom, and other "great powers" while remaining remarkably silent on the history of the secondary powers that have helped to serve the interests of capital and the hegemonic ambitions of the United States. They also have the propensity to explore the state without examining the businesses involved in the space-faring enterprise. This omission flows, in part, from the classified nature of defence-related work; however, disparate sources can help to connect the dots between governments and their surveillance contractors.

Tug of War draws upon interviews I conducted with MDA's founders, employees past and present, and government patrons during 1992–93, and prior to MDA's larger leap into the secret world of international defence/ military contracting. Once transcribed, the tapes of those interviews produced an oral history of more than 1,000 pages. As I reread and reflected on that oral history after the heady dot-com boom had busted, terrorists had flown airplanes with sophisticated flight information systems into the World Trade Center and Pentagon, and the US government had stepped up its war footing, ultimately invading Iraq in 2003 on manipulated intelligence derived from military briefings and private contractors, I knew I had a larger story to tell. I therefore turned to archival material at Library and Archives Canada (LAC), some of it received through several requests under the Freedom of Information and Protection Act, as well as publicly available business records, government documents, and other sources that could place MDA's trajectory within the larger context of surveillance capitalism's expansion, the Cold War's emphasis on permanent military preparedness and continental integration, and the rise of the North American security state. Interviewees who spoke about MDA's first decade focused on the excitement of their technological innovations. Those who discussed the 1980s and early 1990s emphasized the business strategies and structures MDA had instituted to survive the winds of technological change and global competition, including the pull of military contracting. And documents collected after MDA went public in 1993 disclosed the ways in which the firm capitalized on neoliberalism, systems integration, and the expansion of the world's surveillance architecture. Together, these sources have given me the luxury of hindsight, an increasing appreciation about the concatenation of events that pulled MDA into surveillance capitalism and a larger tug of war, and a better understanding about the ways in which time, memory, and selective amnesia shape the histories we tell ourselves and others over time.[30]

The MDA case therefore demonstrates that historians have much to contribute to the field of surveillance studies, particularly when they search for sources that allow them to trace how those asserting no particular interest in gaining military power nevertheless get drawn into the promises of space exploration, larger state objectives, and the US military-industrial complex.[31]

THE MILITARY CONTEXT FOR MACDONALD, DETTWILER'S PARTICIPATION IN SURVEILLANCE CAPITALISM

The ascendancy of the United States as the world's most powerful military-industrial power set the stage for MDA's participation in the expansion of surveillance capitalism. Creating a feedback loop between military and business interests, US policymakers conceived and initially developed computer and satellite technologies through the military. Thereafter, they hoped government procurement contracts would encourage the private sector to enhance American hegemony by developing additional products and services for military and commercial purposes. As the Cold War evolved, policymakers then justified further public expenditures on businesses both large and small by stressing the need to maintain the US role as "policeman" in an increasingly competitive and dangerous world. National securities scholar Joan Johnson-Freese maintains that such military-industrial strategies continue to matter to our understanding of the United States' "heavenly ambitions." While most policymakers throughout the world see outer space activities as capable of providing a win-win situation, at least in terms of "over-lapping economic and commercial interests," US policymakers do not. Instead, they remain mired in a "Cold War, zero-sum political perspective," she argues, where "one country's advances must be at the expense of someone else." Thus, the US government has consistently provided rationales for increased military spending, upgrades to surveillance capabilities, and additional corporate clusters to serve the country's agenda to remain the dominant military force on Earth and in outer space.[32]

Despite his own faith in the promise of the United States to revolutionize the world for the better, US President Eisenhower articulated a countervailing argument that would emerge among those who worried about what *Sputnik* and *Explorer* had unleashed. In his prophetic farewell address to the American people on 17 January 1961, Eisenhower argued that "only an alert and knowledgeable citizenry can compel the proper meshing of the huge industrial and military machinery of defense with our peaceful methods and goals so that security and liberty may prosper together." He therefore cautioned "against the acquisition of unwarranted influence, whether sought or unsought, by the military-industrial complex."[33] Extending Eisenhower's warning, later critics argued that the US military establishment and the corporations that received federal spending to build systems and develop regional markets for American expansion had created a permanent war economy as well as a form of monopoly capitalism, a way to absorb the surplus productivity of labour and capital without threatening capital's interests.[34] Economic historians Michael Bernstein and Mark Wilson recently explained that early critics of the military-industrial complex also understood what later revisionist work would reveal: that governmental support for the military-industrial complex "socialized risk, privatized profit, and gave corporations undue influence over U.S. domestic and foreign policy." The government also pulled research universities into the military-industrial complex through various grants, contracts, and other incentives.[35]

Historians have long recognized the role of the military in capitalist expansion and technological innovation; by the time he published a 2000 study of high-tech firms in California's Silicon Valley, however, Stuart Leslie could still argue that absent from "virtually every account of freewheeling entrepreneurs and visionary venture capitalists is the military's role, intentional and otherwise, in creating and sustaining Silicon Valley" and Stanford University's researchers who formed many of the Valley's computer-based firms on the strength of government procurement contracts.[36] Leslie and others have noted similar omissions in coverage of the Massachusetts Institute of Technology (MIT) and its high-tech corridor along Boston's Route 128, as well as other hot spots of innovation, where technological "family trees" have emerged from the military's connections to research universities, government contractors, and national plutocrats. They have also shown how clusters of government agencies, technology firms, venture capitalists, lawyers, and research universities pulled scientists, engineers, and other workers into the project, created opportunities for amateur computer coders to expand the effort, and profited from the commercial products military contracts allowed them to develop and then sell to consumers around the world.[37] Scholarship on the computer industry has reshaped our understanding of the government's role in linking scientific research, technological development, and business expansion to military ambitions; however, the larger satellite-based space industry remains understudied in the historical literature, with military connections rarely receiving sustained scrutiny, even in histories that establish early linkages.[38]

Although the United States led the North American effort to employ satellites for military as well as commercial purposes, and Canadians prefer to celebrate their role as purveyors of peaceful space applications, MDA's history reveals that Canada has long associated itself with the American military-industrial complex and the creation of global surveillance networks, as both political ally and the United States' largest trading partner. John Vardalas has argued that "military enterprise was the primary force behind Canada's early participation in the digital electronics revolution," with World War II thrusting "Canada into a position of geopolitical prominence that otherwise would have been inaccessible to it."[39] According to Laurence Mussio, Canada was additionally "enmeshed in a series of international arrangements" between 1945 and 1975, "in which it had to define its interests as a middle power."[40] One of those interests soon surfaced in the form of telecommunications, an industry Mussio and others have traced to Canada's military agreements with the United States and the launch of *Alouette-1*. Remote sensing emerged as another, with the federal government nurturing firms such as MDA in the business of Earth observation for commercial as well as military purposes.[41]

Canada's association with the military-industrial complex stretches back to 1940, when US President Franklin D. Roosevelt and Canadian Prime Minister W.L. Mackenzie King signed the Ogdensburg Declaration of Defence Cooperation. Other wartime agreements then guided future intelligence sharing programs, defence procurement policies, and production sharing arrangements between the two countries, including the 1957 North American Aerospace Defense Command (NORAD). Although such agreements did not always go as smoothly as both sides hoped, they ensured that Canada would become a component supplier for the US military-industrial complex as well as a significant, albeit subordinate partner in the business of continental integration. By the time the United States launched *Explorer* during January 1958, Americans and Canadians had firmly established their military-economic relationship as Cold War allies. Canadian policymakers had also learned many valuable lessons from their historical relationship to the British Empire and the United States, including the ways in which both superpowers had used public dollars and various policy instruments to quicken the pace of industrial development. Canada had first attempted to catch up to that pace following political independence from Britain in 1867 by invoking the strategies of the United Kingdom and the United States: to stimulate economic development, the Canadian federal government erected tariff barriers, provided charters to private companies, created public authorities to oversee critical areas of the economy, and took state control of industries either limited by the size of the domestic market or threatened by aggressive competitors.[42]

Emerging as members of a sovereign nation following World War II, Canada's policymakers also drew upon the Keynesian model employed by most Western nation-states during the Great Depression and World War II, including its focus on economic growth and the creation of the welfare state. As it turned out, however, the organizations Canada joined and the agreements it entered into prompted Canadian policymakers to abandon the strategies that had created the context for British, then American hegemony. Rather than protecting their infant industries, Canadians joined in the neoliberal project that began during World War II, sealing the country's dependence on the United States, a nation that has proven itself as interventionist and protectionist as Canada, if not more so, by creating clusters of innovation linked to key military bases and national laboratories.[43]

CANADA'S AMBIVALENT PLACE
WITHIN THE CONTINENTAL DEFENCE MARKET

Despite Canada's commitment to the Cold War, during the 1950s and 1960s Canadians began to articulate anxieties about the United States' increasingly dominant role in the world, including what many perceived as the expanding problem of American investments in Canadian firms. In response to mounting concerns about Canada's vulnerabilities vis-à-vis the United States, the federal government convened special commissions, held hearings, and asked interested Canadians to investigate the problem of American influences on Canada's economy and culture. Gathering evidence and reports from business consultants and technical experts, the federal government underwrote studies that ultimately culminated in a National Policy Convention during 1970. "There can be no doubt that Canadian political independence is threatened by the pervasive effect of foreign ownership and control of the Canadian economy," one contributing report to the conference argued. Summarizing the collective mood of those who dominated the conference, the report stressed that foreign capital control precluded the "likelihood of Canadian talent being harnessed towards research distinctly beneficial to Canada." The report also noted a "considerable lack of adequate entrepreneurial and management talent on the part of Canadians. The lack of enough *major* solely Canadian controlled industries has denied this training to Canadians and has instead afforded it to foreigners." The federal government had provided insufficient research funds for universities and various industries, the report claimed, thus creating a "distinctive lack of original Canadian research in new and developing fields" as well as mounting trade imbalances with the United States. "Canada is losing skilled personnel to other countries," the report chided, a brain drain of technological know-how that threatened Canadian sovereignty. Surely, the report suggested, the federal government needed to revisit its taxation and export incentives as well as its government procurement policies to wrest these vitally important industries from American control.[44]

Some government-sponsored reports argued that Canada needed to bolster current or create new Crown corporations – state-owned enterprises operating at a remove from government but with various parliamentary ministers responsible for the corporations' activities and accountability to the public. Others argued that, in the case of computing and other emerging fields devoted to the military and commercial applications of space, policymakers should follow American strategies, stimulating the development of private-sector initiatives from coast to coast. Those arguments prevailed. Rather than taking direct control of entire industries, the federal government initially planned to provide public support for the development of Canada's computing, communications, remote sensing, and other space-based industries. Once Canadian firms had established themselves, policymakers then hoped that the private sector could stand on its own. Recognizing the limits of Canada's domestic market, they additionally argued that the federal government should provide ongoing funding only for firms and technologies with export potential, ones that promised to create strong, diversified Canadian multinational corporations that could compete with other global firms, particularly American ones. Arguing that such firms operated in the national interest, they planned to employ established and new firms as well as the scientific community as policy instruments for Canada's larger ambitions to become a major force in the world and a significant player in the neoliberal project. By spreading risks and benefits widely, policymakers stressed that the federal government could play a part in developing regional hubs for economic expansion. In turn, they hoped the private sector would create jobs and bring the nation together in a common cause despite regional disparities, provincial squabbles, and other issues threatening the country's unity.[45]

To make the case for private-sector involvement in the Canadian space sector, policymakers pointed to SPAR Aerospace, a firm formed by a merger of De Havilland Canada's Special Products Division (the builders of *Alouette-1*) and Avro Canada's Applied Research Unit (whose personnel had built Canada's CF-105 Arrow to serve the Royal Canadian Air Force). SPAR began to issue shares to the public in 1967, quickly created a hub for the development of other firms in Ontario and Quebec, and emerged as the darling of Canada's aerospace industry. Intending to develop SPAR into Canada's prime contractor for all space-based work, the federal government changed Canada's procurement policies, pushed work out from government laboratories and into the private sector, encouraged university scientists to direct more of their research to the "practical needs" of industry, and provided funding to build SPAR's expertise in the business of surveillance. The federal government also encouraged SPAR to work with smaller Canadian firms, developing the latter into subcontractors with capabilities SPAR lacked. They then expected SPAR to increase its shareholdings in such firms, eventually even acquiring them. "While recognizing the significant contribution that will continue to be made by small companies in high-technology industries," one commissioned report for the federal government later argued, the government should "actively foster the formation of large Canadian-owned firms through mergers and consolidations (as in the case of Spar) in order to achieve production volumes necessary to compete in both domestic and export markets."[46]

By 1970, the federal government also created several agencies to coordinate the efforts of Canada's space-based sector. One was the Communications Research Centre (CRC), an arm the Department of National Defence charged with improving indigenous expertise in satellite-based communications. Another was the Canada Centre for Remote Sensing (CCRS), a branch of the Department of Energy, Mines, and Resources established to promote private-sector research and development so that Canadians could capitalize on the country's remote sensing expertise in the international market. Although the United States could "mount the kinds of programs" Canada could not "afford," one prominent Canadian geophysicist argued, "the CCRS put Canadian companies in a unique position to receive and process satellite information on the ground and to develop remote sensing applications worldwide" long before other countries could do so.[47]

Perceiving that space-based initiatives would involve multiple government ministries, departments, agencies, and laboratories, as well as firms
and universities, during 1971 the Canadian government created a new
Ministry of State for Science and Technology (MOSST) to coordinate Canada's scientific and industrial efforts. Inspired by the international Organisation for Economic Co-operation and Development (OECD) reviews of
the Canadian economy, and affectionately dubbed "The Ministry of the
Future," MOSST and the departments and agencies that fell within its portfolio then guided the role that space-based entities would play in Canada's
hoped-for future. Although Canada lacked the scale and scope of the United States' domestic market, MOSST emulated the US plan to turn scientific knowledge and scientists into useful policy instruments as well as stimulating private-sector expansion through government procurement and
spending on space and defence.[48] At the same time, Canadian politicians
and other interested parties developed strategies to differentiate Canada
from the United States, including those that allowed Americans to shoulder the burden of military adventurism so that Canadian businesses could
operate "unseen in the background" as component suppliers to US contractors while the government simultaneously highlighted Canada's role
as a stable, open, and business-friendly nation-state converging on international economic development and peacekeeping missions. As Jerome
Klassen's recent work on the Canadian political economy argues, those
strategies and the internationalization of capital "made Canada an important command and control centre for the world economy."[49] They also
shielded MDA's owners and rank-and-file technologists from the geopolitical consequences of their work, at least initially.

Canadian strategies resonated with the era's increasing emphasis on the
role that scientists and engineers would play in the economic development of "useful knowledge" and the new technologies that promised to
engender the "creative destruction" Austrian economist Joseph Schumpeter hailed as the hallmark of capitalist innovation and entrepreneurship.[50] When management consultant Peter Drucker popularized the
term *knowledge economy* during 1969, as part of his "guidelines" for dealing with the "discontinuity" created by such "creative destruction," he provided key concepts to management consultants, policymakers, members
of the media, and technological enthusiasts that they could apply to their
own experiences. They then normalized Drucker's term into everyday par-
lance and, by extension, reality, as the status of engineers rose in a "new"
economy that required their technical expertise. As the ideas and practices
of "creative destruction" and the "knowledge economy" spread with

advances in computing and space-based technologies, scholarly studies and popular writing on entrepreneurship and strategic management provided to MDA a raison d'être as well as an ideological framework that the firm's young associates could employ to explain their circumstances and the role they might play in and for Canada. Although MDA did not initiate most of the disruptions that have shaped the post–World War II era, members of the firm certainly participated in them. MDA also served the national interest by creating an important regional hub for the creation of Vancouver's high-tech corridor and Canada's evolving role in the larger world order.[51]

Canadian historians have engaged a spirited debate about the federal government's role in the economy. Best exemplified by Canadian historian Michael Bliss, detractors have argued that, by "forcing the pace of change," the federal government has participated in an unending history of corruption, "dubious economic reasoning," ineptitude, waste, and increasing deficits. In the case of policies developed during a high-water mark of Canadian nationalism in the 1970s, Bliss has additionally noted that, "within a remarkably short space of time," the "'knights of the new technology' joined the knaves of the old on the public teat, that extraordinarily free-flowing nipple from which weaning seldom takes place." Comparing his interventionist Canada to an imagined laissez-faire United States, Bliss has both downplayed the role that American policymakers have long played in setting the pace and location for economic development as well as justified American intervention where "national survival was at stake."[52] Although MDA's history confirms many of the results Bliss and his followers cite, including MDA's inability to wean itself from government support, to survive as players in surveillance capitalism, Canadian policymakers followed the American lead, seeking strategic locations across the country on which to build a national economy, and mitigating the risks of disunity by pushing most computing and space-based work out to the private sector. In these strategies, Canadians were no more protectionist and nationalistic than their counterparts on the continent and around the world.[53]

Recent scholarship on the Canadian political economy has revised the Bliss school and pushed the boundaries of H.V. Nelles's classic works on Canadian business-government relations, resource development, and continental integration. For example, Bruce Smardon's work on the shifting terrains of capital accumulation demonstrates that "contrary to the claims of 'untamed markets' and 'laissez-faire capitalism' before World War II," twentieth-century American and Canadian developments "involved systematic state interventions and forms of market regulation that were integral to supporting the transformation of the economy," including the "structured developments after 1945" that ultimately paved the way for "neoliberal developments" and the further consolidation of capital. Smardon and others have also illustrated the central role that the government's "selective liberalization" played in Canada's post–World War II political economy.[54]

MDA's stages of development reinforce much recent work on Canada's business-government relations, but they also demonstrate that surveillance capitalism forced Canada's pace of change following World War II. Chapter 1 explores the foundations laid for MDA's participation in surveillance capitalism and continental integration, including the defence sharing and trade agreements that Canadian policymakers signed with the United States and others, the changes they instituted, and the institutional supports they provided to the private sector prior to MDA's founding. Thereafter, the book focuses on MDA's stages of development, and how its history mirrors the bargains Canadian policymakers struck to attach themselves to the power of the American state, the military-industrial complex, and the neoliberal project.

THE STAGES OF MACDONALD, DETTWILER
AND ASSOCIATES' DEVELOPMENT

MDA's role in the expansion of surveillance capitalism took place during three discrete stages (1969–82, 1982–93, and 1993–2012), with each stage connected to the chief executive officers (CEOs) who guided the firm's transitions: John Spencer MacDonald; John W. Pitts; and Daniel (Dan) E. Friedmann. Each company CEO had received training in engineering but employed a different leadership persona. As shareholders heavily invested in the firm, each aspired to power and influence, and intended to make plenty of money from his association with MDA. The firm's developments reflect those aspirations, as well as the ambitions of Canadian capitalists and federal policymakers. They also expose the unintended consequences of technological innovation as well as the tumultuous road the firm and nation travelled from youthful exuberance to maturing uncertainty.[55]

Part 1, "The Technology Enthusiasts," explores the period from 1969 to 1982, when MDA focused on research and innovative technology firsts but neither the geopolitical context of the company's work nor the business structures required for long-term profitability. "There was no big venture capital start up," one long-time employee recalled. "It was a creeping evolution, one body at a time," with decisions based upon the individual interests of the company's founders and the young engineers MDA recruited from universities. John MacDonald, one of the firm's founders, guided MDA through these early years. He grew up in northern BC and ascended the ranks of academia on his exceptional skills in physics and engineering, ultimately earning a PhD in electrical engineering from MIT. Accepting a faculty position at the University of British Columbia (UBC), MacDonald hoped to turn Vancouver from a place dominated by fish, lumber, and tourism and into a world-class engineering hub. As a technological enthusiast and charismatic weaver of possibilities, he drew on his experiences and relationships at MIT, and created the team that set MDA on its longer-term journey into surveillance capitalism. Under MacDonald's leadership, MDA employed a sweat-equity formula (the uncompensated overtime efforts of its young associates) and government contracts to seed the firm's development. MacDonald also failed to make MDA a profitable business, a situation that ultimately forced him to step down as CEO during the economic recession of the early 1980s. Prior to the recession, MacDonald put up personal guarantees and a mortgage on his home to save the firm from ruin. In return, he received an increasing percentage of shares and control over MDA's direction.

During MDA's first decade in business, the company took on projects that included a great deal of software work, such as supervisory control systems for the telecommunications, oil, and gas industries, flight operations computer systems for commercial airlines, mobile data communications terminals for the Vancouver police department, and anything else a bright and able employee suggested. With each engineer managing and working on the projects that interested him, the firm's young associates worked long hours and saw themselves as full participants in the firm. "I thought we were building something for the future," one former employee recalled, "that we were putting in all this effort to achieve something. I didn't know what it was," he stressed, "but I wasn't just working for a firm. I was putting part of my soul into that company in exchange for something in the future that wasn't really defined."[56] Chapter 2 examines MDA's business launch, the local mentors who assisted the young associates, and the various software projects that fostered the firm's sweat-equity formula.

In 1971, MDA also received its first opportunity to build a satellite ground receiving station for Canada's Centre for Remote Sensing. Once firmly attached to government procurement contracting, MDA expanded rapidly into the business of remote sensing, gaining recognition for its pioneering ground station work and drawing attention as the first commercial firm to produce detailed digital images of the Earth from synthetic aperture radar (SAR). Earth observation work taught people at MDA how to collaborate with government partners, first in Canada and then elsewhere. By the end of the 1970s, technocrats in government also helped the firm to capture most of the global market for ground stations by selling MDA's services in the export market. MDA's young recruits gloried in their technological successes and the sense of ownership they derived from working on their own projects and the government contracts that MacDonald and others had acquired for the firm. Chapter 3 explores changing procurement policies and the government contracting paradigm that influenced MDA's most exciting period of technological innovation and laid the foundations for the company's future as a systems integrator.

As one long-term employee reflected on MDA's first decade in business, he argued that "there was a special synergy, a special gathering of the right people at the right time." John Macdonald "in particular," he recalled, "was like a messiah figure, saying to each and every one of us, 'This way to the Promised Land.' And if he had walked over a cliff, everybody would have lockstep followed him right over it."[57] Many of them nearly did. Between 1977 and 1982, the firm struggled under the weight of a larger economic recession, costly software project overruns, failed diversification and product development plans, and the manifold problems attended by rapid and undercapitalized expansion. During the crisis, SPAR offered to purchase a share in MDA to save the firm from bankruptcy. When MacDonald spurned SPAR's overtures, some of those who wanted to save the technologies they had developed left the firm, thereafter creating start-up companies linked to their experiences at MDA. Others hoped that MacDonald could convince the federal government to save the firm from catastrophe. Chapter 4 examines the outside forces and internal challenges that created MDA's near-death experience.

Part 2, "The Investor-Business Strategists," explores the changes that took place after outside investors, the federal government, and a new business executive arrived to save MDA from the dustbin of history. As one of those investors and MDA's new CEO, John Pitts guided the firm's evolution from 1982 to 1993. Pitts grew up in an elite household on Vancouver Island. Trained in mechanical engineering, he pursued a Harvard master of business administration (MBA) rather than a technical path. He had previously run several manufacturing businesses, had familial relationships with and connections to significant policymakers in Canada and the United States, had no illusions about what firms must do to compete in a capitalist universe, and positioned MDA to profit from the firm's technologies. MDA's employees had to accept a sea change in organizational temper when the firm shifted from MacDonald's personal to Pitts's professional management. MDA's founders had started MDA to create a business where they could enjoy their work. Pitts and venture capitalists got in for the purpose of getting out, in circumstances meeting the goals that motivate such people: a massive financial return in five years or thereabouts. Pitts negotiated the refinancing of the firm, introduced cost controls, reduced MDA's inefficiencies, and set up three divisions as profit centres. By introducing these structures, Pitts hoped to generate consistent revenues from the systems side of the business so MDA could ripen its products for larger-scale manufacturing. He additionally pooled all engineering resources into a matrix management structure, forcing MDA's individualists to work on projects that needed them rather than on ones they wanted to pursue. Once done, MDA stood ready to team with Canada's prime space contractor, SPAR Aerospace, and other firms that could help MDA to win larger government procurement contracts in and beyond Canada.

Under Pitts's leadership, MDA entered the American military market by developing an automated weather distribution system (AWDS) for the United States Air Force, a project that turned MDA into a significant government contractor for space-based work worldwide. Long-standing defence sharing agreements between Canada and the United States set the stage for MDA's participation in the development of AWDS, while the company's strategy to win the work involved courting American military contractors then chasing the US budgetary boon created by Ronald Reagan's "Strategic Defense Initiative" (SDI; created March 1983).[58] To win the AWDS contract, Pitts had a consulting firm inventory MDA's personality types, which quickly identified the need to hire personnel who understood the discipline and specification environment of military organizations. New military hires embraced Pitts's strategies, and ambitious managers jumped at the chance to climb the corporate ladder. Others found a niche in new areas, particularly in robotics and geographical positioning systems. When older workers missed technology shifts, managers shuffled them to other areas, preferring instead to hire new and hence cheaper recruits who could help them to rationalize budgets. Older employees grumbled, but few quit. As more students graduated from research universities during the 1980s, MDA had plentiful choices for the company's technical and management tracks. The firm quickly hired more engineers to work on new technology projects, managers to watch those projects, and marketing strategists to expand MDA's (and hence Canada's) surveillance expertise and global economic reach. Chapter 5 explores the changes that Pitts introduced during MDA's refinancing and restructuring, and the reactions that such changes engendered. It also examines the AWDS pursuit as well as some of the painful lessons MDA's personnel had to learn from their first experience as a contractor for the US military.

Pitts also attempted to turn MDA into a mass manufacturer of products outside of government control. To finance the manufacturing plan, Pitts and MDA's board members agreed to seek more capital, including an investment from SPAR Aerospace. No matter his negotiating savvy, business experience, and political connections, however, Pitts fundamentally misunderstood the difficulties of turning expensive systems into manufactured products for a mass audience. He also underestimated what keeping rather than firing the company's founders might mean for the firm's future, particularly ignoring MacDonald's aversion to manufacturing and his abilities to launch behind-the-scenes rebellions of Pitts's plans. Chapter 6 examines this tumultuous period, and the dilemmas Pitts (and MDA) faced with product development.

When the manufacturing plan collapsed, and MDA failed to win a follow-on AWDS contract with the US military, the costs associated with both placed the firm in a tenuous position once again. The loss of the AWDS contract also revealed that MDA's technological enthusiasts and new military hires had failed to see that newer, more efficient machines and software tools had rendered obsolete the mainframe computers and programs MDA had long employed, that MDA had lost its technological edge. At the same time, desires for liquidity mounted among venture capitalists and others who had invested in MDA. Pitts thus busied himself with finding an exit strategy for the private investors who had risked their capital on MDA during the firm's 1982 financial crisis. During 1992, SPAR Aerospace also offered to merge with MDA, but when negotiations ultimately fell apart at the bargaining table, MDA's board members decided to list MDA's shares on Vancouver's Stock Exchange. Chapter 7 chronicles the events that prompted MDA to "go public" for the first time.

Part 3, "The Systems Integrators," examines the period between 1993 and 2012, the era that pushed MDA more deeply into surveillance capitalism and government contracting for militaries worldwide. While Pitts and other investors put together plans to liquidate their holdings, young and aggressive marketing managers and new investors looked for opportunities to profit from the technologies the firm had developed in the previous two decades. Dan Friedmann guided MDA's third stage of development, first as a business area manager, then chief operating officer, and finally CEO. Born into an elite Chilean family and raised in Vancouver, Friedmann completed a degree in electrical engineering and physics at

UBC. Arriving at MDA during 1979, Friedmann initially joined in the enthusiasm of his fellow technology workers, but he wanted to head the firm one day. He therefore pushed himself into management, eventually fusing MacDonald's space-based formula with Pitts's cost-cutting strategies and moving MDA into the evolving world of defence contracting, intelligence work, and secrecy. Friedmann also engineered MDA's first major labour cuts. One new manager justified MDA's austerity measures by arguing that "we're big enough now that we're attracting attention, there are a lot of predators out there, and we are very much like food to a lot" of them so "we have to work really, really hard to protect ourselves," with people at MDA "feeling a lot more pressure to be more efficient." Moreover, he stressed, "We had to change because the world's changing."[59]

By 1995, with the Canadian government slashing defence budgets and MDA's share performance less than satisfactory, Pitts negotiated the sale of MDA to a US competitor, Orbital Sciences Corporation (a satellite manufacturer and launcher heavily involved in American defence). After investing in MDA, Dan Friedmann also emerged as CEO of Orbital's MDA subsidiary. He then helped Orbital to negotiate the acquisition of the robotics division of MDA's major Canadian rival, SPAR Aerospace, which had numbered its days as an independent entity by overextending its own expansionist plans. Pouncing at a propitious moment, Orbital's SPAR acquisition gave MDA the rights to SPAR's *Canadarm* technology and made Orbital's Canadian subsidiary Canada's new aerospace darling. MDA additionally received SPAR's interest in Radarsat International, the data distributor for Canada's *Radarsat* satellites. At the same time, Friedmann moved MDA into the financial, insurance, and real estate services sector by creating a property information business unit to profit from the dot-com, e-business boom. When the dot-com bust forced Orbital to divest several of its subsidiaries during 2001, MDA then returned to a Canadian-owned business. Chapter 8 explores MDA's evolution between 1993 and 2001 and the lessons its executive team learned from the company's role as a US-owned subsidiary.

On increased demands for the development of drones as well as surveillance technologies for the US "Total Information Awareness" (TIA) program following the terrorist attacks of 11 September 2001, MDA expanded more deeply into intelligence gathering and information products for the financial services sector, enjoying the profits associated with the "war on terror" and the global real estate boom. As MDA and its profits became more visible during the early twenty-first century, the firm also came under increasing scrutiny. As MDA's professional staff began to grumble about increasingly lucrative executive packages while their own wages declined and working conditions deteriorated during 2006, MDA experienced its first labour strike. With the Canadian government reviewing several proposals for surveillance work, MDA quickly settled with its workers, but the strike foreshadowed increasing discontent at MDA. By January 2008, MDA also sparked a national controversy when Friedmann announced that board members had voted to sell MDA's surveillance business to an American weapons manufacturer, Alliant Techsystems (ATK). Several of MDA's employees resigned in protest, publicly citing ethical concerns about the proposed sale. Members of the public then joined in the protest, noting that the proposed acquisition would include *Canadarm-2* as well as *Radarsat-2*, the Earth observation satellite MDA had developed, and into which Canadian taxpayers had invested some $430 million before the satellite's launch from Baikonur, Kazakhstan, on 14 December 2007. As pressure mounted, the federal government announced that it had decided, for the first time in the twenty-three-year history of the Investment Canada Act, that the sale of a Canadian firm to a foreign entity was "not in the national interest." Federal Industry Minister Jim Prentice argued that the decision flowed from the critics who had argued that the deal "handed over taxpayer-funded technology and, in the case of *Radarsat-2*, gave away technology designed to protect Canada's sovereignty."[60] Chapter 9 examines MDA's post-9/11 developments as well as the sovereignty issues exposed by the firm's increased visibility.

As MDA wobbled under renewed uncertainty following the real estate meltdown of 2007 and financial crisis of 2008, Friedmann developed strategies to reduce costs, including more labour cuts. Another strike among professional staff followed during 2009, but once again MDA settled the strike and did nothing about salary concerns and conditions of employment. At the same time, Friedmann arranged for the sale of MDA's property information business, and by January 2011, MDA's executive team once again refocused on the surveillance business the company had tried to sell to ATK just three years before. One year later, David Ebner argued that Ottawa's veto of the proposed sale, on "national security grounds," was "a lucky escape from a near disaster." Ebner also noted that "MDA would have suffered if Stephen Harper hadn't intervened."[61] By the end of 2012, Harper's intervention then allowed MDA to acquire California's Space Systems/Loral (SS/L). Although MDA's fate remained uncertain during federal budget negotiations during the winter of 2012–13, Prime Minister Harper stepped in again, securing for the Canadian Space Agency and MDA "hundreds of millions of dollars in new funding to move the next generation of *Radarsat* satellites off the drawing board and into production."[62] Chapter 10 examines MDA's evolution from 2008 through 2012 and the role that the federal government continued to play in the firm's survival and eventual success in the global space sector.

The decision to pursue space and defence contracts flowed from MDA's work in remote sensing during the 1970s, the experience the firm gained in managing large, complex software development projects and the military specification environment during the 1980s, and an aggressive corporate strategy implemented during the 1990s. Like their counterparts elsewhere, people at MDA and in Canada found it difficult to balance their peaceful intentions with larger ambitions. MDA's history therefore provides an additional opportunity to examine debates over critical issues, including the escalating commercialization and militarization of outer space that threaten the sustainability of the Earth and its people. "Unseen, in the Background" explores the trajectory of surveillance capitalism, military contracting, and the rise of the security state, as well as the lessons we might draw from the MDA experience.

1

"A Permanent State of 'Cold War'"

Preparing the Environment, 1940–1968

Between 1940 and 1968, larger world events and the structural forces of capital prepared an environment conducive to launching systems engineering firms in Vancouver, even if Canada's largest West Coast city seemed an unlikely node for the expansion of surveillance capitalism. During World War II, Canada's relationship with the United States deepened through military and economic agreements. In the postwar reconstruction period and first twenty years of the Cold War, additional security and trade agreements then furthered the integration of the North American defence production base, thereby laying the foundations for the expansion of a neoliberal project dominated by the United States as well as pulling Canada into a place of prominence in world affairs. Those agreements also created the context for Canada's increasing dependence upon American business models and policy decisions centred on the privatization of outer space.

At the same time, Canadians faced several unique circumstances of increasing concern. With a population one-tenth that of the United States, Canada's domestic market remained small when compared to other industrialized countries, and its businesses vulnerable to takeover and control, particularly by American capital. With many Canadians working for American subsidiaries, policymakers argued that Canada lacked the infrastructure and managerial skills to compete with more established nation-states. The rise of a separatist movement in the Province of Quebec, regional disparities, and other internal problems also threatened national unity. With the United States and USSR threatening mutually assured destruction, Canadians also worried about their Arctic region, particularly its seaward reaches. If Canada wanted to secure its place as a significant world power, policymakers argued, the country needed to find ways to work with their southern neighbours while simultaneously attempting to unite the country's citizens in common cause. National unity, they argued, depended upon Canada's ability to reconcile national planning with economic liberalization, and to differentiate Canada from the United States through peacekeeping activities, bilateral and multilateral agreements with other nations, incentives to develop domestic expertise and export markets, and the redirection of science and scientists toward the practical needs of industry, urban and regional planning, and international relations.[1]

By 1968, one Science Council of Canada report argued that it had become increasingly "evident that in an era when science and technology are expanding so quickly, change becomes the natural state of human society, and that the institutions and patterns of social organization which characterize that society must either adapt to this change or disappear."[2] Influential Canadians had no intention of disappearing from the world stage, so they began to adapt to the realities of surveillance capitalism, abandoning what political scientist Bruce Smardon has emphasized as Canada's "historical focus on the Canadian domestic market along with their support for tariff protection and domestically centred accumulation strategies."[3] As John MacDonald and Vern Dettwiler wended their way from college freshmen in 1954 to engineering consultants by 1968, they experienced and benefited from that changing focus.

WORLD WAR II AND CANADA'S "SPECIAL ROLE IN THE NORTH AMERICAN DEFENCE INDUSTRIAL BASE"

World War II fundamentally altered Canada's orientation away from its long history as a member of the British Empire and toward a deepening relationship with the United States. As a member of the Commonwealth of Nations, Canada declared war on Nazi Germany during 1939 and quickly mobilized military personnel for the British effort. By 1940, however, some argued that if Britain fell under German control, Canada could quickly follow. US president Franklin Delano Roosevelt therefore reached out to Canadian prime minister William Lyon Mackenzie King, proposing a plan to protect the North American continent should Germany invade Britain. Affixing his signature to the Ogdensburg Agreement, at a meeting with Roosevelt in Heuvelton, New York, on 18 August 1940, King committed Canadians to a "Canada–United States Permanent Joint Board on Defence." Canadian military historian Jack Granatstein has argued that Ogdensburg "marked Canada's definitive move from the British military sphere to the American" one. Although the exigencies of the moment prompted the Ogdensburg Agreement, it quickly deepened Canada's integration into the US economic orbit as well.[4] During 1941, King met with Roosevelt again, this time to formalize arrangements for cooperation in defence production through the Hyde Park Declaration. King justified the declaration by announcing that neither Canada nor the United States had a choice, given the "growing danger of possible unnecessary duplication of production facilities on the North American continent, with consequent undue pressure on scarce labour and materials if Canada and the United States each tried to make itself wholly self-sufficient in the field of war supplies."[5] No matter the critics who worried about the consequences of such an asymmetrical alliance, Roosevelt and King had crafted a strategy that would guide the two nations' military-industrial relationship during and after the war, in what one Canadian ambassador later described as "Canada's special role in the North American defence industrial base."[6]

Shoring up Canada's "special role," King tapped the energies of Clarence Decatur (C.D.) Howe, the powerful Liberal Party Cabinet minister known as the "Minister of Everything" for the role he played in mobilizing Canadian industry to supply the Allies with war materials. Born in Massachusetts in 1886, Howe graduated from MIT in 1907. Making his way to Canada in 1908, Howe soon turned his attention to grain elevators, serving as chief engineer for Canada's Board of Grain Commissioners and founding an enterprise that eventually became the global engineering firm C.D. Howe and Company. As business prospects waned during the Great Depression, Howe entered the political arena, where he quickly exemplified the expanding role that scientists and engineers would play in the federal government's economic development plans.[7]

A member of Parliament from 1935 to 1957, C.D. Howe became the first engineer to serve in the Liberal government and the only businessman in Prime Minister King's Cabinet. Championing the expansion of private enterprise in the Canadian political economy, Howe surrounded himself with Canada's corporate elite and expanded the use of the Crown corporations that had long advanced national goals that seemed beyond the abilities or interests of Canada's private sector. As Canada's minister of munitions and supply from 1941 through 1944, Howe created twenty-eight additional Crown corporations for war production, from those manufacturing machine tools and synthetic rubber to others managing secret research and development projects for national and North American defence.[8] Howe also coordinated the efforts of those working in other federal ministries and agencies, including the National Research Council of Canada (NRC). Established in 1918 to advise the federal government on science and industrial research during World War I, the NRC became Canada's military science and weapons research organization during World War II, where scientists worked with their UK and US counterparts on signals intelligence, optics, radar, submarine detection, chemical and germ warfare, and other war-related projects. Although intelligence gathering remained within the purview of the NRC, Howe orchestrated the transfer of many military research activities to Canada's new Defence Research Board (established during 1946). As minister of reconstruction (1944–48), Howe then dismantled most wartime Crowns, created new ones to serve particular Canadian needs, and expanded the mission of others to encompass profit for international expansion as key to survival. Working with Canada's banking and industrial elite on plans to pull scientific activities and computer-based statistics into Canada's economic growth plans, Howe and others in government also encouraged more private-sector involvement in the business of postwar continental defence.[9]

Canada's participation in world trade organizations exemplified Canada's shifting orientation toward the United States as well. Canadians attended the Bretton Woods Conference in New Hampshire during 1944, where forty-four Allied nations agreed on the rules that would govern monetary policy among independent nation-states and prepare the way for rebuilding the international order under the International Monetary Fund (IMF) and World Bank. Joining the United Nations as a founding member during 1945, Canada then formed Export Development Canada (EDC), a Crown devoted to providing credit to Canadian companies making foreign investments, and created the International Development Bank (IDB) as an arm of the Bank of Canada to foster a Canadian presence in world markets and help small businesses convert from military production to peacetime operations. Howe then bolstered the federal government's commitment to the ongoing liberalization of the Canadian economy by pushing for the creation of the Canadian Commercial Corporation (CCC, formed in 1946), a Crown with a mandate to facilitate international trade on behalf of Canadian industry and direct Canadian capital and aid to war-torn Europe. Howe also announced the creation of another Crown, Canadian Arsenals Limited, the "fourth" service of the nation's armed forces and part of Canada's industrial preparedness planning. Howe argued that Canadian Arsenals, along with the Canadian Army, Navy, and Air Force, would carry joint responsibility for mobilizing Canadian forces "if called upon by the Security Council" and "to keep her covenant" with the UN. Canada kept its covenant with the United States as well, in defence sharing

agreements that specifically restricted Canadian Arsenals from taking profits and ensuring Canada's subordinate role to the United States in continental military-industrial expansion.[10]

While some Canadians discovered oil in Alberta during 1947, others
participated in the UN Conference on Trade and Employment, in meetings that ultimately ushered in the first US-dominated General Agreement on Tariffs and Trade (GATT, in force on 1 January 1948). Along with
twenty-three other Allied nations, Canadians signed on to the GATT in the
hope of "raising standards of living, ensuring full employment and a large
and steadily growing volume of real income and effective demand." As
minister of trade and commerce (1948–57), Howe and other Canadian
policymakers then pledged their allegiance to the GATT's neoliberal agenda by agreeing to a "substantial reduction of tariffs and other trade barriers to trade and to the elimination of discriminatory treatment in international commerce" as well as an increased emphasis on export-driven
strategies and free trade agreements with larger, more established nation-
states rather than state-led, domestic projects and the protection of infant
industries. Because its code on government procurement excluded departments related to national security, the GATT allowed Canada and the United States to expand the North American defence sector without either
country violating its international obligations. Those loopholes then set
the stage for the privatization of Canadian Arsenals and other Crown corporations so that they too could operate like American profit-taking firms
associated with the military-industrial complex.[11]

To increase Canada's international prestige as a "middle power" in
world affairs, Louis St Laurent, the Liberal lawyer who succeeded King in
1948 and served as prime minister until 1957, enthusiastically supported
Canada's role as one of the twelve initial members of the North Atlantic
Treaty Organization (NATO, founded on 4 April 1949). NATO's member
states vowed to increase their expenditures for collective defence and,
under Article 5, to aid any other member state subject to armed attack.
Although NATO did not invoke Article 5 until the terrorist attacks of 11
September 2001, and Canadians hoped to focus on the UN's approach to
international reconciliation, when the USSR completed its first nuclear
test on 29 August 1949, the United States built larger nuclear stockpiles,
and policymakers on both sides of the US-Canadian border amplified the
importance of the defence sector. Canada's federal government thus transformed its Defence Research Board's Communications Branch into the
Defence Research Telecommunications Establishment (DRTE), where scientists embarked upon the radar projects that ultimately led to the development of Canada's *Alouette* satellite.[12]

Between 1950 and 1952, Canada's "special role" expanded even further, with North American agreements increasingly focused on the protection of classified military information, cross-licensing of patents and inventions, sharing of technical know-how, and the standardization of arms and related equipment for continental defence. To manage these agreements, the Canadian government passed the Defence Production Act of 1951 and created a new Department of Defence Production (DDP) to oversee procurement as well as the organization, mobilization, and conservation of Canada's resources to meet current and prospective commitments to continental defence. The federal government also founded new Crown corporations, including the NRC "spin-out," Atomic Energy of Canada (AECL, 1952). Canada additionally entered the Korean War, maintaining a presence in the conflict until the war's end in 1953. Jerome Klassen has argued that the GATT, NATO, and other world trade bodies and military alliances positioned Canada "among the core group of powers that dominate the world system." Even if Canada did little more than supply component parts for the expansion of the US military and its government contractors, joining that group meant increasing government expenditures on the expansion of a Canadian defence sector.[13] As a result, some Canadians began to worry about the forces that had pulled them into increasingly visible military alliances with the superpower United States.

"WHAT SOLDIERS CALL DEFENCE IN DEPTH": CANADA'S AMBIVALENT COLD WAR ALLIANCE

After the United States dropped atomic bombs on the Japanese cities of Hiroshima and Nagasaki during August 1945, George Orwell coined the term *Cold War* to depict an emerging bipolar world order soon dominated on one side by the United States and its allies in NATO and the capitalist West, and on the other by the USSR and its allies in the Warsaw Pact and the communist East. With the two superpowers possessing nuclear weapons that threatened mutually assured destruction (MAD), Orwell argued, "few people have yet considered [the] ideological implications – that is, the kind of world-view, the kind of beliefs, and the social structure that would probably prevail in a state which was at once *unconquerable* and in a permanent state of 'cold war' with its neighbors." Emerging from World War II as members of a sovereign nation, Canadian policymakers had hoped to focus on resource extraction and heavy manufacturing, the peaceful reconstruction of Europe, multilateral security, world trade, and political reconciliation. As a result, deepening Cold War connections worried those already ambivalent about their southern neighbours, particularly when they considered Canada's geographical position vis-à-vis the United States and USSR. Hearing their concerns, Prime Minister St Laurent appointed the Royal Commission on National Development in the Arts, Letters and Sciences (commonly known as the "Massey Commission"), with Canadian diplomat and lawyer Vincent Massey as chair.[14]

When members of the Massey Commission released their report on 1 June 1951, they cautioned that "Canadians, with their customary optimism, may think that the fate of their civilization is in their own hands. So it is," they stressed, "but this young nation, struggling to be itself, must shape its course with an eye to three conditions so familiar that their significance can too easily be ignored." With fears of continentalism and American annexation guiding their deliberations, the Massey Commission report first reminded Canadians that the US population had surpassed 150 million during 1950 while Canada's "population stretches in a narrow and not even continuous ribbon along our frontier – fourteen millions along a five thousand mile front." Furthermore, it warned, with an English-speaking country of "far greater economic strength" attempting to influence Canada in ways "as pervasive as they are friendly, we have not even the advantages of what soldiers call defence in depth." To meet such population, linguistic, and economic challenges, the Massey Commission report therefore made several significant recommendations to avoid "the very present danger of permanent dependence" on "formidable" American influences, including what they perceived as an "invasion" by the American media. "It is in the national interest to give encouragement to institutions which express national feeling, promote common understanding and add to the variety and richness of Canadian life," the report stressed. Future events would test all such assumptions, especially in whose hands Canada's fate depended, but the Massey Commission report convinced many policymakers that Canada needed economic planning and increased federal funding for a Canada Council for the Encouragement of Arts, Letters, Humanities and Social Sciences, scientific research, and universities, highlighting that scientific research "is essential to material well-being and nation security," with universities "the principal sponsors of research in most branches of science, both fundamental and applied."[15]

Inspired by the commission's findings, St Laurent called for immediate funding to Canadian universities. Following a brief economic recession during 1954, the federal government then formed the Canada Council to encourage the country's unique capabilities, thwart American influences on Canadian culture, and avoid a potential brain drain of Canadian technical know-how and talent. Together, the policy priorities of St Laurent and his Liberal government boded well for young John MacDonald and Vern Dettwiler as they embarked upon university careers.[16]

"A PROPER SECOND HOME":
MACDONALD, DETTWILER, AND THE COLD WAR UNIVERSITY

When they entered university in 1954, John MacDonald and Vern Dettwiler encountered an environment that reflected Canada's deepening relationship with the United States as well as the anxieties and prescriptions of the Massey Commission. In Vancouver as elsewhere in Canada, the federal government's commitment to university expansion made it possible for returning World War II veterans to benefit from increased funding for higher education at the University of British Columbia (UBC). Founded in 1908, UBC's enrolment rose from 3,280 in 1940 to 9,374 by 1947, with war veterans constituting half of that number. UBC administrators thus began to construct more than twenty new buildings to accommodate the expansion of the arts and sciences, create new schools and faculties for commerce, forestry, nursing, engineering, pharmacy, and medicine, and recruit new faculty members eager to enhance research opportunities as well as increase enrolments. With a population surpassing 350,000 by 1954, Vancouver's long focus on fish and lumber had also changed. Promoting the city's beautiful location amid harbours and mountains to global tourists, Vancouver's cruise ships announced the birth of an "Orient Line," which included Vancouver in their itineraries for the very first time. To add urbane attractions near the city's 1,001-acre Stanley Park, developers opened the city's first "cocktail bar" at the Sylvia Hotel to welcome tourists and businessmen alike. Vancouver's suburban Richmond converted from a manual telephone system to a dial exchange, and cable television arrived in Horseshoe Bay. The *Province* newspaper commissioned the first composite photo-map of Vancouver's entire Lower Mainland as well, with George Challenger completing his relief map of British Columbia using one million hand-cut pieces of plywood. And UBC completed new buildings to house its facilities for physics, engineering, and the biological sciences.[17]

While eighteen-year-old MacDonald and twenty-one-year-old Dettwiler completed their first semester at UBC during December 1954, they began to navigate Vancouver's evolving environment for economic development, even if neither acknowledged the larger forces preparing them for life as Canadian scientists in the service of capitalist expansion. Indeed, both claimed they had more pressing concerns that year, chief among them how to get home for the winter break. While making their respective plans, neither college freshman knew of the other's existence, but they shared many common traits: both had grown up in northern British Columbia; each had a keen interest in mathematics, the sciences, and engineering; and, as small-town boys, both found city and university life somewhat onerous during their first semester at UBC. Nevertheless, UBC's wide-eyed undergraduates sensed exciting change in the air and hoped to flourish in the new environment created for technological enthusiasts like themselves. As fate would have it, each young man also booked passage on the same train home from Vancouver, initiating a friendship with long-term implications, including those involving new adventures in travel and map-making that transformed not only their own lives, but also those of people in Vancouver and across the world. These and other memories they then shared, in autobiographical accounts that became their foundational narratives, the stuff of myth-making on which they would form MDA, nurture their young recruits, and build the company's cultural tropes.[18]

Born in 1936, John Spencer MacDonald was raised in Prince Rupert, BC, a fishing port on Kaien Island, some thirty miles southeast of Alaska, just north of the mouth of the Skeena River, and linked to BC's northern mainland via a short bridge and the Yellowhead Highway. Canada's "gateway to Alaska" and home to the third-largest ice-free harbour in the world, Prince Rupert had long accommodated ocean-going vessels carrying military personnel venturing into the northern Pacific as well as commercial traffic in coal, grain, lumber, mineral ore, pulp, sulphur, and other cargo destined for international markets. Reared in such a world, MacDonald discovered his penchant for things electronic and the wonders of radio communication. One by one, and initially to the consternation of his family members, MacDonald dismantled and then reassembled every electrical device in the house. Following that, he turned to fish-boat radios. Dismantling and reassembling those, MacDonald soon found work as a repairman; and by eighteen, he had taken on the responsibility for installing the area's fishing fleet LORAN sets, those long-range-navigation, low-frequency radio transmitters noted for their sensitivity to any form of water, and largely displaced by global positioning systems (GPS). As word of his technical prowess spread, MacDonald also realized his calling: he wanted a career in electrical engineering, a profession then gathering momentum as *the* place for those with innate abilities in physics and a knack for electronics. Leafing through literature, MacDonald then found his "proper second home" – UBC's electrical engineering department, which promised proximity to his family, another BC waterfront playground, and faculty members anxious to mentor young men interested in the latest technological developments.[19]

A boat's journey between Vancouver and Prince Rupert traverses a breathtaking 942 miles of coastline through the Strait of Georgia and Queen Charlotte Strait. As a teenager, MacDonald spent many memorable days travelling the spectacular waterway separating Prince Rupert from Vancouver and the larger world. By 1954, however, he decided he should travel on more sophisticated forms of transportation; having never taken a train before, MacDonald thus jumped at the opportunity to ride the rails.[20]

Unlike MacDonald, Vern Dettwiler was a seasoned train traveller, for the rails had long represented the only affordable means for transporting him from his home in BC's interior to other exotic places. Born in Switzerland during 1933, Dettwiler immigrated to Canada with his family during 1945. Making their way west, the Dettwilers eventually settled in Smithers, a small farming community founded in 1913 on the banks of the Bulkley River as the divisional headquarters of the Grand Trunk Pacific Railway. With its site nestled into the foothills of the Hudson Bay Mountain, Smithers ran to the rhythms of the railroad's clock and emerged as a key location for the regional extraction of mineral and agricultural resources. Once there, Dettwiler recalled, mineral resources, railroad timetables, and the stars above nurtured his passions for mathematics, physics, travel, and the many mysteries of the larger universe. He also boasted that railroads played a central role in sustaining his "Swiss propensity for precision and detail."[21]

The train trip between Vancouver and Prince Rupert, by way of Jasper, Alberta, and Smithers, BC, totals some 2,015 kilometres. The first 1,610 kilometres to Smithers devours two full days and nights, with the final stretch a lonely one for those travelling on to Prince Rupert. In December 1954, however, many university students followed the rails, and few found the trip a solitary one. Perhaps some of those travellers even established lifelong friendships. According to shared memories, Dettwiler and Mac-Donald certainly did. The future founders of MDA first met in the dining car, where, amid the clanking plates and chattering crowds, they found common ground in their mutual interest in science and technology. Once returned to UBC for the spring semester of 1955, they resumed the myriad technical debates they had launched during their first train trip together. Throughout their undergraduate studies, the young men then continued those debates, particularly while on the job at UBC's physics laboratories, where both had secured employment to help fund educational expenses and social activities.[22]

Whether cognizant of the transformations taking place around them, MacDonald and Dettwiler had wandered into a university with administrators, faculty, and students revealing at least some interest in Cold War technologies and business speculation. Much of that interest flowed from the US 1944 Servicemen's Readjustment Act (GI Bill), which provided benefits to returning World War II veterans and the larger military-industrial-academic complex transforming scientists and mathematicians into useful Cold War expansionists. In her study of Cold War universities in the United States, Rebecca Lowen has chronicled the ways in which "generous contractual terms provided universities by the federal government during World War II made university administrators eager to perpetuate the relationship with the federal government after the war." By the early 1950s, those administrators included Stanford University's dean of engineering, then provost Frederick Terman, who hoped to build from such relationships a Western high-tech centre that could compete with MIT. Promoting the creation of Stanford Industrial Park, Terman encouraged faculty and graduates to lease land from Stanford so they could win more research contracts from the US Department of Defense. Those firms and their defence contracts then gave birth to Silicon Valley, the incubator for many high-tech firms. Together with other Cold War universities, Stanford thus bequeathed to the world what Lowen has described as "a pervasive scientism, the triumph of the ideal of apolitical expertise. As one of the top recipients of Defense Department patronage," Lowen argued, Stanford became among "the first universities to forge close relationships to private industrial concerns, many of which were developing war-related technologies." US government incentives, as well as Stanford and its Silicon "family tree" of researchers and firms also provided an economic development model for Canadians to emulate.[23]

Developments in postwar computing additionally tied major American corporations to the military-industrial complex. International Business Machines (IBM), for example, had long served as a US government contractor, maintaining employment records for its Social Security Administration. With World War II providing the impetus for the development of the first general purpose electronic computer for the US Army, IBM quickly moved to the forefront of the computer industry. By 1957, IBM sold its first compiler for the FORTRAN scientific programming language. In the years that followed the launch of *Sputnik*, IBM then emerged as an important NASA contractor to support space exploration. As IBM entered the

Canadian market, it dominated Canada's computer industry as well, populating the country with subsidiaries for continental projects and those interested in constructing the architecture of global surveillance.[24]

"STRAIGHT CONTINENTALISM":
SPUTNIK AND SURVEILLANCE CAPITALISM IN NORTH AMERICA

While John MacDonald and Vern Dettwiler settled into their studies at UBC, Canada joined the secret "Five Eyes" intelligence operation, as part of the United Kingdom–United States of America Agreement (UKUSA). A multilateral arrangement between the United Kingdom, United States, and then Canada, Australia, and New Zealand, the Five Eyes community quickly became what Canada's Brigadier-General James S. Cox has described as "the world's most exclusive intelligence sharing club."[25] During 1956, John Diefenbaker also took his place as leader of Canada's Official Opposition and Canada entered into a Canada-US Defence Production Sharing Agreement (DPSA) to guide future cooperation between the two nations. Solidifying their relationship as North American partners in NATO, Canadians and Americans additionally agreed to promote an integrated industrial base, including the interoperability of military equipment, removal of obstacles to free trade in defence, information and technology exchanges, and reciprocal contracting opportunities. The Canadian Commercial Corporation (CCC) then became prime contractor for Canada's defence production sharing procurement, administering all US military service contracts in Canada and deciding which Canadian firms would qualify to join the defence production pool. Promising to level the playing field for all firms demonstrating competitive pricing and technical competence, the CCC nevertheless favoured large corporations, those with the potential to develop export markets for Canadian economic expansion. Together, the DPSA and the CCC thus confirmed Canada's progressive commitment to the United States and its expanding military-industrial complex. In turn, the United States provided the rationales and models for Canada's increasing focus on scientists as useful policy instruments for the expansion of the defence sector as well as other projects deemed central to Canada's interests, including a larger presence in the global economy, the expansion of private-sector involvement in government contracting for defence- and surveillance-based work, and the eventual privatization of many Crown corporations.[26]

Despite these deepening connections, during 1957 Diefenbaker's Progressive Conservative (PC, or Tory) Party won its first minority government in twenty-seven years on promises to reduce trade dependence on the United States and reassert closer ties to the United Kingdom. Toward those ends, Canada participated in the creation of the UN's International Atomic Energy Agency to promote safe, secure, and peaceful nuclear technologies. During 1958, while fears of an escalating arms race prompted the first international protest demanding a ban on nuclear weapons, Diefenbaker then called for another election, promising to open the Canadian North to research exploration and settlement, work more closely with the provinces to create a united Canada, and foster a new "One Canada, where Canadians will have preserved to them the control of their own economic and political destiny" not in an east-west vision but rather in a "Canada of the North." On 31 March 1958, those promises allowed the Tories to win the largest majority victory in Canadian history.[27] Diefenbaker's "One Canada" vision did not slow continental integration, however; indeed, the history of the "Avro Arrow" demonstrates that it expanded.

Prior to *Sputnik*'s launch, Canadians had built a robust aerospace industry, with A.V. Roe Canada (Avro) emerging as the third-largest company in Canada and a major global manufacturer of aircraft. During 1953, Avro's secret design department began to develop an interceptor plane (known as the CF-105 Arrow) for the Royal Canadian Air Force. Armed with missiles, the Arrow promised to serve as a significant Canadian contribution to NATO's Cold War efforts into the 1960s. Unfortunately for those working at Avro, Canada's evolving relationship with the United States quashed the Arrow's completion. "If *Sputnik* was the bait in a propaganda war," historian Michael Sherry has argued, "leading Americans swallowed it whole, naively or for calculated purposes."[28] The military establishment thus shifted its gaze from conventional interceptors to the development of intercontinental ballistic missiles (ICBMs). On 12 May 1958 political officials in the United States and Canada then announced that the two countries had formalized NORAD, the organization charged with "cooperative air defense arrangements as a government-to-government bilateral defense agreement" to protect shared continental interests and assets. Furthering "the political connections which would make possible the longevity of the Canadian-U.S. aerospace defense relationship into future years," the NORAD agreement also resulted in the 1958 Canada-US Defence Production Sharing Programme (DPSP).[29]

Signing the NORAD and DPSP agreements mere months after the United States launched its *Explorer* satellite, Diefenbaker's Conservatives agreed to concentrate Canadian industrial efforts on the production of specialized component parts for the American military rather than attempt to build their own weapons systems, and to waive the federal sales tax for Canadian companies contracting with the US government in defence production. In exchange, the US government waived its 1933 Buy-American protectionist restrictions as well as duties on Canadian defence product imports. Under the DPSP, Canadians and Americans then built radar stations in northern Canada to monitor Soviet activities and warn of possible aerial attacks on the continent. "On both the military and economic sides of this security relationship," one Canadian ambassador recalled, "our policy in Canada has been one of straight continentalism," with the DPSP crystallizing "into something like a common market" for defence cooperation.[30]

Although Diefenbaker cancelled Canada's Arrow fighter aircraft program shortly after Avro Canada began flight tests in 1958, he did not formally announce the decision until 1959, in a speech where he disclosed that a US-built fighter aircraft would fulfill Canada's role in nuclear strike reconnaissance for NATO. Nearly 15,000 employees lost their jobs at Avro, and others in Canada's supply chain and support networks soon followed. The Arrow's cancellation also prompted many of Canada's aerospace engineers and scientists to leave Canada, with some of them accepting employment at NASA. While many decried the loss, others argued that Arrow's cancellation would allow Canada to focus on peacekeeping initiatives rather than further military spending the country could ill afford. Complicating the situation, Canadians began to experience a recessionary period, which lasted through the early 1960s, prompting more ambivalence about Canada's American allies and fuelling increased economic nationalism among those seeking to distance the country from the United States.[31]

Under Diefenbaker's leadership from April 1957 to April 1963, members of the federal government attempted to assuage fears of continentalism by signalling their intention to stimulate business "in the national interest." They provided funding to complete important infrastructure projects, including the transatlantic telephone cable, Trans-Canada Highway, St Lawrence Seaway, and University of Calgary and York University to further Canada's emphasis on applied research in developing industries, including oil and gas as well as computing and satellite communications. Policymakers additionally encouraged border crossings among business representatives as well as scientists, arguing that porous borders promised to transfer experiences and know-how from American businesses, universities, and government laboratories to Canadian ones. During 1963, the Department of Defence Production (DDP) became the central purchasing agency for the federal government's military and civil departments, and made it abundantly clear that "an essential prerequisite to the long term success of the Production Sharing Programme is participation by Canadian companies in Research and Development (R&D) leading to the production of modern defence material." To ensure that Canadian companies improved their participation numbers to serve Canadian sovereignty and economic growth, promoters of the DDP also advised that Canada needed to borrow heavily from American business models to expand Canada's high-technology expertise, particularly in the private sector.[32]

Among the American models Canadians embraced, few stood out more during the late 1950s and early 1960s than those focused on employing science not purely for knowledge's sake, but rather to advance national economic and social goals, and adopting an engineering creed conceived broadly as individualistic, capitalistic, and status conscious. According to Edwin Layton's seminal study of the North American profession, many postwar engineers hailed from small towns and farms, or emerged in cities as outsiders, from immigrant enclaves, first in Northern and Western Europe, and later from other parts of the world. Many arrived from less well-off segments of the population, with fathers who either tended farms and small, localized businesses, or worked in blue-collar and clerical jobs. As a result, engineers in training hoped to scale the ladder of middle-class respectability by capitalizing on their technical abilities and engineering knowledge. Layton's engineers also prided "themselves on being hard-headed practical men concerned only with facts." Seemingly apolitical, they nevertheless tended to share an ideological positivism, including the belief that "material achievements benefit humanity and advance civilization," with scientific methods and technological advances leading "toward universal peace and the brotherhood of man." Additionally, engineers often assumed that, as "professionals," they had a "unique and vital role to play in social progress," utilizing the leadership and "creative role of the technical expert" for capitalist expansion. Still, by the end of the 1950s, engineers perceived themselves as undervalued in status terms: "if only the public were properly informed of the engineer's merits, he would be accorded the deference that was his just due."[33]

When MDA's future founders graduated from UBC in 1959, Dettwiler with a B.Sc. in mathematics and physics, and MacDonald with a B.A.Sc. in electrical engineering, they found a world ready to receive them as well as policymakers anxious to advance Canada's maturing vision of itself in world affairs. Funding more research and development at the University of Toronto and elsewhere, providing summer internships and full-time employment in places such as Atomic Energy of Canada and the National Research Council of Canada, and encouraging Canadians to attend American universities so they could transfer technical and managerial know-how from the United States to a Canadian setting, the federal government had already begun to assemble the institutional architecture for the professional choices and connections that would ultimately determine the roles Dettwiler and MacDonald would play as they wended their way from university laboratories to the founding of MDA.[34]

GETTING "PAID TO DO JIGSAW PUZZLES": DETTWILER LAUNCHES A COMPUTING CAREER

Vern Dettwiler followed the computer's electrical current into software consulting. According to his biographical account, Dettwiler intended to undertake graduate studies in mathematics and physics at UBC following graduation in 1959; however, the moment graduate school commenced, UBC purchased its first "ALWAC III-E" (a computer used as a server to four remote terminal clients of the US National Security Administration between 1954 and 1956). UBC offered no computer courses, but the University's ALWAC III-E sparked one of those rare moments that many successful people experience and later recall as their turning point. Dettwiler's moment arrived in 1959, when, at age twenty-five, he visited UBC's embryonic Computer Centre and sensed an approaching technological tidal wave he very much wanted to ride.[35]

In our age of instant technological gratification, it is easy to forget that the genesis of integrated electronics took place during World War II, with the military playing a decisive role in the development and expansion of the computer industry. Another decade passed before government contractors conceived the "monolithic integrated circuit" – a bar of pure silicon that Texas Instruments' Jack St Clair Kilby fabricated into the first semiconductor circuit during the summer of 1958 – but with the monolithic integrated circuit forming the heart of computers and other electronic gadgets, IBM introduced its first third-generation computer, the 360, during 1965. Thirty years later, global users worked on eight million personal computers, half a million large computers, and millions of microprocessors integrated into other devices. At the dawn of the twenty-first century, that number had expanded more than tenfold. And now, most people find it difficult to imagine a world not intimately wired to global networks, along with a host of personal devices on which to access them.[36]

When UBC's new Computing Centre stirred Dettwiler's imagination, the excitement generated by the new technology made his choices crystal clear: he withdrew from graduate school, took a full-time position with UBC's Computing Centre, and absorbed himself in coding the university's first machine. "If someone would have said, 'We can have this much computer power,' as we have in the PC today, I never would have believed it. That was just beyond all imagination," Dettwiler mused. "In the old Soviet Union, they didn't have as much computer hardware as North Americans had, so they had to do a lot more thinking about how to do some of the calculations. When you have too much hardware," he stressed, "you don't bother thinking, and you just put more hardware on it. We need to take a step back and ask, 'What is the actual problem we're trying to solve?'" An important question indeed, but one Dettwiler asked as part of a reflection on a thirty-five-year career, a hindsight he developed when he realized what his participation had produced. During 1959, Dettwiler noted, he simply "fell in love" and looked forward to what a career in computing promised.[37]

As he began his computing career, Dettwiler saw himself as an apolitical actor, a person interested in solving technical rather than economic or geopolitical problems, but his career received several boosts from the political economy he inhabited, the first of them the unintentional consequences of Canada's recessionary environment. By 1961, high unemployment, a balance of trade deficit with the United States, and an inflow of foreign capital began to alarm Canadians who equated direct investment by American firms with a "branch-plant economy" that seemed to profit the United States at Canada's expense. As evidence, policymakers pointed to a review Canada had received from the OECD, an entity devoted to increasing private-sector involvement in the world economy, and which Canada had joined as a founding member. Cautioning that Canada needed to achieve "a rate of growth of output sufficient to provide full employment for the rapidly growing labour force of the country," the OECD review advised, "While the inflow of foreign capital, accompanied by 'know-how' and new techniques, has contributed to the fast growth of the Canadian economy, foreign direct investment on the scale experienced by Canada may also create problems." To solve such problems, Canadian policymakers needed to re-evaluate the ways in which they managed the economy, the OECD review suggested, including the need to place a greater emphasis on stimulating indigenous industries.[38]

Prior to receiving the OECD's 1961 review, Diefenbaker had appointed a Royal Commission on Government Organization, with Grant J. Glassco, a prominent chartered accountant, as chair. Charged with looking for ways to "improve efficiency, economy, and service in the dispatch of public business," members of the Glassco Commission undertook a study of Canada's government operations, visited the United Kingdom and United States, and released a five-volume report during 1962–63. The Glassco Commission recommended that "government operations can be improved by adopting the methods that have proved effective in the private sector," particularly those centred on the US defence contracting model. It also stressed the need for private-sector advisers and government technocrats to help produce Canada's national science, research, and development policies.[39] Industry leaders concurred, noting that the United States had established "a position of world leadership" in new industries by supporting the transfer of military and space-based research to the private sector. "It is therefore most unlikely that Canadian industry could develop a similar position" in world markets, they noted, "without some government support. Government-supported research is currently undertaken by Canadian universities and government institutions," they stressed, "but the primary thrust of these activities is directed towards scientific advancement rather than being in support of industrial development." As a result, they advised, Canada's "scientific research should be directed toward 'the practical needs of industry.'"[40]

Unfortunately, the Glassco Commission warned, "the most striking fact to emerge from a comparison of defence research expenditures in Canada, the United Kingdom and the United States is the astonishingly small degree to which Canadian industry shares" in the programs that "production for defence might make to the economy as a whole."[41] A later report additionally stressed that the US government "gets about 72% of its R&D done in industry vs. 28% in-house. In Canada, it is done 27% in industry vs. 73% in-house." As a result, "in a composite ranking of four performance indicators of technological innovation in ten countries," the United States "placed first and Canada last."[42] Policymakers therefore recommended that Canada "contract out" more research and development from government laboratories to the private sector, and adopt a national science policy to improve communications and collaborations between government departments and agencies, universities, and industry.[43]

In the meantime, "Diefenbaker's recession" allowed Lester B. Pearson and the Liberals to regain control of the government during 1963. By the time he emerged as prime minister, Pearson had already gained international prominence. A professor of history turned civil servant and diplomat, Pearson became Canada's first director of signals intelligence and secretary of state for external affairs in St Laurent's Liberal government, playing a significant role in the founding of the UN and NATO. Heading the Canadian delegation to the UN from 1946 through 1956, Pearson also won the Noble Prize for proposing and sponsoring the resolution to create the UN's emergency force that ended the 1956 Suez Crisis. Once elected prime minister, Pearson and his Liberal minority focused on international peacekeeping and the rule of law as well as national unity and security to quell a rising Quebec separatist movement. To build national unity, the federal government introduced many significant changes in Canada, including a universal health care system that soon became the envy of the world, a Canada Pension Plan, and the Order of Canada to recognize outstanding achievements and service to the nation. The first Canadian prime minister to make a state visit to France, Pearson also spearheaded Canada's Royal Commission on Bilingualism and Biculturalism, and began to implement Glassco Commission recommendations as well as the neoliberal policies of the US-led GATT, which included the creation of the Economic Council of Canada, a Crown corporation established under the Economic Council of Canada Act of 1963 to provide advice on how to improve Canada's economic standing in the world.[44]

As the Canadian economy began to rebound under Pearson's Liberals, it once again appeared that the federal government planned to implement national policies to distance Canada from American influences. The federal government increased funding for higher education and provided generous student loans as antidotes to the potential of an American-induced brain drain of Canadian talent. During 1963, it also created a Department of Industry, which quickly absorbed many of the Department of Defence Production's industry development responsibilities to reconcile an increasingly liberalized market with government intervention to advance Canadian objectives. The creation of a Science Secretariat followed in 1964, inaugurating what Canadian policy analysts would later describe as a "golden age of science policy in Canada." Canada also joined the International Telecommunications Satellite Consortium (Intelsat), a public-private partnership headquartered in Luxembourg and involving Canada, the United States, and sixteen other countries. During 1965, NASA then launched Canada's *Alouette-2* as well as *Intelsat-1* (nicknamed *Early Bird* for "the early bird gets the worm," the first commercial satellite placed into geostationary orbit over the Atlantic Ocean at the equator, and starting a process that provided nearly global communications coverage by 1969, in launches that allowed more than 600 million television viewers to witness the first American to set foot on the moon on 20 July 1969).

Although *Alouette-2* and *Intelsat-1* required the launch facilities of NASA, both reflected Canada's desire to negotiate agreements that could provide a fairer share of space-based profits to a nation lacking the scale and scope of the domestic market Americans enjoyed.[45]

Pearson also signed the Canada–United States Automotive Agreement (Auto Pact) during 1965. According to historian Dimitry Anastakis, the Auto Pact "completely integrated the two nations' sectors, knocking down the tariff walls that had once protected Canada's industry from its gigantic southern counterpart." With automakers in Canada no longer representing branch plants in the traditional sense, Anastakis argues, "foreign ownership and continental economic integration were the very reasons that Canadians were able to expect and extract their fair share of the industry." Anastakis's insightful work has demonstrated "how states of asymmetrical military or economic power interact and negotiate outcomes beneficial to their own interests." In many ways, however, the Auto Pact merely furthered relationships already operating within the North American defence sector, one focused on computing, satellite launches, and defence-related work that ultimately rendered traditional manufacturing sectors less significant to the country's economic future and priorities. Indeed, two years prior to the Auto Pact, Canada entered into the Defence Development Sharing Arrangement (DDSA) with the United States, not only to increase Canada's "fair share" of defence production and stimulate satellite developments and the computer industry, but also to improve Canada's cross-border trade balance with the United States.[46]

The escalating conflict in Vietnam provided additional opportunities to create more autonomy for Canada. Among the strategies deployed during the bipolar struggle for global supremacy, the United States and USSR engaged in widespread and ongoing use of psychological warfare, proxy wars, espionage, propaganda campaigns, conventional and nuclear arms races, and rivalries associated with the space race. Canadians fought in the Korean War, but when the Vietnam War commenced, the federal government attempted to remain neutral, even if it did little to stop the flow of military supplies, raw materials, and intelligence to the United States. Still, relations between the two nations began to deteriorate. During 1964, Pearson officially announced that Canada would not participate in the military conflict in Southeast Asia. The following year, when he received the World Peace Prize at Temple University, Pearson then increased tensions by giving an acceptance speech that included a mild rebuke of American policy and bombing in Vietnam. Thereafter, Pearson's Liberal Party encouraged highly skilled American Vietnam War draft dodgers to relocate to Canada, stimulated university research and the proliferation of Canadian-owned firms focused on "useful" science, abolished capital punishment in Canada, and promoted arms control through the UN. Together, these developments fostered an economic boom in Canada: unemployment fell to its lowest rate in more than a decade, and the federal government began to institute a forty-hour work week, mandatory two-week vacations, and a minimum wage.[47]

Asserting the "national interest," Pearson's government created the Science Council of Canada during 1966 (formally incorporating it in 1969), charging the new entity with hiring consultants from the scientific community and industry to produce studies aimed at Canadian sovereignty in defence, aerospace, and computing. Science Council reports quickly provided Canadians with a "regular 'diet' of technology policy studies" recommending that Canadian autonomy depended on funding more industrial and university R&D so that Canadians could "become more creative and develop more wealth." Federal funding, they promised, would create plentiful employment for Canadian scientists and engineers, generate new income, and stimulate the "spin-off effects" that American companies and regions enjoyed from government-funded research and development under US defence and space programs.[48]

Among the plethora of reports produced during the mid-1960s, one examined the computer industry. Although the global computer industry remained in infancy, one minister argued that it had already emerged as "the world's fastest growing and may well surpass even the giant automobile and petroleum industries before the turn of the century." While Canada rapidly became "one of the world's best *customers* for computing systems and software," he observed, it had not gained "a commensurate share of the *world market* for computer products and services. Of perhaps greater concern," he stressed, Canada had not developed "*indigenous Canadian skills* in the application of computers to meet our particular business and industrial needs." In computer products and systems alone, Canadian trade imbalances with the United States had reached $85 million, he stressed, with some predicting that if Canada did not develop its own industry the imbalance would reach $450 million by 1975.[49] "In 1949 Canadians owned abroad $4 billion less than foreigners owned in Canada," another minister argued; by 1967, however, that figure had reached $24 billion, making Canada "more vulnerable than it is often supposed. If foreign owners decide to repatriate large parts of their holdings in Canada," he warned, "their move would have a very depressing effect on the value of the Canadian dollar."[50] Others additionally raised the spectre of the Avro Arrow and the brain drain it had engendered. "Due to the strong multinational nature of [the computer] industry, there had been considerable difficulty in providing sufficiently challenging and productive jobs, with a promising future in Canada," one analyst observed. Consequently, "many of our highly trained and competent people tend to move to other countries," creating "a wide gap in entrepreneurial skills available in Canada," he stressed.[51]

Federal discussions about developing "indigenous Canadian skills" in computing arrived at an auspicious moment for Vern Dettwiler, who spent one of his twelve years at UBC's Computing Centre as department head. While running the organization between 1964 and 1965, Dettwiler witnessed increasing industrial demand for the computer knowledge housed within UBC's Computing Centre. That demand soon turned into opportunities for moonlighting as a computer consultant. As his consulting work increased, Dettwiler also discovered that solving industrial problems satisfied him more than his role as the centre's principal administrator. Before a year had passed, he stepped down as department head and requested a position better suited to his personality and talents: director of the Computing Centre's new projects group. The road from neophyte computer programmer, through administrator, and on to director of new projects took eight years and some soul searching, but at age thirty-three, Dettwiler had learned important things about himself. Perceiving himself as a gifted "techie," Dettwiler concluded that he definitely lacked the desire and agility for administration. He also noted the increasing pleasure he derived from his love of computer knowledge, his desire to acquire much more of it, and the possibility that consulting provided to make his knowledge useful to industry.[52] Whether or not he appreciated it at the time, Dettwiler had powerful champions in the federal government among those crafting policies and incentives to turn his dreams into reality.

By 1968, Dettwiler thought it possible that a creative consultant such as he could build a company based upon his expertise in the computer industry, one that might allow him to get "paid to do jigsaw puzzles," make enough money to "do neat things" in software and hardware development, and enjoy the status his technical expertise accorded.[53] For many young technological enthusiasts turned Dettwiler disciples, "Vern" also emerged as an ideal mentor, a generous sage who enjoyed explaining technical concepts no matter the hour or time involved. One engineer argued that he and others "learned more at Vern's elbow than anybody" they had ever worked with, and in ways that "certainly stood" them "in good stead in years later, both in hardware and software."[54] Dettwiler also displayed some of the classic attributes of the creative genius. Solitary in many ways, often disorganized in his work habits, and preoccupied with technical problems, Dettwiler knew he needed a different kind of visionary if he wanted to realize his expanding dream about launching a company based on his technical expertise and consulting experience. He found that someone in UBC alumnus and old friend John Spencer MacDonald.[55]

"A GRAND, ALBEIT PREMATURE DREAM": MACDONALD LAUNCHES AN ACADEMIC CAREER

In a land of introverts, the extrovert is king, and in contrast to many scientists, engineers, and technocrats, John S. MacDonald casts an impressive shadow. At six feet, five inches, MacDonald has towered above the crowd since his teens, attracting people's attention with his probing gaze, booming voice, boisterous laugh, boundless enthusiasm, and confidence in his own abilities and ideas. Along with his technical expertise, that self-assurance promised to carry MacDonald down any path he hoped to travel. MacDonald later claimed that by the time he entered his second year of study in UBC's engineering program during 1955, he knew what he wanted to do with his life: teach, at the university level, where he could spread the technical faith he had imbibed from his own experiences and professors in his midst. As he tutored fellow students as an undergraduate, putting innovative technical ideas together and finding it relatively easy to convert those around him, MacDonald also discovered his affinity for the role. Thus, MacDonald pursued an academic career with a singleness of purpose unmatched by others in his cohort, applying to graduate school as his undergraduate studies came to a close. Although he remembered being accepted by several engineering departments in Canada and the United States, MacDonald gravitated toward MIT, where the technical excitement in and around Cambridge promised to catapult him into worlds far beyond Vancouver.[56]

When he entered MIT during the fall of 1959, MacDonald found himself at the centre of the United States' most important Cold War university, an institution Vannevar Bush and others had already turned into the largest US academic defence contractor. An electrical engineer, Vannevar Bush played a leading role in the development of the atomic bomb while heading the US Office for Scientific Research and Development (OSRD). During 1950, he then participated in the creation of the American National Science Foundation (NSF), the US government agency charged with supporting non-medical research "to promote the progress of science" and "to secure the national defense."[57] As a professor at MIT, Bush trained many young men interested in systems devoted to American military-industrial expansion, including Frederick Terman, the engineer long associated with William Shockley and the birth of Silicon Valley. According to Adam Brate, Bush also "popularized the idea that machines could solve the problem of *information overload.*" Bush worried about what might happen to digital records once created, but he also hoped his proposed technologies could thwart their uses for unethical and immoral purposes. As his OSRD legacy suggests, however, the best of intentions can lead to dire consequences; and when MacDonald walked the halls of MIT, he not only entered a world full of Vannevar Bush's hope for a better tomorrow, but also the world's most significant "war technology think tank."[58]

While studying at MIT between 1959 and 1964, John MacDonald also lived in a country experiencing extraordinary political change. *Sputnik* and other Soviet feats had increased American efforts to sell the NASA space program, in ways best exemplified by presidential candidate John F. Kennedy's famous nomination acceptance speech at the 1960 Democratic National Convention. "We stand today on the edge of a New Frontier – the frontier of the 1960s, the frontier of unknown opportunities and perils, the frontier of unfilled hopes and unfilled threats. Beyond that frontier are uncharted areas of science and space," he stressed, as well as "unsolved problems of peace and war, unconquered problems of ignorance and prejudice, unanswered questions of poverty and surplus."[59] Defeating Republican challenger Richard M. Nixon on his soaring rhetoric, Kennedy ascended to the presidency of the United States. In 1961, Dwight D. Eisenhower then delivered his cautionary farewell address about the military-industrial complex while Kennedy got on with the business of the New Frontier, which soon included plans to reach the moon within a decade. "No nation which expects to be the leader of other nations can expect to stay behind in this race for space," Kennedy argued. He therefore called for increased funding for NASA and other space-based initiatives; and, on 31 August 1962, Kennedy signed into law the US Communications Satellite Act, with the stated goal of establishing a US-led satellite system in cooperation with other nations.[60]

The vast majority of Americans rallied to Kennedy's positive message rather than Eisenhower's pessimistic warning, reaching to popular science and history for inspiration about American exceptionalism. Gregory Schrempp has argued that popular science writing has provided "a primary arena for the creation of contemporary mythology" and "an ultimate moral ground, a validation and justification of an accepted or prevailing way of life and scheme of values." In a chapter devoted to Carl Sagan's *Pale Blue Dot*, "a manifesto of support for continued space exploration and for humans ultimately colonizing the cosmos," Schrempp demonstrates the ways in which the "glitzy" visual aids of the Earth that NASA and Sagan produced helped to promote the role of science, engineering, and space exploration as significant to our sense of destiny as a species. The space race also supplied the rationale for American military expansion, with *democracy* and *freedom* the code words that allowed members of the American military-industrial complex to pursue their ultimate goal: the demolition of alternatives to capitalism.[61]

Many Canadians embraced a different sense of destiny, evidenced by their reactions to NASA's 1962 launch of *Alouette-1*, the satellite that promised to reveal the unique characteristics of radio communication in the Canadian North. Members of the SPAR division of de Havilland Aircraft of Canada had developed missile components and other advanced aerospace products, but during the construction of *Alouette-1*, SPAR built the satellite's mechanical frame and Storable Tubular Extendible Member (STEM) products, the satellite antennas that gave SPAR its start in the commercial space sector and Canadians a reason to celebrate their country's role as an international power broker interested in the peaceful applications of space. Reflecting those self-perceptions during 1962, Prime Minister Diefenbaker opposed the apartheid policies in South Africa, encouraged the sale of wheat to the People's Republic of China, initially refused to put Canadian forces on alert during the Cuban Missile Crisis, and declined the invitation to accept nuclear weapons from the United States. Ultimately, however, the Canadian government acquiesced; Canada maintained its military alert status with the United States, and Prime Minister Pearson decided to accept nuclear weapons for armed forces during 1963. Under Diefenbaker, Canada also established an annual Defence Program High Technology Conference to provide Canadian industry with opportunities to participate "in new cooperative programs in NATO and the developed world, as well as increased sales to friendly countries in the third world."[62] Diefenbaker's government additionally foreshadowed the inherent difficulties Canada and other small countries would face when attempting to extricate themselves from more powerful allies by signing the Canada-US Defence Development Sharing Agreement (DDSA) "to jointly fund research and development" activities.[63]

With the USSR exposing the contradictions between American perceptions and postwar realities, the Civil Rights Movement also peaked during MacDonald's final days at MIT, ushering in challenges to racial discrimination, segregation practices, and other forms of political and social inequality in the United States. The choice between Cold War priorities and domestic issues created unending imbroglios for Kennedy and his successors, as Lyndon B. Johnson tragically learned when he assumed the presidency following Kennedy's assassination in 1963. Although Johnson could point to his Great Society program, complete with the Civil Rights Act of 1964 and legislation for public broadcasting, federal funding for education, and the "War on Poverty," his administration escalated American involvement in Vietnam (from 16,000 advisors and soldiers in 1963 to 550,000 combat troops by 1968). These compromises not only tarnished Johnson's accomplishments, but also revealed the limits of American power and the government's control over the military-industrial complex.[64]

In the meantime, John MacDonald completed his graduate work in 1964. During his five years at MIT, MacDonald's interests had ranged widely, but the larger environment he inhabited, as well as the passions he developed, ultimately pushed him toward optics and biological systems, experimental studies of handwriting waveforms and signals, electronic simulators, and the long-term potential of the human-machine interface. Undertaking much of his doctoral work at MIT's interdepartmental Research Laboratory of Electronics, MacDonald also found plentiful funds to complete his PhD, with his doctoral thesis acknowledging the US Army, Navy, and Air Force grants that supported his research. Suggesting that he remained apolitical during and beyond graduate school, MacDonald could not have failed to notice the connections between the expansion of the American military-industrial-academic complex and his own scholarly activities and research agenda. He and other engineers would eventually have to reconcile such complex and sometimes contradictory connections, no matter where they travelled after graduation, from MIT and other schools focused on Cold War technological developments.[65]

During graduate school, MacDonald also joined an expanding throng of bright and eager young men anxious to fulfill their promise as professional engineers and teaching-scholars. According to his recollections, MacDonald's keen intellect and winning personality gave him a critical edge, and he quickly rose through the ranks of graduate teaching assistants and instructors. Honing his skills as an orator, MacDonald also recalled that he quickly drew a following, among undergraduates and graduate students alike, as well as professors in multiple disciplines.[66] When he received his PhD from MIT during 1964, his star rose even higher, into a prestigious, two-year post-doctoral teaching fellowship from the Ford Foundation, whose leaders wanted to help the United States win the Cold

War's "technology contest" against the USSR by investing in applied science and universities undertaking military projects.[67] MacDonald's fellowship included a tour of other universities, instituted by the Ford Foundation as a way for young hopefuls to realize full-time, tenure-track positions at top-flight engineering schools. During 1965, MacDonald visited Stanford and other schools, but he also signed on for one at his alma mater, UBC. In many respects, he viewed his journey to the Pacific Northwest as little more than a paid trip home to see his parents. When he arrived at the end of February, however, Vancouver had matured substantially under the thirteen-year stewardship of W.A.C. Bennett, British Columbia's premier, leader of the province's Social Credit Party, and "pay-as-you-go" fiscal conservative whose governments had created several provincial Crown corporations during MacDonald's absence, including BC Hydro, as well as extended the reach of post-secondary education to BC's second and third degree-granting universities, the University of Victoria and Simon Fraser University.[68]

With a metropolitan population surpassing 800,000, a city hall proudly displaying Canada's new flag, and Simon Fraser University nearing completion on Burnaby Mountain, Vancouver was on the cusp of more change when MacDonald arrived for his interview at UBC. He also found the city experiencing one of its revered early February springs, complete with sun shining, flowers blooming, and people in shirt sleeves lolloping along the seawall. Thus, when UBC's head of electrical engineering offered MacDonald a position as an assistant professor, the newly minted doctor of philosophy and Ford Foundation scholar claimed that he paused only seconds before accepting the post. Packing up his young family during the summer of 1965, MacDonald returned to Canada and a tenure-track career that commenced at UBC in September. According to MacDonald, he returned to Vancouver with a "grand, albeit premature dream. I had this vision that one could build a world-class technical entity at UBC analogous to what I had experienced at MIT. I did, in fact, realize the dream," he stressed, "but not in the way I had intended." During 1965, circumstances along Vancouver's Trans-Canada Highway differed markedly from Boston's Route 128: although a good school, "UBC was no MIT"; and Vancouver was not yet a world-class city like Boston. Neither school nor city had the infrastructure to advance MacDonald's vision, including government contracts to bolster technological development, and the critical mass of engineers, venture capitalists, and expansionists to drive such dreams. In distant Vancouver, UBC had only just begun to capture some of Canada's share of resources for advanced research. And, importantly, Mac-

Donald lacked the experience and networks to pull resources, people, and ideas together. Like many idealists, MacDonald was also impatient for results, often alienating some of the people he thought should help him. Finding scarce resources to realize his expansive research agenda, never mind his more expansive dreams, MacDonald had to satisfy himself in the classroom, at least for a time.[69]

As MacDonald settled into his academic career, Lester Pearson announced his decision to step down as prime minister following the 1967 International and Universal Exposition (Expo 67) in Montreal, and SPAR became an independent, private firm, soon emerging as the chosen instrument for securing Canadian sovereignty in telecommunications. At the 1968 Liberal leadership convention, Pierre Elliott Trudeau bolstered SPAR's new role by announcing, "Liberalism is the philosophy for our time, because it does not try to conserve every tradition of the past, because it does not apply to new problems the old doctrinaire solutions." Trudeau additionally asserted his willingness "to experiment and innovate" on the assumption that "the past is less important than the future."[70] Embracing the neoliberal project associated with the GATT and OECD reviews, Trudeau's forward-looking philosophy helped the Liberal Party to gain a majority government and to define Canada's destiny as a country seeking peaceful solutions to the world's many problems, including a preference for détente and the non-proliferation of nuclear weapons, as well as a welfare state capable of implementating universal health care and regional development programs as critical for maintaining Canadian independence, unity, and a more just society.[71]

Although Canada emerged as the world's sixth-largest exporter of capital for overseas investments and loans by 1968, just behind the United States, United Kingdom, France, West Germany, and Switzerland, members of Trudeau's government argued that the country needed to tackle the problem of foreign direct investment in key Canadian industries and resources. As a result, the federal government established the Canada Development Corporation (CDC), a Crown devoted to the stimulation of Canadian industry. Trudeau then appointed Cabinet Minister Herbert ("Herb") Gray to craft legislation to monitor foreign investment and control of Canadian firms. And the Liberal Party began to reform Canada's income tax structure, including incentives to encourage the further development of Canadian-owned firms. The federal government also unified the Canadian Navy, Army, and Air Force under the Department of National Defence, reorganized several ministerial and department responsibilities, and announced the creation of the Department of Supply and Services (DSS), which absorbed most branches of the Department of Defence Production. Thereafter, the federal government established the Canadian Radio-Television Commission (CRTC) to guarantee Canadian ownership and control of its broadcasting system. Perceiving that international trade agreements had created winners and losers, the federal government also established a General Adjustment Assistance Program (GAAP) "to assist firms adversely affected" by the sixth session (known as the Kennedy Round, and named for the assassinated US president) of the GATT's trade negotiations in Geneva between 1964 and 1967. The GAAP helped to reorganize Toronto's faltering Consolidated Computers, Inc., allowing the firm to increase export sales, conserve "230 jobs" for highly skilled technologists in a "critical industry sector," and establish "a base for further domestic development of computer technology." The early success of GAAP and other assistance programs then provided incentives to form computer-based, Canadian-owned companies elsewhere in the country.[72]

While the Canadian government instituted changes promising to increase Canada's ownership and control over the nation's future, John MacDonald's academic frustrations increased; still, it took three critical issues to arouse in the young professor a desire to push his MIT vision from UBC into the private sector. First, it seemed that no matter his fervour, UBC's administration blocked MacDonald's ambitions and caused disappointment no end. Second, the assistant professor started to realize that he "was really made to build systems," but UBC had neither the facilities to house nor the money to fund such adventures. Unlike what he had experienced at MIT, including plentiful and cutting-edge machinery on which to test his theories, UBC often supplied obsolete equipment. When resources finally arrived, rather than a cadre of graduate students to assist him, callow undergraduates constituted MacDonald's labour force. "Because these kids were doing everything for the first time," he recalled, "of course they screwed it up," bungling assigned tasks or breaking the few pieces of equipment he had received. Looking for systems challenges, MacDonald ultimately decided to let private clients fund his efforts.[73]

Like Dettwiler and others before him, MacDonald began to moonlight as a private consultant, dabbling in various projects, including an electronic slot machine design. Once involved in what he deemed "not only proper engineering but also fitting creative work," MacDonald began to rethink his future. His third concern then sealed the imperative of change. While teaching, MacDonald observed that he had many gifted students, "real hot rocks," he called them. Yet, once they graduated, those talented students had but two choices: either they had to leave Vancouver (often

BC, and sometimes even Canada) for want of challenging work; or "they disappeared into" public utilities, "never to be heard from again." Knowing the talent existed, and fearing his best students might suffer the utility fate, MacDonald thought about starting a business where his able students could take on the imaginative, challenging work they craved. He claimed that seed capital, in the form of government incentives and contracting work, did not enter into his calculations during 1968, but the labour of students certainly did. Inspiring his students to work with him on consulting jobs, MacDonald soon decided that he might realize his MIT dream after all, not through UBC but rather by starting his own firm. His ideas also meshed with government debates on science and industrial policies, including the brain-drain concerns then percolating throughout Canadian society and at all levels of government.[74]

In their volume on entrepreneurial activity, strategic management professors Claudia Bird Schoonhoven and Elaine Romanelli have argued, "New organizations do not emerge *de novo* from the idiosyncratic and isolated inventions of individual entrepreneurs." Rather, their "ideas for new organizations, their ability to acquire capital and other important material and human resources, and their new organization's likelihood of survival derive from the contexts in which individuals work and live." The experiences of MacDonald and Dettwiler resonate with these findings, even if many of their contexts were far from local. Still, both young men learned much about business opportunities from local consulting work, educational organizations, and friendships that predated the formation of MDA. Moreover, both possessed the intellectual and ideological leanings, ethnic and personal qualities, and technical talents that caught the attention of local businessmen willing and able to pull them into larger networks.[75]

When he returned to Vancouver, John MacDonald looked up old friends, including Vern Dettwiler. By 1965, Dettwiler was well established at UBC, running new projects, moonlighting as a computer consultant, and teaching a course in multiprocessor systems. MacDonald sat in on Dettwiler's course, and the two had lunch together now and again. By 1968, as MacDonald's frustration increased, lunches with Dettwiler became more frequent, as did the idea of forming a company. Over time, it seemed they talked of little else. One summer's evening, MacDonald then found himself in Dettwiler's living room, where his old friend sat visiting with two other men, each of whom ran a small company in Vancouver. After MacDonald and Dettwiler had exhausted the other two with endless banter about the possibility of launching a technology firm, one of Dettwiler's friends could take it no more. Remembering the scene with great fondness, MacDonald recollected that when a short silence provided an opening, Dettwiler's friend barked, "For God's sake, why don't you guys get off top-dead centre and do it!" Why not indeed? With a little imagination, it seemed clear to both MacDonald and Dettwiler that they could get some business advice, start a small company, hire bright students, have fun doing work they enjoyed, and maybe even make some money. After all, they had secure jobs at UBC, could start part-time, and see what happened. "The objective was to do the kind of work we wanted to do," MacDonald recalled. "I knew there was all this horsepower that wanted to stay here, so I thought we could hire these bright kids to join us, we could do work at a world-class level, and that was really all there was to it in the beginning stages."[76]

That founding vision and the unbounded possibilities it offered quickly infected those who encountered MacDonald, Dettwiler, and their young associates. On maturing reflection, one former employee also saw MacDonald as very shrewd: "Basically, you have in Vancouver a very desirable place to live. If one emigrates from Europe with no previous connections in Canada, and if you look at a map and the statistics, you may decide you want to move to Vancouver." As a result, "there was and is a continuing availability of talent, not only homegrown, but also immigrant." Before MDA's launch, "you had to leave to get a job." John MacDonald "perceived that the talent wanted to be here, and he believed that there was no reason why you couldn't do engineering here as well as elsewhere." MacDonald and Dettwiler buttressed that perception by giving their associates the "room to demonstrate their own kind of excellence."[77] The door to that first "room" soon opened, not in Vern Dettwiler's living room, but in John MacDonald's basement. Chapter 2 explores the firm's basement beginnings and the early software work that set the stage for the kind of firm MDA might become.

PART ONE

The Technology Enthusiasts

2

"Our Knowledge Is in the Holes"

Software Consulting and the
Sweat-Equity Formula, 1968–1977

In business, as in life, timing is critical, with many firms founded in precisely the right place at precisely the right time. No different, MacDonald and Dettwiler found themselves in a city and region "bounded by the resources and cultural understandings of the local," which included business networks established by members of Vancouver's infant electronics industry as well as civil engineers aplenty but few heavy manufacturing facilities, never mind capabilities to design computer systems and software programs. Still, by 1968, British Columbia's population surpassed two million (with more than one million clustered in the Lower Mainland), and Vancouver's new $32 million International Airport had opened for use, both of which expanded opportunities to solve problems attended by change. The wider world was also poised upon a watershed moment in the computer industry, where hardware and software separated into distinct business lines, thereby ushering in the rapid expansion of the software sector. MacDonald's and Dettwiler's technical expertise and university affiliations thus gave them instant credibility among those searching for the competitive edge that software solutions might provide.[1]

Canada's increasing integration into a North American defence-industrial base, along with concerns about American ownership of the Canadian economy, provided additional incentives to MacDonald and Dettwiler as they ventured from academic moonlighting to business careers. Supporting private-sector involvement in research and development to encourage Canadian sovereignty, the federal government introduced assistance programs to foster the creation of domestic computer and communications sectors, including those associated with the 1967 Industrial Research and Development Incentives Act (IRDIA), which provided tax-free grants or credits against federal income tax liabilities for scientific research and development in Canada. According to one working group on "Stimulation Policies to Increase the Canadian Presence," IRDIA's programs "enabled many small firms to remain in business that would otherwise have collapsed."[2] The federal government additionally commissioned a plethora of business-friendly panels and study groups with linkages to the Departments of National Defence and Supply and Services, charging them with making recommendations on how best to stimulate Canadian exports. One report on telecommunications, for example, argued that government supports for Canadian exports could "insure" that "a rapidly growing industrial research and development organization in Canada" would become "primarily a burden to the Canadian tax payer rather than to the individual company."[3] In remote Vancouver, the federal government's commitment to tax incentives and public funding for the privatization of industrial research and development in computing and telecommunications thus signalled that policymakers intended to reward those who could apply their scientific knowledge for economic development.

The discovery of oil and gas in Alberta during the 1950s also set the stage for an economic boom in Western Canada and strategies to protect the mining, oil, and gas sectors as key national interests. To safeguard Canadian-controlled companies in these and other industries, the federal government passed a bill to establish the Canada Development Corporation (CDC), the "vehicle through which Canadian entrepreneurs, investors and managers may significantly influence the future development of Canada for their benefit and the benefit of all Canadians." Created to address the problem of foreign ownership in the Canadian economy, the CDC generated opportunities for those who could provide computer solutions for Canada's public utilities and resource sector as well as regional development and diversification plans. Those opportunities also helped to lure technical personnel to the private sector from the security of academic jobs and the public dissemination of scientific research as well as employment focused on government laboratories, Crown corporations, public oversight, and collective interests.[4]

Imbibing an engineering culture framed by wilful innocence, sweat equity, technological "cool," and unstructured workplaces as the cornerstone of organizational change, MacDonald and Dettwiler began their business careers in a Cold War environment where few challenged capitalism's "creative destruction"; indeed, most in their cohort bolstered its expansion by making research-and-development "skunk works" organizationally "hip," and uncompensated work the badge one wore and price one paid to participate in exciting technological change. MacDonald's MIT experiences and maturing vision reinforced those trends. When they invited university students and others into MacDonald's basement, MacDonald and Dettwiler transformed their young associates into extended family members as well as "partners" on the technological "frontier," in a universe where one's commitment to engineering excellence dominated. Between 1968 and 1969, MacDonald and Dettwiler undertook their first important consulting job with two other young associates, made important business and legal contacts, began to hire UBC students, learned how to run a small software consultancy, and found a niche in supervisory control systems. In the process, John MacDonald also found the leadership role he craved to connect his university-based vision with Vancouver's and Canada's expansion.[5]

Officially incorporating their little firm in February 1969, MacDonald, Dettwiler and Associates (MDA) expanded into more complex software development projects between 1970 and 1977, creating computer systems for Vancouver's burgeoning telecommunications sector, Western Canada's oil and gas industry, and other businesses. With each consulting job requiring increased levels of complexity, the firm hired more technical staff and a general manager to handle day-to-day operations, some of them from Vancouver, and others from John MacDonald's far-flung networks at MIT and in Ottawa. Perceiving themselves as apolitical actors, practical men with an interest in solving little more than technical problems, MDA's technological enthusiasts worked with anyone willing to contract with them and provide opportunities to acquire new skills. They also learned how to negotiate contracts, first locally, then regionally and internationally. On expanding demands for the company's expertise, MDA built its first generic product for future pipeline work, and then ventured into automated systems for map-generation, manufacturing, publishing, data collection, and prescription delivery firms, as well as the airline industry. As a result, MDA helped to expand Vancouver's industrial base and planted the seeds of the region's computer-based industry. The firm confronted new issues as well, including those centred on the problems attended by under-bidding on jobs and the use of sweat equity to make up for the financial losses that early expansion engendered. Although few at MDA seemed to appreciate the geopolitical environment in which they worked, they also served Canada's national interests, as a computer-based, economic development tool. Eventually, circumstances forced the firm's employees to recognize their larger role, but during the company's first decade, technological feats mattered more than any other reality.

"SYSTEM BUILDER":
SUBTERRANEAN OPERATIONS AT THE LOCAL LEVEL

While larger circumstances created the context for MDA's founding, Mac-Donald and Dettwiler perceived the opportunities presented to them, in what Richard Florida has identified as the localization of intellectual capital and the knowledge clusters already present within their larger environment. They also recognized they could solve a company's problems with creative and affordable computer solutions. When their patrons realized returns in the form of a competitive edge, they increased demand for MacDonald's and Dettwiler's off-campus activities. Sometimes they worked together, but more often than not, Dettwiler worked alone and MacDonald employed student researchers to extend his efforts. No matter the blend, however, consulting proved a win-win proposition: local companies increased productivity and lowered costs; MacDonald and Dettwiler made their scientific knowledge productive; and university researchers as well as students gained valuable industry experience. Whether they could sustain a business on their industrial activity remained another question. They needed test cases. The first one emerged in moonlight form during the fall of 1968.[6]

The opportunity for MacDonald and Dettwiler to create a full-fledged business came from Lenkurt Electric Company of Canada, a Vancouver-based telecommunications manufacturer owned by British Columbia Telephone, which wanted a better supervisory control system to oversee the operation and performance of telephone microwave links, pipe and power lines, and other conduits. If something went wrong or a fault occurred on the line, the supervisory control system watching the main system sent warning signals to operators along the line. Before the computer's introduction, however, relays and hard-wired logic technologies dominated the supervisory control field; and this situation forced Lenkurt to employ traditional technologies when providing supervisory control systems for BC Tel's microwave links. Perceiving a threat from rivals, but having neither real-time computer expertise nor plentiful funds to hire from outside Vancouver, Lenkurt Electric searched locally. As an assistant professor, Mac-Donald involved himself in myriad local activities, among them a membership in Vancouver's chapter of the Institute for Electronics and Electrical Engineers (IEEE). Jack Abas, a salesman for Lenkurt Electric, also attended many IEEE meetings. One evening, Abas approached MacDonald and explained Lenkurt's dilemma. As prime contractor for BC Tel, Lenkurt had received a contract to build the Northern Interprovincial Radio System (NIPRS) alarm and control system. BC Tel wanted a system controlled by Vancouver's main machine as well as from remote locations throughout the province. Lenkurt had supervisory control expertise, but the company lacked the necessary know-how to complete a computer-based project.[7]

Exploiting his own reputation as well as Dettwiler's, MacDonald proposed that Lenkurt hire the two consultants and two young research associates he had hired to work on a university-based project: Ken Morin, a software specialist; and Ron Spilsbury, a digital circuit technician. "Lenkurt really stuck its neck out for us," MacDonald recalled. "The company put its bets on four guys with no industrial background. If the computers didn't work, the system wouldn't work. They could easily have gone elsewhere, but they were willing to take a calculated risk."[8] For the Lenkurt team, however, the benefits of collaborating with two technical experts from UBC far outweighed any costs associated with their lack of business knowledge; and that calculation convinced MacDonald and Dettwiler that they could form a small company to do the work. It also settled a few other matters. On the one hand, the young team had no capital start-up costs, because Lenkurt supplied the PDP-8I computer used on the project, but they needed a workshop to house it. They thus set up the computer in MacDonald's basement, because his was larger than Dettwiler's. On the other hand, they needed money from their first contract to build up a bank account for their fledging operation, so they decided to forego paying themselves beyond small compensation for each person's efforts. None of them minded the deferral of financial returns, for at last they had something they could call their own, challenging and fun work in an underground bunker where they could spend evenings and weekends programming the PDP-8I.[9]

Enthusiasm overflowed the informal basement setting as the four consultants embarked on their first task. During the conceptual stage, they came up with an innovative technical idea, one MacDonald labelled the "system builder" and Lenkurt later coined the "51G." Behind the concept lay the promise of customization for telephone technicians, a "system builder" they could program themselves to meet their specific needs. MacDonald designed the system interface. With Spilsbury's assistance, Dettwiler developed the software. And Morin planned and implemented the "51G." The system builder's successful implementation made programming accessible at remote locations, increased operating efficiencies, reduced costs, and established the consulting group's competencies in designing and developing supervisory control system software. Work on the project also resolved issues about the company's formation.[10]

As technical innovators, the four consultants quickly learned an important business canon, which MacDonald liked to cite: "To be creative, you have to be an optimist. To be a businessman, you have to be a realist."[11] Despite MacDonald's magnetic personality, and Dettwiler's aptitude for solving industrial problems, the group's environment revolved around creativity and optimism. According to the firm's founders, they designed it that way, as part of MacDonald's long-term dream for UBC and Vancouver, and on MacDonald's and Dettwiler's desire to create an environment where they could undertake exciting technical work. Still, the associates started their business as a part-time operation, a basement skunk works. To survive, they needed a leader, someone willing to coordinate the project as well as act as ambassador for the team. Because they had based their work on MacDonald's and Dettwiler's reputations, Morin and Spilsbury soon found themselves relegated to technical paths. Dettwiler knew his bent and wanted little part in management. That left MacDonald. Although he had no more business experience than his partners, Mac-Donald clearly wanted control, had the connections and personality for the role, and declared his willingness to take on the responsibility. With the NIPRS project providing the gratification they craved, MacDonald's partners therefore consigned their control to the thirty-three-year-old professor, selecting him as the group's commander and giving him ultimate authority over – as well as the responsibility for – business decisions. All hoped to achieve consensus, but they also agreed that MacDonald could make the final call if and when disputes surfaced.[12]

Moonlighting on the NIPRS project, and the group's need for an official name to receive the first payment provided the incentive for MacDonald to seek legal counsel and a business mentor. As an undergraduate, Mac-Donald had roomed and cultivated a friendship with Peter Butler, a young man who soon took his place among Vancouver's pre-eminent litigation lawyers. By late 1968, Butler's brother, Michael, had moved to Vancouver as well, from a corporate law practice in Toronto. As a member of Canada's East Coast constitutive legal environment and former director and lawyer for the Canadian subsidiary of one of Silicon Valley's high-tech ventures, Michael Butler had experience with technical innovators and understood that lawyers do more than simply launch corporations. They also create corporate tropes and what sociologists Mark Suchman, Daniel Steward, and Clifford Westfall have described as the institutional framework for "understanding and reproducing socially constructed reality," the environmental "toolkit" of "institutional scripts and labels" that undergird basic knowledge about what constitutes a contract, intellectual property rights, and other agreements.[13] Michael Butler arrived in Vancouver, and at John MacDonald's home, in this privileged position, and during his first meeting with MacDonald, Butler knew he had found a special client, a person worth nurturing. Exceptionally bright, MacDonald radiated promise, and although he rarely saw the others, Butler sensed that Dettwiler was some sort of a technical genius MacDonald had "locked away in the cupboard somewhere" in the basement to work on portentous projects. Thus, when MacDonald asked for help, stating that the young technological innovators had no money and needed a name, Butler proffered his services as legal counsellor.[14]

MacDonald "was very good at exposing what he was doing to the world," Butler argued, and together with Dettwiler, the young academic had created "a genius environment. It was a creative environment. In other situations, I would call it entrepreneurial, but I would call this one creative. Entrepreneurial includes creative, whereas creative doesn't necessarily include entrepreneurial." As legal counsellor, "gatekeeper," and "matchmaker," Butler proposed a low-cost package that convinced the young associates they needed federal incorporation, advice that stemmed, at least in part, from Butler's recent arrival in Vancouver. Not yet comfortable with the British Columbia Companies Act, Butler promoted the federal one. But Butler also recognized that if MDA wanted to survive, the company needed the critical imprimatur of federal incorporation to position itself for federal grants and potentially lucrative government contracts in the export market. Butler's legal package reminded all concerned that the infant enterprise remained very much a local entity; however, federal incorporation helped to push the young associates into dreaming about an appropriate name for a more expansive future.[15]

With Butler's advice, the group pitched to Canada's Consumer and Corporate Affairs several possible names, including "Maverick" and other fun and attention-grabbing novelties. Following each proposal, however, word came back that the associates had suggested a name either too vague or already in existence as an American firm. In the end, with Lenkurt's goading and clever name ideas dwindling, Ron Spilsbury suggested that the group should capitalize on the names of their senior partners. They thus submitted the more formal "MacDonald, Dettwiler and Associates Ltd." MacDonald worried that his own common name would prove a sticking point, but Consumer and Corporate Affairs at last issued the decree: permission to use the name if the young computer consultants promised to take responsibility for any confusion that might surface with Dettwiler's butcher shop in Montreal. The distinction seemed clear enough; ergo, on

3 February 1969, the group received their letters patent incorporating "MacDonald, Dettwiler and Associates Ltd" as a private company. Although they appreciated the value of capitalizing on the reputations of MacDonald and Dettwiler, the name "MacDonald, Dettwiler and Associates Ltd" still seemed too stiff for what the founders perceived as an innovative and free-wheeling firm. Thus, founders as well as people who came into contact with the young associates dubbed the company MDA, a moniker that endured. The name aside, MacDonald, Dettwiler, and their young associates had started a *real* company. They retained Butler as legal counsel, hired an accountant, and elected officers (MacDonald, president; Dettwiler, executive vice-president; Spilsbury, first vice-president and secretary-treasurer; and Morin second vice-president). MDA then opened a bank account, Lenkurt paid the first invoice, and MacDonald concentrated on getting other sorts of business advice. As it turned out, several would-be mentors awaited his calls.[16]

MacDonald searched for business mentors among people in the electronics industry who might volunteer their assistance; and in the company's infancy, two local entrepreneurs played particularly significant roles. Jim Spilsbury, Ron's father, came forward first. A radio devotee who ran a small communications business called Spilsbury and Tindall (later Spilsbury Communications), Jim Spilsbury wanted to assist his son and the young professor. MacDonald respected the elder Spilsbury and called often for advice; however, his second local advisor, William H. (Bill) Thompson, became both the company's abiding business coach and MacDonald's closest confidant. When MacDonald returned from Boston, Bill Thompson had established himself as Vancouver's electronics "guru," "business community mentor," and father confessor to young industrial hopefuls. As president of L.A. Varah (Vancouver's main electronics component distributor), Thompson made sure he knew every person connected with the industry and chaperoned many business pursuits. As each technical parvenu arrived in town, Thompson reached out to offer career, business-related, and personal advice. When he met MacDonald, Thompson already had a cluster of young men in his stable of business advisees. But he delighted in making room for another, especially one whose energy positively shook the scales. At the same time, Thompson impressed MacDonald beyond measure. In Thompson, he not only found a personable businessman (something many technical people, including MacDonald, deem an oxymoron), but also someone who seemed to understand and sanction his vision.[17]

MDA's youthful exuberance, part-time bootstrap activity, and skunk-works operation made it conspicuous among Vancouver's start-up firms. MDA's founders and first recruits were all technically talented, "extremely bright, wide-eyed innocents without an ounce of business experience." Technology-obsessed, they worked with little supervision, if any, and according to those who watched MDA during early years, they were also "very genuine," "eager to please," and "high-energy" individualists who saw themselves as "horizon gazers." Their enthusiasm made them fun to work with, but when Mac-Donald realized what that dynamic might entail over time, he turned to Thompson, the only real businessman he knew as a trusted friend. Older than the others, initially detached from MDA's underground operations, and familiar with business strategies, Thompson shared his wisdom with Mac-Donald and remained a company luminary throughout MDA's first thirteen years, initially as a helpful outsider, then board member.[18]

MDA's young partners agreed that they needed Thompson's guidance, but they could not afford to pay him. Thompson therefore offered to exchange his services for a say in the company, arguing that, given the risks involved, he preferred to consult rather than invest in the fledgling firm. As a result, when they met at their first board meeting on 10 April 1969, MDA's founders appointed Thompson as a non-shareholding company director. They also allotted themselves shares. With 995 Class B shares at one dollar each, MacDonald bought 345, making him MDA's largest share-holder (with 34.7 per cent). Dettwiler procured 260 shares, giving him a 26.1 per cent stake in the firm. Morin and Spilsbury purchased what remained: 214 shares (21.5 per cent), and 176 shares (17.7 per cent), respectively.[19] For MacDonald, that April meeting gave MDA new meaning. At last, his lofty dreams seemed within reach. Thompson's age and business experience gave him a quiet confidence, and over the years he helped many engineering innocents realize their business and leadership potential, inside as well as (and especially) beyond MDA. He also confined himself to the familiar and never involved himself in technical issues. Unfortunately, as an older man without computing expertise or a financial stake in the firm, Thompson found much of his business advice rebuffed, and his soft-spoken, unsolicited exhortations frequently fuelling resentment among MDA's expanding set of youthfully ebullient technology enthusiasts, most who preferred trial-by-fire over Thompson's more conservative approach. It therefore took years, and a few good blazes, before Thompson's wisdom finally stuck. Nonetheless, he made his presence felt, particularly during MDA's early years.[20]

One summer evening during 1969, as he stopped by to check on the Lenkurt project, Thompson found MacDonald, Dettwiler, Spilsbury, and Morin, as usual, going at their tasks "hammer and tong." After the associates regaled him with their latest exploits, Thompson realized they had begun to erect something beyond the "system builder" concept. They had launched a systems-based company. Tough by any measure, systems projects are expensive, take years to develop, and do not necessarily lend themselves to product development for mass consumption. Still, by late spring, other requests for MDA's services emerged, first from Lenkurt, and then from another firm. Fearing that the four associates had begun to stretch their capacity, Thompson took MacDonald aside, telling the young scholar that with technology and the market in constant motion, every company must eventually enlarge its operations to take advantage of economies of scale. Failing that, he warned, firms shrink in scale, scope, and influence while competitors follow the logic of Joseph Schumpeter's "creative destruction." Thompson also explained that if a firm expands, the company inevitably outgrows each person's abilities to direct it. Once those realities seemed to sink in, Thompson then predicted the order in which MDA would outgrow its founders' abilities to manage expansion, with MacDonald last in the chain. The young professor thought Thompson's words made theoretical sense. More portentously, he clung to the prediction that he represented the "last" founding manager, for last had no boundaries. Taking solace in his longevity, and invigorated by the evening's chat, MacDonald returned to his basement skunk works less apprehensive about the future. After all, he reflected, his MIT-based vision not only remained intact; potentially, it also meant that MacDonald could employ an infinite number of his most promising students.[21]

MacDonald savoured time spent with Thompson, for whenever they talked he found fresh ideas connected to his vision; however, he had not envisioned the need to discuss business expansion. Indeed, neither MacDonald nor Dettwiler began with aspirations of building a big company. "When we started the company, making money was not a primary concern," Dettwiler recalled. "Money was a means to an end, and the end was to have fun." As a result, from MacDonald's first exchange with Thompson, most debates at MDA centred on the expansion Thompson envisioned, which included diversifying the company base to include product development. Whether they liked it or not, however, Thompson understood that the little firm was born to a world where MDA's founders had to expand, particularly if they wanted to sustain the research-oriented environment both MacDonald and Dettwiler craved. Moreover, although business expansion and product development were neither inevitable nor a foregone conclusion, events quickly confirmed that MDA's early business advisers had laid the foundations for both.[22]

"I KNOW HOW TO FIND A GOOD ENGINEER": CREATING A RESEARCH-ORIENTED TEAM

Following MDA's incorporation, word about the company's university-affiliated expertise spread swiftly in Vancouver's small electronics community. If computing problems posed market barriers, people heard what to do: call UBC or knock on John MacDonald's basement door. While many colleagues encouraged the young innovators and the university tolerated their activities, MacDonald and Dettwiler argued that UBC did not expressly champion the MDA cause. Regardless, UBC donated significant help, even if on a much smaller scale than what MIT and Stanford provided to their spinoff firms. To enhance national and provincial ambitions for more university-industry collaborations, UBC's Computing Centre undertook some commercial work with MDA and hired Dettwiler and MacDonald as faculty consultants. UBC administrators also permitted them to use the university's computers and facilities free of charge, saving the infant consulting firm a sizeable capital expenditure as well as the weight of substantial debt. UBC additionally provided MDA with scholarly cachet and an expanding supply of workers eager to participate in the company's projects. Indeed, MacDonald told his best students that he and Dettwiler had formed MDA so they could provide an exciting, Vancouver-based employment option. Looking to gain industry experience, most of MacDonald's students, and then others beyond his classrooms, jumped at the opportunity to participate in the firm's success.[23]

Within six months, Gil Hobrough, owner and president of Hobrough Ltd, a firm subsequently called Gestalt and ultimately acquired by SPAR Aerospace, provided MDA with its first chance to hire one of MacDonald's promising students. In his mid-fifties during 1969, Hobrough developed techniques for ortho-photographic generation (automating the map-generation process). Like Lenkurt, Hobrough perceived the need for an automated computer control system to manufacture his products, but he had no in-house computing expertise and encountered market barriers that motivated him to seek the assistance of consultants with the skills he lacked. MacDonald assured Hobrough that MDA could solve the problem, but Hobrough argued that he needed an in-house consultant. As a result, MDA offered Barry Crawley, one of MacDonald's students, a chance to

"live" inside Hobrough, so he could gain valuable experience while helping Hobrough move his original invention through production for manufacturing. The Crawley hire did nothing to cramp MDA's workspace in
MacDonald's basement, but Dettwiler recalled that it certainly induced
new concerns: "It was like buying your first house. You put in the offer,
the offer is accepted, and then you say, 'Well, now what are we going to
do?'" For the first time, salaries, unemployment insurance, and income tax
deductions became tangible issues. Despite nervous moments, however,
the associates soon learned the process, and their first hire proved a boon
to the young consulting firm. Hobrough appreciated Crawley's skills, and
within a short time, he hired him away from MDA. All concerned agreed
that Crawley's success at finding a job within Vancouver validated Mac-
Donald's vision and completed a milestone for MDA: the young company's first asset transfer.[24]

MDA hired its second university student, Stanley Semrau, in the summer of 1969. MacDonald first met Semrau when the sixteen-year-old
entered his computer programming work in the 1968 Vancouver Science
Fair, the first of its kind in BC and part of the Canada-wide science fairs
that debuted in Ottawa during 1962. Semrau's project won him first
place, and MacDonald took an immediate interest in the teenager's
work. MacDonald always believed MDA's ultimate success depended on
its ability to do quality work, and that implied hiring world-class people.
He has also boasted that he "always had a nose for technical talent. My
performance in selecting accountants, and things like that, is very
mediocre," he conceded, "but engineers, I know how to find a good engineer." Thus, when staffing requirements on the Lenkurt project necessitated additional hands during the summer, MacDonald approached Semrau. While not MacDonald's student, Semrau knew Dettwiler from UBC's
Computing Centre, wanted to work with the Swiss technical master, and
seemed a natural for MDA. Exceptionally bright, self-motivated, thor-
oughly naive, and already in his second year in computer science and
mathematics at UBC, Semrau found MacDonald's basement and "system
builder" work intoxicating. He therefore decided he could adapt to the
consultants' subterranean operation.[25]

Semrau emulated the exertions and idiosyncrasies of his elders, and his
hire marked the first recognition that MDA was a curious mutation. It fast
became an underground research laboratory, start-up business, and quirky
extension of John MacDonald's family, a place where Semrau and other
technology enthusiasts could see themselves as "pragmatic problem-
solvers," "pioneering" champions of progress, and an "entrepreneurial,"

"extremely committed," "self-confident," "loyal," and "desperate-to-deliver" bunch of "shoot-from-the-hip cowboys" who "embraced problems" and "never really believed that anything was impossible." During the summer of 1969, Semrau spent most daylight hours working under the trees in MacDonald's backyard. At nightfall, he descended into the basement. When classes at UBC resumed in the fall, he continued to work part-time, after the others had gone and as MacDonald's young family slept overhead. Remaining in the basement, Semrau often worked through the night. If exhausted, he "slept several hours on the nearest couch, or went upstairs and crawled into a vacant bed." Coming and going as he pleased, Semrau began to suspect that he and others had an "unusual" employment arrangement. As professional engineers and members of Peter Drucker's new knowledge economy, MDA's young associates believed that their technical expertise gave them an ownership stake in the company's future.[26] Living on the West Coast, MDA's engineers also tended to decry the establishment (meaning Toronto, Ottawa, and Ontario-centred government contractors such as SPAR Aerospace). The young associates nevertheless conformed to the engineering creed Edwin Layton has described. In a deliberately unstructured environment focused on, even obsessed with individualism, professional status, and technological firsts in the service of research and development, engineers at MDA generally expressed conservative assumptions about labour and other challenges to the status quo, with MacDonald and later company leaders declaring that "a union would ruin the whole thing. If you were to take a poll," MacDonald declared, "95 per cent of [us] would say, 'I quit' if you brought a union here."[27]

Management professor Diane Burton has argued that such "early employment related choices – which crystallize organizational culture, authority relations, and routines concerning work – are among the most difficult to undo." As company president, MacDonald nurtured that sense of shared professional destiny, in ways that had a lasting influence over the firm and the high-tech community that MDA's basement beginnings launched.[28] Not only could individual eccentricities exist at MDA. MacDonald and Dettwiler encouraged them to flourish, for such quirks promised to bootstrap MDA's endeavours on the part-time efforts of its founders and the all-consuming energies, cooperation, and sweat equity of university students and recent graduates. Although many of MDA's engineers failed to appreciate (or at least to admit) that many engineering firms started this way during the 1960s, their own version of engineering "cool" emulated the casual dress and other accoutrements of the counterculture washing over the United States, Canada, and the rest of the expansionist West. Indeed, their unconventional work style served capitalism very well as they began to conform to an expanding standard of sweated work and planned obsolescence in the service of the status quo.[29]

While MDA settled into this routine, Lenkurt's NIPRS project answered two important questions about the firm. First, did MDA have a viable business? By the time they had finished the Lenkurt project in November 1969, the associates had two additional jobs booked, which convinced MacDonald there was demand for the business. Thus, while Vancouver's Lower Mainland population finally surpassed one million, Boeing's 747 jumbo jet debuted in Everett, Washington, and the Don't Make a Wave Committee (the precursor to Greenpeace) organized throughout Vancouver to protest underground nuclear testing in the United States during 1970, the associates decided that they had a business concept they could nurture on the Pacific Northwest's expansion and the energies of a new generation of stargazers and MDA disciples. Second, did they know how to run a business? The answer to the second question was not so obvious. As MacDonald later recalled, however, "The answer was more 'no' than 'yes'"; the MDA team therefore decided that if they wanted to establish themselves as members of a serious business (one others would take seriously), the time had arrived to move above ground as well as hire a general manager to run the business and help them to negotiate expansion. Whether they realized it or not, the federal government had provided support structures and incentives for both moves.[30]

"THE FULL MEANING OF START-UP":
TELECOMMUNICATIONS AND THE EXPORT MARKET

During 1969, the federal government established the Export Development Corporation, a Crown charged with developing Canada's export trade, making loans to foreign buyers of Canadian capital equipment and services on terms and conditions competitive with those of other major trading nations, insuring Canadian firms against non-payment on products and services sold abroad, and guaranteeing financial institutions against investment losses. One year later, the federal government supplemented the EDC by passing both the Regional Development Incentives Act (RDIA) to subsidize firms investing in less-developed regions of Canada, as well as the International Development Research Centre Act, which established the International Development Research Centre, a Crown with a mandate to initiate, encourage, support, and conduct "research into the problems of the developing regions of the world" by adapting Canadian "scientific, technical and other knowledge to those regions."[31] Still, as one federal minister cautioned, "Ottawa's efforts should not be regarded as a crutch" or "a substitute for dynamism on the part of Canadian business and industry. It is there to assist momentum and initiative, imagination and innovation, expertise and excellence," particularly in the one "area in which there seems to be a falling down on the part of Canadian industry, and that is in the field of development and research." With the assistance of their governments, he noted, industrialists in Japan and the United States had conducted some 60 and 70 per cent of their country's total research and development, respectively, compared to Canada's 37 per cent. This, the minister argued, had to change if Canada hoped to compete. He therefore recommended the creation of better linkages between industry and university researchers so that all could focus on the useful applications of technological developments rather than scientific knowledge for its own sake.[32]

Although policymakers expected business to take the lead in research and development in the days ahead, the federal government established the Canadian Radio-Television Commission during 1968 to ensure Canadian ownership and control of the nation's broadcasting system. With the formation of the Department of Communications, the federal government then passed the Telesat Canada Act of 1969, creating Telesat Canada to provide satellite services to all of Canada. As Laurence Mussio's work reveals, Canadian policymakers embraced the computer as a "national utility," devoting energy and funding to telecommunications as a key industry in the service of the national interest.[33] To spur the development of a Canadian telecommunications sector, the new minister of communications also set up the Telecommission to provide a series of studies that drew inspiration from Peter Drucker's work on the "knowledge economy" and the OECD's 1969 review of Canadian science policy. One of those reports noted that the rapid development of telecommunications and computer technologies, "and the fading distinction between them, would lead to what was variously termed the post-industrial or information society," thereby giving "rise to profound social, economic, and perhaps political changes." Because the OECD review had recommended the creation of a "Ministry of the Future" to nurture the development of national science policies as well as articulate the significance of private-sector and university-based research for economic development, both federal and provincial governments also set up task forces "to equip themselves with as much expertise as each could afford."[34]

By 1970, Trudeau's Liberal government additionally initiated a National Policy Convention, a forum to address the computer's priority in Canadian life as well as the foreign takeovers that had created the context for perceived brain drains and a lack of entrepreneurial and managerial talent in Canada's high-technology sectors. As plans for the conference unfolded, many argued that Canada needed to supplement the 1965 Program for the Advancement of Industrial Research, as well as IRDIA and RDIA, to develop an indigenous computing capability, not only for domestic purposes but also to reach more deeply into the export market. Following the Government Organization Act of 1969, the federal government then attached the Science Secretariat to the Treasury Board, the Cabinet committee of the Queen's Privy Council of Canada responsible for accountability and ethics, financial, personnel and administrative management, comptrollership, regulations, and most orders-in-council. The federal government also approved the incorporation of the Science Council of Canada to serve Canada's evolving industrial strategy.[35]

These and other federal initiatives created the context for MDA's aboveground operations and expansion into the telecommunications sector. Ken Morin selected the company's new premises, a small second-floor office in Vancouver's Film Exchange Building on West 12th Avenue and Yew Street. Located kitty-corner to a brewery, the Film Exchange housed a photographic laboratory, dance and bridge clubs, parapsychological associations, and what MDA's associates considered "other peculiar enterprises" that fit perfectly with their unconventional operation. The new office encompassed a space approximately 20 feet by 10 feet. Within the area's centre, the "office" contained a general manager's suite-in-miniature. It lacked a window to the outer world, but at least it had a door. The second-floor office came at the right price as well, and was available for January 1970. The partners only had to sign a one-year lease, so they concluded that if anything went wrong, at least they could minimize their losses. Moreover, because none of the four founding members believed that their initial accomplishments warranted giving up the security of their full-time jobs, they deemed the office an ideal size to house any full-time employees they might hire. If MDA expanded and the space proved inadequate, they could always lease more of it.[36]

Established contacts proved beneficial in securing full-time staff for the second-floor operation. This time, MacDonald extended his reach, first to people he encountered at MIT between 1959 and 1965, and then to others he met in Ottawa, at Atomic Energy Canada Limited, the federal Crown corporation charged with managing Canada's national nuclear energy

and research development program. MacDonald had secured employment at AECL during the summers of 1958 and 1959, the intervals between his third and fourth year at UBC and between his graduation and
arrival at MIT. Most people he met on those jobs were deeply invested in
the computer revolution and Cold War capitalist expansion, including
Jack Richardson, a former MacDonald student at MIT who provided MDA
with its first full-time technical employee. By late 1969, Richardson had
emerged as second-in-command at Digital Equipment Corporation (DEC)
of Canada, an Ontario branch of the firm MIT's Ken Olsen and Harlan
Anderson had formed along Boston's high-tech corridor during 1957.
Like DEC's founders, Richardson tapped into his MIT networks and DEC's
international offices when his Ontario operation needed employees.
Thus, when MacDonald told him that MDA needed a good person,
Richardson immediately offered, "The guy you want is Bill Renwick."[37]

A former DEC employee with solid credentials in software engineering,
William (Bill) Renwick had just completed his master's degree in electrical engineering at Imperial College, London. Having nothing to offer
Renwick in the Canadian subsidiary, Richardson attempted to find something at DEC headquarters, but Renwick rejected the prospect. Originally
from Vancouver and wanting to return to the Pacific Northwest, Renwick
decided that MDA could provide him with a viable alternative to American employment. When MacDonald sent him a letter of offer during the
latter part of 1969, Renwick agreed to meet with MacDonald and his associates when in town during December. Like MacDonald before him, once
in Vancouver, Renwick needed little convincing. He returned to Ontario,
packed his bags, moved to Vancouver, and commenced his work at MDA
during the latter part of January 1970.[38]

As MDA's first full-time engineer and occupant of the company's new
office, Renwick spent his first work day in shock. Arriving from a well-
established Ontario firm via an elite British university, both of which furnished all the amenities, Renwick opened a space with "one and a half
rooms, and both absolutely bare, save for a pile of semi-rotten curtains"
deposited in one corner. Initially asking, "What have I done?" Renwick
quickly adjusted his expectations. "The view from the university was that
the only place you could get work was at UBC, BC Hydro, BC Tel, or in the
US," he remembered, but "you'd start to hear about this place called Mac-
Donald Dettwiler, that John had a company out there, somewhere, doing
something, and you didn't really know much about it, but that was sure
as heck the place to be." Renwick thus cleared the hurdle of "learning the
full meaning of start-up" and immersed himself in a much-needed shop-

ping spree. He bought a desk and office supplies, arranged for MDA's first telephone connection, and settled into his new role at the Film Exchange. Hired to work with Dettwiler on the company's Lenkurt job, Renwick learned how to duplicate Dettwiler's systems code and convert the original NIPRS software into "something the rest of the world could understand." The ability to make "sense" of Dettwiler's code while also setting a standard for high-quality workmanship made Renwick an important figure in the technical realm. For MDA to survive its early expansion, however, the company also needed a full-time administrator.[39]

When he began to search for someone with management experience, MacDonald turned to Colin Lennox, a person he had met during his summer work at AECL in Ottawa. By 1965, Lennox had moved from Ottawa to AECL's Whiteshell Laboratories in Pinawa, Manitoba, where he directed a group working on control systems and small transportable nuclear reactors for Canada's Arctic. Trained as an engineer, Lennox drifted into management, where he became an able strategist for the government. As part of his AECL responsibilities, Lennox recruited students from Western Canada's universities. While doing so, he learned that he could count on MacDonald to recommend top-notch engineering graduates. From 1965 forward, the two met regularly and developed a strong friendship. Thus, when MacDonald realized he needed to hire a full-time manager during the NIPRS contract, he immediately thought of Lennox.[40]

In a series of long-distance telephone calls between Vancouver and Pinawa, MacDonald and Lennox compiled a "likely candidate" list, and MacDonald came up with most of his ideas about whom MDA should hire just before bedding down for the night. That meant he called Lennox around 11 p.m. (or 1 a.m. Manitoba time). Lennox endured the little eccentricity, but the process and late-night calls dragged on, with MacDonald complaining that the few he could afford to hire lacked lustre, while most of the candidates he liked thought the West Coast venture too risky or Vancouver too parochial. Even the few willing to take a chance on the embryonic firm either wanted more money than MacDonald could afford, or MacDonald refused to provide them with a share in MDA's ownership in exchange for their management expertise. And on the issue of ownership and control, MacDonald could not and would not compromise. After weeks of disappointment and discussions with his associates about the gloomy outlook, MacDonald decided that he should try to hire Lennox. Ending one last discouraging interview as midnight approached, MacDonald called Lennox, ostensibly to talk things over. But when Lennox answered the telephone, MacDonald bellowed, "I've gone through the list, and nobody wants the job! What do I do now?" Still half asleep, Lennox said, "Well, if things are that bad, maybe I'll have to come out myself and do it." Once fully awake, Lennox thought MacDonald would rebut with "get lost." But instead MacDonald simply grumbled, "Yes, maybe that is a good idea. Why don't you come out and have a look; then we can decide."[41]

A British immigrant and technocrat with government experience but an aversion to risk, Lennox promised to be an agreeable counterpoise to the small-town, high-flying MacDonald. During May 1970, Lennox flew to Vancouver, talked with MacDonald and his associates about the software work they had done for Lenkurt, and decided he should accept the challenge. First, however, MacDonald wanted Lennox to meet Bill Thompson and Jim Spilsbury. MacDonald flew Lennox to Vancouver, and Thompson and Spilsbury conducted the interview on Spilsbury's boat. Once assured that Lennox could look after MacDonald and his young associates, Thompson and Spilsbury sanctioned the hire. Without a moment's reluctance, MacDonald then transferred the headache of dealing with lawyers, accountants, and the "basic daily grind" to Lennox. Once done, MacDonald seemed to relax into what he truly enjoyed: solving the technical labyrinths that intrigued him, marketing his vision, and hiring Vancouver's young engineers to emulate the winning formula he had witnessed and participated in at MIT. Taking on the company's day-to-day activities, Lennox busied himself with turning the small firm into a sustainable operation. Despite his background in what MacDonald deemed "the government's rigid bureaucracy," Lennox also instituted several programs that strengthened MDA's structure, including flexible hours to let people work when it most suited them, and profit sharing schemes whereby the company could make loans to employees so they could purchase shares in the capital stock of the company. Soon after Lennox's hire, Spilsbury decided to leave the company to pursue other interests. Lennox bought Spilsbury's shares and became a director on MDA's board. With a substantial interest in the company's future, Lennox administered all company business transactions, left it to MacDonald to sell the company's image, and, provided the books balanced, allowed his younger associates to work on the creative projects they enjoyed.[42]

Lennox's first assignment at MDA presented him with his first challenge in contract negotiations, particularly explaining to MacDonald and Dettwiler how they worked. Confident that they could procure another contract with Lenkurt, MacDonald and Dettwiler invited Lennox to accompany them to a meeting to discuss the follow-on work. When they arrived, however, Lenkurt representatives told them that MDA had overbid, had provided an unacceptable proposal, and would not receive the follow-on contract. While the first contract had proven cost-effective, Lenkurt representatives claimed that MDA's new premises had obviously increased their costs, which meant Lenkurt could no longer afford their services. The news stunned MacDonald and Dettwiler, but Lennox explained that Lenkurt had to economize and people at MDA needed to remember that technical ideas do not always sell themselves. To win the contract, they had to spell out the details and list those details against proposed prices. Encouraged by such a "novel" strategy, Dettwiler and MacDonald rewrote the proposal, talked to people at Lenkurt about their specific needs, and received the second contract within two months.[43]

The second Lenkurt contract allowed MDA to produce the entire software package for the computer-based supervisory reporting system as well as assist in the design of Lenkurt's hardware interface. As part of the General Telephone & Electronics Corporation (GT&E) International Incorporated subsidiary of US-owned GT&E, Lenkurt then exported the entire system to Iran. Then a Central Intelligence Agency (CIA) asset of the United States, Iran planned to develop nuclear power stations throughout the country, and then use Iranian oil revenues to finance the development of South Africa's fuel-enrichment technology in exchange for enriched uranium. A computer-based supervisory reporting system promised to accelerate those plans. Such systems also enhanced Canada's export sales, which increased from 12 to 40 per cent of GNP between 1960 and 1970 on automobiles as well as aerospace, electronic, and oil-based products.[44]

Lenkurt presented MDA with its first exposure to the international market, even though the small firm had no direct involvement in the export to Iran, the furtherance of South African apartheid, or the moral dilemmas either might engender. Members of MDA who recalled the sale never focused on the controversy sparked at MIT over Iran "investing its oil wealth in setting up special arrangements with United States universities" to train nuclear and other engineering specialists.[45] Instead, they emphasized debates over MDA's business expansion. MDA's move into the international market "was quite a traumatic experience," MacDonald recalled, "because we were really quite overwhelmed by the idea." Still, "we went ahead and did it anyway. And that, in many ways, has been very characteristic of the company," he claimed. "We have never really believed that anything was truly impossible." The firm's entrance into the international marketplace also stimulated MacDonald's interest in export sales, for he realized that much of Lenkurt's success rested on its ability to develop a system in Canada and then sell it abroad, despite student protests over nuclear proliferation, faculty worries about academic freedom and integrity, and other political and professional concerns made public in the wake of such arrangements. And that became the central lesson of MacDonald's early business career: by engineering a split between the moral, political, and business implications of any job, MDA, like other capitalist enterprises, should sell to anyone willing to purchase one of the firm's systems.[46]

"THAT'S HOW WE DO BUSINESS":
PROCESS CONTROL AND THE SWEAT-EQUITY FORMULA

MDA's next lesson in the export market resulted from the company's move beyond British Columbia's borders and into larger regions, where Bill Renwick helped to expand the company's supervisory systems expertise from BC's telecommunications control business to the oil and gas industry, first in Alberta, then the United States. A Calgary-based firm, Western Electronic Systems, had a project with Aquitane Company of Canada to produce a control system for a major natural gas–processing plant in western Alberta. Western Electronic also hoped to lure potential clients by showcasing their expertise at a booth in a petroleum show hosted by Calgary's booming oil and gas sectors. Those at Western envisioned liquids flowing through pipes and valves that could open and shut on command, but their company lacked the computer expertise to mount a demonstration. When Western's representatives heard about MDA's supervisory control capabilities, they called for help. Renwick produced what they needed, and Western's demonstration emerged as the petroleum show's star performer. Western's success also translated into additional work for MDA, including a contract to design a supervisory system for Quindar, an electrical apparatus, equipment supply, and construction firm headquartered in Calgary, but with its Westronic Engineering distributor housed in Vancouver. Westronic's premier salesman, Terry Graham, monitored Renwick's progress, liked what he saw, and convinced MacDonald to propose Renwick for Quindar work. When Quindar decided to bid on a large supervisory system for Westcoast Transmission, a company designated to run a gas pipeline from Northern BC to Vancouver, Graham not only secured for Quindar and Westronic a multi-million-dollar contract, but also delivered to MDA the entire $90,000 software development subcontract (worth approximately $557,000 in 2016), a project that ushered in MDA's first real phase of expansion.[47]

Lennox learned many valuable lessons from Graham, not the least being that MDA had a valuable asset in Renwick. At one company meeting, an oil and gas executive from Houston called Lennox into an inner office and advised, "I've talked with my local Calgary manager, and MDA will get the contract provided you guarantee that Bill Renwick works the project." Lennox offered to bring Renwick in so he could explain details, but the Houston executive cut him off: "I don't need convincing that Renwick can do the job. Will you put him on it?" Remembering what Graham had taught him, Lennox took a gamble: "I'd be glad to, on one condition. I want 30 per cent, cash down, before Renwick starts." When the Houstonian barked, "Where do you get the idea you can get paid with cash up front?" Lennox claimed, "It's the only way we do business west of the Rockies. I know that you're east of the Rockies, but that's how we do business." Speculating on Renwick's reputation and the executive's disinclination to check on the "West-of-the-Rockies policy" paid off. After the executive confirmed MDA's address, he called Houston: "Cut these guys a check for 30 per cent of the contract cost, and mail it right up to Vancouver." Although MacDonald and Dettwiler had exploited their contacts and technical expertise, Renwick revealed that MDA could work with a major hardware supplier and had a niche to fill, one for which clients might gladly pay hard cash. That handshake deal thus convinced Lennox that MDA could get the work its associates wanted, the way they wanted it. The sweat equity of MDA's workforce could also enable the company to survive for the longer term, he hoped.[48]

Taking the whole of his experience on those first few oil and gas projects, Renwick built MDA's first generic product, a modification of the original Asynchronous Tasking Supervisor (ATS) Dettwiler had designed for Lenkurt, which MDA then used on all its subsequent pipeline work. Applications that previously required a clock to track the passage of time could employ the ATS, assuring a micro-second alarm response to conditions along the line and saving MDA's clients precious time and superfluous expenses. The product also solidified MDA's reputation as a competent software consulting firm and reliable developer of hardware interfaces for monitoring systems. That combined expertise then made MDA eligible for development grants and tax incentives administered by the Canadian government.[49]

While Renwick helped to establish MDA as a competent software consulting firm, the company looked for additional staff to supplement the expanding operation. They found them at UBC. As business prospects increased, MDA needed a secretary, someone who could keep up with the demands of the company's full-time and part-time associates. During 1970, Janice Price worked at an IBM office down the hall from Dettwiler's office at UBC, where she organized a computer conference called "Session '70." Price talked with Dettwiler about his new company and agreed to work on projects for MDA. Dettwiler found her work impressive, and by the time "Session '70" finished in July, MDA offered her a full-time posi- tion. The small firm's first female employee and "Girl Friday," Price answered telephones and typed up manuals to document MDA's software projects. Lennox also put her to work running the office and keeping the books while he made sure everyone else produced what they promised to clients. Price soon began to hire a small army of women to work as recep- tionists and secretaries to serve the expansionist needs of MDA's founders and young male colleagues. Over time, as computing began to displace many traditional secretarial roles in the corporate office, women also found work at MDA as word processing operators, assembly plant workers, human resources personnel, and technical writers. Slowly, MDA addition- ally began to recruit female computer analysts, engineers, and scientists. Still, MDA's early male-dominated "system builder" environment contin- ued to guide the firm and those the associates recruited.[50]

With future prospects looking rosy in the fall of 1970, MDA's founders and new team members also decided to hire another promising young engineer from UBC. Vancouver's Pacific Press executives wanted to trans- form their newsprint line so that they could automatically divert newspa- per bundles to the correct truck, with each truck's newspapers customized for specific street drop-off points. Some of MDA's young associates had already decided that they wanted to pursue such work, and had no doubt they could win the contract. As a bonus, the contract would allow Det- twiler and Morin to become full-time employees of MDA. When Colin Lennox returned from a trip to Toronto late in September, however, John MacDonald met him at the airport with shocking news: MDA had lost the Pacific Press bid. The loss bruised the collective MDA ego, and MacDonald wondered if the company could survive the loss. MacDonald recalled that he told Lennox, "Maybe we should pack it in after we finish the work we have," then revealed that MDA had another problem: he had already offered the Pacific Press job to Neil Thompson, a second-year graduate student at UBC. Not realizing MacDonald had offered conditional em- ployment, and excited about the prospect of a full-time job at the fledg- ling firm, Thompson accepted the position on the spot. He also withdrew from the master's program in electrical engineering so that he could show up bright and early for his assignment on 1 October 1970. For the young recruit, day one at MDA was a nightmare: fifteen minutes after he arrived at the Film Exchange, Thompson became MDA's first layoff statistic.[51]

The Pacific Press loss discouraged MacDonald; however, serendipity assured MDA another chance in business as well as the laid-off Neil Thompson the professional opportunity he had quit graduate school to pursue. Helmut Eppich, a tool-and-die manufacturer in Vancouver, had an idea for launching a new business on the automation of data collection at his Vancouver-based EBCO Industries, so he could enhance his abilities to keep track of the shop floor, discover work delays, control workflow, and remain competitive. Eppich developed an innovative mechanical card reader for such a business, but he lacked the expertise to develop an electronic, computerized version of it. As a result, Eppich enrolled in a digital computer course at the recently opened BCIT. Very soon, however, Eppich knew he had insufficient time to learn how to code software; he therefore asked his instructor if he knew anyone who could help. The instructor gave Eppich two local telephone numbers: one belonged to Klause Deering, a manufacturer and potential competitor to EBCO; and the other to John MacDonald. Fearing that a competitor might steal his idea, Eppich tossed Deering's number and called MacDonald.[52]

As EBCO's president and major shareholder, Eppich guarded his ideas carefully, but he knew that his company's hostile environment of welding machines, electricity, grime, oil, and field dust needed a more robust controller than the one he had engineered mechanically. Eppich decided that if MDA could fix his controller problems, he could also trust the little firm with his electronic card reader idea. He therefore offered MDA a small $4,900 contract, which provided just enough capital to pay Neil Thompson's salary and establish MDA's presence at EBCO. As a result, MacDonald informed Thompson that MDA could rehire him, provided he could commence work at EBCO immediately. Anxious to remain in Vancouver and considering MDA special, Neil Thompson decided against telling Mac-Donald to "take his job and shove it." He also took Eppich's original mechanical controller, re-engineered it with an electronic version, and added a plug-interchangeable circuit board. If any faults occurred, Eppich could simply unplug the faulty board, plug in a new one, and wait for the factory to fix the old board. Thompson's electronic board allowed machine-room efficiency and cost savings in one important area, which convinced Eppich that he could trust MDA to keep his secrets.[53]

Eppich told Lennox and Dettwiler about his plans to launch a new business on his mechanical card reader, showed them his design, and gave MDA an additional contract to find a card reader for his factory's environment. Worth not $4,900 but $68,000, that second contract seemed like a windfall for MDA's modest operation. Dettwiler took charge of the project, but other commitments soon forced him to transfer the job to Neil Thompson. Worrying that Thompson might find it difficult to complete the assignment on his own, MacDonald decided to look for another technical employee. He had no difficulty in finding one. Vancouver had two "high-tech" companies, Lenkurt and MDA, but most "techies" wanted to join the younger firm, where they could work with their charismatic professor, Vern Dettwiler, and Bill Renwick. Ken Spencer quickly emerged as one of those technology-obsessed students. When he received his PhD from UBC, Spencer received two job offers: one from Bell Northern Research in Ottawa, Canada's premier telecommunications research and development organization; and the other from MDA. Knowing that many people considered him an abrasive young man, Spencer believed he would fit best with people he already knew in Vancouver. Moreover, MDA had only four permanent staff, and Spencer had ambitions to find a niche working on projects that suited him. He thus joined Thompson at EBCO.[54]

Thompson and Spencer first searched for an appropriate card reader for Eppich's plant; finding none, they decided to design one for him. After several false starts and two years' work on the project, Dettwiler's young team produced a programmable computer for Eppich's office and a wall-mounted version for EBCO's machine shop, which promised Eppich the chance to receive information from his machine shop two floors below his office. Eppich took possession of MDA's prototype during October 1973, and then called MDA to request that Lennox and Dettwiler attend an acceptance test at EBCO. Knowing Eppich was a tough customer, Dettwiler and Lennox arrived at the acceptance test with devices to satisfy any test Eppich might conduct. But Eppich had no interest in their gadgets. He went over to a grinding machine, picked up a handful of iron filings, and poured them down the card slot. That done, he walked over to the EBCO coffee machine and mixed a concoction that contained no cream but plenty of sugar. Eppich then poured the entire cup of coffee into the card reader. While Lennox and Dettwiler expected a tough test, neither predicted Eppich's next move.[55]

While Dettwiler and Lennox looked on in horror, Eppich reached into his jacket pocket, pulled out a punched IBM card, and said, "I've put a code on this card, and if the computer in my office doesn't read this, I'm not paying you." Dettwiler had designed the computer to read every number five times. If it read three out of the five numbers correctly, a green light would signal that the computer had the data. Dettwiler believed in the efficacy of his design; however, when he glanced at Lennox, neither knew what might happen next. Gleefully acknowledging their unease, Eppich jammed his card into the reader. After additional coffee and filings poured out, he pulled the doused card all the way through and watched for the light. When it turned green, Eppich reached into his pocket again, pulled out a cheque, handed it to Lennox, and chortled, "That's it fellows. I'm now on my own." Eppich developed his system, launched Epic Data in 1974, and later argued that Vancouver became "one of the most important areas of telecommunications and systems software" because "we had a combination of people who allowed for cross-seeding of ideas, excitement, enthusiasm, and creativity." Still, he conceded, "We also had the support of the government" in the form of tax incentives, industrial research grants, and regional development programs.[56]

MDA's liaison with Helmut Eppich profited both parties and helped to build Vancouver's industrial base. Eppich saved MDA from its demise, the associates learned a great deal about data transmission, and MDA established itself as a competent process control consultant. In return, Eppich received what he needed to launch Epic Data. Their collaborations also pushed Epic and MDA more deeply into the development and expansion of surveillance capitalism. By 1993, Epic Data had installed more than 500 data collection systems on five continents. Still headquartered in Richmond during the twenty-first century, Epic continued to supply data collection systems for global clients in aerospace, heavy manufacturing, and the military.[57]

Losing the first Pacific Press job also changed MDA's focus, allowing the associates to acquire the expertise they needed to pursue more lucrative work in process control. Just nine months after Neil Thompson's disastrous first day on the job, Pacific Press executives conceded that they had made a mistake with the contractor they had originally hired. MDA bid on and won the replacement contract, one much larger than what the firm had originally proposed during 1970. By 1972, MDA's second chance with Pacific Press also allowed Dettwiler and Morin to join the firm as fulltime associates, provided the opportunity to hire more promising UBC students, enhanced MDA's credibility in process control, and proved the company could do things on a mini-computer previously possible only on large and expensive machines.[58]

MDA's Pacific Press bid and other job proposals flowed from individual employee interests and each person's desire to enhance his status as a member of the computer industry's professional vanguard, all within a deliberately unstructured environment that allowed the young associates to do whatever the customer asked of them. Such an environment additionally provided plentiful sweat-equity opportunities and the hazards associated with cost overruns. Indeed, as one long-time employee remembered, "It was a pretty freewheeling company because it was quite small, and most of us knew each other from UBC. There are all sorts of stories" in MDA lore "about how Vern would come around and say, 'Charge the customer four hours for this,' and it would take us four days."[59] If they thought they could build a system at an affordable price, they took on the project. Only after project completion did they decide if they could profit from it or turn it into follow-on work. "We didn't worry about insurance, or shipping, or anything in those days," one employee remembered. "I guess we weren't really aware of all the risks, but that's the way we did business." To offset the risk, "people worked extremely long hours. Their whole private lives were intimately related to the company. It wasn't unusual to come to work in the morning to find people sleeping at their desks, because they'd worked right through the night and would have just curled up on a bench somewhere and fallen asleep." After waking those colleagues, "We'd go out for breakfast, come back, and continue working. The dedication was extreme."[60]

With immediate financial returns mattering less than engineering feats and the challenges and professional status that new projects promised, MDA employees bid on other specialized systems without doing market research. Those blunders soon forced them to confront the realities that elegant technologies do not in themselves create further demand and that tricky software challenges can imperil young firms. For example, a Vancouver entrepreneur named Brian Hayden had an idea for automating the delivery of prescription drugs to eliminate drugstore paperwork as well as make Canada's health-care services more efficient and less costly. But he quickly found that he wanted to use a minicomputer that was incompatible with the large data disks he used to store patient information. Jumping at the opportunity to solve another difficult technical problem, Semrau and Spencer offered to build a special disk interface for Hayden's start-up firm. MDA's young engineers eventually solved a variety of complicated technical problems during the course of the project, but it took valiant efforts (nine prototypes and hundreds of hours) before the team could read patient data. Indeed, that problem stumped even Dettwiler, the company's best troubleshooter. After many different people had "blunted their pick" on the UniDrug problem and determined that MDA would deliver as promised, MacDonald finally stepped in. Delegating other technical tasks, MacDonald "took two or three whacks at the problem, and finally solved it." The toughest technical problem he had tackled, MacDonald kept the final prototype, placing his last circuit board on MDA's wall of history, as a tribute to a long, drawn-out accomplishment.[61]

The MDA team expected the project to take two engineers and no more than three days to solve; however, it consumed numerous engineers over several months. Still, until later projects forced their hands, MacDonald and Dettwiler took comfort in the knowledge that one of them could, "at least from a technical point of view," fulfill MDA's contractual obligations. MacDonald later confided, "I probably held that dream long beyond its reality. But in the early days it was certainly true, and it is certainly not true today. Somewhere in between I realized that this was no longer the case, probably at least three or four years after it had truly ceased to be."[62]

The company managed to swallow early cost overruns, not because MDA had a surplus cash reserve, but because MacDonald and Dettwiler had engendered in their young staff a level of dedication that allowed MDA to run on sweat equity. With the combination of MDA's underestimated contracts and the reality that the firm had fast become *the* place for electrical engineers and other technology enthusiasts to work in Vancouver, employees often clocked sixteen to twenty hours a day to meet project deadlines. MDA's young associates not only loved the work; many also remembered that they initially preferred uncompensated overtime at MDA to a job with a utility company or, worse still, to finding themselves replaced by another engineer. Moreover, most MDA projects initially involved only one or two people, and the esprit de corps begat energy as well as competition for the affection and esteem of the firm's founders. For example, when Stanley Semrau joined MDA as a full-time employee during 1973, the firm's competitive environment pushed him to invent MDA's eight-day week. Semrau started Monday morning at eight o'clock, worked for 20 hours, went home for 8 hours, and returned on Tuesday at noon. By the time the clock turned 10 p.m. on Saturday, Semrau had engineered a Sunday reprieve and the accumulation of 100 hours (an "eight-day week" involving 12.5-hour days). After six months, Semrau had worked 2,400 hours, amassing the equivalent of a fifteen-month year. Semrau tended to the extreme; however, his efforts reflected the general pace at MDA.[63] In their work on technology start-up and spinoff firms, Philip Auerswald and Lewis Branscomb have confirmed that most infant technology companies start this way, relying on employee enthusiasm, sweat equity, "trust, incentives, and shared objectives," with "innovation in all contexts" centred on a "capacity for collective entrepreneurship."[64]

No matter their "capacity for collective entrepreneurship," concerns mounted at MDA about problems attended by underestimating the time required to complete projects as well as overtime work. Colin Lennox attempted to solve the overtime problem by finding a way to compensate MDA's engineers for their dedication, and in 1973 he instituted a share-option plan and profit sharing bonuses for all company employees. If employees left the firm, they had to transfer their ownership to someone else. For those who remained, however, the idea of ownership had a tremendous psychological effect, even if most employees failed to see actual returns. With a tangible stake in the company's future, overtime work no longer seemed so onerous. Those in government shared their perceptions that fortunes would rise as the computer industry flourished. During 1973, the new minister of communications predicted that "the current situation is no more than a take-off position for developments which may make computer services universally accessible and the industry one of the largest in the world."[65]

A shared stake in the future of a company whose services seemed to know no bounds also ensured that few MDA employees connected their own reality as sweat-equity workers with capitalist expansion and the shrewd management of salaried knowledge workers that many firms adopted as part of a larger process of global competition and an increasing focus on short-term profits, shareholder value, and labour-saving schemes, including the very eight-day weeks and control devices MDA's young enthusiasts helped to engineer.[66]

"GO FOR IT!":
MDA'S SOFTWARE EXPERTISE TAKES FLIGHT

MDA's last milestone in software development during the company's first decade flowed from an airline office dispatch problem that pushed the young associates more deeply into the aerospace industry. By 1974, with Vancouver International Airport's expanding business opportunities in the Lower Mainland, MDA's young enthusiasts found themselves negotiating with Pacific Western Airlines (PWA) to build an automated system to assist airline dispatchers with preparing flight plans, scheduling crews, and routing other operations. MacDonald and Dettwiler heard about PWA through Westronic's president and salesman Gordon English, a likeable man who proved himself an excellent contact for MDA, a champion willing to go out of his way to find an opportunity for MDA at PWA. Bob Burrow, PWA's chief dispatcher and the company's main computer advocate, wanted to develop a computer-based airline dispatch system that could replace the telex machines on which the industry had long relied. Minute-by-minute weather information from around the world, notices to pilots about runway closures, and communications with air traffic control and company stations deluged offices, with operators receiving information they had no way to share. When Burrow met with English, he asked if people at Westronic knew of companies that could help PWA to automate its offices. Already working as a consultant for MDA, English recommended the firm.[67]

From MDA's earliest days at the Film Exchange, Lennox had instituted Friday afternoon happy hours for employees to blow off steam, talk about technical issues, and discuss future prospects. One afternoon, English joined the happy-hour crowd and mentioned his discussion with Burrow at PWA. Previously content to take on whatever assignments came his way, Neil Thompson had never pushed to work on any particular project. But when it looked as if Lennox might assign PWA to someone else, Thompson intervened. A pilot himself, Thompson declared that he was the only man for the PWA job, and later claimed that the contract revealed his own moment of professional clarity. On that Friday afternoon, Thompson knew what he wanted: the PWA contract, for the prospect of heading up the project carried with it suggestive overtones about his future. Lennox and MacDonald agreed that Thompson deserved the chance to prove himself, but if they had any doubts, Thompson's later meeting with Burrow assuaged their concerns. Thompson understood the airline industry, and Burrow considered him a natural bridge between airlines, pilots, and the computer industry. Burrow therefore declared that he wanted Thompson on the job; and Thompson became an instant champion for Burrow, PWA, and the airline industry as a whole.[68]

Thompson convinced Burrow that he could supervise the project, but many at the airline deemed his proposed solution impossible for the complexities of airline dispatch. Before committing to the project, PWA executives thus requested a demonstration of MDA's capabilities. A successful demonstration required more equipment than MDA had; as before, however, the young team soon found someone willing to help. By 1974, MDA had started to purchase computers from InterData (a firm founded in New Jersey during 1966, producing a line of mini-computers that attempted to replicate and compete with the IBM 360). InterData's local salesman, Barclay Isherwood, hoped to make future sales to MDA; he therefore agreed to loan the necessary equipment. Thompson came up with the concept, and with help from Dettwiler and other young engineers, the MDA team produced a demonstration model. Over the next three days, Thompson showed MDA's system to PWA as well as Canadian Pacific Airlines, Air Canada, and Transport Canada. By the end of the third day, Burrow declared, "You know what we want and you can do it." The MDA team spent the next year negotiating what became a fixed-price contract worth $400,000 in 1976 (equivalent to nearly $1.7 million in 2016). Thereafter, Neil Thompson commenced work on a new Airline

Information and Dispatch System (AIDS), MDA's largest software project at the time. AIDS quickly turned into the company's first real maintenance contract as well, one requiring a larger team than either MDA's managers or Thompson originally envisioned. Within a short period, however, Thompson put together a small team of recent software recruits who promised to create a splash in the airline industry.[69]

Demonstrating a capability is one thing; building a large and complicated software system quite another. Within no time, the AIDS project had grown beyond anyone's ability to control it. While Thompson had a clear sense of the project and tremendous rapport with PWA's representatives, he carried most of the programming information in his head. At the same time, no one had allocated enough people to do all the coding necessary for on-time, on-budget completion, and Thompson remained a one-man show while AIDS required a six-person team. As a result, when the project ended in 1977, MDA carried an enormous overtime bill and a major cost overrun.[70] MDA was not alone in the history of such software development crises. Engineers have long estimated poorly, while schedule slippages and cost overruns have plagued many computer projects. As Frederick P. Brooks argued in *The Mythical Man-Month* (a book many at MDA soon read and cited), "All programmers are optimists. Perhaps this modern sorcery especially attracts those who believe in happy endings and fairy godmothers ... Perhaps the hundreds of natty frustrations drive away all but those who habitually focus on the end goal. Perhaps it is merely that computers are young, programmers are younger, and the young are always optimists. But however the selection process works," he emphasized, "the result is indisputable: 'This time it will surely run', or 'I just found the last bug.'"[71]

MDA's first major cost overrun foreshadowed bigger ones to come, while "I just found the last bug" became an oft-repeated rationalization at the firm. Although MacDonald found the $400,000 cost overrun "unpleasant," he never deemed it an "unmitigated disaster." In fact, he considered it quite the opposite. "Our profits weren't very good that year, but it had been very, very successful as a system. PWA was keen as hell about it." MDA had delivered its first dispatch system and built a successful system for PWA, a company within an industry normally closed to outsiders. Thompson had come up with some excellent solutions to PWA's problems, and the small team eventually delivered an exemplary system with every bell and whistle the airline requested. Neil Thompson and MDA also earned reputations that travelled quickly throughout the airline business. PWA "started showing it off to the other airlines," MacDonald boasted, "and we came to conclude, on the basis of all that information, that this was something we could make into a product."[72] Anticipating the development of systems capable of creating considerable savings for intermediate-sized airlines, the MDA team convinced themselves that they had learned all the lessons they needed to know from the first contract. They also believed that resources lost on the AIDS system would soon turn into large dividends for the company's employee shareholders, many of whom had begun to grow impatient for returns. Only one small matter remained. AIDS already existed as an acronym for another airline data recorder. Thus, AIDS changed to FOCUS, shorthand for MDA's new Flight Operations Computer System. By 1977, with a glimmering hope that the company could finally take one of its software development products into worldwide markets, MDA thus began to develop the system.[73]

With the assistance of PWA, three different airline companies showed interest in MDA's FOCUS: SwissAir, Texas International, and Belgium's Sabena. Assuming that development work on one system could pay for production on the other two, MDA bid for and won contracts from all three airlines. "It's as clear today as if it just happened yesterday," MacDonald recalled. "Ken Spencer came into my office and explained that the total of the three contracts was fixed at $5.3 million," with each promising to generate monthly progress payments to offset development costs. "I remember thinking, we priced PWA at $300,000, and it cost us $700,000. With three contracts at $5.3 million, what could possibly go wrong? So I said, 'Go for it!'"[74] Even if no one inside the firm knew it at the time, FOCUS became more than MDA's largest software project; it surfaced as an important instrument of change.[75]

In the meantime, Lennox's general management, Renwick's example, talented young engineers, and expanding software capabilities cemented MDA's short-term future. When sufficient work allowed both Dettwiler and Morin to join the company as full-time associates during 1971, MDA had already emerged as a small yet vibrant organization on which to build. MacDonald found it more difficult to make a full-time commitment to MDA, however; only someone special, offering something unique, could settle that issue. That someone arrived during 1971, in the form of Dave Sloan, a radio astronomer who walked through MDA's door with opportunities to enter the remote sensing field and the global space industry. Chapter 3 charts the remote sensing projects that paralleled those taking place in software development at MDA. Between 1971 and 1979, as the forces of surveillance capitalism firmly attached MDA to the global space race, MDA experienced its most exciting period of technological innovation, laying the foundations for what kind of firm MDA would become.

3

"Innovation in a Cold Climate"

Remote Sensing and the
Government Contracting Paradigm,
1971–1980

Vern Dettwiler's decision to leave the security of UBC had been easy. He enjoyed working on software problems, and when sufficient work justified it, he jumped at the chance to join the firm as a full-time associate. MacDonald's decision was more complex. Although his frustrations at UBC had motivated him to start MDA with Dettwiler, MacDonald had invested many years in graduate school. Not yet tenured, he knew that if he found a business career equally frustrating, or worse, if MDA failed, he stood a bleak chance of obtaining another tenure-track faculty position. He recognized that if he wanted to remain MDA's leader, eventually he had to make a choice, but McDonald also deemed himself a system builder, a "hardware" system builder. If MDA stayed the course in software, he might never have a chance to do what he most enjoyed. Thus, while others expressed their optimism about MDA's future, MacDonald continued to hesitate. What if he could still erect something similar to MIT at UBC, could find a way to link his experiences along Route 128 to Vancouver? He needed something more tangible, something solid to convince him that he could actually attain what he and Dettwiler had first conceived. That something did not take long. Through a concatenation of haphazard events during 1971, a bearded young scientific eccentric named Dave Sloan lured MacDonald into full-time employment with MDA by providing the only stimuli MacDonald ever needed: the opportunity to build hardware systems, a chance to join the space race, and a powerful governmental prop for his dream.[1]

"SPACE FEVER":
NASA, REMOTE SENSING'S PROMISE,
AND THE CANADIAN PARTICIPANTS

Knowledge about remote sensing existed only in the military and selected scientific quarters prior to the late 1960s. Fewer than four generations ago, the creation of satellite images for capitalist expansion was neither feasible nor fully envisioned. Once orbited, however, Earth observation satellites and the ground stations that received and processed their data changed cartographic applications and introduced the commercial promise of remote sensing. Developments in Canada followed the rapid expansion of NASA after 1958, Canada's launch of *Alouette-1* in 1962, and early successes in the development of satellites for telecommunications during the mid-1960s. As many scientists and engineers from around the world drew near to NASA's flame, they soon participated in the "myth of geography's end," sharing in what sociologist Vincent Mosco has described as a "view that communication makes space infinitely malleable, the logical extension of a process of freeing people from spatial constraint with all of its confining economic and social implications." The development of earth observation satellites furthered that view.[2]

Prior to his meeting with John MacDonald, Dave Sloan already had what he described as a NASA-induced "space fever." Working on a physics degree at UBC during 1966, Sloan and his best friend, Peter Kuijt, shared a passion for space exploration that prompted them to propose a rocket club at UBC. UBC administrators opposed them, on the grounds that rocket-club launches posed a threat to the larger community. Disappointed but undeterred, the two searched for tamer projects associated with NASA's first weather satellites, *Tiros* (Television and Infrared Observation Satellite) and *Nimbus* (named for a cloud formation). Launched during 1960, *Tiros-1* carried television cameras to photograph the Earth's cloud cover. Four years later, NASA sent the larger, more complex *Nimbus* into orbit, where it flew ahead of reconnaissance satellites to identify cloud-free areas for high-resolution photography as well as transmit images to remote locations. Once Sloan and Kuijt realized that anyone could build a ground station to receive satellite images, they built their own. Although the Canadian government had already constructed a weather office in Toronto, Sloan and Kuijt's 1966 ground station emerged as Canada's first amateur station and the first commercial weather receiving office in Western Canada. More importantly, once operational, the ground station allowed Sloan and Kuijt to see the Earth from the sky and to capture pictures of clouds. As a result, both determined to spend the rest of their lives following the magic of satellites and to participate in other space-based firsts.[3]

Between 1967 and 1969, the Canadian government provided more incentives for Sloan and Kuijt to pursue their interests. Seeking to avoid becoming a permanent satellite of the US economy, Lester B. Pearson's government had laid the foundations for Canadian sovereignty in space by encouraging studies on science policy. Commissioned by the Science Secretariat, *Alouette* builder John Herbert Chapman and his colleagues produced the first special study of space-related activities. In its presentation to the Science Council in January 1967, the Chapman Commission noted that "experience in the U.S. and other countries shows that a stable, continuing and imaginative space program attracts much of the best technical talents and resources of the country." The report conceded "it could be argued that this would have a deleterious effect on other areas of technology of importance to the country," but "without a major, challenging, stimulating and advanced technological program, many of Canada's technical resources will be attracted elsewhere. The problem," it noted, "is to learn how to couple this activity to other sectors of the economy where there are national needs, and where the civilian sector, both at home and abroad, can benefit." Citing the OECD's emphasis on spinoff effects, the report recommended that Canada establish a national advisory committee on research and development, with scientific representatives from government, academia, and industry helping to formulate policies for satellite communications, remote sensing, and other space-related activities.[4]

Chapman Commission recommendations quickly led to the incorporation of SPAR Aerospace, whose 340 staff had worked on military projects at de Havilland and Avro. While still a division of de Havilland in the early 1960s, SPAR's team had already begun to shift from military projects into non-military space applications. Participating in the development and construction of *Alouette-1* (1962) and *Alouette-2* (1965), they built powerful antennas that enhanced Canada's role in space communications. Officially incorporated on 27 October 1967, SPAR became the major firm on which the Canadian government would depend for sovereignty in space, with its principles emerging among the consultants hired to study other space-related opportunities. With SPAR's scientists promising to rebuild Canada's aerospace industry in the wake of Avro Arrow's cancellation, the federal government formed the Panarctic Consortium, where other Canadian corporations and a few international partners joined SPAR to explore oil and gas in the Arctic and the Northwest Territories as a step toward protecting one critical component of Canadian sovereignty. The federal government also instituted changes to the Bank Act to encourage Canada's financial institutions to direct more of their capital to Canadian industry. Pearson then appointed a special task force to study foreign ownership of Canadian industries, which argued that Canada had "a greater degree of foreign ownership of our resources and manufacturing industries than desirable for the sound development of an independent country."[5]

When he became prime minister in 1968, Pierre Trudeau furthered Pearson's efforts by declaring that his government's "paramount interest is to ensure the political survival of Canada as a federal and bilingual sovereign state. This means strengthening Canadian unity as a basically North American country."[6] While prime minister from 1968 to 1979, Trudeau and his Liberal government included five national interests as part of Canadian unity and sovereignty: economic development and expansion; a harmonious natural environment; quality of life; social justice; and peace and security. Within that context, Canadian sovereignty and unity connoted less dependence on the United States, a country that seemed to be careening out of control in Vietnam and whose government officials seemed to be losing their abilities to manage economic, environmental, and urban problems. As a result, Canada welcomed college-educated Vietnam War draft dodgers and lower-income deserters who, together, added an estimated 40,000 draft-eligible Americans to Canada's immigration rolls. Although many American draft dodgers and military deserters had already sought refuge in Canada, Pearson's government had refused to take them, on the grounds that these Americans had no proof that they had received proper military discharge papers. As anti-war protests gained traction, however, Canadian immigration officials ultimately received alternative orders; and on 22 May 1969, Trudeau announced that they could no longer ask immigration applicants about their military status. Many of those young men and their family members found employment in established firms, while others ultimately made their way west to Vancouver.[7]

Trudeau's government additionally intended to further Canada's sovereignty efforts by seeking a closer relationship with Europe as well as more contact with and increased aid to developing nations, which included diplomatic relations with Cuba (then China and other communist countries). Among his many signature pieces during 1968, Trudeau signed into law the Official Languages Act and supported the international Nuclear Nonproliferation Treaty. The federal government also established the

Canadian International Development Agency (CIDA) to manage the country's foreign aid program. The next year, Canada consolidated the Ministry of Industry and the Ministry of Trade and Commerce into the Ministry of Industry, Trade and Commerce to coordinate the nation's industrial strategies and policies. During 1969, the federal government formed Telesat as well, to deliver live, intercontinental satellite television transmissions, and established a new Department of Communications, transferring all of the Defence Research Telecommunications Establishment from the Defence Research Board to the Department of Communications' Communications Research Centre (CRC) to coordinate the space-based activities of government departments and the National Research Council. Trudeau's Cabinet additionally decided to encourage the Department of Energy, Mines and Resources to coordinate and fund an ongoing research program in the field of remote sensing, to study Canada's natural resources and environment (with the CCRS officially established in February 1971).[8]

Following oil strikes in Alaska and widespread mineral exploration in the North, Canada asserted its sovereignty over Arctic waters. Passing the Arctic Waters Pollution Act during April 1970, the federal government declared Canadian rights over a 100-mile pollution control zone around the Arctic islands. Although Americans objected to the Act, Minister of Indian and Northern Affairs Jean Chrétien argued that "Canada has four primary interests in the Arctic: the security of Canada, the economic development of the North, the preservation of the ecological balance, and the continued high stature of Canada in the international community." The Act also provided a rationale for the development of a remote sensing capability to monitor and manage Canada's land and ocean resources as well as the environment.[9] Canada additionally asserted its sovereign right to enter into agreements on its own, by officially recognizing the People's Republic of China two years prior to the United States. And Trudeau made further international news with his handling of the "October Crisis" of 1970, an event precipitated by the kidnapping of British diplomat James Cross and Quebec Cabinet Minister Pierre Laporte by the Front de Libération du Québec. Responding to the crisis, Trudeau announced to the world his posture on terrorism by invoking the War Measures Act, which gave the federal government extraordinary powers to investigate, arrest, detain, and censor suspects.[10]

In the meantime, Sloan and Kuijt left UBC in 1967, the same spring during which Expo 67 got underway in Montreal and large anti–Vietnam War protests and peace marches took place in Vancouver and elsewhere across the world. Receiving his master's degree in radio astronomy, Dave Sloan accepted a position with TRIUMF, a university-affiliated research institute. At TRIUMF, Sloan participated in the hardware design of the computer data acquisition and control system for UBC's Cyclotron (a particle accelerator, or "atom smasher"), the largest facility of its kind in the world when completed in 1972. Managers at TRIUMF also learned the value of employing sweat equity to promote Canadian expertise in selected quarters. As one Interdepartmental Committee on Space reported, "Great advances have been made [at TRIUMF] on small budgets using the enthusiasm and cheap labour of graduate students and scholarship holders, and with some costs 'hidden' in departmental budgets."[11]

While Sloan provided some of that "cheap labour" at TRIUMF, Peter Kuijt took a drafting job at Wright Engineers, one of Western Canada's most significant mining firms. Kuijt's job then provided the platform on which he and his friend Sloan could build. When it published "At Long Last, ERTS Is on the Way" during 1969, *Electronics* magazine reported that NASA intended to launch its first Earth Resources Technology Satellite (renamed *Landsat* in 1975), a program developed out of the philosophy that one could take unclassified pictures of the Earth and then use them for resource management and peaceful purposes. From program beginnings in 1965, NASA had encouraged other nations to use its satellite's data, but with the possibility of remotely sensed satellite photographs recording spaces outside the United States, NASA decided to establish an International Participation Program for the *Landsat* project. The prelaunch program not only convinced representatives from other nations that NASA had benign intentions, but also encouraged them to build their own ground receiving stations.[12] "At Long Last" thus stimulated global interest in the commercial applications that might flow from the satellite's launch, including the competitive edge that mining companies might enjoy if they had access to the satellite's processed imagery. The technical, kickoff meeting in Annapolis, Maryland, during March 1970 then played the decisive role in determining which Canadians would participate in Canada's contributions to the ERTS/*Landsat* program.[13]

Private-sector involvement in Canadian remote sensing had its genesis within the Department of Energy, Mines, and Resources (EMR). Following World War II, EMR's chief geophysicist, Lawrence (Larry) Morley, organized Canada's airborne survey industry through government procurement contracts, which privatized much of the federal government's aerial reconnaissance work. When remote sensing satellites became a potential reality, Morley then encouraged the development of a Canadian aerospace industry similar to that of the airborne survey. With the assistance of Philip Lapp (a promoter of SPAR, consultant on the Chapman Commission, and Morley's fraternity brother as well as former co-worker at Gulf Oil), Morley emerged as a leading member of the team that supported the proposal to form the Canada Centre for Remote Sensing (CCRS). As part of larger effort to build Canada's infant commercial space industry as a participant in NASA's ERTS/*Landsat* program, Morley and others argued that Canada needed its own remote sensing capability, not only to protect the country's Arctic sovereignty, but also to monitor and manage changes in the environment. Morley's arguments also resonated with defence production sharing agreements between Canada and the United States, and with Canadian obligations under Five Eyes, NATO, NORAD, the GATT, and other international bodies. As a result, when Morley and others attended the Annapolis meeting, Morley had set the stage for Canada to participate in its first five-year, cooperative agreement with the United States on the development and expansion of remote sensing from satellites and aircraft.[14]

Looking for ways to connect themselves to NASA, Sloan and Kuijt convinced Wright Engineers' P.F. O'Sullivan that the company needed representatives at the ERTS kickoff meeting in Annapolis, where they could make the case for the firm's interest in the commercial applications of space exploration. As Kuijt's boss, O'Sullivan needed little convincing. He therefore suggested that the three enthusiasts pack their bags. When they arrived at the first session of the conference, NASA revealed its intentions and Morley announced that the Canadian government had reached an agreement with the United States to build a ground station in northern Canada to receive ERTS data. Sloan and Kuijt exhausted the next two days asking for interviews with Canadian representatives, but deeming them no more than "a couple of young second-raters," the Canadian agency's officials took a necessary precaution: "They simply gave us the cold shoulder," Sloan recalled. But neither young man, nor O'Sullivan, intended to suffer such a slight. According to Sloan, at the next day's plenary session, O'Sullivan stood up and declared, "I'm representing a group of Canadian mining companies that would like to build a ground station, and what's NASA doing to allow private companies to get the data?"[15] NASA representatives explained that while O'Sullivan's question had merit, technical reasons precluded such involvement. Perhaps that was so for NASA, but the moment the meeting closed, Morley and other members of the government approached O'Sullivan and his two young colleagues. "We'd like to talk to you," they trumpeted. "In fact, we'd like to hear about these ideas you have!"[16]

"Impressed by O'Sullivan's chutzpah" and Sloan's technical expertise, Morley invited Sloan to attend CCRS planning meetings in Ottawa. Although still employed by TRIUMF, Sloan made several surreptitious visits to Ottawa. Once there, however, Sloan learned that the University of Toronto, with its plan for a sophisticated new computing facility, would acquire the work for Ottawa's main processing centre. Sloan despaired, but at an early planning meeting, he met Ron Barrington, a scientist who was then part of Canada's other federal agency involved in remote sensing work, the Communications Research Centre. While a member of Canada's Defence Research Telecommunications Establishment, Barrington had participated with the team that built *Alouette-1*. With orbits, antennas, and transmitter power in common, Barrington and Sloan got on marvellously well, and Barrington decided that he wanted to work with Sloan. By the end of the planning meetings, it also became apparent that Morley's main interest was in Ottawa's processing centre. As a result, Barrington and the CRC fought for and won the federal contracts for Canada's ground station work.[17]

Contracts in hand, Barrington searched for a place to build a ground receiving station. The CRC team selected an abandoned radar laboratory, complete with a large antenna, in Prince Albert, Saskatchewan. Barrington subcontracted with the University of Saskatchewan's Space Engineering Division to convert the radar laboratory into a satellite receiving station. He then explained to Sloan the government's plan for a "Make or Buy" policy, which would allow the CRC to buy equipment for the Prince Albert station from the private sector. Revealing that the CRC would seek products similar to those used by NASA, Barrington confided that one piece of equipment, the demultiplexer (a mechanical system used to scan the Earth's surface continuously) was available only through Hughes Aircraft of California, but that Hughes also charged an exorbitant US$500,000 (US$3.2 million in 2016) for it. He therefore suggested that Sloan make a much lower bid for a subcontract, one the CRC could employ as a "Make or Buy" test case.[18]

While the prospect of winning the demultiplexer subcontract excited Sloan, he realized that, as just one person working at TRIUMF, he needed a patron. He therefore approached Bill Thompson, the only business person he knew and trusted in Vancouver. After Sloan finished explaining ERTS as well as his opportunity and dilemma, Thompson declared, "The only company that would be interested in doing this is MacDonald, Dettwiler. John MacDonald and Vern Dettwiler have this little start-up," and "while theirs is strictly a software operation, I know that John wants to get into the hardware business. This seems the perfect opportunity."[19] On Bill Thompson's advice, Sloan paid John MacDonald a visit. MacDonald needed no convincing. He already knew Sloan "by reputation," as a "radio astronomy genius, weather satellite ground station builder, TRIUMF wizard, and space buff." He and Sloan also had many common contacts, including Bill Thompson as a trusted business mentor. MacDonald additionally revealed that he had a long-standing interest in human vision and image processing, and by the time he completed his MIT dissertation on muscular control, the idea of looking at the Earth from space had started to fascinate him as well. With backgrounds, friends, mentors, and professional interests in common, MacDonald decided that Sloan would make an excellent addition to MDA. When Sloan proposed that they might like to work together on the demultiplexer project, MacDonald's interest reached peak voltage, even if Sloan's proposal presented a problem for MDA. The company had just secured the EBCO manufacturing contract, MacDonald explained, and he could ill-afford to hire Sloan on the spot. When Sloan claimed that he had found a second opportunity for MDA, however, MacDonald confessed his desire "to do this," and proposed that "MDA bid on the two opportunities identified." Remembering that meeting as a turning point in his life, MacDonald recalled that he beamed at Sloan and roared, "You help us write the proposals, and if we win even one of them, you and Kuijt can join us and we'll do it! We'll play!"[20]

Sloan wrote the two proposals and MDA lost one straightaway, but Barrington pushed the CRC to award the demultiplexer work to the young, Vancouver-based firm. Still, one other thing stood in the way: MDA's size. Procurement officers at the Department of Supply and Services had reservations about giving a small, unknown firm such a large federal subcontract. After much discussion in Ottawa, however, Barrington finally convinced people at the DSS that they should at least investigate MDA's operation. Colin Lennox then received the call that soon altered MDA's future, with the DSS representative simply growling into the phone that MDA could expect a visit from a government auditor within one week.[21]

Lennox and MacDonald knew that winning the subcontract depended, at the very least, on a credible-looking office. They thus rented some additional space in the Film Exchange building, borrowed the photographic laboratory's space for the inspection, asked Bill Thompson to loan them some electronic test equipment, and quickly assembled the makeshift office. After he turned MDA's little operation upside-down for three days, the DSS auditor declared that he had reached a decision. With MacDonald and Dettwiler busy at UBC, the auditor took Lennox and Bill Thompson to lunch, announcing that MDA could have the job, provided the company took care of one "fatal flaw." The auditor's phrase stunned Lennox. What fatal flaw could MDA possibly have, he wondered. But Thompson, slightly more detached than Lennox, asked, "What's the problem? We'll fix it for you." Leaning forward, the auditor replied, "You don't have a quality assurance group, you've never built any hardware, and frankly, I don't trust you to get it right the first time." Lennox retorted, "Whom would you consider qualified as a quality assurance group?" Turning to Lennox, the auditor winked, "Lenkurt Electric, of course."[22]

With that moment linking the local to the national, MDA to Ottawa, and a wider connection to the global if MDA could deliver on its first major federal subcontract, Lennox excused himself from the table, jumped into his car, drove to Lenkurt, and asked to see Ray Heron, Lenkurt's president. Although Heron barely knew Lennox, when Lennox explained he had an urgent situation on his hands, Heron agreed to chat. After Lennox explained MDA's quality assurance dilemma, Heron claimed, "I don't think we can do it either, but you certainly don't stand a chance unless you take our advice. And you won't do that unless I charge you, so I want $3,000, hard cash, on the day you get the contract." Overjoyed, Lennox exclaimed, "Great! Will you put that in writing?" Heron wrote a letter and signed it. Letter in hand, and one foot out the door, Lennox turned back to Heron and asked, "Why are you doing this for us? You could bid on the job and subcontract to MDA." Smiling, Heron replied, "Because the most important thing MDA can do for Vancouver is to become as large as Lenkurt one day. I cannot hire people from the East," he stressed, "because when they come out for an interview, they say, 'If I don't hit it off with you guys, where can I go?' I want a vibrant electronics industry on the West Coast, and frankly, you're my best chance." Lennox understood: MDA needed friends, and the firm's young associates had no right to spurn what they deemed "inferior" electronics companies such as Lenkurt or employees who "merely cranked out telephone systems." Lennox claimed that he never forgot Heron's important message and that powerful moment. Moreover, with the help of Heron and others, he soon developed a vision of his own: one centred on MDA participating in the construction of something important in and for Vancouver, in particular, and Canada, in general.[23]

By 1971, after the skeptical DSS auditor had left, MDA received the demultiplexer subcontract from the federal government, Sloan became MDA's eighth full-time employee, and the company retained Kuijt as its draftsman and artist.[24] Worth $68,000 (approximately $403,000 in 2016), that first subcontract from the Communications Research Centre gave

MDA a foothold in Canada's infant remote sensing industry, the federal government's research and development funding stream, and the global surveillance community. In addition, as MDA's first remote sensing product, Sloan's multispectral scanner demultiplexer made a splash. It matched the quality of Hughes Aircraft's more expensive equipment, and provided to Barrington and the CRC a Canadian-developed device at nearly one-eighth the cost of what Hughes charged. The little firm's feat also appeared to justify other changes the government had initiated, including the decision to create a new ministry to increase domestic innovation, rationalize the Canadian government's bureaucracy, and enhance the nation's competitive presence in world markets.[25]

"MINISTRY OF THE FUTURE":
THE NEOLIBERAL CONTEXT FOR ACCELERATING
THE PACE OF CHANGE IN CANADA AND AT MDA

On 14 August 1971, Canada announced the creation of the Ministry of State for Science and Technology, marking "the birthday of Canada's 'Ministry of the Future' as recommended by the OECD" review of the Canadian economy in 1969. Alastair Gillespie, the parliamentary secretary to the Treasury Board, assumed responsibility for MOSST. Gillespie had long voiced concerns about Canada's future, arguing, "Our difficulty is that we appear to be mesmerized by the problems, preoccupied by change and uncertainty, and indeed with a transition from an age of continuity to [Peter] Drucker's discontinuity." The "linear planning" of the 1940s and 1950s had produced "many of the problems of the 60s," he emphasized, including "urban sprawl, pollution, traffic congestion," inflation, unemployment, the relative stagnation of traditional manufacturing, and "the question of Canadian ownership, industrial growth, the handling of science and technology, and the use of energy resources." Gillespie therefore recommended that Trudeau focus on opportunities rather than problems, developing a closer relationship with the business community and making it clear that the Liberal Party intended to expand the interests of capital.[26]

Trudeau assured Gillespie and others that he agreed, particularly about the urban problems Gillespie and others had identified. "It has been forecast that by the end of this century, more than seventy per cent of our total population will be living in twelve major centres," Trudeau observed. The "cost of urban land and transportation will continue to spiral at an accelerated rate ... there may indeed be dangers of increased social unrest, and

... fiscal pressures on municipalities will intensify." On 30 June 1971 the federal government therefore established a Ministry of State for Urban Affairs to foster the cooperation of the provinces and municipalities as well as their public and private entities. Although feelings of alienation surfaced within the Western provinces' business community, Trudeau pledged the government's commitment to nurturing regional interests through bilateral and multilateral agreements aimed at maintaining the country's prominence in various fields, including traditional manufacturing, oil and gas, telecommunications, and remote sensing of the Earth and its environment. The government also established MOSST, he stressed, to stimulate the acquisition of managerial skills in Canada's private sector.[27]

Once minister of MOSST, Gillespie argued that he and his team would not involve themselves "as the traditional departments of government are involved, in the implementation of programs"; instead, MOSST's small staff would work with university- and industry-based consultants to recommend priorities "for the application of science and technology in support of our national interests." The culmination of twelve years of studies and the government's centralized advisory structure, MOSST also became Canada's body for formulating national science and technology policy, working with leading federal agencies for research and development: the National Research Council and Supply and Services Canada; and the Departments of National Defence, Communications, Energy, Mines and Resources, Industry, Trade, and Commerce, Fisheries and Oceans, and Agriculture. Gillespie also advocated for contracting-out policies that could push more research and development from government departments and agencies to industry.[28] To effect that change, Gillespie went on a fact-finding mission during MOSST's first operational year. He culled earlier reports, visited Canadian government laboratories, universities, and other high-tech entities, met with those formulating science and technology policies in the United States, organized a scientific mission to Japan so Canadians could witness the "Japanese economic miracle," hosted scientific representatives from Europe, participated in a trade mission to China, and conducted an employment survey to learn more about the supply and demand of talent in Canada.[29]

From early surveys, Gillespie discovered that "the accelerating pace of change in the scientific and technological field, coupled with a national emphasis on higher education in the 1960s," had produced "hundreds of thousands of highly skilled and trained graduates." The country continued to fall behind other industrial nations, however, because Canadians still lacked training for the realities transforming the world, he cautioned. Canadians perceived the demand for new graduates as "everlasting," he argued, but it was not. "Supply soon caught up with demand, creating a job crisis for certain highly skilled Canadians," while a specific shortfall in the supply of computer scientists, systems engineers, and other technology workers made it increasingly difficult for industry to find Canadian graduates with the skills they required to compete. "Our task as a nation is to continue to provide the science and technology that will assist private enterprise to become competitive industrially in the pursuit of national goals," Gillespie emphasized, and "to rationalize the quantity and quality of research and development performed in the private, government and university sectors." He therefore urged the Canadian government to reorganize research and development to end the "adhockery in science spending in Canada."[30]

Gillespie argued that the Science Council of Canada had already "expressed 'alarm' over the deterioration of technology-based industry" and "warned that, unless Canada carves a place for itself in the world market, it is in danger of falling back into its old role of being primarily an exporter of raw materials. The creation of new jobs is urgent," he emphasized, "because the supply of technical manpower is increasing by 9 per cent per year while the demand over the past 3 years has been static." He also noted that "recent lay-offs of scientists and engineers in the chemical industry, particularly by the Polymer Corporation and Shawinigan Chemicals," had "resulted in a flood of letters to Members of Parliament," along with "many applications by Scientists for employment in the government." Rather than lose that talent to NASA and other American-based entities, Gillespie suggested that federal and provincial governments provide incentives for Canadian industry to absorb them.[31] Others concurred, but additionally stressed the insufficiency of focusing on scientists to avoid a potential brain drain. "If Canada is to continue to develop and expand its scientific effort," one argued, "it is essential that there be a dynamic and progressive program for the support of engineering in Canada. Without innovative industry in the area of sophisticated engineering," he warned, "it will become increasingly difficult for the scientific community to convince society that science is a good thing and deserving of support." Although scientific "understanding of complex systems bids fair to make substantial contributions to the understanding of systems in other fields," he emphasized the "unique body of knowledge, which is engineering knowledge" as more conducive to solving the "uncertainty" Canadians faced.[32]

From what he had learned on tours of other countries, Gillespie stressed that Canada "had a lot to learn from our more advanced neighbours and partners," especially the United States, where policymakers already knew that "one of the most powerful tools available to government, to encourage R&D, innovation and the consequent growth of a competitive industry, is its purchasing power."[33] Gillespie therefore suggested that the federal government revisit its criteria for government procurement.[34] "Government requirements for R&D can encourage the formation of new research facilities, especially with respect to new product development through contracts for R&D," Gillespie stressed. He and other policymakers added that "Canada's future needs dictate that more needs to take place in industry for the spin off benefits in the market place."[35] "Since Canada is too small – its population is one-tenth that of the United States – to support large-scale technological ventures on its own," one news source reported, "it has welcomed the subsidiaries of many foreign-based corporations, notably those from the United States." As a result, "Canada is in the unique position of being the only industrialized country that is neither a major producer of technology nor part of a large trading bloc." To correct those problems, the federal government would need to "encourage the development of more Canadian-based multinational corporations to create markets large enough to support innovative R&D. This is related to the nation's new foreign policy," the news source stressed, "which is aimed at expansion of world trade ties and decreased vulnerability to fluctuations in the U.S. economy."[36]

Policymakers had cause for concern about Canada's vulnerability to the United States. As the war in Vietnam dragged on, inflation rose and unemployment increased, first in the United States, then in Canada. Just one day after the debut of MOSST, President Nixon announced his "New Economic Policy" to "create a new prosperity without war." Anticipating an eventual end to the conflict in Vietnam, Nixon's address identified three critical tasks the nation needed to undertake: create more and better jobs for returning veterans, through tax cuts that promised to stimulate the economy; end inflation, by instituting a ninety-day freeze on prices and wages; and protect the US dollar from "attacks of international money speculators" by suspending the dollar's convertibility into gold. Stephen Ambrose has argued that the suspension initiated the end of the Bretton Woods system and the eventual ascendance of the "Group of Six" (with finance ministers and central bank governors from France, Italy, West Germany, Japan, the United Kingdom, and the United States during 1975, and becoming the G7 when Canada joined the group in 1976).[37] Nixon's speech also threatened cutbacks in military and aerospace programs, including those of NASA. Fearing such restrictions, NASA had previously proposed international participation programs that exchanged NASA's assistance and expertise in space-based work with promises by other nations to share the costs of the American space program. According to a spokesperson for SPAR, NASA's interests extended beyond searching for ways to defray costs, however; they also hoped to expand "the base of support for the program on the premise – an astute one, as it later turned out – that it would be more difficult for U.S. politicians to kill a project later if it had attracted significant international co-operation." NASA then applied that premise to *Landsat*, arguing that the US government had already entered into a five-year renewable contract with Canada to enhance "prosperity without war." Still, many Canadians worried about Nixon's intentions and NASA's future.[38]

To lessen Canada's dependence on NASA, some Canadians argued that the federal government needed to move quickly to create a national space agency. Representing those views, one 1972 editorial argued that a "$31-million Canadian communications satellite will start to circle the earth this fall; yet the country still lacks either a space agency or a space policy." Furthermore, it stressed, "the taxpayer is footing an annual $27-million space bill, but the various space programs are scattered throughout five ministerial departments and one agency." As a result, "Only a national space authority can shove such programs along with the necessary single-minded vigor, and decide if Canada should agree to share in the U.S. 'Space-shuttle' project," which it "suspected of having more to do with military planning than with space science and in any case is likely to prove wildly expensive." Gillespie's MOSST "ought to waste not another moment before speaking out firmly for the creation of a space agency." Despite such arguments, federal ministers ultimately deferred that decision, arguing that the country had insufficient resources to fund a space agency immediately. Instead, they suggested that MOSST continue to coordinate the efforts of the National Research Council and other agencies to nurture Canada's space initiatives and enhance the country's sovereignty and economic future. In Vancouver, those efforts then provided opportunities for MDA to participate more deeply in regional developments and Canada's larger bid to play a prominent role in the commercial development of global remote sensing.[39]

"QUICKLOOK":
THE GOVERNMENT CONTRACTING PARADIGM

While the government began to craft policies for Canada's hoped-for future during the fall of 1971, Ron Barrington approached Dave Sloan about negotiating a second contract with the CRC, this time for a ground station device called "Quicklook." Perceiving in his new Vancouver subcontractors a hunger for a piece of the action in Ottawa, one that motivated their willingness to work day and night for little financial return, Barrington hoped MDA could help him to solve a pressing problem. Because the CRC had placed its ground station in Prince Albert, Saskatchewan, Barrington worried that he had no way of knowing whether or not he would receive valuable data. The Prince Albert station could record the data, but the newly created Centre for Remote Sensing's processing centre stood some 1,800 miles away in Ottawa. Already well behind schedule, data processing work in Ottawa promised to take months, and Barrington wanted instant results. With Canada's population surpassing 21 million, that of the United States exceeding 205 million, and Canada's new "Make or Buy" policy in the offing during the fall of 1971, Barrington announced that the CRC had decided to give MDA a small, $110,000 subcontract, one that would allow MacDonald and Sloan to build a Quicklook display system, complete with a Polaroid camera to convert Barrington's raw data into a quasi-television image others could then photograph.[40]

The demultiplexer hardware project and the Quicklook display system changed John MacDonald's life and MDA's direction. It seemed that Sloan could generate ideas on demand, and together that MacDonald and Sloan could implement them quickly. Finally finding in Sloan a technical person who shared his interests, MacDonald thus began to devote all of his energies to MDA's acquisition of remote sensing expertise, later remarking that, in terms of instant gratification, his years with Sloan represented MDA's (and his own) "salad days. It was a marvellous, heady time. Dave and I complemented each other well, and in this case, the whole was certainly greater than the sum of its parts." Idealistic, enthusiastic, and totally inexperienced in the ravages of market realities, MacDonald finally had a tangible goal, one that gave his life meaning and promised the possibility of securing the ends for which he and Dettwiler had created MDA. Invigorated by Sloan's presence, and busy selling *his* company's image, MacDonald also began to spend more time at the office and less time at UBC. While he had always generated an unparalleled zeal among his students, according to many people involved in MDA, MacDonald's personality seemed to take on messianic qualities, with his life and vision as well as MDA's mission becoming wholly indivisible while he worked on the Quicklook project.[41]

While the MDA team worked on the Quicklook display system, Mac-Donald received *Innovation in a Cold Climate*, one of the Science Council of Canada's many advisory reports. Contributing to a series of ongoing warnings that Canadian research and development, particularly in the manufacturing sector, had fallen far below that of other industrial nations, the report argued that without some form of government-industry collaboration, Canada's ability to compete in international trade promised to decline even further. As a result, the report recommended that "every effort should be made to transfer to industry, wherever practical, any work now carried out in-house by the government that may lead to industrial innovation." Furthermore, "both federal and provincial governments should explore the possibility of creating new mechanisms for supplying capital to new and small companies."[42] MacDonald not only shared the report's view, but also declared that he had found the formula on which to expand his vision as well as MDA's business opportunities and Canada's industrial expertise. Thus, MDA's board approved the incorporation of a wholly owned subsidiary, Synaptic Systems Ltd, MDA's "job shop," to assemble Quicklook and other hardware devices on which MacDonald planned to build some of that expertise. MacDonald nevertheless wanted everyone to know that MDA had no intention of competing in the manufacturing world. In May 1972, he publicly declared, "A large portion of our business is with manufacturers. We never want to be taken for one. So at MDA we don't make anything. We buy everything, put it together, and make it work." MacDonald's declaration marked the first public statement about the pro–systems engineering and anti-manufacturing identity developing at MDA, a collective aspiration that continued to guide the firm no matter later advice, opportunities, or threats to the company's survival.[43]

With the government funding initial research and development, Mac-Donald hoped that MDA could take on all the interesting projects it could find, give current employees the exciting work they craved, and perhaps even start to incubate Vancouver's high-tech community with engineering graduates from UBC and elsewhere. Employing such a future as his backdrop and conversational prop, MacDonald began to talk and travel, with anyone and to anywhere he could find an audience. He spoke in Vancouver. He spent time in Ottawa, giving "lectures" at CCRS, the CRC, and Bell Northern Research (then Canada's premier telecommunications research and development organization). He stumped for MDA while among federal ministers, offered to give interviews, and encouraged Sloan to persuade Barrington to give MDA more work.[44]

Given Canada's expanding ambitions for SPAR and the subcontractors it might nurture, Barrington and others needed little convincing. Since its founding, SPAR had emerged as Canada's chosen instrument for securing sovereignty in telecommunications. With the use of Canadian content an important feature of Telesat's mandate, during 1970 SPAR received a significant subcontract from Hughes Aircraft, the US firm Telesat had hired to build the structure for its Inuit language–inspired *Anik-1*. The world's first national domestic communications satellite project, *Anik-1* also provoked a national debate on Canada's technological sovereignty. According to SPAR's official history, many people interested in Canada's aerospace industry "argued that awarding *Anik* to a U.S. company represented a fundamental threat to Canada's technological future. Comparisons were drawn to the cancellation of the Avro Arrow," the history stressed, and "the chairman of the Science Council of Canada said it would be 'complete madness' to throw away Canada's growing expertise in the field." Hughes prevailed, but the political debate over Canadian content prompted the American firm to approach SPAR about participating in *Anik*'s development. SPAR's president, Larry Clarke, negotiated the terms, demanding that SPAR also receive a chance to learn the ropes from Hughes so that its engineers could transfer all they would learn about managing large space contracts to the Canadian setting. Hughes accepted SPAR's terms, and by the time *Anik-1* launched on 9 November 1972, SPAR had developed credibility as an exemplary satellite component parts builder as well as manager of large-scale government contracts. As a reward, influential friends in the federal government then pushed for SPAR to become Canada's only satellite prime contractor for the country.[45]

"By a series of mergers and support from the federal government," one reporter noted, SPAR quickly developed into "a manufacturer of subsystems for communications satellites, and of earth-stations and transmission equipment." As a result, members of the Canadian government "decided that SPAR, with its experience as a subcontractor in earlier Canadian space programs, [should] be the prime contractor" for Canada's future communications satellites and the country's space manufacturing sector as a whole. SPAR's success in supplying satellite components allowed the firm to acquire other firms and products, which solidified its future as Canada's prime space contractor as well as MDA's principal rival in the remote sensing industry.[46] Although MacDonald and other self-proclaimed "western mavericks" remain loath to admit it, MDA and other high-tech firms in Western Canada survived and flourished, thanks to the nationalist policies of Ottawa and the very Toronto-based, "eastern establishment" firms that people at MDA decried as "tin bashers" and "stuffed shirts." "There was a lot to learn" from SPAR, one employee recalled, "in terms of dealing with the government, and negotiating your rates and contracts, knowing the people, getting things done, particularly through the Treasury Board."[47]

While SPAR expanded its reach, MDA completed the Quicklook display system, Barrington immediately saw whether or not he had received quality data, and the Canadian government purchased MDA's device at a much lower cost than American firms charged. As one of the scientists, engineers, and industrialists offering expertise to MOSST, Barrington thus recommended changes that quickly led to Canada's new "Make or Buy" policy. Officially announced by the federal government during August 1972, "Make or Buy" instructed all government departments and agencies "to contract out government-funded research and development to private industry" as a rule, rather than exception. Initially, exceptions included work in fields related to particular national security issues, where no suitable capability existed in the private sector, or where in-house R&D supported regulatory functions, national standards, and departmental competencies. But wherever possible, "Make or Buy" made it clear: the Canadian government would increase opportunities for engineers and scientists in private industry to participate in research and development procurement to meet Canada's national aims and interests within an international environment.[48] By further liberalizing the Canadian economy, policymakers promised that "Make or Buy" would make Canadian firms more competitive with their American counterparts by bolstering their managerial capabilities in R&D. Those promises then extended the ambitions of the Defence Industry Productivity Program (DIPP) to "enhance the technological competence of the Canadian defence industry in its export activities by providing financial assistance to industrial firms for selected projects" with "civil export sales potential."[49]

"Make or Buy" encouraged those in industry and at universities to share their expertise and needs with MOSST and Canada's departments of National Defence, Communications, and Energy, Mines, and Resources. Representing a "shift in emphasis from an inward in-house activity to an outward for and with industry approach," the policy both furthered the significance of the engineering profession in the promotion of Canadian economic development and promoted the federal government as investor in and buyer of private-sector initiatives. Americans had earlier suggested such efforts by stressing a perceived lack of an entrepreneurial spirit in Canada. For example, one American management consultant who addressed the parliamentary secretary to the prime minister argued that

Canadians suffered from a "hangover of British conservatism." Canadians lacked imagination and self-confidence, avoided risk, and had become the "most psychologically insecure people on Earth." Although he claimed to like Canadians, the consultant maintained that Canada needed to emulate the strategies the US government had employed to create its entrepreneurial culture. This, he argued, would encourage Canadian businessmen to change their attitudes and behaviours in fundamental ways, including an end to what he identified as their "over-simplified, naïve view of profit making." Instead, he argued, Canadians needed to adopt a more "sophisticated, profit-oriented view," and the federal government needed to provide tax and other incentives as well as better business curriculum to stress the benefits of "thinking big," including the nurturing of more aggressive corporate strategies. Once done, he promised, Canada would emerge as a more powerful, competitive nation, one worthy of its place in the capitalist world core.[50]

Alastair Gillespie and others assured their US friends that Canada had already adopted many of the aspirations outlined in US President Nixon's 1972 speech, "The Importance of Our Investment in Science and Technology." "There are many engineers in Canadian universities who could launch new enterprises if there were reasonable inducements available," one government official noted, and "there is little reason for believing that Canadians are, as a group, any less competent managers than a similar group in the United States."[51] Members of the Treasury Board also stressed that Canadians could not "be all things to all men. We must be specialists," in areas where Canadians already excelled or could develop expertise, particularly in transportation, communications, and the infant commercial space sector.[52] Canada could not "be expected to compete in every venture with the larger nations of the world," they noted, but Canadians "have the expertise and by our geography some specific resources that can be exploited more economically and conveniently than other nations." As a result, government representatives and their industry consultants articulated the oceans as a unique opportunity for Canadians to pursue more aggressively, along with increased efforts to exploit the Arctic region.[53]

Gillespie also argued that Canadians could be more aggressive without having to emulate every feature of the United States; he therefore urged the government to apply scientific research and development not only "in support of economic growth (and jobs!), but also in "quality of life objectives, including a harmonious natural environment."[54] Toward those ends, MOSST sponsored the elimination of the federal sales tax on all research and development equipment purchased for industrial research, and worked with several Canadian government departments and agencies, including the CRC and CCRS, to encourage the expeditious adoption of "Make or Buy." During 1973, the federal government then created the Foreign Investment Review Agency (FIRA) to screen all proposed takeovers and ensure that the foreign acquisition and establishment of businesses in Canada would serve Canadian interests and bring "significant benefits" to Canada. If they could not do so, the federal government planned to create spinoff opportunities by cultivating Canadian multinationals and small businesses.[55]

In the meantime, with the federal government promising future contracts to meet the specific needs of the remote sensing sector during the spring of 1972, MacDonald knew he had to make a decision. On the one hand, he had not lost enthusiasm for teaching, but he had spread himself too thinly across too many obligations. On the other, he had definitely lost interest in the publish-or-perish schedule, which he found increasingly difficult to keep. Still, he had trained himself as an academic and needed to find out whether he could make the switch from a professor to the life of a full-time businessman. Rather than quit his secure position, MacDonald decided to take a year's leave of absence during academic 1972/73 so that he could temporarily join MDA as its full-time president and ambassador for Quicklook and other projects.[56]

When NASA launched *Landsat-1* on 23 July 1972, completion of the CCRS processing centre in Ottawa still remained months away; however, MDA's Quicklook device set up at the Prince Albert station provided to Canadians their first real glimpse of pictures of the country from outer space. Numerous Canadian dignitaries attended the official opening, and excitement filled the air as *Landsat-1* made its first pass over Canada. Anxious to witness the results of the project he and the CCRS had done so much to support, Larry Morley flew from Ottawa to oversee the operation. Although a seasoned veteran, Morley could not contain himself. Taking charge of the Polaroid camera, and as the antenna tracked each pass, Morley pulled the film, seized the picture, and exclaimed, "Look at this one! Look at this one!" Passing the photographs to a cheering crowd of technology enthusiasts, he then pulled the film again, seized each additional picture, and continued to burst, "Look at this one! Look at this one!" The quality of the Quicklook images could never compare to a full process, but Canada emerged as the first country to achieve instant results from *Landsat-1*. Quicklook transformed MacDonald and Sloan into engineering celebrities, gained publicity for Canada within the international remote sensing community, and ensured that MDA had all the follow-on work its team could handle. With a third subcontract from the CRC arriving by the end of 1973, MDA received the chance to build a backup system for the Prince Albert radar laboratory. Morley's efforts at the CCRS also pushed MDA into other areas, including those focused on Cold War efforts to monitor land masses as well as the oceans.[57]

"POTENTIAL OF WORLD WAR III": WORKING ON BOTH SIDES OF THE COLD WAR ON LAND AND AT SEA

MacDonald's leave of absence from UBC coincided with a "Make or Buy" subcontract from the CCRS to build an airborne data acquisition system (ADAS). Offering the young firm a $137,000 contract during December 1972, Morley and the CCRS allowed MDA to learn how to integrate new hardware, software, and digital recorders into one project. Unfortunately, ADAS cost twice as much as the company had estimated, and once again, MDA had to absorb the cost. Nevertheless, the success of the initial project led to more work with the federal government, including another small ($46,000) contract to build an ADAS for a Canadian research submarine. Work on the submersible system then promised to solidify MDA's position in both sky and sea.[58]

As a derivative of the company's airborne work, MDA's submersible data acquisition system led to MDA's first direct contract negotiation with a bureau of a foreign government, the USSR's Institute of Oceanology of the Soviet Academy of Sciences. Working with Export Development Canada, North Vancouver's International Hydrodynamics had agreed to supply the USSR with three of its Pisces submersibles for scientific research of the deep sea. International Hydrodynamics had previously built Pisces for the newly created US National Oceanic and Atmospheric Administration (NOAA, formed on 3 October 1970), and hoped to export its expertise to other governments around the world. The Soviet order represented its first opportunity, but the contract, worth nearly $4 million in 1974 (or $19.5 million in 2016) quickly ran into snags. Originally negotiated through a Canada-US defence sharing agreement during 1971, the Canadian government had an obligation to inform the US government about the planned export sale, for the foreign "disposition" of the Pisces was based on "significant USA content," including its pressure tanks. Following an interagency review of the proposed contract, representatives of the US government raised security concerns about possible "Soviet exploitation of sensitive USA origin submarine technology" and "clandestine use of highly classified USA underwater defensive arrangements." Those concerns also revealed the power of the American military-industrial complex to influence decisions on both sides of the border.[59]

During 1971, the *Wall Street Journal* had reported that a dozen US corporations had built more than thirty research submarines since 1964, "in anticipation of a boom in underwater work. By one estimate, $50 million [US$307.4 million in 2016] was spent on these 'submersibles,' their tender vessels and their crews." US contractors expected the American government to set up a "wet" NASA, spending "as much as $2 billion a year by 1979"; unfortunately for General Dynamics, Grumman Aerospace, Lockheed, and other military contractors, the director of Westinghouse Ocean Research Laboratories reported that "the last time one of our submersibles was wet was a year ago last September." With NOAA established the year before, "it's hardly a wet NASA," the *Wall Street Journal* contended. "Oceanographic spending never went higher than $500 million, and it is almost all spent on surface vessels. NOAA expects to spend no more than $700,000 for undersea research this year," it claimed. As a result, American military contractors lobbied their representatives in Congress, US government officials put pressure on Ottawa, and the Canadian government killed the International Hydraulics deal. Although the Canadian firm managed to renegotiate the sale of two submersibles for the USSR in 1975 (via the Department of Fisheries and Oceans rather than through defence sharing agreements), and built others for US contractors, by 1978, competitors forced International Hydrodynamics into receivership.[60]

While representatives of the Canadian government began the process that eventually cancelled the initial submersible export sale to the USSR, some members of the negotiating team learned the strategies Americans were willing to employ in the foreign export market. Noting that Americans had sold US-manufactured computers to the Soviet Nuclear Research Centre with only "random spot checks" on the technology involved, Canadian export negotiators questioned whether the United States had "imposed" a "double standard of security requirements." In a snide telex, one Canadian representative in Moscow argued that he "would have thought nuclear research more sensitive than oceanology and supply of computer more significant to Soviet progress in critical areas than supply of [a] submersible."[61]

Despite such tensions, MDA's successful prototype of the data acquisition system convinced Canadian officials to approach the USSR about investigating MDA as a possible electronics supplier. Adhering to MacDonald's principle that MDA should work with any client who promised to spread the company's name and influence globally, the MDA team drafted a proposal to the Institute of Oceanology of the Soviet Academy of Sciences for a $51,000 project. Recalling that proposal, Lennox and MacDonald stressed the importance of their first secret project for the Canadian government and the recognition that their work might have important strategic implications for Canada's role in the Cold War. Still, they mused, the chance to work on another new technology mattered more to those working at MDA than any geopolitical manoeuvring beyond their control. Just one item stood in the way. When the Soviet liaison for the institute looked at MDA's quotation, he informed Lennox that the Soviets could accept the bid only if MDA dropped the price by 10 per cent. Although Lennox and MacDonald had decided that MDA must bid more realistically, they argued that they had proposed the exact amount that they thought the system would cost. Declaring wiggle room impossible, Lennox and MacDonald apologized profusely and shared with each other their fears about losing the contract. In this instance, however, their negotiating naïveté seemed to pay off. When the institute's representative returned to MDA's office, he said, "We'll pay you the price you asked for. We don't think you're like typical North American companies that inflate their prices 10 to 15 per cent for foreigners." But the Soviets had a problem. "We don't have contract documents appropriate for you, because our contract person works for our ship-building industry and the conditions are different. I'm sorry, we can't give you a contract."[62]

Failing to perceive that ship-building documents might also represent a strategic move arranged by political operatives in Ottawa and Moscow, Lennox proposed, "What if we took the Soviet forms and photocopied MDA's terms and conditions on to their sheets?" While Lennox claimed that the Soviets found Lennox's request unusual, the steamship contract negotiator agreed to it. By July 1975, the assistance of government agency advocates and representatives of Export Development Canada then made it possible for MDA to win the Soviet subcontract. Shortly thereafter, Lennox sent Ken Spencer, by then the company's budding young ground station contract estimator, "to the world behind the 'Iron Curtain'" to build a submersible data acquisition system for the USSR.[63]

According to MDA lore, most employees claimed they had little interest in the politics of the work; that is, until the MDA team invited a Russian representative to attend an acceptance test. As it turned out, on the day scheduled for the Soviet visit, other members of the firm had scheduled another acceptance test for a Texas-based firm. When they arrived at MDA, the Texans immediately introduced themselves as members of the John

Birch Society, a right-wing American political advocacy group supporting anti-communism. To avoid what MDA's young associates laughingly described as "the potential for World War III," some members of the MDA team took the Russian representatives on a boat trip in Vancouver's harbour while others hosted the Texans in the firm's one large systems room. Although MDA's associates avoided an international incident in Vancouver, some recognized that their acceptance tests for both the Soviets and Americans had helped to put the company's founders and followers at the heart of the Cold War and the political intrigues of global surveillance.[64]

Beyond ensuring that the company received its first export contract, MDA's original ADAS further enhanced the young firm's reputation as a credible subsystem contractor. Impressed by MDA's increasing capabilities and the credentials the young associates had earned during their first few years, Larry Morley and other members of the Canadian Advisory Committee on Remote Sensing invited MacDonald to participate in a Sensor Working Group. There, MacDonald learned about opportunities in signal processing and sonar systems, two significant fields in the expansion of global surveillance. At working group meetings, MacDonald also got better acquainted with many central players in Canada's remote sensing community, including the working group's chairman, Philip Lapp. Although ADAS initially convinced MDA's neophyte industrialists that they had entered dangerous waters, not geopolitically but by working on too many innovations on a modest budget, meetings with Lapp confirmed that MDA could "go global." With MDA building credible systems for the CRC as well as the CCRS, the remote sensing agencies' representatives wasted little time in marketing the Canadian firm at every opportunity, confirming that the federal government's salesmanship and networking contacts mattered as much as its purchasing power.[65]

While attending NASA's international participation program meetings, Canadian agency boosters advertised MDA capabilities to many foreign countries, particularly in the developing world, where governments had begun to realize the significance of building their own ground stations to receive images from *Landsat-1*. By 1972, those countries included Brazil and its prime contractor, Bendix. When members of the CCRS told representatives from Bendix about what Canada's inexpensive demultiplexer and Quicklook display had accomplished, Bendix sidestepped a relationship with the more expensive American Hughes Aircraft, and instead gave MDA a $230,000 subcontract (worth approximately $1.24 million in 2016) to build another low-cost, ground station subsystem. Once MDA completed the project for Brazil during 1973, Hughes retreated from international demultiplexer competition, a departure MacDonald employed as the evidence he needed to tender his resignation at UBC.[66] The Bendix project also provided a lesson about the delicate touch needed for clients in developing and hence less technically advanced markets. After MDA completed the job for Brazil, a visitor carrying a demultiplexer under his arm asked to see MacDonald. "We had a lightning strike and the demultiplexer doesn't work very well," he announced. "Can you fix it?" Because the visitor had flown all the way from Brazil, MacDonald promptly put the demultiplexer on a bench, tested it, and discovered that a lightning strike had blown a chip in the system. MacDonald replaced the chip and sent the Brazilian on his way. Dettwiler witnessed the scene, and from that moment forward, both he and MacDonald vowed that MDA's staff must look after every client in similar ways, no matter the hour or day of the week. They also promised each other that they would hire only the kinds of people both willing and able to go that extra mile.[67]

MacDonald's decision to join MDA full time assuaged the concerns of many employees and board members. With government contracts expanding from 40 per cent of sales in 1972 to nearly 63 per cent in 1973, the company needed full-time contact with Larry Morley, Ron Barrington, and other Ottawa-based agency representatives, a reality that demanded John MacDonald's full-time attention. Still, his presence required a few adjustments. For one thing, he paced while thinking. For another, he talked while designing and his voice boomed throughout the tiny office. Not even the door to his inner office improved the situation. Several employees thus appealed to MacDonald's wife for relief. She quickly commissioned staff to place foam-rubber padding in every nook and cranny of MacDonald's office, after which she covered the walls with grey flannel. While hardly an archetypal executive suite, MacDonald's grey flannel office allowed others to work in peace. Moreover, the new surroundings seemed to suit MacDonald's personality, MDA's "maverick" élan, and many of the "countercultural" styles then dominating engineering start-up firms and bolstering capitalist expansion, particularly in the technology sector. For many technology enthusiasts, getting the job done mattered more than how, where, under what conditions, or at what time people chose to accomplish that end.[68]

MacDonald has argued that "engineers who are designing stuff" should "work from midnight until nine in the morning, or whatever they want to do. We've certain things that have to be done at certain hours, because that's what the business world demands." Beyond that, however, "as long as the person delivers, as long as they do what they say they're going to do, when they say they're going to do it, I don't give a shit how they do it."[69] At the same time, a spouse's entrance into the office revealed other things about MDA, including the gendered expectations and stereotypes that continued to guide the engineering professions, despite the developing second-wave feminist movement. MDA was a boy's club, one where men created technological solutions to industrial problems, with MacDonald's wife the mother called in to solve domestic rather than business or technological issues within the firm. As a result, while MDA gained a solid reputation in software and hardware development, it also solidified rituals associated with male bonding, including the ways in which "boys and their toys" worked.[70] Moreover, by the end of 1973, that bonding convinced MacDonald that he had discovered the formula for MDA's long-term success: by employing the company's first three remote sensing contracts and MDA's sweat-equity formula to expand business opportunities, he hoped to avoid the stain of permanent "ward status." Although anathema to MacDonald, many free traders, and other pro-business advocates who have enjoyed the fruits of government contracts, subsidies, tax breaks, handouts, and other forms of largesse in the United States, Canada, and other capitalist societies, MDA quickly became a ward of the state, in a government contracting paradigm its associates ultimately found very hard to shake. Regardless, MDA used its first government contracts to develop further ground station products, then exported its expertise abroad in the hope of cashing in on the seed capital the government had provided.[71]

With MDA's expanding team of engineers gladly putting in uncompensated overtime as the badges "western mavericks" wore to celebrate technical challenges and achievements, MacDonald argued that he viewed the financial side of the business in terms of "self-sustainment, about rewarding people for taking the risk," with government contracts enabling the firm "to support the kind of environment where people can be happy, where people can be productive, where people can enjoy what they do, feel challenged, feel that there's a purpose." During the 1970s, Colin Lennox "used to answer the phone, 'Hi, MDA. We're never closed!' And this would be at midnight sometimes," MacDonald recalled. Twenty years later he boasted that MDA's employee commitment never waned: "There's a young girl who works just kitty-corner in the [industrial] park here, and she said, 'You know what I notice about MDA? The parking lot: it's never empty, twenty-four hours a day.' That was something for a company of 750 people," MacDonald stressed, but "it was another thing when we were just seven [or] ten people."[72] No matter the number, government contracting and the firm's sweat-equity formula became the firm's central paradigm:

to work on the cutting edge, produce value for the money, work night and day to get the job done, "learn to do things, and then build businesses around them." Such a paradigm also served those in the government with ambitions for Canada.[73]

Because the government had underwritten its early development, MDA's low-cost, high-quality Quicklook and ADAS products promised to give MDA and Canada a strong competitive edge in the international market. Still, MDA faced fierce competition as it expanded its ground station products, from installations for General Electric and Bendix in the United States, through Computing Devices in Canada, and, by the late 1970s, on to Ford Aerospace, Hitachi and Nippon Electric Corp. in Japan, and Messerschmitt-Bölkow-Blohm in Germany. Although the company remained small when compared to rivals across the world, MDA's staff had confidence in their friends at the CCRS and CRC. They also trusted those promoting improved procurement and other policy levers that promised to open new markets, avoid small firm failures and a future brain drain of Canadian talent, help Western businesses to create spinoff opportunities, develop Canadian corporations into multinationals, and protect Canada's information, technological, Arctic, and space-based sovereignty. With such goals as their backdrop, MDA's hopefuls intended to mount a competitive international sales campaign and vie with companies such as SPAR, which had just received two major subcontracts from the Defence Industry Productivity Program. Estimated at $90 million ($468.5 million in 2016), those subcontracts allowed SPAR to commence work on a remote manipulator system (RMS) for Canada's participation in NASA's Shuttle Program. People at MDA thus believed that they had the chance to expand their operations in similar ways, through the small subcontracts they had received to develop ground station products for the burgeoning Earth observation industry.[74]

From technology developed through 1973, MDA captured additional hardware work worth $1.2 million, $800,000 of it in the export market. For a small firm, that figure seemed like an international bonanza, convincing MDA executives that the company stood a fighting chance to win larger prizes. As evidence, they noted that after MDA successfully completed the Brazilian contract, Hughes and Bendix decided to exit the ground station business. During 1974, Italy planned to build its first ground station, and Canada's Computing Devices won the Italian job, giving MDA a small subcontract for another demultiplexer. Computing Devices saw the Italian ground station through to completion, but thereafter also decided to withdraw from the market. A complex variety of motivations and concerns prompted others to quit the business, including problems with estimating costs and generating profits, but people at MDA read their departures in positive terms, assuring themselves that they had achieved an invincible position within the global remote sensing community. With most of the ground station prime contractors out of the way, and MDA's future looking bright, the firm thus set a corporate objective to supply full ground stations to every future *Landsat* station. Still, the company needed a government champion to convince international customers that a small firm could deliver sophisticated systems. In addition, without venture capital, MDA also needed the government's financial support. Later that year, Larry Morley secured for MDA what the young firm needed.[75]

"THIS WAY TO THE PROMISED LAND": THE UNSOLICITED PROPOSAL PROGRAM AND PORTABLE EARTH

During 1974, while Canadians celebrated Global Television network's first broadcast, the US House of Representatives Judiciary Committee commenced formal impeachment proceedings against President Richard Nixon, and India successfully detonated its first nuclear weapon, Larry Morley busied himself with work on the CCRS's contribution to the Unsolicited Proposal Program. Initiated in 1974 to provide bridge financing for projects suggested by underdeveloped private companies, the UPP helped many Canadian firms to build significant business areas. As an adjunct to the "Make or Buy" policy and other "contracting out" initiatives, one reporter noted, the UPP "encourages the private sector, particularly small business, to submit written proposals containing unique ideas or opportunities to support government objectives in the areas of research and development."[76]

The UPP also allowed members of federal government agencies to support select firms without the nettlesome problems of adhering to competitive bidding and low-bid contracting, and provided to larger firms such as SPAR the opportunity to expand their multinational plans. At the same time, the UPP offered a chance for members of the private sector to dream up proposals for projects they wanted to pursue, with government dollars reducing the risks and costs associated with early research and development. With Larry Morley planning to nurture MDA as one of the small companies through which SPAR could subcontract, Dave Sloan told John MacDonald that he wanted to employ the UPP to build Canada's second Earth observation receiving station, this time a turnkey ground station in a portable trailer. Sloan argued that the Prince Albert station could never cover the entire nation, evidenced by the ways in which it always bypassed small parts of the Maritimes and Newfoundland. A portable station could solve that coverage problem; and, moreover, Sloan argued, MDA could probably build it for no more than $2 million. When he compared his $2 million plan to NASA's $25 million system, Sloan concluded that the portable ground station could secure for MDA the international market the MDA team craved. Armed with knowledge gleaned on the Prince Albert and Brazilian projects, MacDonald embraced Sloan's technical concept as plausible, even exciting.[77] Thanks to the SPAR model and Canadian ambitions, MacDonald thus developed a "presentation where he tracked small, early contracts that MDA had gotten from the government, and showed the spinoff into huge amounts of business, to help justify a Buy Canada program, to help justify the Unsolicited Proposal Program," one employee recalled. "He'd talk basically to anyone who would listen, mostly at CCRS and at Treasury Board."[78]

Demonstrating his abilities to speak with anyone who would give him the time, MacDonald accepted an invitation to attend a CCRS-sponsored symposium on remote sensing at the Empress Hotel in Victoria, BC. During a gathering of distinguished remote-sensing professionals in one working group's hospitality suite, MacDonald began a boisterous discussion with a government procurement officer. Voice booming and long arms waving this way and that, MacDonald began to draw the attention of everyone in the room, including Philip Lapp, a co-author of Canada's evolving space policies. Lapp had resolved to linger in the hospitality suite as nothing more than a fly on the wall, but as he listened to MacDonald sell his ideas and eavesdropped on the general conversation, Lapp noticed that MacDonald began to exchange thoughts and doodle at the same time, moving "things in and out with the rubber eraser on his pencil, changing this, changing that." Moreover, the Department of Supply and Services "guy and I thought this was a very strange selling technique because the [DSS procurement officer] didn't know one end of an electron from another." He "just worried about fair competition and whether or not the price was right. But, being polite, he listened very carefully as John described and drew what turned out, in the end, to be a diagram of the original PERGS station."[79]

On that night, no one in the Empress hospitality suite understood the technical concept behind MDA's Portable Earth Receiving Ground Station (PERGS); after MacDonald explained the details, particularly the low costs associated with building it, however, Larry Morley and the CCRS gave to MacDonald and Sloan what they wanted. "NASA used to tour these poor people from the Third World through Goddard" Space Flight Center in Greenbelt, Maryland, MacDonald recalled, explaining "to them that a ground station was a $25-million project. These guys from the Third World, their eyes would sort of roll back into their heads," he chuckled, "while NASA representatives said, 'But you need one of these.' Dave and I figured you could do it for $2 million, so I basically sold this damned thing."[80] MacDonald conceded that neither he nor others at MDA had learned much about pricing and cost negotiations, but they had discovered how to generate excitement about what they could accomplish on a shoestring. Although they had previously met, MacDonald also won Lapp as an important ally that night at the Empress, and within months MacDonald secured MDA's first UPP contract through the CCRS. Valued at $1.3 million, the contract emerged as the most significant milestone in the company's early history. Smaller than the original $2 million the company had proposed, the contract nevertheless provided a chance for MDA to show the world it could build a turnkey system. As the only Canadian firm then building earth observation ground stations, MDA thus secured a privileged position at the CCRS proposal evaluation table and MacDonald gained a niche beyond the technical realm. Through his performance in Victoria, he solidified his role as a new West Coast voice within national as well as global surveillance circles.[81]

MacDonald's presentations not only affected Lapp, but also interested policymakers and engineers in other quarters, including those housed within MDA. MacDonald had always drawn candidates from UBC to work at MDA; by the time he sold Morley on PERGS, however, technical people working elsewhere wanted in too, if only for the opportunity to work with MacDonald, Dettwiler, Sloan, and other of MDA's talented engineers. MDA's innovative firsts and the research-oriented engineers gathered under its roof made it a special place for like-minded spirits. Indeed, Ray Maxwell and Dan Gelbart recollected that they had joined the firm under the guise of working on process control systems for MDA, but both made it a goal to work with MacDonald and his remote sensing crew. They not only sensed an important harmony at work among Dettwiler, Lennox, MacDonald, Sloan, and Spencer in particular, but each recognized in MacDonald something more.[82] Reflecting on his early engineering career, Ray Maxwell summarized a common perception about MacDonald, Dettwiler, and the firm they had founded. "There was a special synergy, a special gathering of the right people in the right place," he recalled. "Those were really magical times. John in particular was a kind of messiah figure," he stressed, "saying to each and every one of us, 'This way to the promised land,' and if he had walked over a cliff, everybody would have lockstep followed him. He had this charismatic way of describing his vision and imparting it, and everybody bought into it just 'Ka-bang!'"[83] Colin Lennox, MDA's general manager, agreed, adding that people at MDA "had high aspirations, we were doing the very latest technology, we were into hardware *and* software, and we had a glamorous technical leader." John MacDonald "was not just in the academic community, but well-known in the government as somebody who could produce quality, difficult, instrumentation systems."[84]

With that kind of technological energy driving the company forward, PERGS revolutionized the ground station industry. MDA built PERGS, which had its own antenna, on a leased plot of land near Vancouver's International Airport. A 10- by 40-foot trailer housed the entire ground station. Electronics, receivers, demultiplexers, and film recorders filled one end of the unit, and the other housed a darkroom. After successful project completion, MDA transported the station to Shoe Cove, Newfoundland, where it recorded data for seven years. Once MDA's self-contained ground station could receive imagery, process the images, and produce a film version on the spot, MDA further reduced ground station costs. Economical in both size and price, and a unique product formed under Sloan's vision, MacDonald's salesmanship, and government assistance through the UPP, PERGS became MDA's first major showpiece. Sloan had long argued, "We know how to do this, and we can do it for a lot less money, and a lot better" than American firms. When MDA unveiled PERGS, Sloan remembered, others conceded, "We finally believe you."[85] PERGS also involved a tremendous amount of overtime. Sloan recalled that one engineer who worked on the project "estimated that it was more than double the actual amount of time that was actually invoiced and billed, so people were working roughly 100 per cent overtime on the project without being paid."[86] Still, PERGS and other technological challenges at MDA became "almost like a game," another engineer remembered. "You're given this opportunity to build something, which is going to have a visible or tangible output, and you get paid for it. That's a real high."[87] Many who worked at MDA also agreed with another employee who argued, "If you're doing something you really enjoy and you get paid for it, then you're very lucky." During the next few years, such "luck" continued as MDA expanded into the international ground station market.[88]

"PLUG AND PLAY":
APARTHEID SOUTH AFRICA AND THE INTERNATIONAL
GROUND STATION MARKET

By 1975, with hopes of capturing the international remote sensing market for ground stations, MDA board members decided that the company needed to invest in a good salesman willing to work on commission. They found that someone in Barclay Isherwood, a computer salesman for Inter-Data. John MacDonald met Isherwood while the young man completed his degree in geophysics at UBC. As MacDonald got to know him, he noticed that Isherwood had special technical talents, but when Isherwood became a computer salesman, MacDonald also realized that the UBC alumnus had an uncanny knack for brokering a deal; in fact, Isherwood had become a monumental closer. Never satisfied with what they had purchased from InterData, the MDA team called Isherwood each time a problem surfaced, vowing that they would also cancel further orders. But when he arrived to attend to his friends, Isherwood always managed to sell another InterData product to someone at MDA. After several of these incidents, MacDonald decided that he needed to hire Isherwood, not only to free MDA from InterData, but also to have Isherwood sell MDA's ground stations. The savvy young Isherwood agreed to join MDA on one condition, however; he wanted a percentage of the sale for every ground station deal he closed.[89]

Isherwood had no more international selling experience than anyone else at MDA, but he wanted to make money – and plenty of it. During 1976, Isherwood then solidified his marketing prowess by selling a complete ground station to as well as negotiating a $1.3 million contract with the Republic of South Africa. Although many at MDA attributed the sale to Isherwood's persuasive strategies, the negotiation underscored several realities, including that other nations had begun to boycott business transactions with the apartheid government. MDA's global reach also depended upon the help of government technocrats at the CCRS and CRC as well as export negotiators at the EDC, whose assistance to the young firm provided MDA with the "critical route for getting foreign contracts."[90]

With the CCRS and EDC paving the way at remote sensing International Participation Program meetings, people at MDA decided that the firm should capitalize on South Africa's pariah status. After all, Isherwood advised, in accordance with MacDonald's argument that MDA should do business with anyone willing and able to advance the company's ambitions, the large South African contract could allow MDA to develop additional ground station features, all of which the firm could sell to others. Sloan polled employees about working with South Africa (or other international customers), but only one engineer voiced political or ethical qualms about doing so. As a result, MDA bid on and won the job, designing a generalized linescan receiving and processing system that could read data from both *Landsat* and Europe's first weather satellite (*Meteosat*), a project scheduled for launch in 1977 by the new European Space Agency. According to people at MDA, "A few years later, Americans finally made an arrangement with South Africans to receive data" from *Landsat*. But "the Americans, for many years, never figured out how it was the South Africans were able to process the data the day after they got the permission to read it out. It was all there. It was all set up." Of course, Lennox noted, South Africans could process the data because MDA had built the ground station for them.[91] The South African contract also resulted in MDA's first "plug-and-play" export, prompting company promoters to anticipate other applications. Those soon emerged. Within the next four years, five other international remote sensing program participants (Japan, Sweden, Argentina, Indonesia, and Thailand) entered into trade agreements with the United States and Canada, thereafter contracting with MDA so that they too could read data from NASA's *Landsat* and the European Space Agency's (ESA's) ERS-1 satellites. Together, that work enhanced MDA's competitive position in the expanding business of monitoring the globe's weather, resources, and people. It also gave Canadians a more prominent seat at the international remote sensing table.[92]

Reflecting on South Africa and other politically problematic sales, including to antagonists in the Middle East, MacDonald stressed, "I'm the exact opposite of a person who believes in apartheid, but I've always taken the attitude that business is business," a philosophy that continued to guide his career. At a 2004 conference talk before the United Nations Institute for Disarmament Research, MacDonald declared that "a customer is a customer," and "the commercial sector should not concern itself with the applications of its products, whether peaceful or non-peaceful." He added "that the three major civilian applications of space infrastructure – communications, Earth observation and navigation – have significant military uses." As a result, "outputs of the commercial sector could either greatly enhance quality of life or severely damage it, depending upon the decisions of governments."[93]

Regardless the rationale, few at MDA could have failed to appreciate or at least notice MDA's expanding role in the geopolitics of surveillance capitalism. Most focused on something they deemed infinitely more important, however: *their* firm had a chance to emerge as a serious competitor to SPAR. As evidence, they noted that, prior to 1976, potential international customers had worried that a small, Vancouver-based company could not deliver a full ground station. MDA overcame its problems of size and location, they argued, by specializing in value-added, custom solutions for anyone willing to pay for the company's products and services, and for whom Vancouver was as central a location as anywhere else. Of course, as one former government procurement officer affirmed, "MDA would not have been able to go ahead without the contribution of CCRS and the unsolicited proposals and contracts" that provided seed capital for ground station product development. "At CCRS, I had my marching orders," he recalled. MDA "got their contracts. Through the *Landsat* international working group meetings," members of the CCRS, CRC, and DSS "always pushed MDA systems and MDA hardware. We did a lot of selling for them in Australia, South Africa, Brazil," and elsewhere.[94] Government representatives could also sell MDA's expertise because the Department of Energy, Mines, and Resources had negotiated three significant agreements during 1975: the Canada/US Earth Resources Survey Agreement, in force through 1980; a memorandum of understanding between NASA and EMR for the United States' planned *Seasat* satellite, the first Earth-orbiting satellite with an onboard, space-borne SAR designed to extract high-resolution images of the Earth's oceans from deep space; and a software exchange agreement with Japan.[95]

Following the five-year extension of the Canada-US ERTS/*Landsat* Agreement during 1975, MDA quickly received contracts from the CCRS to upgrade Canada's ground receiving stations at Prince Albert, Saskatchewan, and Shoe Cove, Newfoundland, so that Canada could "cope with the increased data rates" anticipated in future *Landsat* launches. When ESA launched *Meteosat* in 1977, the CCRS and ESA also signed a five-year agreement to exchange information and personnel. During 1978, they then extended that agreement into an "ESA/Canada Cooperative Agreement," which made official Canada's involvement in ESA's long-term planning and general studies program. As part of a larger ESA agreement on the "peaceful purposes of space applications," Canada initially agreed to participate with "observer status" only, which included contributing to technical studies and sharing the costs of those studies "on the basis of its average national income" as well as 1 per cent of fixed common costs. Members of the CCRS began to reassess their liaison role with ESA as well, to ensure that "Canadian industry receives its share of ESA contracts." Canada nevertheless remained an observer, then associate member, for an additional four years before emerging as a full member during 1982. The CCRS also developed an information exchange agreement with the Japanese Space Agency, and undertook cooperative projects with other countries. "As in the past, it is CCRS's policy to have as much of the development and production work as possible done in industry so as to help establish a strong Canadian industrial capability in remote sensing," one long-term plan argued. Furthermore, "Industrial participation in projects through the Unsolicited Proposal fund of DSS has resulted in unique products being developed" at MDA and elsewhere, "which have contributed to the mission of CCRS and, in addition, have produced a multifold return in export sales."[96]

Internalizing the formula they had learned through contracting opportunities at the CCRS and through Isherwood's marketing plan, MDA's engineers offered new features, which they could then charge to each new customer. In the process, MDA improved its ground station expertise, enhanced the company's reputation in the international remote sensing community, and boasted that the firm had supplied complete systems or subsystem components to all non-US ground stations built during the second half of the 1970s. Because the MDA team had learned valuable technical lessons, if not necessarily economic or political ones on the PERGS and South African jobs, the company made profits on every subsequent ground station sale, which promised to cover other project overruns and fund further development into ground station product lines as well as diversification plans. MDA's success in reading ESA's *Meteosat* data additionally convinced the CCRS to fund another weather image processing system, MDA's new meteorological product called WIPS. MDA completed its first WIPS contract with Atmospheric Environment Service Canada. Once it was installed for the Canadian government, Isherwood negotiated a further twelve export contracts, including WIPS for Sweden, Czechoslovakia, and Indonesia as part of détente, and one for the Israeli military. That ability further convinced MacDonald that MDA had found in government contracts the perfect formula on which to expand.[97]

During the second half of the 1970s, MDA no longer had to defend its place in the global remote sensing community: it had built solid systems to show potential clients worldwide; and the company's ground station capabilities received broad acceptance among nations anxious to participate in the business of Earth observation. During 1977, newly inaugurated president Jimmy Carter then enhanced the expansion of the ground stations that could receive imagery of the Earth and its resources by signing legislation that created the United States Department of Energy. In that same year, while Carter pardoned Vietnam War draft evaders (many of them living in Canada, and some of them working at MDA), the first Apple II series computers went on sale and the first oil passing through the Trans-Alaska pipeline system reached Valdez, Alaska. Fifteen countries (including the United States and USSR) also signed a nuclear non-proliferation pact, and Anwar Sadat became the first Arab leader to make an official visit to Israel. Canadian policymakers and capitalists took an interest in all of these moves and made a few of their own. They ended Canada's nuclear relationship with India, signed a framework for economic cooperation with Japan as part of Ottawa's attempts to diversify Canada's trading portfolio into the Pacific Rim, and engineered a successful bid to become a permanent member of the G7. With Canada's international prestige solidified on multiple policy decisions, MDA could count on Ottawa to smooth the way for other sales with Canadian allies.[98]

American contracts remained elusive to the Canadian firm, but by 1980, MDA had provided complete systems to four of the five additional ground stations built worldwide. From all he had learned from his mentors in Ottawa, MacDonald grasped that Americans rarely had to "go global," given their own large domestic market, while "what is important as far as the Canadian advanced technology industry is concerned is that Canada has to think internationally." As a secondary power seeking a larger place within the surveillance community, Canada represented that global norm, and excepting the United States and parts of Western Europe, MacDonald observed, "everywhere else is more like Canada." Moreover, as long as Canada and other nations remained dependent on *Landsat* data and agreements with NASA, Canadian policymakers made clear, Canada would have to upgrade its capabilities constantly, for US "space policies could magnify the difficulty of receiving current data received by U.S. resource and oceans-related satellites, and could thus render Canada's resource satellite receiving station obsolete." Such fears of obsolescence boded well for MDA's future, not only as a ground station provider but also as the first commercial firm to produce digital images from synthetic aperture radar.[99]

"REALLY NEW STUFF": SYNTHETIC APERTURE RADAR AND THE EXPANSION OF SURVEILLANCE CAPITALISM

While the use of synthetic aperture radar (SAR) reached the public consciousness only during the 1991 Persian Gulf War, the American military had developed the technology during the 1950s as the best way to retrieve images from deep space. When the US government declassified its SAR documents during the 1970s, many policymakers and surveillance experts saw in SAR another significant commercial opportunity, one that the US government planned to transfer to the expanding space industry as an important reconnaissance tool. At MDA, those opportunities led to another significant moment in the young company's history, and introduced members of the firm to the complexities of the American military-industrial complex. John MacDonald first learned about opportunities in SAR through Larry Morley, who had invited MDA's president to Sensor Working Group meetings in Ottawa, which met to discuss the need for better information processing capabilities to detect, identify, and classify targets in harsh environments, and technologies that could apply sound navigation and ranging (sonar) acoustic wave systems to radio and ranging (radar) wave systems for digital signal processing (an enabling technology that transmits signals and information contained in many different physical, symbolic, and abstract formats).[100]

From MDA's earliest days, MacDonald hoped to hire John Bennett, an extraordinarily bright PhD student who had produced a UBC dissertation on communications theory, computing, and the conversion of signals from analog to digital form. MacDonald considered Bennett one of his star students, but the recently minted doctor of digital signal processing decided to take a position not at MDA but with Bell Northern Research, the joint University of Québec–Northern Telecom initiative that became to Canada what MDA hoped to become to Vancouver. Still, MacDonald's participation in the Sensor Working Group convinced him that he could steal Bennett away. After all, he reasoned, he had already recruited another of his PhD students, Denis Connor, from Bell Northern. Once he became responsible for hiring, Connor then drew on the talent gathered there, particularly MacDonald's former students who disliked Ottawa's winters. Intending to work Vancouver's mild winter strategy on Bennett, MacDonald courted him every time he drifted through Ottawa. Bennett had previously passed on offers from MDA, but MacDonald knew that he had finally found a project Bennett could not resist. During his next trip to Ottawa, and while Bennett's supervisor worked in the office next door, MacDonald burst into his star's workspace and proclaimed that the time had arrived for Bennett's West Coast return. At first, Bennett resisted. In the middle of the action in Ottawa, and still dubious about MDA's ultimate abilities to survive in remote Vancouver, Bennett reminded MacDonald that Bell Northern had trusted him with a strategic project in the development of computerized telephone switching machines. Eventually, however, MacDonald's persuasive arguments prevailed; he hired Bennett, and Bell Northern gave MDA a subcontract to keep Bennett in Ottawa until July 1974.[101]

By the time Bennett joined MDA during the summer of 1974, Simon Fraser University had just launched the *Canadian Journal of Communications* and hired Pauline Jewett, the first female president of a major Canadian university. David Suzuki had just made his debut as host of *The Nature of Things*. And, importantly, Canadian policymakers had entered into negotiations with NASA about Canada's participation in *Seasat*. Part of the Canada-US defence production sharing arrangement and other agreements focused on ocean management and "maintaining a watch" over human activity and environmental phenomena in North America, the *Seasat* program committed the CCRS to ground station modifications at Shoe Cove, Newfoundland, so that both countries could receive processed imagery from deep space.[102] With *Seasat* covering parts of the Arctic, NASA planning the expansion of SAR-based satellites if the *Seasat* launch proved successful, and concerns over Canadian sovereignty emerging in the debate over Canada's participation in the program, policymakers and their consultants agreed that Canada needed to develop its own SAR processor to protect Canadian interests. After all, they argued, Canadian industry had acquired a SAR capability, or could do so, even if Canada might have to license some of the sensor technology from the United States. As a result, champions at the CRC, CCRS, and other agencies encouraged Canadian-owned businesses to participate in SAR feasibility studies. "Not only will such studies expose Canadian engineers to the ideas and developments in other countries," they noted, "but they provide a means of keeping the door open to future cooperation in the operational phase of a satellite surveillance system" with the United States.[103]

While NASA began to transfer its interest in oceanographic research to NOAA during the mid-1970s, the CRC's George Haslam argued that one could digitally process *Seasat* data for military as well as commercial purposes. Unhappily for Haslam, his views represented a professional anomaly. Most researchers believed in the theoretical possibilities of a digitally processed SAR, but few thought it offered a practical solution to *Seasat*. Conventional wisdom held that airborne sensors, using the optical processing techniques developed at the University of Michigan and through laboratories inside the Environmental Research Institute of Michigan (ERIM), provided the only plausible means for extracting images from deep space. As a professional dissenter, Haslam thus determined that if no American institutions found his ideas interesting, he should find a Canadian company to do the work. After an extensive tour of North America,

Haslam found himself at MDA. At a meeting with Dettwiler, MacDonald, and Sloan, Haslam explained his SAR idea. No one at MDA knew anything about SAR; therefore, Haslam decided to stay in Vancouver for several days, to talk about the technology and its implications for *Seasat* and Canada. With other projects pending, Dettwiler quickly dropped out of the meetings, but MacDonald and Sloan devoted the remainder of two additional days to absorb all Haslam had to teach them. By the end of day two, Sloan understood the key scientific concepts: mathematically, SAR applied techniques similar to those employed in his field of radio astronomy and was, quite simply, radio astronomy in reverse. After the third day, MacDonald started to grasp the heart of SAR as well. Looking out instead of in, SAR used the Earth's rather than the spacecraft's motion to create an image.[104]

Once Haslam had satisfied himself that Sloan and MacDonald understood the work, he suggested that MDA should "consider making a proposal to the Canadian federal government to build a digital processor for [the *Seasat*] satellite." However, there were "two rival factions developing for control over all of the SAR development in Canada," Bennett recalled. "One of them was CCRS and the other was CRC," the latter having "moved under the Department of National Defence." Bennett also argued that "DND actually tried to block giving MDA the contract. They could see a civilian agency developing this technology, and they wanted control of it." As a result, Bennett had to "attend roundtable" meetings in Ottawa at the CRC/DND, with "technical experts firing questions, one after another" at him, "trying to poke holes" at his assumptions and MDA's proposal. Fortunately for MDA, Keith Rainey, a foremost authority on SAR processing, had joined the CCRS and "jumped into the fray" to defend MDA's proposal."[105] Shortly thereafter, while Canadian policymakers strengthened the foreign investment review process to avoid a replay of the automobile industry's branch-plant dilemma in the computer industry and "the potential that U.S. firms may distort the Canadian market through predatory pricing in order to gain a dominant foothold in a region like BC," the CCRS offered MDA another small contract.[106]

With Bennett tasked to other work, and the contract stipulating that two employees had to spend a year in Ottawa to learn about SAR, MDA sent Bill Renwick and Douglas Seymour to work with Haslam on a feasibility study for digital "synthetic radar processing. This was really new stuff," Seymour recalled, "so we were working on something that nobody had ever done before." Furthermore, "all the processing in the world on synthetic aperture radar had, for the most part, been done as a military application so it was hidden from us. It was pretty exciting," he stressed, especially since he and Renwick had the opportunity to discuss the project with MacDonald and Sloan when they travelled to Ottawa to attend monthly progress meetings. Within the year, Renwick and Seymour had amassed experience in SAR and learned how to work with the government. Unfortunately for those at MDA, no sooner had Renwick and Seymour returned to Vancouver from Ottawa than Canada "got kicked out of the consortium politically. There were some problems between Canada and NASA. I never really understood it," Seymour recalled, "but there was a rumour that the US military felt that this satellite could see too much." Another story surfaced that "Canada wasn't holding up its end in the joint funding, and for what they were getting out of it, they weren't paying enough," he noted.[107]

Despite rumours, delays, US secrecy, and questions about Canada's financial commitment to *Seasat*, the two countries' government officials settled their differences, and Bennett reminded MacDonald that he wanted to work in the digital filtering field. Thus, when Morley called about an Unsolicited Proposal Program idea centred on SAR, Bennett lobbied for the work and MacDonald supported his ambitions to manage the proposal. It took Bennett some time to nurse the plan through government channels in Canada and the United States, but by late 1976, MDA received a contract from the CCRS to build the world's first SAR processor, and Bennett hired a team of highly trained mathematicians and scientists to make the system work. As rivalries deepened between the CCRS and CRC, Bennett remembered, representatives of the CRC/DND team refused to participate in the project, began to develop their own processor, and ultimately generated "competition around the world, because everyone soon knew that we were all doing this in parallel, so the race was on to see who could produce the first image." Moreover, like so many other projects at MDA during those early years, SAR "was an adventure. You could design new things, build them, make them work, and deliver them, and the idea that you would fail never really entered your mind," Bennett recalled, even if "the technical risk was very high. But somehow the customers, primarily Canadian government people involved in the research laboratories" and the CCRS, "seemed to appreciate the risk."[108]

Even if Bennett appreciated the technological uncertainty and MDA's customers in government understood the politics of *Seasat*, both realities initially escaped the notice of many people at MDA, including John MacDonald. For the moment, it was enough that the federal government had provided the opportunity to undertake yet another cutting-edge project. In retrospect, however, MDA's lawyer Michael Butler observed that government risk-takers and their disregard for "the bottom line requirements of the company, tended to lull John [MacDonald] and others, certainly others on the board, into a sense that nothing could ever go wrong."[109] If he had any doubts, by April 1978, MacDonald received an unsolicited opportunity to learn about how much his firm had gambled. While attending a National Research Council meeting in Ottawa, MacDonald ran into an eminent physicist who quickly castigated him, declaring that MacDonald "had no idea what MDA had taken on" and would never get a digital SAR processor to work. Although confident in MDA's abilities when the conversation with the physicist began, MacDonald started to lose his nerve. Perhaps the physicist was right, MacDonald mused. "After all, he would know," and MacDonald had not involved himself in daily SAR activities for over a year. As a result, when he returned to Vancouver, MacDonald summoned Bennett to his office, growling, "Are you ever going to get an image out of that goddamn thing?" "Oh yes," Bennett calmly replied. "When?" MacDonald demanded. "During November," Bennett promised.[110]

On 28 June 1978, NASA launched *Seasat* with instruments designed to return a plethora of information from the world's ocean surfaces. Managed by NASA's Jet Propulsion Laboratory (JPL), and carrying the first space-borne SAR onboard, *Seasat* orbited the Earth fourteen times daily, penetrating cloud cover and collecting data on sea-surface winds and temperatures, atmospheric water, internal waves and wave heights, sea-ice features, and ocean topography. The satellite remained in orbit for three operational months, and then died under mysterious circumstances. Some speculated that the American government "turned off" *Seasat*, for it became clear after launch that *Seasat* not only saw through cloud cover, but also showed air bases and detected the wakes of submarines. "The problem is you can't hide anything" from *Seasat*, one physicist explained. "One of the images was of Cuba, and you can actually see Cuban air bases with all the aircraft on the ground and all the military installations." He also confirmed that *Seasat* showed "the US Seventh Fleet. You can see an aircraft carrier and five surface destroyers, and you can see another thing, just a wake, but it's the attack submarine that travels with the pack," he reported. "You can actually detect a submarine down to a level of about 1,000 feet with this thing – very powerful."[111] A consensus thus developed that US military officers feared the implications of *Seasat*'s commercial development. Some argued that a hardware failure in the power supply had triggered *Seasat*'s demise, but that rationale gained little traction. Regardless, by the time the short circuit in the satellite's electrical system ended its mission in October, *Seasat* had gathered forty-two hours' worth of data, enough to keep engineers and analysts busy for many years. Because MDA had sent an employee to the PERGS station in Shoe Cove at the same time that *Seasat* made one of its initial passes over Canada, the firm managed to acquire four tapes of data, enough to create a *Seasat* image of Trois-Rivières, Quebec.[112]

With sufficient data to process an image, MacDonald made a public announcement: "MDA will produce the first synthetic aperture radar image on November 13," 1978.[113] Some worried that MacDonald had set up himself for an embarrassing failure, but Bennett trusted his team, including a SAR system implementer named Peter McConnell. Young McConnell had fully immersed himself in the implementation stage of the work, had confidence that MDA could produce images, and recalled that respect for and dedication to Bennett meant that members of the SAR team "were just going like a bat out of hell to meet this date for him." Still, implementation required an enormous technical effort, overtime hours, and an unending series of data searches. "One of the problems," McConnell explained, "was that processing synthetic aperture radar is extremely computer intensive." Unlike the real-time images we have come to expect on all of our portable devices, just one *Seasat* image "took forty hours of computer time" to process. "Getting computer time" represented another daunting challenge, McConnell recollected, "because other people were using the [mainframe] computer in the daytime, so we pretty much were relegated to using it at night."[114]

While members of the implementation team raced to meet MacDonald's deadline, the computer overloaded on each run, while computer disks shook apart and ultimately failed from intensive use. As pressure mounted and disks continued to crash, McConnell and his colleague Ron Fielding decided that they had best work a sixteen-hour swing shift. Seven days a week, starting at four in the afternoon, they worked until eight the following morning. Occasionally MacDonald checked in on his shift workers, offering encouragement as well as pizza and beer. After nearly three months on the night shift, McConnell and Fielding opted to overlap their efforts. At 10 p.m. on one overlapping shift, McConnell and Fielding thought that they might produce an image, nursing it by hand through every process. At 2 a.m., McConnell then went home to nap. When he returned six hours later, McConnell walked into a small room with six people peering at a screen, and many more filing in. In the time it took for Dave Sloan to find a television monitor, more than thirty people had stuffed themselves in, where they witnessed one failed attempt, followed by success in the form of Trois-Rivières in every glorious detail, including three ships under its bridge and a nuclear power plant.[115]

MDA produced its first SAR image on 28 November 1978, five months after *Seasat* launched and just fifteen days later than MacDonald had predicted. By December, MDA's SAR team also produced an entire Trois-Rivières scene. Creating the first image took approximately 100 hours' worth of computing time, involved intensive overtime, and required resources more than double what MDA had proposed. As usual, employees waived their overtime, declaring that their technical feat provided its own reward. Eventually, the MDA team also produced "a bigger image. We made it with all four looks, and we submitted it to a magazine called *Aviation Week and Space Technology*," McConnell recalled, which a "lot of people" at MDA and elsewhere "call 'death from above' because of its war-like stance." War jokes aside, however, everyone at MDA, including MacDonald, declared the accomplishment more significant than extra hours, cost overruns, and any concerns that "death from above" might engender.[116]

Within the year, JPL repeated MDA's accomplishment, but Dettwiler boasted that "we beat the US by nine months, which we were pretty pleased about."[117] Delivering the world's first digitally processed SAR image from a spacecraft, MDA attracted the attention of the German Space Agency, European Space Agency, and especially the US military. Indeed, McConnell remembered that after MDA published its "four looks" of Trois-Rivières, "all of a sudden, two guys from the National Security Administration came up" to Vancouver, "wearing government-issued black patent leather shoes and thick, black-rimmed glasses" to see precisely what people at MDA had discerned. Whether or not they wore such things, representatives from the United States' NSA already knew what *Seasat* SAR images showed: air bases, military installations, aircraft carriers, surface destroyers, submarine wakes, and other classified information. Regardless, MDA's SAR success convinced MacDonald and his disciples that the company had a viable strategy for the future, one with technical abilities, employee dedication, and government contracts, all of which promised to fasten MDA's hold on the germinating SAR movement.[118]

While busy with *Seasat* work, MDA received another CCRS contract to build an airborne digital processor. The CCRS had purchased an older radar system from Michigan's Environmental Research Institute, which it planned to install on a Canadian aircraft to explore SAR's commercial applications. The US radar contained an old, optically correlated system; however, Keith Rainey, the CCRS's SAR guru, had also worked in Michigan and "knew the radar inside-out." As a result, Rainey gave MDA his mathematical calculations, and helped Bennett to design the new processor. Rainey "just came out and basically said, 'Here's the design for it, I know this radar intimately, and this is what the processor has to look like,'" Bennett recalled. "So, from a mathematical, theoretical point of view, he just handed us the design, which helped a great deal." With Rainey's assistance, and the cooperation of a network of engineers and scientists working on SAR, MDA's first airborne radar project became a huge success. The moment MDA's team installed the airborne processor, "the plane took flight," and within just a few hours, "it produced its first image." That experience logged in, the MDA team then looked forward to exporting SAR and airborne radar just as they had exported their ground station expertise.[119]

"We're not interested in bolting metal or shuffling paper," MacDonald declared. "We're interested in real technology development, something we can build and exploit." Noting that MDA had moved into hardware during 1971, built its first satellite ground receiving station in 1972, and emerged as the first commercial firm to process a digital SAR image just six years later, MacDonald stressed that MDA engineers had learned how to work and negotiate with the Canadian government, and had entered the export market as "a kernel of our business. Do it here first," he stressed, "then try and export it. One of the things that I believe very strongly is that every company in Canada that's in the technology business should think export from the very beginning. We started thinking export in the mid-1970s. We had no idea how to go about it," he confessed, but "with the privilege of hindsight, I say, 'Everybody should be doing this.' That's how we're going to build this country in the next century. If we don't do something like this," he cautioned, Canada will "go down the tubes, because the old paradigm doesn't work anymore."[120]

During 1971, MDA had neither the resources nor the credibility to build a robust international business in surveillance. As a result, Phillip Lapp observed, Larry Morley, chief architect of the CCRS, quite literally "put MDA on the remote sensing map" and solidified the firm's systems house integrity.[121] MDA also owed its initial success to Canada's "Make or Buy" policy, the Unsolicited Proposal Program, and procurement contracts envisioned and then provided by Morley and his successors at the CCRS as well as Ron Barrington, George Haslam, and their associates at the CRC, all of whom introduced MDA to the wider possibilities of defence sharing work.[122] MDA augmented Canada's governmental ambitions as well, providing to policymakers an important example of what national policies might develop, including a small firm that could help to cement Canada's international reputation as a core centre for surveillance work. According to Colin Lennox, people at MDA also told their government friends precisely what they wanted to hear, "stroking them, letting them know things were working, that jobs in Canada were being created" because of the federal government's help. Moreover, the UPP worked well because people at the CCRS made shrewd political as well as financial choices. Those at the CCRS knew that MacDonald shared their technical insights, and over time they also came to appreciate that MDA's eager staff could rise to any technical challenge. Whether or not they knew or cared about overtime bills and cost overruns associated with that challenge, for the moment they basked in the glow of MDA's technical accomplishments and the ways in which the firm had helped to place Canada in the remote sensing limelight.[123]

While John MacDonald, Vern Dettwiler, and their talented young associates lured other technology enthusiasts into MDA, the exciting work, promises of future government contracts, and the ability to live in Vancouver kept them there. With remote sensing and government contracts linking MDA to the expansion of surveillance capitalism, people in the firm could boast that they knew how to solve industrial problems, build ground stations to receive and process satellite data, and push the envelope in synthetic aperture radar. Drawing interest from the US government, their innovations laid the foundation for the company's future as a member of a North American military-industrial complex, even if few at MDA noticed such connections.[124]

Despite these early accomplishments, however, many at MDA feared a limited export market for ground stations and worried what might happen if the Canadian government turned off the contracting tap. With the federal government promising to assist small firms with the development of computer-based products through grants and tax incentives, some also believed that the company's future resided not in systems but in manufacturing products for mass consumption. MDA's management team thus attempted to diversify, and the firm's board of directors approved projects that promised to produce repeat sales, particularly on exciting but potentially risky and costly work in flight information computer systems, mobile data terminals, business computer systems, meteorological monitoring, airborne radar, and electro-optical products. To enter those markets and build customized solutions for their remote sensing clients, the MDA team also tended to underestimate (and hence to underbid) the effort required to complete projects. This meant that the firm fuelled much of its early expansion on the sweat equity of its young engineers, many of whom later recalled that they had worked sixteen- to twenty-hour days, nearly year round. They undertook these herculean efforts because the exciting technical work consumed them, because as Neil Thompson put it, "I was not just working for a firm, I was putting part of my soul into the company in exchange for something in the future that wasn't really defined."[125]

Few had the time or inclination to think about specific definitions of the future, never mind the implications of their work, yet, as MDA evolved during the second half of the 1970s, the firm's founders and employees had to confront some of the harshest realities of capitalism, including the boom-and-bust nature of "creative destruction" and the fact that the costs of expansion can quickly spiral out of control. As chapter 4 reveals, the first real crisis at MDA pivoted on an unintended consequence of early success: as an expanding business, MDA needed more capital than John Mac-Donald had envisioned and would require even more if the firm hoped to survive the late twentieth century's highly competitive and volatile markets of change.

4

"Two Things Went Wrong at Once"

Financial Crises, Mythical Man-Months, and the Near-Death Experience, 1975–1981

On 29 October 1975, MacDonald composed a provident letter to Peter Meyboom, Canada's assistant secretary of the Industry Branch at MOSST, detailing the projects that had flourished under the guiding hand of "Make or Buy" and the Unsolicited Proposal Program. Arguing that Canada's long-term industrial strategy had "been far too much a scatter-gun approach," MacDonald cautioned that "we must realize that because we are only twenty-two million people, we do not have the financial resources to stand at the forefront of all areas of technology." He therefore stressed that Canadians "must choose well and become the best in the world at what we have chosen."[1] Whether MacDonald appreciated it or not, politicians, technocrats, consultants for MOSST, and other policymakers in Ottawa already understood this reality, but as Colin Lennox, MDA's first general manager and self-proclaimed technocrat noted, MacDonald had written to Meyboom because MOSST could "become" MDA's "eyes and ears, hold" MDA's "hand, and give references" to help "MDA to move into the international plane, at a level where credibility was 'guaranteed' by the Canadian government."[2]

No matter his motivations for writing the letter, MacDonald argued that, in its relationship with MDA, the federal government had quickened innovation in Canada, despite the nation's harsh climate. He therefore encouraged Meyboom to promote more funding for private sector firms so that Canadians could avoid what MacDonald and other technical innovators describe as the trap of "vulture" capital. MDA had not yet turned a profit, MacDonald confessed, but it had expanded its technological innovations exponentially, made enough money to survive, and found a modus operandi that Meyboom could advertise as an example to other Canadians.[3] Touting MDA's successful Portable Earth Receiving Ground Station

(PERGS), MacDonald pointed to what *Electronics Communicator* reported: "With a growth rate averaging over 80% per year, MDA is currently achieving one of its objectives – to put the BC electronics industry on the high-technology world map." *Electronics* noted, "Dr MacDonald is the first to admit that MDA's marketing has, in the past, consisted of 'responding to the needs of people who come in through the front door,'" but "with the increased emphasis on market development, both nationally and internationally, MDA has already made a unique contribution to the growth of Canada's electronics industry on the Pacific coast, and much more will be heard of the firm in the years ahead."[4] As this chapter reveals, government officials, bankers, and others did hear a great deal more about the young firm in the days ahead, not all of it quite so bullish.

Between 1975 and 1981, while MDA's sales expanded from $2.3 million to more than $20 million, and its staff increased from fifty to nearly two hundred, the firm's escalating expenditures involved costly diversification and product plans, a move to a larger facility to house more projects, and dangerous cost overruns. All of this unfolded during a general economic downturn, while conflicting visions of the company's future fanned the flames of business disagreements that ultimately engulfed MDA in permanent personal rifts, the resignations of talented engineers and managers, and the loss of valuable technologies. Several programs, including those within the Department of National Defence and the National Research Council of Canada's Industrial Research Assistance Program (IRAP) emerged to assist technology companies with the development of promising commercial products; however, as the 1973 oil crisis and subsequent economic recession washed over North America during the second half of the 1970s, government officials made it clear that no one could save companies that refused to absorb the realities of the changing world order. People in government stressed that they had an interest in the technologies MDA had developed for Canadian surveillance, but they also revealed that they had alternatives and contingency plans, particularly those centred on SPAR Aerospace, the chosen instrument for stimulating Canada's space-based industry.[5]

Waiting in the wings as MDA overextended itself, SPAR offered Mac-Donald a safety net, in the form of an investment the larger company expected to exchange for a share in MDA. When MacDonald rejected the offer, he quickly learned that he could count on neither loans from the bank nor further support from government. As a result, near-ruin arrived at MDA's door during 1981, in a financial crisis that ultimately forced Mac-Donald to step down from the presidency of MDA to avoid bankruptcy and the firm's descent into the dustbin of history. Although many people at MDA blamed the firm's problems on cost overruns associated with FOCUS (MDA's Flight Operations Computer System), they misdirected their gaze. The software project simply exemplified MacDonald's confusion about ownership versus control, and the unintended consequences of undercapitalized expansion following the company's early technological success. As in the past, world events created the context for MDA's painful lessons in capitalist expansion and the changing geopolitical environment.[6]

"A PUBLIC FRIGHTENED ABOUT ITS SAFETY": THE ENERGY CRISIS AND CANADA'S FALTERING ECONOMY

Although initially shielded from the oil crisis that began on 15 October 1973, when members of the Organization of Arab Petroleum Exporting Countries declared an oil embargo in response to American assistance to the Israeli military during the Yom Kippur War, Canadians began to feel the pinch of the energy crisis as economic hardships wended their way west from Ontario's industrial centre. Oil reserves quickly turned Alberta into the richest province in the nation, but money flows into western Canada failed to reach Vancouver. Inflation reached 11 per cent in both the United States and Canada during 1974, with stagflation and the economic recession quickly following. As Dimitry Anastakis has documented, with the crisis hitting the automobile sector immediately, the Canadian government intervened to save jobs. It then bailed out firms such as Massey Ferguson and Dome Petroleum, created new Crown corporations such as Petro-Canada as an antidote to further branch-plant domination by the United States, and purchased de Havilland and Canadair to avoid another Avro Arrow fiasco.[7]

The energy crisis prompted the Canadian government to place greater emphasis on alternative energy sources, including nuclear power, which quickly embroiled Canada in a diplomatic crisis as well. After the Indian government exploded an atomic device during 1974, US Secretary of State Henry Kissinger, already angry about Canada's resurgent nationalism, denied that the United States had contributed nuclear material for an Indian nuclear bomb. Instead, Kissinger blamed Canada and AECL's export business for creating another nuclear weapons state. Kissinger's accusation alarmed many Canadians, and prompted renewed calls for changes to government priorities that could tame inflation, quell strikes, and maintain Canadian independence from what they perceived as an increasingly aggressive United States. With Quebec separatist, Canadian nationalist, and organized labour movements, along with calls for state intervention in the economy picking up momentum, it once again appeared that Canada intended to distance itself from its continental relationship to the United States, even if declassified documents later revealed that the relationship expanded rather than contracted during the second half of the 1970s.[8] Meeting with members of the Canadian Manufacturing Association on 30 January 1975, Alastair Gillespie, by then minister of industry, trade and commerce, argued that Canada had three "paramount challenges" to meet: inflation, decreasing industrial productivity, and "the pitfalls of protectionism. Canada depends," he stressed, "upon access to foreign markets and world trade for its high standard of living." As a result, he encouraged the federal government to focus more on export-driven strategies.[9]

Conceding that Canadians expected government "to reasonably regulate business," the deputy minister for industry, trade, and commerce nevertheless argued that the Canadian "people do not want an all-out confrontation with business for fear of damaging the economy." Surveys revealed that ongoing economic and political crises had created a public "frightened about its safety," thereby justifying cuts to government spending in external aid, social programs, and unemployment insurance. At the same time, policymakers called for increasing expenditures on surveillance technologies and policing, energy programs, urban congestion and management, and the spatial distribution of population and economic activities to protect the Canadian people from threats internal and external to the nation.[10] As Canadians prepared a mission to the European Economic Community during 1975, he also asserted that government priorities needed to include a review of and amendments to acts focused on foreign investment, national defence, government organization and scientific activities, national industrial and regional development, and trade-industrial linkages to Western Europe, Japan, the Middle East, and the USSR. European manufacturers had long "relied on American suppliers of mass-produced advanced components who have led world technology and achieved economies of scale thanks, in part to the immense size of the US Federal Government market," he argued, but Canadians could tap into new opportunities in the computer, communications, and remote sensing industries by emulating the "stimulus provided" by the United States' "research and development under defence and space programmes."[11]

To maintain Canadian sovereignty and security, some policymakers suggested that innovation should flow from procurement "practices designed to stimulate Canadian controlled industry," which could lead to "new concepts in our national identity."[12] Others proposed that capabilities in remote sensing would allow for the "exploitation of Canada's natural resources with minimal damage to the environment."[13] Stressing the need to reward "those firms who have out-performed others – even if their price is not the lowest tendered," others argued that increased funding for industry could retain "creative Canadian engineers and scientists in Canada" as well as foster the rapid automation of financial institutions as a critical sector of the national economy. To increase "the presence of Canadians at the management and policy levels in important industrial elements in our economy" as a national goal, members of the federal government also noted the need to "develop Canadian talents and open employment for our rising young technologists," highlighting that "systems engineering and systems management are at the centre of this high technology, knowledge-based, world economy."[14] Canada's national goals boded well for MDA's future, but if the company's associates wanted to pursue all the "knowledge-intensive" opportunities presented, they needed to find ways to manage expansion.

"THE PERSON WHO TAKES THE RISK MAKES THE DECISION":
BOOTSTRAPPING REVISITED

By 1975, MDA had extended its bootstrapping beyond the usual limits, but as Bill Thompson had warned MacDonald while others still worked in his basement during 1969, when MDA and its founders moved beyond initial stages, they would need to seek investments from outside the company. By the time firms implement strategies for a sustained effort to support expansion, he cautioned, the concern over finding and acquiring more capital would continue to mount. Moreover, MDA's initial success in government contracting never guaranteed more of it, which also meant that the associates needed to nurture new relationships to extend their ambitions. Beyond courting personal connections with influential representatives in government agencies devoted to remote sensing work, MDA did neither.[15] "The quality of one's life is related to enjoying what you do. It's not related to making a lot of money," MacDonald maintained. "I've always had the view that if you enjoy what you do, you will make money, but if you focus on the money, you may make it, but you probably won't be happy." He conceded that "profit is necessary to sustain an environment, but it doesn't have to be a huge profit. The primary thing is to be the best in the world at what you do. To me, that's been more important than the financial side of the business."[16]

When MacDonald and Dettwiler recruited staff, they hoped to attract people who believed the technical paths they had chosen mattered more than logging hours, receiving immediate payment for their efforts, or the economic and geopolitical environments they entered. In this they were successful. With a median age of thirty-three, MDA's staff consisted largely of talented individualists and guileless idealists. Energetically cavalier, seemingly apolitical, eager to please, and anxious to receive recognition for their deeds no matter the personal cost, MDA's staff desperately wanted to deliver systems that could put them on the global map as world-class technical aficionados. Indeed, as one long-time employee recounted his interview with MDA, which took place at a company barbecue, "People at MDA lived and breathed the technology. And probably the ones who were keenest on the technology were not at the barbecue. They were probably working that night. They were workaholics, but socially oriented," he remembered, "and totally consumed with analyzing things. It was like getting married, joining a family. Do they like me? Do I like them? Do you take him to be your lawful employee until death does you part?" But in all seriousness, he argued, "it was and is a company that expects and demands high loyalty." Others agreed, noting that such loyalty allowed MDA to bootstrap its expansion on the strength of employee dedication.[17] MDA's hiring practices, promotion decisions, and expansionist plans also confirm the "connectability of social capital" Pamela Walker Laird identified. "After years of their touting the virtues of modern objective methods," management consultants failed to note how much "upward mobility still required, more than anything else, the personal endorsement from someone in authority" and "gatekeepers' subjective notions of who merited opportunity to join their networks."[18]

While MDA tried to accommodate everyone hired, when someone could not or would not consummate the marriage, MDA quickly arranged an annulment. MDA's "misfits would just get ejected out of the company," one former employee recalled, with those who remained "putting the job as number one in their priorities."[19] As the company's first general manager, Colin Lennox strengthened that bond by introducing Friday night happy hours, company sailing voyages, flag-raising ceremonies on MDA-sponsored climbing trips, and frequent social gatherings that included spouses, significant others, and children. As a result, the lines between business and family, work and play, and the public and private blurred. When expansion required the services of someone to manage a project, MDA promoted from within, among "family members" who had demonstrated their loyalty to the firm, and could continue to privilege the noble callings of scientific research and technological development over what MacDonald and others perceived as the less-than-savoury image of those who merely crunched numbers and seemed to care only about the bottom line.[20]

Accepting MDA's founding philosophy and company shares in lieu of the financial rewards of overtime pay, MDA's staff meticulously logged their hours and looked forward to when the company could compensate them fully. John MacDonald, Vern Dettwiler, Ken Morin, and Stanley Semrau received full compensation for their early overtime, while others received shares based on their positions in and contributions to the company. Only a few early employees actually received those initial shares, but MDA's 1975 profit sharing scheme allowed every single employee to receive a yearly bonus, pro-rated to salary and based on a percentage of MDA's profits. Most agreed that profit sharing could provide significant returns; and if, in what most deemed an unlikely event that the company had a bad year, they declared their willingness to forego the bonus.[21]

With some associates owning a stake in the company and all pinning their hopes on future bonuses, MDA initially survived its ad hoc procedures and neophyte mistakes. According to those who study high-tech firms, MDA had good company, for many companies employ such sweat-equity formulas at the outset. Once technical and business development involves increasingly complicated structures, however, companies must look for capital from other sources. In a typical small business, originators acquire seed capital, first from passive, informal investors (including family members), later moving on to active but still informal investors such as personal acquaintances and employees. Once capital requirements exceed the funds available from such sources, they usually move into a "pre-venture" phase, seeking capital from outside their personal spheres, including potential suppliers and customers, banks, and the government. When those supports no longer suffice, they must then turn to people with the skills, capital, and influence they themselves do not possess. Ultimately, that means more powerful outside investors, including the institutional venture capitalists, lobbyists, and other experts MacDonald hoped to avoid. At this stage, company founders must usually relinquish some ownership of the firm, a step many cannot take, or take only on the brink of extinction, because they equate loss of ownership with loss of control. But without a realistic plan for expansion, including large capital infusions, many business founders find themselves losing both. As Mac-Donald, Dettwiler, and Lennox later conceded, while the lessons seemed simple, implementing them was not.[22]

From the beginning, MacDonald had a clear vision of what he wanted for and from MDA: a community based upon his MIT experience. He extended that vision to include MDA as a Canadian exemplar of technical excellence and an internationally recognized engineering presence. While he recognized that MDA needed to hire a general manager and people with legal and accounting expertise, he deferred many important business and marketing decisions, noting that such a strategy had served him, his associates, and the firm's followers pretty well during MDA's first several years. "I think it was John MacDonald's ability to gather excellence around him, and focus it, and make it go forward that built the company," one former employee recollected. MacDonald "was the person who had enough vision, enough momentum, enough status, and enough integrity to carry [the firm] forward," while others accepted his aversion to business as the price one paid to follow a trail-blazing strategy on the technological frontier.[23]

On the strength of MacDonald's vision, MDA's board made a firm decision to expand; however, expansion required capital, and plenty of it. For each new employee, the company had to pay salaries and fringe benefits as well as acquire space, furniture, a telephone, computer equipment, and all the assorted amenities that expansion entailed. Moreover, the company continually won more bids than expected, so MDA had to hire additional people and bid on additional jobs to protect employees from future lay-offs. The company's *1975 Annual Report* indicated that if the company wanted to take advantage of all the opportunities its board members and staff had identified, MDA needed sufficient working capital to finance expansion. But the report also confirmed MacDonald's conviction that increasing the company's working capital (from $118,800 during 1974 to $197,000 in 1975) should prevail as the essential means to secure a larger line of credit at the bank, the only institution other than the government MacDonald planned to employ to finance the company's future. During fiscal year 1975, MDA's sales increased from just over $1 million to nearly $2.3 million, while its staff increased from thirty-eight to fifty. MDA also acquired its first bank loan: a $350,000 obligation the company incurred to develop its ground station market, start development work on FOCUS and other potential products, hire more employees, and lease additional space and equipment to house the company's swelling operation as well as vehicles and other management perks to reflect the firm's larger professional status.[24]

Despite increased pressure for working capital, MacDonald convinced himself that MDA's winning sweat-equity and government contracting formulas, combined with a new relationship with the bank, could ensure MDA's survival. At the same time, some people argued that the company had become too dependent on government contracts and ground station sales. "The feeling was that we didn't know how long the satellite ground station business would last," Lennox recalled. "We could see an end to how many countries would want a satellite ground station or an end to our dominance in the supply of them, and we had shown that we were capable of growing by a factor of 100 per cent per year, bootstrapping ourselves."[25] Conceding that the "ground station business has been the backbone" of MDA "and has supported all sorts of folly on the part of management," MacDonald agreed that "anybody who knew the business in those days said that we had to diversify because the ground station business couldn't last." Thus, as MDA ground station sales began to dwindle during 1975, several of MDA's board members began to argue that the company needed a more balanced organization for long-term expansion, one that could exploit other opportunities the firm had received, particularly to create generic products derived from work already underway.[26] Many members of consulting firms reached similar conclusions. Having succeeded by providing intangible services, some see the company's future prosperity linked to tangible products. Indeed, ever since industrialization began in Britain during the late eighteenth century, aspiring industrialists have jettisoned custom solutions in favour of possible fortunes in the economies of scale associated with mass manufacturing, including Henry Ford, who repudiated luxury, hand-crafted cars in favour of the Model T.[27]

Specific products developed for customized systems provided MDA with opportunities and a rationale to begin manufacturing universal products for use in all future systems. Still, like many technology start-ups, especially those not founded on one specific product, MDA encountered overwhelming roadblocks as it attempted to straddle the transition from a customized systems environment to a manufacturing domain. While some firms completely abandon their role as consultants in favour of production for major market penetration, most first try to fuse the two environments under one roof. MDA chose the latter strategy, even though the firm lacked the resources to "tool up" for the manufacturing challenge. MDA's board members thus engaged in heated discussions with MacDonald and others about maintaining and then expanding the Synaptic Systems subsidiary MDA had created to assemble hardware. Engineers on the remote sensing side of the business often thought that the expenditures to build a manufacturing facility wasted company resources. Conversely, those who championed the manufacturing cause saw little benefit from, and even less future in producing, one-off systems. Some firms manage to surmount such hurdles; however, many small firms do not possess the capital reserves and political clout to survive the transition. As a result, product champions tend to develop diversification plans and begin to make the case for venture capital.[28]

Although MacDonald sanctioned MDA's diversification plan, he stood his ground on the issue of ownership. Fearing that venture capital and outside investor participation on MDA's board would dilute the company's original goals, MacDonald convinced board members to use ground station profits and bank loans to fund MDA's development plans beyond what government grants, contracts, and tax-based subsidies could absorb. In addition, MacDonald announced that, if necessary, he would rather put up personal guarantees than forfeit ownership control. Later recalling, "I have always had the philosophy that the person who takes the risk makes the decision," MacDonald stressed that he preferred personal risk to bequeathing to others ultimate decisions about MDA's future. As a result, even dubious board members acquiesced, ushering in a period where MacDonald soon learned how much his risk might mean, to him as well as to MDA.[29]

"MORE MONEY, PLEASE":
THE STRAINS OF DIVERSIFICATION AND PRODUCT DEVELOPMENT

By 1976, MDA's board members had identified several product areas the company should develop for the firm's evolving diversification plan. It also became clear that diverse areas also signalled diverse foci. One group proposed that MDA should stay the course in scientific systems, ground station products, and research and development linked to their remote sensing work and the expansion of complex and increasingly expensive surveillance networks. They therefore proposed derivative products such as off-the-shelf multi-spectral scanner test generators, line-scan processing systems, and weather image processing systems for the booming satellite business, all of which promised opportunities in weather forecasting, twenty-four-hour news coverage, and other innovations associated with the launches of Cable News Network (CNN) in 1980 and The Weather Channel (TWC) in 1982. Another group suggested moving more deeply into micro-processors to compete with established firms such as IBM and start-up companies like Bill Gates and Paul Allen's Microsoft Corporation (officially founded in Albuquerque, New Mexico, on 4 April 1975). They thus argued that MDA should develop remote job entry terminals for business applications. To exploit Canada's increased emphasis on expanded policing to secure the nation, still another group proposed development of surveillance-based tracking and mobile data communications systems for police and other security forces. And, finally, those working on PWA argued that MDA could sell similar systems to airlines worldwide.[30]

To exploit all (or even several) of the opportunities they identified, MDA's board members also decided to restructure the company into separate profit centres. Contentious debates took place over how many divisions to create, but eventually the board settled on three. One division focused on scientific systems and ground station products, including development work on SAR, meteorological systems, and imaging; and the other two centred on the commercial business systems and mobile data terminals MDA had started to develop through government procurement contracts and small grants. They also agreed that if Neil Thompson's PWA project proved successful, they would explore product developments for the larger airline industry.[31]

With the 1971 cooperative Canada-US agreement on remote sensing extended through 1981, members of the scientific systems division argued that the CCRS's plans to expand their remote sensing efforts justified product development beyond ground station work. Indeed, MDA had just received the opportunity to work on synthetic aperture radar for the proposed *Seasat* launch, and the CCRS planned to support more such work over the next decade. Although "the need to manage, control and sell its natural resources could justify the 180 million dollar cost of a purely Canadian satellite," members of the CCRS argued that "it is more likely that Canada will seek partnership in an international system. In order to be accepted as a 'responsible' partner and to ensure technological sovereignty in remote sensing," they stressed, "Canada will have to maintain state-of-the-art expertise in a number of selected technical areas, including satellite data reception and processing, image analysis, synthetic aperture radars and optical scanners. This course of action," they noted, "will allow Canada to negotiate from a position of strength, and preserve the option of a purely Canadian satellite if international negotiations are not satisfactory." People at CCRS also boasted that procurement policies and the UPP fund had already developed a "specialized Canadian industry," with MDA a prominent member of its core. Pointing to what MDA had already accomplished, members of the CCRS additionally argued that MDA could not only meet "increasing domestic needs," but had already "been successful in exporting several million dollars' worth of equipment and services abroad."[32] Such praise thus prompted MacDonald to approve expenditures on the systems side of the business to develop technologies of interest to the CCRS. Eventually, those expenditures included work on a film recording dilemma that had stumped many inventors.

Dan Gelbart, one of MDA's most talented engineers, envisioned a way to solve the film image problem to enhance MDA's position in the ground station market. According to Ken Spencer, the engineer who had risen through the ranks to become MDA's ground station manager during the late 1970s, Gelbart became one of Canada's "most multi-skilled" engineers, among its most "prolific in invention, in understanding the breadth of technologies," and someone who could "have a patent a day if he wanted to" apply for all of those flowing from the ideas he generated.[33] Gelbart also bucked some engineering trends. With micro-processors gaining popularity in the second half of the 1970s, most engineers agreed that the electronics industry would soon generate a convergence between hardware and software solutions, but Dan Gelbart had taken an intense disliking to software. He also began to realize that his interests lay in optics and mechanics rather than electronics, an epiphany that came to him when his wife delivered their first child. Deciding he should follow in his father's shoes, raising his son at home in the same way his father had raised him, Gelbart knew he had to dream up a project that could rationalize his desire to work in the "solitary confinement" of his own basement. Happily for all concerned, John MacDonald understood subterranean work, MDA had already established flexible work schedules, and Gelbart knew that if MDA wanted to maintain its competitive edge in remote sensing, the company needed to find a way to create higher quality ground station images.[34]

MDA employed another company's film image recorder to fulfill its contractual obligations for Sweden's Kiruna ground station during 1978. Two companies bid for that work: one proposed an extremely accurate but slow machine, and the other proposed an extremely fast but less accurate machine. The MDA team chose the faster one. Unfortunately, the Swedish contract had a penalty clause associated with accuracy specifications for the film image recording unit. When MDA's subcontractor failed to deliver a recorder acceptable to the specifications, the Swedish client invoked the penalty clause, which cost MDA $75,000. The inferior film image recorder had created trouble enough on the Swedish contract, but other clients had also started to demand similar specifications, and then more stringent ones for future ground station work. Called in to meet with MacDonald and knowing that he had to sell the company president on the idea that MDA needed to send him (rather than someone else) away to work on the film image recording problem, Gelbart announced that he thought he had found a solution employing mechanics and optics rather than electronics. The idea intrigued MacDonald. He therefore suggested that he and Gelbart should talk it over with Ken Spencer. When the three finally met to discuss options, Gelbart claimed that he could solve the problem, but only if he worked on it at home. When MacDonald and Spencer asked him why, Gelbart explained that he wanted to raise the perfect child. While neither MacDonald nor Spencer understood the rationale, Spencer surprised Gelbart by proclaiming, "If MDA gets what it wants, I don't see any problem with that arrangement." Just one more hitch remained.[35]

While Gelbart's solution piqued his interest, MacDonald argued that others had tried to develop the recorder technology without success; moreover, with other product development setbacks and cost overruns imperilling MDA's future, he was in no mood to gamble without assurances. MacDonald therefore authorized a $100,000 allocation to Gelbart and his project. "If you can make a black-and-white film image recorder work in three months, I'll give you more money," MacDonald promised. Otherwise, the flow of money would stop.[36] From MacDonald's perspective, Gelbart was an excellent risk. "He's one of the most meticulous engineers in the world," MacDonald later explained. "He always does little experiments to prove his ideas are correct before he starts spending big dollars on them." As a result, MacDonald had no qualms about fronting money to Gelbart for his proof-of-concept work. Elated that MDA had given him the chance to oversee the development of a significant technology as well as his own son, Gelbart shuffled off to his basement. Within two weeks, Gelbart had made excellent progress on the film recorder problem; however, when his son unplugged a crucial wire in the middle of an important test, Gelbart decided to seek the services of a reputable daycare centre. Once sequestered at home without distractions, Gelbart easily met MacDonald's deadline. Within three months, Gelbart produced a prototype that worked, and MacDonald gave him the money promised to develop what became MDA's black-and-white film image recorder (FIRE).[37]

Two-thirds of the way through development work on the black-and-white FIRE, Gelbart approached MacDonald once more, this time declaring, "I think I have an idea for a colour machine; and I need more money, but I can demonstrate that it will work." Producing colour images posed difficulties beyond those associated with black-and-white ones, and this MacDonald knew. Again, he needed assurances from Gelbart. Choosing brown for the difficulty it poses to colour synthesis, MacDonald chuckled, "OK Dan. You spend a little bit of money, but unless you can produce brown light out of this thing, I'm not sure you're right. I want to see brown light." Leaving that meeting in high spirits, Gelbart once again descended into his basement. After several months passed, Gelbart entered MacDonald's office once again, presenting a slide with a brown spot in the middle of it and beaming as he pronounced, "Here, more money please!" MacDonald authorized the money required, and Gelbart disappeared into his subterranean laboratory.[38]

Beyond product development on the systems side of the business, the Commercial Business Systems division seemed to offer an excellent opportunity for diversified expansion. Work on commercial systems stemmed from a small grant MDA had received in 1972 from the National Research Council's IRAP to investigate industrial applications based on micro-processor technologies. MDA's new batch communications controller (called the 4880 and designed to reduce data entry costs) promised to seed business systems products for the government as well as the private sector.[39] Consultants to government had encouraged MDA's optimism by arguing that the development of an indigenous computer industry could improve Canada's balance of trade. "We now have an annual trade deficit of more than five hundred million dollars per year in computers and office equipment," one Canadian analyst observed in January 1977, producing "our fastest growing product trade deficit. Future Canadian computer purchases will amount to billions of dollars," he warned, with the "the resulting trade deficit" having "serious consequences if we continue on our present path."[40] Other analysts concurred, noting that Canada "has the second-highest per capital number of programmers and systems engineers in the world. And we are second only to the United States in the per capital number of computer installations." As a result, they suggested, "international links are already being established which provide the potential for massive data exchange activities."[41]

Responding to opportunities in the computer sector, policymakers stressed the need for more private-sector involvement in research and development to enhance Canada's "information sovereignty" so that Canada could avoid the "storage of Canadian information in foreign locations beyond the reach of Canadian law." They also hoped to deploy defence and space programs to generate a "greater entrepreneurial and business thrust in the less developed parts of Canada."[42] Focusing on the faltering economy, international competition, information sovereignty, and the equalization of Canada's disparate regions also suggested the need

for "Buy Canada" initiatives and the creation of a more attractive environment for Canadian venture capital investments in Canadian industries
from coast to coast. The Department of Industry, Trade, and Commerce
also emphasized the need to socialize the Canadian people for the significant role that technology-based firms and venture capitalists would need
to play in Canada's future. "Post-industrial society will be a knowledge
intensive society, in which cognitive labour will displace manual labour,"
the department declared. As a result, "the computer will be a key instrument in storing, manipulating and making knowledge available."[43]

The third product division, Data Communications Systems, resulted
from a Communications Research Centre (CRC) procurement contract
MDA had received to develop a mobile radio data system (MRDS) for the
Vancouver City Police Department. Prior to that work, "most of the projects that we had done involved highly trained, technical sorts of users,"
Stanley Semrau recalled, "so this was new for the company, in that there
were these front-line, technically unsophisticated employees who would
be using the system." What was more, the police mistrusted computer
technology and considered the project "somewhat of a threat to the
policemen" who perceived the introduction of a computer system "as a
way of keeping track of them, disciplining them," and "making fools" of
rank-and-file officers. Ultimately, people at MDA assured the Vancouver
police force that the proposed MDA system would not threaten them, but
rather that it could serve as "a useful tool" to keep track of others, a break-
through that could also connect the Vancouver Police Department to a
"nation-wide system of the RCMP," one that ultimately connected the
RCMP to the Canadian Police Information Centre, then the Canadian
Security Intelligence Service (CSIS). The Vancouver City Police Department project helped people at MDA "learn a lot about selling at the municipal level" and to those involved in domestic surveillance. It also began to
cement a relationship with law enforcement that furthered the government's capacity for data mining and MDA's abilities to work with other
governmental entities on similar projects.[44]

While members of the three divisions commenced their work, Mac-
Donald decided to look for a new office location. MDA already occupied
every available space and had knocked out every possible wall in the Film
Exchange building on 12th Avenue in Vancouver's West End. The company started out in one room on the second floor, took over that corner
of the building, and began to knock down walls and build rabbit warrens
to accommodate further expansion. As soon as each tenant moved out,
MDA moved in. When the firm finally occupied half of the building, it

could expand no more. Like metropolitan areas elsewhere in North America, central Vancouver had become prohibitively expensive in relationship to its less-well-developed suburban communities. Thus, longtime tenants announced that they intended to renew long-term leases they could still afford.[45]

With the assistance of MDA's Commercial Systems Division manager, MacDonald finally found a suitable facility for MDA's expansion near Vancouver's International Airport in Richmond. Recently constructed and buildings still vacant, Richmond's Shellbridge Industrial Park had plenty of room to accommodate the company's expansion. It also had other strategic advantages. Inflation, along with a housing boom in the Lower Mainland, had started to make life difficult for young people thinking about making the move to an increasingly expensive Vancouver. Thus, after MacDonald visited the facilities at Shellbridge, he took out a real estate map of the Lower Mainland, looked at housing prices, and decided that the Richmond suburb still remained affordable for MDA's young staff and potential recruits. The facility's proximity to the airport and accessibility from a wide range of housing also promised to provide convenient access to MDA's expanding number of global clients. Moreover, as the facility's first tenant, MDA could negotiate excellent terms on a three-year lease, as well as a right-of-first-refusal on additional space within the industrial park. Convinced that the Shellbridge location could save MDA money in the long run, MacDonald quickly signed a deal.[46]

While MacDonald arranged for MDA's move, Bill Thompson and others continued to worry about MDA's escalating expenditures. To make the case for venture capital, Thompson also decided to interview MDA employees, ultimately bequeathing to history an investigation that targeted MacDonald's refusal to seek outside capital as the root cause of what Thompson perceived as a problem of "sagging morale within MDA." Thompson's investigation cited management credibility problems, broken promises, and employee complaints that MDA had badly planned the three divisions. He also reported that employees complained that "people are putting more into their work than they are receiving in return from the company," and that, despite the thrill of taking "technological dares," cost overruns, uncompensated overtime, and a "lack of management talent" to deal with critical issues had begun to "infect" the entire firm. Thompson therefore concluded, "It is time for management to face up to the fact that the present management is comprised of technocrats, not managers in the business sense." This, he argued, could not continue, and many of MDA's problems could "be eased considerably by seeking additional equity. If we are to continue to ride the crest of opportunities," he cautioned, "the company must have more capital. If equity capital is not to be increased then our rate of growth must be cut back." Despite such warnings, however, MDA persevered; and by the time employees arrived at their new, open-space office, MacDonald had allocated sections to reflect each division's expansion as well as space for FOCUS.[47]

MDA moved during the December holiday. The moment employees settled into their new offices in January 1977, MDA needed more space; thus, employees began to knock down walls, build more rabbit warrens, and demand additional buildings. Within the year, it seemed clear that MDA had made a geographically wise move, perhaps even an excellent economic one, but in the short term, the costs associated with relocation placed additional financial burdens on the firm.[48] "As usual in business, you're OK unless two things go wrong at once," Ken Spencer, then MDA's ground station manager later recalled, "and two things went wrong at once." First, "the scientific, the core business, didn't make as much money as we had projected," and expenditures on Gelbart's FIRE machines strained ground station reserves. Second, the computer business and mobile systems areas "lost money faster than the remote sensing business could make up" for the loss.[49] While seasoned business people usually spend up-front time on market analysis and pencilling the costs associated with diversification and product development plans, most engineers and scientists have trouble moving beyond Emerson's rationalization for innovation: if technological visionaries "build a better mousetrap, the world will beat a path to [their] door." MDA's executive-engineers were no different. They spent little time on market research, learning only later that the product technologies that had enticed them personally did not always create their own demand. The federal government's UPP, IRAP grants, and other incentives furthered MDA's myopia, evidenced by the company enthusiasts' failure to recognize that government decisions, political expedients, and international agreements had often created one-time or short-term demand for the company's technologies and the government funding it received to develop them.[50]

Exacerbating these dilemmas, MacDonald's desire to maintain financial control over his vision prompted heated debates over the company's future, creating fissures between MacDonald and his shrinking pool of allies on the board of directors versus those who called for outside investment capital and the need to build structures to manufacture proprietary products. Ultimately, all of those debates centred on power – who had it, who wanted it, and who might lose it. At the same time, those who enjoyed creative and sophisticated systems engineering work often collided with their product-oriented colleagues. Many of the former argued that the latter needed to remember why MacDonald and Dettwiler had created the company: to extend their experience with university research and development, to work on the cutting edge of technological innovation, not to produce widgets. Some board members furthered that vision by encouraging employees to pursue ideas that seemed interesting without first analyzing the market for the products they planned to develop, which fuelled more rancorous arguments among and between divisional heads and MDA's rank-and-file engineers.[51]

"IF ONE GROUP MAKES A CLANGER": THE DEMISE OF MDA'S PRODUCT DIVISIONS

Within less than two years, the strains of undercapitalized expansion, an expensive move, insufficient market research, and a deepening recession forced MDA to abandon its product divisions. Soon after MDA moved into its new facilities during 1977, ledgers showed inadequate resources to continue development on the business computer system that MDA had hoped introduce as a competitor to IBM machines. Making matters worse, IBM introduced a lost-cost micro-processor that quickly rendered obsolete the effort MDA had already expended. The division's revenues of $3.5 million, expenses of $3.6 million, and a net operating loss of $53,901 thus forced MDA to shut down the Commercial Systems Business area as well as the company's Synaptic "job-shop" subsidiary, thereafter subsuming the latter operation into the company's whole.[52]

When MDA folded Synaptic into the larger firm, assembly plant employees felt nothing but relief. As part of a subsidiary, they felt alienated and experienced the kind of class fractions that began to surface between new technology workers and traditional manufacturing employees. Once absorbed into the parent firm, however, Synaptic employees began to feel part of the MDA team. The Synaptic experience also revealed important traits in both John MacDonald and the firm's founding vision. Mac-Donald never mentioned the assembly side of the business when he talked about MDA, because it never represented the original goal of pursuing and doing the exciting technical work that he and Dettwiler had articulated from basement beginnings. Indeed, MacDonald deemed it little more than a necessary evil because clients had asked MDA to build hardware systems. Nor did a manufacturing environment comport with the status that members of MDA's engineering team expected to enjoy as part of Peter Drucker's "new knowledge economy" and their membership in the technological vanguard. As increasingly hostile rivalries developed between the technology workers of the parent firm and the manufacturing team in Synaptic Systems, MDA's engineering elite thus asserted their educational and hence cultural if not necessarily economic capital over the assembly plant workers, against whom they sought to distinguish, distance, and detach themselves. They also used consumption to set themselves apart from the working-class assembly team: buying sailboats, taking flying lessons, collecting old technologies, purchasing equipment for skiing expeditions, and sporting countercultural clothing and hairstyles to reflect their perceptions of what constituted a systems builder.[53]

During 1978, with staff increasing to ninety and financial resources wanting to develop the mobile data terminal, further undercapitalized expansion also forced MDA to spin off the Data Communications Division. As Philip Auerswald and Lewis Branscomb have argued, "For technology entrepreneurs within corporations seeking to advance 'radical' technologies not directly tied to the core business, frustration is common," and spinoffs usually occur among employees equally "frustrated with their employers." MDA was no exception.[54] MDA's Data Communications manager, Tom Purdy, had long seen the promise in one of the prototypes Dan Gelbart had developed while working on the Vancouver Police Department project. When Purdy realized that MDA could not afford to develop Gelbart's wireless data modem, he approached Bill Thompson, and together they decided to free the technology from MDA so that they could launch one of the world's first data systems vendors. Raising most of the start-up capital from Ventures West, Vancouver's first real venture capital firm for technology companies on the West Coast, Purdy and Thompson formed Mobile Data International (MDI). As part of the negotiation, MDA retained an option, receiving $3 million for the mobile data technology, and accepting some up-front cash, subsequent payments, royalty rights, and a portion of MDI's shares. In addition, MDA loaned to MDI several of its key employees to see the technology's development through its final stages. Given his new duties at, fiscal responsibilities for, and loyalties to MDI, Bill Thompson withdrew from MDA's board. MDA retained its ownership in MDI for a number of years; however, when the firm needed additional working capital to fund operations during the early 1980s, MDA sold its royalties and shares to MDI.[55]

MDI struggled for several years, but it had plenty of venture capital behind it and had begun as a firm whose senior executives understood and embraced the logic of product development and capitalist expansion within Canada. Moreover, when financial problems finally culminated in Barclay Isherwood's decision to resign from MDA, Purdy and Thompson asked the young marketing virtuoso and business strategist to join MDI as company president. Before he accepted the offer, Isherwood undertook a thorough market study and identified a niche in radio dispatch, not just for law enforcement entities, but also for package tracking and delivery. Happily for Isherwood and many other former MDA employees who took positions at MDI, Isherwood secured a contract with Federal Express (founded in 1971) to automate their tracking system. Isherwood then accepted MDI's offer to join the firm on the condition that its employees receive 33 per cent of the company's shares. That deal sealed, Barclay Isherwood became MDI's president in January 1982. By 1988, regardless its own expansion problems, MDI returned its investors' capital and then some. In that year, Isherwood engineered a bidding war that resulted in Motorola's acquisition of MDI and its mobile data terminals. As its largest competitor, Motorola purchased MDI for US$107 million (or $190 million in 2016). Many of MDI's shareholders became millionaires overnight, including more than a dozen ex-MDA employees who followed Isherwood to MDI during or shortly after MDA's tumultuous period of undercapitalized expansion. Unfortunately for others, MDI disappeared from Vancouver following the takeover, and many MDI employees quickly lost their jobs.[56]

As he reflected on the demise of MDA's two product divisions, Colin Lennox conceded that "MDA was not a product-oriented firm. It was still searching for its product." MDA "had custom-written software products, it had the demultiplexer and Quicklook as the hardware products, but they weren't ordered in large quantities." Moreover, "everyone who ordered one wanted all the latest new features that the other people didn't have, and therefore you were always doing a lot of customizing." The challenges of customization, he argued, exemplified "what MDA people found fun. They didn't want to have boring product jobs being churned out. That wasn't what they came to MDA for." Large, complex, and expensive systems projects made "it fun to work at MDA – fun, but very stressful." To finance the company's general expansion as well as its abortive product developments, MDA thus incurred a cash-flow crisis as well a deteriorating esprit de corps "because as the company got larger, the consequences of any mistake were felt by everybody," Lennox stressed. "If one group made a clanger on a job, everybody suffered."[57]

Although the company's core business in ground stations continued to turn a profit, MDA took a beating from its product misadventure. The company's strategy became increasingly disjointed between MacDonald's systems vision and the product champions who called for the investment of venture capital to support the company's endeavours, which raised, in the most glaring terms, the spectre of ownership versus control. It also confirmed that, with the exception of remote sensing, MDA could not count on the Canadian government as its main product customer and ambassador.[58] Thus, while the Canadian Broadcasting Corporation became the first in the world to employ an orbiting satellite for television service (thereby linking Canada "from east to west to north"), the US dollar plunged to record lows against European currencies, and worldwide unemployment rose during 1978, MDA began to crash with the deepening economic recession. To recuperate its losses, MDA bid on further scientific systems jobs, with past performance and friendly government officials securing the firm many contract wins. Making the case for Canada's and MDA's further participation in the Landsat program, one corporate planning group in government argued that "Canada has benefited industrially from early and continued involvement," with MDA establishing "a prominent international reputation. Several industrialized countries" had "purchased receiving and analysis equipment" it noted, and MDA had generated "sales of $11.9 million in international business. From experience and credibility gained in supplying" the ground station upgrade to the Canadian Shoe Cove station as well, it stressed, MDA promised to gain a "reasonable share of export sales to 1984 at more than $38 million, provided commercial advantages can be maintained" on future Landsat upgrades.[59]

The CCRS also announced that it planned to extend its efforts into remote sensing applications for forestry and agriculture as well as ocean and land management, all of which promised to help MDA develop additional remote sensing products. Furthermore, MDA's patrons at the CCRS promised to fund additional research that would allow MDA to develop products based upon SAR, including ones that would fall under the global crop information agreement the Canadian and US governments had recently signed. "Current developments indicate that the period 1985–2000 will see a world-wide earth observation system, made up of several polar-orbit satellites in complementary orbits," CCRS noted, but "Canada's ability to manage, control and sell its natural resources requires guaranteed access to data from both the multi-spectral scanner and SAR instruments" MDA had developed. Moreover, Canada had already entered into negotiations or discussions with several partners, including NASA, ESA, and the Japanese Space Agency, to participate in an international "surveillance satellite program."[60] They therefore recommended that the government continue to fund MDA's systems efforts.

Promises of future work did not solve MDA's pressing cash-flow and management problems, however, and that reality quickly forced John MacDonald to take a personal risk so that MDA could draw on the account of one of its export ground station contracts. During early 1978, the Royal Bank had threatened to call MDA's loans. Determined to see his vision realized and fearful about relinquishing a share of his ownership in MDA, MacDonald found the means to satisfy bankers: $1 million in personal guarantees.[61] He "put his own house and everything else on the line," Dave Sloan recalled, "and in exchange for that," MacDonald gave Vern Dettwiler and other large shareholders an ultimatum: "'You guys can join me in this personal guarantee, or I want your shares.' And I guess Vern was unwilling to take that risk," Sloan speculated, so Dettwiler relented. In return for his promissory note, MacDonald also demanded that the board pass a resolution to give him official control of the company. As a result, MacDonald acquired 55 per cent of MDA's shares and a full 60 per cent of the firm's voting privileges. "From that point on," Sloan stressed, "John was going to run" MDA the way he saw fit, and "he didn't want to hear other people's advice."[62]

MacDonald's personal guarantees saved the company from immediate financial ruin; however, debates over from where capital investment should come continued, creating further cracks in MDA's management structure, revealing that MDA no longer had a clear direction, and suggesting that the company had finally expanded beyond its founders' abilities to manage the firm. With his increased ambassadorial activities at the CCRS and elsewhere, MacDonald had neither the time to solve technical issues nor the desire to immerse himself in day-to-day management problems. Even if he had the time, he had no interest in hearing bad news, particularly if it involved questions about his leadership abilities. As often happens during such crises, those toting day-to-day responsibilities began to resent that their input had little or no influence on the financial future and direction of the firm. Unfortunately for MDA, increasing frustration finally trumped loyalty to either MacDonald or Dettwiler. Concluding they could no longer agree to disagree over the issue of control, some resigned, while MacDonald asked others to leave. As financial, managerial, and cost overrun crises escalated, MDA lost some of its most valued senior technical staff, leaving further voids in the company's organizational structure and a revolving management door that entailed discontinuities in the day-to-day operation of the firm and dangerous project vacuums. During 1978, Colin Lennox, the only general manager MDA's employees had ever known, resigned. By 1980, both Dave Sloan, MDA's hardware grandfather, and Ken Spencer, the company's ground station manager, joined the ranks of departing employee-managers no longer able to withstand the force of MacDonald's resolve. Shortly thereafter, Barclay Isherwood, MDA's marketing maven quit to join the MDI start-up. And in 1981, Neil Thompson, the company's FOCUS project leader, as well as Doug Seymour, a manager who had taken over the ground station and synthetic aperture radar areas after Spencer's departure, resigned as well.[63]

For the firm's employees in general, and the disciples of MacDonald, Dettwiler, Sloan, and Spencer in particular, "We had the feeling that [we] were participating in a classic Greek tragedy," Dan Gelbart recalled. "It was at that point when the harmony between these four people kind of fell apart." In early years, "there was harmony between them, and when Barclay got added, there was still harmony, so there was logical decision making." But when "things fell apart and some of these senior people left, the harmony was lost and you could feel that." Non-managerial engineers were "exactly like the kids" in a bad marriage. "Technically, I had no problems, because I was only affected by things made out of metal," he joked, "but when Barclay left, John MacDonald came to my house and tried to explain to me what had happened, because he was actually very concerned that it would affect the technical people badly."[64] Such feelings put on full display what Pamela Walker Laird has described about climbing the rungs of the corporate ladder: "What was most prized was one's fit into a firm's subculture and knowledge of its idiosyncrasies, both human and procedural." Harmony between those who had ascended from within reflected "all the comforts to be found with the familiar and predictable." Its breakdown thus threatened the "intertwining of personal and business ties," and promised the "discomforts of testing and integrating the unfamiliar." Over time, MacDonald, more than anyone else, sensed those sources of danger.[65]

Because many of MDA's managers had also played important company directorship and shareholding roles, their departures caused more than a loss of harmony, institutional memory, and technical expertise. They forced expensive changes to the company's board composition and shareholding structure. MacDonald's increased ownership role eventually convinced Lennox and Bill Thompson to leave the board. MacDonald replaced them with people who seemed to sanction his vision. Philip Lapp, the Toronto remote sensing consultant who participated in the creation of SPAR and aided in the construction of the CCRS, emerged as

MDA's most important new board member, the hoped-for link to federal government networks, grants, and work.[66]

Undercapitalized expansion forced MDA to relinquish control of some of its potentially lucrative product opportunities as well, including the data tracking device moved to MDI when MDA needed to unload the Data Communications Division to raise capital for other projects. But when Bill Renwick decided to leave MDA during 1978, the firm also lost its asynchronous tasking supervisor (ATS) technology. Renwick realized that neither MacDonald's vision nor MDA's resources could support his pipeline work. Despite his influence in the company, he also gathered that if he pushed for the further development of the ATS, the company could and probably would go under. As a result, Renwick negotiated a deal: as compensation for his earlier overtime efforts, he received the rights to his tasking supervisor technology so he could venture on his own. Although Renwick had never fancied himself an entrepreneur, he wanted to save the technology he had created. Thus, when MDA spun off the tasking supervisor, Renwick formed a small company called KADAK Products Limited, a firm that survived into the twenty-first century. Renwick's MDA experience taught him a great deal about what he wanted for and from his technology. He therefore chose minimal expansion, internal development, and survival. His reward was a loyal and expanding following of clients who appreciated Renwick's technical prowess and personal touch.[67]

MDA lost more than critical personnel, technology, and windfall profits by spinning off its sophisticated data tracking device and the ATS; by abandoning the product cause, MDA lost the confidence of the larger business community. It also inadvertently began to seed Vancouver with experts and technologies that could compete with MDA as Canadian policymakers struggled with national unity issues and an economy that made North America, in general, and Canada, in particular, an increasingly risky and expensive place to do business. MacDonald thus began to realize his larger dreams of turning Vancouver into a world-class engineering hub, even if that transition gave the Canadian government alternative actors to nurture as the 1970s closed.[68]

"EQUITY RATHER THAN SYMMETRY":
CANADA AND THE INTENSIFYING NEOLIBERAL PROJECT

Between 1978 and 1980, the Canadian government offered little hope to a small firm that had just abandoned its product divisions; indeed, Canada's defensive posture, future plans, place within the neoliberal order, and changing relationship to the continental integration project appeared to threaten MDA's very survival. With many corporations downsizing their North American operations and shifting production facilities to less-developed parts of the world so they could lower their labour costs, Canadians found themselves engulfed in an escalating economic crisis. By 1978, that crisis already included the rise of the Parti Québécois and the migration of anglophone businesses to Toronto as well as rising unemployment, particularly in southern Ontario's manufacturing sector. The Liberal government also had to contend with a loss of confidence in the Canadian dollar, and an increasingly heated debate over the decision to create Petro-Canada as a way to solve Canada's energy and security problems, which independent Calgary firms and the Progressive Conservatives led by Albertan Joe Clark not only vociferously opposed, but also intended to use in the next election as evidence of Trudeau's irresponsible government policies. Critics additionally pointed to Canada's continuing dependence on American corporations as well as what many perceived as an "inadequate level of research and development" in Canadian industry, despite billions of public dollars spent to enhance the nation's position within the international market.[69] With the GATT's 1973–79 Tokyo Round nearing conclusion, Canadians faced the reality of further reductions in tariff barriers as well, including those that had allowed for import substitution to encourage local production for local consumption. Worse still, although Canadians worried about Canadian job losses, they seemed to care little about who manufactured the consumer products they craved.[70]

As domestic capital headed elsewhere, particularly to the United States, Canada's deepening crises prompted yet another debate over Canadian sovereignty, foreign subsidiaries, and the structural issues that seemed to serve the interests of US capital rather than Canadians. "Despite the recent misguided enthusiasm for the 'Post-Industrial Society,'" one government consultant argued, "it should be recognized that at least 60% of all jobs in the service sector are dependent on the goods-producing sector. The main thrust of future policy," he stressed, "must be to reverse the chronically adverse trends through the attainment of a much higher degree of 'Industrial Self-Sufficiency.' This effort should not be limited to so-called 'high technology,' but rather should extend across the entire spectrum." Sharing the belief that Canada's future depended upon a strong manufacturing sector, he argued for "more than a mere conglomeration of *ad hoc* sectoral strategies." Otherwise, he warned, Canada would soon drift from an American "Branch-Plant Economy" to a "Warehouse Economy."[71]

The Science Council's John Shepherd also raised the spectre of yet another Avro Arrow disaster if Canada did not immediately integrate its industrial and defence projects for diversified operations, commercial product development, and job creation. "A strong, competitive and innovative industry requires a national commitment to produce a climate favourable to industrial development," Shepherd argued, and "the policies of government at all levels must reflect this commitment." Moreover, "the historical evidence available in Canada and in other industrialized countries shows that, over the long period, domestic control encourages a greater intensity of R&D and more meaningful employment than do other types of enterprise." Pointing to the United States, where the Department of Defense and NASA had stimulated the commercial development of computers and other space-based industries, he urged policymakers to nurture "indigenous industrial development as an essential underpinning to a healthy economy."[72]

To address such concerns, Canada held its first Federal-Provincial Conference of First Ministers on the Economy during 1978. Alastair Gillespie, then minister of energy, mines, and resources (EMR), opened the conference by noting, "In most other industrial nations 50 to 65% of the R&D is performed by industry," while Canada's "comparative figure is 40%. If we are to sustain and build a competitive economy in Canada, we need to find ways to stimulate a competitive level of R&D investment in Canada by Canadian firms." Heeding his advice and the arguments of others, the federal government thus promised to expand tax credits, use the "lever of government procurement" to "promote and strengthen technology intensive industries," encourage closer coordination between the NRC and provincial governments through the creation of Centres of Excellence that could transfer technological capabilities from universities to industry and "make the most efficient use of scarce resources," as well as organize working groups under MOSST to prepare a national action plan to monitor Canada's state of industrial R&D.[73] Bruce Smardon has argued that, as the voice of "private capital began to argue more aggressively for market-oriented policies promoting greater international competiveness," MOSST's abilities to effect a state-led, national action plan waned in all areas but those that had guided its policy priorities since its founding in 1971: in oceans and space, both of which depended upon budgetary allocations to the DND and its affiliated agencies within the Departments of Communications and EMR.[74]

Prime Minister Trudeau stressed that private capital had little to fear from his Liberal government when he announced a tight fiscal outlook for

1978–79. "Despite cutbacks in some federal research activities, the government remains committed to giving increasing priority to research and development," Trudeau argued, with a target of "1.5 per cent of gross national product by 1983." In striving for this objective, he noted, "The government is looking primarily to an improvement in private sector R&D spending, the area in which Canada, compared to other industrialized countries, has by far its greatest shortfall." As a result, the federal budgets for 10 April and 16 November 1978 included new tax incentives for business investors as well as expanded procurement opportunities for those who could provide the $4 billion worth of annual purchases the federal government made in goods and services.[75] In 1979, the Board of Economic Development ministers reinforced Trudeau's promises by dismissing calls for more government control of the economy. Although energy self-sufficiency emerged on their list of national priorities, thereby paving the way for the 1980 National Energy Program, the ministers once again devoted themselves to the liberalization of the Canadian economy, defence sharing agreements with the United States, expansion of contracting-out policies, and mechanisms that promised "to ensure that federal procurement" could "promote industrial development as well as other socio-economic objectives, consistent with Canada's international obligations." They also approved plans to transfer more university research into the private sector, and noted that "the Defence Industry Productivity Program includes a section which provides contributions to defence or defence related R&D," all "repayable out of the profits generated from the sale of the products." Ministers noted that all government activities needed to meet GATT obligations, but additionally assured investors that the government intended to provide "financial assistance to firms to develop and implement rationalization plans, including mergers or acquisitions."[76]

With government ministers focused on the interests of capital and rationalization plans of large firms, the world was on the cusp of additional change that promised little relief to financially troubled MDA. In 1979, the USSR invaded Afghanistan, Margaret Thatcher became the first woman elected prime minister of the United Kingdom, the Ayatollah Ruhollah Khomeini returned to Iran after a fifteen-year exile, Joe Clark ascended to the prime ministership of Canada on promises of tax cuts, and the Conservatives formed a minority government. According to Armand Mattelart's study of global surveillance, "Margaret Thatcher came to power as the paragon of monetarist policies, which steered the world economy towards neo-liberal economic principles." Deregulation, in particular, he stressed, "was consummated the following year with the election of

Ronald Reagan as president of the United States," which "dissolved the concept of politics into market logic, with the doctrine of free trade inaugurating a new mode of governability." Although Canada already had a long history of free trade in the continental defence sector, larger events confirmed that Thatcher had not yet convinced everyone that everything should "dissolve" into the "market logic" of deregulation.[77]

While a fire sparked the Three Mile Island nuclear accident in Pennsylvania, anti-nuclear activists called for and then received new regulations in the nuclear industry. After sixty-three Americans found themselves hostages at the American Embassy in Tehran, a new era in US-Iranian relations began, in economic sanctions that ultimately weakened long-standing ties. President Jimmy Carter's handling of the crisis allowed Ronald Reagan to win the presidential election during November 1980. And following a nine-month term in office, with continuing budget deficits, high inflation, unemployment, and the decision to institute an eighteen-cent per gallon gasoline tax, Joe Clark and his Conservative Party received a vote of no confidence. The Liberal Party thus returned to power in March 1980, and Trudeau regained the helm on the promise of a more activist government, which included the creation of the National Energy Program. When Reagan took the oath of office in January 1981, his administration immediately retaliated against the NEP, making it clear, as Bruce Smardon has argued, that Americans would not "tolerate an autonomous stance by the Canadian federal state" in economic matters of interest to both nations. With other problems distracting Trudeau and Parliament (particularly the referendum on Quebec sovereignty, a bitter conference involving a constitutional settlement and the hotly debated Canadian Charter of Rights and Freedoms, and provincial rancour over the direction of the Canadian economy), Canada acquiesced, thereby reinforcing a long-term trend in the Canadian defence industry to push for "further continentalism," with Canadian firms "even more concerned to maintain access to the American market with as few restrictions as possible."[78]

During November 1980, the US Department of Defense also released its Directive 2035.1, "Defense Economic Cooperation with Canada," which signalled the American desire to maintain a "long-term balance [of trade] at the highest practicable level in the reciprocal purchase of items of mutual defense interest," while also reminding Canadians that "this relationship is based on the principle of equity rather than symmetry." The directive recognized "the differences in capabilities and capacities of the defense-oriented industries in the two countries and the relative sizes, structures, and materiel requirements of the U.S. and Canadian armed forces," but it also stressed that the US government intended to strengthen its grip on the continent.[79] In his work on Petro-Canada, John Erik Fossum argued that "the move toward tighter continental integration reduced the ability of individual state actors to launch comprehensive and coherent interventionist programs."[80] With the directive threatening Canadian autonomy, the federal government formed an Interagency Committee on Remote Sensing to protect Canada's Arctic, information, and technological sovereignty. Members of the CCRS then promised to provide more work to MDA, in contracts involving the agency's thirteen affiliated departments, including the Department of National Defence.[81] The distractions of a faltering economy, geopolitical instability, and asymmetrical relationships mattered less to people at MDA than the CCRS's plans to provide more work. Indeed, MDA's optimists pointed to eighteen profitable months in the systems business following the decision to abandon products during 1978. Unfortunately, they ignored the business cannon MacDonald once liked to cite: "To be creative, you have to be an optimist. To be a businessman, you have to be a realist."[82] By late 1980, any realist could see that MDA was about to implode. The FOCUS project provided the final spark.

"THE BUZZ SAW CALLED FOCUS":
MYTHICAL MAN-MONTHS AND MDA'S ESCALATING CRISIS

By the end of 1980, the FOCUS software project was out of control, financially and technically. MDA contract negotiators had estimated that, of the three FOCUS contracts it had undertaken with SwissAir, Sabena Airlines, and Texas International Airlines, one could pay for the development costs of the other two. When he reviewed year-end statements for 1980, however, MacDonald discovered that from the $5.3 million received for all three contracts, MDA had already accepted $5 million in progress payments but completed only half of the initial development work. Spending the $5 million on salaries and other things to keep the rest of the company's operations afloat for two years, MDA's board members and managerial staff had no financial reserves on which to draw. With project completion well behind schedule, Texas International then threatened to sue. Unfortunately, MDA had neither the financial backing nor the business structures to handle any of these problems, including the Texas International threat. Thus, when Philip Lapp visited the firm during the crisis and "had the opportunity to talk to some of the key people" involved, he "found everybody in a state of shock about the company, where it was going, the concern" that FOCUS would "drag everything down" and destroy all "they had worked so hard to build."[83]

The FOCUS project team also generated more than the usual amount of "mythical" man-days and months, particularly into what Frederick Brooks Jr has described as the "second system syndrome."[84] MDA's team "put 500 man-days into the month, adding 600 man-days on to the end of the plan," one former employee recalled, "so obviously they weren't making any progress, and in fact they were regressing."[85] Eventually, MacDonald had to ask Dettwiler to step in, with FOCUS "probably the biggest rescue job that Vern ever got involved with. The buzz saw called FOCUS," MacDonald recalled, "had taken about 90 per cent of the money, we were about 50 per cent of the way through, and we'd spent the money on wages and everything else. The hours had been put in," he noted, "but the completion!" was nowhere in sight.[86] And no one seemed capable of taking ownership of the problem. "It was bigger than any of us," one employee stressed.[87] Another employee who had travelled to Brussels to install the Sabena system recalled, "I got a call from my wife" declaring that another MDA employee had called to ask if he was "charging out all of his expenses on his own personal American Express card." When his wife replied that she thought so, the other MDA employee cautioned, "Call him, and tell him to be careful. MDA may not be able to cover those expenses. They may not even be able to make payroll." In response, the employee in Brussels told his wife, "I've got to just go on faith." After all, he reasoned, "If the company was going to stay afloat, we had to do the installation."[88]

"It wasn't all FOCUS's fault," one former employee recalled, "although FOCUS certainly takes all the blame. It pointed out all the various management weaknesses," and "all of a sudden, it was apparent that there wasn't any one person who was in control," anyone who could "make the hard decisions."[89] FOCUS also reflected the difficulties inherent in attempting to manage larger forces regardless of the individual decisions made. "It was a cultural thing, born of the systems house mentality," another former employee noted. "A systems house is one that produces custom solutions, and the systems business is a tightrope act. If you do everything right, you make money, but if you do something wrong, you lose badly. And in FOCUS," MDA "fell off the tightrope."[90] Eventually, John MacDonald agreed. "I've decided that this type of company cannot do anything but grow or shrink – there's no such thing as stability." Furthermore, throughout MDA's history, "we would go out and bid a bunch of jobs, not expecting to get them all, and we'd end up getting more than we expected." Thereafter, "we'd hire a bunch of people to do it, and now we've got to go and bid still more. And that gets kind of scary at times," so much so that some managers and board members pressured MacDonald to abandon FOCUS.[91]

"Whether we dumped FOCUS or not, we would have had to refinance the company," MacDonald later affirmed. "There were no ifs, ands, or buts about that."[92] MacDonald therefore refused to "dump" FOCUS because, as one employee emphasized, "he's a very honourable man. He would rather put the company under than default." Moreover, representatives of SwissAir "knew he wouldn't take the money and run." They also "trusted Neil [Thompson] because he understood what they wanted. They trusted that we could do it, trusted that John MacDonald would see it done somehow."[93]

MDA's decision to expand without a major capital injection had created management rifts over the company's direction, the void into which FOCUS fell, and the necessity to abandon potentially lucrative product opportunities that profited others but ultimately not MDA. By September 1982, MDA's staff had increased to 200, but the company had also incurred a net loss of $1.85 million for fiscal year 1981. Still, most employees continued to delude themselves. "There are two kinds of success," one employee observed. "There's success measured by the shareholders, which includes some employees, and that would be a market float on MDA." But "the majority" of MDA's employees "wanted a continuation of the greenhouse environment, where they could feel the excitement of working in a company that had no bounds." They also wanted "the excitement of being able to do something for the first time, and if you fail you fail, if you succeed you succeed." Although high-quality workmanship and "let's do it our way" continued to define MDA's "core," he conceded that "that form of success was what got MDA into [financial] trouble in the first place."[94]

No matter the overtime spent or dedication to a job well done, when vendors visited to remove leased potted plants, accounting staff revealed that the company could not pay for leased cars and rental equipment, and rumours spread that MDA could not meet payroll, never mind overtime obligations, MacDonald's devoted employees finally realized that MDA could fail. Knowing that senior managers had begun to prepare layoff lists to decide who could stay and who had to go, employees who lived through that "horrendous" time also confirmed the consensus that emerged among MDA's creatives turned realists: "An optimist is a guy who brings lunch."[95]

Some continued to believe that the "government would stand behind John MacDonald," would offer a bailout package, but most began to cite Bill Thompson's assertion that "every night the assets of the company walk out the door" in the systems business, "and you should hope that they'll walk back in on Monday."[96] After too many of MacDonald's "assets" failed to return on too many Mondays in a row, and following more painful discussions with a host of employees and board members, Vern Dettwiler, Philip Lapp, and others finally convinced MacDonald that the time had arrived to seek outside equity. They also advised MacDonald to step down from his presidential role. As Bill Thompson had predicted many years before, the company had finally outgrown even MacDonald's ability to manage MDA. During a painful interview session in 1993, MacDonald reflected on Thompson's advice and the decision he had to make. "Once I thought about it, it was clear that was the thing to do, but it hadn't occurred to me. You have to have those things pointed out to you. I guess what was happening was I wasn't having fun anymore. I mean, certainly it wasn't very fun during all of this."[97]

"A SAFETY NET":
SPAR'S OFFER, MACDONALD'S REJECTION,
AND THE FINAL CRISIS

Much of MDA's history with SPAR had its roots in the FOCUS crisis, with Philip Lapp encouraging John MacDonald to accept SPAR's investment and management expertise to save MDA from ruin. During 1977, cooperative NASA agreements had allowed SPAR to receive two critical contracts from the Canadian government worth some $90 million (or nearly $356.5 million in 2016), the first to design the remote manipulator system (RMS) for the space shuttle, and the other to build a simulation facility for the RMS. At the same time, SPAR received defence sharing production contracts from the Canadian and US militaries to undertake infrared research and development for ship-borne surveillance systems, a project that soon became a full-scale development program between the two countries. Although SPAR initially lacked a major electronics base, it acquired one through Radio Corporation of America. When RCA decided to sell its Canadian space and communications division during 1977, members of SPAR reached out to the Canadian government. Knowing that those in government already had grave concerns about Canada's telecommunications industry and the branch-plant structure of the country's electronics and other sectors, SPAR found allies among those who wanted to keep RCA's technology in Canada. Under a tacit agreement with John Chapman, head of Canadian space operations in Ottawa, key ministers agreed to massage the deal. SPAR still remained small by world standards, but its acquisition of RCA's telecommunications business finally gave the firm the electronics expertise it required to play a critical role in Canada's aerospace industry.[98]

With SPAR's sales reaching $70 million by 1977, and its expertise as a prime contractor solidified by 1979, Lapp and other government consultants produced a report encouraging the federal government to turn SPAR into Canada's chosen instrument for all space-based work. "About 100 Canadian firms specializing in high technology have sales ranging from $1 million to $50 million a year," the report noted. "Most of them fall in the lower half of that range, but assisted by funding programs and tax measures, have developed strong technical capabilities in specialized areas." Those smaller firms also had weaknesses: "Most of them are so small that they lack the financial resources and, in some cases, the managerial skills that would enable them to engage in systems development for larger projects." Thus, "It would clearly be advantageous for Canada if the existing structure could be condensed into a small number of large firms able to compete internationally, to ensure that the new systems are designed and manufactured by Canadians in Canada." The report argued that other countries already had "buy national" programs that Canada could emulate, including the US Department of Defense, which had long provided "a vast stimulus for domestic industry," with capital assets "said to exceed those of the 100 largest corporations in the country. 11 states have enacted 'buy American' laws, and another 17 adopted regulations that have similar consequences for foreign manufacturers." The report also noted how Japan's "insistence on buying Japanese is holding up the current GATT negotiations." As a result, it recommended that the federal government "foster the formation of large Canada-owned firms through mergers and consolidations (as in the case of Spar) in order to achieve production volumes necessary to compete in both domestic and export markets." With the Tokyo Round ultimately producing the GATT's first government procurement agreement, the report stressed exemptions rather than inclusions, which provided much room for the Canadian government and SPAR to manoeuvre.[99]

Despite a "tight fiscal outlook" during 1979, the federal government quickly acted upon many of the report's recommendations, including the adoption of a special Source Development Fund for Major Procurement, with an initial ceiling of $25 million but promises to increase it to $40 million in 1980/81 and $50 million in 1981/82. The fund would provide additional incentives to Canadian industry in "areas of national interest," policymakers argued, to avoid fragmentation of the industry, create spinoff opportunities, and intensify subcontracting opportunities to benefit smaller Canadian businesses. The federal government also noted recent American developments that had prompted the decision to create the fund, including a lowered US tax rate applied to capital gains from 49 per cent to 28 per cent and "technological innovation" incentives that had reached US$51 billion compared to Canada's $2 billion. Employing procurement as a policy tool, the government hoped that space and defence contracts would "open the door to new markets and keep the Canadian supplier at the forefront of technology." Canada's first year's $25 million for major procurement under the fund thus went to SPAR, allowing the company to bid "sole source" as the prime contractor for Telesat's next series of satellites rather than performing as a subcontractor to US Hughes Aircraft. It also helped the SPAR team learn "how to be a prime contractor" and "develop a competitive space industry in Canada." Those in government who assisted SPAR with winning the bid also noted that "continuing government business will be required to develop Spar to the point where it will be fully competitive as a prime contractor," one capable of expanding into a multinational firm with a host of subcontractors located in Canada and around the world.[100]

By 1981, SPAR had the experience, expertise, and government support to help (or take over) MDA. SPAR also became MDA's bête noire and emerged as the focus of MDA's "resentment about all things eastern and status quo" when the larger firm's executives offered investment capital to save MDA from failure. Recalling SPAR's 1981 overture, Lapp stressed that "SPAR intended to provide MDA with a safety net, so that [MDA] couldn't crash," but that safety net "would have involved SPAR coming in and effectively running, or helping to run" MDA, or "perhaps call the shots on the financial side until the company was solvent again." Furthermore, Lapp argued, such an arrangement would "essentially let the current management work its way, or earn its way back into independence." Although Lapp and others considered the SPAR proposal "a pretty good one," John MacDonald and his disciples at MDA "didn't like it at all, because they didn't like the thought that they might lose the company" to SPAR, an entity they considered inferior technologically as well as an undeserving favourite of the federal government. People at MDA also complained that SPAR had inherited RCA's draconian purchasing staff, which made life miserable for other Canadian contractors. Additionally, SPAR employees had a union and negotiating muscle, whereas MDA had neither.[101] In MacDonald's view, SPAR's offer was nothing more than a "predatory move," a clever ploy to acquire the superior, innovative, and high-flying MDA. Fearing the implications, and with the backing of most employees, MDA's board rebuffed SPAR's offer.[102]

Unfortunately for those at MDA, the recession and Canada's high interest rates made it impossible to attract investors other than SPAR. MacDonald's search for capital thus became long and frustrating. Eventually, however, a capital injection from outside the firm, including funds from private investors, venture capitalists, SwissAir, and the Canadian government, saved MDA from extinction. As part of the bailout package, outside investors insisted that MDA replace MacDonald with an experienced business person. Within hours, MacDonald's ownership control plummeted from 60 per cent to less than 20 per cent, and he had to "promote" himself from president and chief executive officer to MDA's chairman of the board.[103] Chapter 5 explores the business-investor strategies that transformed MDA from a technology-obsessed firm for which profit constituted a means to continue, into a company that slowly, sometimes grudgingly, yielded to the discipline inherent in the principle that profit *is* the goal of capitalist enterprise. John W. Pitts guided that transition. He first orchestrated a refinancing package to stabilize MDA for the near term. He then introduced the firm's employees to a disciplinary structure to build the project management expertise MDA would need for further expansion into European markets, the global space industry, and the American military environment. Time would tell whether either MacDonald or his vision could survive the change.

PART TWO

The Investor-Business Strategists

5

"Unscrambling the Mess"

Financial Restructuring, Management Discipline, and the Military Contracting Formula, 1981–1987

During the winter of 1981–82, while Vancouver's population surpassed 1.25 million, bankruptcy loomed at MDA. Employee sweat equity and the indispensable support of the federal government had already allowed MDA to extend its stay in a bootstrap environment far beyond what most companies can endure; and after twelve years in business, those reinforcements could no longer secure MDA's future. Having rejected SPAR's safety net, and with FOCUS continuing to spiral out of control during 1980 and 1981, MDA's ability to make its payroll became less and less certain, a situation exacerbated by the Canadian recession increasing in severity and slamming the Lower Mainland's economy particularly hard. By 1982, Vancouver's "construction bubble burst, pricked by the needle of 20-per cent-plus interest rates and a global recession that shrank the demand for British Columbia's natural resources" and real estate. An article examining Vancouver's problems noted that housing "prices tumbled by a third and in 1982 unemployment rose to 12 per cent. Locked in the economic doldrums, the city was just four years away from its 100th birthday." John MacDonald was also in the doldrums and running out of time, particularly when he considered that the Royal Bank planned to call the loans on which he had risked his personal assets.[1]

MacDonald spent nearly a year searching for friendly investors; however, as such prospects dwindled, he reached out to officials in Ottawa in a desperate attempt to secure a federal loan. When the government turned him down, MacDonald turned to Toronto's Bay Street bankers. After several aborted efforts in Toronto, MacDonald thought he could secure financing through the venture capital arm of the Canada Development

Corporation. At the last minute, however, the CDC cancelled the proposed deal, informing MacDonald that, with interest rates climbing from 15 to a breath-taking 20 per cent, investments in small technology-related firms represented an impossible risk for the federal government and Bay Street investors. "To this day, I hate to walk down Bay Street," MacDonald later remarked, and "I avoid the Toronto transit system because I spent so much time in it" during that long year."[2] While MacDonald exhausted his options, word spread inside the firm that MDA would probably go under. As a result, several small groups formed to ponder their options. John Bennett, MDA's SAR and airborne radar champion, pulled one group together, saying, "We want to make sure that MDA lives, but, if it doesn't, we ought to have Plan B."[3] Others had additional plans, including Bob Hamilton, the firm's ground station manager, who told another group that he would "start his own company to do ground stations and to employ all those people" working on them.[4]

In such a tangle, MacDonald had few choices, but events conspired to help as receivership neared. In a classic eleventh-hour bailout, several investors emerged, each with a different motivation for underwriting MDA's near-term continuation, but all hoping to profit from long-standing defence sharing arrangements with the United States and new federal incentives for Canadian venture capitalists. They also believed that MDA's promising technologies could provide substantial returns if managed properly. The negotiated bailout additionally guaranteed to MDA a necessary component for longer-term survival: an experienced business person named John W. Pitts, who had the bottom-line administrative expertise, political clout, and negotiating skills to refocus MDA's operations. "John [Pitts] really did save the company," one employee recalled. Prior to his arrival, "things really began to come apart at the seams. I remember calling back from" a business trip in "Europe, just hoping that they would answer the phone, because we were told things were that bad, that we might not get paid next week. There were horrendous rumours running through the place, so the fact that [Pitts] showed up, was able to gather the monies together, and basically put the company back on its feet, I don't think has been recognized."[5]

An executive anxious to blend MDA's innovative firsts with the logic of capitalist expansion, Pitts hoped to profit from military contracts as well as the products he and others planned to manufacture on the strength of MDA's most promising technologies.[6] Whereas MacDonald and Dettwiler had emphasized technological excellence above all else, Pitts planned to realize shorter-term financial returns by making MDA attractive to future investors, and the sooner the better. Pitts first arranged for the refinancing of the firm. He then introduced cost controls and a disciplinary management structure to transform MDA from a freewheeling operation to an enterprise focused on profit. During the first five years under Pitts's leadership, MDA gained capabilities in project management on the systems side of the business and captured a major share of the international remote sensing market, which allowed the firm to move more deeply into radar and sonar surveillance, as well as control and logistics systems. The West German Space Agency and the European Space Research Institute purchased MDA products, and the firm built the European Space Agency's Central User Service system for ESA's ERS-1 satellite. Additionally, MDA won awards for innovation in geocoded image correction, laying the foundation for its work in geographical positioning systems (GPS). Finally, the company built a complex military system for the US Air Force, which distinguished MDA as a systems contractor capable of supplying and integrating large and complex projects. Such transformations rarely happen without difficulty, and the years spanning 1982–1987 encompassed a conversion that posed enormous challenges to MDA. Additionally, like other founders before and after them, neither John MacDonald nor Vern Dettwiler received guarantees about his future within, or even with, the newly refinanced company. Only John Pitts could make that call.[7]

"BACK ON ITS FEET":
JOHN W. PITTS, THE ELEVENTH-HOUR BAILOUT,
AND FINANCIAL RESTRUCTURING

Born on 13 October 1926 in Victoria, BC, John W. Pitts grew up in an establishment family with connections in government and business. His father Clarence, a prominent lawyer on Vancouver Island, suffered from multiple health problems, including tuberculosis contracted during his service during World War I. As a result, shortly after his birth, young John Pitts moved with his family to Ashcroft, BC, a small railroad town near Kamloops. Although he raised his children in remote Ashcroft, Clarence Pitts had ambitions for his son. He therefore sent young John to Vancouver Island, where the teenager could receive a classic education at Brentwood College, a prestigious private boarding school in Victoria. After high school, Pitts served in the Canadian Armed Forces until World War II ended. He then embarked upon his university career.[8]

Like John MacDonald after him, Pitts decided to take advantage of Canada's eastern networks and the porous border dividing his homeland from the United States. Casting his gaze toward the centre of power near Ottawa, Pitts made his way to Montreal and McGill University, where he decided to study the mechanical arts. Very soon, however, he realized that he had more interest in business than engineering. Graduating in 1949, Pitts pushed his way south, to Cambridge, Massachusetts, and Harvard University's Graduate School of Business, where many ambitious young men had travelled to rub shoulders with North America's business-political elite and the graduates of the world's first Master of Business Administration program. In the whirl of postwar prosperity, and with Harvard's 1949 graduates quickly becoming "the class the dollars fell on," the Business School's cachet and the success of its MBA graduates convinced Pitts that he had made the right professional decision.[9]

Receiving his MBA from Harvard in 1951, John Pitts quickly married a young Minneapolitan named Margaret Erling Brunsdale, a woman from a well-heeled American family who had travelled to Boston to complete her formal training in art and design. Through his marriage, Pitts cemented a relationship with important and influential American family members, including Margaret's sister Anne, who had moved to Washington, DC, during 1950 to begin a career with the Central Intelligence Agency. Thereafter, Anne Brunsdale took her place as a resident fellow of the American Enterprise Institute (AEI), where she founded the free trade and pro-deregulation magazine *Regulation*. During Pitts's tenure at MDA, Brunsdale also received an influential appointment from President Ronald Reagan, a seat on the International Trade Commission (which she chaired from 1989 to 1990). With his own family's financial resources, influential Harvard alumni, and new family members behind him, Pitts catapulted himself into the vanguard of North America's expanding business networks. He received several employment offers in Eastern Canada and the United States, but Pitts wanted to make his mark on the West. He therefore returned to Vancouver, a city rapidly developing on the completion of Lougheed Highway and population expansion. Taking a managerial position at Vancouver Iron and Engineering Works (VIEW), the young "Harvard man" proved himself an able administrator. He also acquired an itch to make money for himself rather than for others. Thus, in fewer than three years at VIEW, Pitts decided that he had acquired sufficient experience to venture on his own.[10]

During 1953, while the Korean War ended, Avro's secret design department began development work on the Arrow, and John MacDonald and Vern Dettwiler prepared for life at UBC, twenty-seven-year-old Pitts left VIEW, vowing he would never work another day for anyone but himself.

Ambitious to generate wealth and create a diverse portfolio, Pitts spent the next decade buying or founding several small companies, among them Vision Manufacturing Ltd, a remanufacturer of black-and-white television picture tubes. Endowed with influential connections, business acumen, experience in manufacturing environments, and much luck, Pitts sold his firms at precisely the right time, netting profits that allowed him to expand his holdings. By the mid-1960s, he also earned for himself a reputation in Vancouver's Lower Mainland as an excellent executive as well as a disciplined and formidable negotiator. Employing the proceeds of his Vision Manufacturing sale, Pitts purchased a large share in Okanagan Helicopters, a Penticton, BC–based company that had moved to Vancouver in 1949, thereafter emerging as the world's largest commercial helicopter operator. By October 1970, forty-four-year-old Pitts had elevated himself to Okanagan's presidential suite; and two years later, he secured his place as the company's chairman of the board. By the time he appeared on John MacDonald's radar ten years later, Pitts had expanded Okanagan from a local entity with revenues of $7 million into a worldwide operation with revenues exceeding $85 million (or nearly $192.8 million in 2016). His success at Okanagan extended Pitts's influence in Vancouver, allowing him to invest in other firms, serve on the boards of some of them, and participate in local fund-raising.[11]

Despite his accomplishments, during February 1982 Okanagan Helicopters ousted the Harvard graduate in what was, at least for Pitts, a hostile takeover by Calgary's Resources Services Group Ltd (RSG). Instant termination prompted Pitts to file a wrongful dismissal suit against RSG, which he eventually won in a BC Supreme Court decision that awarded him a small but significant $146,046 settlement. Pitts's legal battle attracted the attention of local newspapers and venture capitalists, including Winslow Bennett. A founder of Equity Mining with interests in and around Vancouver, Bennett considered Pitts an important friend and business associate. He therefore offered Pitts some office space so that the former Okanagan executive could re-establish himself in downtown Vancouver. With a deepening recession and enfeebled economy, Pitts accepted Winslow's offer and began to explore investment opportunities in several start-up companies, hoping to acquire at least one of them at a bargain-basement price.[12]

In the meantime, Vancouver's Ventures West Management Inc. expressed interest in MDA. By 1982, Ventures West held shares in a number of Vancouver-based businesses, including MDI, the spinoff company that resulted from MDA's inability to finance the further development of its

Data Communications division. Ventures West had pursued MDA from the firm's earliest subterranean days, but John MacDonald had consistently rebuffed the advances of Vancouver's "vulture capitalists," including Michael J. Brown, a high-flying UBC graduate in economics and Oxford University Rhodes scholar who co-founded Ventures West, became its president, and propelled the firm into a significant provider of private capital for early-stage technology companies. Although he had long prided himself on his abilities to avoid Brown's overtures, by 1982 MacDonald needed Ventures West. Local news coverage had also introduced Mac-Donald to Pitts's legal battles; and with Pitts looking for investment opportunities, MacDonald thought he had finally found a solution to MDA's woes. From Ventures, MacDonald merely wanted money. From Pitts, MacDonald wanted money as well as the talents of a seasoned businessman, someone who could help to save and then manage his floundering firm.[13]

Prior to April 1982, Pitts had never heard of MDA; within twenty-four hours, however, several people called to talk about the company's technological promise, managerial bungling, and financial troubles. Michael Brown was one of Pitts's sources of information about MDA; John Mac-Donald was another. Brown had seen articles about Pitts's lawsuit against Okanagan and called to ask Pitts if he had any interest in MDA. Already briefed by Brown, Pitts agreed to meet with MacDonald. In the narrative he crafted about that first meeting, MacDonald recalled saying, "I hear you're interested in buying into a company and running it," to which Pitts replied, "Yes, I am." MacDonald then asked, "What do you want out of it, for yourself?" Pitts responded, "I want to make some money and have a challenge." Leaping to his feet, MacDonald cried, "Jesus, do I ever have the job for you, the challenge part anyway!" According to Pitts's recollection of that same meeting, he warned MacDonald, "Now, you know, all those [computer] boffins you've got out there, there'll be no more of this high-falutin stuff." Relieved beyond belief, MacDonald exclaimed, "You don't have to convince me, John. Anything!" After what seemed like an eternity to MacDonald, Pitts then offered, "I've talked to Ventures West, and if they're prepared to go in, I'm prepared to go in. And I have some friends who would be prepared to invest with me."[14]

At Pitts's office on that spring day, MacDonald had no bargaining chips left to play. He shook Pitts's hand, called Michael Brown, described his visit with Pitts, and declared himself ready to make a deal on behalf of MDA. With bankruptcy looming and the Royal Bank poised to call MDA's loans, the company's finances presented the most pressing problem.

Brown and MacDonald thus asked Pitts to accept a position as MDA's new CEO to placate the bank. Pitts agreed to review MDA's books with Brown, and to consider investing in MDA. Pitts and several of his business and personal associates (later known as "The Pitts Group"), as well as Michael Brown and his partners at Ventures West, viewed MDA as Vancouver's best high-technology venture opportunity. MacDonald's new "partners" also had specific exit strategies: by capitalizing on the age-old adage "Buy high, sell low," they looked to a time in the not-too-distant future when they could sell the companies they acquired and move on to other investment opportunities. Pitts and Brown also adhered to the capitalist belief that those who succeed in business manage their risks by employing their money to accumulate a lot more of it, and that risk management means knowing a firm's profit potential, its bottom line. Although many technical innovators find the venture philosophy and its profit-maximizing vision discomfiting, MacDonald had to accept that engineering elegance could no longer carry the day, and that MDA's new investors would care only about those technologies that promised a sizeable ROI.[15]

Once Pitts and Brown reviewed the books, pencilled the costs, and inventoried MDA's technical assets, they concluded that the company needed an immediate injection of $6.5 million. At the same time, they perceived in several technologies unexploited opportunities to minimize their risks. Like institutional venture capitalists elsewhere, they had no plans to remain active in MDA after they had returned their initial investment ten times over, which they expected to do within five years. Indeed, they invested in MDA precisely because they perceived untapped product opportunities that MDA could not exploit as the result of management gaffes rather than scientific or engineering inadequacies. Unlike some venture capitalists, however, they also invested in MDA before the firm's founders had created coherent business structures, defined a viable marketing strategy, and built a production facility capable of achieving the economies-of-scale on which large-scale manufacturing depends. Nevertheless, MDA's remote sensing success had opened the door to several niche markets. The new investors therefore believed that MDA could return their equity within the standard venture timeframe.[16]

Only one other issue remained: Pitts realized that he could place himself in an untenable position if he accepted an executive position with MDA. During 1982, the BC Labour Code clearly made all directors and executives jointly and severely liable for meeting company payrolls, and with obligations well over $1 million, MDA could not meet its commitments. "It didn't seem to be very prudent to become an officer of the company," Pitts argued. Consequently, before he committed to MDA's executive suite, Pitts knew he needed to secure more capital to resolve the immediate crisis of the FOCUS cost overrun. Ventures agreed to participate in the capital injection only if Pitts could reschedule MDA's bank loans and secure additional financing from the Canadian government as well as SwissAir. Brown and Pitts then met with executives at the Royal Bank, reminding them that they too had a powerful incentive to see MDA survive the crisis. MDA owed the bank over $3 million, and, if it went under, the bank would lose its stake in the firm. Moreover, if the bank called the company's loans, MDA's accounts receivable would become worthless, and neither Texas International, SwissAir, nor Sabena had any intention of paying for partially completed FOCUS systems if MDA declared Chapter 11. Thus, if the Royal Bank wanted to receive repayment, its representatives had few and limited options. They therefore decided to work with Pitts, his investor group, and Ventures West, agreeing to defer the loan call if MDA installed Pitts as president and chief executive officer the minute Pitts had financing in place.[17]

During June 1982, MDA retained Pitts as a consultant to manoeuvre around the liability associated with the BC Labour Code. Spending the next two months examining MDA's organization, Pitts first concentrated on a capital infusion plan. He then negotiated deals, first with MacDonald and then with MDA's major shareholders, arguing that if he could arrange additional financing from the Canadian government and Swiss-Air, members of the Pitts Group and Ventures West were prepared to put up $1.8 million in exchange for preferred shares in MDA. With the venture capital commitment in place, Pitts then turned to raising the remaining $4.7 million from the Canadian government and SwissAir.[18]

The federal government's motivations for helping MDA differed from those involved in the Pitts Group and Ventures West. Following the US election in 1980, the Reagan administration focused its attention on implementing supply-side economics (particularly tax cuts, deregulation, and the negotiation of free trade agreements). But Reagan also accelerated the reversal of détente and the escalation of the Cold War with the USSR by ordering a substantial buildup of the US armed forces and stimulating the further expansion of the American military-industrial complex. In a January 1981 report to Congress, Caspar Weinberger, Reagan's secretary of defense from January 1981 to November 1987, discussed Reagan's proposed missile defence system and what his administration expected from NATO allies. "The unremitting Soviet military buildup of the last several years has meant steady annual increases in Soviet defense expenditures of 4–5 per cent in real terms," Weinberger warned. To deter "or directly meet this threat, the Western allies must devote substantial additional resources to defense. It is also important that this increased overall burden be shared in a relatively equitable fashion by alliance partners." Members of NATO as well as Japan had agreed to "increase defense expenditures by an annual fixed rate of at least 3 per cent," and to commit themselves to rationalization and standardization within NATO. "This administration will take the lead in securing the willing participation of all allies in this endeavor," he promised.[19]

Seeking Canada's participation in the US missile defence plan, Weinberger arranged a meeting between Reagan and Trudeau to discuss the Defense Authorization Act of 1981 that would appropriate US$53 billion for government procurement, research and development, civil defence, and other military expenditures as well as the Defence Production Sharing Arrangement between the US and Canada. Reagan visited Canada in March 1981, and despite strained relations and ongoing issues, he and Trudeau reaffirmed both countries' commitment to the DPSA, NORAD, and NATO. They also reviewed cross-border trade in defence, which influential policymakers in Canada deemed "important not only from an export viewpoint but also necessary to maintain a strong Canadian defence base. This would further support US endeavours, in having a viable additional source of supply for their Preparedness Program," they argued.[20]

As DPSA trade imbalances neared $550 million in favour of the United States by the end of 1981, Trudeau extracted from Reagan a memorandum of understanding that would allow Canadian firms to serve as prime contractors on several joint initiatives, including a continuation of SPAR's role on infrared surveillance, tracking, and detection systems for the Canada-US Navy development program, as well as the development of an automated weather distribution system (AWDS) for the US Air Force. With 2,000 employees and abilities to deliver its first robotically controlled *Canadarm* to NASA established in 1981, SPAR had the technical and managerial capabilities to bid as prime contractor for the joint Canada-US development program. As a result, an officer of the US Department of Defense attended a briefing with SPAR during November 1981. Three years later, SPAR received an US$86 million contract to develop the system. MDA's work on FOCUS and SAR had demonstrated the firm's technical abilities to develop AWDS and other all-weather systems, even if the company lacked the necessary management structures for such work. AWDS additionally promised the possibility of a production contract to install approximately 160 AWDS at American military bases across the world. Seeking to exploit the US government procurement system and acquisition market so that Canadian firms could penetrate the massive US defence market and help to protect Canadian sovereignty as well, influential members of Canada's own military-industrial establishment thus pushed the federal government to save MDA so that it could participate in AWDS.[21]

At the same time, with the NEP in place, energy minister Marc Lalonde deemed MDA an integral part of Canada's bid to promote conservation and "green technologies" within the nation's industrial sector. Viewed by many as environmentally clean as well as important to the country's overall Western Energy Program, MDA's technologies seemed to guarantee several different kinds of return on any government investment. Concerns over the potential for creating global electronic waste (e-waste) from technologies then viewed "green" never entered the discussion; however, the desire to protect Canadian sovereignty and quell dissent in the Western provinces certainly did. With the United States withdrawing from an East Coast Fishery Treaty with Canada and the UN Law of Sea Conferences, several policymakers argued that Canada needed better safeguards for the oil and gas sector as well as its Arctic regions and ocean resources. MDA's expertise in land, sky, and sea promised to contribute to those efforts.[22]

Several Canadian policymakers also argued that the federal government had already made a considerable investment in MDA, with the young firm generating employment in BC and representing a significant West Coast connection to SPAR and the surveillance industry. Members of the CCRS additionally stressed that Canada's continued participation "in the development of image analysis systems for land-based resources" depended on its abilities to upgrade "the reception stations at Prince Albert and Shoe Cove." MDA's ground stations had therefore made a significant contribution to Canada's "leading role in multi-lateral deliverations among industrial countries regarding global earth observation systems expected in the 1980s. Should Canada fail to upgrade her technology to current standards," they warned, Canada's remote sensing "prominence and ability to influence future developments will disappear. Other countries would have sole control of ways of acquiring data of Canada, and we ourselves would have less comprehensive and timely access to data on our own resources."[23]

With a Canada-US Airspace Systems agreement in negotiation, MDA's expertise promised to give Canada continued leverage, one confidential report noted. "Prima facie, the economics look good. The USA will be spending $10 billion over the next ten years; Canada will be spending $3

billion over the next twenty. Given the strains in the bilateral relationship, the prolonged recession," and "growing protectionist sentiments in
the Congress," any Canadian proposal "would need to be put to the
Americans very carefully," it advised, and would "have to be seen by all
players in the U.S. that" preferential treatment toward Canada "was at
least as much in their interest as it was in Canada's." But "the question
will quickly become what we are prepared to give up to gain access to the
U.S. market," the report emphasized.[24] By mid-1982, policymakers
answered at least part of that question by privatizing some Crown corporations, including Canadian Arsenals. They also concluded that "the
national interest" necessitated delivering MDA and its technological
know-how from the jaws of bankruptcy. Rather than lay off 200 people,
as well as lose an important subcontractor for SPAR and potential prime
contractor for AWDS, the Department of Industry, Trade and Commerce
therefore agreed to award to MDA a no-strings-attached grant of $1.7 mil-
lion through its Industry, Energy, Research and Development Program
the moment Pitts convinced SwissAir to provide the additional $3 mil-
lion needed for the financial rescue.[25]

     Pitts had already developed a campaign to deal with SwissAir, for he
knew that all other commitments could fall apart without the airline. He
also understood that MDA's 200 employees working through the tumultuous months of July and August depended on his negotiating skills.
Although the strains of looming bankruptcy, board conflicts, and "sagging
morale" among employees had started to show on MacDonald as well, he
convinced others that his own negotiation with Pitts had demonstrated
that Pitts could bring SwissAir onside. "John Pitts is the best negotiator
I've ever had anything to do with," MacDonald argued. "If I wanted to have
the perfect business, I'd make Barclay [Isherwood] the salesman and Pitts
the negotiator. I've sat on the other side of the table from John once, and
I never want to be on the other side of the table from him again." No matter MacDonald's confidence, SwissAir represented a formidable challenge, and no one understood that more than John Pitts.[26]

     During late July, Pitts travelled to Zurich, along with John MacDonald
and Elizabeth Harrison (Michael Butler's successor as MDA's legal counsel). MacDonald and Harrison knew MDA's operations and had negotiated previously with SwissAir. As the proceedings' only outsider, Pitts thus
positioned himself as uncompromised, no matter the outcome. He
reminded the airline's executives that if they refused to invest, MDA would
have to declare bankruptcy and SwissAir would have to start all over again
with another contractor, a situation that would cost much more than the

$3 million proposed. "I was in a great position to play hardball," Pitts remembered, "because if they didn't agree to put up this initial money, then they would have nothing. They saw the wisdom in that, and eventually agreed" to MDA's terms, "with some caveats," which included the creation of a subsidiary to exploit FOCUS and shield the main company from potential liability, as well as an option to send a SwissAir manager to supervise FOCUS completion. Pitts and Harrison agreed to launch MDA Aviation Systems, Inc. to include SwissAir in the future profits of MDA's systems business, and Pitts welcomed the insertion of SwissAir management expertise, which he deemed a boon to MDA's operations. By the end of the meeting, SwissAir agreed to inject $2.1 million into MDA and to trade the remaining $900,000 owed to them for MDA shares as their stake in the company's future. SwissAir also exercised its option, sending to Vancouver a man named Godi Bowman. Later the head of the airline, Bowman became an important ally to Pitts and MDA. The deal's completion was "a source of considerable relief, and a great satisfaction to all of us," Pitts recalled, "because SwissAir's people were excellent, nice people, and beloved by all at MDA by the time they went back to Switzerland."[27]

With MDA's rescue in sight, MacDonald bothered himself little about other events taking place during that sweltering summer of uncertainty, including 700,000 demonstrators gathered in New York City's Central Park to protest the proliferation of nuclear weapons, a rejection of a nuclear freeze resolution by the US House of Representatives, and a special conference called by Canada's ten provincial premiers to draft a comprehensive plan for national economic recovery. Instead, MacDonald focused on his apprehension prior to leaving Vancouver for Switzerland, his continued loathing for Toronto's financial centre on Bay Street, and especially the miracle he believed he had witnessed at the SwissAir negotiating table. Perceiving in Pitts and the SwissAir team the saviours of his vision, MacDonald rejoiced in MDA's new beginning. MacDonald's remaining apostles at MDA hoped upon hope that he had placed his faith in the right sorts of people, for their future prospects depended on them as well.[28]

As MDA's new leader, Pitts had to make important decisions about MDA's founders. Dettwiler had already chosen a technical path, and MDA team members loved to work with him. Pitts knew he could capitalize on loyalty to Dettwiler and saw no reason to change his role. But Pitts worried about MacDonald. With his control issues and merry band of followers, MacDonald might emerge as a problem. An instinctively private person, Pitts also preferred to linger in the background; thus, as he contemplated his own unhappy departure from Okanagan while *Time* magazine declared "The Computer" the *man* of the year (the first object in history to receive the distinction) and the Soviet spaceship *Vanera-13* landed on Venus, Pitts decided to retain MDA's charismatic government ambassador and technology leader. Although he had experience in running complex manufacturing establishments, MDA's sophisticated technologies represented new challenges; Pitts therefore decided that MacDonald would remain important to maintaining company morale.[29]

After he established MacDonald's new role, Pitts turned his attention to restructuring MDA's board to reflect the company's new owners; and during a dramatic closing on 15 September 1982, he brought all investor groups together to sign the appropriate legal agreements. On 17 September, MDA's board members then installed Pitts as the company's new president and CEO. Two representatives of Ventures West became majority shareholders, together owning 26 per cent of MDA. Pitts obtained a $10,000 monthly salary, options on additional shares, and management incentive bonuses that resulted in a 15.6 per cent ownership stake in the company by the middle of 1984. Three of Pitts's associates from Vancouver's and Seattle's business elite took their respective places on the board, while John MacDonald (left with 20 per cent of MDA's shares) and a representative of his choice gave the restructured firm continuity with the past. Despite his antipathy toward SPAR, MacDonald chose Philip Lapp for his connections to Ottawa as well as the friendship and support Lapp had displayed throughout the FOCUS crisis. Although his shares plummeted from 60 to 20 per cent during financial restructuring, MacDonald recognized the prudence of change. "We were not yet completely out of the glue," he remembered, "but for me, at least, someone else now had the responsibility of unscrambling the mess." Thereafter MacDonald became "chairman of the board," to "handle the company's public relations, and direct technological development, all the things" he liked doing. "Pitts's arrival was one hell of a relief, it really was," MacDonald stressed.[30]

Even if he had no choice, MacDonald argued that "the decision to transfer the executive responsibility for this company to a professional business person was the best decision I ever made. I wish that I had done it five years before, when the first tremors hit." Unlike many companies founded by technical creatives, the firm that Dettwiler and MacDonald formed had extracted from Pitts, the Canadian government, and other investors another chance to carry on, this time under the direction of an experienced business executive. That lesson logged, members of the executive team thereafter looked to financial investors rather than engineering experts to serve on MDA's board. In the meantime, MDA's restructured board passed a resolution to create employee and management share option plans. By offering a limited number of common shares to employees, at one penny a piece, the board acknowledged employee contributions and dedication during MDA's crisis (for, barring the management exodus, only a few technical employees quit the company during the recession). "Throughout the FOCUS fiasco and all the troubles, and the hand-to-mouth, pay-cheque-to-pay-cheque operation that went on, we did not lose, aside from Neil Thompson, any key technical people that I can recall," MacDonald argued. Others who had lived through the ordeal confirmed most of MacDonald's memories; however, they also noted that many engineers had scarce employment options during 1981–82, save for Bill Renwick, Dave Sloan, Ken Spencer, Barclay Isherwood, and other engineering managers who had departed during the crisis after doing so much to make MDA a technological success. Still, they remembered, common share offerings gave employees another incentive to stay.[31]

Pitts recognized the basic philosophical divergence between himself and MDA's creative founders, yet he continued to value their input. Instead of removing them from the company's operations, Pitts allowed MacDonald, Dettwiler, and their technology apostles to find a niche and, in the process, to promote the new direction into which Pitts hoped to drive the firm. Time would test the prudence of that decision, but for the moment, Pitts ascertained that he really had no other choice. Some engineers had already made it clear that "if they had little to no work experience" prior to joining MDA, they had "even less interest in business. As a matter of fact there was a pretty derogatory outlook by the engineers on management" even before Pitts arrived, one former employee argued, increasingly deriding those who inhabited the executive suites of "Mahogany Row" as "the suits" and "bean counters." Once Pitts and his management team occupied those suites, however, MDA's employees also encountered new and irksome management changes, including the demand that they retroactively sign disclosure agreements and adhere to the discipline of formal correspondence about the progress of the projects on which they worked.[32]

"WATCHED MORE CLOSELY": CREATING COST CONTROLS AND A DISCIPLINARY FRAMEWORK

When Pitts arrived during 1982, MDA had elegant technologies but neither the management nor disciplinary framework on which to maximize profits for capitalist expansion. Adhering to Andrew Carnegie's maxim from the 1870s that if you "take care of the costs, the profits will take care of themselves," Pitts quickly zoomed in on the operational side of the business, introducing cost controls to reduce MDA's inefficiencies, and setting up three divisions as profit centres with incentives for each to compete for the resources of the firm.[33] Through these basic structures, Pitts hoped to generate consistent revenues from the systems side of MDA, so that the company could generate cash reserves to ripen products for mass manufacturing. The manufacturing plan would soon test his assumptions about MDA's future, but "for a company like this to survive, it has to have cost controls and engineering and operational management methodologies in place so it can carry on fixed-price, software development projects on time and on budget," one new manager stressed. "And that's the rigour that John Pitts introduced to the company."[34]

Interviewing MDA's customers and employees, Pitts unearthed a variety of problems, from a dearth of cost and management controls to duplication of effort in key project areas. "MDA's philosophy was to do good, solid, imaginative engineering work, but there was little or no emphasis on the subject of profit," Pitts observed, "and even if there had been an emphasis on profit, there were no control systems in place in the company." That meant that none of MDA's "managers could monitor on a week-to-week and month-to-month basis. There were some financial statements that came out," Pitts noted, "but to me they were meaningless, because you couldn't put them all together and get an end result, and they needed something to show the changes in financial position," a measure MDA's staff did not seem to appreciate. Pitts conceded that people at MDA had learned at least one important lesson from the FOCUS fiasco, however: "In taking on a major contract, they did not have proper project management controls," and that "was true for almost everything that went on in the company. It just showed up blatantly on a large contract which extended over a period of time." At the same time, Pitts sensed that many of MDA's original technical staff viewed him with suspicion. Although relieved that the company had survived its crisis, a number of MDA's key staff signalled fears that his button-down Harvard profile, along with the attitude it implied, could rapidly corrupt the company's original goal of doing fun, exciting technical work. Pitts thus moved cautiously, at least at first, so he could find a "balance between management control and engineering creativity. When it tilts too far one way, you have this jungle that's completely out of control," he explained, "but if it tilts too far the other way, you have an over-cultivated desert. So you have to find a middle way, where there's the balance you find in a well-tended garden."[35]

Analyzing the management structure at MDA, Pitts first identified redundancies. Where three divisions could do, he discovered five, all run as fiefdoms. Each area had its own staff members, all of whom project managers tended to hide from others if their own project had no current use for them. As often happens in such circumstances, divisions rarely transferred information, and each business area had its own set of managerial, sales, and technical employees. To correct business and marketing inefficiencies, Pitts thus brought together the company's area managers and encouraged them to adopt a matrix management structure, common resource pools, and standardized cost and management controls. Infusing the management structure with the kind of discipline he had learned while serving in the Canadian military and then put into practice during his business career, Pitts insisted that project managers submit quarterly reports on their division's progress, which they had never done before. He also forced them to create manageable engineering work packages, project schedules, and budgets. As they learned how to consolidate their resources, Pitts hoped that surviving project managers would begin to see the synergies between MDA's systems expertise and the business goals he envisioned.[36]

MDA's staff initially opposed Pitts's matrix structure. Under MacDonald's leadership, a person "motivated and ambitious to learn new things" had "fabulous opportunities, despite the pressure that was always there, the panic that one was always in," one former FOCUS engineer recalled. He also deemed the disciplinary framework Pitts introduced as "in part, a knee-jerk reaction to FOCUS, which was – and how shall we put it? – mildly disorganized." He conceded that Pitts's reorganization was "good from a business point of view," but stressed that change "came at the expense of future potential innovation and future ideas."[37] Others agreed, but one employee who ascended from the engineering ranks into management saw things a little differently. "I sometimes shudder at the amount of freedom I was given" during the 1970s, he recalled. "The pro was that your job was more varied, being kind of your own person, and having to look after more than just the engineering process itself." Lamenting the "bureaucracy increasing quite a bit," with "many more rules" and "requirements" making it more difficult for "a more junior project engineer" to innovate because "he's going be watched more closely," he nevertheless wondered if he would "be prepared to give a junior guy that much freedom" under Pitts's "new regime." But watching MDA's star-gazing employees more closely was precisely what Pitts and other investors hoped to achieve.[38]

The orchestration of cooperation and structural cohesion towered as the greatest challenge Pitts faced during his first two years at MDA's helm. Once he persuaded a sufficient number of MDA employees that a new, more practical structure for allocating the company's resources could benefit everyone involved over the longer term, however, MDA's engineering teams slowly began to adopt and adapt to the concepts of managing by matrix. As a result, they soon completed proper work package breakdowns before beginning new projects and attempted to control costs to effect long-term profits. That process first took place within the systems side of the business, where project managers seemed keen to avoid the "mildly disorganized" chaos FOCUS seemed to have engendered "at the expense" of their devotion to the ground station business. Pitts thus consolidated all ground station, meteorological, and space-borne synthetic aperture radar activities under the Systems Division to capitalize on the firm's systems products, turnkey projects, and data-mining work. Once he had proven the efficiencies and logic of his management structure, Pitts hoped to focus most of his attention on why he had invested in MDA in the first place. By building project management expertise to capitalize on the company's opportunities in large-scale systems projects, and plowing the profits from Systems into a manufacturing vision based upon the development of some of MDA's most promising products, Pitts envisioned expanding MDA into an investment bonanza. He therefore established two other divisions – Airborne Radar and Electro-Optical Products – to exploit product opportunities that he and other investors had identified. He also launched a Corporate Division to house the administrative functions of MDA's expanding bureaucracy, including groups focused on finance, management information and training, computing, and corporate development.[39]

As he combined his profit-oriented product strategy with MacDonald's systems vision and MDA's employee dedication to engineering excellence between 1982 and 1984, Pitts composed MDA's first substantive five-year plan, a strategic roadmap designed to yield a sustained and sizeable ROI. The plan included exploiting MDA's technical concepts to cultivate a diverse portfolio of products from current divisional efforts and through corporate development schemes. Whether the company could transcend its original environment and learn to focus on profit-oriented product development remained another issue. The Systems Division provided the first test case for project management control and innovation in MDA's new climate. It also presented an opportunity for MDA's personnel to acquire better negotiating skills.[40]

"YOU WATCH WHAT WE DO":
NEGOTIATING CONTRACTS TO PROFIT FROM
TECHNOLOGY TRANSFER

The FOCUS crisis and the SwissAir negotiation demonstrated to Pitts that, without the addition of better negotiating skills, MDA's large projects could once again imperil the company's future. Although MDA had few technical rivals in remote sensing, and its project groups had grown from small cliques into project teams of ten to thirty people, Pitts found that MDA's pricing skills had deprived the company of profits on many remote sensing projects. Two problematic jobs in particular, one for the European Space Agency and another for the Israeli military, thus convinced him that MDA needed an in-house training program in contract negotiations, project pricing, operational management, and the vagaries of international intellectual property law. Pitts's decision bloated the administrative structure MacDonald and Dettwiler had always hoped to avoid, but MDA's early SAR and meteorological work had set the stage for such a program.[41]

After MDA delivered its *Seasat* and airborne processors to the Canadian government during 1978, SAR gained worldwide appeal and placed the company in an enviable international position. Planning to build an export business based on SAR, members of MDA approached the Canadian government about development funds to build a real-time processor for future applications. When *Seasat*'s failure and the economic downturn prompted the Canadian government to decelerate plans for SAR development, MDA's associates had to look elsewhere for seed capital, which ultimately made it difficult for the firm to protect its intellectual capital. By early 1979, MDA received two small contracts from the US Jet Propulsion Laboratory (JPL) to design a more advanced SAR processor. At the same time, the European Space Agency decided to launch its own SAR satellite and requested technology development proposals from its member countries. The Canadian government had just signed an agreement with ESA to "establish the framework for the co-operation of Canada in the Agency's activities as an important step toward closer relations" with the European community. As the only non-European "observer-status" member of ESA, Canada initially received little more than rights to information in contract reports for its participation in studies, as well as a promise that ESA would consider Canada for associate membership during 1981. In exchange for representation in meetings and two delegates who could advocate for a fair share of the industrial returns from its participation,

Canada also agreed to contribute 1 per cent annually to the fixed common costs for ESA studies.[42]

MDA's proven expertise in SAR made it a natural to participate in studies and bid on several ESA development contracts, including one to build a real-time SAR processor prototype for use on board ESA's first satellite, ERS-1. Alas for MDA, Canadian proposals ran into European protests, the most vociferous coming from aerospace representatives of Marconi Company in England, Dornier Consulting in Germany, and Alenia Spazio in Italy, all of whom objected to ESA awarding such critical work to Canada and its young technology company. Eventually, MDA won a development contract, but, in an effort to appease European members, ESA put limitations on the Canadian firm. After MDA completed the 1979 design phase study and submitted a phase two proposal to build the SAR processor, ESA stipulated MDA had to team with European industrialists. Anxious to win their first prime contract from ESA, MDA's negotiators agreed to ESA's terms, and during late 1979 the company sent John Bennett to Europe to investigate potential subcontractors with whom MDA could work. After five weeks, Bennett decided that MDA should team with Marconi as well as with a small firm in Italy, but when he made his recommendation at headquarters in Paris, ESA representatives announced that they wanted MDA to team with Germany's Dornier and Italy's Alenia Spazio. Flabbergasted, Bennett demanded, "Why didn't you tell me this five weeks ago?" ESA representatives simply replied, "We were hoping you'd come to the same conclusion on your own." The news stunned Bennett, but MDA's negotiators acquiesced. After all, they reasoned, if MDA wanted to work in Europe, MDA's technology enthusiasts had to award the subcontracts to Dornier and Alenia Spazio.[43]

ESA's subcontracting structure included a clause that guaranteed the transfer of MDA's entire system design documentation to Dornier. In the midst of the FOCUS crisis and a larger recession that threatened to capsize the firm, MDA's neophyte negotiators thus provided written assurances that the Canadian firm would realize no margin return on a significant technology transfer. ESA "just wanted to pick our brains, and then transfer MDA's technology into European industry," Bennett recalled, "but we were starving for work, and the Canadian government wasn't funding anything, so we went along with it." That rationale confirmed Pitts's fears that many MDA engineers had not yet grasped the competitive nature of the global economy their efficiencies had done so much to accelerate. If Europeans wanted to compete in the space and technology sector, they, like others, needed to find ways to lower their costs, acquire key tools, and work with anyone who could help them advance their own geopolitical interests in an increasingly cut-throat marketplace. MDA's bungling provided one crucial opening Europeans sought. Seeing it, they seized the opportunity. As a result, MDA's credulous negotiators ushered in a harsh lesson in property rights, while the company's original research environment and callow pricing practices contributed to a transfer of technology without MDA reaping any gains from its intellectual seed corn. Pitts could do nothing about a system MDA had delivered during 1981, but he determined that the company would never again suffer a similar blow.[44]

Pitts also encountered problems in customer-driven systems. Anxious to please anyone who promised to pay them to push technological boundaries, MDA's young associates rarely renegotiated projects when additional customer requests invariably increased system development costs. As a result, no sooner had Pitts worked out an equitable arrangement with SwissAir than he found himself embroiled in a second thorny negotiation, this time involving a weather imaging system called WIPS II. Barclay Isherwood had managed to sell twelve WIPS I systems after MDA completed its first imaging contract during the late 1970s, but MDA's meteorological group soon got the company into additional financial trouble when its members designed a second-generation weather imaging system for what many at MDA considered "a hard-driving air force customer" in the Middle East.[45]

Signed during 1980, the WIPS II contract with the Israeli government represented MDA's first direct project for a foreign military. As before, members of the Canadian government massaged the deal. Barclay Isherwood and Doug Seymour (the original WIPS product champion) then negotiated the contract and seemed to understand MDA's relationship with the Israeli Air Force (IAF). When they concluded the negotiations, Isherwood and Seymour agreed that MDA would allow two IAF officials to "live inside MDA" so that they could monitor progress on the second-generation meteorological system Seymour planned to manage and MDA's young enthusiasts promised to build. Unfortunately for engineers left behind to complete the project, Isherwood and Seymour tendered their resignations at MDA just shortly after they had signed the contract to complete the Israeli system. With FOCUS demanding the attention of MDA's senior managers, the responsibility for WIPS II development fell to less experienced personnel. Halfway through the project, an Israeli official demanded that MDA apply military rather than commercial specifications to the WIPS II performance tests. MDA's technical staff tried to accommodate the customer's requests; however, by the time Pitts arrived at MDA, they had not only violated the original agreement but had also increased development costs and created technical difficulties that forced the meteorological group to call on Vern Dettwiler to rescue the project. Dettwiler nursed WIPS II through to completion, but the contract infringements entailed a $200,000 cost overrun, an additional burden that a struggling MDA could ill afford to absorb.[46]

With the customer driving most of the technical changes and refusing to accept the system without each additional modification, Pitts decided to hold a meeting at the Israeli Consulate in New York. Travelling east with Heinz Schulthess (MDA's new WIPS II project manager) and Elizabeth Harrison (the firm's lawyer) during 1983, Pitts had a tough negotiation ahead of him. When the MDA team arrived at the consulate, they received a quick lesson in negotiating with clients from regions of the world unfamiliar to them. Ascending to the meeting in an elevator, they shuddered before the television cameras watching their every move. Experiencing others "watching the watchers" should not have surprised the team from Vancouver, but it did. Once they reached their destination, an armed guard stationed behind a one-inch-thick, plate-glass window greeted them. The MDA team then had to undergo a full search before they could enter what they remembered as a "large, semi-dark room" where Israeli negotiators awaited them. MDA had participated in the creation of the very surveillance networks and systems the team faced, but rather than reflecting on the irony of the situation, they linked the intimidating encounter with the security state to life beyond North America and Europe, in places where people did not seem to enjoy the freedom of movement they had come to expect in Vancouver. Such assumptions were far from rare at MDA and elsewhere. At the same time, although Harrison had seen Pitts negotiate in Switzerland, had herself encountered obdurate negotiators, she wondered if even Pitts could surmount such an arduous challenge.[47]

Somewhat rattled by the encounter at the Israeli Consulate, Pitts nevertheless knew that if he wanted to gain from his investment in MDA, he had to stand his ground when threatened by a "tough customer" turned formidable adversary. "We are not going to continue with this project unless we get more money," he fumed. "You're making all these changes, and refusing to pay for them, so we're going to refuse to do any more work." Following a declaration that "You can't do that!" by an IAF negotiator, Pitts retorted, "The hell we can't. You watch what we do!" Caring more about his personal exposure and equity risk capital than what he perceived as an idle threat, Pitts initiated arbitration proceedings against the IAF that very day. He also made sure that MDA had a new contract and an additional $325,000 to complete the WIPS II project before his team left New York City.[48]

Witnessing Pitts turned young Schulthess into an ardent champion of MDA's new CEO, whom he thought others should respect as a leader who could shepherd the company's future. When he returned to Vancouver, Schulthess spread the news about Pitts's negotiating feat and persuaded many people in the remote sensing group that the divisional restructuring plan represented positive change. Before long, the consulate story became a central narrative in MDA lore, not only about Pitts, but also how the company lost its innocence and learned to negotiate with a hard-hearted military customer. As news circulated around Vancouver about Pitts's negotiating prowess and business savvy, he solidified his reputation as one of the city's best high-tech business brokers. His negotiating skills reinvigorated MacDonald, Dettwiler, and their engineering apostles at MDA as well. Now, they argued, their elegant technologies also had a brilliant new CEO to negotiate for the company and sell its expertise and products worldwide. They also boasted that, although they still had their collective "eye on the sky," they had planted their "feet" firmly "on the ground." Pitts's financial restructuring, stringent cost controls, matrix management structure, and negotiating skills promised to move MDA from a firm centred on research and one-off systems and into a business that could begin with an early-stage, conceptual research contract for government and transform the results into profitable products. Foreseeing a workforce focused on evolving technological breakthroughs and a management team capable of anticipating and benefiting from satellite launches as well as data retrieval to service the demands of an expanding number of commercial, manufacturing, military, and nation-building clients around the world, Pitts also provided opportunities for MDA's ambitious engineers in the Systems Division.[49]

"INSTRUMENT OF CHANGE": MILITARY HIRES, AMBITIOUS MANAGERS, AND THE SYSTEMS STRATEGIC PLAN

After his successful negotiation with the Israeli Air Force, Pitts decided to hire consultants who could train company managers in budget preparation and large-scale project administration, as well as identify those with the management and marketing skills MDA desperately needed. He thus retained Western Management Consultants (WMC) "to try to understand who would be the next round of leaders" at MDA. "I think it was completely unnecessary," one former engineering manager recalled, "but I think that Pitts eventually got tired of sitting back, and he wanted to do something to provide an instrument of change. He wanted to see MDA a $100 million company by 1988, with an excellent track record for profits," an ambition Pitts shared with others who expected a five-year return of "ten times what they paid" as an investment in MDA.[50] Inventorying the firm's personality types, WMC's representatives argued that "all the people" at MDA had "basically grown up with the company," one member of the Pitts's new management team recalled. Summarizing MDA's staff as "introverted, strong engineers, who know MDA but that's all they know," WMC therefore suggested that MDA needed to "diversify a little bit," look at resumés "differently," and take "a chance" on people MDA would not "ordinarily hire to stimulate the organization" and change the company's direction.[51]

Some of the people MDA had not ordinarily hired included former military personnel who understood both the military specification environment and the discipline of its organizations as well as the government's ambitions to secure Canadian sovereignty through the use of surveillance technologies employed by the US military and its NATO allies. With free trade agreements in the offing, Europe's reinvigorated role in international affairs established, and Israel's increasingly robust alliances with the United States, Canada, the United Kingdom, and other nations developing or on the horizon during the early 1980s, those new hires also emerged as critical actors in MDA's evolving relationship with the American military-industrial complex and its strategic surveillance-security partners. They thus took on leadership roles at MDA that they had learned in officer training programs such as those provided by the Royal Military College of Canada in Kingston, Ontario. Important allies to Pitts, the WMC team also helped to transform MDA from a technical creative's haven to a bureaucratically structured enterprise, one based on business and marketing strategies, rather than what Pitts perceived as a propensity for MDA's engineers to pursue whatever fetching technological puzzles that seemed challenging and fun.[52]

MDA's technology purists found the transition difficult; however, under what many employees considered the constrictions of a new and unwelcome bureaucratic structure, Bob Hamilton found his calling within the Systems Division. John MacDonald had hired Hamilton during 1971, to work with Ken Spencer on the process control job for Pacific Press. Following his first assignment, Hamilton then moved into remote sensing.

Arriving with a master's degree in electrical engineering from UBC, Hamilton displayed remarkable technical competence, even during the company's early years. Over time, his belief in MDA's systems capability flourished into a sophisticated vision about MDA's business potential. With an expanding self-perception that his talents best suited management, Hamilton moved into marketing. By the time the FOCUS crisis threatened the company's very survival, Hamilton also decided that, if MDA failed, he should start his own business, one that could resurrect MDA's remote sensing group under his leadership. He had shared these ideas with other engineers, but when Pitts arrived, Hamilton perceived in the new management structure a lower-cost way to implement his business ideas from within MDA. As a side benefit, Pitts seemed to recognize his business acuity. Jumping at the chance to prove his worth to Pitts and MDA, Hamilton thus lobbied for the senior management role of the Systems Division, so he could position himself to ascend on the new engineering and management methodologies he had learned from Pitts and WMC. According to Dan Friedmann, "although John Mac[Donald] has always had the vision of what remote sensing could do, to change the world, Bob took it in steps that made business sense."[53]

Demonstrating a canny understanding of the global remote sensing market as one full of long-term opportunities in data mining and surveillance, Hamilton promoted the acceptance of Pitts's management philosophy and lobbied for increased expenditures on research and development within the Systems Division. Hoping to augment MDA's edge in spaceborne SAR, meteorology, and ground stations, he argued that the company could build integrated, turnkey systems. *Landsat-4* and *-5*, France's *Satellite Pour l'Observation de la Terre* (SPOT), and the planned ERS-1 launch program developing within the European Space Agency also promised opportunities to process data from new satellites as well as in international procurement. With the intensity of this expanding vision guiding his every move, Hamilton surrounded himself with people who believed in the Systems cause. When Pitts promoted him to vice-president of the Systems Division, Hamilton then decided to nurture two budding talents, George Cwynar and Daniel (Dan) Friedmann. He promoted Cwynar to manager of operations and Friedmann to manager of marketing, encouraging both young men to share their ideas and promote or hire people with management skills MDA needed.[54]

The first opportunity to expand the scope and influence of the Systems Division emerged with the launch of more powerful satellites. By 1976, NASA's first three *Landsat* satellites could produce only eighty-metre resolutions, with each element covering little more than one acre. Although considered remarkable for their day, early satellite images quickly created the demand for deeper Earth observation capabilities and sensors with different spatial, spectral, and temporal resolutions. To meet demands for finer resolutions of land surface details to map areas affected by forest fires as well as atmospheric, geological, and hydrological change, the United States launched *Landsat-4* on 16 July 1982, just two months before the board officially installed Pitts as MDA's new president. *Landsat-4* carried many new features, including Hughes Aerospace's thirty-metre-resolution Thematic Mapper sensors, which improved scene accuracy from under 75 per cent to over 83 per cent, facilitated greater mapping precision, and broadened the range of applications for land and marine image detection and categorization.[55]

Anticipating the launch of France's first *SPOT* satellite (which entered orbit in February 1986), French scientists and engineers then enhanced scene accuracy even further. "*SPOT* had a very nice feature," one engineer explained, for "it didn't only look down" like *Landsat* did; "it had a mirror that could look to the side." The French had built *SPOT* "to do this particularly, because people knew that height is the piece of information that is the hardest to extract." Furthermore, he argued, "in order to do accurate mapping, you had to have the height information, and up to that time, the only way you could do it was by sending survey crews, setting up surveying equipment, and measuring things." In remote, inaccessible areas, such measurements remained "impossible, never mind expensive." The development of *SPOT* thus "showed the promise of being able to do terrain height calculations for everywhere on Earth," but remote sensing satellites continued to have two major disadvantages: they could not produce images through cloud cover or at night. Users of Earth observation data therefore began to demand other kinds of sensors. MDA's early work on meteorological systems as well as radar technology, specifically high-definition SAR, gave MDA a distinct competitive advantage when bidding on multiyear design and development contracts to retrieve digital images, "night or day, rain or shine, and independent of cloud cover." MDA's radar specialists therefore argued that the firm should develop generalized synthetic aperture radar (GSAR) systems for all future ground stations, as new installations or upgrades.[56]

During 1982, while The Weather Channel aired in the United States and ushered in the twenty-four-hour "weather forecast that will never end," MDA received from Environment Canada its first contract to develop a meteorological data analysis system (METDAS). Designed for the Pacific

Weather Centre in Vancouver, METDAS emerged among the first weather analysis systems employed by local television networks. As MDA fine-tuned its capabilities, Hamilton perceived that increased demands for other services could place MDA at the centre of continuous global monitoring, with ground stations receiving valuable data for weather analysis and resource management, as well as urban planning, domestic surveillance, and international security.[57]

With GSAR and METDAS development underway by 1983, global mapmakers and those interested in geographical information systems (GIS) also began to demand GPS that could correlate satellite imagery with actual map projections. As potential international customers emerged in petroleum and mineral resource exploration, forestry, land management, and especially the military, the Systems Division started work on several image analysis projects, and Hamilton encouraged Pitts to turn his attention (and the company's resources) toward the creation of products focused on geocoded image correction for satellite mapping, meteorological data analysis, and automated weather distribution.[58] Under a series of three separate contracts totalling $15 million, MDA began to develop a multi-observational satellite image correction system. Called Mosaics, the system "produced what we call geocoded images, which means that every dot on that picture has a specific position on the Earth's surface that's known," Dan Friedmann explained. As one of the principal architects of Mosaics, Friedmann also noted that the work "allowed all the remote sensing data to be put into digital databases" and prompted MDA to develop a generic product called Geocoded Image Correction System (GICS). Originally commissioned by the CCRS, to process *Landsat* Thematic Mapper and *SPOT* data, as well as produce digital images using geocoding techniques, GICS became the world's first commercially developed geocoded image correction system and set the standard for processing, displaying, and producing raw satellite image data as geographically corrected images aligned with standard map projections. Although MDA never profited directly from the development of consumer gadgets based on GICS, the original work allowed MDA to increase the precisional accuracy of surveillance equipment, thereby furthering the company's hold on the international remote sensing market's demand for more ground stations in the days ahead.[59]

While working on GICS, the MDA team also received an opportunity to develop a satellite mapping system called Meridian. Again, the firm began with a contract from the federal government, this time from the Canadian Atmospheric Environment Service to design an ice mapping system. Once

MDA completed its development work, Meridian emerged as "the first completely digital map generated from space-borne imagery for the commercial market," Friedmann boasted, and eventually evolved into a system comprising three of MDA's application software programs. Together, those programs then allowed potential customers to process, analyze, interpret, and manipulate data from multiple satellite and sensor sources. Designed for mutual compatibility, either as stand-alone units or for inclusion in MDA's ground stations, GICS and Meridian promised to enhance the company's traditional ground station business so the firm could develop systems for new market expansion and larger-scale projects.[60]

Mosaics, GICS, Meridian, and other projects confirmed the importance of Pitts's strategy to house MDA's remote sensing capabilities under the Systems Division, where engineers began to develop important methodologies that soon formed the heart of all future MDA systems work. MDA's geographical mapping and tracking systems also helped to define the contours of surveillance capitalism and its geographical positioning systems. As geographer Mark Monmonier has confirmed, the US Department of Defense first developed GPS "to help troops and missiles find themselves on maps," but as an "efficient technique for entering new information – field observations as well as remotely sensed data" – GPS ultimately provided a way to connect any "portable ground station to a cell phone," and became a significant "instrument for tracking employees, children, parolees," and others. "Whatever the ethics and pragmatics of location tracking," Monmonier has observed, "the unintended consequences of GPS call for skeptical awareness of our brave new globe and its plausible threats to personal privacy." Although those threats remained well "under the radar" during the 1980s, at least to the general public, GPS also laid the foundation for MDA's future work with the US military.[61]

While IBM and their competitors introduced the world to the personal computer and Microsoft settled into its new headquarters in Bellevue, Washington, Hamilton sensed that MDA's expanding role in remote sensing for governments worldwide could turn the company into a profitable enterprise in any economic environment. As a result, he ignored those policymakers who continued to raise concerns about Canada's abilities to retain technical experts, achieve better trade balances, and improve the country's R&D performance no matter the federal dollars spent while the world recession "amply" demonstrated "the paucity of new market opportunities, particularly in the Third World." Instead, he focused his energies on the philosophy that Dave Sloan had long articulated, that MDA's future resided in the remote sensing business and not in products, and in selling repeat hardware systems rather than retooling the company for mass manufacturing. In the process, he fostered and expanded the Systems Division in ways that blended John MacDonald's vision with Pitts's management discipline.[62]

Larger world events and the neoliberal project seemed to justify Hamilton's judgment. With manufacturing plants increasingly off-shored, and spending on defence on the rise, those involved in the integration of North America's military-industrial complex continued to call for increased spending on surveillance. As one confidential briefing on technology transfer during 1983 articulated, influential Canadians in the defence sector had prompted the government to focus on negotiating enhanced defence sharing agreements so that Canadian firms could gain better access to classified information in the United States and more American procurement contracts. "Western lead times of five to seven years" over the Soviet-led Eastern Bloc "had, within the past decade, been reduced to two to three years," the briefing stressed. President Reagan would also continue to shift resources from welfare programs to strategic defence initiatives, the briefing predicted. To take advantage of that shift, Canadian policymakers therefore decided to expand their own "contracting out" efforts. As a result, the briefing encouraged Canada's new Scientific Research and Experimental Development tax credit program to promote the creation of Canadian networks of firms, universities, and other research institutions so that Canada could play a larger role in American military markets linked to NATO. It also noted that Trudeau's 1981 meeting with Reagan, along with Canada's ongoing commitments to the DPSA, NORAD, and NATO, had foreshadowed such collaborations.[63]

At the same time, the protracted recession, billion-dollar deficits, Quebec's opposition to the Canada Act of 1982, protests by Western Canadians over the NEP, and other problems convinced Trudeau to step down as prime minister on 30 June 1984 rather than face defeat by the Progressive Conservatives. Although John Turner, finance minister from 1968 to 1975, became prime minister following Trudeau's departure, his term lasted just seventy-nine days. After spending nearly a decade outside of government as a Bay Street corporate lawyer, and overly optimistic about the Liberals' chances for victory, Turner quickly arranged to have Parliament dissolved and an election called for September. Utilizing Turner's bumbling as well as feelings of voters in the Western provinces and his native Quebec, PC leader Brian Mulroney promised a new constitutional agreement for Canada and a better deal for Quebec. On 4 September 1984, the Progressive Conservatives then won their first election in twenty-six years and the largest majority government in Canadian history. That win also set the stage for Thatcher- and Reagan-inspired changes in Canada, including the ongoing liberalization of the economy through free trade agreements and regulatory reform as well as further tax cuts, austerity programs, and concentrations of capital.[64]

Under the leadership of Mulroney, the PCs also came to power on promises of cuts to the federal bureaucracy (particularly the welfare programs Trudeau's Liberals had introduced), lower deficits, the privatization of Crown corporations, an end to the NEP and the Foreign Investment Review Agency (FIRA), and friendlier relations with the United States. As Bruce Smardon has documented, the success rate for FIRA applications among foreign firms interested in taking over Canadian ones had already climbed under the Trudeau Liberals, from 79 per cent in 1981–82 to 90 per cent in 1982–83; however, when Mulroney became prime minister during 1984, his PC government redefined FIRA "within the context of closer relations with private capital and ideological commitments to promoting greater trade and investment links with the United States." Promoting "foreign investment through an 'open for business' policy," the Investment Canada Act (ICA) of 20 June 1985 empowered the federal government "to forbid foreign investments" of "significant" size only if they did not present a "net benefit to Canada. The acceptance rate for takeovers" therefore "increased to 98.5% in 1985–86 and 100% for new establishments in that same year," Smardon noted. Foreign investment in Canada then rose from approximately $100 billion in 1985 to nearly $600 in 2010, with the ICA rejecting only 1 of the 1,638 foreign acquisitions it had reviewed. That rejection took place in 2008, when the ICA invoked its right to block the sale of MDA to US-based Alliant Techsystems, as "not in the national interest." In the meantime, the Mulroney government kept other election promises: it abolished the NEP and began to privatize a host of Canadian Crown corporations.[65]

The PC party realigned Canada's foreign policy toward Europe and created warmer relations with the United States, a process that flowered in Quebec City during March 1985. There, at "The Shamrock Summit," Prime Minister Mulroney and President Reagan committed both countries to increased trade liberalization and the controversial Canada-US Free Trade Agreement (signed in 1988, put into force during 1989, then superseded by the 1994 North American Free Trade Agreement). Although Mulroney had promised to lower the deficit and shrink government spending, both expanded. Canada's further integration into the US military-industrial complex and the world's capitalist power core also provided Bob Hamilton with incentives to fortify the Systems' cause. By employing business concepts to profit from surveillance-based work under the DPSA, NORAD, and NATO, Hamilton developed strategies to proliferate, extend, and exploit MDA's remote sensing expertise while simultaneously revitalizing his engineering team's desire to strive on the technological edge. MDA's GSAR, GICS, and Meridian mapping system formed the heart of Hamilton's plan, but he also drew lessons from the FOCUS software project and earlier meteorological work to create a business and marketing structure that promised to give MDA's Systems Division the strength it required to bid on large-scale development projects involving both software and hardware. By 1984, Hamilton's plan then helped to secure two important contracts that furthered his own goals and buttressed Pitts's ambitions to create a well-tended garden. The European Space Agency awarded the first of those contracts; and the United States Air Force quickly bestowed the other one.[66]

"ALTITUDE, OXYGEN!":
NEW LESSONS IN MANAGING EUROPEAN SUBCONTRACTORS

During 1984, earlier work for ESA finally paid off. Impressed by MDA's generalized SAR, geocoded image correction, and Meridian work, ESA awarded MDA a contract to build a turnkey ground station in Kiruna, Sweden, so that member countries could receive data from the proposed ERS-1 satellite (which launched on 17 July 1991). Having learned humbling lessons through several bungled technology transfers, MDA's managers hoped that the ESA project could allow them to gain the project management expertise they needed for future ground station work. Pitts additionally hoped to employ the contract to rebrand MDA as a profit-oriented company with excellent negotiating skills.[67] Working with ESA's member nations involved new challenges, however; as the European equivalent of NASA, ESA represented the interests of twelve countries, all of which wanted a piece of the ERS-1 project. Through German lobbying, Dornier Systems thus won the prime contract for the entire ERS-1 project and MDA received a co-contract to build the ground station segment, with the SAR processor its main responsibility. Arguing that Canada lacked full member status, ESA's representatives also demanded that MDA subcontract some of the ground station software to European participants. Thus, MDA had to negotiate four subcontracting arrangements with representatives from different nations, establish rapport with representatives from non-English-speaking countries, and set up an office in Switzerland to monitor each subcontractor's progress.[68]

Given the complexity of the ESA project and the multiple management issues he needed to sort out elsewhere, Hamilton decided to hire an experienced manager for the Kiruna project. Cameron (Cam) McDonald arrived in Vancouver from Ontario Hydro, a provincial hydroelectric power commission as well as hybrid of a government department, Crown corporation, and municipal cooperative that coexisted with private companies until its reorganization into five separate companies during 1999. By the early 1980s, Ontario Hydro's purchasing department undertook some $2.5 billion worth of business annually, and McDonald personally handled $40 million in contracts each year. When he arrived at MDA, however, McDonald found that his Vancouver colleagues deemed a $2 million contract "a big project," he chortled; indeed, even a $400,000 contract caused gasping "Altitude, oxygen!" pleas. Despite such outbursts, McDonald told Hamilton that he planned to negotiate a fixed-price contract for the Kiruna project. Still reeling from the FOCUS experience, Hamilton initially refused, arguing that fixed-price contracts had endangered MDA in the past and promised to do so in the future. Over time, however, Cam McDonald convinced Hamilton and others to trust him; and by the end of 1984, he delivered on his promise by securing for MDA the largest contract the company had yet received. Worth $35 million, the ESA contract established McDonald as a credible negotiator for MDA. Despite earlier misgivings about working with Europeans, the synergies that developed among project staff also generated unparalleled enthusiasm for working with ESA.[69]

Arriving in Vancouver from Ottawa via his native Scotland, the good-natured yet no-nonsense McDonald nurtured many technical personnel, and turned MDA's new challenges into opportunities for a group of up-and-coming MDA project managers. At the same time, he selected the project's personnel from a pool of people comfortable with the idea of moving to Switzerland for an extended period of time, including Vern Dettwiler, Heinz Schulthess, and Pietro Widmer, all of whom had emigrated from Switzerland to Vancouver. These three project members, in particular, added lustre to MDA's co-contractor role when McDonald revealed that each of them also spoke French, German, and Italian. Their technical skills and translation abilities then allowed MDA to surmount many of the cultural obstacles and misunderstandings that a Canadian presence threatened to engender. McDonald's decision to capitalize on such useful and profit-generating assets also signalled a maturing vision of MDA's future, one centred on project management expertise for the expansion of space-based surveillance. From 1984 through September 1987, as McDonald's team learned how to manage several European subcontractors, they integrated MDA components with those of the subcontractors, built MDA's first documentation libraries, and gained credibility with ESA's European members.[70]

Meeting all of ESA's challenges, MDA delivered its first major fixed-price contract on time and on budget, the only one of ESA's six co-contractors to do so. As a result, when Widmer and Schulthess made their final design review presentation at the European Space Technology Centre in Noordwijk, the Netherlands, Europeans responded not with their usual confrontations but with an unprecedented ovation. The ERS-I ground station segment work and a happy European reception to it gave the MDA team new confidence as well as a firm hold on the European surveillance community. The experience with project management controls also convinced them that fixed-price contracts could yield profits surpassing the firm's earlier cost-plus work. ESA's reception additionally highlighted that MDA had achieved a "recognition factor in Europe higher than in Canada," one member of the team remembered. Indeed, Europeans seemed to appreciate more than their Canadian counterparts how much MDA had involved itself in work "changing people's lives" across the world. But even if they felt underappreciated in Canada, members of the Systems Division no longer felt that way in Europe, he observed. With success in Europe confirming that MDA could successfully complete large-scale project management contracts, MDA secured the major market share of all future ground station installations in Europe as well as the Middle East and Asia.[71] In the meantime, MDA also received its first opportunity to enter the large American military market by developing an automated weather distribution system (AWDS) for the United States Air Force. As a complement to MDA's work in Europe, AWDS represented the firm's largest contract at the time. Initial development work also offered the company the chance to employ engineering methodologies learned on FOCUS and meteorological systems to manage large software development projects, navigate the USA's defence procurement system, and work with major American military contractors.[72]

"IT WAS *THE* LEARNING EXPERIENCE":
RECEIVING AN EDUCATION IN US MILITARY CONTRACTING

Long-standing defence production sharing agreements between Canada and the United States set the stage for MDA's participation in the development of AWDS, while the company's strategy to win the work involved courting American military contractors then chasing the US budgetary boon created by Ronald Reagan's Strategic Defense Initiative (SDI; created March 1983, and derisively labelled "Star Wars"). "It is testimony to the power of the SDI myth," Vincent Mosco has argued, "that, with nearly two decades of demonstrable technical failure, it continues to live on in American political mythology," with its most libertarian supporters dreaming that such projects could "end politics as we know it," with government disappearing or at least dismantling the welfare state so that it could "operate like a business" and promote the "privatization ethic." Such dreams also made their way into Canada and other parts of the world, where neoliberal policymakers, military contractors, technological enthusiasts, and consumers of surveillance capitalism's derivative products believed they had joined a new world order and economic opportunities without end. Although widely criticized, SDI nevertheless promoted a massive investment in ground- and space-based systems, with the US government investing well over $100 billion in the project and other space-related research, testing, and follow-on work during and after Reagan's eight years in office. The Defense Advanced Research Projects Agency (DARPA) stood at the centre of Reagan's initiatives. Created during 1958, in the wake of the *Sputnik* humiliation, DARPA has had a mission to make strategic investments in innovative technologies for national security to avoid future "strategic technological surprises." By 1980, it had also combined its early nuclear monitoring and materials science research with cyber-technology efforts to establish a new Defense Sciences Office, thereafter directing its attention to the acquisition of technologies that could advance American military and industrial ambitions.[73]

Through DARPA's commercialization plans, US investments in the business of permanent war preparedness made their way into American universities, national laboratories, and government contracting firms, but they also promised windfall opportunities to American allies. Although Canada later rejected direct participation in Reagan's SDI, policymakers had no qualms about providing logistical support, particularly when it promised to increase opportunities for Canadian firms working on space-based technologies following the reaffirmation of the Canada-US Defence Production Sharing Agreement. When Trudeau's Cabinet approved a Defence Review during July 1982, Canada's deputy ministers on foreign and defence policy also argued that "a defence base policy would likely be popular with both the government and the public mainly because such a policy appears supportive of sovereignty and Canadian industrial development at a time when both are issues of high priority."[74]

Allan Gotlieb, undersecretary of the Department of External Affairs, Canada's ambassador to the United States, and an ardent champion of more friendly relations between Canada and the United States, noted that Canada and the United States "had about US$88 billion in two-way trade in 1982," with "Canada a market for 19 per cent of total U.S. products." Furthermore, "Canada is more important to the U.S. as an export market than either Japan or the countries of Western Europe. Last year the U.S. bought $49 billion from Canada," creating a market that accounted for "nearly 70 per cent of the total Canadian exports. In addition to our business dealings," he emphasized, "the military linkages between our countries are very numerous," with more than "800 defence agreements of widely varying magnitude struck in the last 70 years." As a result, Gotlieb encouraged Canadians to bid on defence procurement work with the US government as one way for Canada to improve its balance of trade and lower its budget deficit. "Canadian companies should recognize that large parts of the U.S. Defense Procurement [system] are open to Canadian bids," Gotlieb advised. "It is estimated that over one-third of the roughly 90 billion dollars annual U.S. military procurements is accessible for Canadian competition on a regular basis." Although Canadians face limited opportunities to participate in "programs of a highly classified nature and in those programs which have high visibility in U.S. Congress," he stressed that "an initial review of the defence industries area in Canada suggests that it is structured with a focus on the aerospace, electronics, vehicle and ammunition sectors."[75] As a result, when Pitts became MDA's CEO, he deemed the company a natural for such work, and AWDS a way to realize his larger product development and manufacturing plan.

Representing the next generation of international data handling stations, the AWDS opportunity emerged from a long-standing assumption that Canada and the United States would each agree to pay 50 per cent of contract costs in joint security initiatives. In the case of AWDS and SPAR's participation in NASA's space shuttle program, Trudeau had already extracted from Reagan a promise that Canadian firms would act as prime contractors on several projects under an expanded Defence Development Sharing Agreement (DDSA), with experienced American military suppliers serving as Canadian subcontractors. Members of Canada's Department of National Defence also hoped that the arrangement would help to overcome US assertions of extraterritoriality "with respect to Canadian sales to the East Bloc and Cuba," so that Canadian contractors could receive more information about US classified programs and technologies as well as generate profits by employing Canadian research projects to create products "for which there would be a follow-on US government demand." Whether they could later justify such projects for civilian uses remained a thornier issue.[76]

By participating in joint research and development projects with the United States expanding program in space-based surveillance, members of Canada's military-industrial establishment stressed that "Canadian firms would acquire experience in the management of technology" and the American government procurement system. "It is likely that such participation would result in some acquisition of technical data not otherwise available," they noted, but since the DDSA "deals with a service, research, rather than a good," any joint project used by the military for national security would also fall outside "the GATT and its Procurement Code." The promise of an expanded exchange between Canada and the United States thus prompted Canadian policymakers to promote Canada's "willingness to pursue economic cooperation with the USA" and further liberalization of the Canadian economy to create "beneficial spillover effects." In previous projects, the Canadian government had appointed prime contractors for all defence sharing initiatives; during 1982, however, it ran an open competition for the AWDS project and relied upon experienced American military subcontractors to court Canadian firms as potential primes.[77] Because MDA had not previously bid on a US defence contract, members of the MDA team thought their bid was a long shot, particularly when they considered their more-established competitor, Toronto's Litton Systems. But when Florida-based Harris Corporation, an American military contractor and established supplier in the US weather market, approached MDA about teaming on the project, they began the proposal process.[78]

"We were really dragged into [AWDS] screaming in some respects," one MDA employee recalled. "Harris came to us. They wanted to win, and because it was a joint US-Canada program, the only way they could win it was to do it with someone in Canada." As a result, "they came knocking at our door and dragged us into this thing." For people at MDA, "it was a big step, because we were very non-military, so there was nobody here who was really interested in military systems. On our own initiative we would never have gone into it," but "it was a huge software project, and our feeling was that [Harris] could protect us from a lot of the military nonsense." AWDS also represented "another new market," the employee recalled, and allowed "us to go after the benign pieces of the military business, because we would learn all their standards and protocols. So it was a good decision." As a weather system, "we weren't making weapons guidance systems. You couldn't really argue that it was an offensive system. It was a support system. And yet," he quipped, "we'd supply toilet paper to the military if they wanted to buy it. It's just logistics support."[79]

Although representatives from Harris had already attended briefings with the USAF and understood the project's requirements, the AWDS proposal presented an enormous challenge to MDA. Neither accustomed to reducing their engineering methods to writing, nor familiar with the rigours of writing proposals to military specifications, the MDA proposal team had to look to Harris for support, which became "a great enabler for us to go after military things," according to one employee.[80] "We would have scoffed at those projects earlier," another employee offered, but AWDS "grew us substantially, got us into other high-reliability" systems work.[81] Unbeknownst to most at MDA, their perceived abilities to learn the ropes from Harris also confirmed the faith that the Canadian government had placed in the firm by investing in the bailout package so that MDA could undertake the AWDS work.

Whether dragged into the process or not, Western Management's recommendations convinced John Pitts that MDA should place its new military hires at the centre of the AWDS proposal project. In addition, because the contract promised the company future sales exceeding $150 million, Pitts wanted former military personnel to guide MDA's reluctant engineers into a more disciplined environment, one that could help them to navigate the transition from MacDonald's freewheeling environment to Pitts's vision of a profit-oriented firm focused on the American military-industrial complex. According to Dan Friedmann, the AWDS project represented the "big leagues"; if MDA could win the first contract, development work would place the company in a unique position to build the AWDS production systems that the American government subsequently planned to install at every US military base around the world.[82]

The AWDS opportunity involved more than writing the proposal to military specifications. In writing the proposal, people at MDA had to come to terms with doing business with an American contractor like Harris. They also had to understand the US Air Force, the Canadian government agencies that provided half the money for the project, and Litton Systems of Toronto, their main competitor. Still, as one AWDS proposal team member argued, people at MDA had "this tendency to think that you can get really chummy with large corporations" like Harris, "that they'll stick by you when the going gets tough." But MDA discovered that "Harris is only about 100 times bigger" and will "do whatever the hell they want. I think they had 60,000 employees" to MDA's 500, "to give you some idea of the relative dimensions." As a result, MDA also had to learn that "just because you deal with a big company like Harris, and they're your partner, they're not in bed with you."[83]

No matter the lessons learned, by the time MDA submitted the proposal during May 1983, the firm had added expertise in writing defence contract proposals to its repertoire, and had gained much more experience in the use of stringent project documentation, card keys, disclosure agreements, and other security measures. The USAF also expected MDA to provide its "dirty laundry and wave it in public. They wanted a complete list of projects done in the past, which didn't even have any relevance to AWDS," another member of the AWDS team recalled. Working with the American military thus taught MDA that they "had to be careful on each and every project, because you're only as good as your last" one.[84] The contentious look into MDA's past troubled those who did not want to participate in military research and development, but like it or not, Canada's ambitions, as well as MDA's, had foreshadowed the eventual embrace of the American military-industrial complex, one Pitts, Hamilton, and others intended to profit from by stimulating a deeper connection to it. As a result, those who opposed that connection would either have to "disappear" or "mould" themselves to such work.[85]

Although MDA faced new challenges and lost the more "free and open" environment that some people continued to crave "before military contracts" became part of MDA's core competencies, teaming with Harris proved effective for expansion. By 1984, in response to President Reagan's argument that NASA should remove obstacles and encourage more private-sector involvement in its space programs, NASA created a new Commercial Space Policy that promised to stimulate more research and development networks by providing seed money to businesses and universities via academic commercial grants, space commerce announcements of opportunity, and industry space commercialization grants. Andrew Butrica has argued that US space policies assumed "a symbiotic relationship between commercial and military interests," and demonstrated that a "key tool for promoting private ventures in space was government itself through privatization (Landsat) and NASA." Thus, while MDA awaited the outcome of the AWDS proposal, the Reagan administration prompted NASA to enhance opportunities for future work, not only between firms like MDA and Harris, but also between private and public universities, as well as government agencies and the military-industrial complex. Canadian policymakers soon followed the American lead.[86]

During April 1984, people at MDA received news that the MDA-Harris team had won a $20 million, twenty-eight-month, cost-plus contract with the USAF to develop two automated weather distribution systems, one permanent, the other portable. Between 17 and 19 April, an officer of Canada's

Department of External Affairs joined representatives of the USAF at MDA to brief the team on the contractual management review structure of the AWDS project. Two months, later, the Canadian and US governments then made further progress on joint economic defence cooperation, removing technology transfer restrictions from the United States to Canada and broadening the scope of earlier agreements to include the export of both defence-related and "similar" commercial high-technology products.[87]

In the original AWDS bid, the MDA team proposed a thirty-six-month project with a $37 million price tag, but when members of the USAF reminded the team that the contract could not exceed twenty-eight months, MDA managers adjusted the price downward. Some things are hard to unlearn; and, as before, MDA's technology enthusiasts worked plenty of overtime to accommodate changes the USAF requested. No sooner had the project run six months than MDA was six months behind on the promised completion date. The USAF threatened to cancel the project, and those who remembered the FOCUS fiasco once again cited passages from *The Mythical Man-Month*. By 1986, however, John MacDonald and John Pitts managed to persuade the USAF to renegotiate the contract for a fixed price of $40 million. Thus, while Sally Ride became the first American woman in space, Mikhail Gorbachev called for glasnost and perestroika, scientists discovered a hole in the ozone layer, the *Challenger* space shuttle exploded, and a nuclear accident unfolded at Chernobyl, Pitts's negotiating prowess received another boost.[88] Regardless of the feat, however, representatives of the USAF insisted that MDA improve its abilities in the military specification environment to avoid future dilemmas. Thereafter, they also sent to Vancouver several technical advisors from Mitre Corporation, a private, not-for-profit firm spun out of MIT and charged with providing engineering and technical services to the USAF, particularly its Semi-Automatic Ground Environment system for continental air defence. Together with Harris, Mitre's technical advisors thus provided the assistance MDA required to complete the AWDS project, which included additional training in writing systems documentation to military specifications.[89]

By the summer of 1987, with the development phase of AWDS completed successfully, MDA reached a corporate milestone and the Systems Division demonstrated that the company could deliver large-scale software development systems. Dave Caddey, MDA's first military hire and member of the firm's new management team, argued, "We learned an awful lot about managing large contracts" on the first AWDS project. "We lost a lot of our naïveté on big programs and software development, learned a lot about the military specification environment, military standards, and so on. We really did have to come face-to-face with them and work through them." At the same time, "We developed a fair bit of confidence and lost some of our naive view of the world. But on the other hand," he suggested, "I think we developed a willingness to get in the trenches and go for it."[90] Adding to Caddey's list of lessons learned, one former employee quipped that AWDS also taught MDA about "how many forests it takes to produce the documentation." Regardless, the experience set the stage "for doing the big projects we've done since then. AWDS was *the* learning experience."[91]

Delays, financial and management changes, threats of project cancellation, and the novelty of meeting military standards created many anxious moments at MDA, but under the renegotiated contract the firm finally delivered an excellent system to Eglin Air Force Base in Florida, on time and on budget. The USAF rewarded MDA's efforts through additional contracts to upgrade AWDS as well as train Air Force personnel on the system's operation and maintenance. Reinforcing the importance of discipline and working to external standards, the follow-on contracts provided valuable experience in software development review and inspired confidence in what MDA could accomplish. Although many of the technical staff on AWDS had come from the scarring experience of FOCUS, they no longer questioned Pitts's abilities to negotiate on their behalf. Nor did they worry about their own abilities to compete for and complete complex, high-quality software projects for the American government. Still small when compared to SPAR or the more mammoth Harris, MDA nevertheless turned a critical corner.[92]

With something significant to show other potential customers in space and defence, aviation, and meteorology, members of the Systems Division suggested that MDA's long-term success resided in following the "real money" they perceived in government guarantees, particularly those attached to military spending. Still, as AWDS made MDA more visible, some Canadians questioned the company's new direction. When newspapers reported that MDA would win a sole-source contract to upgrade the South African station during 1985, anti-apartheid protestors descended upon the firm. Pitts turned to his PC friends in government, but they refused to intervene. Prime Minister Mulroney, they argued, opposed the apartheid regime in South Africa, and they had to defer to him, even if his policies put Canada at odds with leaders in the United States and the United Kingdom. "Mr Holier-Than-Thou Mulroney said that Canadians were not allowed to export strategic material to South Africa," John Pitts complained. As a result, rather than listening to the protesters who had arrived at MDA's door, Pitts blamed the Canadian government for the loss of an

$8 million-plus contract with South Africa, one French engineers ultimately gained.[93]

"The AWDS contract and the kerfuffle last fall over MDA's alleged plans to sell a satellite weather system to South Africa both raise questions about Pitts's apparent strategy to steer MDA toward defence work," one reporter argued. That work additionally raised "questions about Pitts's balancing skills, as he teeters between innovation and regulation." Regardless of the distractions that the arrival of anti-apartheid protestors and news coverage posed, by 1987 Pitts made it clear that praise from the USAF had ultimately tipped him toward defence contracting and "the discipline of the work package." Indeed, he argued, his exit strategy depended on both. MDA thus began its work on the AWDS production proposal and the possibility the contract represented: revenues in excess of US$100 million.[94]

"A FAIRLY WATERSHED BUSINESS PLAN":
LOOKING TOWARD AN EXPANSIONIST FUTURE IN SYSTEMS

While MDA commenced work on the AWDS production contract proposal, the world population reached five billion, Soviet Secretary Gorbachev and US President Reagan signed the Intermediate-Range Nuclear Forces Treaty to reduce nuclear stockpiles, and the Israeli-Palestinian conflict erupted into the First Intifada in the West Bank and Gaza. At the same time, Bob Hamilton and his Systems Division managers decided to write a new five-year plan that incorporated marketing strategies for expansion in geographical information, space and defence, and aviation. Arguing that the division could take its skills into other areas, Hamilton, his protege Dan Friedmann, and others in Systems had already undertaken an extensive review of their operation. By 1987, as they perceived future success in all areas of remote sensing, the strategic planning team argued that their division could diversify the company's offerings on significant repeat sales they had generated on systems developed during the early 1980s. The Canadian International Development Agency (CIDA) bought a meteorological data analysis system for installation in Peru, they noted, and the division had sold Meridian systems to the CCRS as well as other significant international clients in the United States, Australia, Thailand, India, and Saudi Arabia. In addition, the West German Space Agency and the European Space Research Institute, two key European clients, had purchased MDA's generalized synthetic aperture radar product.[95]

From the company's early work on mobile data terminals and FOCUS, in addition to project management expertise gained on the AWDS phase one contract, the five-year plan declared that Systems could pursue significant work in the aviation business, supplying flight operations, aeronautical information, and flight data processing systems to a host of international customers. From development work during the 1980s, the plan targeted new opportunities in space and defence systems as well, to supply governments with systems engineering and integration expertise. The Systems Division also embarked on a "value-added" strategy for ground station upgrades. And because overseas installations had solidified MDA's international reputation as a government contractor capable of supplying and integrating large, complex, turnkey systems for governments and the military, MDA promised to enhance Canada's position in the evolving world order of surveillance capitalism as well as provide yet another example of what Canadians could accomplish. Such success also promised to maintain Canadian sovereignty in a new era of free trade.[96]

"That was a fairly watershed business plan. We completely changed the mission statement of the company," Friedmann boasted. "We looked at our strengths and said, 'Let's focus on our strengths and see what markets develop.'" Reducing those strengths to writing, the division articulated its intention to pull the rest of the firm into a "systems engineering company for selected market niches with worldwide operations."[97] MDA's board approved the new five-year plan as 1987 closed, which included the creation of new sales, service, and marketing support offices in Ottawa, the United Kingdom, Malaysia, and Australia. "A lot of good things came out of those planning sessions," one participant observed. "We'd always done international business, but we realized that if we were going to have growth, we couldn't just depend on the Canadian market. There wasn't enough room. Secondly, we wanted to try to get away from just being purely dependent on ground stations." With the production contract to install approximately 160 AWDS at American military bases across the world standing at the centre of the plan, Friedmann noted that "we [also] started looking at things like the Meridian image analysis system, and taking our core competencies in large software development projects and project management competencies in systems engineering, and applying it to other areas, particularly defence."[98]

Between 1982 and 1987, MDA's staff expanded from 232 to 609, while gross revenues climbed from $16 million to over $63 million. As 1988 opened, the Systems Division alone housed 397 of MDA's staff members and had gross revenues nearing $44 million. Those numbers paled in comparison to their expansionist neighbours at Microsoft (whose employees had reached 1,816 and year-end sales had climbed to nearly US$346 million in 1987), but MDA had finally matured into a mid-sized, high-technology company with the kinds of expertise it could showcase to customers across the world. From all they had learned in remote sensing, Systems Division staff created a solid foundation for continued expansion, generating important revenues and evolving from a remote sensing entity into a full turnkey systems provider. Moreover, through the new five-year plan, Hamilton, Friedmann, and other key Systems personnel hoped to extend John MacDonald's vision as both brake and booster upon MDA's original technology concepts as well as the basis for further military contracting and surveillance work.[99]

In the meantime, other divisions concentrated on generating profits through products under Pitts's larger manufacturing vision. That effort culminated in one of the most challenging moments in MDA's history, testing MacDonald's original vision of the company, the strategies of Pitts and other new investors, and MDA's relationship with SPAR Aerospace. Chapter 6 examines the developments that finally forced MDA's investors to concede that Systems *was* and would probably remain the company's core for the future. Still, it took another trial by fire and more scar tissue for MDA's product promoters, especially Pitts, to appreciate how much his manufacturing vision might cost.

6

"The Systems Vision Was Too Hard"

Investor Strategies, Product Development,
and the Demise of the Manufacturing Vision, 1982–1988

When John Pitts arrived at MDA during 1982, he appreciated the exacting nature of the systems business and worried about its abilities to generate the financial returns he and other investors hoped to enjoy. Forecasts often change with each systems project, and when a one-off systems engineering company bids and wins more projects than predicted, its managers often find their projects understaffed until they hire additional employees to meet the needs of that particular project. Conversely, if a systems operation fails to win a key project, or contract "wins" represent only half of those anticipated, vulnerabilities emerge, with overstaffing problems and possible layoffs looming. Worse still, if a systems company loses a large bid, or is late on major project deliveries, revenue projections change overnight. For those who invested in MDA with Pitts, this exposure to the vagaries of such a cyclical boom-and-bust, feast-or-famine environment thus promised to present special problems as they contemplated the future investors they planned to attract. MDA's product potential seemed to offset the gamble they had decided to take; Pitts therefore argued that he and others invested in MDA because they believed in the promise of MDA's product opportunities, even if they suspected managerial incompetence among some of the firm's founders and principal engineers.[1]

Pitts additionally shared concerns about the export market for ground stations as well as what might happen if the federal government's Centre for Remote Sensing cut off the flow of money to MDA. The protracted recession and world debt crisis had significantly slowed the development of countries on the periphery, making it more difficult for them to embark upon many planned activities, including satellite-based surveillance. Economic growth plans among wealthy nations also contracted, while mushrooming deficits in Canada prompted the government to scale back its commitment to the expansion and maintenance of its own ground station operations. During 1982, with NASA increasing its *Landsat* service charge to the CCRS from $50,000 to $600,000 per annum as well as Canada's usage fee for the Prince Albert, Saskatchewan, satellite receiving station from $200,000 to $600,000 per annum, members of the CCRS proposed that the federal government close the Shoe Cove, Newfoundland, receiving station that Canada had established to record the *Seasat* data and on which MDA had developed its synthetic aperture radar capabilities. Although the director general for Environment Canada's Atlantic Region argued that the station constituted "a valuable, if small, core of expertise and capability in a region that sorely needs it," and warned that closing Shoe Cove would result in the "loss of coverage," infrastructure, and jobs for Atlantic Canada's "future land and sea resource management needs," Trudeau's Cabinet approved the station closure on 10 June 1982. Three months later, Pitts then took his place as MDA's new CEO.[2]

When he moved into MDA's "Mahogany Row," Pitts assumed that Shoe Cove exemplified some of MDA's frailties. Systems embodied the company's strengths, but the closure and FOCUS overrun magnified Pitts's perceptions about the contrasts between systems and product companies. "When John Pitts came into the company, he wasn't really comfortable with the systems business," George Cwynar, the Systems Division manager of operations recalled. "He thought it would be good to have something steady, like a products business, which would complement systems and give the whole company a stronger revenue and cash flow." Products also represented what Pitts knew best. With his equity capital fastened to the company's future, Pitts thus hoped to reshape MDA into a more diversified company that could accommodate new products derived from MDA's systems. He also hoped to tie MDA's systems expertise to opportunities with ESA, North American defence efforts, and Canada's SPAR Aerospace, in teaming projects that could provide financial support for his larger manufacturing vision.[3]

After he inventoried MDA's assets, Pitts decided that the firm could turn its state-of-the-art technologies into repeat sales in several significant areas: the flight operations computer system (FOCUS) for worldwide airline sales; the SAR processor-based integrated radar imaging systems (IRIS), with potential applications in small aircraft surveillance and resource management; and especially the high-speed remote sensing film image recorder (FIRE) products that MDA had begun to develop during 1978. The FIREs promised profits in graphic arts, the printed circuit board industry, geophysical data processing, and other areas beyond remote sensing, a diversified portfolio of electro-optical products that could guarantee the strategy of selling MDA within five years at a ten-fold return on investment, so that Pitts and others could move on to other ventures. As insurance against risk, Pitts formed both MDA Aviation Systems, Inc. and divisions to house Airborne Radar and Electro-Optical Products. He also approved expenditures for research and development in robotics.[4]

Convinced that Electro-Optical Products (EOP) could become MDA's largest wealth-producing division, Pitts championed FIRE as his best chance to realize a sizeable ROI. FIRE and other products developed under the EOP Division also presented Pitts with a tremendous manufacturing opportunity, provided all went according to plan. As a result, from 1982 to 1988, Pitts fought endless battles to secure for the EOP Division whatever capital, tools, and employees he believed it required to further his investment-exit strategy. Realizing the potential incompatibility of MDA's systems focus and a manufacturing environment, Pitts also determined to wean EOP from the parent company so it could tool up, capture large markets, and return his as well as others' investment capital. With plans for success in all three divisions, and the eventual sale of EOP, Pitts personally hired EOP's management staff, people from outside MDA's borders who shared his product vision and arrived with experience in manufacturing environments. On the basis of his reading of management literature, Pitts's exit strategy made sense. It also represented the classic vision of post–World War II manufacturers bent on expansion. Under Pitts's guidance, people at MDA thus spent more than five years and an enormous amount of capital trying to develop products to reach the ends for which Pitts and others had invested.[5]

Unfortunately for Pitts and those who believed in his vision, the product adventure failed, even if under circumstances very different from what MDA had tried to orchestrate during the 1970s. Problems flowed in some ways from impatient venture capital, but they also revealed larger dilemmas, including the reality that many North American manufacturers had begun to consolidate their interests, de-industrializing in favour of the service economy, and off-shoring their remaining manufacturing plants to poorer parts of the world where they could exploit cheap labour costs and lax environmental regulations. Pitts thus pushed his manufacturing vision into a Canada that had begun to decline as "a market on which foreign capital casts an envious eye. Our market is still affluent," historian Duncan McDowall argued during 1992, "but in comparison with those of the new trade blocks, insignificant. As the smallest 'G-7' member with a population of only 27 million," he stressed, "Canada contends on the one hand with the fear that it is about to be swamped by huge trading blocks, and on the other hand with the unavoidable need to restructure its own economy to meet these global shifts."[6] Beyond such dilemmas, Pitts met resistance from MacDonald and his devoted followers, many of whom continued to nurture the system builder, research-oriented vision that had catapulted MDA into the centre of surveillance capitalism. "There was always the belief that the systems business was too hard," Dave Sloan argued, but MDA employees "were a bunch of systems people trying to do manufacturing, and I don't think Pitts" and his investor-business strategists "realized that was a different culture. They just assumed" manufacturing "was easy, because it looked easy at a distance."[7]

The forces of capital accumulation, global competition, and divergent visions of MDA's future thus fostered yet another tumultuous era in MDA's early history; and as each product endeavour floundered, then failed, the quandary over MDA's future resolved itself in significant and prophetic ways. For starters, product failures showed the problems associated with tackling the challenges of creating a manufacturing environment in a larger systems house. "We thought that one could build manufacturing businesses out of the place, and that this could kind of be a research and systems core. It took a long time for me to understand, and I daresay for most of us to understand," John MacDonald argued, "that you just couldn't mix the two types of businesses, that the same executive group could not run the two types of businesses. They are just culturally and in every other way too different. And that was a long time in coming, I confess."[8] Failed product launches also demonstrated the pull of surveillance capitalism, with the Systems Division's financial success pushing the firm and its expanding number of employees more deeply into the world of government procurement contracting for the global space industry and the expansion of geographical information systems, satellite surveillance, and tracking systems for the American-centred military-industrial complex. As a result, MDA's future as a systems integrator became inextricably bound to the expansion of a post-Soviet world order centred on the United States, but with new and aggressive competitors surfacing worldwide, particularly in Asia.[9] A significant step down that road, and one that Pitts inadvertently helped to pave, took place first inside MDA Aviation Systems, Inc., the entity that housed FOCUS.[10]

"YOU HAVE THREE CHOICES":
FROM FLIGHT OPERATIONS TO AVIATION SYSTEMS
AND DRONE SERVICES

Following his negotiations with SwissAir during 1982, John Pitts unveiled MDA's first subsidiary since Synaptic Systems: MDA Aviation Systems, Inc., to protect the parent firm from the liability the FOCUS project presented. As the firm entered the 1980s, few doubted that FOCUS had been the catalyst for MDA's financial disaster; however, Neil Thompson's original design for PWA also represented an exceptional technological achievement. Indeed, many in the airline industry and at MDA argued that FOCUS could eventually overpower all competitive products in the market once the firm finished its obligations to SwissAir, Sabena, and especially Texas International Airlines. With TIA threatening to sue MDA over FOCUS, Pitts first visited TIA's Houston operations as a consultant for MDA, where he quickly proved his worth as an excellent negotiator for the imperilled firm. With the Congressional passage of the US Airline Deregulation Act of 1978, the American airline industry began to experience significant uncertainty, particularly among smaller airlines struggling to compete in a more volatile market. The Act ultimately placed airline employees in a difficult situation as well. Three years after its passage, the Reagan administration defeated the Professional Air Traffic Controllers Organization (PATCO) in its strike of August 1981, a watershed that triggered the firing of air traffic controllers involved in the strike, the decertification of PATCO, and the decline of the American labour movement as a whole. With competition increasing and labour's muscle contracting, consolidation swept over the American airline industry. By 1982, that sweep included TIA's takeover of Continental Airlines, which soon placed TIA's employees at risk. As a result, when Pitts arrived to discuss the FOCUS fiasco, MDA's team had less to fear about losing their jobs than those at TIA.[11]

According to one engineer sent to Houston to install FOCUS, when representatives from Texas International threatened to sue MDA, Pitts immediately barked, "You have three choices. You can pay us another $1 million and we'll finish this contract, you can take the system as-is, where-is, and we will send a team of people to try and help you try to finish it, for six weeks," Pitts suggested, "or you can sue us, bankrupt us, and you won't get a penny, because we're bankrupt as is. Take your pick."[12] As the negotiations unfolded, TIA ultimately signed an "as-is" agreement with MDA, the firm completed the work, and some suggested that FOCUS had a future beyond the first three contracts. Because MDA had already completed and installed one satisfactory system for Sabena, and Pitts had negotiated Swiss-Air's financial commitment to the product, members of the board and Pitts's inner circle convinced themselves that experienced marketing personnel could identify new customers for the FOCUS product.[13]

As deregulation of the airline industry spread from the United States to Europe between 1982 and 1984, marketing representatives at MDA Aviation Systems made significant global contacts. By the time the company delivered the SwissAir version of FOCUS in 1985, however, it had become obvious that those involved directly in the airline industry might have more success at selling MDA's flight information products. As a result, MDA abandoned its direct sales efforts and Pitts negotiated an agreement that gave to SwissAir all rights to MDA's FOCUS technology in exchange for a royalty on future systems sales. SwissAir sold one FOCUS to Canadian Airlines, and although Sabena, SwissAir, and Canadian Airlines continued to use and then promote the system into the early 1990s, SwissAir's first product sale represented FOCUS's final launch. New technologies on the market, although less elegant than FOCUS, also cost financially strapped airline companies far less than the system Thompson had originally designed. Indeed, MDA's history in flight information systems demonstrated the point in practical terms. Neil Thompson, MDA's airline industry champion, understood the industry's structure and realized he could exploit his original design within his own small organization. Resigning from MDA in 1981, Thompson formed ATI Aero Technology Inc. Like Bill Renwick before him, Thompson had amassed a specific expertise in software development and had an aversion to large project teams. He thus limited his vision and created a slow-growth, three-person firm that generated just enough revenue to outrun or keep pace with competitors. After Thompson resigned, MDA also lost its most important link to the airline market and had to return to its former status as an industry outlander in a narrowing and highly competitive field. With two important strokes against it, MDA thus drove itself out of the airline market as quickly as it entered it.[14]

In the end, no amount of capital injection could save FOCUS from oblivion, but MDA ultimately benefited from FOCUS in unanticipated ways. The Systems Division learned how to refine the software development process from the FOCUS experience, and finally came to terms with the pitfalls in running complex software development projects. As a result, FOCUS gave MDA a strategic advantage on future contracts involving similar systems, particularly for clients focused on the American military-industrial complex. That knowledge they then applied to the automated weather distribution system designed and built for the US Air Force. Resurrecting its FOCUS proficiency also gave the Systems Division an opportunity to build a profitable business area in aviation systems, one that could combine software, hardware, experiences gained from the company's original work on the mobile radio terminal technology, and the management know-how MDA acquired on its AWDS and ESA projects. Over time, that expertise then provided an opening for MDA to move more deeply into the business of unmanned aerial vehicles, in work that ultimately included flight operations, maintenance, and training as well as imaging archives for data exploitation and change detection.[15]

"A RICH COUNTRY'S MILITARY TOOL":
FROM AIRBORNE RADAR TO INTELLIGENCE GATHERING SYSTEMS

During 1985, MDA launched its Airborne Radar Division to exploit an integrated radar imaging system (IRIS) product the company had developed between 1982 and 1983. Building on MDA's earlier SAR work, IRIS became a real-time, all-weather, high-resolution radar surveillance system for use on small aircraft. After MDA delivered its first commercial IRIS system for ice reconnaissance in the Canadian Arctic during 1983, MDA's investors and systems managers hoped to market the product as a tool for border and sea-ice surveillance, maritime patrol, and geological exploration. By March 1985, MDA received one contract from the CCRS and another from Intera Technologies, a Calgary-based firm interested in developing geological programs to isolate radioactive waste. Placing MDA's surveillance product on a company-owned aircraft, Intera embarked upon a whirlwind tour to promote the IRIS system in Finland, Sweden, Germany, and Taiwan. In addition, MDA and Intera made joint non-aircraft presentations to representatives from the governments of India, Pakistan, and South Korea. By 1986, with Intera's enthusiasm for IRIS established, and gross revenues of $606,000 realized from their first sale, the MDA team hoped to advertise IRIS for future applications in agriculture, forestry, hydrology, and oceanography. Because the CCRS had already recommended MDA and several of its technologies to MOSST and other government agencies for such applications, MDA's management team also decided that the IRIS product needed a divisional structure to optimize its market potential. With two IRIS contracts in hand, Pitts thus moved the ten-person IRIS team to its own premises, where MDA expanded its presence into a fourth building within the Shellbridge Industrial Park and increased the company's leasing expenditures.[16]

As MDA's corporate restructuring unfolded, John Bennett emerged as the obvious candidate to manage Airborne Radar. With a burning desire to see the IRIS technology succeed, MDA's signal processing guru put his heart and soul into the new division, and by 1986, he had convinced some of his allies in the Canadian government to co-fund further technological development on the product. Bennett's efforts ultimately gained the division a $5 million contract through Canada's Defence Industry Productivity Program (DIPP), the federal program charged with promoting research and development of technologies that promised to contribute to Canada's strategic objectives in space and defence as part of Mulroney's agenda to establish friendlier relations with the United States. That seed money also allowed Airborne Radar to expand from ten to twenty-six employees. By early 1986, IRIS had fuelled interest elsewhere as well, including at Intera, where the product's champions offered MDA two additional IRIS-based contracts.[17]

Unfortunately for the Airborne Radar team, neither Bennett's efforts nor DIPP's assistance and Intera's enthusiasm could save the IRIS product from failure, and no one saw it coming more dramatically than John Bennett. While putting together a business plan for the Airborne Radar Division during 1988, Bennett realized that IRIS would fail unless MDA identified "some new markets, because there just wasn't a big enough remote sensing market for the technology." He and his team thus "identified the military market" as MDA's best chance to realize profits from IRIS, which involved "several years roaming the world trying to convince the militaries of the world to buy the system," Bennett recalled. Although gross revenues for IRIS peaked at $3.8 million in 1986, over the next two years they dropped precipitously. At the same time, gross research and development expenditures rose from $475,000 in 1987 to over $1.1 million during 1988, which represented nearly 50 per cent of the division's revenue. The product had potential applications, but civilian users once again found less expensive technologies to meet their needs. The technology's surveillance capabilities intrigued governments as well, but Bennett soon learned that only the richest among them could afford to employ IRIS as a military tool. MDA's only other target market, the vast swath of less-developed countries and emerging economies, foresaw marginal benefits from IRIS; and even if they wanted the technology just to own it for future purposes, struggling countries could not justify IRIS on a cost-benefit basis. "The bottom line was that IRIS was a rich country's military tool," Bennett conceded, and the United States in particular had already developed similar products for such a use.[18]

Although MDA had identified at least part of IRIS's business in "the militaries of the world," further expansion of the product would have to wait for the rise of the BRIC countries: Brazil, Russia, India, and China. Alas for the technology's enthusiasts at MDA, the company could not afford to wait that long, and IRIS simply had no real market in the late 1980s. MDA therefore closed the division in 1990, rolling Airborne Radar and the IRIS technology into the Systems Division.[19]

The IRIS experience paralleled the FOCUS failure in a number of key ways; yet, like FOCUS, it benefited the Systems Division and pushed MDA more deeply into the development of larger surveillance systems. When coupled to other remote sensing products, IRIS allowed the Systems Division to bid on and win important image analysis and mapping work, including an ice data integration and analysis system for Environment Canada's Ice Centre. Intera's world tour of IRIS additionally established global contacts for MDA's future ground station upgrades and the image analysis, mapping, and reconnaissance systems that have come to dominate global relations and everyday reality through the Internet and interactive technologies. Work on IRIS also helped to expand MDA's presence in Asia, particularly after MDA won a contract to upgrade China's airborne imaging radar system as part of an effort to improve China's flood monitoring, natural disaster relief, and military capabilities. Signed in 1993, the Chinese contract extended MDA's market share in geographical information systems as well, which ultimately emerged as the company's largest business area during the mid-1990s.[20]

"A DEAL BETWEEN CANADA AND NASA": FROM MUSCLE ACTUATOR RESEARCH TO SPACE ROBOTICS

In another effort to harvest products, MDA hired Guy Immega as the firm's manager of new product development. Immega had worked for MDA off and on during the 1970s, in areas that meshed nicely with MacDonald's intellectual interests and MDA's vistas. Immega understood vision systems and had a burgeoning desire to join the up-and-coming field of robotics. Impressed by Immega's work and long-range vision, MacDonald recommended him to Pitts, and in 1984 MDA hired Immega to ascertain whether or not the company could adapt existing technologies to new business areas or modify new technologies to Pitts's product mandate. Although MDA's board members had made theoretical commitments to move more deeply into robotics, Pitts argued that expenditures on the AWDS pursuit and product development precluded another large capital investment.

Nonetheless, he authorized a small investment for Immega's projects. Immega quickly identified several technologies worth exploring, and by 1986, his small research team thrust the company into the development of a robotic muscle actuator called ROMAC.[21]

The evolution of surveillance capitalism, Canada's deepening integration into the American military-industrial complex, and the promise of lowering manufacturing costs through automation provided the context for MDA's involvement in the development of ROMAC. During his 1984 State of the Union address to the American people, President Reagan announced that he had directed NASA to build an International Space Station (ISS) by 1994. SPAR had already delivered Canadarm-1 to NASA in 1981, and when NASA began its aggressive campaign for international participation in ISS during 1982, its representatives focused on Canada. As before, NASA's representatives hoped to appease congressional members who wanted to defray some of the costs associated with the US-centred program, while Canadian policymakers saw SPAR's participation as a way to increase Canada's prominence in the global space industry. As a result, the Canadian government launched another series of studies to review and rationalize the benefits of ISS to the Canadian economy. As the designated prime contractor for all space-based work in Canada and the firm best positioned to become a significant multinational enterprise, SPAR became heavily involved in the Canadian review. Its executives also began to search for acquisitions that would allow SPAR to penetrate the US government procurement system and emerge as Canada's complete systems supplier for worldwide military and commercial customers. During 1984, SPAR then purchased California's Commercial Telecommunications Corporation to extend its reach into the use of satellites for commercial communications, particularly in banking and the media. Anticipating Canada's participation in ISS, SPAR also pursued and received several significant procurement contracts from the US Department of Defense that promised significant expansion into the US communications market.[22]

During 1985, the Canadian government announced its commitment to the ISS project, and "NASA welcomed the money that Canada's contribution would bring into the program," SPAR's official 1992 history asserted, because "the manipulator system represented roughly $1 billion (Canadian)." Both governments "had seen the potential for stimulating the development of advanced Earth-based applications of these new technologies," the history continued. As a result, intense negotiations took place "to hammer out the technical details of Canada's contribution," which eventually included an agreement to spread the robotics work between several companies on both sides of the border. With the National Research Council designated as Canada's co-signer of a memorandum of agreement with NASA, SPAR became the prime contractor for the ISS mobile servicing system, then sought bids from other Canadian firms interested in serving as subcontractors for the *Canadarm* project.[23]

In the meantime, Prime Minister Mulroney assigned new responsibilities to the Ministry of State for Science and Technology, including a 1985 mandate to conduct annual reviews of Canada's science and technology activities and the effectiveness of federal expenditures on new federal-provincial agreements. Collaborations between the federal and provincial governments furthered Canadian economic liberalization and encouraged promotion of a more "science-oriented culture" to improve the diffusion of industrial innovation and technology across Canada. The federal government also reorganized MOSST to reflect the changes Mulroney hoped to effect as part of his commitment to negotiating a free (and hopefully fairer) trade agreement with the United States, including four sectors policymakers most wanted to enhance: Government Research and Universities; National Science and Technology; Industry, Trade and Technology; and Space Policy. While MOSST published a background paper as part of a national forum on science and technology, the Task Force on Program Review released its *Government Procurement "Spending Smarter"* report.[24]

Together with a bevy of other studies, "*Spending Smarter*" called for the further expansion of Canada's "contracting out" policies as well as a greater focus on industrial and regional development linked to the private sector and its university partners. "In 1984–85, the value of contracts for goods and services issued by the federal government exceeded $9 billion," the report noted, with most of it devoted to the "acquisition of high technology equipment" for the DND. Invoking the spectre of the Avro Arrow, the report also asserted that the presence of an increasing number of American subsidiaries undertaking DND's work explained both the "relative decline in the technology base of Canadian industry" as well as Canada's "increasing deficit. Canada is unique among its major defence partners in the export dependency of its defence industry," "*Spending Smarter*" claimed. The report therefore suggested that Canada needed to improve its domestic "procurement lever to support industrial development" and "the competitiveness of Canadian-based industry in world markets" to reduce the country's technological and financial dependency on the United States. The report then identified projects that task force members deemed "critical over the next 10 to 15 years": space-based radar; communications satellites, particularly mobile ones; a *Radarsat* satellite with an onboard SAR processor; and robotics for the ISS. Absorbing the report's proposals, the federal government privatized the DeHaviland Crown in 1986 and adopted American space policies as well as the OECD's concept of "science policy as a science and technology/innovation strategy" to encourage greater mobilization of entrepreneurs, private-sector firms, provincial research organizations, venture capitalists, and university researchers involved in applied science as the central stakeholders in Canada's policy future. The federal government then selected SPAR to lead Canada's "critical" mega-projects into the next decade.[25]

After NASA and MOSST had signed the MOU outlining Canada's participation in the larger ISS program, Canada attached its signature to an agreement with the United States, ESA's member states, and Japan to design, develop, build, and maintain equipment for ISS. During March 1989, the Canadian government then committed the country to a Crown for Canada's space program and participation in ISS by establishing the Canadian Space Agency (CSA). "At the start of my interest in robots," Guy Immega explained, "there was no particular or obvious space connection to be made, but then Canada made this commitment as an international participant and shareholder" in ISS "to supply robots, and that opened up opportunities" for MDA.[26]

As early as 1986, ROMAC looked promising as an internal technology transfer from Immega's new product research operation and into the Systems Division for further development, but the transition quickly represented new challenges for MDA. If few company engineers gave much thought to the ethics of and synergies developing between robotics and the military-industrial complex, or the potential for automation to change the geographical location for production and employment, fewer still contemplated the shifting terrain of power relationships and the law. Obsessed with yet more exciting work on the technological edge and seduced by the possibilities further space exploration promised, the MDA team simply wanted to pursue another potential innovative first. Over time, they also hoped that plans for the ISS would provide plentiful opportunities for MDA to participate in the development of robotics. Combining naïveté about the realities of global production trends with a woeful lack of experience in the vagaries of patent law, MDA thus managed to botch yet another product opportunity. Immega lost ownership of his inventions, and MDA became embroiled in expensive legal proceedings with a former employee who applied for a patent on the ROMAC technology.[27]

Although a very unpleasant lesson in the realities of patent law, ROMAC's development furthered John MacDonald's vision of turning

Vancouver into a high-tech centre. When ROMAC died at MDA, Immega decided he wanted to seize something positive from an otherwise devastating experience. He spoke with MacDonald, and together they agreed that Immega should take advantage of opportunities that MDA could not afford to pursue. MDA thus "spun-out" Immega, and in March 1991 he formed a small company called Kinetic Sciences, Inc. MacDonald took a seat on KSI's board and positioned MDA to work closely with Immega on joint efforts for the ISS and other projects. MDA board members also decided to fold all future robotics initiatives into the Systems Division. Once the division's managers absorbed the lessons of the ROMAC debacle, they paid more attention to protecting MDA's research findings and development work, as well as the company's position in robotics, in projects that ultimately formed the heart of the company's interactive surveillance services, particularly the drones developed for "strategic partners" that would expand government expertise in robotics on the strength of military demands, defence sharing arrangements, and trade agreements.[28]

In the meantime, Immega pursued emerging opportunities in robotics, hired four staff, and retained university researcher-contractors to assist him. By 1992, Immega received $500,000 in procurement contracts from the CSA and DND, the seed capital KSI needed to create autonomous robots for use on the ISS. Initially conceived to serve governments, the ISS project transformed Immega's life and turned Canada's public universities into technology incubators for the private sector and the interests of global capital. The ISS effort also took more than ten years to develop and thirty years to assemble, in work that eventually involved more than US$150 billion in taxpayer dollars as well as the energies of scientists and engineers representing five space agencies and fifteen countries. Russia's first segments and the first US-built components launched in 1998. Although no one at MDA foresaw where the ISS might carry them when Immega began to follow the promise of robotics during the mid-1980s, capitalists, policymakers, technological enthusiasts, and space writers eventually normalized the kinds of partnerships that the ISS represented, employing the space-based mythologies that helped global workers to adjust themselves to the "privatization ethic" Vincent Mosco explored in *The Digital Sublime*.[29]

MDA's ROMAC experience also demonstrated the ways in which procurement contracts have socialized business owners to perceive themselves as wealth- and job-creating drivers of change, and to see government as a necessary but bloated evil rather than an essential provider of the safety nets that capitalism and its agents fail to provide. Immega initially contracted with the federal government to create economic stability for KSI so that it could build a commercial business with products and proprietary technologies for use in other applications. During 1993, Immega then planned "to wean" KSI from such "contracts, because they won't last forever." Twelve years later, however, that weaning had not taken place, and KSI built many experimental robots for the ISS on seed capital provided by government procurement contracts. KSI also created robots to clean up nuclear waste, and Immega fashioned a miniature fingerprint sensor for cell phones, but even these depended on the support of taxpayer dollars. When Immega sold KSI's intellectual property to a California-based firm during 2005, he launched a new career as a science fiction writer and nonfiction essayist. Engaging in a little historical amnesia about the role that government had played in his own career, Immega crafted stories about promising technologies that required little more than a plucky inventor-engineer and the private hand of "vulture" capital to develop.[30]

"FIRE IS THE STANDARD":
FROM ELECTRO-OPTICAL PRODUCTS
TO A NEW RELATIONSHIP WITH SPAR

MDA's difficulties with FOCUS, IRIS, and ROMAC taught members of the MDA team important things about themselves and their environment, but it took the company's major effort, the Electro-Optical Products Division, to transform MDA's relationship with SPAR and demolish Pitts's larger product development and manufacturing dreams. When MDA unveiled Dan Gelbart's black-and-white FIRE during 1981, the technology revolutionized the remote sensing industry. Not only fast, FIRE produced accurate images, thereafter setting the standard for ground station film image recorders. "Almost everyone in the production processing of film, from imaging spacecraft, be it JPL with the Interplanetary Program, or the Canada Centre for Remote Sensing, or the Australians, or the American processing system, they all use FIRE," John MacDonald recollected. "FIRE is the world standard, there's no question about it."[31]

While Gelbart continued to develop the Colour FIRE during 1981, MDA hired a ground station salesman named Daniel (Dan) Murray, a young man destined to replace Barclay Isherwood but who became an instant champion of MDA's electro-optical products mere moments after he witnessed the Colour FIRE in action. With its abilities to show shades of colour (light green for diseased trees, for example), Murray perceived the Colour FIRE's potential to detect timber disease as well as mineral deposits and other resources. He therefore convinced Pitts and several members of the board that MDA could power the technology into the remote sensing market for various kinds of work. Starting his job at MDA during the company's financial crisis, Murray devoted himself to FIRE sales, quickly making one for inclusion in the upgrade to MDA's South African ground station and shortly thereafter making another to the University of Alaska for use in the production of satellite data. When MDA displayed the Colour FIRE during 1982, the machine received an industrial research award, a feat that allowed Murray to sell four more black-and-white and colour machines with relative ease.[32]

Although grateful for MacDonald's earlier support of his FIRE developments, Gelbart linked the FIRE's research award to Ray Maxwell's assessment about MDA's "special gathering of the right people at the right time" during the 1970s. "We each had done little things, but this was a team which did together something quite major, all done with young people, unbiased by any previous experience, so everything was a fresh start." But Gelbart also argued that they accomplished such feats because young engineers could build on the "special synergy" that radiated outward from "MacDonald, Dettwiler, Sloan, and Spencer." Working on technology's edge, they could venture into uncharted spaces and possibilities as well as realize the fulfillment of the technical creative's fondest dreams. Thus, when Pitts restructured the firm, Gelbart resigned. Indeed, he left MDA precisely because he wanted to further the synergies he had developed with Ken Spencer, MDA's former ground station manager. During 1983, Gelbart and Spencer thus launched CREO, one of Vancouver's most successful high-tech ventures, to follow opportunities in optics and digital printing. Dave Sloan and others had followed Barclay Isherwood and Bill Thompson into MDI for similar reasons. No matter their later destinations, however, the energy and commitment they developed in MDA's seemingly unconventional and apolitical environment had allowed them to adhere to the discipline of a Cold War ideology that rarely forced them to think about where their technological firsts might lead; and Pitts's embrace of procurement contracting for the US military changed those perceptions.[33]

In the meantime, Murray continued to demonstrate MDA's FIRE at trade shows during 1983, which prompted interest from clients outside the remote sensing field. Murray's initial sales from those demonstrations then convinced Pitts that MDA should launch the Electro-Optical Products Division to power the technology into several markets that could create the sorts of mass demand on which Pitts and other investors could realize their five-year exit strategy. Pitts also retained the services of a California-based consulting firm, whose principals soon predicted that the Colour FIRE could capture a sizeable share of the graphic arts and printing market as well as generate revenue through the circuit board industry by automating the process via artwork rather than the common practice of taping boards together. By adding photographic software tools to the original film recorder, FIRE thus promised large manufacturing companies that they could reduce costs by duplicating film masters of coloured artwork and circuit boards. At the same time, a Houston-based firm, Western Geophysical, showed interest in the FIRE technology for plotting and archiving seismic data. Dreaming about windfall profits and quick returns in electro-optical imaging for graphic arts and the printed circuit board industry as well as in geophysical data processing, MDA's restructured board decided to pursue product development work in all three areas.[34]

For those in the Pitts Group and at Ventures West, it appeared that EOP products might pay off quickly. By 1984, EOP had already hired seventy employees and realized gross revenues nearing $4 million (about $9.2 million in 2016). Although EOP's R&D costs had also increased to $3 million during the same year, Pitts argued that the Systems Division had generated sufficient profits in remote sensing and on the AWDS phase one development project to make up for the loss. Pitts and other product champions therefore encouraged the board to approve expenditures for further developments. With EOP entering into new market areas beyond remote sensing, they also argued that MDA would need more capital to build a manufacturing facility as well as create production and distribution channels. Unfortunately for Pitts and his allies, while MDA's Washington neighbour Microsoft celebrated its tenth anniversary and sales figures reaching US$140 million during 1985, EOP's capital requirements translated into a net company loss of $3.5 million. When he reviewed MDA's year-end results, Pitts also realized that EOP's development and manufacturing costs had begun to eat away at the profits of MDA as a whole. Still, Microsoft's accomplishments suggested a future with enormous profit potential if MDA stayed the course in manufacturing. As a result, Pitts and other product champions convinced members of the board to authorize further internal capital infusions as well as a search for more outside investment, some of which Pitts secured from associates in Scotland, to move the EOP Division and its expanding number of staff members to a manufacturing location several miles away from corporate headquarters. Phillip Lapp also approached members of SPAR about the

EOP dilemma. SPAR thus offered MDA another lifeline – this time an investment in exchange for more seats on the board and a share of the company's profits.[35]

Although MDA had spurned SPAR's advances in the past, by 1985 the company needed capital to build EOP's manufacturing facility, and Pitts shared none of MacDonald's qualms about the larger firm. Moreover, with the Mulroney government shifting its gaze from single-company grants to the development of innovation clusters and networks of excellence, MDA could not count on non-repayable research grants or development assistance for EOP. MDA thus took the plunge, and SPAR purchased 11 per cent of MDA. As part of the investment package, SPAR promised to provide important subcontracts on the ISS and other major projects, including work on *Radarsat*, a proposed remote sensing satellite with onboard SAR. SPAR also stipulated that Pitts and MacDonald had to sign a right-of-first-refusal agreement, which essentially guaranteed that if they sold MDA, SPAR had first options on Pitts's and MacDonald's shares. Furthermore, neither Pitts nor MacDonald could sell any of his shares without first offering them at the same price to SPAR. The agreement gave MDA a much-needed capital injection; however, it put other investors in a tenuous position. By 1985, with John Pitts, John MacDonald, and SPAR each owning approximately 11 per cent of the company, those at Ventures West (then owning 23 per cent of MDA) faced the reality of losing their plurality should a takeover come to pass. But *Radarsat* promised government guarantees, additional work, and stability while investors waited for the windfall profits the EOP Division seemed certain to generate. Thus, Michael Brown and his partners at Ventures West agreed to the deal.[36]

Radarsat work began in the early 1980s, but "the project had a difficult birthing process," SPAR's President Larry Clark later confirmed. On 28 January 1986, the US *Space Shuttle Challenger* exploded just seventy-three seconds into its flight, killing five NASA astronauts and two payload specialists. "The disasters of 1986 made for a rough year in the satellite business all over the world," Clark observed. "There was a desperate shortage of launch capacity, and users just wouldn't give commitments" to purchase satellites.[37] Facing a budgetary pinch as well as the *Challenger* disaster, the Canadian government thus shelved *Radarsat* as a high-risk venture Canada could ill-afford. That decision then placed SPAR (and by extension MDA) in a tenuous position: SPAR's revenues of $233 million in 1985 dropped to $191 million in 1986, and its profits fell from $25 million to $8 million during the same period. Eventually, however, sovereignty concerns prompted the federal government to rescue the country's aerospace industry; work on the project thus commenced at SPAR, and Canada's prime contractor slowly began to recover.[38]

By 1987, newspapers noted that members of the federal government had encouraged cooperation between SPAR and MDA because the country needed an east-west connection to protect Canada's Arctic sovereignty. "Detecting violations of Arctic waters will now be easier following the federal government's approval of a $725-million remote sensing satellite project, the *Globe and Mail* reported. "Dubbed Radarsat, it is scheduled to be launched from the United States in 1994 and will have a five-year life span," the paper noted. SPAR received the prime contract for *Radarsat*, and MDA garnered a subcontract to provide "ground equipment and many other components." Frank Oberle, Canada's new minister for industry, science and technology, stressed that *Radarsat* "is not a spy satellite. But he didn't rule out the possibility that data it collected on ships in Arctic waters would be passed on to the military," the paper stressed. "Recent intrusions of Arctic waters by US and Soviet submarines have made Arctic sovereignty a political issue"; thus "*Radarsat* will enhance our claim to Arctic sovereignty by providing daily surveillance of the Arctic islands and waters," no matter cloud cover or degrees of darkness and shadow, the paper claimed.[39] With SAR promising to provide a powerful technological solution for Canada, the Canadian government then signed the 1988 Arctic Pact to encourage US recognition of Canada's sovereignty claims. Unfortunately, once signed, "the agreement did nothing to bring the two nations any closer in their dispute over Canadian Arctic waters," ethicist Phil Smith-Eivemark argued. Indeed, he stressed that "Arctic militarization" proceeded "against the expressed wishes of the Canadian people."[40]

In the meantime, things went from bad to worse in Richmond, despite MDA's entrance into an important accord with SPAR and another restructured board to reflect MDA's capital requirements and SPAR's financial interest in the firm. At MDA headquarters, an increasing number of employees, particularly within the Systems Division, argued that the company needed to prioritize its work on *Radarsat* rather than expend more money on EOP. Reminiscent of the earlier Synaptic Systems "them versus us" problem, relationships between EOP and Systems employees began to deteriorate just before the manufacturing group moved to its new facility in 1986, which initiated squabbles on the board and increased the isolation of EOP staff. Pitts and other FIRE champions then ran further afoul of Systems as EOP struggled to find an appropriate manager who could generate business and profits beyond the remote sensing field.[41] Murray managed to sell forty-four Colour FIRE 240s in the remote sensing market between 1984 and 1988, all of which turned consistent profits every year on the strength of the machine's dominance in that market; by 1988's end, however, the other three product lines consistently lost money, even with initial marketing success in the United States, Europe, and Japan.[42]

In graphic arts, technical difficulties delayed a major product introduction until 1987, and when MDA finally entered the market, it faced fierce competition from companies with deeper pockets, long-established manufacturing facilities, and a larger domestic market in which to sell. Those firms included Kodak, the famed multinational that had dominated the imaging and photographic equipment, materials, and services sector since its founding in 1889. MDA's problems in the graphic arts industry revealed that the Canadian firm had no competitive advantage vis-à-vis Kodak and other US competitors. MDA installed FIRE machines within colour studio and advertising markets in London, New York, Chicago, and Los Angeles, but the firm lacked sufficient funds to create more robust American channels for effective marketing and distribution. As a result, MDA failed to capture an adequate share of the market to profit from the FIRE's graphic arts applications.[43]

In the printed circuit board (PCB) industry, MDA over-designed its FIRE machine, even when it had few competitors as it entered the market. Called the FIRE 9000, MDA's product incorporated computer-aided design and software tools to create a "photo tool" that could marry photographic and chemical processes into a "sandwich." Traditional technologies had taken forty hours to produce one printed circuit board, whereas MDA's FIRE 9000 could accomplish the same task in just ten minutes. MDA's technical achievement earned another industrial research award for the firm, and the FIRE 9000 soon dominated the market in North America. The product also made inroads into Europe and Asia. Unfortunately, the efficiencies of the FIRE 9000 drove other PCB manufacturers out of business with relative ease. Had MDA installed a timer and increased the machine's speed over time, the company might have exploited the product more fully. But the decision to showcase the FIRE 9000's high-speed performance immediately destroyed the very market MDA hoped to penetrate. Moreover, the FIRE 9000 was very expensive, a reality that made the machine far too costly for other potential applications.[44]

In the seismic market, where MDA hoped to sell its GeoFIRE, a machine that could "plug into" companies such as Shell Canada and Western Geophysical, the EOP Division entered into its first contract without undertaking a thorough market study. By the time EOP's team sold six machines to the first customer, the GeoFIRE saturated the market, exposing to the world that MDA lacked the knowledge required to market sophisticated and expensive machines. As a result, MDA never sold another GeoFIRE. Complicating the situation, its sales took place while Western nations de-industrialized and the global economy became increasingly digitized. Foreign direct investment, capital mobility, labour migration, and labour-intensive manufacturing thus moved from Canada to less developed regions.[45]

"WE HAD NO IDEA WHAT IT WAS GOING TO TAKE": THE PRODUCT VISION'S FINALE

Retrospectively, several former EOP devotees realized that MDA fundamentally misunderstood the FIRE's power, had no idea what to do with it, and expanded the EOP Division even when it never made enough money to justify a continued effort. Licensing agreements, for example, might have generated profits for the firm; however, no one at MDA, not even Pitts, proposed such a strategy. In addition, each EOP commercial product cost more than $100,000 to develop and manufacture, which placed all but the largest companies beyond MDA's marketing reach. And all of the firm's FIREs required a sophisticated sales-and-service network, a capability MDA lacked no matter the market. These realities limited sales from the start, allowing larger firms to profit more from MDA's products than the neophyte manufacturer ever did or could.[46] "Your objective as a shareholder is not to create employment," one senior management team member argued. "It is to generate a return on investment. When we entered the market" to sell FIRE products, "we were trying to build on an assembly-line basis a bunch of boxes, and we were making changes to those boxes as we went. We had absolutely no idea how to engineer in a product environment, no idea of the effort and commitment it would take to build a service network around the world to service that equipment, and no idea what it was going to take to build a marketing and distribution network around the world."[47]

In addition to technical and marketing problems, MDA's attempt to wed two different kinds of businesses fell apart. While Pitts continued to defend the product cause, Systems employees arrived at board meetings to appeal to directors, arguing that EOP had strapped MDA with financial and other losses at the very time when globalization had already dismantled the manufacturing imperative in places like Canada. Hamilton, the Systems Division head, "had no opposition to anybody trying to build Electro Optical or anything else," Dan Friedmann argued, "but he certainly was opposed to doing that at the expense of the Systems business." Indeed, from the moment he joined MDA during 1976, Hamilton argued that MDA had uniquely positioned itself to make systems a profitable, expansion-oriented business. When Pitts introduced a disciplinary framework to meet that end, Hamilton set for himself the task of turning his own vision of what MDA could become into a reality. As he rose from remote sensing's marketing manager to a company vice-president, Hamilton thus built upon MacDonald's original vision of MDA as a firm operating at a world-class level of engineering excellence through government contracts to seed long-term expansion. Turning Systems into the firm's most consistently profitable business, Hamilton fought a long, hard battle on behalf of remote sensing and systems integration. Expressing concerns that expenditures on product development would ultimately erode MDA's systems expertise, Hamilton vigorously and openly reminded board members that Pitts steadily captured important internal research and development funds from Systems while EOP and Airborne Radar managed to devour the company's marketing resources. Significantly, Hamilton also had a champion in John MacDonald as well as financial backers in the Canadian government and the United States, particularly among enthusiastic supporters of continental integration. EOP had neither.[48]

Pitts had set the stage for such a conflict, but it took further dissension among MDA's rank-and-file employees and between board members, along with the financial uncertainty of the late 1980s to convince Pitts that he had no choice but to give up on his manufacturing vision. And by 1987, the Systems Division had decisively won the battle for MDA by introducing new technologies and a system integrator capability that enhanced MDA's revenues, while EOP and other product divisions drained the company's lifeblood to the point of anemia. Hamilton and Friedmann had also composed the prescient five-year plan that could secure a greater share of the space-based market through large-scale systems integration projects, more disciplined engineering work packages, and a razor-sharp focus on governmental budgets for surveillance work at home and abroad. When he presented the new plan during 1987, Hamilton persuaded MDA's board that the company's expansionist potential lay in diversifying out of remote sensing and into large-scale systems engineering and integration projects based on the company's existing skills and government contracts. Changing markets, dreams of worldwide digital webs, and the increasing integration of the global economy then sealed the fate of the manufacturing plan. Thus, with $17.5 million in gross revenues, 160 employees, and a net loss of $550,000, the EOP Division went up for sale. A lengthy and costly search for a buyer followed, but the decision to abandon products allowed MDA to rebrand itself as a systems house guided by the five-year plan crafted by the Systems Division.[49]

The demise of MDA's product adventure flowed from multiple sources, including overly optimistic market forecasts, expensive over-engineering of prototypes, and a failure to understand the complexities of product development, from initial research through the manufacturing stage. Product failures also reflected the adaptability of capitalism, which included its abilities to accommodate space-based technologies for further expansion. Despite his earlier success in manufacturing, Pitts found himself out of step with capitalist expansion as well as the manufacturing shift from North America to less-developed parts of the world. As a result, EOP's supporters tackled myriad manufacturing challenges within a firm that had received only outside support for an increasingly networked future. Even if MDA had the capacity to learn how to make manufacturing pay in such an environment, MDA's new investors had short-term investment-and-exit goals rather than a long-term, patient vision for the firm and its workers. Neoliberal ideologues, scholars in business and engineering schools, policymakers, and popular business writers had normalized the need for such short-term investment vistas. Thus, despite more herculean efforts by MDA staff, Pitts had to concede that he could not transform MDA into a product-oriented firm. Product failures under Pitts's leadership foreshadowed more to come, when periodically someone came forward with a plan to turn other systems designed for the military into products for other uses. Initially, those plans generated enthusiasm and dreams of windfall profits; ultimately, however, they too failed, as did any plans to change MDA's systems house environment.[50]

Nearby neighbour Microsoft had adjusted to surveillance capitalism, developing the kinds of products larger American government procurement and global consumer markets could absorb, all in a nation with a population ten times that of Canada's. As president of a US government contractor, Bill Gates also understood his firm's larger role. He therefore connected his mass-manufacturing vision with the US government's ambitions to win the Cold War and make the world safe for American-style capitalist expansion by employing cheap labour abroad and middle-class consumers wired for increased surveillance and product obsolescence. North of the border, MDA had nothing to offer those everyday consumers as the 1990s drew near. Even if it did, MDA lacked state protections to develop a domestic market.[51]

Thus, while astronomers at the University of California reported that they had witnessed the "birth of a giant galaxy," Reagan signed a secret order permitting the covert sale of arms to Iran, and the Dow Jones average closed at over 2,200 for the first time, Pitts also had to admit, "We are regarded as world leaders in imaging satellite ground station technology," not manufacturing mavens. He also confirmed that MDA achieved and maintained its leadership "largely through the support and encouragement of the federal government."[52] After more than seventeen years in business, John MacDonald finally conceded the point as well. "John MacDonald is the first to admit the company might never have been in the remote sensing business if it hadn't been for Canadian government support through procurement starting back in the early 1970s," Andrea Gordon reported in the *Toronto Star*. Indeed, "Companies involved in aerospace work don't get anywhere without government, he says, because they are the major buyers in the world." Still, "The CCRS (Canada Centre for Remote Sensing) at the time was run by some very farsighted bureaucrats," MacDonald offered, "and their investment has certainly paid off for Ottawa." Despite MacDonald's back-handed compliment to his friends at the CCRS, however, Gordon additionally noted that government contracting had transformed MDA from "a firm that did all its initial business in Canada to one that exports 80 per cent of its products and has eight offices around the world." Thanks to the encouragement of Phillip Lapp as well as others at the CCRS and Export Development Canada, one of those offices included a strategic one in Ottawa, where MDA's management team could learn how to lobby at the government and gain better access to procurement officers at the DND and DSS.[53]

Friends in the Canadian government had already delivered to MDA its first prime contract in the US government procurement system, with the automated weather distribution system (AWDS) project foreshadowing more such work to come if MDA could learn how to sell its expertise in what one employee dubbed the firm's "golden triangle" of systems engineering, software engineering, and project management.[54] The Systems Division's five-year plan also urged a greater focus on marketing if investors and employees alike hoped to survive the winds of change. MDA also needed to fine-tune its methods for technology transfer if the company's stakeholders were to profit from internal research and development. And the firm needed to turn its systems into more dynamic profit spinners if the company wanted to maintain its place in the competitive world of digitization. On the one hand, Pitts had lost the struggle. On the other, and despite Friedmann's argument that "Hamilton built the Systems Division from scratch in 1982 to $25 million by 1987, turning a profit every year," Pitts had created the context for MDA to mature from a skunk-works operation into a profit-oriented business focused squarely on the expansion of surveillance capitalism. With Hamilton supervising its development, Systems then started to maximize on MDA's core capabilities by incorporating MacDonald's original vision and extending it to secure profits in new business areas created within the infrastructure that grew out of Pitts's disciplinary efforts during the 1980s.[55]

Still, two important issues lingered. Throughout its second misadventure in product development, MDA had lost its technological and hence competitive edge as it focused on products at the expense of systems research and development. Between 1984 and 1988, the company's gross revenues expanded from $21.3 million to $63.4 million ($15.7 in the domestic market and $47.7 in exports). Its staff also increased from 294 to 609, while common shareholder equity climbed from $2.5 million to $9.0 million. But rising labour costs and soaring inflation in Canada, when coupled to new global competitors and emerging technologies during the late 1980s, also compelled more people at MDA to recognize that other firms (including Microsoft) had beaten them in the race to profit from new technology. Board members therefore concluded that MDA needed to create a leaner operation and better marketing strategy to remain viable. At the same time, the investors' dilemma remained: Pitts and his associates, those at Ventures West, and a host of employees past and present wanted to liquidate their holdings in MDA.[56] As chapter 7 reveals, those challenges created another pivotal moment in the company's history.

7

"One Amorphous Mass"

Systems Integration, Strategic Planning, and the Search for Liquidity, 1988–1993

Between 1987 and 1988, members of the Systems Division expanded MDA's horizons by generating banner profits, despite the firm's product losses. With mounting political, environmental, and economic pressures to reduce military spending in Canada and elsewhere, the Systems management team assessed trends, set crucial goals, and began to target areas removed from but still essential to the weapons business, particularly in geographical information and aviation systems, as well as space and defence. Having completed the company's first major projects for the European Space Agency and United States Air Force during 1987, MDA quickly won three systems integration contracts from Italy, Spain, and Canada, and received a second contract to work on ground station components for ESA's ERS-1 satellite. During 1988, the Meridian system won an industrial research award for technological innovation in geocoded image correction. Combining that expertise with synthetic aperture radar, the Systems Division bid on and won contracts to supply systems for Canada's Atmospheric Environment Service as the foundation for all future meteorological applications with Canada's Department of National Defence. The division additionally won a SAR-based contract with the Republic of Korea, which promised to enhance MDA's (and Canada's) position in Asian markets. In the United States, the firm received an opportunity to work with Lockheed on a satellite data acquisition system for the US Navy Tactical Environment Support Service. MDA's performance at the automated weather distribution system acceptance tests in Florida also led to additional USAF contracts to enhance the system and provide user training to Air Force personnel.[1]

On the strength of Systems' abilities to profit from Canada's connections to ESA and Reagan's strategic defence initiatives, MDA's board authorized the five-year plan during 1988. Bob Hamilton and his Systems management team then began implementation. With product divisions disassembling and ground station sales declining as MDA began to work on new contracts in aviation as well as space and defence, many of the firm's government allies, shareholders, and employees began to argue that the Systems Division had articulated, perhaps for the first time in the company's history, the core business expertise MDA had begun to develop after Dave Sloan first walked into John MacDonald's office in 1971. Neither a remote sensing nor a product company, MDA had evolved into a systems integrator employing software development and off-the-shelf hardware to serve the interests of governmental entities worldwide. From that moment forward, and with engineering processes reduced to writing, the company came together under a vision that finally married Pitts's profit-oriented focus to MacDonald's technical concepts, which laid the foundations for Dan Friedmann's ascent within the firm. Although more than five years later than expected, that vision also provided a chance for many of MDA's investors to liquidate their holdings. MDA travelled a difficult road as the firm adjusted to the realities of another economic downturn, changing government priorities, and the five-year plan's painful restructuring. But as they gained experience in the vagaries of defence contracting and an increasingly deregulated global economy, people at MDA settled into their roles as systems integrators for the expansion of surveillance capitalism and a military-industrial-academic complex centred on the United States.[2]

In his work on the globalization of surveillance, Armand Mattelart has observed that the trend toward increased budgets for defence surfaced amid increased funding for new network technologies and the commercialization of space during the Margaret Thatcher–Ronald Reagan era. Thatcher, Reagan, and their allies had already argued that spending on the social safety nets that emerged in the 1930s and expanded through the 1970s had created the recessionary period of the early 1980s. Decreased social spending and a more deregulated economy to protect capital's interests, they argued, would spur recovery and power further economic growth. Following George H.W. Bush's ascendancy to the presidency of the United States in January 1989, the Thatcher-Reagan strategy then flowered with the fall of the Berlin Wall on 9 November 1989, the Persian Gulf War from 16 January through 6 April 1991, and the formal dissolution of the USSR on 26 December 1991. Into the power void of a one-world order, the US government, whether dominated by Republicans or Democrats, developed strategies to maintain American hegemony. US policymakers promoted further deregulation, increased efforts to privatize the public sphere, implemented austerity programs, and supported initiatives emphasizing American dominance of global information and the techno-security systems associated with C4ISR (Command, Control, Communications, Computing, Intelligence, Surveillance, and Reconnaissance).[3]

Canadian reactions to Reagan's paradigm furthered MDA's focus on procurement contracting between 1988 and 1993. By the early 1980s, many members of the Canadian establishment embraced Margaret Thatcher's famous motto, "There Is No Alternative" (TINA) to economic liberalism, a slogan that underpinned a belief that modern societies can survive only through free markets, free trade, and globalization of the capitalist ethos. A devoted Thatcherite, Reagan employed the same ideological framework to justify his "trickle down" approach to the economy and the burgeoning deficits his Strategic Defense Initiative engendered during his two terms in office (1980–88). Heterodox development economist Ha-Joon Chang has demonstrated that TINA provided more than an effective catchphrase for neoliberalism, however; it allowed its adherents to engage the world in collective historical amnesia. Global elites in government, business, and academia rewrote history, crafting a free market mythology that erased the ways in which the United Kingdom and then the United States had achieved their hegemony: through tariffs and other protectionist policies. Once the United Kingdom and United States could stand on their own, members of each country's status quo then called for military expansion to protect their interests and free trade agreements with less-developed regions, in a strategy Chang has described as a "kicking away the ladder" development strategy.[4]

As former colonial subjects of the British Empire, Canadian policymakers might have seen the ladder falling away from them after World War II, but they did not. Instead of protecting their infant industries as a way to overcome their dependence on natural resources and American capital, they looked to the United States and the OECD for Canada's policy framework. In an effort to maintain political sovereignty while simultaneously seeking greater entrance into export markets, particularly in government defence procurement, Prime Minister Mulroney and his PC government thus welcomed the possibility of a free trade agreement with the United States. Reaching a final agreement on 4 October 1987, Mulroney and Reagan made the Canada-US Free Trade Agreement (CUFTA) official on 2 January 1988. Thereafter, members of the Canadian government, whether Conservative or Liberal, planned to enter into agreements with less-developed nations so that Canada could maintain its place as a member of the G7 core.[5]

Bruce Smardon has linked the CUFTA to the framework established by the Glassco Commission during the 1960s, but he also suggests that Canadians had many chances to change course, particularly during the 1970s and early 1980s, when the Liberals had enough power to establish the NEP, social movements emerged to oppose economic liberalization, and Trudeau had several important dissenters in his Cabinet (including Herb Gray, who took charge of the Foreign Investment Review Agency). "What the opposition to the trade deal failed to realize," however, was that CUFTA "was only one manifestation of a deeper and longer-term pattern in which the context of social forces had precluded the formulation of meaningful federal policies to deal with Canada's dependent position vis-à-vis the United States," Smardon argued. After Thatcher articulated TINA, Canadian policymakers no longer bothered to debate "a state-led approach to restoring economic growth and controlling prices." With Trudeau's Liberals moving "decisively to rebuild ties with Canadian capitalists as the key means of getting out of the crisis" of the recession, Canadian politicians "followed a pattern that existed more generally in the Western capitalist world, in which the way forward was defined in terms of a closer articulation of the actions of the state with the interests of business." Following their election in 1984, Mulroney's Conservatives merely accelerated those trends. With dissenters focused on little more than workers' immediate concerns about potential job losses and the protection of "existing Canadian cultural capital," they watered down "more radical proposals of change in order to gain greater support from private capital more generally." Unfortunately, Smardon emphasized, "greater autonomy from the United States could be gained only through explicit forms of anti-capitalist mobilization that stressed the need for more democratically based institutions of finance and investment in the Canadian economy," but that failed to happen.[6]

By 1988, if few Canadians perceived the CUFTA's connection to the Glassco Commission, fewer still could identify Glassco's genesis in World War II and the military-industrial agreements that had laid the foundations for Canada's dependence on the United States. Indeed, as anti-capitalist sentiments waned in Canada, even those who could see through the cloud cover and darkness, including MDA's technology workers, had little interest in opposing free trade. At MDA, the CUFTA promised more work on *Radarsat*, the first remote-sensing satellite designed and built in Canada, the International Space Station, other exciting C4ISR projects, and especially the automated weather distribution systems MDA planned to install across the US Air Force's global network. The follow-on

AWDS contract provided the first test of MDA's new five-year plan; however, ultimately, it also challenged MDA's assumptions about how the CUFTA might work.[7]

"THE BIGGEST MARKET IN THE WORLD": MDA'S HUMILIATING LESSON IN MILITARY FREE TRADE

With AWDS forming the heart of MDA's new strategic plan, people throughout the firm foresaw a rosy future as 1988 dawned. MDA had served as prime contractor on the AWDS design and testing phase of the multistage program for the USAF, and its personnel had learned much about American military specifications. MDA's expectant staff thus looked forward to winning the production contract that would allow them to install approximately 160 AWDS at American military bases across the world. Although members of the MDA team conceded that they remained woefully inexperienced in American military operations, many of them also failed to understand that Trudeau's original agreement with Reagan provided no guarantees about the role that Canada might play in future work for the USAF or any other branch of the US government. Indeed, when officials in Canada and the United States negotiated the deal that ultimately allowed MDA to receive its first opportunity to lead a US defence procurement project, they agreed that Canadians could serve as prime contractors on the design and testing phase, but that more experienced American firms would have to take charge of any AWDS installations that followed. Members of MDA therefore had to switch roles with Harris.[8]

Emboldened by their initial AWDS success, MDA's employees and shareholders worried little about their role reversal with Harris; instead, they confidently boasted that their acceptance test and follow-on contracts virtually guaranteed the team's production contract win. *The Wednesday Report: Canada's Defence News Bulletin* seemed to agree with MDA's assessment. Reporting on the firm just two months after the CUFTA went into effect, the *Wednesday Report* argued that MDA had gained sufficient experience to undertake much more defence-related work. The firm had partnered with others to conduct "the initial feasibility studies on the DND's Space-Based Radar (SBR) project," worked with "imaging sonars for mine countermeasures (MCM) for Defence Research Establishment Pacific," and "won a $40 million development contract for the U.S. Air Force for the Weather Distribution System (AWDS)," the *Report* noted. With defence-related work reaching "about 25 per cent of MacDonald Dettwiler's business over the past few years," MDA's management team expected "the defence-related part of our business to grow substantially," one new business area manager predicted. "I could see it grow to being 50 per cent of our business over the next three or four years," he told the *Wednesday* reporter. Although the naval "community in the world is really small," he conceded, MDA hoped "to establish its bonafides into future mine countermeasures worldwide."[9]

Anticipating an AWDS production contract worth approximately US$63 million (or just over US$128 million in 2016), as well as more defence-related work, MDA's board members authorized a plan to raise equity capital through the sale of the EOP Division. They also approved expenditures on a new facility designed to the company's specifications, one that could house all the facilities and new staff members that a swelling number of anticipated procurement contracts for AWDS, *Radarsat*, the ISS, and other projects would require. As construction on the new building began during 1988, the *Province* reported that MDA's "classy" new "home," a $16 million, 180,000-square-foot facility to "house 525 corporate office, research, and engineering staff," promised to improve the company's efficiencies as well as entice potential investors.[10]

Unfortunately for its expectant staff and investors, just two months prior to MDA's scheduled move to its new facility during January 1989, members of the AWDS team received a call that few had anticipated: their team had lost the AWDS production contract to install AWDS systems across the USAF global network. "We had a misfortune in the follow-up," John MacDonald argued, "and of course this was all aided and abetted by the Canadian government who kind of arranged all this in the first place, had run the competition, and expected us to go and get the production contract and make them all into heroes," he groused. Additionally, "the Americans really pulled a fast one" on MDA, MacDonald stressed. "Instead of it just being a contract to supply the system, it became a contract to supply and operate the system."[11]

Although many people at MDA agreed with MacDonald's assessment, one new senior manager crafted a little more nuance into the narrative. "I think what left people incredulous was the fact that we got beaten by orders of magnitude on the pricing," Bob Wallis argued. "We were running this race, thinking that we had a chance to win, and thinking that we had a good chance to win, and we didn't have any knowledge at all that there was some other runner out there, so far ahead of us, that we could never hope to catch them." Rather than the United States pulling "a fast one," Wallis allowed, "it was our complete lack of awareness of the whole procurement process and exactly where [MDA stood] in the US" that sunk the bid. Moreover, he noted, MDA needed the win more than Harris did, so while the loss devastated people at MDA, the American firm's personnel took it in stride. People at Harris also knew that other contractors with better technologies as well as more experience in operations and maintenance for the USAF could outbid the Harris-MDA team. When asked what valuable lessons MDA learned from the experience, Wallis noted that the firm learned all too little. "We went back into" the US market "again, and did exactly the same thing two or three years later. We bid on a large FAA [Federal Aviation Administration] procurement in the United States. We spent a lot of money, and once again, we were seriously underbid. After those two thrashings," MDA finally decided "to pull out" and "learn the process," he argued, "but we had to do it once again to convince ourselves" that the United States "is the biggest market in the world," with many more competitors, lobbyists, and insiders influencing who might win the country's lucrative defence procurement contracts.[12]

Beyond their naïveté about how US defence procurement worked, people at MDA neglected to allocate sufficient funds for a market study and assumed that the technological elegance of their initial design would prevail, no matter the procurement contract's specifications. Although MDA had delivered two systems and won a contract to support those systems, when the USAF announced its request for proposals (RFPs) for the phase two work, it articulated the need for bidders who could accommodate 100 such systems. Wedded to their original mini-computer architecture, MDA's engineers never bothered to track the shift taking place from the use of mainframe computers to distributive networks. Indeed, as a critical factor in the follow-on contract, the USAF cited the military's expanding need to offer new, lower-cost, microcomputer solutions for the integrated systems they planned to install worldwide. But that was not the only specification people at MDA failed to see or chose to ignore.[13]

The USAF's initial RFP for AWDS had clearly stated that the multi-phase project would include a $40 million, ten-year maintenance subcontract on each operational site. Neither MDA nor Harris had this expertise. Harris had plentiful experience in US defence procurement, including work to provide tracking and other data services for NASA, large Wall Street banking houses, and a host of American companies, agencies, and universities tied to the military-industrial-academic complex. But Harris had no strategic advantage vis-à-vis procurement contractor ConTel Corporation, the largest US independent telephone company prior to the deregulation of the US telecommunications industry in 1996. By the second half of the

1980s, ConTel had acquired a number of US government-preferred computer system and software companies as well as cellular communications and satellite data network providers. Prior to the competition for the AWDS phase two project, ConTel had also received a significant operations contract for the USAF. Understanding the importance of networked communications on USAF bases, ConTel proposed a microcomputer solution rather than what one engineer described as MDA's "dinosaur" mainframe architecture. ConTel thus won the production contract as well as received a maintenance contract that enlarged the scope of the project, in work ultimately worth US$103 million. As they reflected on ConTel's "win" and their "loss," a dejected group of employees and investors finally had to admit that MDA "couldn't compete," John MacDonald recalled. Failing to "track the technology shift" additionally signalled that if MDA wanted to win future defence procurement contracts in the United States and elsewhere, the company needed to invest in a computer infrastructure "based on micros," he stressed.[14]

Caught off-guard by their gaffe, MDA's staff found themselves with neither contract, as well as the daunting challenges of retooling their operations for microcomputers and finding ways to fill their new building with projects that could make up for the financial loss and professional humiliation. "We were so sure that we were going to get that contract," one employee recalled, "that the letdown and disbelief were just tremendous. We've won and lost contracts over the years," she observed, but AWDS "was the one that really sort of devastated everybody, because" people throughout the firm "thought they had it." Still, she conceded, "it was a big US contract, and it's not easy to win a US government contract."[15] Such rationalizations did little to console the AWDS production proposal writing team who had taken on the task as a "labour of love," Dave Caddey, MDA's first military hire and AWDS manager recalled. "That's all we did, day and night," for nearly a year. "We really thought we were going to win" but "we got hosed. We got crushed. Everybody went to the end," and the USAF "picked the three lowest bidders. So, all this talk about price realism didn't make a lot of difference in the end," he stressed. For Caddey and others, "it was one unbelievable shock," because "we already had the project started, had the team already going, and had spent about $700,000 on the pursuit. It was a massive pursuit budget," he emphasized. "We wanted to book that business and we missed it by a mile, so it was pretty embarrassing, a pretty humbling experience."[16]

Although the March 1989 creation of the CSA promised to provide work with SPAR, the AWDS defeat revealed that MDA lacked the experience·

to serve as a prime contractor within the US government procurement system, that the "great open market to the south" would remain closed to the company unless and until MDA could assert its comparative advantage to customers involved in the evolution of the security state. Additionally, people at MDA had to admit that they "weren't really prepared to go into the US at that time. It's very competitive," one employee argued. "There are a lot of entrenched people already there, who know the customers better, and we don't bring a lot of uniqueness to the US." On the other hand," he reasoned, "when we compete with US people abroad, we seem to have no problem with them. The US ability to sell internationally is not very good," he asserted. Reflecting perceptions of Canada's place in the world, he also argued that Americans "are far too arrogant. They don't understand other people's cultures. They're always trying to impose their ways on others, whereas we are a lot more willing to understand their culture." Moreover, he stressed, "Canada's not a colonial power and we're a lot more trusted internationally."[17] Still, as Pitts cautioned the dejected AWDS team, as the most powerful nation in the world and Canada's closest and most significant trading partner, the United States had the upper hand. "We continued to blunt our pick a few times, to try to penetrate the US market," Pitts allowed, but he also argued that if people at MDA wanted to succeed in rather than merely complain about the continental relationship, they had to learn more about low-bid contracting and what it might take to "win" in the "bloody red oceans" of global competition.[18]

The effort expended on AWDS also put the company in a tenuous financial position again, for Pitts had not yet completed the sale of the EOP Division when the AWDS news arrived. Aviation Systems had booked an important job to build a national aeronautics information processing system (NAIPS) for the Australian Civil Aviation Authority, but with MDA "wedded to" an obsolete "design," their NAIPS would soon confront competition from newer technologies. Indeed, some competitors had already appeared in remote sensing, Pitts noted, which meant that for the first time MDA had lost its competitive edge within its core area of expertise. For most in the firm, MDA's new high-tech office felt empty without cutting-edge computers and the expansionist promises provided by the AWDS production contract. Making matters worse, members of Aviation Systems needed more development funds for the Australian project and MDA required marketing resources to foster new relationships. "We thought we could save money by staying with the same hardware," MacDonald explained, but the AWDS loss revealed how much that decision had cost.[19]

Just one year before, Expo '88 had highlighted the promise of Vancouver, including its expanding number of technology firms linked to MDA, particularly CREO, the digital printing company formed by former employees Dan Gelbart and Ken Spencer. Behind Expo's glitter lay several significant challenges, however; Canada's relative labour costs had risen throughout the 1980s, the country's inflation had edged up toward uncomfortably high rates, and other countries (the United States, in particular) had become more cost-competitive through the off-shoring of production facilities as well as wage suppression as union bargaining power declined. To meet such challenges, Canadian investors sent their funds abroad rather than put their money into Canadian-owned firms, particularly risky high-tech ventures such as MDA, a company with withering product divisions, obsolete technology, declining revenues in remote sensing, and, by implication, no corporate strategy. Staggering in the midst of such competitive pressures, the Systems Division began to lose important contracts as well, including those for ground station work.[20]

Bob Hamilton and Dan Friedmann convinced Pitts that MDA needed to focus on information processing and reconnaissance as the business areas the company most needed to pursue if it wanted to remain in business following the AWDS fiasco. Their five-year plan had already recommended aviation systems as well as space and defence markets as the best way to expand the company's business and reduce its risks in remote sensing. As they drew on the company's seventeen years in remote sensing and the AWDS blunder, however, they increasingly stressed the need to link MDA's expertise with the longer-term development and integration of systems for C4ISR and the techno-security state. Hamilton and Friedmann also cast their gaze toward potential markets in air traffic management, where MDA's expertise in FOCUS, AWDS, and meteorological systems had already provided the NAIPS opportunity. With board approval to expend MDA's limited resources in these areas, the firm thus began development on airspace management and flight operations systems for global civil aviation authorities and departments of defence.[21]

With the $13 million NAIPS project signalling MDA's entrance into contracting work for the larger Five Eyes intelligence club and its security collaborators in the United States, United Kingdom, Canada, Australia, and New Zealand, the Canadian government provided MDA with three significant defence-related contracts to develop target detection, communications, signal processing, and electronic countermeasures systems. Those contracts saved MDA in the near term and promised further work, if MDA could harness its expertise for the effort. Employing the formula that had pushed the firm from ground stations to synthetic aperture radar and image analysis work, "We took our expertise in geocoding, our software expertise out of AWDS, and some of our airborne radar expertise, and all that infusion went into space and defence," Friedmann noted, so that MDA could develop "a number of businesses" focused on radar and sonar surveillance as well as control and logistics systems. Still, he conceded, before the company could profit and investors could realize their return, MDA needed to restructure its overhead. Anxious to execute a company overhaul, Friedmann lobbied for and received the restructuring job that lowered MDA's prices and made the firm attractive to investors.[22]

"OUR PRICE WAS TOO HIGH":
DAN FRIEDMANN AND THE SYSTEMS RESTRUCTURING PLAN

Born in Chile on 19 September 1956 and raised in Vancouver, Daniel (Dan) Friedmann arrived at MDA during the late 1970s. His father had prospered by turning his attention from engineering to business, ultimately emerging as a CEO of an international coal mining company. Young Friedmann shared his father's inclinations and ambitions. Graduating from UBC with a degree in engineering and physics during 1979, Friedmann swiftly applied for a position with MDA. An excellent engineer, Friedmann ascended the ranks on the mathematical formulas he developed for the company's geocoded image correction system. He also made it clear that he had ambitions beyond the technical realm. When asked at his first performance review, "What are your career goals?" Friedmann matter-of-factly replied, "I want to become president of MDA." Despite his executive dreams, however, Friedmann also wanted to showcase his technological achievements; thus, he published his GICS formulas in scientific circles, a decision that put his intellectual capital and MDA's proprietary knowledge at risk. Castigating the young engineer, Bob Hamilton told Friedmann that profiting from his engineering expertise would depend upon carefully guarding rather than sharing his findings, particularly if he wanted to move into management. Friedmann admitted that he absolutely wanted an executive position rather than an engineering job at MDA, for the former connoted money, power, and influence. Satisfied that Friedmann understood what future actions might mean to his career, Hamilton decided to take a chance on the young engineer. After all, he reasoned, Friedmann had demonstrated his abilities as a self-promoter, a quality Hamilton thought he could harness to market the Systems vision.[23]

Mentoring Friedmann from 1979 to 1986, Hamilton ultimately promoted his protegé from Systems engineering research jobs to the manager of business development. Hamilton also encouraged the firm to underwrite Friedmann's graduate education. As he understudied Hamilton and completed his master's degree in engineering physics, Friedmann realized that he shared Hamilton's vision about MDA's future: that its profit potential resided squarely in the expansion of surveillance systems linked to space and defence. Thus, Friedmann lobbied for and received the chance to market the strategic five-year plan. Together, Hamilton and Friedmann plotted the strategy, Friedmann analyzed markets, and Pitts watched carefully. When illness forced Hamilton to resign during 1989, Pitts took Hamilton's protegé under his wing, and Friedmann seized the opportunity to ascend. In June 1989, Pitts then promoted Friedmann to company vice-president and general manager of Systems. Friedmann's elevated stature came with his first important executive task: the restructuring of the firm into a one-division operation, an assignment that gave the up-and-comer an opportunity to prove his worth to Pitts, the company's investors, and MDA as a whole.[24]

Looking for areas where MDA could cut costs, Friedmann first turned toward corporate overhead. Between 1982 and 1988, the company had created a large infrastructure to support its three product divisions. With MDA refocused as a systems integrator by 1989, Friedmann argued that the company no longer required many of its administrative services. During October 1989, on a day employees called "Black Thursday," Friedmann lowered the boom, first on MDA's Management Information Systems department, which, under Pitts's direction, had outstripped the company's Research and Development section in size and cost. After he inflicted deep cuts to that department, Friedmann pruned corporate public relations and accounting. While many MDA employees considered it a drastic, even draconian measure, Friedmann argued that the company had no choice. "It made a lot of people unhappy, and in fact we had some layoffs for the first time" in the company's history, Friedmann remembered, but cuts took place "not in engineering, but overhead. The overhead we were carrying would have forced us out of business. We had to drop our prices," he stressed, "which we did first, because we just were not getting any business. We halved our overhead costs, and that allowed us to pass on about 5 to 10 per cent discounts to customers. Previous to that," he argued, "we had analyzed the losses, the win ratio, and it had dropped to an unacceptable level. If it drops too low," he explained, "you basically go out of business, because you don't have enough marketing money to do it. And the number one reason it had dropped to an unacceptable level was that our price was too high."[25]

After wielding his axe on the company's corporate division, Friedmann transferred MDA's remaining staff into three business areas: Geographical Information Systems (Geo-Info), Aviation Systems, and Space and Defence. The company also created a military-inspired Integrated Logistic Services (ILS) department to pool engineering resources, train customers, and provide support services to the firm and its clients. During December 1989, as the newly established CSA set up its headquarters in Longueuil, Quebec, to coordinate the country's civil and space-related policies and programs, MDA's board members authorized a plan to operate EOP as profitably as possible while Pitts continued to seek a buyer. Friedmann closed the division's international sales offices and folded Airborne Radar into the Geo-Info business area. Two months later, Pitts promoted Friedmann to executive vice-president, putting him in charge of the company's operations and long-term strategic plan. Friedmann then assembled a young and aggressive management team, which included long-term employees who had proven their allegiance to Systems as well as recent hires with military and business backgrounds. MDA's new team "became more aggressive," one manager recalled, "because the world" became "more aggressive."[26]

Happily for MDA's new management team, Pitts also found a buyer for the Electro-Optical Products Division: California's Cymbolic Sciences Inc. By selling EOP to Cymbolic at its 1990 book value of $5.5 million just one year after the Berlin Wall fell and as the larger economy tipped into another recession, MDA gained a much-needed capital injection at precisely the right time. Cymbolic assumed MDA's employee obligations and outstanding repayments on the FIRE's development work and guaranteed preferential pricing on the remote sensing FIRE, which gave MDA continuing access to the technology it needed for systems integration projects. EOP's departure reduced MDA's staff by an additional 15 per cent, but Friedmann argued that the division's sale allowed MDA to apply employee skills to areas the company knew best, and where several key contracts provided the opportunity to standardize the company's expertise so that each new sale no longer represented a customized, one-off system.[27]

One former employee likened Friedmann's aggressive management style and efficiency measures to the American military, and the creation of the ILS pooling department a way "to supply his army." Whereas Pitts had regularized and categorized workers, Friedmann determined to create "one amorphous mass," where the "discipline of the work package" and "compartmentalization" of former teams triumphed at "the expense of innovation."[28] Although many who aspired to management roles had accepted Pitts's framework, one sixteen-year-employee Friedmann had recruited to serve as a management "general" reflected the mood of many long-time MDA employees following Friedmann's elevation within the firm. "I would hate to start at MDA now," he argued, for "you end up in this 250- or 300[-person] engineering pool, and to find your way out of that is a formidable task."[29] According to another senior manager, many engineers also began to see their professional status waning in the face of cuts and the company's reorganization. "There used to be a lot more" innovation and professional pride, he argued. "Now it's a job more than a vocation." Although the new management team selected several people "in a senior engineering group" to focus on innovation, most MDA employees increasingly found themselves "paid to make sure their work packages [came] in on time and on budget," he stressed.[30]

Painful as restructuring seemed to MDA's employees, particularly those displaced by it, the leaner organization paid off in operational terms. Between 1990 and 1991, gross order backlogs increased from $47.5 million to $96.3 million. Between 1990 and 1993, MDA's staff members also climbed from 455 to 777, and gross revenues nearly doubled from $46.8 million to $85.2 million. One senior manager therefore stressed, "We're big enough now that we're attracting attention, there are a lot of predators out there," and "we have to work really, really hard to protect ourselves," with people at MDA "feeling a lot more pressure to be more efficient. We had to change, because the world's changing." With the fall of the Soviet Union during 1991, he noted, MDA faced new competitors who planned to launch satellites of their own, so that they too could protect their own sovereign interests and challenge the hegemony of the one-world order the United States had achieved and planned to maintain through its powerful military-industrial complex, trade agreements, and surveillance-security networks. But new competitors also provided opportunities for MDA to harvest its technologies and regain market share.[31]

"NO LONGER SO EXCEPTIONAL":
HARVESTING TECHNOLOGIES TO GAIN MARKET SHARE

By 1991, sufficient contract wins allowed Friedmann, Pitts, and MDA's board members to turn their attention to plowing revenue back into technologies for use in future engineering systems work rather than manufacturing dreams. Two products within the company's Research and

Development department enticed MDA's management team and members of the board for a time; however, in the end, both groups decided to keep those technologies as trade secrets, ones the company could employ in future systems design work. In another instance, MDA spun off a software package developed to recalculate images using the concept of spreadsheets. Dubbed "Y_0" to create "why not?" scenarios, MDA's personal-computer-based technology reduced the time necessary for image calculation testing. Rather than develop it, MDA's legal team negotiated a licensing agreement with David Kauffman, one of the company's former marketing employees. Kauffman then formed a company called FACET Technologies. MDA's first profitable technology transfer spinoff, FACET Technologies marketed the Y_0 product for use in remote sensing and other applications. Although the lure of product development continued to surface throughout MDA's business areas, the firm's senior managers had their marching orders from Friedmann: in the future, they would encourage employees to pursue licensing options and patent protection applications for their technologies rather than develop them internally.[32]

By capitalizing on its expertise and employing new technologies, MDA regained its dominance in the ground station market, which allowed the firm to bid on and win two contracts to build national remote sensing centres for Indonesia and Taiwan. On the strength of those two contracts, Friedmann orchestrated a generalized ground station upgrade program (GSUP), and merged the meteorological systems business area with Geo-Info to improve marketing efforts in the emerging geographical information systems market. By 1991, with SAR innovations in digital elevation model extraction and artificial vision systems realized, MDA received a contract from the European Space Agency to build ESA's Central User Service system, and MDA won a contract from Brazil to build a SAR processor for that country's ground station. Following the Tiananmen Square protests of 1989, MDA also secured work from China to upgrade a ground station to receive data from *Landsat-6*, *ERS-1*, and Japan's new *JERS-1* satellite.[33]

New work for developing nations posed challenges for MDA, but as its employees adjusted to the firm's maturing marketing focus, they learned how to lobby members of government more effectively, including Canada's policymakers. In post–Tiananmen Square China, for example, Pitts argued, "We had a problem, because we got the order, and then we couldn't get an export permit" because members of the federal government "said, 'You can't sell that stuff to the Chinese!'" As a result, Pitts employed MDA's expanding expertise as political leverage. Reminding government officials that such work could enhance Canada's presence in Asia, Pitts "managed to get enough political support in Canada to get the thing through." The federal government then worked to ensure that MDA booked all available ground station contracts, which allowed the firm to provide nine more generalized upgrades across the world. Realizing that they had an old technology on their hands, MDA's management team also began an aggressive campaign to harvest GSUP, selling it off at low prices to regain MDA's market share.[34]

In Aviation Systems, MDA's consolidation of FOCUS, AWDS, and meteorological systems, as well as work on Australia's NAIPS, led to a $68 million contract with Transport Canada to build the Canadian Automated Air Traffic System. As part of a teaming arrangement with Hughes Canada, the 1991 CAATS contract gave MDA an additional connection to the global airspace management market. According to John Bennett, MDA's SAR and IRIS champion, that contract also gave MDA "some security." As the company's then largest "win" and "71 per cent of the company's bookings in 1991," CAATS represented a safer way to diversify, Bennett argued. Large government contracts such as CAATS, "which go on for five or more years, when there's so much revenue per year – almost like bread and butter," gave MDA "a security base" as well as "diversification," Bennett stressed, "so that if the ground station business turns down one year, air traffic may pick up, and so on," he explained.[35]

Contracts emerged in Space and Defence as well, with MDA receiving an $18 million contract to design the operations and management control software for the Canadian Space Station Program, a multi-year project promising to give the firm some of the "bread and butter" it required to nurture other areas. Part of the ISS's Freedom project, Canada agreed to contribute *Canadarm-2* for the mobile servicing system. As the builder of *Canadarm-1*, SPAR acquired the prime contract, thereafter awarding to MDA the control software subcontract. According to many at MDA, work on *Canadarm-2* gave MDA the recognition its founders and employees had long coveted in Canada: "Suddenly we were a major subcontractor," Bennett argued.[36] Another engineering manager observed that the ISS allowed SPAR and MDA, "despite earlier and ongoing difficulties," to "develop accords in specific areas."[37] Philip Lapp confirmed that "one of those accords involved *Radarsat-1*, in which SPAR and MDA agreed that MDA would do the ground segments and SPAR would do the space segments."[38] During 1987, SPAR had received the $725 million prime contract for *Radarsat-1*, thereafter awarding several major subcontracts to MDA, Ottawa's Canadian Astronautics Ltd, and Saskatoon's SED Systems as part of the

CSA's desire to spread work across the nation. MDA also purchased a 30 per cent interest in Radarsat International Inc., a venture created in 1989 by SPAR and its subcontractors to process, market, and distribute data from the CSA's *Radarsat* satellites. By 1991, with *Radarsat-1* scheduled for launch in 1995 and an expanded program on the horizon, MDA's *Radarsat* subcontracts increased the company's prestige as well as its employees' confidence. Indeed, as Larry Morley, MDA's long-time patron at the Centre for Remote Sensing argued, "MDA became the definitive designers of SAR processors, and the basis of *Radarsat.*"[39]

Until the early 1990s, most had equated Earth observation with a "spacecraft orbiting the Earth and making images," John MacDonald argued. The uninitiated believed "there's a ground station and a ground segment necessary to not make the spacecraft lonely, or something like that," but "it's becoming an information business, and the spacecraft is incidental," MacDonald stressed. Thus, "we are trying to position ourselves to assume a leadership position" as "the best company in the world in developing infrastructure to feed information to people who need it out of these types of spacecraft. It is our view that we can become a prime contractor for those systems and do subcontracting to the space people" like SPAR, he opined, "which is kind of a role reversal that SPAR has trouble getting its head around."[40] Moving from a technology development company to a systems engineering and integration firm could not guarantee MDA's long-term future, but Pitts's work discipline and Friedmann's systems integration plan allowed MDA to bid "on larger contracts. We're in a different league now than we were" in the 1980s, one investor noted.[41]

Looking at those changes from another angle, one engineer argued, "Until recently, the company relied on technology and capability developed in the early days, and I feel for the last say five to ten years, it has almost been coasting on its reputation and the talent and the technology that was developed" through the mid-1980s. "The company has to begin to rely on something else, for it's no longer so exceptional technically that our technology will carry the day. Maybe that day's gone whereby technology will carry the day for anyone," he noted, but "the world is no longer enamoured with high-technology, and doesn't buy it for its own sake. They buy technology now because it will do something and save them money," he mused.[42] No matter the rapidity of change, however, world events had simply pulled MDA into the larger orbit of surveillance capitalism and its unending logic: governments and businesses buy technology because it promises to save money, not because they are simply "enamoured" with it. The trick is how to sell that technology as a necessity to the public and a larger collection of customers and consumers.

Perceiving these realities, Friedmann argued that the decision to prune and pool resources allowed MDA's new business area managers to concentrate on marketing the company's expertise, and the board to authorize funding for research and development as well as an extensive training program. Founding "MDAU" (for MDA University), senior managers planned to "enhance" employee skills, "rationalize" the company's workforce, and "turn software development" into "an engineering discipline in the company as opposed to an art." In keeping with other professional gatekeepers, MDA's new management team additionally stressed that, despite their desire to promote from within, if they failed to find the "right sorts of people" to climb MDA's reorganized corporate ladder, they needed to look to business school graduates, military personnel, and others with deep connections to defence procurement, particularly in the US military-industrial-academic complex.[43] "If we can find somebody here who's got half the skills" in engineering "and can acquire the other half" in government contracting, business, and marketing, "we go that way," Friedmann argued. "We try to bring the new ones in at the bottom, from university, but we've had to hire a lot of senior people because we just can't grow" that class of employee "fast enough."[44]

"I don't think we're the most creative company in the world," one marketing manager noted, but "I still think we deliver value for the money." Furthermore, "You need some bureaucracy when you get bigger," he stressed. "The board and the senior management of the company are interested in controlled growth, and when you choose that kind of path, you're a little more risk-averse than you would be if you were just going for the gusto" technologically. But "you don't go belly-up as easily," even if such a strategy "doesn't really lend itself to the individual, demented scientist who one out of ten times comes up with something that's really useful." As a result, MDA began to "hire all these guys who have this high-achieving track record" at university, "and the first we do is have them write code," telling "them that 'in two years' time you'll be writing code very well.' I don't know why they put up with it," he noted, but MDA "trades on the fact that there's no real opposition in this part of the world. I think we'd have a higher turn-over rate, for instance, if we were in Toronto," he offered.[45] With MDA's local dominance in mind, Friedmann insisted that managers focus their team's energies on generating revenue for the company's future expansion and demands for liquidity among the firm's largest investor groups. Friedmann's long-term focus on merging a disciplined workforce with shareholder value over employee creativity thus began. Although some additionally argued that Friedmann would pursue the company's long-standing "policy to get rid of government contracts" as well, MDA never did. Indeed, Friedmann's consolidation of resources into a one-division firm made government contracts critical to the company's future in aerospace, surveillance, military reconnaissance, and the systems business as a whole. Only MDA's most oblivious employees could have failed to appreciate what such a future implied.[46]

With new business generating profits in all business areas, as well as Friedman controlling costs and the everyday management of MDA, Pitts finally had the opportunity to concentrate on why he had invested in MDA in the first place: working with shareholders to realize their desire for liquidity and a reasonable ROI. Pitts also spent his days at the negotiating table, on acquisitions to expand MDA's expertise in surveillance technologies for governmental entities worldwide. To that end, Friedmann transferred George Cwynar to Ottawa, so that the seasoned systems operations manager could assemble a team to market MDA's systems integrator approach to the federal government, particularly at the Departments of National Defence and Supply and Services, as well as the newly created Canadian Space Agency.[47]

After nearly ten years with MDA rather than the five he had envisioned, Pitts negotiated the firm's first major acquisition during October 1991: 50.1 per cent of Earth Observation Sciences Limited. Headquartered in the United Kingdom, EOSL promised a more efficient way to service MDA's expanding set of European clients. Although MDA employees were proficient in at least twenty-five languages and several dialects, Pitts wanted to secure a strategic position in an English-speaking country with close ties to Canadian ambitions in the United Kingdom and emerging European Union. EOSL thus seemed like a perfect choice to launch such an initiative. Moreover, EOSL worked on space and defence contracts in areas similar to MDA's Geo-Info business. The acquisition therefore removed a significant competitor in an area where MDA had aspirations.[48]

Once he had completed the EOSL acquisition, Pitts turned to Australia, Malaysia, and other strategic locations, where MDA could acquire firms or set up offices to "distribute sales geographically" as well as put employees "closer to the customer" and its "needs and procedures." The strategy included an increased presence of MDA's sales and engineering staff as well as "national value-added agreements" aimed at lowering information and labour costs, hiring locals, and pushing Canada's surveillance expertise and corporate world view into host countries. Embedding offices in key geographic areas also expanded MDA's ability to provide a robust array of services to future customers, particularly governments focused on liberalizing their economies and willing to enter into free trade agreements, foreign investment promotion and protection agreements (FIPAs), and other arrangements with Canada. Between 1990 and 1993, as members of the federal government negotiated the terms of the North American Free Trade Agreement, Canada also entered into FIPAs with Poland, Argentina, and Hungary. Once in force, those FIPAs sought to diversify Canada's (and by extension MDA's) expansionist plans.[49]

"THE USES OF HEAVEN":
ALTERNATIVE VISIONS OF MDA'S FUTURE

During 1991, MDA had the opportunity to expand in several different directions, but the areas the firm ultimately pursued reflected, as they had before, Canadian attempts to remain prominent in the world's power core. During the Persian Gulf War, Canada allied itself with the United States, employing SAR and other space-based technologies to launch the most devastating air assault in history. If the Gulf War served as the technology's introduction to the public, with newscasters and military experts explaining that the United States could not see missiles under cloud cover, scientists and engineers at MDA knew better. Indeed, MDA's work on SAR had made those details abundantly clear fourteen years earlier.[50]

Even if "unseen" by most, MDA's early work on SAR had demonstrated to policymakers that Canada had many of the technological capabilities it would require to ascend in a post-Soviet world dominated by the United States. Thus, just months before Mikhail Gorbachev's resignation as the Communist Party's general secretary on 24 August 1991, Canada renewed its commitment to the United States and NORAD, extending the relationship through 1996. "Although the Cold War" would soon come to an end, one mini-review of the NORAD renewal agreement stressed, "both countries believed it prudent to maintain their cooperation in aerospace surveillance because of the uncertainties of the future." Over the next few years, Canada continued to grapple "with the implications of the still evolving post–Cold War world order and of developments in missile defence," the review argued, but "since the end of the Persian Gulf War, the United States abandoned the Strategic Defense Initiative" in favour of "defence against theatre ballistic missiles like the SCUDs used by Iraq. The deployment of missile defence systems in the late 1990s could have implications for Canada's roles in NORAD, NATO, and the United Nations," the review cautioned. "As the 1994 *White Paper on Defence* states, the issue cannot be ignored, because weapons of mass destruction, including missiles with nuclear, chemical or biological warheads 'already or may soon threaten Canada's friends and allies in Europe and elsewhere,'" the review stressed. As a result, "Canada may want to retain the option of deploying forces to areas where they could face such weaponry."[51]

Time would tell whether Canada would retain its deployment option, but the renewal of NORAD signalled that much of MDA's work would flow from Canada's participation in NATO, the Five Eyes Program, free trade agreements, the OECD, and the GATT (superseded by the World Trade Organization on 1 January 1995). Once done, MDA then sought greater entrance into and visibility among governments focused on military-industrial and surveillance expansion, particularly those allied with the United States and its government procurement contractors. The decision to focus on geographical information and aviation systems as well as space and defence therefore gave MDA the chance to expand, as well as a golden handcuff to American-centred surveillance, even if only a few at the firm recognized or cared about the potential consequences of that decision. But the moment MDA incorporated restructuring into its larger, long-term plan, the firm received important contracts from the Canadian federal government, with most of them linked to the DND.[52]

Just six months prior to the formal dissolution of the Soviet Union in December 1991, the *Economist* had articulated the kinds of work MDA could expect to receive as a government procurement contractor. In a special issue devoted to the emerging "Uses of Heaven" the Gulf War anticipated, the *Economist* produced a special issue on the future commercialization and commodification of outer space. "Earth observation satellites will not make a lot of money," the *Economist* argued, "but they will change the world. The use of space has transformed communications by allowing any point on the map access to every other point," thereby "changing the ways that wars are fought and prevented, by allowing generals to know what is going on and to communicate with forces spread across the globe." At the same time, "the planets have been transformed, by robot explorers and surveyors, distant blurs into strange new worlds," while the "birth and death of stars and galaxies have been watched," along with activities on Earth. And "this activity provides business opportunities." Moreover, with members of the American military "jostling for control in a new arena, Air-force publicists coined the term 'Aerospace' to convince everyone that was the business of those who fly in the air," the *Economist* noted, which helped the public to accept and normalize "aerospace" into the country's "language, perhaps because President Eisenhower's alternative, 'the military-industrial complex' sounded much more sinister." Regardless, "the growth in satellite use (particularly by armed services) made space a respectable business in its own right."[53]

With "space a respectable business" by 1990, "annual sales of space hardware" became "bigger than those of civilian aircraft" in the United States, the *Economist* reported. What was more, after the US government deregulated "its communication satellite (comsat) industry" between 1972 and 1986, that business also "thrived. Afraid to leave high-technology industry entirely in American hands," the European Space Agency "developed its own family of rockets and fostered European industry's capacity for building spacecraft" as well, to "keep up-to-date," the *Economist* reported. With Europeans, the Japanese, and other component suppliers such as those in Canada fully immersing themselves in the ISS and other space-based projects, the "military potential of space" then revealed itself "for the first time and to great effect, in the Gulf War." The *Economist* also stressed that "the third space age, if it lasts as long as the other two" (the first from 1957 to 1972, and the second from 1972 to 1986), "will end in the auspicious year 2001." Thereafter, it prophesied, "space-flight will be, just as it is now, a mundane but indispensable aid to business and to the other concerns of the Earth: one component among many that keep the global culture of technology hanging together." The special issue additionally predicted that "without the spur of competing with the Soviet Union, the old dreams of men in space, and of new frontiers, may be able to wither, leaving a purely pragmatic programme. Such a course has much to commend it," the *Economist* cheered.[54]

Decision-makers in Canada and at MDA took note of these trends and positioned themselves to cash in on the "purely pragmatic" and potentially lucrative uses of outer space, but they also appreciated the challenges the *Economist* described. "Any country that wishes to be able to throw its weight, or warhead missiles, around on a large scale needs to know what the world looks like." As a result, "Military-observation satellites could do well in the 1990s," creating "a perpetual picture of the Earth. It's a powerful, if frightening vision, an inverted panopticon, with the periphery constantly scrutinizing the center from every angle," the *Economist* warned. "The question of how such data should be made available is under discussion. Scientists are eager for the findings to be shared openly," the *Economist* stressed, but "governments will not be happy for everyone to be able to see what they are up to, although they are keen to have the availability for themselves." MDA's work on SAR and other C4ISR projects thus prepared the firm to do business with anyone willing to pay for the privilege of seeing what others might not want them to see. "It is in making satel-lite data useful, not in providing the stuff, that an industry waits to be born," the *Economist* predicted, one that would "make the present use of satellite imagery by town planners, resource specialists, geologists, and a few others (fast-food companies spotting booming suburbs for new out-lets, for example) pale by comparison."[55]

Although military applications promised to generate the kinds of ROI that MDA's shareholders envisioned, mounting environmental concerns prompted several members of the firm to argue that MDA should centre its efforts on the more peaceful "uses of heaven" that the *Economist*'s spe-cial issue had identified, including environmental management systems. During 1983, they noted, the UN had asked Gro Harlem Brundtland, Nor-way's first woman prime minister, to lead a World Commission on Envi-ronment and Development." Seven years later, US Democratic Senator Al Gore Jr presided over a three-day conference where legislators represent-ing forty-two countries proposed the creation of a "global Marshall plan, under which industrial nations would help less developed ones grow eco-nomically while still protecting the environment."[56] Gore failed to win passage of such a plan from the US Congress, but Prime Minister Mul-roney perceived opportunities that meshed with Gore's views. As a result, in 1990 his government published a *Green Plan for Canada*, a roadmap for Canadians who hoped to become "trustees of a unique, beautiful north land." Arguing that Canada could lead the "go green" movement, the plan envisioned the creation of "tools to exercise our 'stewardship' over this nat-ural patrimony."[57] Some people at MDA therefore hoped to develop infor-mation technologies for land, resource, and mapping systems within the Geo-Info business area, where they had secured a contract to develop a land information infrastructure system for the Province of BC. Mulroney's support, they stressed, could lead to similar contracts elsewhere.[58]

As members of the firm absorbed the information provided by the *Econ-omist*, some argued that the possibilities of a worldwide web might provide another opportunity for a future decoupled from military contracts. In her study of the Internet, Janet Abbate has documented the genesis of the World Wide Web from the Advanced Research Project Agency Network (ARPANET), a Cold War project designed to protect the US Department of Defense's communications network, even if under nuclear attack. From project beginnings in 1968, work at universities and research laboratories extended those efforts, and during 1975, the DoD placed ARPANET under the control of the US Defense Communication Agency. By 1983, the agency then separated the network into two areas: one for use by the military, and the other for civilian purposes. When the US government decommissioned ARPANET during 1990, Senator Gore quickly introduced a bill in Congress calling for an "information superhighway," a mission that prompted the Congressional passage of the US High Performance Computing and Communications Act of 1991 and the creation of the National Information Infrastructure. With these developments underway, those interested in what they perceived as more peaceful uses of outer space thus argued that Geo-Info had positioned the firm to cash in on an expanding commercial demand for global geographical information systems once the US government decommissioned the National Science Foundation's NSFNET (which finally took place during 1995).[59]

As the environmental movement spread and opportunities associated with the decommissioning of NSFNET neared, MDA's board members agreed to set up an office in Boulder, Colorado, as an entryway to the world's largest Earth observation market. As a reward for that move, MDA received an important contract from the US Geological Survey's Mapping Division to develop a national archive processing system for *Landsat* data.[60] On the strength of that contract, some members of the firm argued that MDA should expand its efforts into the environmental consciousness movement. Indeed, John MacDonald argued that MDA "located in Boulder" precisely because the remote sensing market had changed "very rapidly" and would "be driven by our requirements to measure the characteristics of the planet for a long time to come from outer space. To do it properly," MacDonald argued, MDA would need to lead the effort to "organize the information," which he perceived as "one of our big opportunities in the future."[61]

Although Pitts and Friedmann agreed about the future of data mining and the opportunities arising from the need to organize information more efficiently, they disagreed with those who hoped to join the environmental movement. MDA "spent a lot of money chasing what I think is a rainbow," Pitts argued. "I'm not suggesting that there isn't money to be made in the environmental business, but it's the guys who are in the clean-up area, and provide filters and chemical contamination reduction schemes" who will make it. "The only thing MDA can offer is observing, from the skies," he suggested, "and most of that can be observed from the ground as well." As board members evaluated all of the opportunities a restructured MDA could pursue, Pitts's assessment of MDA's future prevailed, and the "environmental business" failed to gain traction.[62] MDA's ultimate rejection of the environmental movement had much to do with the federal government's changing priorities as well as the company's embrace of networked technologies and the "aerospace industry." With work underway on the CAATS contract it had secured from the Canadian government, MDA took its expertise "on the road" with yet another "good reference from Canada," Friedmann argued. During 1992, the Australian Civil Aviation Authority then enlarged the scope of its national aeronautics information processing system, awarding much of the work to MDA. The firm's successful NAIPS system also captured the attention of the Norwegian Civil Aviation Authority (NCAA). As members of the first nation outside of the United States to connect to the ARPANET, Norwegian policymakers needed a more sophisticated information processing system. Once Canadian government officials assured them that MDA could do the work, the NCAA provided a contract to MDA, increasing the firm's as well as Canada's visibility in Europe.[63]

Beyond "aerospace," MDA received an opportunity to join a Canadian naval consortium led by Montreal-based SNC-Lavalin (Canada's largest engineering and construction firm following the 1991 merger between Surveyer, Nenniger, and Chenevert Consulting Engineers and its long-time but failing competitor, Lavalin Civil Engineering). As a member of that consortium, MDA thus received a $75 million systems engineering contract from the federal government to provide mine countermeasures technology for the Canadian Maritime Coastal Defence Vessel (MCDV) program. Representing MDA's largest contract award during 1992, MCDV pushed the company's remote sensing techniques into larger sonar applications and promised to "lead to future Canadian Navy contracts." The contract also signalled a significant pivot in Canadian strategy. To remain a prominent player in the future of surveillance capitalism, Canadian policymakers had decided to push the national interest beyond North American borders, particularly into strategic defence program relationships with developing powers such as China, Brazil, and Russia. Canadian officials therefore increased the federal budget for Arctic sovereignty, bilateral trade agreements, and a more robust military apparatus to protect both.[64]

Thanks to the assistance of friends in government, MDA secured its role as prime contractor capable of subcontracting to major Canadian firms focused on missile systems, cyber-security, and civil-military aircraft manufacturing as well, including American-owned Raytheon Canada and Canada's Bombardier Inc. (which acquired Canadair in 1986 and de Havilland Aircraft during 1992). Once again, MDA relied on the Canadian government to kick-start its efforts, first in Canada and then beyond the country's borders. "It just so happens that all the stuff we're into" in missile systems and cyber-security "is funding-sourced by the government, one way or another," one marketing manager noted. Although he complained that "the trouble is that the whole space industry is government controlled," he conceded that MDA's success had always relied on government contracting and control, even if the scale and scope of both had changed.[65]

"There are a number of philosophies, or paradigms that we followed," no matter the size of the project, another marketing manager recollected. "The first is 'Do it first in Canada, make sure it works, and then take it on the road.' And that" always did "a couple of things for us," he explained. It gave the firm "a nice, secure, safe home base. If we first did it in Korea, and then screwed up, the Korean government would have no compunction about putting us into bankruptcy. At least the Canadian government's a benign customer," he observed. "They're also closer to us, culturally, we speak the same language. Doing it first in Canada," he stressed, began with "ground stations." Thereafter, "We did it with weather, and now we're doing it with CAATS. We're now exporting that technology, and we're just starting to do that with MCDV. But the philosophy," he argued, simply followed the paradigm begun in the early 1970s. The strategy relied "a lot on the Canadian government's help, not from a financial point of view," but "always politically," he conceded. "We need the Canadian government's help. It starts in the field, in defining what we need" on international projects, "and then back here" in Canada "we'll get in touch with the appropriate minister."[66]

All of these moves, in Canada and abroad, demonstrated MDA's widening linkages to political deal-making and its executives' maturing abilities to lobby members of Parliament. Such connections also confirmed Canada's deepening integration into an increasingly globalized military-industrial complex, even if MDA and other procurement contractors continued to supply little more than component parts, "good reconnaissance" and "good logistical support" to American space, data mining, and security industries. Recognizing such trends, one long-time employee argued that "the founders are still fundamental at MDA," but "the difference now is that there's very little fat, and we're market-focused," with projects coalescing around government procurement contracts. By 1992, few could fail to see how much they had helped to fashion MDA's new action plan on the strategies employed by their long-time rival SPAR. For for those who remained unconscious of those connections as John Pitts turned his attention to business acquisitions and increasing demands for liquidity among MDA's shareholders, however, SPAR soon made its long-term goals and the foundations it had laid for MDA's future crystal clear.[67]

"THE PRICE MEANS MORE THAN MONEY":
SPAR ATTEMPTS TO ACQUIRE MDA, ONE LAST TIME

Expanding into strategic geographic locations from 1989 forward, selling the EOP division during 1990, and acquiring EOSL in 1991 enhanced the original exit strategy outlined by Pitts and others who had invested in MDA during 1982. New systems engineering offices worldwide provided critical connections to American defence procurement contracting, the European Economic Community, and Asian markets, all of which promised the chance for shareholders to liquidate their holdings.[68] Thus, at the instigation of Ventures West (then holding 23 per cent of MDA's shares), SPAR made yet another bid to acquire MDA. SPAR had grown substantially since it purchased an 11 per cent share in MDA during 1985. Indeed, as it entered its twenty-fifth year in business during 1992, SPAR could boast that it had more than 4,000 employees, $500 million in space revenues alone, and $3 billion when it included operators and users. With exports in excess of 75 per cent of its business over the past five years, and more than 5,000 Canadian suppliers served, it also had international recognition for its expertise in "robotics, resource management, communications, remote sensing, environmental monitoring, [and] surveillance."[69]

Although SPAR's leaders conceded that their firm remained "fragile by international standards," in a global space industry with revenues in excess of $90 billion (with Canada representing $430 million and SPAR $323 million of the country's total), they noted that SPAR had received $275 million in government contracts during fiscal year 1991. In that same year, they had made key acquisitions as well, including Leigh Assets (1990) and Prior Data Systems (1992), which promised to enhance SPAR's "real-time systems software and digital communications expertise – the enabling technologies of the future for the design of end-to-end systems solutions via satellites." SPAR had additionally invested in Telesat (which the Mulroney government privatized during 1992), a strategic move that expanded SPAR's end-to-end communications capabilities. Repositioning itself from an "inward, almost secretive company," SPAR's 1992 briefing to the federal government declared, the company "had adjusted its strategy to the competitive realities of the 1990s," and "emerged as a truly publicly traded, shareholder-directed, professionally managed" and "higher-margin, communications, informatics, and software-driven company using space as its enabling technology." Still, SPAR lacked some of the expertise MDA had acquired, including the smaller company's software and information-processing capabilities. An acquisition of MDA thus promised to prepare SPAR for larger plans to acquire an American leader in digital technology to gain greater access to "advanced U.S. markets, and enhance" the company's "competitiveness in world markets." SPAR thus made an overture, and Pitts agreed to commence negotiations.[70]

While discussions got underway during March 1992, Philip Lapp realized that as a director of SPAR and John MacDonald's representative on MDA's board, he had a conflict of interest. After several sleepless nights and long discussions with MacDonald, Lapp decided to tender his resignation from MDA's board. His departure was painful, especially for MacDonald. Lapp had provided crucial assistance to MacDonald during the FOCUS crisis and for more than a decade had proven himself a valuable director and ally. But Lapp's resignation opened an additional door for Dan Friedmann to further his own ambitions at MDA. With Lapp vacating his seat on the board, MacDonald needed a new ally and saw in Friedmann his obvious, nay only choice. Under Bob Hamilton's mentorial wing, Friedmann had, perhaps more than anyone else, understood MacDonald's vision. By consolidating MacDonald's desire to work on technology's cutting edge with Pitts's focus on business and marketing strategies, Friedmann had also exploited MDA's promise into a profitable systems integrator capable of reaping the benefits of an expansionist future in surveillance.[71]

As negotiations proceeded in the summer, SPAR and MDA signed a memorandum of understanding that described how the companies would work together and the roles each would play in Canada's *Radarsat* program. The MOU also flowed from SPAR's desire to eliminate a competitor while simultaneously developing into an end-to-end systems engineering company with capabilities in communications as well as remote sensing. Believing they could secure the deal, and given the earlier right-of-first-refusal agreement MacDonald and Pitts had signed, SPAR's board members made MDA an attractive offer. From negotiation's beginnings, however, Lapp questioned the viability of a merger; and, as it turned out, members on both sides failed to act upon his suggestion that "cultural problems stemming from a), the East-West thing; and b), the early history of SPAR's attempts to acquire MDA" during the early 1980s "warranted significant discussion." Instead, discussions began to centre on SPAR's 4,000 employees dominating Canadian firms chasing the country's space-based contracts, while MDA, the country's second-largest aerospace contractor, still had fewer than 600 employees, only $60 million in revenue, and little national recognition. As a result, MacDonald's fears about MDA's autonomy mounted; and by the time the final SPAR offer arrived at MDA's board meeting, he hesitated at the bargaining table. Pitts soon followed.[72]

The conflict between SPAR and MDA resonated with a much longer history of regional dissension between east and west, in what MacDonald had always perceived as "the Toronto establishment" versus "western mavericks" such as those he and Vern Dettwiler had assembled at MDA. MacDonald conceded that the MOU helped to establish an excellent working rapport between the two companies, but emotional energies and deal-quashing innuendos spread swiftly throughout both firms, and particularly into MDA, where many concluded that the two firms could never effectively get along, could never really merge. "MDA people are basically software people, they're quiet, soft-spoken, competent, high-mentality West Coasters," Lapp explained, while "SPAR's employees are seen as a bunch of tin bashers, in the eyes of MDA certainly. SPAR has its own software people too, but they started in the aircraft business, and the hard-knocks electronics business, and they're a different breed." Lapp also confirmed that "it is common to a lot of other stories that have the same cultural basis. A lot of people don't understand that until they actually live them," he argued, but "I'm one of the privileged few who have been able to live on both sides, been able to recognize the differences. I've also reached a stage in my life where I see that they're pretty close to irreconcilable." Thus, as soon as MDA's executives "could find an alternative way, such as going public," they seized it.[73]

In the end, no amount of good will, hand holding, or cajoling by members of either party could make the merger work. Irrespective of MacDonald's respect for SPAR President John McNaughton, and what MacDonald called "the noble dream" McNaughton had attempted to engineer, MDA terminated negotiations with SPAR. "I could have walked out of it with several million dollars in my pocket," MacDonald argued, but "the price wasn't right, and price means more than money."[74] People at MDA had long defined and then asserted their identity through their perceived differences from SPAR, an assessment shared by many West Coast champions who agreed with MacDonald's assessment that, to compete in the international market, SPAR relied far too much on government support, whereas MDA did not. Whether MDA could compete without the government's financial and political support remained uncertain; however, by the summer of 1992, one thing was undeniable: the deal to merge SPAR and MDA had died. Thus, with his desire for liquidity firmly established and Friedmann's abilities to run a profitable business demonstrated, Pitts promoted the thirty-six-year-old Friedmann to MDA's chief operating officer. "Dan is a very quick learner, and he's learned a lot from John [Pitts], as he learned from me in earlier years," MacDonald declared. He also argued, "I think that my role in the next five years is to develop Dan, because he may be capable of taking over from both of us in the end." Friedmann concurred; he therefore spent the next two months preparing MDA's staff for inevitable change.[75]

With SPAR's failed acquisition behind them, MDA's major stakeholders called for a special board meeting, where they adopted a shareholder protection program and moved forward with plans to pursue a public listing. At the same time, because MDA's ground station upgrade program had created cash reserves in excess of the company's working capital needs, Pitts recommended that MDA reduce its reserves by $11 million through a special dividend of $1 per common share. Once done, company representatives then got to work on the listing prospectus that would alter MDA's future. During March 1993, MDA also moved its CAATS development team out of corporate headquarters and into a new home shared with a Canadian subsidiary of American-owned Hughes Aircraft. MDA thus transitioned from a small business to a medium-sized, "threshold" firm capable of teaming successfully with other major players in the aviation field, a turning point that most specialty technology firms never have a chance to make. Over time, few could fail to notice that Canadian government support and influence made that turn possible.[76]

During November 1992, *Canadian Business*'s Bill Knapp had anticipated MDA's transition by including the firm among Canada's new "Masters of the Universe." Canadians had long "resigned to thinking of themselves – and having the rest of the world see them – as the most inward-looking people around," Knapp argued, "but on the eve of the constitutional convention" and as "the end result of an eternity of navel-gazing, something very curious happened – Canada succeeded in putting its imprint on The Great Beyond," Knapp reported. "It may come as a shock to a lot of Canadians," Knapp stressed, "but Canada is rapidly moving to the forefront of a huge and growing international space industry," with the National Research Council and SPAR intending "to provide unprecedented levels of precision guidance to robots such as the *Canadarm*. Officials at NASA are anxious to incorporate it into plans for the international space station to be launched by several countries, including Canada, in the late 1990s." Although SPAR had long maintained its position as "the undisputed patriarch of the sector," Knapp argued that it received that role "to prevent the fledgling industry from tearing itself apart [by] competing for the very contracts that were intended to help it grow." The "federal government designated SPAR as the prime Canadian contractor for major projects," which then channelled "work through a small group of major subcontractors," Knapp noted, including Vancouver's MDA and Cambridge, Ontario's, ComDev Ltd, both of which "developed into major international players who now dominate global niche markets." As a result, MDA had captured "85% of the world market for the ground stations that receive and process signals from earth observation satellites and spacecraft carrying sensors that measure atmosphere, ocean and land surface conditions on a global scale." Knapp also observed that MDA's expanding expertise had created the opportunity to provide "operations management software" for SPAR's *Canadarm*.[77]

Although Knapp asserted that "most of the industry's privately held companies have weaned themselves away from a dependence on government contracts," MDA's pre-public listing promotional literature disputed such claims: "We know who our customers are. We know our markets. They are either big governments or big contractors." In the longer term, the firm also promised to focus on technical innovation, business structures, and a marketing policy that would further tether MDA to the American military-industrial complex and the expansion of surveillance capitalism. With more complex programs involving teaming arrangements, MDA thus planned to optimize what had long been the heart, soul, and source of profit for MDA, even if few employees understood that reality. MDA's gross revenue increased from $52.6 million in 1989 to $85.2 million at fiscal year 1993's end (or $127 million in 2016); and with consolidated revenues increasing 18 per cent year-over-year, MDA's *1993 Annual Report* emphasized that the company's flirtation with products had decisively ended. The report therefore assured potential investors that MDA had firmly established itself as a systems integrator, government contractor, and survivor in the "knowledge-based world" economy.[78] As chapter 8 reveals, MDA's survival as a publicly traded systems integrator would continue to depend on the vagaries of the world economy as well as the government's decisions and assistance.

PART THREE

The Systems Integrators

8

"This Company Will Be Sold"

MDA's Public Offering, Orbital's Acquisition, and the Dot-Com Bust, 1993–2001

While the new US president, William Jefferson (Bill) Clinton, pushed the Omnibus Budget Reconciliation Act of 1993 through Congress without a single Republican vote, thereby cutting taxes for 15 million low-income families, raising taxes on the wealthiest 1.2 per cent, and mandating spending restraints and budget cuts, MDA and Canada prepared for another critical moment in the history of surveillance capitalism and continental integration. On 9 August 1993, MDA announced its initial public offering on the Vancouver Stock Exchange, with its shares listed at just under $5.00 each. Less than three months later, the Liberals won their most significant election since 1949. Taking 179 seats in Parliament, the Liberals virtually obliterated the Tories, who suffered the worst defeat on record by a governing party. On 4 November 1993, Joseph Jacques Jean Chrétien, a party insider and influential Cabinet minister since 1965, then became prime minister on promises of reducing the deficit and the national debt he had inherited from Trudeau and Mulroney, reforming the unemployment insurance system, renegotiating or cancelling NAFTA, and investing $6 billion on Canada's infrastructure to stimulate the Canadian economy. Chrétien also made his hostility to defence spending well known, declaring that in a post–Cold War world, Canada needed to reduce its military budgets.[1]

This chapter traces the uncertainty that MDA faced during 1993 and the policy decisions that transformed the firm from an independent Canadian entity to a subsidiary of US Orbital Sciences Corporation during 1995. It also explores the ways in which the more powerful American firm helped its MDA subsidiary to acquire SPAR's robotics division and rights to *Radarsat* during the recession of the 1990s. The acquisition pushed MDA into yet another product adventure, this time in a property information business unit linked to the deregulation of the financial services sector and the Internet bubble that ultimately threatened the future of both Orbital and MDA. Once again, MDA survived because the Canadian government, along with Canadian shareholders and taxpayers, stepped in to save the firm from disaster.

"BIG FISH IN A SMALL POND":
REFLECTING ON MDA'S NICHE AS THE PUBLIC OFFERING NEARED

By the middle of 1993, MDA had cemented its direction as a systems integrator with plans to extend the reach of Canada's ambitions in the global space industry. "We're no longer a products company. We're no longer a remote sensing company," one member of MDA's new senior management team argued. "If you look through our literature since 1989, you will always see this company pitched as a systems engineering company. Prior to that, we gave a lot of different messages as to what we were." During 1989, "if you would have asked ten different employees, you might have gotten twelve different ideas as to what we were." They would say, "We sell some boxes, and also we sell other things," he noted, "but if you walk around the hall" now and "ask ten people what business we're in, at least seven of them will say, 'We're in the systems engineering business.'" Apparently the other three had not paid attention.[2]

With MDA consistently pitched as a "systems engineering company" as Pitts prepared the firm for its initial public offering, some people speculated about the company's future, while others reminisced about its past and how best to judge MDA's worth to Vancouver and the larger world. On the one hand, MDA had achieved a reputation for world-class engineering excellence, many noted, with MacDonald securing his position in the international remote sensing community when the governor general conferred on him the Order of Canada in 1988. The order designated MacDonald an eminent person in science and technology and honoured him for "improving the policy environment within which industry and science work together" and the "model" he bestowed to "the new breed of 'high-tech' engineers."[3] With the assistance of the Canadian government and other local electronics firms, MDA had also established an "anchor" for Vancouver's high-tech community "at a time when there wasn't very much" in the way of technology-based firms. Few considered the company a success in return on investment, but many agreed with one former employee's assessment of MDA's value: "If you look around" Vancouver and note what "spun out of that collection of the first thirty or forty people at MDA, they're the leaders in the industry. They're not necessarily the biggest and most powerful companies, but they're still making exciting stuff happen."[4] One on-again, off-again employee also confirmed that "it's almost gotten to the point where you don't work for a company now, you work on a project" for MDA or one or more of its progeny. Vancouver's technology core members had the luxury "to move among companies" in Vancouver, he reported, because "everything that everybody does" in the systems business, "all their tools are behind their ears." Each company's "physical assets" also had "feet" that could travel from one firm to another, once Vancouver had a sufficient number of high-technology firms.[5]

MDA also retained university students who might have gone elsewhere in search of work, and helped to create spinoff opportunities for local manufacturers, including MDI (acquired by Motorola), CREO (later acquired by Kodak), CSI (eventually acquired by Canon Japan), and a host of other smaller firms started by former MDA personnel. With MDA creating opportunities that the company chose not to exploit or could not employ to its advantage, MDA had helped to attract more venture capitalists to British Columbia's Lower Mainland as well. On the other hand, MDA still remained small when compared to companies in California's Silicon Valley, including those started long after MDA's founding that reached a size 15 to 100 times that of MDA by 1993. By that same year, nearly twenty start-up companies in Seattle had already reached US$100 million in sales, a feat MDA had not yet achieved. Although Vancouver's venture capitalists and former employees turned high-tech owners argued that MDA remained "a big fish in a small pond," they agreed that MDA did well relative to its position within the global economy. Ken Spencer, Dan Gelbart's co-founder at CREO, stressed that "the financing of the business, making it profitable, getting liquid, as they're finding out, is really tough, so they picked, out of ignorance or out of interest, a tough business, and they've done very well at it, given the nature of the business." He also confirmed that MDA remained "a big employer, and to have grown like it has, relative to the Vancouver scene, it's done very well." Still, "there were two other companies that started in 1969, and they're in the multi-billion-dollar range now, so it depends on how you're measuring it. In think the only difference between MDA and Intel," for example, "is that Intel picked a product and MDA picked systems."[6]

While his product/mass manufacturing vision for MDA ultimately failed, Pitts also noted that he had turned the company into a profit-oriented business that could secure some of the bounty promised by the expansion of the global surveillance networks braided into an increasingly securitized world. As MDA's leader, Pitts had established himself as one of Vancouver's leading citizens as well, chairing the city's Science Fair, extending charitable fund-raising activities, and working on ventures that aided and abetted Vancouver's reputation as a global city that could attract technology workers from around the world. Among his accomplishments, one gave Pitts great pleasure: he "railroaded through the first individually sponsored by-law change in the City of Vancouver" to protect his neighbourhood from over-development. He talked to his city councillor, "hired a couple of architects and lawyers, drafted a by-law, and by getting the neighbourhood to support it," financed another sort of milestone for Vancouver. Wealth and status, he noted, could buy many things. When asked about MDA's financial ups and downs, the firm's value to the community under his leadership, Pitts simply replied, "700-plus people employed, paying taxes, buying houses, raising kids, and all that good stuff."[7] Still, a former employee recognized that MDA continued to have a "real conflict between the shareholders' ideas of success and the employees' 'Gee whiz, let's have fun, this is a neat company' kind of success." Although each notion of success met "with a major contract," he increasingly found that it had become, "'When can the company be sold? When can it spin off? When can the company receive some sort of return on investment?', running head-on into what kind of bureaucratic structure is going to be imposed on the company to try to meet that original structure" the company's founders had envisioned. Pitts never solved that dilemma, he argued, but Friedmann determined to do so. After all, "What is a company, really? It's a collection of individuals and a collective memory, influenced heavily by potential future events."[8]

Different definitions of success and critical historical turns mattered less than what MDA's accomplishments promised, Dan Friedmann argued. MDA had a new management team, all under the age of forty-five, and they looked not to the past but to a future of government contracts in space and defence. "If I were to look ten years down the road," Friedmann predicted, "I could see us getting to somewhere between half a billion and $1 billion in some markets, with operations all over the world, become a multinational. I think our target is to have 70 per cent of business outside of Canada, to grow strongly in Systems." He confided that "not everyone agrees with me on that one, but until somebody tells me to do something differently, that's what I'm doing." Apparently, no one with any clout ever did. As MDA prepared for life in a post–Cold War universe, another change took place along "Mahogany Row": Friedmann fulfilled the ambitions of his first annual review in 1979, becoming MDA's new leader while John Pitts slipped into the background as a director and deputy chairman of the board.[9]

Friedmann's future status would ultimately depend on his willingness to make a significant financial investment in MDA; however, as members of the management team reflected on the transitional era they had entered, they crafted a statement that would guide MDA into the uncertainty of the "Great Beyond." "The end of the Cold War, coupled with increasing constraints on government budgets, has led to shifts in space and defence spending." As a result, they promised that MDA would focus "on surveillance, simulation and management information systems, rather than weapons. This translates into systems built largely through systems engineering and software expertise rather than through manufacturing capabilities." The report also noted that the "need to react to rapidly changing world situations has led to a dramatic increase in the requirement for effective command and control systems," all of which would "rely on data base management, data fusion, information extraction, and an efficient human-machine interface." The report additionally stressed that "large defence budgets have also been allocated to support the efficient management and deployment of military resources," a market "that shows great compatibility with [our] strengths" in surveillance and other defence-related offerings.[10] Finally, the report noted that MDA's new direction had finally provided an opportunity for shareholders to realize their financial return. Time would tell whether Friedmann could realize his vision, and how long a return on various people's investments might take, but as one senior executive argued eight months before MDA announced its public listing on the Vancouver Stock Exchange, "SPAR made an offer and we rebuffed it," but "the fact is that" Ventures West "went out and enticed SPAR. Our major shareholder wants out. In fact, most of our major shareholders want out," he argued, "and there's going to be a change. One way or another, this company will be sold."[11]

John MacDonald, still holding 10 per cent of MDA's shares, also appeared to "want out," as he contemplated his own future during 1993. "We have gotten to the point now as a species where we have to learn how to create a sustainable economy, an environmentally sustainable economy," he argued. "We have to continue to build wealth, and better people's lives, and all those kinds of things, but at the same time we've got to do it in a way that is sustainable in the long run," he stressed. "We can't cut off the CO_2 generation overnight. We can't just destroy everybody's economy by taking what has evolved out of the industrial revolution and stopping it," he noted. "We're in this transition period between doing things that are not very good for the planet and the sustainable development era," he emphasized, with information "an enormously important tool" for the transition he envisioned, and "many critical decisions needed over the next century. That's the kind of time scales in which I think," MacDonald stressed "I'm going to make whatever contribution I can to putting that system into place. I'll be ninety years old before anything is really happening" by the 2020s, he allowed, but "it's important to make a start. This is part science, part politics, part salesmanship, part management, part engineering. It's all those things rolled into one," he advised, "but I believe we can manage data and information in order to manage this planet. It's going to take a very long time from where we are today, which is primitive to the kind of thing I envision for the future." Nevertheless, "that's what I'm going to work on. Now," he chuckled, "that could all change tomorrow of course." Only time would tell what might change any of MacDonald's immediate tomorrows, but he had numbered his days at MDA by disclosing that "my role in the next five years is to develop Dan" Friedmann.[12]

Vern Dettwiler also thought "it would be nice if we'd get a little equity" return on what he, MacDonald, and their engineering apostles had accomplished, but he also worried about the path MDA had chosen. "We need to take a step back," Dettwiler advised, "and ask, 'What is the actual problem we're trying to solve?'" He still loved "solving jigsaw puzzles," but he also seemed to want something else. "People have asked if I would be willing to start over again," the sixty-year-old Dettwiler disclosed. "I look at the time frame and say, 'Look. I'm not that young any more' and don't know if I'd be willing to go through another ten years of" building another firm, "because my family did not see much of me during" the years devoted to MDA. As he had done before, Dettwiler thus consigned control of the company's future to others, setting his sights not on grand visions but on doing something valuable and without fanfare as he entered his seventh decade. Travelling to Switzerland for MDA had allowed Dettwiler to "discover" his roots, "and I got very interested in it," he claimed. Dettwiler also confided that he planned to remain at MDA for several more years but had settled on Switzerland for the longer term, because "we should be able to learn from each other's cultures," both "the good and the bad." In particular, he marvelled at Switzerland's public transportation system and argued that the "Swiss learned a long time ago how to manage forests, which BC still hasn't learned. The Swiss have learned that forests are a very precious resource, and consequently, nobody, not even the government, is allowed to clear a forest. If they have to clear it for some reason," he observed, "they must plant another one somewhere, in concentration."[13]

No matter MacDonald's and Dettwiler's visions or plans for the future, a central focus on sustainability appeared to have no place in MDA's plans. It therefore seemed clear that anyone interested in the environment would have to leave. Again, only time would tell whether or not the "price was right" for MacDonald, Dettwiler, or others in an increasingly competitive and dangerous post–Cold War era of deregulated capitalism centred on the United States, but they received their first test of the company's value to others shortly after 9 August 1993, the day they made their initial public offering under the trading symbol "MDA."

"A STRONGER PRESENCE IN THE US MARKET": MDA'S PUBLIC OFFERING AND THE CANADIAN CONTEXT

When MDA "went public" on the Vancouver Stock Exchange during August, the company's shareholders hoped to attract investors as well as gain "a stronger presence in the U.S. market." As a result, MDA's *1993 Annual Report* highlighted the firm's 18 per cent increase in revenues from $71.9 in 1992 to $85.2 million during 1993, as well as its "special dividend of $1.00 per common share, reducing cash reserves by $11.0 million." Throughout "North America, Europe, and most of the developing world, there is building pressure for government to provide cost-effective services in response to alarming budget deficits and debt burdens," the report advised, but MDA's presidential message boasted that the firm could provide such services "in Canada and internationally" by expanding on "niche markets" it had developed in "earth observation, resource management, land information, aviation, and space and defence."[14] Headquartered in Richmond, BC, with offices in Ottawa and Malaysia as well as subsidiaries in Colorado, England, and Australia, the firm thus issued press releases announcing MDA's "unlimited" capitalization "with no par value of which 10,989,997 shares are currently issued and outstanding" for sale.[15]

Unfortunately for those at MDA, initial trades fell short of the windfall they expected, with shares selling for under five dollars throughout the company's first sixteen months as a publicly traded firm. Increasing their uncertainty, Prime Minister Chrétien and the Liberals offered little initial relief. Indeed, they had won the 1994 federal election on promises that they would renegotiate the North American Free Trade Agreement and end the country's debt burden by reducing defence spending as well as the Canadian deficit to 3 per cent GNP over the next three years. Still, MDA's *1994 Annual Report* expressed the hope that the company's "knowledge of specific applications markets, coupled with proven systems engineering expertise and project management capabilities" could "provide cost-effective systems for the supply of essential government services." MDA's expertise in automated flight systems, data mining, surveillance, first-strike targeting, and robotics also promised "growth opportunities" for MDA as a publicly traded Canadian entity or attractive acquisition for a host of American firms lobbying on the cutting edge of free trade agreements, the deregulation of telecommunications and the financial services sector, and the accelerating privatization of space and defence. Moreover, with the 1993 approval of the CSA's new long-term plan covering activities through 2010, MDA appeared to have plentiful opportunities at home, particularly in the development of *Radarsat* to monitor the oceans and Canada's Arctic as well as work on the ISS. The CSA had also announced that it had moved the headquarters of *Radarsat*'s data distribution, Radarsat International, from Ottawa to Richmond "to be closer to Asia, which is perceived as the prime market for radar images from space." Thus, the report looked forward with confidence, to other lucrative opportunities emerging in the space industry after the introduction of the World Wide Web and global positioning systems.[16]

Despite prospects during 1994, uncertainty remained about the Internet's abilities to connect computer networks and organizational computer facilities across the world as well as the capacity of GPS to transform global air traffic and other systems. Commercial Internet service providers had begun to emerge during the 1980s, but a fully de-commissioned military technology turned commercialized enterprise had not yet debuted as a panoptical "network of networks" consisting of millions of private, public, academic, business, and government users, local to global in scope, and linked by a vast array of electronic, optical, and wireless technologies. Moreover, although MDA's management team had hedged their bets on the expansion of aviation, geo-information, and space and defence systems, the US Department of Defense's satellite navigation system had not yet become fully operational, and much GPS development still depended on government budgets and the future of the world's political economy in a post-Soviet universe.[17]

Happily for those at MDA, the neoliberal project, government procurement spending, industry deregulation, and other public policies helped to bolster both developments. Canada's participation in the world's governing bodies and its policymakers' desires to remain active participants in the global power core made it increasingly difficult for Chrétien to keep his promises to renegotiate the NAFTA and carve out an independent path for Canada. Indeed, Chrétien's Liberal governments (from

November 1993 through December 2003) tightened Canada's political, economic, and military ties to the United States as the best way to create "growth opportunities" and supply "essential government services" to the Canadian people. Canadians had begun the progressive liberalization of the country's economy long before 1994, but the country's full integration into the larger ambitions of the United States climaxed with the NAFTA. Put into effect on 1 January 1994, the agreement superseded the CUFTA and ushered in an era of open (if not necessarily equal) trade between the United States, Canada, and Mexico. In the wake of the USSR's dissolution at the end of 1991, Canada also joined the United States and its allies in the World Trade Organization (established on 1 January 1995). Influential members of the WTO then entered into an unprecedented number of free trade agreements with developing nations.[18] Free trade and a host of foreign investment promotion and protection agreements, along with Canada's membership in the WTO, then further fastened Canadians to an American-centred brand of globalization, with some 75–80 per cent of the country's economic fortunes continuing to rely on the United States.[19]

Emily Goldman and Andrew Ross have demonstrated that globalization "transformed the U.S. defense industrial and information base to a global one," providing opportunities for firms and policymakers interested in the expansion of a techno-security paradigm friendly to the United States. Congress called for increasing missile defence budgetary allocations as part of its 1994 "Contract with America," justifying increased spending on surveillance to assuage fears that Iraq, Libya, North Korea, and China would obtain weapons of mass destruction if unchecked. Although Chrétien declared his intention to reduce Canada's military apparatus and to balance the budget through spending cuts, his Liberal governments committed Canadian taxpayers to further defence spending by signing a 1994 WTO agreement on intellectual property and government procurement that exempted "essential security interests relating to the procurement of arms, ammunition or war materials, or to procurement indispensable for national security or for national defence purposes."[20]

During 1995, interested Canadians also encouraged the renewal of the NORAD agreement, the Shared Border Accord on information pertaining to immigration and customs, and the Canada-US "Chapeau Agreement" on mutual defence. The "Chapeau Agreement" flowed, in part, from the $2.9 billion US defence budget for 1995–96, and its ongoing commitment to missile defence research and development. "Although the Cold War has ended," one policy analyst warned, "arms control advocates and others, including the Canadian government," wanted to maintain the Anti-Ballistic Missile Treaty signed by the United States and USSR, "if only to consolidate peaceful U.S.-Russian relations." As a result, "NORAD could make a major contribution to international stability and the monitoring of missile proliferation if it were to participate in a multilateral surveillance system involving NATO countries and even Russia." Long allied with the Five Eyes program, the Canadian government thus reaffirmed its participation in NATO, renewed its commitment to NORAD, signed a security agreement with the United States to protect classified information of mutual interest, and made billion-dollar commitments to "future force interoperability" between the US Department of Defense and Canada's National Department of Defence. The two nations also signed a memorandum of understanding on Command, Control, Communications, Computers, Intelligence, Surveillance, and Reconnaissance (C4ISR). With that accomplished, both countries could count on further defence and surveillance spending throughout the 1990s and into the twenty-first century, including public funds to support the ongoing privatization of C4ISR capabilities, autonomous, unattended, and unmanned systems, and the world's surveillance system architecture.[21]

Chrétien's Liberals committed Canada to many other projects "in the national interest" through 2010, including those centred on the CSA's plans to fund follow-on work for *Radarsat* and the development of a Canadian rocket to launch small payloads into orbit. Both projects, policymakers argued, could continue to protect Canada's Arctic, information, and technological sovereignty, even if the federal government had decided to forego expenditures on an Arctic subsurface surveillance system as the price Canada had to pay to address "the budget deficit and a peace dividend."[22] SPAR and its subcontractors, many argued, had and would continue to play a central role in Canada's territorial sovereignty efforts, particularly when they considered the multinational's "long association with the Government of Canada through cost shared government/industry research and development." Regardless, they stressed, tackling the budget deficit had to and would remain the federal government's top priority.[23] Thus, when the devaluation of the Canadian dollar made MDA, then SPAR, bargain-basement and hence attractive acquisitions for American providers of space products and satellite-based services, the Canadian government raised no alarms. Instead, members of the Canadian plutocracy gambled that American-owned subsidiaries in Canada could provide greater access to US capital networks, classified information, and the largest defence procurement system in the world.[24]

"A CRITICAL COMPONENT OF US NATIONAL SECURITY":
ORBITAL'S CANADIAN SPACE ACQUISITIONS

Although MDA shareholders lamented the company's lacklustre stock price, which reached a high of $8.13 in 1994, then fell to $5.50 during 1995, foreign investment in Canada became more attractive as the Canadian dollar began its decline during the late 1970s. The Canadian dollar rebounded to a high of 89.34 cents US on 4 November 1991; however, it hovered at 77.5 cents US during 1994 and slid to 72.86 cents in 1995. As a result, several firms began to talk about acquiring MDA, including Canada's CAI Private Equity, a corporation founded in 1989 by two former partners of New York City's Solomon Brothers, Montreal business executive and former chairman and CEO of Alcan Aluminum Company named David Culver, and several other influential investors. Specializing in leveraged "buyouts, restructurings, acquisitions, recapitalizations and other corporate growth initiatives," CAI targeted firms anxious to tap into a "cross-border network" for "Canadian companies seeking to expand in the U.S."[25] With offices in Toronto, Montreal, Vancouver, and New York City during 1994, CAI entered into discussions on a potential acquisition of MDA, which prompted several American firms to show interest in MDA as a good, low-priced buy. Those firms included Orbital Sciences Corporation of Dulles, Virginia, a firm founded in 1982 to "defend" the United States, "provide global communications," "study the Earth," and "explore our solar system and the galaxy beyond."[26]

Investors initially balked at MDA's high asking price, but Orbital's executives wanted to make a strategic acquisition of a firm with capabilities in "advanced space-qualified software, air navigation systems, military electronic systems, and network communications training and consulting." When they learned that John Pitts had transformed MDA from a loose collection of technological enthusiasts into a disciplined workforce primed to manage the military specification environment, Orbital's board members decided to look more deeply into MDA's operation. With NASA offering to launch *Radarsat-1* in exchange for US access to the data retrieved from the satellite via MDA's stake in Radarsat International, news reports also revealed that MDA had elevated Dan Friedmann to MDA's president and CEO. Orbital's board members thus took the plunge, for the acquisition promised to eliminate a potential competitor as well as provide an opportunity to incorporate the Canadian firm's ground stations and "major optical and radar imaging" capabilities into Orbital's "Earth observation satellites" and larger diversification plans.[27]

According to reports on Orbital's 31 August 1995 agreement to acquire MDA "in a tax-free merger to be completed by the end of the year," Orbital would gain access to even larger markets and more powerful surveillance capabilities after NASA launched *Radarsat-1* as Canada's "secret military eye in the sky." *Radarsat*'s images additionally promised opportunities to ride the Internet boom by focusing on the emerging e-business market in mapping, property tax, and legal data. As a bonus, Orbital would acquire Friedmann to run the new US subsidiary. The 1995 purchase price for MDA, a perceived bargain at US$67 million in stock, therefore allowed Orbital to become an international firm for the first time and one of the largest space technology and satellite services companies in the world. In exchange, Orbital provided access to the American market that MDA's executives and shareholders had long craved. Moreover, once Orbital and MDA executed the deal, John Pitts and other shareholders would have a chance to "cash out." Pitts thus stepped down from MDA, other investors exited as well, and MDA delisted its shares on the Vancouver and Toronto stock exchanges.[28]

On 4 November 1995, just two months after Orbital acquired MDA, NASA launched Canada's SPAR-built *Radarsat-1*, a satellite fully equipped with one of MDA's powerful SAR instruments to acquire images of the Earth. By the time it launched, *Radarsat-1* had cost $641 million. Radarsat International (RSI) contributed $10 million as well as the $53 million it planned to pay the CSA in royalties, while provincial governments contributed $57 million. One report also disclosed that MDA owned a 25 per cent share in RSI, with Canada's SPAR and ComDev as well as Lockheed Martin, of Bethesda, Maryland, serving as RSI's other three co-owners. NASA additionally revealed that Canada and the United States had entered into an agreement in 1993 that gave war-industry giant Lockheed Martin the exclusive right to sell and distribute *Radarsat-1* data within the United States. Operational until 2013, *Radarsat-1* passed the Arctic daily, most of Canada every seventy-two hours, and the entire Earth every twenty-four days, collecting images for use by military as well as commercial entities, and providing to the owners of RSI lucrative contracts for the satellite's data. MDA then acquired Halifax, Nova Scotia's Iotek, Inc., "a company specializing in signal and sonar technology for military customers." That 1996 acquisition enhanced MDA's surveillance capabilities and provided to Orbital an increased capability to contract with the Canadian government and sell its systems integration services to an expanding number of military customers worldwide.[29]

In the meantime, SPAR's financial position began to deteriorate on the plans it had employed to become a $1 billion multinational by 2000.

SPAR's troubles became particularly evident within its ComStream subsidiary, a San Diego–based firm and international provider of digital transmission solutions that promised to enhance SPAR's offerings. During 1992, SPAR had received a $67 million contract from NASA for further *Canadarm* and other work, with half of the firm's revenues centred on space communications hardware, 32 per cent on robotics and other space-related work, and 13 per cent on aviation and defence. SPAR additionally entered into agreements to produce mobile satellites to provide isolated regions with mobile communications. As mobile communications expanded in importance, SPAR's board members approved a plan to diversify into the modem manufacturing business. ComStream, a US$30 million company, offered that capability and a chance for SPAR to acquire an important American subsidiary. SPAR thus purchased ComStream for US$58 million during 1992. By 1995, ComStream posted a $10.5 million profit on $250.7 million in revenues, but as competitors entered the digital transmission market with the launch of *MSat-1* on 20 April 1996, the subsidiary staggered and SPAR's losses began to mount.[30]

As SPAR teetered during 1996, deputy prime minister and minister of the environment Sheila Copps came to the firm's defence, arguing that export sales had allowed SPAR's revenues to increase from "$400 million to $640 million" between 1991 and 1995. "Our partnership with the government for research and development has allowed SPAR to concentrate its scarce resources on broadening our international market share and thereby optimizing the return to the Canadian economy." As a result, "I am convinced that in the absence of cost-shared development investment, SPAR would not have grown as quickly or been as successful as it has been in international markets." That partnership had "allowed SPAR to employ a large number of knowledge-workers," with 70 per cent of them among Canada's "highly skilled engineers and technicians." Global competition, other nations making direct investments in R&D, and other "factors argue for a strong national strategy to encourage investment in Canadian research and development," including funds for a proposed National Technology Investment Program to "level the playing field for Canadian firms operating in export markets. It is our hope," she emphasized, "that the government's fight against the deficit/debt will be balanced with the equally important need to invest in Canada's ability to compete in a rapidly changing knowledge-intensive global economy."[31]

Copps's analysis resonated with those who had long stressed the need for better R&D policies to protect national sovereignty, decrease foreign direct investment in Canada, avoid a brain drain of Canadian talent, and encourage more private capital investment in Canadian-owned multinationals. Copps and others additionally argued that the federal government should intervene more directly in the Canadian economy just as the US government had done, by restructuring Canada's research and development capabilities through defence spending.[32] Responding to these concerns during 1997, the federal government gave SPAR a $30 million contract to supply the ISS with two robotic workstations as well as a $170 million "Canada Hand" to support the firm's robotics work. With Export Development Canada's assistance, SPAR also received contracts from American, Brazilian, Malaysian, and other militaries to maintain their Sea King helicopters. No matter such help, however, SPAR's problems continued; and it had to settle expensive law suits involving one of its satellite communications systems, which plaintiffs argued had caused a 1995 satellite launch by Lockheed Martin to fail. Although SPAR rebounded during 1998, posting a $31 million profit on $251 million in sales, its Canadian shareholders experienced a particularly "wild ride" as ComStream's losses mounted, commodity prices tumbled as part of the Asian financial crisis, and the Canadian dollar sank (to 63.11 cents US on 27 August 1998). As a result, SPAR's board members decided to divest their holdings in ComStream.[33]

The US Congress imperilled SPAR's future as well by passing the Commercial Space Act of 1998 "to encourage the development of a commercial space industry in the United States." Signed into law by President Clinton, the Act signalled American intentions to privatize more of the space industry, slash NASA's budget as the result of billion dollar cost overruns on the ISS, and make it increasingly difficult for foreign-owned firms to compete for large-scale contracts centred on the United States. During December 1998, the CSA then made SPAR's untenable position even worse by revealing that it had entered into a public-private partnership with MDA, signing a master agreement that awarded the *Radarsat-2* mission project to the US-owned subsidiary rather than SPAR. The master agreement committed the federal government (and Canadian taxpayers) to a $225 million investment in the project in exchange for the data *Radarsat-2* would provide. MDA promised to invest $80 million, but quickly managed to defray that investment by accepting follow-on contracts. Those contracts ultimately increased the government's share of the costs from 74 per cent to 83 per cent, reduced MDA's costs from 26 per cent to 17 per cent, and expanded government expenditures to an estimated $418.6 million by the time the satellite actually launched during 2007. When combined with a decimated Canadian dollar and the Asian financial crisis (which "extinguished" interest in the "hot spot" markets SPAR had identified), competition from larger manufacturers of space-based systems convinced SPAR's board to refocus the firm to its traditional role as a component supplier for larger systems houses. Despite these changes, SPAR continued to wobble.[34]

By 1999, SPAR was on the chopping block. On 12 January, the press announced that members of American and Canadian investment groups had gained control of SPAR's board and the CBC divulged that SPAR, "once the darling of Canada's aerospace industry, has sold, for $63 million, its *Canadarm*-making division to a U.S. Company," the MDA subsidiary of Orbital Sciences. In a press release issued the day before, MDA announced that it had signed a worldwide sales and distribution agreement for *Radarsat-2* imagery with another of Orbital's subsidiaries, Orbital Imaging (OrbImage), which gave OrbImage an exclusive ten-year licence to sell *Radarsat-2* data everywhere but in Canada, where the CSA retained such rights. By the end of February, MDA then negotiated the full acquisition of Radarsat International (RSI). Although John MacDonald and Vern Dettwiler had retired from MDA in 1998, they finally had the opportunity to join their former associates in celebrating the acquisition of MDA's *bête noire*, in the form of SPAR's interest in RSI as well as its Space and Advanced Robotics Division in Brampton, Ontario. With both acquisitions complete by 10 May 1999, SPAR returned to repairing and overhauling military and commercial aircraft. Two years later, however, L-3 Communications, a New York City–based defence contractor acquired majority stock in SPAR, ending SPAR's forty-one-year history as Canada's iconic, prime aerospace contractor.[35]

Charged with marketing, processing, and distributing data worldwide from the CSA's *Radarsat-1* satellite as well as the planned *Radarsat-2* launch, RSI placed Orbital's MDA and OrbImage subsidiaries in an enviable position, but the acquisitions of SPAR and RSI also put pressure on the parent firm. By December 1999, Orbital announced that it had to sell a 33 per cent stake in MDA's new robotics unit to CAI Capital Partners for US$75 million, so that Orbital could pay down some of its debts. New York–based Peter Restler, a CAI founding partner, took a seat on MDA's board, signalling that MDA's future board composition would represent the interests of capital and those with financial positions in telecommunications, the energy sector, and investment, asset, and real estate management. With CAI's interest in the firm realized, the Canadian government provided the funding needed for MDA to deliver *Canadarm-2* to the ISS (which launched on 19 April 2001) as well as complete *Radarsat-2* (scheduled for launch in November 2001). At the same time, NASA awarded to MDA a $35 million contract to launch two new satellites in 2002. With contracts in hand during 1999, and others on the horizon, MDA then had the clout to become a member of the International Astronautical Federation, the world's foremost space advocacy organization.[36]

According to the observations of one industry insider in 1999, "White House policy formally recognizes what all the commercial satellite imagery industry's players already know – that the health of the industry is a critical component of U.S. national security." US defence procurement contracts thus became even more lucrative to those who could supply security components and advanced robotics, a situation made more explicit by Donald Rumsfeld when he became US Secretary of Defense. In a 2002 speech that followed the 11 September 2001 terrorist attacks on the World Trade Center in New York City and the US Pentagon in Washington, DC, Rumsfeld argued, "We must promote a more entrepreneurial approach to developing military capabilities – one that encourages people to be proactive, not reactive, and to behave less like bureaucrats and more like venture capitalists." Few had so potently linked war and surveillance to the profit motive, while defence and national security contractors had rarely had so much economic and political influence, both of which they planned to employ as private agents to the government. Indeed, as the Canadian Centre for Policy Alternatives (CCPA) argued in 2006, through the privatization of the *Radarsat* program during the 1990s, Canadian taxpayers footed "almost 90% of [the] $1.15 billion bill" for both *Radarsat-1* and *Radarsat-2*, which CCPA deemed "Canada's largest single contribution to the militarization of space and to U.S. war-fighting."[37]

By 2000, those working at Orbital's MDA subsidiary understood the trends others later articulated: *Radarsat* data could provide "a variety of logistical and planning" tools. As a result, MDA received many more "defence intelligence" orders from the American government as well as "unnamed defence and intelligence agencies" ranked among the world's top customers for *Radarsat* data. Although some reports noted that *Radarsat-1* had the potential to track ice flows and monitor agriculture, from the late 1990s forward, most *Radarsat* sales centred not on environmental applications but on military enhancements that promised to generate "most of the company's revenues." Those included ongoing upgrades to the USAF's Eagle Vision family of systems to meet military demands for digital imagery to support air- and carrier-based mission planning and intelligence gathering, as well as aeronautics systems that enabled worldwide clients to "track mobile assets like trucks and aircraft, as well as to manage mobile workforces."[38] *Radarsat's* powerful images also promised to provide a platform for MDA to ride the dot-com boom into information products and e-business applications focused on property tax and legal data, as well as other sensitive private and public information, that began to create the privacy concerns that have continued to plague legal communities and the public since individual and group dossiers ascended into outer space.

"SIGNIFICANT OPPORTUNITIES FOR US": E-BUSINESS, DEREGULATION, AND INFORMATION PRODUCTS

As the construction of Al Gore's "Information Highway" got underway following the birth of the Internet, MDA's senior executives and board members decided to launch a property information products business on a budding e-business market. Introduced in 1995, the e-business market expanded rapidly after the US government deregulated its communications and financial sectors, both of which paved the way for unprecedented corporate consolidations, the privatization of many public utilities, and a dot-com boom. Signed into law by President Clinton, the US Telecommunications Act of 1996 allowed media cross-ownership and the deregulation of the broadcasting market, which "let anyone enter any communications business – to let any communications business compete in any market against any other." By 2001, as the International Telecommunications Satellite consortium that had contracted with NASA to launch its satellites since 1964 faced competition from private telecommunications companies, lobbyists convinced government entities to privatize Intelsat, with public services provided under the oversight of the International Telecommunications Satellite Organization.[39] In the meantime, Citicorp merged with Travelers Group, which swallowed Citibank, Smith Barney, Primerica, and Travelers into the Citigroup conglomerate that combined banking, securities, and insurance services. Although the Citigroup merger violated the Glass-Steagall Act of 1965, which had limited commercial bank securities activities, the US Federal Reserve granted Citigroup a temporary waiver. Thanks to financial services lobbyists, Congress approved and Clinton then signed into law the bipartisan Gramm-Leachy-Bliley Act, also known as the "Financial Services Modernization Act of 1999" (GLBA, and commonly pronounced "glibba"). GLBA repealed Glass-Steagall, made mergers like Citigroup's legal, and allowed commercial and investment banks, securities firms, and insurance companies to consolidate, which led, as many critics of the GLBA have argued, to the 2007 subprime mortgage crisis and 2008 global financial crisis.[40]

No matter the precarity engendered by it, deregulation fuelled the dot-com boom and created another speculative frenzy that confirmed what Vincent Mosco observed in *The Digital Sublime*: "What made the dot-com boom a myth was not that it was false, but that it was alive, sustained by the belief that cyberspace was opening a new world by transcending what we once knew about time, space, and economics." Such beliefs stimulated the 1997 boom, with stock markets in industrialized nations rapidly raising equity values on the expansion of the Internet sector and its tertiary markets. When the United States launched *Landsat-7* in 1999, to provide cloud-free images and update the US Geological Survey's global archive of satellite photographs, its images created even more speculation in e-commerce. While many worried about the Year 2000 Problem (Y2K, the "Millennium bug" caused by the practice of abbreviating four-digit years to two digits), a swarm of Internet and GPS enthusiasts raced to acquire, produce, and purchase new images of the Earth, all of which helped to generate the NASDAQ's 10 March 2000 climatic intra-day trading that opened at 5132.52 and closed at 5048.62.[41]

Few could dispute how much Canadians had tied their destiny to the dot-com boom. At an Industry Canada Workshop on North American Integration in 2000, economist Richard Harris argued that "the phenomenal U.S. growth during the 1990's, with low inflation and low unemployment, has had a two-fold effect." First, "it has quashed a lot of doubts by anti-market proponents as to the performance merits of U.S.-style market capitalism." Second, with the US economy some fifteen times larger than Canadian one, "the fact that the U.S. has done so well relative to Canada has raised the export dependency of Canada on the U.S. and increased the benefits to catch up with the U.S." As a result, he argued, "deeper Canada-U.S. economic integration is the only realistic option for further progress in developing significant export market access for Canadian products." Increasingly, it seemed, most Canadians agreed.[42]

Profiting from the dot-com frenzy and Canada's deeper integration into the US economy during early 2000, Orbital's MDA subsidiary won a number of critical information services contracts, including one from England's National Land Information Services. NLIS gave MDA a seven-year licence, *Canadian Business* reported, which allowed MDA to sell to "data wholesalers," making it much easier for realtors and developers "to access land ownership and property databases." MDA also received a contract "to develop an electronic goods and services exchange for England's Improvement and Development Agency. Thanks to agreements like that," *Canadian Business* noted, "more than half of MDA's revenue comes from outside Canada in a typical year, and its reliance on North America is decreasing." On expanding e-business during 2000, MDA's revenues had also exceeded $401 million, "up" 35 per cent "from $298 million the previous year," and the firm employed 1,700 people worldwide.[43] As a result, MDA secured a $190 million credit line from a banking syndicate for an anticipated expansion in property information products, with the Royal Bank of Canada acting as MDA's lead arranger, book runner, and administrative agent. "The growing international demand for land-related information products and the availability of the Internet," Friedmann argued, had provided the rationale for MDA's expansion "beyond traditional information systems markets." At the same time, "our international experience, our familiarity with land information, and our technical depth in designing and maintaining large-scale information delivery systems" created the context for "for many of our new product endeavours."[44]

According to *Canadian Business*, most of MDA's expansion from 1996 through 2001 derived not from defence procurement but from the investments it had made in products. RSI sold high-resolution pictures and maps to military customers, the news outlet allowed, but once MDA acquired Triathlon Mapping in 1997, the firm provided most of its mapping services to municipalities and industries focused on resource extraction. By 2000, the company had also moved more deeply into the American financial services sector, *Canadian Business* reported. Acquiring US-owned DataQuick Information Systems, MDA added a property data mining division to its holdings, with Home Value Estimator software to assess land and other property values based upon real-time market information. With most of its work in the United States, MDA's DataQuick division promised "to speed up approvals for mortgages," *Canadian Business* stressed, in places such as Freddie Mac, one of the largest mortgage finance agencies in the United States.[45] Looking ahead to 2001, Friedmann predicted, "We will continue to expand nationally in the U.S. with land-related information products and services," as well as "open our U.K.-based land information business." Following delivery of "several systems, including the first components of the Space Station Remote Manipulator System to orbit," he also argued that MDA would "begin a new phase of funded, long-term systems support and enhancements for the duration of the Space Station mission. Finally," the board had positioned MDA "to capitalize on many new international information systems and product opportunities."[46]

Alas for MDA, the speculative dot-com bubble peaked just nine days after the American subsidiary secured its credit line from the banking syndicate. Several days after the 10 March 2000 spike, it became increasingly clear that many of the dot-com companies had valuations far exceeding their actual worth. As a result, the dot-com bubble began to burst. Some companies failed completely, while others, including Orbital and its subsidiaries, found themselves strapped with increasing financial burdens and declining market capitalizations. Shortly after it launched *Canadarm* to the ISS during 2001, Orbital's market capitalization plummeted from US$873.4 million in 1999 to $175.22 million, while MDA's tumbled from US$211.72 million to $118.31 million. Within one short year, Friedmann's prognostications about MDA's future collapsed as well, particularly after the firm absorbed the news that NASA's financial troubles and US fears about potential national security breaches by Canada had prompted the decision to withdraw NASA's participation in the launch of *Radarsat-2*. Although the CSA announced that it had awarded to MDA an additional $160.5 million "to incorporate new requirements to the Master Agreement" for the *Radarsat-2* program so that Orbital's subsidiary could award a subcontract to Boeing's Delta Launch Services as a replacement for NASA, the dot-com bust jeopardized Friedmann's assurances to shareholders that *Radarsat-2* remained "on track for launch in early 2003." It additionally imperilled Friedmann's plans to establish MDA "as the leading civilian SAR data provider" for the company's property information products business.[47]

"RECENTLY DODGED A BULLET": THE DOT-COM CRISIS AND ORBITAL'S DIVESTMENT OF MDA

Long before the collapse of the dot-com boom, Orbital had over-extended itself financially. Indeed, like so many other firms during the second half of the 1990s, Orbital had taken on substantial and unsustainable debt to acquire both MDA and SPAR's Space and Robotics Division, as well as Magellan Corporation and Navigation Solutions, LLC (the latter two purchased to enhance Orbital's expertise in portable, automobile, and handheld GPS devices). Just months after it acquired SPAR's Space and Robotics Division, Orbital announced that its stock had fallen by 64 per cent, a reality that prompted major newspapers to report on CAI's 33 per cent stake in MDA Robotics. Although the *New York Times* confirmed that the deal promised a needed infusion of capital to pay down Orbital's debt, and Canada's *National Post* celebrated the news that Canadians had invested in MDA, Orbital soon had to sell its Magellan subsidiary and divest its MDA shares. Orbital continued to own a majority position in MDA following its initial sale to CAI, but Canadians took control of MDA's board during December 1999 while Orbital sought buyers for Magellan and its other subsidiaries. During 2000, MDA then "repatriated" *Radarsat-2* and offered its second IPO on the Toronto Stock Exchange.[48] Although the Canadian dollar had climbed back to just under 70 cents US, thanks in no small part to the Bank of Canada's decision to raise interest rates following a 1998 low, CBC News reported that Canadians had lost a great deal from Orbital's acquisition of MDA. "MDA was a public company once before. It was listed on the Vancouver Stock Exchange for a few years until it was acquired by U.S.-based Orbital Sciences Corp in 1995 for a mere $86 million," the CBC chided. CBC also complained that "last year Orbital sold a third of MDA to Canadian investors for $112 million. Nice going, Orbital (where were the Canadians?)."[49]

Orbital completed its first and second phases of the MDA divestiture during May and June 2001, selling its shares to a collection of Canadian institutional investors, including CAI, the British Columbia Investment Management Corporation, and the Ontario Teachers' Pension Plan Board. In return, Orbital received a $112 million transfer in May, $38 million in June, and the final $19 million in July. OrbImage also retained its exclusive distribution rights to *Radasat-2* imagery for US customers, while MDA's RSI subsidiary received the "worldwide rights to RADARSAT-2 distribution, except for the US." When combined with the earlier $67 million the company received, Orbital's sale of MDA returned 30.5 million shares to Canadian investors for US$240 million, what many considered an excellent five-year return for Orbital.[50]

No matter who won or lost on the deal, *Canadian Business* writer Matthew McClearn noted that MDA had "dodged a bullet. Orbital's recent history has been characterized by recurring losses and hard times, forcing it to sell its stake in MDA to finance debt repayment and operations expenses." McClearn nevertheless remained bullish on Canada's "new darling" in the space industry and its "myriad businesses wrapped up in a 1,800-employee conglomerate." Emphasizing that "66 consecutive profitable quarters can't be wrong," McClearn argued that "President and CEO Daniel Friedmann and his crack management team have discovered new markets and driven explosive growth (averaging about 20% annually since 1991), while earning an enviable track record of giving clients exactly what they want." Of course, McClearn mused, "there's always the risk MDA will lose focus and drift off into space."[51]

As it turned out, larger events ensured that MDA would probably avoid a potential "drift off into space" as a Canadian-owned firm. Prior to the 2001 terrorist attacks on the World Trade Center and Pentagon, the Canadian government unveiled its plans to fund more "knowledge-based growth" activities, which promised to place MDA at the centre of several "innovation clusters." The CSA also provided more funding for the *Radarsat* mission, and major clients demanded more images for various objectives, including those associated with NATO's aerial bombings in Yugoslavia during 1999.[52] Chapter 9 explores where demands for security and military operations, as well as a wartime, property information boom carried MDA during the seven years following 9/11. It also examines MDA's first serious labour dispute as well as the closer public scrutiny the firm faced as concerned employees, citizens, and policy analysts began to share more publicly their discoveries about MDA's connections to the American military-industrial complex and threats to Canada's sovereignty.

9

"Shades of Grey"

11 September 2001, the Homeland Security Bubble, and Canada's Sovereignty Imbroglio, 2001–2008

At 8:46 a.m., American Airlines Flight 11 crashed into New York City's World Trade Center's North Tower. Within fifty minutes, United Airlines Flight 175 crashed into the South Tower and American Airlines Flight 77 flew into the Pentagon. As worldwide audiences watched the World Trade Center buildings begin to implode, interactive media outlets reported that a fourth plane headed for Washington, DC, had crashed near Shanksville, Pennsylvania. Representing a pivotal moment in world history that soon revealed the limits of the American empire and challenged perceptions about global interdependence, the four coordinated suicide attacks prompted national leaders and ordinary citizens to react immediately. Canadians received 226 diverted flights and the government launched Operation Yellow Ribbon to deal with grounded planes and stranded passengers. Despite countervailing voices calling for peaceful, diplomatic solutions to the terrorist attacks, historian Reg Whitaker also observed that most Canadians "instinctively sympathized with Americans, shared their pain and anger," and supported a military response to 9/11. As a result, Jean Chrétien's Liberal government passed the controversial Anti-terrorism Act of 2001, Canadians joined a coalition of nations in the "war on terror," and business lobbyists formed the Coalition for Secure and Trade Efficient Borders, insisting that Canada reopen "the border for unimpeded commerce," no matter "the political cost."[1] Security Council Resolution 1368 condemned the attacks as well, declaring the UN's readiness to take "all necessary steps" to combat all forms of terrorism in accord with its charter. Following news reports that Al Queda had taken responsibility for the terrorist attacks, leaders in the Middle East and Afghanistan also condemned the violence. Iraq, the notable exception, issued an official statement declaring "the American cowboys are reaping the fruit of their crimes against humanity."[2]

With Iraq's official statement repeated ad nauseam in the mainstream media, many feared how the United States might ultimately respond to any physical or verbal provocation. By the afternoon of 11 September 2001, US Secretary of Defense Donald Rumsfeld had already issued orders to look for evidence of Iraqi involvement, setting in motion a military response to the terrorist attacks as well as a hunt for both Osama bin Laden and Saddam Hussein.[3] According to award-winning journalist Shane Harris, "One of the first themes to emerge from the 9/11 attacks soon became a familiar refrain: The government had failed to 'connect the dots' about terrorism, specifically the Al-Qaeda network." Although it "wasn't widely known that some of the 9/11 hijackers were already on terrorist watch lists when they entered the United States, mysterious phone calls intercepted on September 10, which hinted at the next day's calamity, weren't translated in time to be of any use," Harris reported. "No one – no *system* – had gathered all the pieces of the puzzle and put them together." Thus, "The Watchers," a group of American "mavericks" who had spent most of their careers in American intelligence and national security agencies, knew "better than anyone that the signals of terrorism were out there, waiting to be detected in a sea of noise." For them, 9/11 "resonated on a particularly haunting level. 'The Watchers' had been expecting this moment, had worked hard to prevent it," Harris argued, "and when it happened, they felt emboldened, and entitled, to act."[4]

The War in Afghanistan commenced on 7 October 2001, when US and UK forces initiated aerial bombing campaigns on Taliban and Al-Queda camps. On 26 October, President George W. Bush then signed into law the USA Patriot Act, which prompted indefinite detentions (including those at Guantanamo Bay, Cuba), enhanced surveillance, and increased information sharing across jurisdictional boundaries. The Patriot Act also prompted new privacy and security concerns in the United States and across the world. Regardless, on 25 November 2002 the US Congress passed the Homeland Security Act, which created the Department of Homeland Security, fostered the largest restructuring of the American government in history, and increased the militarization of civilian life, particularly in urban environments. Part of a larger plan to construct a "Total Information Awareness" program at the Pentagon, the Patriot and Homeland Security acts fell under the auspices of the Defense Advanced Research Projects Agency (DARPA). In such a "high-tech spy craft" environment, Harris argued, DARPA quickly received funding and other resources to gather personal information on every American, as well as other "suspects." The Bush administration additionally employed every component in its arsenal to effect "regime change" in Iraq, with or without its traditional Cold War allies.[5]

As fears increased, hate crimes rose in the United States and abroad. At the World Trade Center site, courageous people worked day and night searching for remains, while toxic debris placed thousands at risk, a situation exacerbated by local and federal government misinformation about air quality and environmental safety in Lower Manhattan. Within a week, the American economy stumbled, the stock market tumbled, and shares lost $1.4 million in valuation. Wage losses then mounted, GDP declined, an already struggling US airline industry experienced increasing financial problems, and life became more uncertain for those long involved in a struggle just to make ends meet. Longer term, however, with increased spending on anti-terrorism and the War in Afghanistan, DARPA received the go-ahead to gather all the data it could absorb.[6]

Anticipating profits from what they had learned as members of Orbital, MDA executives readied the firm for the "Homeland Security Bubble." According to a working paper for the New Transparency, by 2006, 9/11 had "opened up a vast [US]$130-billion potential market for small and medium sized Homeland Security (HLS) providers in North America," creating the context for the rise of a "security-industrial complex" as well as the "Homeland Security Bubble."[7] As one of those providers, MDA quickly received contracts from the US Department of Defense and Canada's Department of National Defence to provide monitoring systems for military and commercial purposes. *Radarsat*'s powerful images stood at the centre of those contracts, but as the "war on terror" expanded, MDA received additional funding to build Canada's *Sapphire* military satellite and NEOSsat, the world's first space telescope dedicated to detecting and tracking asteroids, satellites, and orbital debris. The firm also received contracts to develop robotics for unmanned aerial vehicles (UAVs), as well as opportunities to sell property information products to a wider audience, including those who hoped to cash in on patriotic calls for more consumption, home ownership, and economic development. With the company's headquarters in Richmond reduced to two divisions – Information Systems and Geospatial Services (ISG), and Property Information Products – and its Ontario division focused on Robotics and Space Systems, MDA's profits, new executive pay and benefits packages, employee wage stagnation, and relationship to the military-industrial complex and financial sector became more visible as well. As a result, MDA experienced its first labour strike during 2006, followed by prominent and unwelcome national exposure when its board attempted to sell the company's "bread and butter" ISG and robotics divisions (which included tax-payer-funded *Radarsat* and *Canadarm*) to Minnesota's weapons manufacturer Alliant Techsystems (ATK). When Friedmann announced the proposed sale to ATK in January 2008, engineers resigned, critics mobilized, and MDA faced yet another crisis, all under an uncomfortable media spotlight and a parliamentary committee investigation during an economically dangerous year. Under widespread public scrutiny for the first time in its history, MDA, whether unwittingly or deliberately, also exposed many of the concerns that had plagued Canadians since World War II: how to draw a line between themselves and their American counterparts, control Canada's destiny, and assert the country's sovereignty while simultaneously working with the United States to achieve a prominent place within the world's power core. MDA faced new challenges as well, including those raised by concerned policy analysts, citizens, employees, and others who began to scrutinize the company's work more closely and to share more publicly their discoveries about the firm's military contracts, labour disputes, and especially threats to Canada's sovereignty.[8]

"BREAD AND BUTTER":
INFORMATION SYSTEMS, GEOSPATIAL SERVICES,
ROBOTICS, AND INCREASED PUBLIC SCRUTINY

MDA already had a strategic foothold on the American military and intelligence gathering market before 11 September 2001, with *Radarsat* the firm's central offering to worldwide governments seeking to enhance their "mission critical" systems. As a result, MDA consolidated all of its military contracts as well as its portable ground station and small satellite constellation work into one division, and focused the energies of its Ontario robotics team on the firm's civilian space systems. In these areas, MDA had many multi-year contracts that promised to provide the sorts of "bread and butter" security that had guided MDA's strategic plans since the early 1990s, so that others in the firm could concentrate on the riskier business of property information products. Among those multi-year contracts, MDA had received an important one from the US Air Force while Orbital arranged for its final divestitures of MDA in mid-2001: to develop a system to "ingest" various forms of digital terrain, elevation, and "air navigation data (such as the locations of navigation aids, runways, buildings and towers), and to build a virtual model of the physical environment surrounding an airport" so the USAF could display as well as "modify the approach procedure through a drag-and-drop user interface." At the end of

August 2001, Orbital's *OrbView-4* – a high-resolution commercial satellite that promised to visit each location on Earth in fewer than three days – exploded on launch, forcing the USAF to turn to other contractors who could collect data from *Radarsat-1* and future satellites. The USAF thus awarded to contracts to Northrup Grumman's Electronic Sensors and Systems Division, and Boulder, Colorado's, Vexcel Corporation to provide information gathered at MDA's wholly owned *Radarsat* data distributor, Radarsat International (RSI). After 9/11, Northrup and Vexcel then promised to deliver an unending series of requests for imagery.[9]

Perceiving the "longer-term changes in the marketplace" that the "tragic events of Sept. 11 and the failed launch of *OrbView-4*" had engendered, MDA's executives quickly reported on the shifting "priorities" of the USAF and "some of the company's customers" who would provide "longer-term opportunities for our various intelligence, defence, surveillance, policing capabilities and information products." During December 2001, MDA also reported that it had acquired Earth Satellite Corporation of Maryland (EarthSat), a firm that had pioneered the use of remote sensing for petroleum, mineral, and groundwater exploration. With annual revenues of US$20 million, EarthSat had the potential to expand MDA's "ability to extract land information from satellite images" for various uses, including "change detection," urban planning, and property assessment. Friedmann also assured MDA's shareholders that the acquisition "significantly expands our market reach as it gives us access to" EarthSat's US "customer base."[10]

The Canadian Space Agency also stepped forward to assist MDA's expansionist plans in February 2002, by announcing that it had awarded MDA a contract to extend the mission feasibility study for a constellation of small *Radarsat* satellites to "strengthen Canada's leadership and expertise" in the "growing market" of Earth observation. A system representing "the most advanced spaceborne land information and mapping mission ever conceived," the CSA boasted, the constellation promised to include applications for ice monitoring, disaster management, ocean and Arctic sovereignty, and, by implication, military engagement.[11] Thanks to the CSA contract as well as others from worldwide customers, MDA's 2002 *Annual Report* reported, "We have come out of a challenging year with a strong backlog in our systems business." The report also highlighted MDA's 2002 acquisition of Dynacs, Inc., a Houston-based software and engineering services provider with wide-ranging contacts in the "largest systems market in the world." When combined with EarthSat, Dynacs instantly expanded MDA's "reach into key U.S. government agencies and prime contractors." Dan Friedmann therefore summarized the year by emphasizing that MDA's "business with defence and defence-related agencies continued at a steady pace," particularly for the "geospatial information products from satellite imagery" that MDA would continue to provide through its current capabilities as well as via *Radarsat-2* and the constellation of satellites once launched.[12]

Employing data gathered from national agencies and private government contractors around the world, along with the Bush administration's insinuations that Saddam Hussein possessed or was attempting to produce weapons of mass destruction, "The Watchers" managed to convince members of Congress to pass the Authorization for Use of Military Force against Iraq Resolution of 2002. Although never made explicit, the Bush administration also used Grand Jury testimony from the earlier 1993 World Trade Center attack to create a false impression of the connections between Iraq and 11 September 2001. Anti-war protestors and long-time allies challenged the legality of invading Iraq (including members of the UN Security Council and the governments of Canada, France, Germany, and New Zealand). Regardless, on 19 March 2003, the United States began its military occupation of Iraq, with a stated policy of "regime change." Ultimately the voices of reason and a series of investigations discredited claims about Iraqi weapons programs and links to the 9/11 terrorists, but the tide had already turned. The Bush administration prepared the world for a protracted struggle in the Middle East and the potential of permanent war. One month later, MDA announced the completion of "an important order" for the US National Imagery and Mapping Agency, "a multi-level land cover database for more than 50% of the Earth."[13]

During his last year in office, Prime Minister Chrétien refused to support the American "coalition of the willing" in Iraq, declaring that the 2003 invasion lacked the sanction of the UN Security Council. Chrétien's government nevertheless authorized Canadian "peacekeeping" missions in Afghanistan (the first of them secretly arriving as part of Joint Task Force 2 in October 2001). Although most news outlets continued to argue that Canadian support for Chrétien's 2003 anti-invasion decision remained strong, those with continental business interests complained that his position hurt their relationships in the United States. They had little to fear. US Homeland Security spending continued to soar, Canadian components continued to flow into the US military, and continental defence sharing continued in the form of rebuilding efforts, logistical support, "mission critical systems," and eventually military personnel. And unlike during the Vietnam era, American war resisters could count on no safe haven in Canada.[14]

By the time defence policy analyst Steven Staples visited CANSEC 2003, Canada's largest defence and security trade show, he found that "the timing" of the Iraq invasion "could not have been better for arms manufacturers to gather in Ottawa." As a representative of the Polaris Institute, a research and advocacy non-profit that challenges the influence of corporations on public policy, Staples argued that while "U.S. troops were tearing down statues of Saddam Hussein in the middle of Baghdad," American "lawmakers were approving President Bush's request for $80 billion in new military spending, and Canada's military had just been handed its largest spending increase in more than a decade." Lobbyists representing the Canadian Association of Defence and Security Industries seemed unusually "upbeat" as they moved through CANSEC's trade show aisles, Staples noted. With more than 150 corporations and a record 3,600 delegates in attendance, CANSEC's "distinctly military focus" had attracted "U.S. defence heavyweights" and "Canadian heavies eager to ink contracts," including CAE, Magellan, and MDA, Staples reported. "The war against Iraq has given the arms industry unprecedented promotional opportunities for its high-tech weapons courtesy of around-the-clock coverage by CNN," he added, with the corporate media "embedding" reporters with an "all-volunteer" military and turning Iraq into a media spectacle of C4ISR capabilities without the nettlesome problems of roving photographers capturing the detritus of body bags, collateral damage, and civilian casualties.[15]

According to Staples, MDA stood out among those showcasing C4ISR offerings at CANSEC. With Canada's defence industry increasing by 47 per cent since 1998 and valued at $7.5 billion by the time the trade show got underway, Staples argued that the "growth of Canada's arms industry and its deep integration into the U.S. military-industrial complex is an issue of increasing concern for Canadians, many of whom are opposed to the war on terrorism." MDA's visibility at CANSEC therefore pitted several citizen groups against the firm, Staples reported, including a small group of protesters made anxious by British Columbia's recent contract with MDA "to administer its voluminous databases of information on citizens, despite objections from civil liberties advocates." Linking earlier WTO, G8 summit, and anti-war protests to the Canadian arms industry, and predicting more dissent and civil disobedience to come, Staples noted that "100 demonstrators blocked an entrance" to the CANSEC building, "resulting in four arrests."[16]

The small CANSEC protest failed to faze MDA's executives, whose success at winning more defence procurement contracts in Canada and the United States seemed to confirm what trade negotiators for Canada's Department of Foreign Affairs had argued during 2001. "In a world that feels markedly less safe than before 11 September," Michael Hart and William Dymond observed, "military preparedness, the capacity to gather and analyze intelligence, and resources available to police and other enforcement bodies assume new priority." Providing the tools for those new priorities, MDA and other defence contractors had merely tapped into the Cold War's "dense network of cooperative arrangements that have quietly proven their worth over the years," particularly among those who could navigate the procurement process for NATO, NORAD, Five Eyes, and Canada-US defence production sharing agreements. "Protestors, nationalists, environmentalists, human rights activists, and other 'civil society' groups have captured the government's attention out of all proportion to their weight in society," they asserted, but unfortunately "the government has been reluctant to accept that many of these groups are animated by values and preferences that most Canadians do not share." Indeed, they stressed, "Canadians have come to terms with the post-CUFTA atmosphere of trade liberalization and closer Canada-USA trade and investment ties," an assertion that had allowed business leaders to find "their voice and become increasing insistent" that Canada "achieve a seamless market governed by a single set of rules implemented and administered by the two governments to achieve their common interests in a well-functioning and secure North American economy."[17]

Moving through CANSEC and other venues with information systems and geospatial services to sell, during 2003 MDA posted a "record year" in "defence intelligence. Our company is continuing to make inroads into operational strategic U.S. defence projects, as we provide mission-critical systems to this growing market," Dan Friedmann reported. Those systems included more work with the US Army Space and Missile Defense Command to "enable global coverage and imaging under all environmental and lighting conditions," and to deliver data "within 90 minutes of collect, preferably via direct downlink to an existing military mobile ground station." The firm received "total orders of about $70 million" for information alone, Friedmann noted, particularly from unnamed customers seeking access to the powerful images collected by *Radarsat-1*.[18]

"MISSION CRITICAL":
SOARING PROFITS, EXPANDING EXECUTIVE PAY,
AND MDA'S FIRST EMPLOYEE STRIKE

Between 2003 and 2006, ongoing war, demands for *Radarsat* data and "mission critical systems," and environmental destruction created even wider opportunities at MDA. As a result, the firm began to develop its small satellite-based information mission capabilities to "provide a source of long-term revenues."[19] MDA additionally began to develop robotic applications for unmanned aerial vehicles. MDA's entrance into the drone market began, in part, from work the firm received from NASA. The *Challenger* disaster, problems with the Hubble Space Telescope (HST), and budgetary cuts had imperilled many of NASA's initiatives during the 1990s, but public support for the HST program convinced members of the US Congress to fund one final servicing mission to save the space telescope. Given the work of SPAR, then MDA on *Canadarm*, NASA turned to Canada, and by 2005, NASA awarded to MDA US$154 million to develop a "robotic grapple arm" to rescue the HST. Anticipating that award, Friedmann argued that the grapple arm represented MDA's first major opportunity to develop space robots for work beyond the ISS, "as the world leader in extending human reach in hostile environments with great precision and reliability." Although NASA eventually cancelled the HST program, MDA's early drone work provided yet another "new major source of long-term revenue," as well as a chance to "transition from the development of major robotics components to long-term systems support and enhancement contracts" for military as well as commercial purposes.[20] To effect that transition, and with a market capitalization of US$661.53 million during 2004 (up from US$106 million during 2003), MDA's board of directors decided to provide better incentives to MDA's senior executives to enhance shareholder value as well: they initiated lucrative compensation packages for those at the top. Executive salaries and bonuses soared by 78.8 per cent and 599.5 per cent respectively, with total compensation increasing 63.9 per cent over 2003.[21]

Although members of Canada's Centre for Remote Sensing continued to sell MDA's surveillance expertise both as a critical component of Earth resource monitoring to avoid environmental catastrophes and as central to the UN's 2000 International Charter on Space and Major Disasters as "the expression of a collective resolve to put space technology at the service of relief authorities in the event of a major disaster," most of MDA's ISG work centred on "military applications," because, as Friedmann claimed, "military forces are becoming increasingly reliant on complex systems of communication and computer devices exchanging information."[22] In the wake of Hurricane Katrina, the deadliest and most destructive storm during the Atlantic's 2005 hurricane season, people at MDA also realized that they could mobilize the company's "resources to support increased informational needs" for the property information products business, so that "insurance carriers" could "cover their customers' losses as quickly as possible." Tapping into those opportunities, MDA's annual reports claimed that the company's market valuation had increased substantially, from just over $661 million in 2004 to $1.75 billion by 2006. The board therefore approved another enhancement to MDA's executive pay and benefits package, as well as resources for the property information products unit and Brampton, Ontario's, Robotics and Space Division to take advantage of the emerging drone market.[23]

By 2004, media outlets confirmed that the aerospace industry had begun to hire an increasing number of employees again, "a reversal of a downward trend that began 14 years ago at the end of the Cold War," the Aerospace Industries Association reported. "Declining defense budgets, industry consolidation, and two commercial market downturns" that began during the 1990s thus came to a decisive end.[24] Unfortunately for MDA's employees, expanding defence budgets and the firm's soaring profits failed to trickle down to workers. As a result, members of Ontario's SPATEA (SPAR Professional and Allied Technical Employees' Association and MDA's only unionized workforce) began to air their grievances publicly.

Engineers, scientists, technologists, contract administrators, and allied technical staff had formed SPATEA in 1977 "to represent employee career concerns in discussions" about company goals and long-term strategies, first at SPAR, and then at MDA. Until June 2006, they managed to reach mutually acceptable agreements; however, as their own status began to decline with increased numbers of technical personnel entering computing and its tertiary industries worldwide, MDA's Ontario-based employees began to organize for a strike for the first time in the twenty-eight-year history of SPATEA. Their collective agreement had expired on 31 December 2005, but six months at the negotiating table had failed to produce a contract acceptable to the labour team. Citing MDA's substantial profits over the past five years – with maximum adjusted stock prices climbing from just $3.95 in 2004 to a decade high of $52.00 during early 2006 – and executive compensation packages increasing more than 70 per cent during the same period, members of the SPATEA bargaining team argued that their members as well as unorganized employees within the firm sought nothing more than improvements in their base salary, which had declined relative to provincial averages. In Ontario alone, they noted, MDA's salaries had fallen some 5 to 10 per cent below national levels. As a result, the bargaining team argued that their salary demands were neither "unreasonable" nor a threat to MDA's "competitive" position.[25]

MDA's senior executives acknowledged the value of their professional employees' "goal" of an increasing share of the firm's profits, but consistently refused to "bridge the gap" in the next three-year collective agreement. Finding themselves "steadily losing to both markets and inflation over the last five years," and with "long-standing and growing dissatisfaction with arbitrary, unilateral-decisions concerning their career goals, working conditions and salaries," SPATEA's bargaining team called for a strike vote. On 16 June 2006, fully 87 per cent of the SPATEA membership rejected the final offer tabled by the firm. They then endorsed the strike. With several key projects looming, on 18 July MDA announced that the firm had entered into a new three-year collective agreement with SPATEA. The strike lasted only one month, and MDA's unorganized employees at other locations did not walk out in solidarity with their SPATEA colleagues in Ontario. Nevertheless, SPATEA's decision to strike signalled a rising, albeit amorphous consciousness among MDA's professional workers, many of whom had long seen themselves as talented individualists rising into the dominant class and superior to non-technical employees, but now had to acknowledge that they might have something to learn from those who comprehended the value of bargaining rights to protect collective interests. Only time would tell if they would come to see their own present circumstances in a much larger historical context, in the series of economic and technological changes that had already produced an endless series of talented individuals and skilled groups in decline.[26]

Cancelled NASA contracts and labour strife aside, the Homeland Security Bubble provided MDA with work for an expanding number of technology workers willing to accept the company's employment terms. National security issues also prompted policymakers to authorize funding for the development of *Sapphire*, Canada's first military satellite. Helping MDA to build on its telescope work, Defence Research and Development Canada additionally provided funding for *NEOSsat*, Canada's "Sentinel in the Sky." The federal government then expanded its Public-Private Partnership (PPP) program for work on unmanned aerial vehicles. As before, MDA's friends in government not only planned to award much of that work to the West Coast firm, but also embraced the interests of capital over labour. As he ascended to prime minister during 2006, Stephen Harper then reinforced policies to bolster both.[27]

"GOLDEN CIRCLE OF THE CROWN": THE DEVELOPMENT OF *SAPPHIRE* AND *NEOSSAT*

Sworn into office on 6 February 2006, Harper began his first term by referring explicitly to Great Britain's Queen Elizabeth as Canada's head of state and linking Canada and the United Kingdom to a "Golden Circle of the Crown," which included a broadening of the Five Eyes intelligence program and Canada's commitment to military expenditures. Before several weeks had passed, Harper also made a surprise trip to Afghanistan, where he greeted Canadian military personnel deployed to the region since 2001 as part of the NATO-led International Security Assistance Force. When the Israel-Lebanon conflict broke out in 2006, Harper then immediately declared Israel's "right to defend itself," further attaching Canada's surveillance and military communities to the national budget, American ambitions in the Middle East, and Israel's place within both.[28]

Multinational security projects created the context for Canada's rapprochement with Israel and MDA's involvement in the development of *Sapphire*. According to Kole Kilibarda's work on the New Transparency project, Canadian and Israeli cooperation surfaced as just one "part of a broader network of knowledge sharing and production relating to the development of 'counter-terrorism' technologies tied to Washington's 'Global War on Terror' since 11 September 2001." Chrétien's Liberals had signed the Canada-Israel Free Trade Agreement during 1997, and Prime Minister Paul Martin's government (2003–06) enhanced the trade zone by formalizing various security agreements, including the 2005 Technology and Science Cooperative Agreement between the Canadian Space Agency and the Israel Space Agency. But Canada's involvement in the Middle East expanded after Harper became prime minister and the Conservatives won a minority government during the 2006 federal election, Kilibarda argued. Thus, the American-centred strategy to involve US allies in "regime change" and the reconstruction of the Middle East prompted Canada to settle its long-standing differences with Israel, and when the "Conservative government assumed office in February 2006," Kilibarda observed, security ties between Canada and Israel "deepened." Thereafter, counterterrorism and crime emergency preparedness emerged as the main foci of agencies linked to the missions of US Homeland Security and the long-standing Five Eyes intelligence program.[29]

Although MDA received the *Sapphire* contract just "months after China destroyed one of its own weather satellites using a missile, leaving a large amount of debris in low Earth orbit and putting other nations on notice that their commercial and military space assets were vulnerable to attack," the desire to "re-establish Canada's contribution to surveillance in space" and rise as a significant "energy power" ultimately surfaced as Canada's raison d'être for building and operating *Sapphire*. Policymakers also cited OECD reports that continued to remind Canadians that they had fallen behind the United States as well as the European Union, China, and many developing nations in the competitive global space race. Through *Sapphire*, Harper believed he could reverse that long-term trend. Thus, between 2006 and 2007, MDA bid on and won more than $76 million in contracts from Canada's Department of National Defence to build *Sapphire*, in a teaming arrangement that also included ComDev International and England's Surrey Satellite Technology Ltd.[30]

Harper's determination to reassert Canada's role in surveillance capitalism provided opportunities for MDA to play a leading role in the country's Networks of Centres of Excellence (NCE) program as well. With his government encouraging more of the university-industrial collaborations Canada had begun to develop during 1989, Harper hoped that the NCE could enhance Canada's "industrial know-how and investment capacity." The NCE's mission also comported well with the new Canada-Mexico-US Security and Prosperity Partnership of North America (SPP; formed on 23 March 2005). In Canada, the new SPP included an investment in *NEOSsat*, a micro-satellite project funded by the Canadian Space Agency and Defence Research and Development Canada. MDA led the effort, with partners including the University of Calgary, the CSA's David Florida Laboratory in Ottawa, Microsat Systems Canada Ltd of Mississauga, Ontario, and ComDev International. Officially announced on 31 March 2008 as Canada's "Sentinel in the Sky," *NEOSsat* promised to circle the Earth every 100 minutes and emerge as the world's first satellite dedicated to detecting asteroids and space debris.[31]

Finally, Harper's focus on rapprochement furthered the Canadian-Israeli connection to the development of aerial robotics for use in unmanned vehicles, including those produced through a Canadian Private-Public Partnerships (PPP) between MDA and its Israeli partners, Israel Aerospace Industries (IAI) and Elbit Systems. During 2008, in an effort to defeat the Taliban in Kandahar province, the Canadian Department of National Defence expanded on previous developments in "joint commander centres for tracking shipments" by awarding to the MDA-IAI team a two-year, C$95 million contract to build drones carrying surveillance equipment. That contract emerged as MDA's "first big breakthrough after five years of work in the burgeoning realm of unmanned aerial vehicles," and positioned the firm to emerge among the world's most sophisticated suppliers of drones for use by military as well as commercial entities. MDA also benefited from the creation of Canada's Institute for Robotics and Intelligent Systems (IRIS), which included MDA as a significant industry partner. As before, policymakers hoped that *Sapphire*, *NEOSsat*, IRIS, and similar projects would help to wean Canada from its long-term dependence on the United States so that Canadian capitalists could further their reach into Europe, Asia, and other parts of the world.[32]

In the meantime, while government contracts for *Radarsat* data, robotics, *Sapphire*, NEOSsat, and other information systems and geospatial services provided much of the "bread-and-butter" on which the firm had long depended, MDA's executive team continued to worry about potential budget cuts and the company's ongoing dependence on the federal government. As a result, they hoped that their work on UAVs would ultimately lead to increased commercial work. To offset the risk, they also focused on the expansion of the property information products business that had begun to boom on deregulation of the financial services sector, increased property valuations, and the expansion of natural disasters such as the 2004 Indian Ocean earthquake and 2005 hurricane season. As the firm's executives mapped out and then executed their larger strategy for property information products between 2004 and 2008, it appeared that the financial services sector could wean MDA from its dependence on government as well as provide windfall profits for the company's shareholders.[33]

"ESSENTIAL INFORMATION":
BANKING ON REAL ESTATE SPECULATION,
AND THE EXPANSION OF PRIVACY CONCERNS

While multinationals worldwide called for more deregulation and better tax incentives on which to expand, Americans fuelled a real estate, development, and credit boom that allowed MDA to move even further into data mining for the financial services sector. In the United States alone, the ratio of debt to disposable personal income rose from 77 to 127 per cent between 1990 and 2007, with mortgage-related activities consuming much of that increase. Following 9/11, loan incentives, easy initial terms, rising housing prices, and "love of country" rhetoric encouraged borrowers to assume increasingly difficult mortgages. Mortgaged-backed securities (MBSS), in particular, allowed institutions and investors from around the world to speculate in the US housing market. Easy credit additionally encouraged an increase in the lower-quality, adjustable-rate subprime mortgages that appeared in 2004 and promised homeowners favourable refinancing terms as well as quick returns on the escalating price of real estate. During 2005, banking lobbyists then celebrated the passage of the US Bankruptcy Abuse Prevention and Consumer Protection Act, which, among other things, encouraged more risk-taking in businesses large and small while simultaneously making it increasingly difficult for consumers to file for personal bankruptcy, even if most of their cases centred on extraordinary medical expenses and job losses. Indeed, "the 2005 changes made clear that certain derivatives and financial transactions were exempt from the provisions of the bankruptcy code that freeze a failed company's assets until a court decides how to apportion them among creditors," the *Financial Times* confirmed.[34]

With such changes providing incentives to those who could provide property information, MDA's executives and shareholders announced that the time had arrived to invest more heavily in the financial services sector. During 2004, the firm had delivered a pilot system to facilitate the e-filing of land title documents in British Columbia. Thereafter, MDA acquired Marshall & Swift/Boeckh, a Los Angeles–based supplier of property information and valuation solutions for the US property insurance sector. MDA then expanded more deeply into the United Kingdom, crafting proposals that won for the firm multi-million-dollar contracts to modernize the National Land Information Service and to decrease response times on land and property information requests throughout the United Kingdom. As a result, MDA "solidified" its "reputation as a supplier of essential information solutions to the U.K.," Dan Friedmann announced, "by increasing our customer base and adding more value to each transaction." On the strength of opportunities in the United States and despite the United Kingdom's sluggish 2005 housing market, MDA's board thus authorized continued expansion in the firm's property information business.[35]

While SPATEA employees launched their strike during 2006, MDA purchased Mindbox, a specialized software tool to provide in-depth analysis of loans. MDA then marketed its Mindbox capabilities to more than 100 financial services firms in the United States, including Countrywide Home Loans and Ford Motor Credit. The firm also acquired xit2 Limited, a UK-based firm serving as a "one-stop data exchange network for all stages in the life of a mortgage," as well as Rochford Brady, a leading property search firm in the Republic of Ireland. MDA additionally branched out into court records and services via its connection to BC On-Line, a database that gave MDA access to the public records of the province's private citizens. The latter purchase created new privacy concerns on Canada's West Coast, particularly when people in BC learned that MDA controlled the rights to data collected by *Radarsat*. Despite protests and legal challenges from the Canadian Bar Association, however, MDA retained its access to the property information that an increasing number of global clients coveted. Dan Friedmann therefore assured MDA's shareholders that the company "will continue to focus much of our efforts in the Financial Services sector, expanding our search business, launching our white label HIP [Home Information Packs] service in England and Wales, and developing our valuation business in the U.K., as well as in Germany."[36]

By diversifying its data mining expertise into property information products between 2004 and 2006, MDA generated revenues amounting to some $500 million annually. According to a website devoted to monitoring what an expanding number of critics dubbed "financially engineered destruction," MDA's Mindbox acquisition also put at risk "tens upon tens of millions who applied for loans with Mindbox programming attached (which is everybody)," with privacy "forever lost to a global surveillance organization." The website also advised that MDA held "many of the defense contracts of the United States" and was "building drones that hover over the Middle East." When aggregated, MDA's information products posed more than privacy and defence-related concerns, however; the mingling of financial services soon threatened banks, mortgage lenders, property insurance firms, and untold numbers of consumers.[37]

The speculative real estate bubble peaked in 2006, on what critics have called a "shadow banking system" of hedge funds and investment banks, many of them disguising their leverage levels from regulators and investors through complex computer modelling, off-balance-sheet securitization (the bundling of assets and debt), and derivatives (including weather derivatives that attempted to hedge the risks associated with adverse or unexpected environmental conditions). Along with others, the shadow banking system took on substantial debt to fuel expansion, including high-risk loans that ultimately made it impossible to absorb large-scale losses such as those associated with MBS transactions and subprime mortgages made to higher-risk borrowers. As interest rates began to rise in 2006 and 2007, housing prices started to fall, and refinancing became more difficult for an increasing number of those who had taken out second and third mortgages to pay for increasingly expensive items, such as vehicles, vacation properties, and advanced education. As adjustable-rate mortgages reset at higher rates, delinquencies and defaults mounted, and mortgage-backed securities lost much of their value. Fearing the soundness of US financial markets, global investors scaled back, credit tightened worldwide, and investments slowed in North America and Europe. In such an environment, the speculative boom created the context for both the subprime mortgage meltdown and the global financial crisis of 2008. It also placed MDA at risk, even if many at the company failed to see the larger structural forces "operating in the background" of MDA's surging property information business.[38]

MDA's 2006 *Annual Report* expressed regret that MDA "saw limited growth" in its US property information business "due to a reduction in mortgage lending activity, as well as lower claims activity in the insurance information business, as a result of a rather benign hurricane season." The report nevertheless argued that MDA's "British Columbia property information business continued to grow through 2006 in a strong BC housing market." With revenues finally exceeding $1 billion, the property information business representing nearly 70 per cent of the firm's total, and revenues from geospatial services declining from 10 per cent in 2005 to 5 per cent during 2006, the report stressed that MDA would "continue to focus much of our efforts in the Financial Services sector." Although the development of *Sapphire* and NEOSsat promised to generate future revenue, MDA had struggled to secure large contracts with NASA and several other US government agencies, and its executive team worried that Harper's Conservatives might not make a long-term commitment to Canada's space program as the government reacted to economic problems in the United States. Indeed, when Harper's Conservatives released their 2006 *Advantage Canada* report, the federal government promised tax, regulation, and debt reduction but little in the way of infrastructure development, save for border security and transportation networks. Those priorities seemed to limit MDA's opportunities in the domestic market. Making matters worse, the US government created renewed uncertainty by increasing its emphasis on the regulation of exports and imports in defence-related articles, services, and technical data, including the satellite and launch technologies it had placed on the protected US Munitions List (USML). Friedmann's executive team thus began to reconsider MDA's future; and their discussions ultimately persuaded the board to approve the sale of the space-based, systems sides of the firm so that MDA could focus on the property information products business.[39]

"EVERY BUSINESS HAS ITS PRICE":
THE PROPOSED ACQUISITION
AND ESCALATING SOVEREIGNTY CONCERNS

With more than 3,000 employees working at locations across Canada, the United States, and the United Kingdom during 2007, MDA began negotiations to "sell some of its assets," specifically its Information Systems and Geospatial Services (ISG) and Robotics divisions. Hoping to persuade American military contractors to purchase its space-based divisions for $1 billion so that MDA could "realize the inherent value" of the firm's surveillance capabilities, MDA's board members argued that the sale would fulfill the promise of the five-year plans the company had pursued since

1993 to gain access to wider opportunities in US defence contracting. The deal would also "permit" MDA's space-based units "to expand in the large U.S. systems market under U.S. ownership," where USML restrictions would not preclude access to classified military information. Such a sale additionally implied substantial returns to the firm's major shareholders, as well as revenues MDA could use to develop its property information products.[40] When the *International Business Times* and *Wall Street Journal* reported MDA's intentions during June 2007, the first argued that "potential buyers are balking at the roughly $1 billion asking price," while the latter reported that "four defense contractors, including Lockheed Martin Corp., Raytheon Co., Northrup Grumman Corp. and Alliant Techsystems Inc. [ATK], expressed interest but opted against a bid, citing people familiar with details," which included concerns that MDA, like so many other firms, had over-valued its worth. As a result, on 14 June, the Canadian Press announced that MDA shares got a "pop" of 11 per cent "on rumours" it planned to sell its "surveillance and space engineering division." Thereafter however, MDA's stocks took a "roller-coaster ride," the *National Post* reported, "shooting up 13% before closing 7% at trading's close." Citing a prominent industry analyst, the *Post* also stressed, "We're inclined to believe that MDA will not divest its ISG as yesterday's rumour suggested. That being said, every business has its price."[41]

Despite reports that ATK had hesitated at the initial asking price, the US firm had designs on MDA's *Radarsat* technologies and drone capabilities. With annual revenues in excess of $4 billion and employees exceeding 17,000 across twenty-one American states, ATK headquartered its operations in Minneapolis, Minnesota, and served the US government as a military contractor and manufacturer of land mines, cluster bombs, missile systems, and combat caravans. Already a strategic partner with MDA, ATK had ambitions to "gain access to classified technologies that MDA previously could not sell outside Canada," *Aviation Week and Space Technology* (*AW&ST*) reported. As a bonus, ATK would also acquire MDA's "large civil space business, deriving about 40% of its annual revenues from the Canadian Space Agency and NASA, and supplying the robotic arms used on the space shuttle and International Space Station." ATK thus offered US$1.3 billion for MDA's ISG business unit, betting "a lot of money" on MDA because "concern about Asat attacks will prompt the Pentagon and intelligence agencies to distribute work among satellites that are smaller, simpler, and much more numerous," *AW&ST* noted. "MDA's leadership in small satellite design," ATK's chairman and CEO confirmed, also emerged as a "key driver" in the proposed acquisition.[42]

Unfortunately for those hoping to close the deal, Canadian sovereignty concerns thwarted the plans of both ATK and MDA, ultimately forcing MDA down yet another "rocky road of reinvention."[43] The public airing of the proposed deal also exposed how much surveillance capitalism and a larger tug of war had drawn Canadian taxpayers into the American military-industrial complex as well as created uncertainty about MDA's role in peaceful Arctic observation and the Canadian government's objectives in outer space. MDA's 2007 *Annual Report* had declared its revenues and earnings "up," because "the diverse product mix and customer base of the Company's business had limited the effects of soft housing and lending markets in the U.S. and United Kingdom." Moreover, the report stressed, MDA wanted to focus its "management and financial resources exclusively on its rapidly growing information products business" for those "involved in real estate–related transactions such as the buying, selling, conveyancing, mortgage financing, and insurance of properties." MDA's total backlog, the report claimed, had climbed from $479 million in 2006 to $641 million in 2007, $500 million of which it attributed to ISG's business areas.[44] Ultimately for ATK, that backlog, the *Radarsat* constellation mission project, and MDA's UAV work became too hard to resist. ATK made the offer and, following the launch of *Radarsat-2* from Kazakhstan's Baikonur Cosmodrome on 14 December 2007, Dan Friedmann announced that MDA had "executed a definitive agreement for the sale of its information systems and geospatial services business" to ATK, with the "$1.325 billion in cash" deal subject to little more than regulatory approval of the two nations' governments.[45] In a separate press release, ATK announced that the acquisition also promised to establish ATK as a "full-spectrum international space company."[46]

Given earlier deals sanctioned by the Investment Canada Act, representatives on both sides of the proposed ATK-MDA deal thought the sale would pass through the regulatory process with relative ease. It did not. The moment MDA announced the sale on 8 January 2008, a political firestorm began, with members of the national press reminding Canadians that their tax dollars had funded MDA's rise from relative obscurity to one of the nation's pre-eminent systems engineering firms. From the mid-1970s forward, local reporters observed, the company had also served as an anchor for the development of Vancouver's high-tech community, including the Lower Mainland's cluster of expertise in information systems, robotics, and space-based intelligence for both commercial and military clients. "Despite his earlier enthusiasm for the deal," the *Globe and Mail* reported, "yesterday the Industry Minister [Jim Prentice] had no comment on the MDA sale." Instead, an Industry Canada spokesman "said it would be improper for him to discuss the pending deal because Mr Prentice is also in charge of vetting foreign investment and officials reporting to him will be scrutinizing the Techsystems bid." The *Globe and Mail* additionally announced that the Harper government had just replaced the head of the CSA, "only nine months on the job," with "Guy Bujold, a former top Industry Canada bureaucrat" who would "take over as interim boss." That announcement provided additional uncertainty, not only about the MDA-ATK deal but also about the CSA's future.[47]

Several MDA engineers also resigned in protest over the proposed ATK deal, citing ethical objections to working for a company that "produces weaponry that kills people indiscriminately – soldiers and civilians alike." Underscoring that Canada had signed the UN 1997 Convention on the Prohibition of the Use, Stockpiling, Production and Transfer of Anti-Personnel Mines and on Their Destruction (commonly referred to as the Mine Ban Treaty), whereas the United States had not done so, one American-born engineer who resigned told reporters that he had moved to Canada to "avoid having my tax dollars go to support companies like ATK." Moreover, he stressed, the sale of a Canadian company to an arms manufacturer violated the Mine Ban Treaty. Another resigning engineer claimed that he had wanted to work on *Radarsat-2* because he and others had assumed that the satellite "would be used for good," for civilian purposes and peaceful Arctic observation. Joining the protest, some Canadians bloggers argued that ATK's gain seemed like a pretty bad deal for Canada. They therefore demanded a national conversation about the "morality" of selling to an American weapons manufacturer the whole of MDA's satellite and space-based units, which included *Canadarm-2* and *Radarsat-2*, the earth observation satellite MDA had developed, into which Canadian taxpayers had invested at least $430 million, and MDA operated following the satellite's launch.[48]

MDA's founding fathers weighed in on the debate as well. Retired from MDA in 1998 and living in Switzerland, Vern Dettwiler argued, "When I was still working" at MDA, "I and most of my fellow workers believed quite strongly that we would not like to work for a defence (or offence) based company, particularly a foreign" one.[49] Also retired from MDA in 1998, John MacDonald countered that MDA shareholders "didn't have much of a choice." With Canadian "advanced technology" firms finding it difficult to "tap into lucrative U.S. government space and defence contracts," MacDonald argued that "free trade with the U.S. is a myth." MDA therefore needed a US parent firm to improve the company's win rate in US government procurement. "If the company wants to fulfill its destiny," MacDonald asserted, "it has to do this. None of us likes it," he lamented, "but the market for the space side of MDA isn't really in Canada. We had a good 40-year run at building one hell of a space program on the West Coast," MacDonald boasted, but he also cautioned that "the government will be responsible for creating a new Avro Arrow disaster" if it killed the ATK deal without "rapidly" increasing "funding for Canada's space program." Indeed, MacDonald stressed that the federal government needed to double the budget of the CSA "immediately" to save the country's space-based industry from ruin.[50]

"UNDERMINING OUR NATIONAL SOVEREIGNTY": PARLIAMENTARY HEARINGS AND THE FOILED ACQUISITION

When Parliament's Standing Committee on Industry, Science and Technology held its first meeting on 29 January 2008, the NDP's Peggy Nash moved a motion calling for a discussion of the MDA sale with Jim Prentice, the minister with ultimate authority to decide whether the proposed ATK acquisition would provide "net benefits to Canada" under the Investment Canada Act. Thereafter, the committee scheduled four hearings to receive evidence from Prentice, university and industry researchers, labour leaders, members of MDA, and other interested parties. Ultimately, the hearings brought to light unresolved concerns that had consumed Canadian policymakers for several decades, including those associated with the potential brain drain of Canadian talent, direct foreign investment in the Canadian economy, and the erosion of Canadian Arctic, technological, and cultural sovereignty. They also had the potential to challenge self-perceptions about Canada's distinctive identity as an international power broker interested only in the peaceful applications of outer space. At the same time, the testimony published for posterity reveals Canada's imperial ambitions and the long-term role it has played in the neoliberal project.

Steven Staples, chair of the Rideau Institute on International Affairs, and Marc Garneau, former president of the CSA, were among those who appeared before the committee on 5 March. Anticipating the concerns of others, Staples argued, "Ironically, in this sale of RADARSAT-2, we may be undermining our own national security. We could be selling off our ability to monitor our coasts and provide our government with the data it needs to make decisions." In addition, he noted that Canada "could be eroding our industrial base and space industries, which will limit our future capacities." He therefore agreed with protestors, arguing "this is a bad deal for Canadians." Others who appeared on that day concurred.[51]

A retired military officer, former astronaut, and engineer-politician, Marc Garneau testified that MDA "is not just another Canadian company being reviewed under the Canada investment act. It's a company that has received significant and deliberate funding from the Government of Canada. The Canadian taxpayer has invested heavily in the growth of MDA to help create a world-class Canadian company capable of building the hardware that Canada needs to meet its national strategic objectives in space," including Arctic sovereignty and the monitoring of the Northwest Passage. "The Canadian government agreed to pay about $430 million of the roughly $520 million RADARSAT-2 price tag," he reminded members of the committee, "to help MDA develop its commercial market for space-based imagery." In return," the Canadian government allowed MDA to "own and operate the satellite, and provide the government with specific imagery. This was a bold move back in the late nineties," he emphasized, one that positioned "Canada as a leader in this developing international market. There is no question that ownership of this satellite by MDA allowed it to get an extremely attractive offer from ATK of over $1.3 billion. In essence," he observed, "the Canadian taxpayer allowed MDA to secure a very lucrative deal for its shareholders, yet the Canadian public, which should be viewed as a shareholder, is giving up a great deal if this sale proceeds." Garneau additionally argued that "the Government of Canada should take into account the fact that MDA is the only space company in Canada capable of building large, complex satellites." As a result, "its sale would mean that from now on, the Canadian government would have to buy future satellites from foreign-owned companies. The bottom line," he concluded, "is that space is a critically important strategic tool for the Government of Canada. That importance will continue to grow as more and more countries head for space" and "Canada will require new and more capable satellites in the future."[52]

Hugh Thompson, a spacecraft systems engineer, testified that he had agreed to speak up on behalf of twelve MDA employees who shared his concerns about the proposed sale. Although he considered himself a loyal employee, Thompson argued that he and other MDA employees feared they would lose their jobs or have to leave the company because, "in good conscience," they could not work for a company like ATK. This problem paled in comparison to other concerns, however, for "when ATK buys the systems division of MDA, they will be buying our intellectual property," he stressed. "When ATK bids new technology developed in Canada for U.S. classified projects, it seems highly likely that this technology will also become classified." He therefore cautioned that "Canada will lose access to technology that has been developed by Canadians in Canada for the benefit of Canada." Finally, he echoed those who had already resigned from MDA over the Mine Ban Treaty: "Although working for ATK might not violate the letter of the treaty, it certainly violates the spirit of the treaty. I personally have a problem with working for a company that violates international law, even if they don't violate the law in their own country." Noting that "many of my co-workers and I, as well as many other Canadians, are against the weaponization of space," he concluded that "the only sensible thing for Canada to do now that we have reached this state is to reject this deal and reject the transfer of the RADARSAT-2 operating licence." Once done, he argued, Canada should "immediately move forward so that MDA can get on with building the things that Canada wants and needs for our security, our sovereignty, and our contributions to global environmental monitoring." That would "continue our tradition of building a healthy, high-tech space industry that is not beholden to whatever the next plans of the U.S. military might be."[53]

When asked if he had previously known about MDA's work on military applications, Thompson conceded that "MDA certainly is involved in military activities and surveillance, and RADARSAT-2 is involved in military surveillance." Regardless, "there's a line that one somewhere draws; everything is shades of grey, but at some point one's involvement is too far beyond what one is willing to accept, and this certainly would push me beyond my line."[54] His "line" reflected a long-standing problem for many Canadians, one they had tried to draw since World War II. "History shows that American control of Canadian space assets is not without precedent," long-time space writer Chris Gainor had argued, "but such a large and unambiguous sale of Canadian space assets will cause Canadian policymakers to look skeptically at further investment in space," he cautioned. Furthermore, "ATK has promised to continue operations in Canada, but the pressure from American authorities that shut MDA out of American military work may also lead to stipulations that such work be done by American workers on American territory."[55]

Following his appearance on 13 March, where he assured the committee that he would "take all the steps necessary to ensure that contractual and other obligations are respected and that the interests of the Canadian taxpayers are protected," Prentice undertook the confidential task of deciding MDA's fate.[56] On 20 March, he then confirmed that he had decided to invoke the Investment Canada Act rule that allowed the minister of industry to delay making a decision for an additional thirty days. On 26 March, after MDA confirmed its 2007 profit of $95 million (nearly 14 per cent higher than 2006), Prentice created an advisory committee for the CSA. Charging several "highly respected business and academic leaders" to work with Guy Bujold to review the CSA's projects "against existing and emerging government and science and technology priorities," Prentice asked the advisory committee to assess the agency's "challenges," provide "strategic advice" to Industry Canada on the CSA's "expenditures and potential for future investments," and recommend "new opportunities where Canadian expertise, science and technology can continue to contribute to maximizing social and economic benefits for Canadians," all to "reinforce the direction of Canada's space program and foster better alignment of its programs with the evolving priorities of Canada and Canadians."[57]

On 1 April, while members of the advisory committee commenced their work, MDA's Dan Friedmann appeared before the standing committee to address many of the questions that had long troubled the government. Would the sale of MDA to a US firm threaten Canadian political independence and control over projects subsidized by Canadian taxpayers? Would it result in a brain drain of Canadian engineering and managerial talent to the United States? Would Canada lose important intellectual property that the government funded to protect Canadian interests? And would the sale adversely affect Canadian researchers working in new and developing fields? The committee also wanted Friedmann to respond to fears that the sale could subvert regulations of the 2005 Remote Sensing Space Systems Act on the distribution of data gathered from *Radarsat-2* as well as damage Canada's reputation as a peaceful nation that adhered to international treaties to avoid the weaponization of space.[58]

Friedmann first addressed questions about *Radarsat-2*, arguing that the "Government of Canada has all the necessary powers and authority" to "exercise full control" over the satellite. "MDA won an open competition to design and build a complete system," with *Radarsat-2* "meeting or exceeding the operational needs of the Government of Canada. This so-called investment by the Government of Canada in the RADARSAT-2 satellite," he stressed, "is a prepayment for data to be delivered to the government over the next seven to ten years." The federal government's right to the data "will continue to be protected under this transaction, and taxpayers will get their money's worth as contemplated," he asserted. "By far the largest growth opportunity for exports is represented by the U.S. space and defence market," he argued, and to gain access to that market, MDA needed "a partner with proven capability to win U.S. government procurements," one "that can and will lever our technical excellence, but without the duplicate capability that could render ours redundant." He also stressed the need for "a partner that employs U.S. citizens with government access and security clearances. Without this partner, we cannot get the work. That is why we have chosen this path," he advised, because it "is a win-win situation for everyone."[59]

On the issue of Canada's total investment "in the neighbourhood of $445 million," with cost overruns "something like $200 million," Friedmann countered that "MDA's original contribution was in the order of $180 million. We just got shortchanged on $100 million of that because we are supposed to pay for all the operations and nobody considers that." MDA "spent more than $80 million on construction," he argued, and "Canada was arranging for a free launch – not be confused with a free lunch – from the U.S. government in exchange for whatever they were going to do with the U.S. government." The US government "did not come to the party as the king with RADARSAT-2," Friedmann chided. Indeed, the Canadian government "made the decision to continue with the program and basically financed the U.S. contribution." When pressed to elaborate on government subsidies and the public-private partnerships that had helped to develop technological know-how and nurture the space industry worldwide, Friedmann maintained that one could not "call it investment." The government "contracted" with firms such as MDA "to do the work in their country. The ownership is all over the place," he argued. "British Aerospace owns the fourth-largest defence contractor in the United States. Most British companies are owned by the French, but they do their work in the countries according to the laws of the countries – another big misconception," he stressed.[60]

Addressing the possibility of layoffs, particularly at MDA's robotics division in Brampton, Ontario, as well as the potential for a brain drain of Canadian talent caused by moral qualms about the deal and ATK's control of the company's payroll, technology, and UAV operation in Suffield, Alberta, Friedmann argued that "the number one reason we picked this option was to maintain the jobs in Canada. That's what I'm trying to do. But the only way you can have jobs in Canada is to have work, and I need work." MDA has "1,500 employees in Canada, and a small percentage have a personal problem with this deal," he noted. Indeed, "I probably have the biggest personal problem with this deal. I lose my dream job" of "twenty-eight years." Regardless, he maintained, "the turnover due to this transaction will be minimal." Only "about thirty people have left since this transaction," he stressed, but "the transaction does not register on my human resources report as a major concern." He conceded that "salary is a concern," but emphasized his "fiduciary duty as the president of the company to get value for my shareholders." When pressed about shareholders profiting by the deal at the expense of employee job security, Friedmann argued that ATK told MDA that "they would keep the work and the technology and export mandate in Canada. They would keep our management staff in Canada and they would keep our management in place." Although he privileged managerial over rank-and-file employment, Friedmann emphasized that no one in the systems business had "job security. We are six months from being out of business. We have to go out and win the business." As a result, "the only job security employees have "is access to work and the absolute vast majority of our employees understand this. I didn't want to rub it in with the news, but we got 99.95% approval from shareholders," he claimed, which included "over 1,000 MDA employees," members of the "government and private pension funds from many provinces," and "many thousands of Canadians," with "Ontario Teachers' Pension Fund" MDA's "largest shareholders."[61]

Friedmann dismissed claims that the government might lose its ability to protect Canada's sovereignty and global reputation if ATK acquired 100 per cent ownership of MDA's space business. Those concerns, he argued, resided with the federal government and the laws, treaties, and agreements that policymakers would choose to enforce. "Canada's future as a space nation is not foremost dependent on the ownership of its space industry," Friedmann claimed, "but rather on the vision, initiative, and space budgets of the government. It is the brilliant work of Canadians who, over the years, have captured the imagination of all of us" and "pushed the frontiers of Canada's space capability avidly," he asserted, "whether owned by Canadians or Americans, whether governed by Conservatives or Liberals." Believing that MDA had positioned Canada "to advance into the next league of the world's stage," Friedmann thus expected the minister of industry to agree to the sale. When the Conservative chair of the committee, James Rajotte asked what benefits ATK expected from the agreement, Friedmann confirmed that the United States would have access to *Radarsat* data, which ATK could sell "over the next seven years." Still, he claimed, "The minister has shutter control. He can close the shutter of the satellite" if and when sovereignty issues arose.[62]

Finally, on 3 April 2008, the committee heard testimony from other groups, including the National Automobile, Aerospace, Transportation and General Workers Union of Canada (CAW-Canada), whose representatives had continuing concerns about the fate of employees at MDA's robotics division in Ontario. Carol Phillips, assistant to the president of the

CAW, argued that "the proposed sale of Canada's leading domestic supplier will erode Canada's national and Arctic sovereignty. It is contrary to existing Canadian law," she asserted, and "will transfer ownership and control of vital technology and data to a foreign nation, contrary to our national security interests. It will wipe out future opportunities for Canada to enhance domestic expertise in space technology and know-how," she argued, would, "once again, as we saw with the Avro Arrow," result "in the emigration of countless high-skilled aeronautical engineering and technical positions to the United States and provide no guarantee for employment levels in Canada."[63] The proposed sale seemed to confirm that Canadians could never escape the spectre of the Avro Arrow employment disaster, but in a display of how much the neoliberal project had altered the conversation since 1959, neither labour representatives nor university researchers and policymakers articulated the idea that the country might have an alternative to the ongoing privatization of the public sphere or the further incorporation of Canada into the American military-industrial complex that had guided the country's integration into surveillance capitalism for more than fifty years. The earlier debate had underscored the Great Depression and the three decades of social experimentation it had engendered, but as Bruce Smardon has argued, despite billions of dollars spent on attempts to improve Canada's R&D ranking within the international community since the 1970s, by the twenty-first century "it was taken for granted that the only way to increase R&D and innovation was to move the federal state ever closer to private capital."[64]

While interested parties awaited the government's final decision about ATK's acquisition of MDA, Canadians registered their opinions on the potential sale, including those who had begun to post comments on CBC's *Quirks and Quarks* blog as early as January. Registering typical complaints about the proposed sale, "Not Impressed" argued that "the ethics of this thing are so upsetting, that despite any personal concerns, I find it very suspicious that" *Radarsat-2*, "paid for by Canadian tax dollars and initially intended for Earth imaging for peaceful purposes, is going to be redeployed to assist in a military effort that we didn't agree to pay for."[65] "MDA Ex-Employee" asked Canadians to remember "when SPAR was bought out by Orbital Science Corp. in '99 (also an 'evil' US firm) and subsequently spat out by them the year after, the company's value was only 63 million dollars." MDA "did a hell of a job in packaging the deal and selling it to an unsuspecting buyer. But then again, MDA is in" the "real estate business too."[66] "Rob" then queried, "Why stop at MDA? We should get our government involved, tell all US companies that make weapons/hardware/devices for the US military that have divisions here in Canada to pack up their offices and facilities and go home. And if they are Canadian companies, shut them down permanently."[67]

Responding to critics of the sale, "Angry Shareholder" fumed, "Maybe you missed that economics class but the only reason a business exists is to generate wealth for its owners and/or shareholders. Like many Canadians," "Angy Shareholder" noted, "I invested in MDA because of its proven ability to secure contracts & consistently deliver 'the goods.' I offer no apology for wanting to make a profit on my investment."[68] On glassdoor.com, an employer-rating site where many MDA employees soon grumbled about their working conditions and low salaries, some even likening the experience to a "sweat shop for engineers," one disgruntled "Employee-Investor" also offered that because "the potential for future military business based on the company's capabilities is now visible, the company needs to reset employee and stakeholder (read: Canadian politicians and taxpayers) perceptions of the company's purpose and business." Another problem, "Employee-Investor" continued, "is the compliant and narrowly focused board of directors. Largely financial in background, none are from the UK (the fastest growing business segment in data sales) or the space business (biggest white bird hanging round Dan Friedmann's neck)," "Employee-Investor" stressed. "The absence of understanding of the company's branding led to the complete failure of a 1.3 billion dollar transaction. Why propose it if it's going to fail," "Employee-Investor" asked, and "why not" sell "the concept like crazy once the critics start sounding off? Somebody needs to get the chop over that." Others shared similar views, in ways that reflect an expanding Canadian belief that corporations have no other obligation to the governments that charter and the taxpayers who financially support them than to generate shareholder wealth.[69]

On 10 April 2008, Jim Prentice announced that critics of the sale could finally stop "sounding off." Sending a formal letter of rejection to ATK, Prentice declared that Canada would not allow the sale of MDA unless ATK could offer "new and compelling" information. "At this point," Prentice argued, "I've made it very clear to ATK the transaction as proposed doesn't meet the net benefits test" of the Investment Canada Act. He then gave ATK thirty days to adjust their proposal in response to his preliminary decision.[70] ATK hired lobbyists, and MDA and its allies continued to make the case for the sale, but on 9 May 2008, Prentice announced that, for the first time in the twenty-three-year history of the Investment Canada Act, the federal government had decided to block the sale of a Canadian firm to a foreign entity as "not in the national interest." Citing pressure from critics who argued that such a deal "handed over taxpayer funded technology and, in the case of *Radarsat-2*, gave away technology designed to protect Canada's sovereignty," Prentice argued that an "extensive and rigorous review process" had confirmed that the sale would not provide a "net benefit to Canada." Prentice then confirmed that MDA would receive a new four-year contract, worth $109 million, for ongoing work on robotic systems for the ISS. Shortly thereafter, scientists, politicians, and the business community called on the federal government to save Canada's space industry. Thanks to those who served on the CSA's advisory committee, the federal government quickly announced that it had increased funding for *NEOSsat* and other space-based projects.[71]

"TOO BIG TO FAIL":
PRIVATIZING THE PUBLIC GOOD AND THE 2008 FINANCIAL CRISIS

As he reflected on MDA's recent history as well as the government's decision to allocate additional funds to the CSA, John MacDonald argued that the ATK deal "got killed by the government and of course that woke up the Canadian Space Agency. The agency now has a guy with a vision of where it should go. And everything's fine now. But it had to have that kind of stimulus to wake itself up." On his own role post-MDA, MacDonald stressed, "after I had 'retired'" from MDA during 1998, "the opportunity came along to work in renewable energy," so he "decided to" found Day4Energy. "The energy business," he predicted, "and the technology behind it will be the major thing that happens in human civilization in the 21st century. We will change our energy system." Still, he conceded, "Many people don't grasp the change in the infrastructure that will be required to make that all work. While the problems are quite solvable," he noted, "the change is major – it is going to take time, it is going to take money. But by the middle of this century, I think our energy system will be dominated by renewables." Just sixteen years earlier, MacDonald had predicted that change by 2026, but he still believed in "making a start" toward the creation of a more sustainable future by 2050. After all, as a science, technology, trade, and industrial policy advisor to Canada's DND Science Advisory Board and the CSA's Advisory Council, no one knew better than MacDonald the lessons systems engineers had learned from the *Mythical Man Month*. Systems engineering involves inevitable delays, even when some optimist declares, "I just found the last bug."[72]

American reporters found Prentice's announcement surprising, particularly when they considered Prime Minister Harper's friendship with the

United States. Conceding that the "proposal raised issues about Canadian Arctic sovereignty that crossed party lines," the *New York Times* claimed that it "also revealed a debate about control of Canada's aerospace industry that stretches back to a 1959 decision to cancel the development of" the Avro Arrow "in favor of purchasing American aircraft." Nevertheless, the *Times* reported, the "announcement was all the more unanticipated because it came from a Conservative government which has sought to improve relations with the United States and has generally opposed nationalist policies."[73] Although Prentice had given ATK thirty days to persuade the Canadian government to reverse its position, an earlier *New York Times* piece reported that "the United States and other countries reject Canada's claim over the Northwest Passage, a potential shipping channel through the Arctic," and "few predicted" the sale as a likely outcome even if MDA had the right to sell its *Radarsat* images "to business and other governments." Citing Dan Friedmann's testimony before Canada's parliamentary hearings, an executive for ATK, and a spokesperson for the US White House Office of Science and Technology Policy, the *Times* also suggested that "MacDonald Dettwiler has its own complaints about the *Patriot Act* and other recent measures in the United States. Their restrictions against foreigners working on crucial projects like satellites" had limited MDA's "bidding on contracts in the United States," the paper reported, which "left the Canadian government as the company's only real customer, a fact that prompted the sale of its space unit" in the first place, the paper stressed.[74]

Attempting to clarify Canada's position, *Peace Magazine*'s Ron Shirtliff summarized the issues that technologies and trade agreements had raised over the past twenty years and more. "RADARSAT I and II are great eyes in the sky," and proudly touted by the CSA "as being Canada's great contribution to the peaceful use of space for the surveillance of the surface of the earth. We are told," he noted, "that they are meant to assist us in keeping track of global warming, and assist in marine surveillance, search and rescue, disaster management, hydrology mapping, geology, agriculture, and forestry. All of this is true," he asserted, but the CSA's "promotion may be a ruse. These ingenious machines also have the ability to act as spies in the sky, and more ominously, to act as a very precise gun sight for missiles launched from air or land, or from space." As a result, Shirtliff stressed, "much of their use depends on who gets the data that they send back to earth." By privatizing a public good, the Canadian government had already stipulated that the country and its people had no real say over what satellites "are meant to assist." Shirtliff conceded that MDA had to pay the operational expenses of the taxpayer-funded satellite following *Radarsat*'s launch; however, he additionally stressed that MDA was then "free to generate revenues by selling the data they collect to commercial interests in other nations," with "no restriction known to prevent them selling the data to the American military."[75]

Shirtliff also disclosed that "in exchange for NASA's launch of RADARSAT I, the US government controlled 15% of the observation time" since 1996, with its agencies "free" to "access to all RADARSAT data over six months old." He additionally reminded readers that many of MDA's own press releases had confirmed that "the U.S. military's 'family' of at least five portable ground stations, called 'Eagle Vision', are specifically designed to use 'Commercial' satellites like RADARSAT I and II. With Americans fearing a breach by Canada of national security," NASA "refused to launch RADARSAT II." As a result, during 2007 "Canadians turned to the Russians."[76] Such complicated relationships in a highly complicated global economy might have shocked those who had failed to pay attention, but should not have surprised anyone who had already connected the dots, including the major media outlets that speculated about the "pending sale of the space division of MDA, the operator of 'Canadian' satellites to an American military contractor." Americans, ATK, and other global strategic partners, Shirtliff stressed, had long invested in MDA's technological reach and international business plans precisely because they expected a substantial return from Canada's military-industrial contractors.[77]

No matter the public airing and eventual failure of the ATK acquisition, MDA continued to receive the government contracting work that Dan Friedmann and the firm's shareholders craved. During August 2008, the Canadian DND awarded a "strategic win" to strengthen MDA's position in the UAV surveillance market. Valued at C$95 million, with a third-year option valued at an additional $35 million, the contract allowed MDA to develop a "long endurance" UAV "surveillance solution" to support Canada's expanding armed forces in Afghanistan. Two months later, *Aviation Week and Space Technology* reported that the Canadian military had received its first Israeli-built Heron as part of a teaming arrangement with MDA. "IAI built the aircraft," *AW&ST* reported, while MDA took on the responsibility for "management, training and maintenance for the Canadian military." *AW&ST* also reported that MDA had received other "strategic wins," to upgrade remote sensing ground systems" for "confidential customers" anxious to receive *Radarsat-2* data for "a variety of surveillance and reconnaissance applications" as well as support the Canadian Navy's Maritime Command Operational Information Network.[78]

In the meantime, "the unthinkable" happened, again: just eight years after the dot-com bubble burst, highly leveraged financial institutions, all "too big to fail," began to collapse. On 15 September 2008, Lehman Brothers, the fourth-largest bank in the United States, filed for Chapter 11 protection, making it the largest bankruptcy in American history. An already distressed financial market quickly plunged into a period of extreme volatility. The Dow Jones experienced its largest one-day point loss, intra-day point range, and daily point gain. Other banks both large and small soon failed as well, creating a "perfect storm" for the largest bail-out in American history, the $700 billion Troubled Asset Relief Program. Approved by Congress, and signed into law by President Bush on 3 October 2008, TARP went into effect just one month before the US presidential election. When combined with the subprime mortgage crisis, the "evaporation of liquidity" among hedge funds, and the collapse of Lehman and other major financial institutions, the downturn in global stock markets ushered in the worst financial crisis since the Great Depression of the 1930s. At its peak during October 2007, the Dow Jones Industrial Average index had surpassed 14,000. By March 2009, it had tanked to 6,600. Some prospered on the volatility, but most lost a great deal, including retirement savings, homes, jobs, and future prospects.[79]

Policy analysts Peter W.B. Phillips and David Castle argued that Canada's well-regulated banking industry initially allowed Canadians to weather the storm pretty well. During 2008, "Canada's income tax treatment for R&D investments was the second most favourable among the G-7 countries for large firms and the most favourable for small and medium sized firms, with implicit subsidies of about 18% and 32% respectively."[80] Along with tax cuts, the exigencies of an immediate crisis, and what Bruce Doern and Alan Maslove have described as the "largesse of a distributive spending game," those subsidies also helped Stephen Harper to win re-election on 14 October 2008, with "a strengthened minority government, but without" Harper's "much desired majority government." Harper "and his Minister of Finance already knew that his surpluses were likely gone in the face of the then occurring banking and stock market crash," Doern and Maslove noted. As a result, Canada began to feel the pinch of the "Great Recession" as well. "The Harper performance after the October 2008 election was among the most incompetent ever seen in Canadian politics," they emphasized. Harper then cut public spending "rather than a needed stimulus, and in a stunningly vindictive way, announced he would eliminate public funding for political parties and bank strikes by federal government workers for two years." As Canada slipped into the global recession, those decisions also forced Harper to prorogue the newly elected Parliament to avoid a vote of no-confidence in the House of Commons.[81]

Economist Robert Samuelson has observed that "the widespread faith – and the sense of security it imparted – that economic management would forever spare us devastating disruptions has been shattered" with the Great Recession. "Just as there has never been a war to end all wars," Samuelson confirmed, "there has yet to be an economic theory that can end all serious economic instability."[82] Canadians were never exempt from these realities, but as chapter 10 reveals, the forces of surveillance capitalism and assistance of Prime Minister Harper allowed MDA to survive, and then thrive, despite the Great Recession.

10

"A Lucky Escape"

The Great Recession, Property Information Divestment, and the Acquisition of a Critical Mass in Satellite Manufacturing, 2009–2012

As MDA neared the anniversary of its fortieth year in business during 2009, the enterprise and its 3,200 employees once again faced an uncertain future. Although MDA's backlog had increased from $757 million in 2005 to more than $1 billion by 2009, the firm's revenues declined from a high of more than $1.2 billion to $857 million in 2008, while its market capitalization fell from a forty-year high of $1.89 billion during 2007 to $1.22 billion in 2009. MDA's shareholders also took a beating, with the company's stocks tumbling from $53.82 in 2007 to $16.85 by 17 October 2008. During January 2008, Dan Friedmann had argued that MDA's potential sale to ATK would "allow the company to focus management and financial resources exclusively on its rapidly growing information products business." Just one year later, however, many conceded that the Canadian government's decision to block the ATK deal had actually saved MDA from ruin, at least for the short term. More dependent than ever on the space business as they waited to hear about the fate of the Canadian Space Agency budget under the country's 2009 Economic Action Plan, MDA's executives once again prepared for layoffs.[1]

Happily for MDA's shareholders, Prime Minister Harper's Throne Speech of 26 January 2009 assured Canada's business community that his government would assist them. In their history of political policing in Canada, Reg Whitaker, Gregory S. Kealey, and Andrew Parnaby suggest that 9/11 "inaugurated a new era of global War on Terror under hegemonic American leadership that parallels in eerie ways the Cold War." With "accountability mechanisms appropriate" during the Cold War environment quickly deemed "patchwork, threadbare, and outdated," Canadians added "emergency powers" to the "state security arsenal," constructing new "suspect communities" and expanding the nation's focus on domestic surveillance.[2] As a result, the Harper government increased spending for the Department of National Defence by 21 per cent and the RCMP by 45 per cent between 2005 and 2010, which provided additional domestic surveillance opportunities for MDA. The federal government also increased its 2009–10 budget from $15.7 to $33.7 billion, and confirmed that the CSA would receive $110 million over the coming three years to develop advanced robotics and other space technologies. The CSA "assessed its programs to ensure they continue to meet government priorities, align with the Government's Science and Technology Strategy and deliver economic benefits to Canada," the Economic Action Plan reported. As a result, MDA quickly won additional contracts to satisfy Canada's UAV commitment to Project Noctua, which leased UAV intelligence, surveillance, and reconnaissance services to Canada's armed forces in Kandahar and elsewhere.[3]

By 17 February 2009, newly elected President Barack Obama and a Congress dominated by Democrats also signed into law the American Recovery and Reinvestment Act, with $787 billion committed to an overhaul of the country's aging infrastructure. The US Act promised to "enhance energy independence, expand educational opportunities, preserve and improve affordable health care, provide tax relief and protect those in greatest need," and included provisions for struggling American businesses against foreign competition. While "not specifically aimed at Canada," Melissa Hausman and David Biette have argued, the new "Buy American" protectionist posture, particularly in government procurement, "was already consistent with the loopholes under the WTO and GATT" and "part of the larger tension between trade and protectionism" that has defined American capitalist expansion. In response, policymakers in Canada therefore began to mention "the possibility of opening up subnational procurement to US firms" while simultaneously announcing to the world that Canada represented a "country on the world stage." It therefore seemed to those at MDA that they needed a stronger strategic partner to gain a critical foothold at the centre of the world's largest procurement market.[4]

"DOUBLE-BACK GUARANTEE":
SOARING PROFITS AND FURTHER LABOUR STRIFE

Bolstered by news that RapidEye had selected MDA as the sole supplier of direct downlink solutions for its constellation of satellites and the global surveillance market (including the USAF's Eagle Vision Program), MDA's stock inched upward during the first half of 2009. The media also confirmed that MDA had won major UAV contracts from the Canadian and Australian air forces, significant *Radarsat-2* contracts from Canada and the European Space Agency, and other security contracts, including one to support the 2010 Olympic Games in Vancouver. On the strength of such work, *BCBusiness* awarded to MDA the province's number one business rating during April 2009, arguing that by completing "its first surveillance mission for the Canadian Forces in Afghanistan with its new unmanned-aircraft service," MDA had developed another new technology to "collect new kinds of data that, in turn, could generate new kinds of data-management services – the MDA model all over again." By the end of September, the firm had additional wins to celebrate at its Brampton, Ontario, facility, when employees unveiled MDA's "next generation" robotic arms for use in future space missions. Reimagining the firm as a total information company, gathering and selling data services related to the expertise it had developed in orbital imaging, and then branching out into new unmanned-aircraft surveillance services, media outlets confirmed the resiliency of the business unit that MDA's board had attempted to sell to ATK. Although revenues dropped by 14 per cent between 2008 and 2009, Dan Friedmann boasted that MDA's profits had nearly doubled during the same period.[5]

All of that news had a different effect on MDA employees, many of whom continued to earn below-market wages or faced the possibility of no job at all. In pursuing austerity measures, employees argued, MDA executives had long refused requests for better pay. As a result, by the end of September 2009, just as their previous three-year agreement terminated and MDA began to respond to several key CSA requests for proposals, some 400 professional engineers and technical staff signalled their frustration by once again walking off the job at MDA Robotics in Brampton. Unlike 2006, however, they did not walk alone; this time, employees at David Florida Laboratory in Ottawa joined them.[6] Engineering services resumed at MDA Robotics after MDA's management team reached a new four-year collective agreement with SPATEA on 26 October 2009, but further labour strife, the engineering strike, and other employment concerns created deepening rifts between the company's senior management team and MDA's rank-and-file employees. Nor did those rifts vanish when MDA's stock got another bump on November's news that the firm had received a multi-million-dollar amended *Radarsat* contract from the CSA as well as several significant contracts to provide satellite solutions for a large range of broadcasting services and expanded flight path safety capabilities for the US Air Force.[7]

By January 2010, just months after the collective agreement went into effect and MDA won a $200 million contract from the Russian Radio Research and Development Institute, *Aviation Week and Space Technology*'s Michael Taverna reported on a "double-back guarantee" that promised to increase MDA's earnings even further. "Two new U.S. and Canadian financing agreements underscore the growing willingness of export credit agencies to match the system of guarantees put in place by France and other satellite and launch suppliers," Taverna noted. MDA had emerged as one of the firms that had "drawn on a financing package from Export Development Canada to build and launch a communications satellite for the Ukrainian space agency," a $254 million deal to supply Ukraine with two ground stations that promised to give the Eastern European country "access to direct broadcast and Internet services without relying on foreign suppliers such as the Russian Satellite Communications Co. (RSCC), the region's largest operator." The project helped MDA to "evolve from a satcom equipment supplier into a prime contractor – a position it already enjoys in the Earth-observation satellite field," Taverna reported. He additionally observed that similar agreements had taken place within the US government, including one to refinance a second satellite for Asia Broadcasting Satellite, which American-owned Space Systems/Loral began to construct "under an authorization-to-proceed arrangement." Significantly, "Space Systems/Loral has manufactured most of Intelsat's satellites since 1994," Taverna observed, "losing only a few key contracts to Lockheed Martin, Orbital Sciences, and Boeing over the past two decades."[8]

In highlighting the financing agreements that MDA and Space Systems/ Loral received, Taverna revealed many of the synergies that would soon form the heart of MDA's evolving strategy to "gain critical mass in the commercial satellite manufacturing industry and better position the company to win U.S. defence and intelligence work."[9] But neither *AW&ST* nor other media outlets connected the dots for their readers or the general public. Instead, Taverna simply noted that "the U.S. and Canadian moves are intended to counter an aggressive financial policy being pursued by France's Coface," a global leader in credit insurance. He also revealed that the governments of China, Germany, Italy, and other countries also planned to aid satellite and launch service sales with public financing. While many private firms profited from such "double-back guarantees" and MDA's executive and board members began to revaluate their "strategic alternatives" in "various businesses to increase shareholder value," global austerity programs began to kick into high gear for those without such assurances.[10]

"A LUCKY ESCAPE":
PROPERTY INFORMATION, DISASTER CAPITALISM,
AND THE BIG SHARE BUY-BACK

During July 2010, media outlets reported that MDA's shares had risen "more than 40 per cent over the past 12 months and 160 per cent from their low in 2008. The shares are now just 16 per cent from their record high, reached in 2007," *Global Investor's* David Berman reported, with analysts "now overwhelmingly bullish on MDA." Berman also reported that refuelling stations "might be just the thing to drive another source of revenue for the company, but the plan is by no means the Hail Mary pass of a desperate company." MDA, "like just about every other company, took a hit during the financial crisis, which shrank its profit in the third quarter of 2009 to a mere 3 cents a share." But "in the first quarter of 2010, earnings rebounded to 71 cents a share, a record for the period," Berman stressed.[11]

With Harper's government announcing support for the next phase of the *Radarsat* constellation mission during August, rumours then surfaced that MDA had begun to explore the sale of company units. On 10 October *Bloomberg News* noted that on "annual revenue of about C$1 billion ($978 million) and a market value of C$1.9 billion," MDA shares had recently "climbed as much as 9.9 per cent in Toronto trading to C$50.69, the highest level since May 2007." *Bloomberg* additionally asserted that MDA had no intention of "running an auction and may decide not to sell itself or any divisions."[12] Fewer than two weeks later, others reported that "speculation now centers on the company shedding its profitable real estate title business" so that the company could "focus on satellite and space opportunities." With few countries able to launch radar-imaging satellites into orbit, financial analyst Doug Mohney argued that "MDA's operation of RADARSAT-2 and a planned supplemental constellation of three satellites is of strategic value" for Canada as well as the firm's shareholders. MDA had also "floated the idea of building a refuelling/servicing platform for satellites," Mohney noted, which promised to allow the firm to leverage its robotics and satellite operations expertise into a floating gas and power station. Citing Dan Friedmann and others, Mohney additionally reported that the "company said 65 satellites – $16 billion dollars' worth of in-orbit hardware – ran out of fuel or failed in the past decade while it will cost another $36 billion to replace 136 satellites expected to be decommissioned early due to running out of fuel between 2012 to 2020." Although satellite operators seemed "lukewarm" on MDA's refuelling "idea," other options had enormous appeal, particularly for those interested in the firm's property information business, Mohney stressed.[13]

On 5 November 2010, the speculation ended; reporting the official news, media outlets confirmed that MDA had sold its property information business unit to TPG Capital, one of the world's largest private equity firms focused on leveraged buyouts, growth capital, and recapitalization investments in distressed companies as well as turnaround opportunities. *Bloomberg News* reported that MDA had agreed to the sale for "about C$850 million ($849.6 million) after taxes," where "the unit, with 1,050 workers and all except 30 of them in the U.S. or the U.K., serves insurance companies, lenders, and lawyers." Friedmann emphasized that MDA would "be looking for M&A opportunities," *Bloomberg* reported, because its executives had "determined that this business should operate under separate ownership going forward if we could crystallize good value."[14] Friedmann also argued that MDA would "leverage our core strengths to further diversify our growing Information Systems and Geospatial Services business into commercial and international markets. As we have done in the past," Friedmann promised, MDA would "continue to provide shareholder value through a combination of organic growth and acquisition initiatives." He additionally stressed that he believed TPG "will provide a good home for our valuable and dedicated employees." Friedmann eliminated the news that MDA's executives could also count on substantial bonuses and attractive compensation packages from the sale; however, he confirmed that MDA's board had "adopted a dividend policy of $1 per share from operating cash to be paid in two equal instalments of $0.50 per share on or about March 31st and September 30th, commencing in 2011."[15]

By January 2011, MDA's executive team had refocused on the information systems and geospatial services units they had tried to sell to ATK just two years before. One year later, the *Globe and Mail*'s David Ebner argued that Ottawa's veto of the ATK sale on "national security grounds" was "a lucky escape from a near disaster. The sale price was handsome," but MDA and "Mr Friedmann would have been left with a company focused on real estate at exactly the wrong time, sales plummeting and profit evaporating." Ebner also noted that "MDA would have suffered if Stephen Harper hadn't intervened." In response to the "lucky escape," Friedmann simply replied, "You readjust." On 2 May 2011, Harper's government then made it easier to readjust after the Conservatives won Canada's first right-wing majority government in fifty years. Although not "widely recognized by most people because it generally operates unseen, in the background," MDA's technology promised to net the firm its "biggest-ever win, a crucial

Phase D contract worth roughly $500-million to build" the *Radarsat* constellation system, Ebner reported. As that contract neared "go-ahead" from Ottawa in March 2012, Ebner argued that MDA had a chance to outpace the "benchmark S&P/TSX index," even if Canadians saw no "Made in Canada" stamp on MDA's technologies they could "cheer."[16]

Among its many technologies operating "unseen, in the background," MDA's satellite radar imagery became an "essential element" of the geospatial information packages used in government communications, defence, and Earth observation, as well as a variety of other businesses. Indeed, Friedmann had earlier hinted that MDA "planned to enter, in a much bigger way, new commercial markets like oil and gas, agriculture," and other extractive industries. British Petroleum's Deepwater Horizon oil spill on 20 April 2010 then provided plentiful opportunities to profit from such industries, with *Radarsat* images making it possible for oil companies to "enhance production and mitigate environmental risks in their oilfields." Those same images could also assist emergency-response teams to see oil and gain area overviews to mitigate even further disaster; however, industry lobbyists and MDA's executives understood more than the general public the many other opportunities provided by oil spills, gasoline prices, tar sands development, the Keystone Pipeline, and especially Prime Minister Harper's 2006 declaration that Canada had emerged as an "energy superpower" on the strength of its vast oil, gas, and uranium reserves. As a result, MDA bid on and won several multi-year contracts to supply "surveillance capabilities" to oil companies, including "a leading integrated" one in Alberta as well as another for Petroleos Mexicano (PEMEX, Mexico's largest oil company) for its "continued monitoring of natural oil seeps and spills in the Gulf of Mexico."[17]

During 2011, MDA also unveiled a new geospatial product, the National Urban Change Indicator (NUCI) to show "if and when an area has undergone a human-induced change sometime in the last 25 years." The US Department of Homeland Security and Federal Emergency Management Agency emerged as MDA's first NUCI customers, *SpaceRef* reported. Thereafter, MDA received contracts to monitor "areas of interest around the globe," including one for Canada's "next generation" *Radarsat* constellation mission, and others from the US National Geospatial Intelligence Agency and Canada's Department of National Defence. Linking its expertise to civil space projects, MDA also secured long-term maintenance contracts for its *Canadarms* and a coveted contract from NASA's Johnson Space Center to "assist in the berthing of unmanned vehicles visiting the space station." From all it had learned on FOCUS, AWDS, and CAATS, the firm additionally received follow-on contracts from the US Federal Aviation Administration to "modernize flight design practices and to harmonize military and civilian air navigation in the long term." Blending its expertise in military and civilian work, MDA then entered into a multi-million-dollar agreement to work with Boeing Space and Intelligence Systems to provide "high-power communications for military and commercial satellite users." Solidifying its bona fides as a full-spectrum, international space company in its own right, MDA also entered into an agreement with Intelsat to build a space-based service vehicle that promised "to create a new commercial space segment for MDA."[18] Geographer Stephen Graham has demonstrated that "change indicators" such as the ones MDA produce have become symptomatic of the ways in which "new military ideologies of permanent and boundless war are radically intensifying the militarization of urban life." Taking lessons from the Cold War era, MDA simply repurposed its technologies to fit the demands of the twenty-first century.[19]

During early May 2011, Friedmann then indicated another change by announcing that MDA planned to buy "a space company" with American "roots or else return to shareholders the $793 million" the firm had acquired from the sale of its property information business. He also "made clear the company is searching for a large target, and not a strap-on acquisition," one that could give the firm "solid entry into the U.S. government market, and a presence in markets where MDA has expertise that could be transferred to a U.S. operation for access to government business."[20] Three weeks later, *cantech letter* reported that the financial crisis had created the context for such plans, forcing MDA down the "rocky road of reinvention" once again. "MDA's fiscal 2010 revenue of $689 million paled when compared to 1.2 billion the company did just three years prior," *cantech* conceded, but "the company is rebounding on newfound success, generating revenue on large satellite contracts," and the "boost" it needed from the sale of its property information business. Putting MDA's "cash to use with recent dividends and share buybacks," but not necessarily pay increases to its "valuable and dedicated employees," MDA's chief financial officer, Anil Wirasekera, told a *cantech* reporter, "It seems that shareholders increasingly embraced the changes going on at MDA," particularly those focused on expanding the firm's communications business and "service business in UAVs." When asked why MDA had sold its property information business, Wirasekera confirmed that MDA executives "saw a prolonged recession in the Property Information market and felt it was time to crystallize on the opportunity and provide value for our shareholders. We plan to know this by the end of the summer," he promised. He kept his word, and by summer's end, others learned that MDA planned to deploy $500 million in what David Ebner described as "one of the bigger share buybacks in Canadian market history."[21]

Within no time, some questioned the numbers MDA had highlighted to show "robust profits growing at double-digit rates" when the company asked investors to tender their shares for the company's summer sharebuyback plan. During October 2011, the *Globe and Mail*'s David Milstead even suggested MDA's numbers "might not paint the clearest picture" of the firm's performance, a situation he declared "ironic, since MDA, as it's known, makes its business delivering high-quality data and information to corporate and government customers." Employing earnings before interest, taxes, depreciation, and amortization (EBITDA) rather than International Financial Reporting Standards (IFRS), MDA noted that its worth had increased 18 per cent, and "operating earnings" had expanded 22 per cent over the previous year. "But, as Veritas Investment Research Corp. Analyst Dimitry Khmelnitsky notes," Milstead reported, such "metrics exclude the costs of stock-based compensation, and operating EBITDA also leaves out corporate overhead." Cautioning investors to "turn to the company's net income figures, which are calculated according to rules laid down by IFRS," Milstead reported that "a one-time disclosure upon its conversion to the IFRS accounting rules" showed "first quarter costs of $19.4 million, up 486 per cent from $3.3-million in 2010's first quarter." This, he argued, revealed a 14 per cent operating earnings decline over the 2010 period.[22]

Milstead also emphasized that Khmelnitsky had found in the securities filings "the number of stock-based awards exercised for cash by MDA's top executives increased by 19 per cent year over year in 2011's second quarter." He therefore stressed that "this double-digit profit grower may actually have declining earnings." Although the Veritas report had allowed its "clients some time to decide whether to tender their shares back to the company for a price of no less than $53," many shareholders "didn't have the benefit of the analysis. MDA now trades at around $44," Milstead reported. During January 2012, David Ebner then confirmed much of what Milstead had reported, additionally adding that MDA's stock had "been stuck in neutral in the past year," even if it had "more than doubled in the past three." As it turned out, MDA's potentially problematic practices were far from alone.[23]

"BUDGET CUTBACKS EVERYWHERE":
SPACE BUDGET UNCERTAINTY AND WORKFORCE RESTRUCTURING

Although the Harper government announced its intention to renew its commitment to the International Space Station during February 2012, by March the media began to report that "preliminary" assessments "suggest" that the Canadian federal budget "doesn't include the money needed for the Radarsat Constellation Mission as envisioned." Citing Canadian Space Agency representatives, however, they cautioned, "It is pretty premature at this time to comment on the budget," and noted that MDA seemed solid, with revenues increasing and a perceived market capitalization of nearly $1.5 billion during 2011 over its 2003 low of $106.17 million. Regardless, MDA's executive team announced that the board had authorized accelerated "steps" to "restructure" the firm's "work force."[24] MDA thus began to shed jobs during May, starting with 100 of them at the firm's Brampton facility, the site of labour organizing and recent strikes over bargaining agreements. The *Brampton Guardian* also disclosed that MDA "expects to lose more this year as a result of cuts to its space-robotics program." It then cited the number for 2012: "50 Bramptom employees" if the "Radarsat [Constellation Mission] does not continue." Uncertainty about the future also prompted other employees to "leave on their own," the *Guardian* reported.[25]

By the time MDA's management team had finished selling off assets and lowering the layoff boom during mid-2012, the company had reduced its workforce by 25 per cent, in what one disgruntled employee labelled "severance avoiding 'Working notices.'" Although most employees agreed that they enjoyed "flex-time," the fellowship of their co-workers, and the challenges projects provided, one employee sarcastically dubbed "quiet hallways" one of the "pros" to working at MDA, because "many good and senior people quit this year," while others got "laid off." In advice to senior management, the reviewer argued, "You can fix this problem, but you must do work. There are many people going to leave if salaries aren't drastically (> 40%) changed." Echoing 1993 interviewees who had argued that management needed to remember that MDA's "assets have feet," the reviewer additionally warned, "You thought this year is bad attrition, just wait until no response from MDA and next year comes." Although "the people are great," another employee advised, the "cons" of working at MDA included "extremely poor compensation, no vision, insecure employment, no opportunities for advancement, and low morale due to feeling a lack of a future" with the firm.[26]

As early as 2009, one former employee at headquarters in Vancouver had already articulated the general mood that later bloggers reinforced: MDA's "pay is the lowest I've heard for a programmer in the area. 9 interns left at the end of the year and no one wanted to go back," while full-time employees quit "to find better pay/treatment." While "the projects sound cool and important," the former employee stressed, "the environment and pay are not worth it." Over time, increasing numbers seemed to agree. By July 2010, one employee addressed mounting concerns that "MDA Corporate Management have a good business model that ensures the survival of the business," but with "only very little consideration for its employees." The employee therefore stressed that "the day MDA Corporate Management realizes the assets it has through its employees, and the day they decide to reward the employees adequately, they will become one of the best companies in Canada." For increasing numbers, that day never arrived. In January 2011, another employee argued that MDA "has long been notorious as a high-tech sweat shop, with salaries now in the lowest quartile (bottom 25%) compared to national averages. This is in" Vancouver, the employee noted, a "city with the highest real estate prices in Canada." As a result, the employee proffered a little advice to engineers elsewhere: "Don't even consider relocating here." Female and minority employees cited deeper concerns. One reviewer argued that MDA remained "chauvinistic, sexist, and nepotistic," while another suggested that "it is difficult to advance" at MDA "unless you are a white male," a problem others have acknowledged as an abiding problem within many North American high-technology workplaces.[27]

Undeterred by Canadian budgetary uncertainty, MDA pursued its plans to acquire a space company; and by June 2012, Loral Space & Communications Ltd confirmed that it had agreed to sell its Palo Alto-based satellite manufacturing subsidiary, Space Systems/Loral (SS/L) "to Canadian communications rival" MDA for US$875 million.[28] Within weeks, some analysts argued that the SS/L deal would "boost" MDA's "earnings in 2013 by 50 per cent," and "give the company a platform to win upcoming space contracts from the U.S. Government."[29] Still, the deal required the approval of both countries' governments, and the failed ATK acquisition reminded both parties that they might have a fight on their hands, particularly with public grumblings about MDA's deteriorating charms. In the midst of the speculation, one employee argued that MDA "was my first employer after graduation." Excited about the prospects, "I thought I had hit a jackpot working as a contractor for the military but my dream was very quickly shattered." "Once a leading edge company," another employee complained, MDA had "fallen to mediocre status." With budget cuts on the table, the employee also noted that MDA "can't rely anymore on the vast sums of Canadian tax payer money it used to receive as this has stopped." Thus, the firm offered "very little" in the way of "salary increases in the past 5 years" but much in the way of "budget cutbacks everywhere," with "many people at the lower ranks losing their jobs through layoffs. People are also walking out the door for new opportunities," even in a recessionary environment. "Unfortunately, there's way too much top heavy management," with "nepotism really high" and "an environment of low morale" few would want to join or purchase, the employee noted.[30]

Raising the Avro Arrow spectre, another employee predicted that even the promised "purchase of US company Loral Space & Communications for 875 million will probably see the further demise of staff and work within all Canadian divisions. MDA's future focus will be with the US commercial satellite market," and "Canadian companies will be gutted as they slash lower rank salaries in order to save money." As a result, the employee advised junior engineers to "use MDA as a temporary training ground for your next job, or stay away. You have been warned." As more professionals began to consider themselves members of the "lower ranks," they not only recaptured the "sagging morale" problem that Bill Thompson had identified during the late 1970s, but also revealed how well MDA's sweat-equity formula had served the company's shareholders and Canada, no matter the economic climate.[31]

The global recession and uncertainty about Canada's federal budget also prompted MDA's largest shareholder, the Ontario Teachers' Pension Fund (OTPF), to "cash out a significant chunk of its holdings" in MDA. Reporting on the sale of 1.35 million MDA shares on 10 July 2012, the *Globe and Mail* confirmed that the OTPF had "realized a huge profit on its initial $14-per-share investment. It sold two million shares in April, 2002, for $27 per share," the paper reported, "another two million shares for more than $47 in May, 2006, and 1.6 million shares for $53 last October." When government budget cuts "slowed the flow of business to a trickle, forcing MDA to cut more than 150 jobs," the paper noted, the company also increased its focus on looking for acquisition opportunities in the United States. With the Loral deal still as uncertain as the federal budget and the health of the global economy, members of the OTPF thus decided the time had arrived to move their investments out of MDA.[32]

Happily for those invested in its pension fund, the OTPF cashed out at the right time, for by mid-September 2012, the US Department of Justice, rather than the Canadian government, "cast fresh doubt" on MDA's "plans to acquire the satellite manufacturing arm" of Loral. Those doubts prompted RBC Capital Markets to lower MDA's rating; and MDA's shares quickly fell 6 per cent. MDA's executive team continued to lobby for the acquisition as well as more work, but the firm's future once again hung in the balance. Only time would tell how many contracts MDA might win, how many layoff packages the firm might issue, how much the CSA and MDA might receive from the federal government to save the *Radarsat* Constellation Mission and other space industry projects, and whether or not the US government would sanction the sale of an American firm to a Canadian one. It only took a few months to settle those issues. As before, the Canadian government stepped in to protect MDA's role as a global communications and information company in the service of much larger ambitions.[33]

"FULL CIRCLE": PRODUCTS OF THE COLD WAR, SPACE SYSTEMS/LORAL, AND THE FULL-SPECTRUM DEAL

On 29 September 2012, the Canadian Space Society hosted 200 dignitaries at its "Canada on Orbit Gala/Gala Canadien à propos de l'orbite" dinner in Ottawa's Canada Aviation and Space Museum, to celebrate the fiftieth anniversary of Canada's first *Alouette* satellite launch. Honouring twenty-five scientists and engineers who had contributed to *Alouette-1*, the gala boasted three major corporate underwriters: Boeing Company (the world's largest aerospace firm); Telesat Canada (the first to launch a commercial, domestic communications satellite); and MacDonald, Dettwiler and Associates. Ron Barrington, the representative of the Communications Research Centre who had done so much to encourage MDA's very first space-based procurement contract with the federal government, conspicuously stood among the "*Alouette* Pioneers" honoured and photographed to commemorate "Canada on Orbit." Several speakers also took to the podium, among them former CSA president William MacDonald (Mac) Evans, who lauded the "*Alouette* Pioneers" for their scientific work and the role they had played in educating the next generation of "space cadets."[34]

Several weeks before the gala, long-time Canadian space writer Chris Gainor argued that *Alouette-1* "was as much a product of the Cold War as its more famous predecessor, *Sputnik,* and it was a forerunner of the communications satellites that have since formed the heart of Canada's space industry." *Alouette-1*, Gainor argued, did not simply advance scientific research, meet the Canadian desire for better communications coverage across far-flung territorial holdings, and "silently" continue to "orbit the Earth on the 50th anniversary of its launch. The work of building Canadian satellites was farmed out to private industry as part of a federal government policy of encouraging high technology businesses" to birth Canada's space components industry, Gainor noted, and "led to the growth of companies such as Spar Aerospace," MDA, ComDev International, and other Canadian procurement contractors. To carry out that policy, and to garner taxpayer support to execute it, the Canadian government also launched Telesat and the Department of Communications. "The Canadian military that created" *Alouette-1* and Canada's opportunities to participate in the American-centred aerospace industry, Gainor stressed, "is re-entering space with the launch of two satellites – *Sapphire*, to provide space situational awareness" for the military and NEOSsat, Canada's "Sentinel in the Sky" to detect and track near-Earth asteroids, satellites, and orbital debris. Fifty years of work in space had helped to create the context for Canada's first military satellite and the world's first space telescope, but both *Sapphire* and NEOSsat, Gainor concluded, "bring the story of Canada's space program full circle back to its roots," as a component supplier for surveillance capitalism and the military-industrial-academic complex's expanding reach.[35]

Although MDA's future remained uncertain during September, the interests of capital, the firm's past performance, and a quick succession of events justified MDA's prominent seat at the gala's corporate sponsorship table. On 18 October 2012, Canada's Department of National Defence announced the "send off" of the *Sapphire* spacecraft, Canada's first satellite dedicated "strictly for military purposes" and scheduled for launch by the Indian Space Research Organization on 25 February 2013. As the primary contractor for *Sapphire*, MDA had managed to build the satellite "for under $66 million," *cantech letter* announced. Moreover, "As space continues to be an important part of the global security environment," Canada's minister of national defence confirmed, "our government believes that this satellite is an essential component of our robust defence for Canada and North America, through NORAD."[36] Beyond MDA's achievement in the development of *Sapphire*, the *Ottawa Citizen*'s David Pugliese reported, MDA received a contract from DARPA's "Phoenix Project to develop and demonstrate technologies to cooperatively repurpose valuable components from retired, nonworking satellites and demonstrate the ability to create new space systems at greatly reduced cost." With MDA employing a robotic on-orbit servicer and components launched alongside commercial satellites, the US program "hopes to transition its developing technologies into sustainable commercial applications that in turn support U.S. Department of Defense (DoD) needs in the future," Pugliese noted. Happily for Canada, he stressed, "MDA is under contract from DARPA to assist with defining this commercial plan."[37]

On 28 October, *SatNews Daily* confirmed that the US National Geospatial-Intelligence Agency had also exercised a one-year option to have MDA continue its software work on overlaying satellite images from multiple dates to identify "changes in land-cover that persist regardless of seasonal changes or weather effects."[38] Three days later, MDA then announced that it had received a multi-million-dollar contract with USAF *Eagle Vision* to provide "near real-time in-theatre access to essential image data," including *Radarsat-2*'s support for the acquisition of other "critical imagery information" and "homeland disaster relief missions." Despite news that the United States planned to leave Afghanistan in the spring and that both the American and Canadian governments planned to review spending on defence, it seemed that MDA had secured its immediate future, even if its employees could not count on similar assurances.[39]

By the end of October, MDA's executives and board members also gained what they had long wanted: a critical mass in the US commercial satellite industry to solidify MDA's status as a leader in information and communications for government and commercial organizations worldwide. On 29 October, several news organizations reported a 10 per cent stock surge on MDA shares, "the top gainer on the TSX" on reports that MDA had received anti-trust approval for its acquisition of Space Systems/Loral (SS/L). MDA formally announced the completion of the acquisition on 2 November 2012, thereafter boasting a market capitalization of $1.95 billion on the TSX and a stock price of $56. With offerings in UAV surveillance services, satellite communication and aviation solutions, actionable information, satellite ground systems, robotics, space missions, and ship surveillance, intelligence, and communication systems, MDA thus emerged as a full-spectrum, multinational space company, with headquarters in Richmond, major manufacturing facilities in Canada and the United States, offices across both nations, and strategic regional operations in Bangalore, Moscow, and Rio de Janeiro. Still, with the American presidential election less than one week away, and plans for spending on the CSA still publicly obscure, defence budgets and the fate of the *Radarsat* mission hung in the air.[40] The federal government had "estimated the project would cost around 600 million Canadian dollars," David Pugliese reported, but "recently declassified documents from Canada's Department of National Defence put that price tag now at more than 1 billion Canadian dollars." With the government announcing that it would reduce the Canadian Space Agency's budget from $424 million to $363 million over the coming year, "the agency's budget is expected to drop back to its regular base level of around 300 million Canadian dollars. That funding level could increase again," but only "if the government approves new space projects."[41]

Budget allocations for the CSA remained uncertain at the end of 2012, but the prime minister secured the *Radarsat* Constellation Mission (RCM) for MDA. On 19 December 2012, the *National Post* reported that "the Harper government has approved funding for Canada's world-beating surveillance satellite program, just as it seemed that it may become the victim of spending cutbacks." Sources, the *Post* noted, also confirmed that "the Prime Minister intervened personally to secure hundreds of millions of dollars in new funding to move the next generation of Radarsat satellites off the drawing board and into production." Conservative Cabinet ministers argued that the RCM project would serve the "national interest" as well as "unlock wealth, secure our coastlines and borders, protect our population, and deliver services. There is speculation in the industry," the *Post* reported, "that the United States is interested in buying Constellation satellites once the project goes ahead." That work secured MDA's near-term future, even if the public did not yet know that MDA would soon receive a $706 million contract for the *Radarsat* Constellation Mission. Policymakers confirmed other long-term priorities as well, which signalled their willingness to socialize the risks and privatize the profits of billions of tax dollars on more surveillance technology as part of Canada's ongoing attempt to protect the country's sovereignty, avoid a brain drain of Canadian talent, secure an important global, never mind regional development tool, and remain a significant player in the geopolitics of the Five Eyes intelligence program, the global space industry, and international affairs as a whole.[42]

Although previous military personnel, government contractors, and reporters (including Canada's naval intelligence officer, Lt Jeffrey Paul Delisle) had exposed government secrets, extra-legal procedures, human rights violations, and establishment propaganda, revelations following leaks by ex–National Security Administration contractor Edward Snowden would soon retest official narratives as well as assumptions guiding enthusiasm for expenditures on information gathering technologies to meet national and global challenges. For the moment, however, MDA received what its shareholders wanted: more work and a Palo Alto–based

facility from where some 25 per cent of US government satellite communication flowed. "Unseen, in the Background" revisits MDA's recent trajectory as well as the lessons we might draw from the expansion of surveillance capitalism and Canada's deepening integration into a North
American market dominated by US military contractors.

"Unseen, in the Background"

A View from the Security State

On global demands for satellite-based communications, Earth observa-tion, and reconnaissance following its acquisition of Space Systems/Loral (ss/l), MDA's profits soared. The firm's revenues climbed from $879.9 mil-lion in 2012 to nearly $2.1 billion by 2014, while order backlogs increased from $2.2 billion to nearly $3.1 billion during the same period. Although its net earnings declined from $83.9 million to $47.1 million between 2012 and 2014, MDA reports stressed a significant increase in market cap-italization, from $1.783 billion to $3.429 billion. MDA's stock prices also surged, from $49.33 on 19 October 2012 to a high of $100.22 on 15 March 2015. Still small when compared to other global conglomerates, by 2014 MDA had become a "global commercial satellite powerhouse," *cantech let-ter* reported, with its 4,800 employees providing communications and drone services to military and commercial customers worldwide as well as support to the oil, gas, and mining industries. *SpaceRef* also placed MDA firmly at the centre of Canada's "military space," with the firm providing *Radarsat-2* imagery to soldiers in the field and customers seeking access to "surface movement monitoring products and services." MDA's executive team therefore reorganized the firm once again, this time into two main business units – Communications, and Surveillance and Intelligence – with global offices and subsidiaries providing a host of systems and ser-vices "to support a wide range of defence and commercial applications," all wrapped into an interactive network designed to expand on government funding for the "next generation" of even more powerful satellites. Earth observation remained central to MDA's business areas, with *Radarsat* pro-jects consistently focused on gaining "critical mass" and more wealth-generating opportunities in the United States.[1]

Protests over Parliament's enactment of the controversial Anti-terrorism Act and the Bank of Canada's announcement that Canada had slipped into recession on 15 July 2015 created distractions and renewed uncertainty at MDA, with shareholders taking another "wild ride" on the Toronto Stock Exchange. When antipathy toward Harper and the Conservatives created an opening, however, MDA and other space-based firms could count on Marc Boucher; as executive director of the Canadian Space Commerce Association, he promised to persuade Canadian policymakers (and the voting public) that Canada had once again fallen behind other countries in science and technology because the Conservatives had not given the CSA and its corporate partners the attention both deserved. Boucher stressed that Canada desperately needed a robust space plan, one that businesses small and large could count upon for at least the next decade, one that would involve the voices of "all the stakeholders," especially *Canadarm*-builder MDA. As a result, members of the aerospace industry exacted from the Liberals and NDP a promise to develop a long-term plan if elected. Liberal Marc Garneau argued that his party would include much more funding for research and development, "particularly with respect to environmental changes that are occurring on our planet and in our oceans." Chiming into the discussion, Peggy Nash reinforced Garneau's promises by noting that the NDP understood that "businesses that are investing millions of dollars in this cutting-edge field – need to know they've got a reliable partner in the government of Canada." Neither Garneau nor Nash mentioned the role that taxpayers would play in that partnership, but other promises of "real change" helped Justin Trudeau and the Liberal Party to win their historic victory on 19 October 2015. Six months later, the CSA received additional funding for space-based procurement, and MDA turned another corner in its history.[2]

On 14 April 2016, after more than twenty years as MDA's CEO, Dan Friedmann stepped down from his position at MDA after the board announced that the corporation needed a US citizen at the helm for further expansion. According to *SpaceNews*, Friedmann "carries the wrong passport (Canadian) for a company whose growth is in part tied to U.S. government contracts." *SpaceNews* also suggested that Friedmann "lives in the wrong place – British Columbia, not Palo Alto, California, where MDA's growth engine, satellite builder SS/L, is located."[3] As a result, Friedmann's successor, Howard L. Lance, became MDA's first American president and CEO effective 16 May 2016. Lance had served as chairman and CEO of Harris Corporation, the firm that had introduced MDA to the US military specification environment. During May 2016, he also served as an executive advisor to the Blackstone Group, one of the world's leading investment firms. Once officially designated MDA's new CEO, Lance thus moved the firm's executive suite to California. Just ten days earlier, on 6 May, *Canadian Manufacturing* had reported that the federal government "is looking to help" MDA "get the next generation of Canadian-made satellites off the ground" by investing yet another $54 million to "develop better radar, speed up satellite-based data transmission and improve cloud-based data processing." Announcing that investment, Navdeep Bains, Canada's minister of innovation, science, and economic development argued, "Companies are struggling to reduce the time it takes to bring great ideas to market, and testing innovations is essential to making that transition." He therefore assured the public that MDA would help several partners, including ComDev International and Magellan Aerospace, to work on new satellite technologies.[4]

Within six months, the *National Post* reported that several Canadian space policy analysts and journalists, including the Rideau Institute's Steven Staples and the Commercial Space Blog's Chuck Black, had raised sovereignty concerns about MDA's management restructuring and new corporate headquarters. With fears of foreign control over Canada's space industry in full view by mid-October, *Ottawa Citizen*'s David Pugliese noted that MDA had, "on its own, significantly altered its corporate make-up to bring it within the U.S. orbit." He also reported that Lance not only led the firm from San Francisco's SSL MDA Holdings, Inc., a corporation registered in Delaware, but had also "made a series of new senior appointments, bringing in a retired U.S. Air Force general with a background in space operations as well as a former U.S. defence intelligence official who had worked for the CIA." As a result, Staples argued that MDA had engineered "a stealth takeover" of "sensitive" technologies "Canadian taxpayers" had funded but that an American corporation and the US government now controlled for their own use. Staples also suggested that MDA had accomplished the "very thing that the Conservative government was worried about" during the 2008 ATK debate. Black conceded that MDA officials had restructured the firm to win "lucrative U.S. military and government contracts, something its Canadian pedigree had hindered," but he shared Staples's concerns, noting that US Honeywell International had already acquired Canada's second-largest space company, ComDev, earlier in the year. With Space Systems/Loral controlling Canada's largest space company, Black emphasized that US "law is now governing vital Canadian security and space assets." Countering that MDA's business in Canada had not changed, Don Osborne, president of MDA's Information Systems group in Canada noted, "From a management perspective, I have a boss who I report to who is in the United States." Moreover, he stressed, "Companies have very complicated legal structures for all sorts of reasons," not the least being "better access" to larger markets. Although Dan Friedmann remained on MDA's board through the transition, on 13 January 2017 MDA announced his resignation from the board, effective immediately.[5]

MDA's incorporation into the larger American military-industrial complex should not surprise, for this is what happens when policymakers privatize public goods and think they can manage the hegemonic power of capitalism. MDA's history also exemplifies Canada's ongoing integration into the North American defence-industrial market, for as John MacDonald argued during the ATK debate in 2008, MDA had no choice but to seek entrance into the United States, given the limits of Canada's market. No matter how one tries to manage it, capitalism is incapable of anything but the valorization of capital. As a result, this study in surveillance capitalism was never about individuals and the choices they made. In the end, Canada's trajectory and MDA's history reveal that individuals, whether policymakers, industrialists, or workers, are products and components of the larger structures they serve. Unless they challenged the universe they had entered, those involved in the MDA story had to rationalize the capitalist imperatives they needed to meet so they could continue to believe that they controlled their own destinies.

Over the past sixty years, policymakers, capitalists, scientists, the media, and technology's enthusiasts have sold remote sensing satellites on their abilities to predict and then limit the most devastating consequences of environmental change. At the same time, they have promoted space exploration, communications satellites, and Internet platforms on their abilities to connect the world in ways that could usher in a "global village" of peaceful consumers anxious to participate in economic growth. Increasingly, they have also pitched military satellites as a necessary component of sovereignty, freedom, and democracy. It was never a question of whether or not government would play a significant role in the development and expansion of surveillance systems. Policymakers accepted that they would. Instead, they worried about how to develop new policies to manage "contracting out" from government to industry so they could socialize the risks of the undertaking while simultaneously positioning themselves to profit from economic growth strategies and perpetual change. Downplaying the role of Earth observation and communications in reconnaissance and military preparedness, space writers and technological enthusiasts enhanced the strategies of policymakers and capitalists by focusing on what outer space exploration and technological development could do to create a healthier and more prosperous world.

As Evgeny Morozov observed during 2011, however, optimism in technology's abilities to change the world for the better is often a dangerous snare: "Reframing social problems as a series of technological problems" distracts policymakers "from tackling problems that are non-technological in nature and cannot be reframed." But when each technology inevitably fails to solve problems, its enthusiasts "are usually quick to suggest another, more effective technological fix as a remedy – and fight fire with fire," he asserts. "This explains why we fight climate change by driving more cars that are more fuel-efficient and protect ourselves from Internet surveillance by relying on tools that encrypt our messages and conceal our identity." These strategies do little more than create "a never-ending and extremely expensive cat-and-mouse game in which, as the problem gets worse, the public is forced to fund even newer, more powerful tools to address it," he suggests. As a result, "we avoid the search for a more effective non-technological solution that, while being more expensive (politically or financially) in the shorter-term, could end the problem once and for all."[6] MDA's history confirms Morozov's findings. We are already in information overload, and have plentiful evidence to confirm that we are damaging the planet, along with the oceans and atmosphere on which we depend for human survival. Providing another $54 million in taxpayer funding to "develop better radar, speed up satellite-based data transmission and improve cloud-based data processing" will not change in any significant way what we already know about what we are doing to the Earth and its people. This is perhaps the most important lesson from the MDA story, but there are others.

"CREATIVE DESTRUCTION":
LESSONS FROM MDA'S HISTORY

Long before the 1962 launch of *Alouette-1*, and no matter the political party in power, members of the Canadian plutocracy had accepted the capitalist ethos, which privileged private property rights and consumption over the collective aspirations of those who called for the protection of labour and public goods. But with the launch of *Sputnik*, Canada's elite quickly learned that without a satellite surveillance capability, they could not compete with their counterparts in the larger American nation. Moreover, they realized that they would "never learn what other nations know about us, which must be viewed as a serious non-military threat" to Canada's political and cultural sovereignty.[7] As a result, they encouraged Canada's surveillance capability through public policies aimed at incubating private businesses and providing ongoing support for technological innovation so that Canadian firms could wend their way from obscurity to international prominence. Canada's political and economic alliances with the United States also created the context for the education Canadians would receive as they entered into complex negotiations with a capitalist system in which government policies incentivized some activities while discouraging others.

Canada's simultaneous efforts to maintain national sovereignty and global influence attached to but separate from the United States also taught people at MDA that they could capitalize on surveillance and the technologies they created for its expansion, not by entering the market on their own, but by fastening themselves to public funding streams, government grants, procurement contracts, and the largesse of political operatives anxious to protect Canadian interests and to expand the wealth and influence of a sparsely populated but resource-rich nation. The Canadian government also encouraged people at SPAR, MDA, and other space-based firms to build something first for Canada, thereafter exporting their surveillance expertise into larger markets so that Canada could maintain its place among the world's capitalist power core. Canadian policymakers, capitalists, and technological enthusiasts consistently raised the spectre of the Avro Arrow disaster as well, arguing that foreign direct investment in the Canadian economy could result in a brain drain of Canadian talent, know-how, and surveillance expertise, thereby imperilling the political independence of the Canadian people and Canadian sovereignty as a whole. To solve such dilemmas, they proposed the further expansion of public funding and "contracting out" policies to stimulate technological innovation in the private sector. Generally well-intentioned and seemingly apolitical, people at MDA got caught up in the excitement of technological development and capitalist ambitions, but it took the stimulus of the state to push them to take a larger leap into remote sensing and the increasingly secretive world of surveillance procurement.

When they entered university during the 1950s and started MDA in 1969, neither John MacDonald nor Vern Dettwiler seemed to understand that they and the young engineers who would join them had come of age during the "great compression," that anomalous period between the Great Depression of the 1930s and the recession of the 1970s when North American inequalities in wealth and income contracted on the strength of post–World War II circumstances. Like their counterparts in the capitalist universe, Canadians began to assemble a social safety net and peacekeeping missions that promised to save capitalism from its own "creative destruction." During 1946, Saskatchewan became the first province to introduce something close to universal health coverage. Other provinces soon followed, and by 1984, Canadians had strengthened quality of care through federal standards guided by the Canada Health Act. Long deemed the envy of the industrialized world, Canada's old age pension scheme, health care delivery system, unemployment insurance plan, and welfare structure became the primary elements of the safety net. Canadians, like Americans, also sought to make education more affordable to more people, on readjustment acts that promised low-cost, low-interest benefits in the hope of a more equitable and peaceful tomorrow. Canadians additionally attempted to gain influence by attaching themselves to the United Nations rather than the United States; in this, however, they were not successful. Signing North American defence production sharing agreements prior to the Cold War, policymakers tethered Canadians to their more powerful capitalist neighbours, in a relationship from which they never extricated themselves. Regardless, that relationship allowed many young men to ascend, particularly those who could make sense of new technologies and present themselves as objective experts interested only in efficiencies and apolitical problem-solving.

Sputnik created an additional opportunity for electrical engineers and computer scientists to ascend, for it accelerated the Cold War and put on full display the bipolar world contest. As popular writers explained the Cold War's capitalist imperative to the public, they amplified the message of policymakers who had already crafted narratives about the engineer's usefulness to space exploration, the "new" knowledge economy, and society as a whole. Members of the federal government had begun to draw scientists and engineers into policymaking bodies during World War II, but the computer's disruptive qualities and the sophistication of new technologies prompted increasing calls for their services and expertise. Once fully ensconced in the capitalist ethos, engineers and scientists with private ambitions thus joined capitalists in the creation of a publicly funded architecture for the expansion of surveillance capitalism. In the process, engineers also achieved the professional and social status they long sought by participating in ongoing decisions that privileged the private over the public, and technological solutions to the nation's economic, political, and social problems over non-technological ones.

John MacDonald and Vern Dettwiler founded MDA within this environment, and assumed that they inhabited a meritocratic society that had

allowed them to ascend on their talents, hard work, and intuitive understanding of a "new" economy they would help to create. As a result, they
began their business with a very specific vision, one where profit represented nothing more than a means to work on the technological edge,
where the elegance of their work could speak for and sell itself. For Dettwiler, that vision encompassed a desire to do exciting engineering work in
an environment where he could find personal as well as professional fulfillment. When presented with an opportunity to try to manage that environment, he declined, preferring to secure for himself a place in MDA's
technical realm. Accordingly, he transferred his control to MacDonald in
exchange for a position as MDA's principal engineer, a post he enjoyed for
thirty years. Motivated by his experiences at MIT, MacDonald extended
MDA's vision to a place where promising young engineers could find challenging employment on the West Coast as participants in a Canadian firm
operating at a world-class level of engineering excellence. MacDonald also
wanted to control that environment. Believing that "sovereignty is a right
which has its roots in the ability of a people to control their own destiny,
to build their own value system and to build their own quality of life," Mac-
Donald hired a general manager to take care of day-to-day business and,
throughout his presidency, MDA avoided outside investors. Equating loss of
ownership with loss of sovereignty and control, MacDonald employed a
government contracting formula and the sweat equity of the firm's young
employees to extend his vision. As it turned out, both served the interests
of capital very well. Indeed, the Cold War focus on re-engineering the
world for the commercial space industry helped to create the business clusters and technology corridors that now girdle the globe, even if individual
participants did not initially perceive the role they would play in the
expansion of much larger structures and ambitions.[8]

Unfortunately for the vast majority, as Thomas Piketty's award-winning
work on the economy demonstrates, inherited wealth rather than merit
has continued to play the decisive role in determining mobility, particularly after the mid-1970s, when wages stagnated and neoliberal policies
resurrected the wealth and income inequality long associated with the
earlier "Gilded Age." As a result, Piketty stressed, "The hope invested in a
more just social order" has collapsed. "Economic growth is simply incapable of satisfying this democratic and meritocratic hope, which must create specific institutions for the purpose and not rely solely on market
forces or technological progress," he emphasized.[9] This is another lesson
from the MDA experience. Although the technical achievements of MDA's
founders and workers placed the firm in the vanguard of remote sensing

worldwide during the 1970s, competition exposed the eternal verity that technical elegance cannot control the process of capitalist expansion. As a result, MDA nearly failed. To save the firm he and Dettwiler had created, MacDonald had to relinquish control so that an experienced executive backed by institutional venture capitalists, deep-pocketed customers, and the Canadian government could push MDA into the next phase of surveillance capitalism. Thereafter, MacDonald's career depended upon his role as a technological enthusiast and policymaker, someone who could serve as MDA's ambassador and one of Canada's pre-eminent technocratic luminaries. As a reward for his participation in policymaking bodies, MacDonald ascended into the ranks of Canada's space-based elite. During 1988, Canada's governor general conferred upon MacDonald the Order of Canada, and in 1993 he emerged as Canada's Eminent Person in Science and Technology. Returning to his roots in 2010, MacDonald then became the chancellor of Prince George's University of Northern British Columbia, where he continued to nurture the world view he learned from his experiences at MIT and MDA.

During 1982, John W. Pitts became MDA's new president and CEO. An executive motivated by acquiring a sizeable return on his investment, Pitts understood and embraced the capitalist ethos. He therefore refinanced the firm, introduced vigilant cost controls, and pushed MDA into military procurement contracting as part of Canada's larger defence sharing agreements with the United States. Once done, Pitts hoped to maximize profits from military contracting and the systems side of the business while simultaneously attempting to develop products from MDA's unexploited technologies. Through that process, Pitts transformed MDA from its original skunk-works operation into a capitalist enterprise for which profit became the ultimate goal. He also restructured the company to meet its investors' exit strategy: a ten times financial return in five years, or the equivalent thereof. From 1982 through 1987, Pitts therefore attempted to reconfigure MDA's original systems engineering focus into a manufacturing environment based on mass production. Ultimately, that strategy failed. Despite his commitment to capitalism and military contracting, John Pitts failed to see many of the forces that would shape the future of surveillance and his own destiny as a man trained at Harvard during the 1950s but ill-equipped to make a full transition from the conservatism of the past to the accelerated pace of capitalism. That pace included the deindustrialization of North America and the off-shoring of operations and work to cheaper regions, both of which made Canada a decreasingly attractive environment for global investment.

Although Pitts failed to transform MDA into a manufacturing bonanza, MDA's systems work soon taught those who wanted to remain with the firm that they had to accept the realities of Canada's defence sharing arrangements with the United States, the continental integration of the military-industrial complex, global capital accumulation, and their place within the WTO and other international governing bodies. Always, their futures depended, they learned, on the expansion and vagaries of surveillance capitalism and Canada's participation in an increasingly integrated North American economy. When MDA failed to win an important US military contract under Pitts's leadership, they also had to concede that their focus on technological elegance had once again imperilled MDA. Having lost their technological edge, some of them additionally came to understand that they had less control of their own destinies than some of them had originally imagined. Indeed, shifting technological requirements depended on the changing world economy, Canadian investments in R&D, free trade agreements, the export strategies of Canadian imperialists, and the evolution of the global space industry under American dominance. To compete in such a world, they would need to improve their marketing abilities and lobbying efforts to keep their interests on the policy agenda. By the early 1990s, these larger forces therefore prompted Pitts to concentrate his efforts on shareholder desires for liquidity while turning MDA's operations over to strategists who fully accepted the neoliberal project, including the role that MDA's systems integration would play in continental and worldwide surveillance.

From 1987 to 2016, Dan Friedmann focused on key geographical areas and the company's core strengths in systems integration. By expanding on MacDonald's original vision, the company's expertise in remote sensing, and Pitts's profit-oriented and disciplinary structures, Friedmann executed a plan that included business structures and marketing strategies centred on profitable, long-term expansion in systems engineering, globalization, and the dawning Internet era. Still, the firm's managers worried about the risks of dependency on government entities. "The thing that could happen to us now is that a major project could be cancelled, the government might decide to freeze spending, and kill something like Space Station, cancel MCDV, cancel CAATS," one project manager observed in 1992. "You cancel three contracts like that and we're finished, so, that might be a bigger risk now, being too close to the government," but "it just so happens that all the stuff we're into is funding-sourced by government, one way or another," he concluded.[10] As it turned out, that did not change in a post-Soviet universe.

Speaking for the aggressive, young management team during 1993, another senior executive stressed that MDA merely needed to spread its risk beyond Canada. "Our objective is to span enough governments worldwide, and in enough entities within those governments, so that we're recession-proof, and I think that it's pretty clear that we are. The recession is incidental to us," he argued. "We're not a consumer business. We don't sell into that market." Instead, "We sell governments which have ongoing needs," and their cycles are very different from economic recession cycles. In fact, there's the thought that governments run contrary to the economic cycle. They spend more in poor times."[11] More than twenty years later, it appears that his perceptions were at least partially correct in articulating that worldwide governments intended to spend more, no matter economic circumstances, not on social programs and other problems, but rather on the expansion of the security state. As a result, MDA's plan to sell its space-based business during 2008 failed on "national security" grounds, its property information product adventure misfired during the financial restructuring of the world economy following the global recession, and its satellite communications, imaging, and reconnaissance business areas thrived as Canada expanded its surveillance as well as military capabilities during the twenty-first century. Still, MDA's survival continued to depend on its access to larger markets, particularly in the United States. Thus, when Americans provided an opportunity to engineer a "stealth takeover" of MDA and its technologies, the firm's management team and board members seized it.

Throughout each successive stage in its development, MDA demonstrated that in a capitalist universe, small, high-tech start-ups can have some part of a lot of different visions, provided the sum adds up to shareholder value, short-term investment strategies, and the ongoing needs of governments. During 1993, John MacDonald argued that "the conventional wisdom in 1969 was that, 'Who the hell could build an aerospace industry in BC, let alone Richmond?;'" but "now it's a high-tech centre," he boasted with no false modesty. What was more, MDA showed, "by example," that one could "build world-class wealth generation, appropriate to the coming times, here in this country," with "only a few things necessary in order to be able to do it." MacDonald emphasized that "one of the key" things Canadians needed was "to think internationally. You can't think you're going to build the kind of business that this country is going to need by just sticking to Canada, or even to just North America, because the great open market to the south is not nearly as open as everybody thinks."[12] When MacDonald received Canada's inaugural John H. Chapman Award of Excellence for helping to position Canada as a world leader in space science and technology, people at all levels of government concurred. They therefore encouraged MacDonald to share his "passion, dreams, commitment," and pearls of wisdom about the importance of space-based surveillance and the export trade with the federal government, Science Council of Canada, National Research Council of Canada, and larger world.[13]

Neither central architects nor passive participants in the ongoing drama of capitalist expansion and the techno-security state, people at MDA simply learned how to adjust to changing circumstances, even if some of the outcomes had nothing to do with what they originally intended. The trajectory of Canada's participation in global surveillance incorporated the Canadian people into the larger objectives of the United States and the interests of capital. The rising status of a global technocracy then made it increasingly lucrative to focus on engineering and science, on more technology as a way to gain more work, increase revenues, pay larger dividends to shareholders, and win the race for procurement contracts. To stay in business, surveillance contractors constantly need to lobby governments and others for more work, all the while increasing pressure to expand commitments to fund surveillance and the military. In such an environment, the professional engineer could argue, just as John MacDonald did in 2004, that "a customer is a customer," and "the commercial sector should not concern itself with the applications of its products, whether peaceful or non-peaceful." In turn, politicians and regulators, often intimately associated with such lobbyists and industry players, and with many increasingly dependent upon the security state for their livelihoods and the regions they serve, habitually run the risk of compromising themselves and their constituents. Even the Canadian government's decision to quash plans to sell the company's space and defence division to ATK in 2008 pointed MDA in the direction of further expansion into security systems, communications satellites, and information gathering for militaries and commercial organizations worldwide. Every move MDA has made, whether strategically successful or bungled, placed the firm more deeply at the centre of systems integration for permanent war preparedness, the further development of UAVs, and information and communications products focused on surveillance and tracking, change detection, and data mining, processing, dissemination, and even manipulation.

The services and products that firms such as MDA provide have increased concerns over the privacy issues and civil/human rights abuses that flow from information gathering and dissemination. They have additionally contributed to mounting anxieties about the ramifications of the techno-security state and created the context for ongoing (even if ultimately ineffective) protests over the outsized influence of major global corporations currently dominating both private and public actions as well as individual and collective imperatives. There are other unintended consequences as well, including those associated with information overload and the distractions it creates (something MIT's Vannevar Bush and others foresaw as a hazard more than fifty years ago). The inability to manage the planet and its resources, no matter the technology, also persists, with the deployment of drones and instruments of war creeping into every aspect of civilian life, along with non-state actors who have managed to slip under the surveillance radar to launch terrorist attacks, including recent ones in Canada. For better or ill, Edward Snowden's security leaks have revealed that public-private partnerships expand the influence of capital and multinational firms on public policymaking, thereby creating an engineered world we all too often ignore but later find troubling.[14]

We can do nothing about the past, but ongoing concerns about orbital debris and environmental destruction, military adventurism and terrorist attacks, widening wealth and income inequality, and government and corporate corruption provide an opportunity to ponder who or what we serve. Dwight D. Eisenhower's prophetic warning about the dangers of the military-industrial complex serves as one place to start. We also have the chance to address his post-presidential speech emphasizing that the search for absolute security "can eventually end only in national bankruptcy."[15] Or we can simply engage in more historical amnesia and the mythical thinking of the past. Engineers provide us with a template for the latter strategy. Seeing and selling themselves as amoral and apolitical actors more interested in solving "real world" problems than in transforming global belief systems in the geopolitical sphere, many members of the "new" knowledge economy intellectually removed themselves from ideological, political, and moral discourses, preferring instead to view the narrative of history as driven from a positivist place, in a meritocratic, technocratic universe where their expertise could drive a better, post-industrial, post-ideological future. Sponsored research, at universities, in government laboratories, and through the privatization of the space industry then extended that faith during and after the Cold War, with technological cheerleaders encouraging non-technical actors to participate. Joined by a host of technocrats, government contractors, industry boosters, politicians, and wide-eyed consumers, the mainstream media promoted the myth of the new economy that now occupies centre stage in the sprawling drama of the equally mythological narrative of human exceptionalism and the power of surveillance technologies and a wired world to solve global problems.

Vincent Mosco has argued, "Myth is not a gloss on reality; it embodies its own reality. These views are especially difficult for people to swallow as the chorus grows for the view that we are entering a new age, a time so significant that it merits the conclusion that we have entered 'the end of history.'" But such myths fail "to consider the potential for a profound contradiction between the idea of a liberal democracy and the growing control of the world's political economy by the concentrated power of its largest businesses," Mosco asserts.[16] A recent *Globe and Mail* article on Vancouver's latest "high-tech" makeover is a case in point.

Writing his piece as MDA's stock surged during March 2015, public relations strategist Richard Littlemore declared, "Every great tech scene has an origin story, complete with a ground zero." In Vancouver, "the point of genesis is the Vancouver suburb of Richmond, in an old shed long since lost in the fog along the Fraser River delta," he asserted. "That's where Professor John MacDonald and physics grad Vern Dettwiler headed on Feb. 3, 1969 after they walked out of the University of British Columbia to set up a little remote-sensing company. They thought they had an interesting technology," he continued, but "were disappointed that the brilliant young scientists and engineers they'd seen go through UBC all seemed to be leaving town." Following the article's publication, John MacDonald's son decided to employ the Comments section on *Globe and Mail*'s website to correct a few of Littlemore's errors before corroborating most of the narrative Littlemore had crafted. MacDonald's son noted that MDA began neither in a shed nor with remote sensing, but rather in his childhood home's basement. Thereafter, however, he repeated much of the story MDA's founders began to articulate more than forty years ago. Both Littlemore and MacDonald's son included the brain-drain concerns MacDonald had identified, but they omitted that Canadians had long articulated such concerns. Their narratives also confirmed that MDA created the nexus for the talented team of ground station builders who later built many of the technology firms that now dot Vancouver's Lower Mainland, but omitted why they left the firm in the first place.[17]

What stands out in Littlemore's narrative, beyond the obvious errors about MDA's founding and tumultuous history, is the complete absence of the government's role in the creation and sustenance of Vancouver's surveillance-contracting corridor; instead, he credits MDA with near-magical powers, including how much other high-technology entrepreneurs had "benefitted over the years from lessons learned at the knee of MDA's masters."[18] One need not fault Littlemore for some of these oversights, or for citing Ventures West as the principal "angel" in Vancouver's high-tech investment community, to see that such pieces illustrate the selective memories we call upon to explain the current and often temporary successes that each new technological wave engenders. Those magical narratives also ignore the policymakers who provide access to taxpayer-funded largesse through federal military contracts, what Stuart Leslie has described as the "biggest 'angel' of them all." They additionally tend to obscure financial and real estate bubbles, those displaced by change, and the socialized risks and privatized profits that flow from ventures serving the larger interests of capital and the military-industrial complex. Littlemore's work is simply symptomatic of a larger phenomenon.[19]

Since the dawn of capitalist experimentation, members of every generation have seen themselves and their world pivoted on the cusp of the new, buoyed by a new economy and a new paradigm of prosperity. It always was, and once again is, the future. With Peter Drucker's invention, it became very flattering to consider oneself a member the "new" knowledge economy rather than, say, the know-nothing economies of the past. But every society bases its economy on the knowledge at its disposal, while the twenty-first century's widening girth of concentrated power owes much to an uncritical faith in cyberspace, satellite surveillance, and science, technology, engineering, and mathematics to produce a future that will allow us to reach the penultimate nirvana we seek. People at MDA, like so many people elsewhere, shared and then helped to spread that faith. Unfortunately, the current generation now lives with the unintended consequences of an earlier confidence in the future, and they are increasingly demanding new answers.

Although many of his own solutions remained technological ones as he continued to ponder his own future as an ambassador for a sustainable economy, John MacDonald has long conceded the importance of making a start, to avoid "doing things that are not very good for the planet."[20] Toward that end, MacDonald returned to his roots on 10 February 2010, accepting the honorary role of chancellor of the University of Northern British Columbia in Prince George. In his 2012 message to the university community, MacDonald declared, "Since leaving the North to pursue an advanced education and several careers, I have learned many things. One of the most important of those is that talent and world-class capability can come from anywhere." Furthermore he argued, "It is important that we ensure that this precious resource – the intellectual capacity of our young people – has access to advanced education at the highest level no matter where they live and grow up." He also cautioned that the "current energy system that powers the prosperity of human civilization is unsustainable. Our global energy system will have to change. It will happen in this century and that is today's big challenge."[21] In a sea of challenges, it certainly stands out as a critical one. As MacDonald's initial 2026 deadline gets closer every year, it may well be time to cast off what he called the "primitive" thinking of previous generations.[22] If we have the kind of human agency he also imagines, we might make the start he envisioned by looking neither to capitalist orthodoxy nor to technological fixes, but rather to the historical record, to see what space exploration, data mining, panoptical surveillance, military-systems integration, and the security state have already wrought.

Vern Dettwiler returned to his roots following his retirement from MDA in 1998 as well, but he took a different path. After his retirement, he did not return to BC's northern interior. Instead, he moved to Switzerland. Living a quiet life in the country of his birth, Dettwiler became a well-known member of the International Club of Berne (ICB), "a keen hiker and an enthusiast of Switzerland's excellent public transport system." When he died suddenly on 16 September 2013, some of his fellow ICB members wrote a moving eulogy for him, where they claimed that "perhaps unknown to most ICB members," Vern Dettwiler had "lived and worked for nearly 40 years in Canada. There in 1969 he co-founded Mac-Donald, Dettwiler and Associates (MDA), a pioneering provider of innovative electronic solutions. In later years," they noted, "MDA expanded into space technology, becoming Canada's foremost specialists in this field and subsequently one of the world's leading communication satellite companies."[23] Some members may not have known that twenty years earlier Dettwiler had also suggested, "We need to take a step back and ask, 'What is the actual problem we're trying to solve?'"[24] With the power structures employed and technologies developed by the current generation sure to shape the circumstances of future ones, and problems in need of solutions that might force us to test our assumptions about the narrative of human progress, perhaps Dettwiler's question is the better place to start.

Notes

INTRODUCTION

1 National Aeronautics and Space Administration (hereafter NASA), National Aeronautics and Space Act.

2 Bromberg, *NASA and Space*; Graham and Hanson, *Spy Satellites*, 14–47; Launius, Logsdon, and Smith, *Reconsidering Sputnik*; Lewis, *Spy Capitalism*, 46; Sherry, *Shadow of War*, 314; Wills, "*Innovation in a Cold [War]*"; and Wills, "Satellite Surveillance."

3 Slotten, "Satellite Communications."

4 During 1967 the United Kingdom, the United States, and the USSR affixed their signatures to the Treaty on Principles Governing the Activities of States in the Exploration and Use of Outer Space, Including the Moon and Other Celestial Bodies (commonly called the Outer Space Treaty, or OST). The new international space law barred state parties to the treaty from placing nuclear or other weapons of mass destruction in outer space. By January 2013, 102 countries had become state parties to the treaty, while 26 others had signed but not yet ratified OST. See United Nations (hereafter UN), Office for Outer Space Affairs, "Treaty on Principles," 3–8; and UN, Committee on the Peaceful Uses of Space, *Status of International Agreements*, 11.

5 Gainor, "*Alouette 1*"; and Rosenblatt and Dickson, "At Long Last."

6 NASA, *NSSDC Master Catalog*. On the European Space Agency's entrance into the space race during the 1970s, see Madders, *New Force*; Suzuki, *Policy Logics*; and Sandholtz, *High-tech Europe*.

7 Jaramillo, *Space Security Index*, 17–18. SSI is part of a larger international program to "improve transparency on space activities and provide a common, comprehensive knowledge base to support the development of national and

international policies that contribute to the security and sustainability of Outer Space." Nations with launching capabilities since 1957 include the USSR, 1957 (from Kazakhstan since 1957, and Plesetsk, Russia, since 1991); the United States, 1958; France (from Algeria), 1965; Japan, 1970; China, 1970; the United Kingdom, 1971 (from Australia in 1971 and abandoned during the late 1970s); the European Space Agency (ESA) consortium, 1979; India, 1980; Israel, 1988; Iran, 2009; and North Korea, 2012.

8 Ibid., 11–12, 27–43.

9 Marc Boucher, "Sapphire: Canada's First Military Satellite," *SpaceRef*, 6 March 2012.

10 Jaramillo, *Space Security Index*, 11, 24–5, 27, 34, 57, 61–8, 137–48.

11 Ibid., 89 (89–104 provides a brief introduction to the development of the commercial space sector and interactions between commercial operators and government contractors).

12 MacDonald, Dettwiler and Associates (hereafter MDA), "About Us"; Spence, "Recognizing Dan Gelbart"; Paul Kaihla, "Hissin' Cousins: BC's High-tech Entrepreneurs Share Corporate Origins, but Fall Short of Being Mutual Admirers," *Canadian Business*, 15 May 2000; Yang, "Magic Mountain," 22; Kapp, "Banging the Gong"; and John Faustmann, "Barclay Isherwood: Prime Mover at Mobile Data International," *Canadian Business*, August 1987, 53.

13 Stephanie Price, qtd in Christopher Donville, "MacDonald Dettwiler Surges as Loral Deal Approved," *Bloomberg News*, 29 October 2012.

14 Eric Lam and Frederic Tomesco, "MacDonald Dettwiler Launches into Orbit on Satellite Boom," *Bloomberg News*, 7 March 2013. In addition, see Michael Taverna, "Double-Back Guarantee," *Aviation Week and Space Technology*, 4 January 2010, 36; Gainor, "*Alouette 1*"; and "MacDonald Dettwiler to Buy Loral Subsidiary for $875 Million," *Guardian*, 27 June 2012.

15 David Ebner, "MDA's Daniel Friedmann Likes the Earth under His Feet," *Globe and Mail*, 6 January 2012.

16 Interview with Dollard (18 January 1993). Despite many of the approaches deployed to describe and define entrepreneurs – from intuition about the market and a desire to generate wealth, through a propensity for risk-taking and the need for achievement, and on to the ability to innovate, motivate personnel, and organize/direct an organization – scholars of entrepreneurship and business management have long conceded that we continue to know very little about entrepreneurship, no matter the plethora of journals, research institutes, and disciplines devoted to the subject. On the continuing debate over definitions of entrepreneurs/entrepreneurship and the managerial strategies and structures of organizations that house them, see, for example, Cunningham and Lisherson, "Defining Entrepreneurship"; Cuff, "Notes

for a Panel"; and Åstebro et al., "Seeking the Roots." For an excellent overview of Canadian entrepreneurship from the perspective of the biographers who have celebrated Canada's "great men" in business as well as the organizational synthesis associated with business history doyen Alfred DuPont Chandler Jr and the structural factors involved in business success and failure, see Bellamy, "John Labatt." Although Chandler's *Strategy and Structure* and *Visible Hand* dominated interpretations of business history during the 1980s and into the 1990s, cultural factors and larger social structures have once again gained traction, particularly in recent scholarship on the history of capitalism. On the educational, legal, political, and social structures and values that have influenced the development of business institutions in the United States and elsewhere, see Cochran's classic *Business in American Life*; and the more recent collection of essays in Landes, Moykr, and Baumol, *Invention of Enterprise*, particularly Baumol and Strom, "'Useful Knowledge' of Entrepreneurship." For a typical celebration of the personal qualities guiding Timothy Eaton and successful entrepreneurship in Canada (as well as an indictment of the personal qualities of the sons who inherited their father's company and drove it into bankruptcy), see McQueen, *Eatons*. On the importance of the socio-institutional context for entrepreneurship in Canada, see Marchildon, *Profits and Politics*. In addition, see Ball and Wood, "Political Economies of Surveillance"; and Laird, *Pull*, 1–50.

17 William L. Fishman, assistant director for international communications, Office of Telecommunications Policy, Executive Office of the President, Washington, DC, Before the Fourth International Conference on Computer Communication, Kyoto, Japan, September 26–29, 1979, Department of Communications, Secretariat to the Computer-Communications Interdepartmental Committee, RG97-F-IV, vol. 418, file 7500-1331-4(2), U.S. Government (hereafter RG97, vol. 418, US), Library and Archives Canada, Ottawa (hereafter LAC).

18 Lapp and Interdepartmental Task Force on Surveillance Satellites (hereafter Lapp and Task Force), *Satellites and Sovereignty*, 13, as well as 7–14, 31–43, and 49–51, LAC.

19 Helpful overviews include Harris, *Watchers;* Mattelart, *Globalization of Surveillance;* and Lyon, *Surveillance after September 11*. On the role of the Royal Canadian Mounted Police in Canada's domestic surveillance programs, see Whitaker, Keeley, and Parnaby, *Secret Service*, 468–520.

20 Canadian Space Agency (hereafter CSA), "Canadian Satellite RADARSAT-1"; Wills, "*Innovation in a Cold [War]*"; and Paglen, *Blank Spots*.

21 Andrejevic, *iSpy*, 94–102; and Lyon, *Electronic Eye*, 1–18.

22 See Foucault, *Discipline and Punish*; Mattelart, *Globalization of Surveillance*;

Andrejevic, *iSpy*; Marx, *Machine in the Garden*; and Adas, *Machines as the Measure*.

23 Parenti, *Soft Cage*, 78; and Foucault, *Discipline and Punish*.

24 Mokyr, *Gifts of Athena*, 297.

25 Mosco, *Digital Sublime*, 25.

26 See Söderberg and Netzén, "When All That Is Theory," 111; and Wills, "Satellite Surveillance," 104–6.

27 White, "Materiality, Form, and Context."

28 Mukerji, "Intelligent Uses of Engineering," 15.

29 Lyon, *Electronic Eye*, 19.

30 Interview tapes, interviewee edited and approved transcripts, and documents provided by interviewees are in the possession of the author.

31 For discussions about surveillance-centred networks in the post–Cold War era, see DeBlois et al., "Space Weapons"; Graham, *Cities, War*; Graham and Wood, "Digitizing Surveillance"; Haggerty and Ericson, *New Politics of Surveillance*; and Lyon, *Surveillance Society*. On the power of interactivity across multiple media platforms, and the synergies between commerce, culture, management, media, surveillance, politics, and war, see, Andrejevic, *iSpy*, 1–51 and 251–68; Parenti, *Soft Cage*, 1–12 and 77–212; and Mindell, *Between Human and Machine*.

32 Johnson-Freese, *Heavenly Ambitions*, 3.

33 Eisenhower, "Farewell Address."

34 Baran and Sweezy, *Monopoly Capital*.

35 Bernstein and Wilson, "New Perspectives," 2 as well as 3–9.

36 Stuart Leslie, "Biggest 'Angel' of Them All," 49.

37 See Leslie, *Cold War and American Science*; Leslie and Kargon, "Selling Silicon Valley"; Berlin, *Man behind the Microchip*, 140–8; Matthews, *Silicon Valley*, 112–46; Heinrich, "Cold War Armory"; Abbate, *Inventing the Internet*; Hounshell, "Medium Is the Message"; Lowen, *Creating the Cold War*; and Noble, "Command Performance." On the creation of technological "family trees" between universities, industries, and the government, see Suchman, Steward, and Westfall, "Legal Environment of Entrepreneurship."

38 De Larrinaga, "Between Blind Faith and Deep Skepticism"; and Huntley, "Mice That Soar."

39 Vardalas, *Computer Revolution*, 278 and 295.

40 Mussio, *Telecom Nation*, 222 as well as 65–8, 92–3, 97–114, and 223–7.

41 Wills, "*Innovation in a Cold [War]*," 129–38; and Gainor, "*Alouette 1*."

42 King, *Canada and the War*; Canada, Department of Defence Production, *Canada–United States Defence Production Sharing*, 7, 23–6, and 67; North American Aerospace Defense Command (NORAD), "Brief History"; Thomp-

son and Randall, *Canada and United States*, 171–98; and Sayle, "Pattern of
Constraint."

43 For an important corrective to the myth of free trade and unfettered capitalism in the development of the United Kingdom, United States, and other
market-oriented societies, see Chang, *Bad Samaritans*, particularly 1–68.

44 Lower Vancouver Island Liberal Association, "White Paper on the Economy,"
National Policy Convention, November 1970, 3–4 and 10, in Mary Keen,
Ministry of State for Science and Technology (hereafter MOSST), R1526, vol.
19, file 11, LAC. Some Canadians focused their attention on the creation of
national cultural institutions as a defence against American incursions, but a
chorus of others, including many policymakers, government technocrats,
capitalists, manufacturers, and scientists turned their attention to the federal
government's need to protect Canada's established and fledgling industries,
including those focused on automobiles and aviation, the potential of
nuclear power, the discovery of oil and gas reserves, and the emerging fields
of computing, telecommunications, and space-based surveillance. Some also
argued that defence sharing arrangements with the United States could help
Canada to overcome American protectionist policies, including restrictions
imposed on Canadian firms by the 1933 Buy American Act.

45 See Lapp and Task Force, *Satellites and Sovereignty*.

46 Consultative Committee on the Implications of Telecommunications for
Canadian Sovereignty (hereafter Consultative Committee), *Telecommunica-
tions and Sovereignty*, 73, LAC; Wills, "*Innovation in a Cold [War]*," 129–38; and
Godefroy, "Canada's Early Space."

47 Interview with Lapp.

48 "MOSST Accomplishments, First Year," 1972, MOSST First Ministry, R1526, vol.
43, file 12, LAC.

49 Klassen, "Canada and the New Imperialism," 177.

50 Schumpeter, *Capitalism, Socialism, and Democracy*, 139. In addition, see
Schumpeter, *Theory of Economic Development*, 93–4, for the traits he identified as central to the entrepreneur, including "the dream and will to found a
private kingdom"; "the will to conquer; the impulse to fight, to prove oneself
superior to others, to succeed for the sake, not of the fruits of success, but of
success itself"; and "the joy of creating, of getting things done, or simply of
exercising one's energy and ingenuity."

51 Drucker, *Age of Discontinuity*, 247. Widely considered the father of modern
management, Drucker continues to preach through his devoted disciples.
See, for example, Rosenstein, *Create Your Own Future*.

52 Michael Bliss, "Forcing the Pace," 116. In addition, see Bliss, *Northern Enterprise*, and *A Canadian Millionaire*, the latter arguing that Sir Joseph Flavelle,

"a particularly lucid small-*c* conservative," exemplified the nineteenth-century entrepreneur whose market-oriented ideas "were only partially congenial to his business colleagues in Canada, so many of whom looked constantly to government for tariffs, subsidies, and other handouts" (viii). A cursory reading of American history reveals that Flavelle's Canadian colleagues were far from alone in looking to government for subsidies and handouts. See, for example, Wills, *Boosters, Hustlers, and Speculators.*

53 For a classic interpretation of Canadian business-government relations and powerful rebuttal to the myth of the "free" market, see Nelles, *Politics of Development*, 495, which argues that the twentieth century "did not greatly alter the pattern of resource development" in Canada. "It did, however, contribute to a reduction of government – despite an expansion of its activities – to a client of the business community. This need not have been so. The failure to bring the regulatory and service functions of the state into the framework of democratic accountability was the failure of parties and politicians to pursue the logic of responsible government into the industrial age." In addition, see Armstrong and Nelles, *Monopoly's Moment.*

54 Smardon, "Shifting Terrains," 147 and 145. Anastakis, *Autonomous State*, 6–8, demonstrates that the federal government's creative and selective trade liberalization in the auto sector, which embraced government bureaucrats, firms, union leaders, and workers as national "instruments of collective action," allowed Canadians to "expect and extract their fair share of the industry" and paved the way for later free trade agreements. Employing Canada's Polymer Corporation (a Crown formed during 1942 as part of the federal government's emphasis on war production) as another example of Canadian selective liberalization, Bellamy, *Profiting from the Crown*, xii, 215, and 220, suggests that "contrary to neoconservative rhetoric, Crown corporations can be both effective instruments of public policy and dynamic and profitable commercial enterprises." Through "Ottawa's willingness to lengthen Polymer's political leash, to let its managers manage according to the dictates of the market and not those of the ballot box," Bellamy argues that policymakers provided a space for Polymer to create a "chemical valley" of firms in Sarnia, Ontario. As an investor in and protector of Polymer, the government helped to blend its military commitments with private initiatives, reverse the brain drain many Canadians feared, and maintain Canada's place in a profitable sector. According to Bellamy, Polymer also exemplified "postwar economic dynamism." In an example of Alfred Chandler's "managerial capitalism," Polymer became "flexible, efficient, and imperialistic." Privatized in 1988, in a strategy that Michael Bliss and other detractors had hoped to engender in various industries, Polymer also became the target of a foreign competitor,

with the German petrochemical giant Bayer AG acquiring Canada's synthetic rubber producer in 1990.

55 Wills, *"Innovation in a Cold [War]."*
56 Interview with Thompson (18 May 1993).
57 Interview with Maxwell.
58 See Kay, "Space Policy Redefined."
59 Interview with Caddey.
60 Jim Prentice, qtd in "Govt Confirms Decisions to Block Sale of MDA Space Division," CBC News, 9 May 2008.
61 Ebner, "MDA's Daniel Friedmann."
62 John Ivisin, "Stephen Harper Steps In to Save Radarsat Upgrade after Budget Cutbacks Threatened Satellite Program's Future," *National Post*, 19 December 2012.

CHAPTER ONE

1 H.H. Brune, Computer/Communications Secretariat, "Comments on the Report 'An Appraisal of the Industrial Development Aspects of the Computer Service and Manufacturing Industry'" (hereafter Brune, "Comments on the Report"), 5 December 1975, 5, RG97, vol. 413, file 7500-1031-2-A-21, pts 1–4, Procurement Policy, 1973–77 (hereafter RG97, vol. 413), LAC.
2 Science Council of Canada, *Towards a National Science Policy*, 3, LAC.
3 Smardon, *Asleep at the Switch*, 14.
4 Granatstein, *Britain's Economic*, 32. In addition, see Dyer, *Canada in the Great Power Game*, 201–11; King, *Ogdensburg Agreement*; Canada–United States Permanent Joint Board on Defence, *Permanent Joint Board*, LAC; and "Master Data Exchange Agreement for Mutual Development of Weapons Systems," 19 March 1984, Department of External Affairs, Block 27, Canada-U.S. Defence Production Sharing Policy, RG25-A-3-C, vol. 12698, file 27-11-2-US (hereafter RG25, vol. 12698), LAC. King ascended as a civil servant, first Canadian minister of labour, and industrial consultant to the Rockefeller family. Through his cross-border connections, King became Canada's dominant political leader from the 1920s through the 1940s, and Canada's longest-serving prime minister.
5 King, *Canada and the War*, 5. In addition, see Roosevelt, "Call to Battle," 582–3.
6 Allan E. Gotlieb, ambassador of Canada to the United States, Notes on an Address, "Canada's Special Role in the North American Defence Industrial Base," Canadian Defence Products Mission to Arizona, Phoenix, Arizona, 24 October 1983 (hereafter Gotlieb, "Canada's Special Role"), 1–2, RG25, vol.

12698, LAC. With ground broken for construction of the US Pentagon on 11 September 1941, the Hyde Park meeting foreshadowed subsequent bilateral defence industry agreements between the two nations.

7 Bothwell and Kilbourn, *C.D. Howe*. During 1908, Howe accepted an inaugural professorship in civil engineering at Dalhousie University in Halifax; and in 1913, he moved into grain elevators.

8 Bliss, *Northern Enterprise*, 527–8. Following Howe's election to the House of Commons in 1935, King appointed Howe to two important portfolios: minister of railways and Canada's first minister of marine (later consolidated into the Ministry of Transport). The federal government nationalized the Canadian National Railway in 1918, not only to save several privately owned but bankrupt railroads in the West, but also to create a transcontinental railway system capable of defending Canadian economic interests against encroachment and control by aggressive American corporations. In 1937, Howe introduced legislation that turned the CNR into a Crown corporation. He then helped to consolidate the government's radio broadcasting activities into the Canadian Broadcasting Corporation, and created Trans-Canada Airlines as a national air transportation service. World War II developments included Canada's work on the US-led Manhattan Project, which produced the world's first atomic bombs.

9 See McDowall, *Sum of the Satisfactions*, 55–8 and 143; Bellamy, *Profiting from the Crown*, xii–xvii, 200, and 215–18; and Bothwell, *Nucleus*, 444–8.

10 C.D. Howe, qtd in H. Reginald Hardy, "Canadian Arsenals Ltd Is 'Fourth' Service of Nation's Armed Forces," *Ottawa Citizen*, 9 February 1946. In addition, see Canada, Department of Defence Production, *Canada–United States Defence Production Sharing*, 7–11 and 79–119, LAC; WSHDC UNTD4248 to Extott DDP/Chell GNG, 30 Jul 82, RG25, vol. 12698, LAC; Chapnick, *Middle Power Project*, 149–56; Sayle, "Pattern of Constraint"; and Mikesell, *Bretton Woods Debates*.

11 World Trade Organization, "General Agreement," 1 and 7; and "Committee of Economic Deputies: Proposal for Joint Development of the National Aerospace Systems of Canada and the United States," confidential memorandum to the under-secretary, 16 June 1982, 2, RG25, vol. 12698, LAC.

12 B. Wooding, Col., defence counsellor, Canadian Delegation to NATO, to David Nicholls, assistant secretary general defense planning and policy, NATO International Staff, Brussels, 11 August 1981, 1–2, Department of External Affairs, Block 27, Defence, Canada-U.S. Defence Production Sharing Policy, RG25-A-3-C, vol. 14605, file 27-11-2-1, pt 17 (hereafter RG25, vol. 14605), LAC; Canada, Department of National Defence, Defence Research Board, *Annual Report*, 1–18; and NATO, "Short History." NATO commitments

averaged some 3.4 per cent of each nation's annual gross domestic product (GDP) by 1981.

13 Klassen, "Canada and the New Imperialism," 163. In addition, see "DND/DOD Master Data Exchange Agreement for the Mutual Development of Weapons Systems" (including "Security Agreement between Canada and the United States for the Protection of Classified Military Information," exchange of letters, 5 August and 15 September 1950; "The Industrial Security Agreement between Canada and the United States," exchange of letters, 6 February, 13 and 31 March, and 5 April, 1952, 1–2; "Aide Memoire," ca 1948, 1; and United States Department of Commerce, International Trade Administration, Office of Industrial Resource Administration, "Defense Materials System and Defence Priorities Systems," January 1981), RG25, vol. 12698, LAC; Canada, Department of Defence Production, *Eighteenth Annual Report*, 5, LAC; Bothwell, *Nucleus*; and Hart and Dymond, "Common Borders," 21 and 31–2.

14 George Orwell, "You and the Atomic Bomb," *Tribune*, 19 October 1945. Founding members of the NATO alliance included Belgium, Canada, Denmark, France, Iceland, Italy, Luxembourg, the Netherlands, Norway, Portugal, the United Kingdom, and the United States. The Warsaw Pact's 1955 membership included the People's Republics of Albania, Bulgaria, Hungary, Poland, and Romania, the Czechoslovak Republic, and the Union of Soviet Socialist Republics. In addition, see Litt, *Muses, the Masses, and the Massey Commission*; Cormier, *Canadianization Movement*, 29–31; and Thompson and Randall, *Canada and the United States*.

15 Canada, *Royal Commission on National Development*, 11, 13, 18, 4, and 135–6, LAC.

16 See Litt, *Muses, the Masses, and the Massey Commission*.

17 University of British Columbia, "Brief History"; Barman, *West beyond the West*, 318–19 and 329–33; and Davis, *History of Metropolitan Vancouver*, 254–98.

18 Interviews with Dettwiler (14 December 1992 and 11 January 1993), MacDonald (7 and 18 January 1993), Maxwell, and Semrau.

19 Interview with MacDonald (7 January 1993); Barman, *West beyond the West*, 6–17, 271–305, 350, 377–83, 411–12, and 443; and John Faustmann, "John MacDonald Had a Firm," *Canadian Business*, February 1986, 60–6.

20 Interview with MacDonald (7 January 1993).

21 Interview with Dettwiler (14 December 1992).

22 Interviews with Dettwiler (14 December 1992 and 11 January 1993), and MacDonald (7 January 1993).

23 Lowen, *Creating the Cold War*, 14 and 6. On Terman's plan, Silicon Valley soon housed Hewlett-Packard, Varian Associates, Eastman Kodak, General

Electric, and Lockheed Corporation. *Creating the Cold War,* 104–5 and 147
also covers federal patronage to MIT. In addition, see Sinclair, "Profession of
Engineering in America"; Noble, *Religion of Technology*; Nye, *American Tech-*
nological Sublime; Adas, *Machines as the Measure*; and Wills, "*Innovation in a*
Cold [War]," 127–8. On the ways in which corporations shape social and
moral consciousness, see Jackall, *Moral Mazes.*

24 Usselman, "IBM and Its Imitators." The Social Security Administration was
created in 1935 following the passage of the US Social Security Act.

25 Cox, "Canada and the Five Eyes," 4. In addition, see "BRC53/P/Final 049"; Littleton, *Target Nation*; and Richelson and Ball, *Ties That Bind.* Publicly
released by the National Archives on 25 June 2010, the UK's declassified documents on the UKUSA Agreement reveal that the top-secret alliance originat-
ed from a 5 March 1946 British-US Communication Agreement that networked the UK Government Communications Headquarters (GCHQ) and the
US National Security Agency (NSA). That agreement then extended to the
Commonwealth realms of Canada, Australia, and New Zealand, with each
country responsible for intelligence gathering and analysis in different parts
of the world. According to Cox, 6–7, explicit assignments remain classified;
however, "research indicates that Australia monitors South and East Asia
emissions, New Zealand covers the South Pacific and Southeast Asia. The UK
devotes attention to Europe and Western Russia, while the US monitors the
Caribbean, China, Russia, the Middle East and Africa." And,

as it did during the Cold War, Canada's arctic territory provides considerable sigint advantage. Canadian Forces Station Alert, on the northern tip
of Ellesmere Island, Nunavut, was originally an arctic weather station, but
began sigint duty by eavesdropping on northern regions of the USSR in
1958. Alert remains active today, collecting information from the interior
of Russia and China. Other Canadian sigint assets reach into Latin America and out into the North Atlantic and North Pacific Ocean. Five Eyes
partners apparently do not target each other, nor does any partner seek to
evade their national laws by requesting or accepting such activity. There is,
however, no formal way of ensuring such eavesdropping does not take
place. Each partner is trusted to adhere to this "gentlemen's agreement"
between allies.

For further information on Five Eyes and its expansion into other countries,
see Andrew, Aldrich, and Wark, *Secret Intelligence.* On Canadian concerns following Edward Snowden's leaks of NSA material to Glenn Greenwald during
2013, see Colin Freeze, "'Five Eyes' Intelligence-Sharing Program Threatens
Canadians Abroad, Watchdog Warns," *Globe and Mail,* 31 October 2013;
"Canadian Spy Agency Sued for Allegedly Violating Charter," CBC News, 22

October 2013; and Stephanie Nolan and Colin Freeze, "Brazil Is Tip of the Iceberg on Canadian Spying, U.S. Journalist Says," *Globe and Mail*, 7 October 2013.

26 Canada, Department of Defence Production, *Canada–United States Defence*, 7–11 and 79–119; and United States Department of Defense, *Directive 2035.1*.

27 Smith, *Rogue Tory*, 280. In addition, see Simpson, NATO *and the Bomb*.

28 Sherry, *Shadow of War*, 314.

29 NORAD, "Brief History," 5. In addition, see Canada, Department of Defence Production, *Canada–United States Defence*, 1–11 and 62–5.

30 Gotlieb, "Canada's Special Role," 1–2.

31 Smardon, *Asleep at the Switch*, 138, suggests that "it was a measure of the strength of the social forces integrating Canada economically and culturally into the American orbit, that both its military and political leadership could see no role for the Canadian air force besides defending the United States from Soviet attack." In addition, see Gotlieb, "Canada's Special Role," 62–5; and Gainor, *Arrows to the Moon*, 15–41.

32 Canada, Department of Defence Production, *Canada–United States Defence*, 11. In addition, see Goldman, "National Science"; White, *Skule Story*, 175–84, 189–200, and 205–14; Lowen, *Creating the Cold War*, 1–6, 9–14, 44, 104–5, 118, 140–7, and 237; Wills, *"Innovation in a Cold [War],"* 122–3; Smith, *Rogue Tory*, 3–25; and McDowall, *Sum of the Satisfactions*. Diefenbaker's "One Canada" vision also flowered in Canada's first Bill of Rights (signed into law during 1960) and the vote for First Nations and Inuit people.

33 Layton, *Revolt of the Engineers*, 8–13, 53, 58–9, 65, and 120.

34 Interviews with Dettwiler (14 and 21 December 1992), and MacDonald (7 January 1993); and Lowen, *Creating the Cold War*, 6–20.

35 Interview with Dettwiler (11 January 1993); and National Security Administration, "Growing Up."

36 Yost, *Computer Industry*, x–xviii, and 55–65; Berlin, *Man behind the Microchip*, 63–101; Vardalas, *Computer Revolution*, 105–80; Chandler, *Inventing the Electronic Century*, 83–97, and 123–57; and Edwards, *Closed World*, 43–74.

37 Interview with Dettwiler (11 January 1993).

38 OECD, *Economic Surveys, Canada 1961*, 5 and 25.

39 Canada, *Royal Commission on Government Organization*, 19 and 21, LAC. In addition, see Hartle, "Report of the Royal Commission," 367–8; Minister of Supply and Services Canada to P. Robinson, a/chairman, Computer/ Communications Secretariat, Communications Canada, Ottawa, 28 May 1976, 2, RG97, vol. 413, LAC; and Stegeman and Acheson, "Canadian Government Purchasing," 442–78. Echoing US president Harry S. Truman's 1947

Commission on the Organization of the Executive Branch of the Government (aka, the Hoover Commission, with former president Herbert Hoover as chair), Canada's Glassco Commission drew much of its inspiration from Eisenhower's implementation of the Hoover Commission's recommendations and Canada's 1951 Defence Production Act.

40 Brune, "Comments on the Report," 5.

41 Glassco Commission, qtd in confidential memorandum to the Cabinet, "Criteria for Government Procurement and Conduct of Research and Development, and Other Scientific Activities," 13 December 1971, 1–2, MOSST, RI526, vol. 30, file 22, LAC.

42 A.W. Johnson, President's Office, Treasury Board, to Druy, re: "Toward a National Industrial Strategy Air Industries and Electronics Industries Associations Paper," 23 August 1971, 34, MOSST, RI526, vol. 24, file 3, LAC. Smardon, *Asleep at the Switch*, 152, argues that the "Glassco Framework" ended "even the pretense that the management of the federal state should be done at a distance from business." The Glassco framework was not radical, however; it emerged as the logical extension of earlier defence sharing agreements.

43 Canada, Task Force on Program Review, *Government Procurement, "Spending Smarter,"* 159 and 123, LAC.

44 See English, *Worldly Years*, 1–67; and McDowall, *Sum of the Satisfactions*, 127–41.

45 Working Group #21, Background and Discussion Paper No. 3, "Turnkey Bidding on Government Tenders by Common Carriers," ca 1974, 1, RG97, vol. 413, LAC; Consultative Committee, *Telecommunications and Sovereignty*, 69, LAC; interview with Lapp; and McLin, *Canada's Changing Defense Policy*. The Intelsat Consortium operated from 1964 to 1973, then became the International Telecommunications Satellite Organization until privatized in 2001. By 2000, seventy countries used Intelsat for international communications.

46 Anastakis, *Autonomous State*, 5–6 and 12. In addition, see Gotlieb, "Canada's Special Role," 6.

47 Stursburg, *Vietnam War*, 217; and Preston, "Balancing War and Peace." As part of the NORAD alliance, Canadians received US defence contracts worth nearly $2.5 billion between 1965 and 1972.

48 Dufour and Gingras, "National Policy-Making," 13–14; and Brune, "Comments on the Report," 5. In addition, see Mussio, *Telecom Nation*, 97–8.

49 "Remarks by the Honourable Jean-Luc Pepin, Minister of Industry, Trade and Commerce, at the Control Data Corporation Press Conference," 14 August 1970, 1–2, MOSST, RI526, vol. 44, file 17, LAC.

50 Alastair Gillespie, "Resume of a Speech on Bretton Woods Agreement, to the House of Commons," 7 March 1969, MOSST, RI526, vol. 19, file 25, LAC.

51 Ish Singhal, "Computer/Communications Industry: A Scenario of Strategies and Mechanisms," 12 November 1974, 16–19, RG97, vol. 407, file 7500-1031-2-A-4, pts 1–3, Working Group No. 4, Increasing the National Presence, Stimulation Policies (hereafter RG97, vol. 407), LAC. Singhal stressed that by "developing Canadian entrepreneurial competence in selected areas of the computer/communications sector, it is likely that we will be able to achieve better returns from our investment in human capital. The market for minicomputers will grow rapidly, especially for process control and other specialized applications. The export market will also expand." Others agreed, but T.M. Chell, assistant under secretary, Defence Programs, to Department of External Affairs, confidential "International Defence Programs Progress Report," including Appendix I, "Canada–United State Defence Production Sharing Procurement, January 1959 through December 1981," 1 March 1982, 8, RG25, vol. 14605, LAC, noted that the government had, since the cancellation of the Avro Arrow, "purchased the majority of its equipment 'off-the-shelf' from foreign companies," particularly American ones. The Defence Production Sharing Agreement sought to correct this imbalance, and confidential government reports confirm that Canadians had achieved a cross-border balance in defence production sharing procurement of some $500 million in favour of Canada between 1959 and 1969. Still, policymakers worried that balance would erode if Canadians failed to increase their own technological base, particularly when they considered the ways in which the US government seemed to protect its small businesses to the detriment of Canadian ones.

52 Interview with Dettwiler (11 January 1993).

53 Interviews with Dettwiler (14 December 1992 and 11 January 1993).

54 Interview with Maxwell.

55 Interviews with Dettwiler (21 December 1992 and 11 January 1993), Druce, MacDonald (7 and 14 January 1993), Maxwell, and Semrau; and MDA, *Our Knowledge Is in the Holes.*

56 Interviews with MacDonald (7 and 14 January 1993); Faustmann, "John MacDonald Had a Firm"; MacDonald, "Science and Technology Policy"; and CSA, "Dr John S. MacDonald Receives First Ever John H. Chapman Excellence Award from the Canadian Space Agency," *SpaceRef*, 16 June 2000.

57 National Science Foundation, "About." With "an annual budget of about $7.0 billion (FY 2012)," the NSF now boasts that it has emerged as "the funding source for approximately 20 per cent of all federally supported basic research conducted by America's colleges and universities."

58 Brate, *Technomanifestos*, 36 and 33; and Wills, *"Innovation in a Cold [War],"* 130–9.

59 Kennedy, "New Frontier." In addition, see McCurdy, *Space and the American Imagination*, 1–92.

60 Kennedy, "We Choose to Go." In addition, see Eisenhower, "Farewell Address"; Eisenhower, "Speech"; and Legislative Note, "Communications Satellite Act."

61 Schrempp, *Ancient Mythology*, 6, 12, and 202; and Slotten, "Satellite Communications."

62 "International Defence Programs: Progress Report," 29 April 1981, RG25, vol. 14605, LAC; Consultative Committee, *Telecommunications and Sovereignty*, 69, LAC; and interview with Lapp.

63 Gotlieb, "Canada's Special Role," 6–7.

64 See, for example, Bernstein, *Guns or Butter*.

65 Interview with MacDonald (14 January 1993); and MacDonald, "Experimental Studies."

66 Interview with MacDonald (7 January 1993).

67 Burke, "Rough Road to the Information Highway."

68 Interview with MacDonald (7 January 1993).

69 Ibid.; interview with Dettwiler (11 January 1993); and Davis, *History of Metropolitan Vancouver*, 299–345. MacDonald reached Vancouver too late to attend the official opening of UBC's new Woodward Biomedical Library, but he arrived in time to witness the openings of Simon Fraser University and Vancouver City College. As Canada turned eighty during 1966, MacDonald also had the opportunity to join other Vancouverites in celebrating both the graduation of the British Columbia Institute of Technology's first 400 students and the unfolding of George Norris's *Spirit of Communication* sculpture. That *Spirit* found ample voice in assistant professor MacDonald.

70 Pierre Elliott Trudeau, qtd in Liberal Party of Canada, "History of Liberal Party."

71 According to Neufeld, "Hegemony and Foreign Policy," 20 and 16, Trudeau reinforced Canadian nationalism by de-emphasizing Canada's "middle-power" strategy in favour of "national aims and interests in the international environment." By rephrasing Canada's role in the world, Canadian capitalists enjoyed "clear benefits" in their "association with American-led efforts toward liberalization in trade and investment regimes. Domestically," Neufeld reported, "concessions were extended" to everyday Canadians, "in the form of the welfare state – to provide a stable basis for capitalist class hegemony within Canadian society."

72 Jean-Luc Pepin to C.M. Drury, 27 June 1972, 1, 6, MOSST, R1526, vol. 44, file 17, LAC; Canada, Department of Defence Production, *Eighteenth Annual Report*, 5–10, LAC; and E.J. Payne, "Developing a Canadian Computer/

Communications Industry," December 1974, 3–4, RG97, vol. 407, LAC. In addition, see Marchildon, "Canadian Multinationals," 1–15.

73 Interviews with MacDonald (7 and 14 January 1993).

74 John MacDonald, qtd in Andrea Gordon, "Canadian Firm Leads the Way to Making 21st-Century Maps," *Toronto Star*, 8 September 1987; and interview with MacDonald (7 January 1993). In addition, see Cormier, *Canadianization Movement*, 29–31.

75 Schoonhoven and Romanelli, "Premises of the Entrepreneurship Dynamic," 2; Burton, "Company They Keep," 13–39; and Ginsburg et al., "Entrepreneurship in Context," 321–2. On the importance of social capital networks, see Laird, *Pull*.

76 Interviews with MacDonald (14 January 1993), and Dettwiler (14 December 1992).

77 Interview with Immega.

CHAPTER TWO

1 Schoonhoven and Romanelli, "Premises of the Entrepreneurship Dynamic," 6. In addition, see Yost, *Computer Industry*, 105–36; Edwards, *Closed World*, 43–74; and Wills, *"Innovation in a Cold [War],"* 128–40.

2 Chairman, Working Group 4, to members of Working Groups 4, 8, and 11, "Stimulation Policies to Increase the Canadian Presence," Appendix D, 26 September 1974, 4, RG97, vol. 407, LAC.

3 National Academy of Engineering, "Telecommunications Research," 20. In addition, see Mahapatra and Rogers, "Empirical Study."

4 "Statement by Finance Minister E.J. Benson before the Commons Committee on Finance, Trade and Economic Affairs, Bill to Establish the Canada Development Corporation," 4 May 1971, MOSST, R1526, vol. 23, file 19, LAC. In addition, see Charles L. Caccia, MP, Davenport, to constituents, April 1972, 1–2, MOSST, R1526, vol. 46, file 9, LAC; "Ottawa's Blind Spot on Takeovers," *Toronto Star*, 16 November 1970; and Lower Vancouver Island Liberal Association, "White Paper on the Economy," 4–5, MOSST, R1526, vol. 19, file 11, LAC; Yergin, *Prize*, 391, 494–8, and 554–6; and Greber, *Rising to Power*, 123–35. During 1970, the federal government blocked the sale of Canadian-owned Dennison uranium mines to a US corporation. With Alberta emerging as a hot spot for exploration from the 1950s forward, the federal government intervened again in 1971, to protect Home Oil from an American takeover.

5 Interviews with MacDonald (7 January 1993), Dettwiler (11 January 1993), and Semrau. For organizational theories on entrepreneurship that emphasize

the importance of local, regional, and professional networks, geographical factors, and governmental support for business start-up and expansion, see Schoonhoven and Romanelli, *Entrepreneurship Dynamic*; Tushman and Murmann, "Dominant Designs"; Zucker, Darby, and Armstrong, "Geographically Localized Knowledge"; and Audretsch and Stephan, "Company-Scientist Locational Links."

6 Florida, *Rise of the Creative Class*. By "creative class," Florida refers to technologically creative people and the capitalists who follow them, rather than artists and musicians. In addition, see Suchman, Steward, and Westfall, "Legal Environment of Entrepreneurship"; Kenney, "Introduction"; Leslie, "Biggest 'Angel' of Them All"; Gray, Golob, and Markusen, "Seattle"; Gray et al., "Four Faces of Silicon Valley"; and Leslie and Kargon, "Selling Silicon Valley."

7 Interviews with Dettwiler (14 December 1992 and 11 January 1993), MacDonald (7 January 1993), Lennox, Thompson (15 January 1993), and Semrau. In addition, see Smith, "Techmaps"; and Atkinson and Coleman, *State, Business, and Industrial Change*, 99.

8 John MacDonald, qtd in L.A. Varah, "Innovation Is the Business," 2.

9 Interviews with Dettwiler (14 December 1992), and MacDonald (7 January 1993).

10 Interviews with Dettwiler (11 January 1993), and MacDonald (7 January 1993).

11 MacDonald, quoting Kip Fuller (creator of a novelty line of toy "Servitron Robots") in Fiffer, *So You've Got*, 9.

12 Interviews with Dettwiler (14 December 1992 and 11 January 1993), and MacDonald (7 and 14 January 1993).

13 Suchman, Steward, and Westfall, "Legal Environment of Entrepreneurship," 365–6 and 377; and interviews with Butler, Dettwiler (11 January 1993), and MacDonald (14 January 1993).

14 Interview with Butler.

15 Ibid.

16 Interviews with Dettwiler (14 December 1992), MacDonald (7 January 1993), and Butler; and Canada, Minister of Consumer and Corporate Affairs, *Letters Patent*. On 4 March 1969, the group designated MacDonald's home in Vancouver the consultancy's headquarters and corporate office, and later registered as an Extra-Provincial Company. See Province of British Columbia, Companies Act, 11 July 1969 and 30 December 1970, and *Annual Report of Extra-Provincial*.

17 Interviews with MacDonald (7 January 1993), Lennox and Price, and Maxwell.

18 Interviews with MacDonald (7 January 1993), Lennox, and Dettwiler (11
January 1993). Adjectives and attributes describing MDA's personnel derived
from interviews with Murray, Sloan, Prentice, Lennox and Price, MacDonald
(18 January 1993), Spencer, Maxwell, Pitts (6 May 1993), Morris, Semrau,
McConnell, and Renwick and Seymour. In addition, see Layton, *Revolt of the
Engineers*, 8–13, 53, 58–9, 65, and 120.

19 Interviews with MacDonald (7 January 1993), Butler, Lennox, Dettwiler (11
January 1993), and Spencer.

20 Interviews with Sloan, MacDonald (7 January 1993), Butler, Lennox, Dettwiler (11 January 1993), Spencer, and Renwick and Seymour.

21 Interview with MacDonald (7 January 1993). On founding visions and motivations germane to the MDA case, see Burton, "Company They Keep," 13–27;
Willard, Krueger, and Feeser, "In Order to Grow"; and Livesay, "Entrepreneurial Dominance." In addition, see Schumpeter, *Theory of Economic
Development*.

22 Interview with Dettwiler (14 December 1992); and interview with MacDonald (7 January 1993).

23 Interviews with Dettwiler (11 January 1993), MacDonald (7 January 1993),
John Bennett, Spencer, and Semrau.

24 Interview with Dettwiler (11 January 1993).

25 Interview with MacDonald (7 January 1993); and interviews with Dettwiler
(11 January 1993), and Semrau.

26 Interview with Semrau.

27 Interviews with MacDonald (18 January 1993), and Pitts (6 May 1993). Mac-
Donald's guiding philosophy is echoed in interviews with Friedmann, Mur-
ray, Beattie, Prentice, MacDonald (4 January 1993), MacDonald (7 January
1993), Lennox, John Bennett, George, Semrau, Maxwell, Spencer, Caddey,
Morris, McConnell, and Renwick and Seymour. In addition, see Layton,
Revolt of the Engineers, 8–13, 53, 58–9, 65, and 120.

28 Burton, "Company They Keep," 13.

29 Interviews with MacDonald (7 January 1993), Maxwell, and Semrau. In addition, see Frank, *Conquest of Cool*, 1–33.

30 Interview with MacDonald (7 January 1993); interviews with Lennox, and
Dettwiler (11 January 1993); and Weyler, *Greenpeace*, 1–90.

31 "Notes for Speech on Second Reading of Bill C-10: An Act to Amend the
Export Development Act," 4 April 1974, MOSST, RI526, vol. 30, file 29, LAC;
Lower Vancouver Island Liberal Association, "White Paper on the Econo-

my"; EDC *Today*, "Export Development Canada"; Business Development Bank of Canada, "Industrial Development Bank"; and Greber, *Rising to Power*, 170.

32 Donald McDonald, "Profiting from Partnership," speech to the Canadian Manufacturers' Association conference, "The Future Is Now," ca 1970, 9, MOSST, R1526, vol. 46, file 16, LAC.

33 Mussio, *Telecom Nation*, 65–8, 92–3, 97–114, and 222–7.

34 Consultative Committee, *Telecommunications and Sovereignty*, 3–4, LAC. In addition, see Science Council of Canada, *University Research*, 3–4, LAC, which recommended special grants to encourage universities and scientists to specialize in key research areas and the "practical needs" of industry; Gerard Pelletier, minister of communications, "Computer/Communications Policy: A Position Statement by the Government of Canada" green paper, 1973, Department of Communications, Secretariat to the Computer-Communications Interdepartmental Committee, RG97, vol. 418, file 7500-1445-1, Green Paper General (hereafter RG97, vol. 418, Green Paper), LAC; Canada, Parliament, Special Committee on Science Policy, *Science Policy*, LAC; Canadian Computer/Communications Task Force, *Branching Out*, LAC, which stressed the need for educational support, national and international standards, and closer cooperation between the government and the private sector and between the federal and provincial governments, with particular emphases on regional balances and Canadian ownership and control of the industry; and Dufour and Gingras, "National Policy-Making," 5.

35 "Remarks by the Honourable Jean-Luc Pepin," 14 August 1970, MOSST, R1526, vol. 44, file 17, LAC. In addition, see Treasury Board, "Change in Organization," 1 April 1975, 1–2, MOSST, R1526, vol. 374, file 73, LAC; and Drucker, *Age of Discontinuity*.

36 Interview with MacDonald (7 January 1993); and interviews with Dettwiler (11 January 1993), and Renwick.

37 Interviews with MacDonald (7 January 1993), and Renwick and Seymour; and Thompson, "MacDonald, Dettwiler & Associates Ltd and Synaptic Systems Ltd Sales Analysis, 1972–1975" (hereafter Thompson, "MDA/Synaptic Sales Analysis"), 4. On AECL and the politics of engineering, see Bratt, *Politics of CANDU*; and Bothwell, *Nucleus*. DEC, headquartered in Maynard, MA, from 1957 through 1992, was acquired by Compaq in June 1998, and merged with Hewlett-Packard in May 2002. For a discussion of DEC's relationship to MIT, see Schein et al., *DEC Is Dead*.

38 Interviews with MacDonald (7 January 1993), and Renwick.

39 Interview with Renwick; and interviews with MacDonald (7 January 1993), Lennox and Price, and Thompson (18 May 1993).

40 Interviews with MacDonald (7 January 1993), and Lennox.

41 Interview with Lennox; and interviews with MacDonald (7 January 1993), and Dettwiler (11 January 1993).

42 Interviews with MacDonald (7 January 1993), Lennox, and Spencer; L.A. Varah, "Innovation Is the Business," 2; and Province of British Columbia, Companies Act, 30 December 1970. On 30 December 1970, the province authorized the company to issue 100,000 shares (50 Class A shares at $1,000 each, and 50 Class B shares at $1,000 each). On 12 April 1971, MDA's board then appointed Colin Lennox the company's fifth director. Spilsbury retained 50 Class B shares and sold Lennox his remaining shares. At the same time, MDA enacted a by-law that allowed the company to provide loans to its employees so they could purchase shares in the capital stock of the company which resulted in the following shareholdings: MacDonald, 332 Class B; Dettwiler, 251 Class B; Morin, 206 Class B; Spilsbury, 50 Class B; Thompson (Bill), 1 Class B and 50 Class A; and Lennox, 160 Class B.

43 Interview with Lennox; and interviews with MacDonald (7 January 1993), and Dettwiler (11 January 1993).

44 A.W. Johnson, President's Office, Treasury Board, to Drury, re: "Toward a National Industrial Strategy Air Industries and Electronics Industries Associations Paper," 23 August 1971, 5, MOSST, R1526, vol. 24, file 3, LAC; "Iran Will Spend $15-Billion in U.S. over Five Years," New York Times, 5 March 1975; "Iran Has Plans for When the Oil Runs Out," New York Times, 9 March 1975; and Klassen, "Canada and the New Imperialism," 166–75.

45 John Kifner, "Iranian Program Debated at MIT," New York Times, 27 April 1975; and interviews with MacDonald (7 January 1993), Lennox, and Spencer.

46 Interview with MacDonald (7 January 1993).

47 Ibid.; interviews with Lennox and Price, and Renwick and Seymour; and Thompson, "MDA/Synaptic Sales Analysis." On Alberta's place in larger global rivalries for oil resources, money, and power, see Yergin, Prize, 371–614.

48 Interview with Lennox and Price.

49 MDA, ATS; MDA, Our Knowledge Is in the Holes; Canadian Electronics Engineering, "Practical Solutions," 32; and interviews with MacDonald (7 January 1993), Lennox, and Maxwell.

50 Interviews with MacDonald (7 January 1993), Lennox and Price, Dettwiler (11 January 1993), and Allan. In addition, see Cohoon and Aspray, Women and Information; and Margolis, Unlocking the Clubhouse.

51 Interview with MacDonald (7 January 1993); and interviews with Lennox, and Thompson (15 January 1993).

52 Interview with Eppich.

53 Interview with Thompson (15 January 1993); Lennox, "Report on Jobs"; Thompson, "MDA/Synaptic Sales Analysis"; and interviews with Lennox, and Eppich.

54 Interviews with Thompson (15 January 1993), Spencer, and Eppich.

55 Interviews with MacDonald (18 January 1993), Lennox and Price, Thompson (15 January 1993), Spencer, and Eppich.

56 Interview with Eppich; interview with Lennox and Price; and *Epic Data*.

57 Interviews with MacDonald (7 January 1993), Lennox and Price, and Eppich; and Epic Data, "About Us."

58 Interviews with MacDonald (7 January 1993), Lennox, Thompson (15 January 1993), and Spencer; and Thompson, "MDA/Synaptic Sales Analysis."

59 Interview with Allan; and L.A. Varah, "Innovation Is the Business," 2.

60 Interview with J. Bennett; and interviews with Lennox, Thompson (15 January 1993), MacDonald (7 January 1993), and Spencer.

61 Interview with MacDonald (7 January 1993); interviews with Lennox, Thompson (15 January 1993), MacDonald (18 January 1993), Spencer, Semrau, and Renwick and Seymour; and Thompson, "MDA/Synaptic Sales Analysis."

62 Interview with MacDonald (7 January 1993).

63 Ibid.; and interviews with Spencer, Semrau, and Renwick and Seymour.

64 Auerswald and Branscomb, "Start-ups and Spin-offs," 91.

65 Gerard Pelletier, minister of communications, "Computer/Communications Policy: A Position Statement by the Government of Canada" green paper, 1973, Department of Communications, Secretariat to the Computer-Communications Interdepartmental Committee, RG97, vol. 418, Green Paper, LAC.

66 Interviews with Louth, Lennox, Dettwiler (11 January 1993), Morris, and Semrau; and Canada Minister of Consumer and Corporate Affairs, *Canada Supplementary Letters Patent*. The share option resulted in a subdivision of the original 80,000 Class A shares into 800,000; and the subdivision of 20,000 Class B into 200,000.

67 MDA, *1977 Annual Report*, 11; and interviews with MacDonald (14 January 1993), and Thompson (15 January 1993).

68 Interviews with Prentice, MacDonald (14 January 1993), Dettwiler (11 January 1993), and Thompson (15 January 1993).

69 Interview with Thompson (15 January 1993); interviews with Prentice, Lennox and Price, Allan, and Morris; MDA, *1976 Annual Report*; and MDA, *1977 Annual Report*.

70 Interviews with Lennox and Price, Thompson (15 January 1993), and Morris.

71 Brooks, *Mythical Man-Month*, 14.

72 Interview with MacDonald (14 January 1993).

73 Ibid.; interviews with Allan, Prentice, Maxwell, Thompson (15 January 1993), and Morris; and MDA, *AIDS, 1976 Annual Report*, 12; MDA, *1977 Annual Report*, 2, 5; and MDA, *1989 Annual Report*, 7.

74 Interview with MacDonald (14 January 1993).
75 Interviews with Lennox and Price, Thompson (15 January 1993), and Mac-Donald (18 January 1993).

CHAPTER THREE

1 Interviews with MacDonald (7 and 18 January 1993).
2 Mosco, *Digital Sublime*, 92; interviews with Sloan and MacDonald (18 January 1993); and Seymour, "Study," 1. In addition, see Macauley and Towman, "Providing Earth Observation," 38–41; "The Uses of Heaven: A Survey of Space," *Economist*, 15 June 1991, 3–5, 16–18; *Interavia*, "Long View from Space," 24–9; "Remote Sensing Sparks a Row over America's Space Policy," *Economist*, 21 July 1984; Lenco, "Remote Sensing"; Arlen J. Large, "Eyes in the Sky: NASA Finds Many Buyers for Satellite Pictures and Plans New, More-Revealing Landsats in '80s," *Wall Street Journal*, 5 April 1979; Rosenblatt and Dickson, "At Long Last"; Science Council of Canada, *It Is Not Too Late*, 97–137; Wills, *"Innovation in a Cold [War]"*; Slotten, "Satellite Communications," 315; Lewis, *Spy Capitalism*, 46; McCurdy, *Faster, Better, Cheaper*, 56–61, 86–95, and 97–137; Mazlich, "Idea of Space Exploration"; Graham and Hanson, *Spy Satellites*, 14–47; Jamison, "Technology's Theorists," 505–33; Bell, *Coming of Post-Industrial Society*; and Bromberg, NASA *and Space*.
3 Interview with Sloan. In addition, see Mack, *Viewing the Earth*, 1–17, 20–2, and 183–95; and *Ubyssey*, "Sciencemen," 2.
4 Chapman et al., *Upper Atmosphere and Space Programs*, 99–100, and 110–13.
5 Dotto, *Heritage of Excellence*, 1–3, LAC; Charles L. Caccia, MP, Davenport, to "Constituents," April 1972, 1–2, MOSST, R1526, vol. 46, file 9, LAC; and Marchildon, "Canadian Multinationals." Those financial institutions included the "big five" – the Royal Bank of Canada, Canadian Imperial Bank of Commerce, Bank of Montreal, Bank of Nova Scotia, and Toronto-Dominion Bank – all of them among the largest multinational enterprises operating outside of Canada.
6 Trudeau, qtd in Potter, *Transatlantic Partners*, 28.
7 Preston, "Balancing War," 73–111. According to Giuseppe Viliante, "Vietnam War Draft Dodgers Left a Mark on Canada," Canadian Press, 16 April 2015, Canada "labeled draft dodgers as immigrants, as opposed to refugees," which resulted in estimates that "up to 40,000 made the journey."
8 Treasury Board, "Change in Organization," 1 April 1971, 2, MOSST, R1526, vol. 374, file 73, LAC; Lapp and Interdepartmental Task Force on Surveillance Satellites, *Satellites and Sovereignty*, 15–23 and 85–6, LAC; G.K. Davidson, Computer/Communications Secretariat, to Department Representatives,

IT&C, CCA, TBS, DOC, DREE, Finance, 10 December 1973, 1–2, RG97, vol. 413, LAC; and Matte, *Space Policy*, 83–5.

9 Jean Chrétien, minister of Indian affairs and northern development, to the House of Commons, on Second Reading of the Arctic Waters Pollution Prevention Bill, 16 April 1970, 1, MOSST, R1526, vol. 23, file 20, LAC. In addition, see Terrance Wills, "Canada's Arctic Claims Worry the U.S.," *Globe and Mail*, 18 April 1970; "Let's Lean on Trudeau," *New York Times*, 18 April 1970; and Department of Natural Resources, "Agreement Relating to the Delimitation of The Continental Shelf between Greenland and Canada," RG45, vol. 356, file 1370-6/0, pts 1.1 and 1.2, CCRS Liaison Cooperation (hereafter RG45, vol. 356), LAC.

10 See English, *Just Watch Me*, 95–104.

11 J.J. Treyvaud to Mrs M. Mersey, re: Interdepartmental Committee on Space, Annual Report, 1972, 1–2, MOSST, R1526, vol. 44, file 2, LAC.

12 Rosenblatt and Dickson, "At Long Last"; Mack, *Viewing the Earth*, 183–95; and United States House of Representatives, "Remote Sensing."

13 Interviews with Sloan, Morley, Lennox, Collins, and Lennox and Price; Alastair Gillespie to Aurele Beaulnes, re: The University Science Issue (ref. no. 6-633-72), 21 June 1972, 1–7, MOSST, R1526, vol. 43, file 3; and J.F. Grandy, deputy minister to Alastair Gillespie, minister of industry, trade, and commerce, 25 January 1973, MOSST, R1526, vol. 30, file 22, LAC; American Institute of Aeronautics and Astronautics, *Collection of Technical Papers*; Butrica, *Single Stage*, 29–31 and 173; Mack, *Viewing the Earth*, 3–4, 9–10, 15–16, 27–42, 183–95; and Rosenblatt and Dickson, "At Long Last."

14 "Canada Centre for Remote Sensing, Long-Term Plan, Fiscal Years 1978/79–1982/83," 2, Canada Centre for Remote Sensing, RG39-A, 68602, vol. 1 (hereafter RG39), LAC; and Interviews with Lapp, Sloan, and Morley. In addition, see Rosenblatt and Dickson, "At Long Last"; *Interavia*, "Long View from Space," 24–9; and Mack, *Viewing the Earth*, 3–10, 15–16, 20–33, 34, 37, and 183–94.

15 Interview with Sloan.

16 Interview with Morley; interviews with Sloan, and Collins; and Mack, *Viewing the Earth*, 189–94.

17 Interview with Sloan; and interview with J. Bennett.

18 Interviews with Sloan, and Renwick and Seymour; and MDA, *ERTS Data Acquisition System*.

19 Interview with Sloan, 30 December 1992.

20 Interview with MacDonald (7 January 1993); and interview with Sloan.

21 Interview with Lennox; and interviews with Sloan, MacDonald (7 January 1993), and Dettwiler (11 January 1993).

22 Interview with Lennox and Price; and interview with Dettwiler (11 January 1993).

23 Interview with Lennox. MDA's expanding local, and then national connections resonate with the chapters found in Schoonhoven and Romanelli, *Entrepreneurship Dynamic*, and confirm the findings outlined in Laird, *Pull*.

24 Interviews with Lennox and Price, and Dettwiler (11 January 1993).

25 Interviews with Sloan, Dettwiler (11 January 1993), and Thompson (15 January 1993); *Interavia*, "Long View from Space," 25–6; *1989 Annual Report*, 4; Seymour, "Study," insert A and table 2; L.A. Varah, "Innovation Is the Business," 2; and Meyboom, "In-house vs Contractual Research."

26 Alastair Gillespie to Jim David, "PM's Speech to the CMA Conference in Toronto, 8 June 1971," 20 May 1971, 2 and 9–11, MOSST, R1526, vol. 24, file 7, LAC. In addition, see Dobell, *Canada's Search for New Roles*, LAC.

27 Trudeau to Alastair Gillespie, minister of state for science and technology, 18 November 1971, MOSST, R1526, vol. 43, file 3, LAC. In addition, see English, *Just Watch Me*.

28 "Notes for Throne Speech: Science Policy and Industrial R&D," 28 January 1972, MOSST, R1526, vol. 43, file 6, LAC.

29 "MOSST Accomplishments, First Year," 1972, 2; Organisation for Economic Co-operation and Development, Restricted, Paris, 13 August, 1971, CMS(71)3, Scale 2, "Meeting of Ministers of Science of O.E.C.D. Countries: Conclusions and Possible Recommendations" (Report by the Committee for Science Policy), 1–13, MOSST, R1526, vol. 44, file 4, LAC; and "Notes for a Speech by the Honourable Jean-Luc Pepin, Minister of Industry, Trade and Commerce to the Victoria Chamber of Commerce, Victoria," 8 May 1972, MOSST, R1526, vol. 44, file 16, LAC.

30 "MOSST Accomplishments, First Year," 3–6.

31 Alastair Gillespie, minister, MOSST, to Aurele Beaulnes, 21 March 1972, MOSST, R1526, vol. 43, file 5, LAC; and MOSST, "SECRET" (handwritten, "Destroy"), Final Draft for the Minister's Approbation, December 1971, 1, MOSST, R1526, vol. 30, file 22, LAC. In addition, see Lapp, Hodgins, and Mackay, *Ring of Iron*, LAC; and Treasury Board, "Change in Organization," 1 April 1975, 1.

32 George Sinclair, "Development of Science and Engineering in Canada," 1 June 1971, MOSST, R1526, vol. 44, file 4, LAC.

33 Alastair Gillespie, "For Publication," *Ottawa Report*, 18 November 1971, MOSST, R1526, vol. 43, file 3, LAC.

34 Confidential memorandum to the Cabinet, re: Criteria for Government Procurement and Conduct of Research and Development, and Other Scientific Activities," 13 December 1971, MOSST, R1526, vol. 30, file 22, LAC; and Gillespie

to Beaulnes, 21 March 1972, MOSST, R1526, vol. 43, file 5, LAC. In addition, see Lapp, Hodgins, and Mackay, *Ring of Iron*; Treasury Board, "Change in Organization," 1 April 1975, 1, LAC; and Beaumier, "Innovation in Canada," LAC.

35 "MOSST Accomplishments, First Year," 1972, 7, LAC; Air Industries Association of Canada and the Electronics Industries Association of Canada, "Canadian Government Spending and the 'Make or Buy' Problem in the Context of a National Industrial Strategy," Ottawa, May 1971, 4–39, MOSST, R1526, vol. 24, file 3, LAC; Alastair Gillespie to MOSST personnel, 30 August 1972, MOSST, R1526, vol. 43, file 11, LAC; Systems Dimensions Limited, "Brief to the Treasury Board, EDP Policy Task Force," 6 May 1971, 5–10, MOSST, R1526, vol. 45, file 15, LAC; "Research and Development in Government and Industry: Targets and Criteria for Make or Buy Decisions," confidential record of Cabinet decision, meeting of 23 May 1972, MOSST, R1526, vol. 30, file 23, LAC; and Canada, Task Force on Program Review, *Government Procurement*, "Spending Smarter," 1, 12, 126–8, and 144–58, LAC. Science Council of Canada, *Towards a National Space Policy*, LAC, anticipated the Make or Buy policy as early as 1968. In addition, see Niosi, Manseau, and Godin, *Canada's National System*, 49–54.

36 "New Science Minister for Canada," *Science*, 12 January 1972, 285, MOSST, R1526, vol. 43, file 3, LAC. J.J. Treyvaud to M. Mersey, re: Interdepartmental Committee on Space, Annual Report, 1972, 13, MOSST, R1526, vol. 44, file 2, LAC, additionally argued, "Means must be found to foster the growth of Canadian-based multinational corporations if Canadian industry is to compete effectively in the international marketplace, and even on the domestic market ... If multinational corporations are to be a fact of economic life in the future, then Canada cannot afford to neglect participating fully in this game too."

37 Ambrose, *Nixon*, 143–50 and 225–9.

38 Dotto, *Heritage of Excellence*, 37–8, LAC. In addition, see Mack, *Viewing the Earth*, 184–93.

39 "Canada Needs a Space Agency," 15 July 1972, in MOSST, R1526, vol. 43, file 13, LAC.

40 Interviews with Sloan, and Dettwiler (11 January 1993).

41 Interviews with MacDonald (7 and 18 January 1993); and interviews with Gelbart, Sloan, Butler, Lennox, Maxwell, Spencer, Semrau, and Renwick and Seymour.

42 Science Council of Canada, *Innovation in a Cold Climate*, 30–1.

43 MacDonald, qtd in L.A. Varah, "Innovation Is the Business," 3; and interviews with Sloan, and MacDonald (7 January 1993).

44 Interviews with Sloan, and MacDonald (7 January 1993); and L.A. Varah, "Innovation Is the Business," 1–3.

45 Dotto, *Heritage of Excellence*, 88–93, LAC.

46 Consultative Committee, *Telecommunications and Sovereignty*, 73, LAC. In addition, see Department of External Affairs, SPAR Briefing (1993), RG-25-A-4, vol. 27446, file 6010-5, MF-13691 (hereafter, RG25, vol. 27446), LAC.

47 Interview with Seymour and Renwick; and interviews with Sloan, and MacDonald (7 January 1993).

48 "MOSST Accomplishments, First Year," 1972, 6–8.

49 Department of Industry, Trade, and Commerce, "Quick Reference on Incentive and Development Programs for Canadian Industry," 8, MOSST, R1526, vol. 44, file 4, LAC.

50 Ian H. McLeod, managing principal, McKinsey & Co., to Barnett J. Danson, MP, parliamentary secretary to the prime minister, "The Canadian Businessman: An American Perspective," 11 October 1971, 3–9, MOSST, R1526, vol. 45, file 20, LAC.

51 Treyvaud to Mersey, re: "Interdepartmental Committee on Space, Annual Report, 1972," 7, MOSST, R1526, vol. 44, file 2, LAC.

52 A.W. Johnson, President's Office, Treasury Board, to Drury, 23 August 1971, 7–8, MOSST, R1526, vol. 24, file 3, LAC; and A. Beaulnes to Alastair Gillespie, 5 May 1972, MOSST, R1526, vol. 43, file 10, LAC.

53 Alastair Gillespie to Mike Gillan, Prime Minister's Office, 29 August 1972, MOSST, R1526, vol. 43, file 12, LAC. In addition, see Gillespie to MOSST Personnel; and "Speech from the Throne Opening of the Fourth Session of the Twenty-Eighth Parliament," 17 February 1972, MOSST, R1526, vol. 45, file 24, LAC.

54 Gillespie to Gillan, 29 August 1972, MOSST, R1526, vol. 43, file 12, LAC; "Notes for a Speech by the Honourable Jean-Luc Pepin, 8 May 1972," 11; A.L. Strange to K. Kelly, 26 July 1972, MOSST, R1526, vol. 43, file 13, LAC; and Office of the Prime Minister, news release, 18 January 1974, MOSST, R1526, vol. 30, file 20, LAC. In addition, see Department of Industry, Trade, and Commerce, "Talking Points" with respect to the Diplomatic Note (Number 62), 17 April 1974, RG97, vol. 418, US, LAC; Payne, "Developing a Canadian Computer/Communications Industry," 9–10, Working Group No. 4 of the Interdepartmental Committee for Computer/Communications Program and Policy Coordination, Restricted, "Report on Foreign Take-over of Canadian Computer Services Companies," Ottawa, February 1975, and Electrical and Electronics Branch, Department of Industry, Trade and Commerce, "An Appraisal of the Industrial Development Aspects of the Computer Service and Manufacturing Industry," September 1975, RG97, vol. 407, LAC; and Canada, Task Force on Program Review, *Government Procurement*, "Spending Smarter," 1–20, 124–67, and 196–222. In addition, see Klassen, "Canada and the New Imperialism," 163–90.

On the development of Statistics Canada (known as the Dominion Bureau of Statistics until 1972) as the handmaiden of public-policymaking and national accounting systems, see McDowall, *Sum of the Satisfactions*.

55 "Discussion Paper: Earth Observation by Satellite – Continued Participation by Canada in the U.S. LANDSAT Program," 4 September 1979, 1–10, RG39, LAC. During 1971, the CCRS proposed a 50:50 cost sharing agreement for joint remote sensing projects between the federal and provincial governments, but the federal government later withdrew the proposal, which some at the CCRS believed delayed provincial engagement with large-scale use of satellite data. According to Dufour and Gingras, "National Policy-Making," 15, "Much of the debate in science and technology policy revolved around tensions between the two levels of government in identifying their respective spheres of interest and influence," but they also noted that the Science Council of Canada had suggested that "effective 'national' science policy may in fact consist in a multiplicity of science policies, each responding to the specific needs of regions or sectors of this country, framed within some broader national perspective."

56 Interview with MacDonald (7 January 1993).

57 Interview with Lapp; and interviews with Sloan, MacDonald (7 January 1993), Lennox and Price, Dettwiler (11 January 1993), and Collins; Lapp and Task Force, *Satellites and Sovereignty*, 1–2, LAC; Evans, "Canadian Space Programme"; Mack, *Viewing the Earth*, 191–2; and United States Congress, *Remote Sensing*.

58 Interviews with MacDonald (7 January 1993), Lennox, Maxwell, Semrau, and Renwick and Seymour.

59 MOSCO 3097 to OTT Ext ECL, Sale of Submersible-USSR, 20 October 1971, SSHDC388 to EXTOTT ECT, "Secret," 31 January 1972, WSHDC 830 to EXTOTT ECT, "Secret," 2 March 1972, 3, and EXTOTT ECT WSNDC to EXTOTT ECT, 30 March 1972, Department of Employment and Immigration, Secret File System, SF-R-69, vol. 956 (hereafter SF-R-69, vol. 956), LAC.

60 T. O'Toole, "'Wet NASA' Left High and Dry," *Wall Street Journal*, 12 December 1971. In addition, see "Subs Left Research High and Dry," *Greeley Tribune*, 20 December 1971; and "Submersibles Sinking Fast," *Medicine Hat News*, 14 June 1979.

61 MOSCO 577 to TT EXTOTT ECT DE LDN, re: Submersibles and Computers for User, 20 March 1972, SF-R-69, vol. 956, LAC.

62 Interview with Lennox; and interview with MacDonald (14 January 1993).

63 Interviews with Lennox and Price, and Spencer.

64 Interviews with Lennox, MacDonald (14 January 1993), Maxwell, Spencer, and Semrau.

65 Interviews with Lapp, MacDonald (7 January 1993), and Lennox and Price.

66 Interviews with Sloan, MacDonald (7 January 1993), and Dettwiler (11 January 1993).

67 Interviews with Sloan, MacDonald (7 January 1993), Lennox, Dettwiler (11 January 1993), and Collins; Seymour, "Study," table 2; and Thompson, "MDA/Synaptic Sales Analysis," 4.

68 Interviews with MacDonald (7 January 1993), Lennox, Maxwell, Semrau, and Renwick and Seymour; and Thompson, "MDA/Synaptic Sales Analysis," 4.

69 Interview with MacDonald (7 January 1993).

70 Interviews with MacDonald (7 January 1993), Lennox, Maxwell, Semrau, and Renwick and Seymour.

71 Seymour, "Study," insert B and table 2; *Interavia*, "Long View from Space," 25–6; and interview with Sloan. Chang, *Bad Samaritans*, 1–68, provides an excellent discussion about the myths of free trade and unfettered capitalism in the development of market-oriented societies.

72 Interview with MacDonald (18 January 1993).

73 Ibid.; and interviews with Sloan, Lennox, Dettwiler (11 January 1993), and Spencer.

74 Interview with MacDonald (14 January 1993); Payne, "Developing a Canadian Computer/Communications Industry," December 1974, and "An Appraisal of the Industrial Development Aspects of the Computer Service and Manufacturing Industry," Electrical and Electronics Branch, Department of Industry, Trade and Commerce, September 1975," 1–27, RG97, vol. 407, LAC; Brune, "Comments on the Report," 5; and J.D. MacNaughton, vice-president and general manager, Remote Manipulator Systems Division, SPAR, "An Address to the Air Industries Association of Canada," 26 September 1978, 1-8, MOSST, R1526, vol. 55, file 18, LAC.

75 Interviews with Sloan, and MacDonald (14 January 1993); Seymour, "Study," 5, tables 1 and 2; MDA, *1975 Annual Report*; *Canadian Electronics Engineering*, "They Know about Us," 37; and *Electronics Communicator*, "MacDonald, Dettwiler & Associates Ltd, Exceptional Talents," 5.

76 "MDA Wins Big Contract," *Richmond Review*, 14 September 1987, reported on MDA's acquisition of more UPP funding for much later work on a meteorological satellite and analysis system for Brunei, an oil-rich nation and the first Asian customer outside of Japan to purchase one of MDA's systems, as well as a $10 million contract from the Canadian government to work on *ERS-1*.

77 Interviews with Lapp, Sloan, MacDonald (7 January 1993), and Dettwiler (11 January 1993).

78 Interview with Seymour and Renwick; and interviews with Sloan, and Mac-

Donald (7 January 1993). In addition, see "Notes for a Speech by the Honourable Jean-Luc Pepin, 8 May 1972," 1, in which Pepin noted, "Almost 44 per cent of us view American ownership of Canadian companies as having an adverse effect on our economy. This compares with 41 per cent two years ago, and 34 per cent three years ago. Strangely enough, while Ontario is normally considered Canada's centre of 'economic nationalism,' the same survey found that the greatest anxiety actually exists in British Columbia, where 53 per cent of the public said U.S. ownership was a 'bad thing.'" By 1972, the federal government had also established an Interagency Committee on Remote Sensing to review the progress of the CCRS, and to provide recommendations for future operational and research needs, including those focused on infant firms such as MDA. The membership of the committee included representatives from various departments, including Energy, Mines, and Resources, Environment, External Affairs, Indian and Northern Affairs, National Defence, and the National Research Council, as well as observers from Treasury Board and MOSST. See "Terms of Reference of the Interagency Committee on Remote Sensing," 27 April 1972, RG39, LAC.

79 Interview with Lapp.
80 Interview with MacDonald (7 January 1993).
81 Interviews with Sloan, Lapp, and Lennox; *Canadian Electronics Engineering*, "Practical Solutions to Difficult Problems," 32; *Electronics Communicator*, "MacDonald, Dettwiler & Associates Ltd, Exceptional Talents," 5; "Canada's Second Ground Station Capable of Receiving and Processing Earth Resources Technology Satellite Images," *Aviation Week and Space Technology*, 20 January 1975; "Satellite Unit Contract Set," *Vancouver Sun*, 28 December 1974; "City Firm Wins Space Job," *Province*, 28 December 1974; and "BC Firm Wins $1.3 Million Job," *Globe and Mail*, 28 December 1974.
82 Interviews with Gelbart, and Maxwell; and interviews with Sloan, Lennox, Spencer, and Renwick and Seymour.
83 Interview with Maxwell.
84 Interview with Lennox.
85 Interview with Sloan; and interviews with Gelbart, MacDonald (7 January 1993), Dettwiler (11 January 1993), Allan, J. Bennett, Collins, Widmer, Maxwell, Spencer, and Renwick and Seymour.
86 Interview with Sloan.
87 Interview with J. Bennett.
88 Interview with Widmer; and interviews with J. Bennett, Sloan, MacDonald (7 January 1993), Dettwiler (11 January 1993), Allan, Collins, and Renwick and Seymour.
89 Interviews with Sloan, Lennox and Price, and MacDonald (14 January 1993).

90 Interview with MacDonald (7 January 1993).

91 Interview with Lennox and Price; interviews with MacDonald (7 January 1993), and Renwick and Seymour; and Commission of the European Economic Communities, "COM(75), 467 Final, Brussels," 10 September 1975, 63–4, RG97, vol. 418, file 7500-1331-3, pt I, European Economic Community (EEC) Mission (hereafter RG97, vol. 418, EEC), LAC. Founded in 1975, ESA emerged from a cooperative space research and technology agreement signed by ten member states: Belgium, Denmark, France, Germany, Italy, the Netherlands, Spain, Sweden, Switzerland, and the UK. In addition, see Craig Couvault, "South African Satellite Carries Earth Imaging System," *Aviation Week and Space Technology*, 21 June 1993, 23; Krige, "Crossing the Interface," 27–50; Mack, *Viewing the Earth*, 15; Carter, "Private Sector," 49–57; Madders, *New Force*; Suzuki, *Policy Logics*; and Sandholtz, *High-tech Europe*.

92 Interviews with Sloan, MacDonald (7 and 18 January 1993), Collins, Maxwell, Morris, and Renwick and Seymour; Seymour, "Study," 2, insert B, tables 1 and 2; and director-general, Policy Directorate, Corporate Planning Group, to Distribution, "Government of Canada Memorandum, re: Earth Observation by Satellite," 11 September 1979, RG39, LAC. By 1977, MDA won a US$1.8 million prime contract to build a ground station at Kiruna, Sweden, to receive data from NASA and ESA satellites. The next year, MDA built a full ground station for Australia as well (an export worth US$4.5 million), in 1979, MDA received contracts to build a receiving station for Indonesia and provide upgrades to the original South African station, and in 1980 MDA won two additional prime contracts, one for Indonesia (worth US$2.8 million) and the other for Thailand (worth US$5.3 million). MDA won every ground station contract it bid during the late 1970s, except for one that flowed from Germany's political ties to Argentina. Within two months, however, Germany's Messerschmitt-Bölkow-Blohm needed help, and they turned to MDA.

93 Interview with MacDonald (18 January 1993); and John MacDonald, qtd in UN, Institute for Disarmament Research, "Safeguarding Space," 4. In addition, see Krige, "Crossing the Interface," 27–50; and Mack, *Viewing the Earth*, 15.

94 Interviews with Sloan, MacDonald (14 and 18 January 1993), and Renwick and Seymour, 18 May 1993; Seymour, "Study," 3; and MDA, *1976 Annual Report*.

95 "Canada Centre for Remote Sensing, Long-Term Plan, Fiscal Years 1978/79–1982/83," ca 1978, RG39, LAC.

96 Ibid., 32–3 and 9.

97 Seymour, "Study," 3; MDA, *1976 Annual Report*, 13; and interviews with Sloan, MacDonald (14 January 1993), and Renwick and Seymour.

98　Interviews with Sloan, and Lennox; and Seymour, "Study," 3, and table 2.
99　Interview with MacDonald (18 January 1993); and Seymour, "Study," 2, insert B, tables 1 and 2.
100　Interviews with Sloan, and MacDonald (7 January 1993); In addition, see Le Chevalier, *Principles of Radar*, xiii–5; and Haykin, Lewis, and Rainey, *Remote Sensing of Sea Ice*, 1–9, 515, and 637.
101　Interviews with MacDonald (7 January 1993), and J. Bennett.
102　Lapp and Task Force, *Satellites and Sovereignty*, 1–3, 43–65, 75, 83–8, and 170–6; "Canada Centre for Remote Sensing, Long-Term Plan, Fiscal Years 1978/79–1982/83," 1–36, RG39, LAC; and interviews with Lapp, Sloan, and Morley.
103　Lapp and Task Force, *Satellites and Sovereignty*, 176. In addition, see Morley, *Canada's Participation in Seasat*; and Shaw, CCRS *Remote Sensing*.
104　Interviews with Sloan, MacDonald (7 January 1993), Dettwiler (11 January 1993), and J. Bennett; Mack, *Viewing the Earth*, 57; Godbole, Haslam, and Vant, "Spotlight SAR Project," 5–8; and Cumming and Bennett, "Digital Processing," 710–18.
105　Interview with J. Bennett; and interviews with MacDonald (7 January 1993), George, and Renwick and Seymour.
106　H.H. Brune, Computer/Communications Secretariat, to C.D. Quarterman, Industry, Trade and Commerce, re: Foreign Take-overs of Canadian Computer Companies, 15 January 1975, 1–2, RG97, vol. 407, LAC; and interviews with J. Bennett, and MacDonald (7 January 1993).
107　Interview with Renwick and Seymour.
108　Interview with J. Bennett; and interviews with Sloan, MacDonald (7 January 1993), George, McConnell, and Renwick and Seymour.
109　Interview with Butler.
110　Interview with MacDonald (14 January 1993); and interview with J. Bennett.
111　Interview with McConnell.
112　Interviews with Sloan, J. Bennett, MacDonald (7 and 14 January 1993), and McConnell; Norris, *Spies in the Sky*, 171–2; Westwick, *Into the Black*, 67–120; and NASA, *Report*.
113　Interview with MacDonald (14 January 1993).
114　Interview with McConnell; and interviews with J. Bennett, and MacDonald (14 January 1993).
115　Interviews with Sloan, Morley, McConnell, and Renwick and Seymour.
116　Interview with McConnell; and interviews with Dettwiler (11 January 1993), MacDonald (14 January 1993), and J. Bennett.
117　Interview with Dettwiler (11 January 1993).

118 Interview with McConnell; Interviews with MacDonald (14 January 1993), and George; and Wills, *"Innovation in a Cold [War]*," 149–51.

119 Interview with J. Bennett.

120 Interview with MacDonald (7 January 1993); interviews with Murray, Prentice, Lennox and Price, Maxwell, MacDonald (18 January 1993), Spencer, Pitts (6 May 1993), Morris, McConnell, and Renwick and Seymour; and COSSA *Space Industry News*, "Industrial Award."

121 Interview with Lapp.

122 Interview with MacDonald (18 January 1993); and interviews with Friedmann, Beattie, Prentice, J. Bennett, George, McDonald, and Caddey. In addition, see Nelson, *Technology, Institutions.*

123 Interview with Lennox and Price; and Morley, *Remote Sensing.*

124 MDA, *1975 Annual Report*; MDA, *1976 Annual Report*; MDA, *1977 Annual Report*; and MDA, *1989 Annual Report.*

125 Interview with Thompson (18 May 1993).

CHAPTER FOUR

1 John S. MacDonald to Peter Meyboom, 29 October 1975, 2. In addition, see John S. MacDonald to Sheila Copps, deputy prime minister and minister of the environment, re: "Arctic Sovereignty and Environmental Protection," 8 December 1994, Department of Communications, Central Registry File, RG108-A, vol. 1248, file 127329 (hereafter RG108, vol. 1248), LAC; and "An Appraisal of the Industrial Development Aspects of the Computer Service and Manufacturing Industry," Electrical and Electronics Branch, Department of Industry, Trade and Commerce, September 1975," 1–27, RG97, vol. 407, LAC.

2 Interview with Lennox.

3 MacDonald to Meyboom, 29 October 1975, 2; interviews with Lapp, Lennox, and Renwick and Seymour; and Meyboom, "In-house vs Contractual Research."

4 *Electronics Communicator*, "MacDonald, Dettwiler & Associates Ltd, Exceptional Talents," 5.

5 Interviews with Lapp, Lennox and Price, MacDonald (18 January 1993), Spencer, and Pitts (6 May 1993); and Dotto, *Heritage of Excellence*, 86–93, LAC.

6 Consultative Committee, *Telecommunications and Sovereignty*, 63–75; Allen H. Wright to Alistair Gillespie, "R&D Success Stories," 7 March 1979, MOSST, R1526, vol. 52, file 15; "Spar Aerospace Limited," MOSST, R1526, vol. 55, file 18; "Action for Industrial Growth: Continuing the Dialogue – The Federal Government's Response to the Recommendations of the Overview Com-

mittee Reviewing the Industry Sector Task Force," ca February 1979, 3–6, MOSST, R1526, vol. 56, file 17; and L. Denis Hudon, secretary, minister of state, science and technology, memorandum to the minister, "Public Information Program for the Announcement of the Source Development Fund," 14 March 1979, MOSST, R1526, vol. 26, file 26, LAC; Faustmann, "John Mac-Donald Had a Firm"; Seymour, "Study," 2; and Thompson, "Investigation."

7 Anastakis, *Autonomous State*, 3–8 and 354–5. In addition, see Marchildon, "Canadian Multinationals"; Bothwell, *Nucleus*, 424–9; and Greber, *Rising to Power*, 183–4.

8 Alastair W. Gillespie, minister of energy, mines and resources, to the Canadian Club, Toronto, "'Energy: Can a Sudden Crisis Happen Here?': (A Report on Canada's National Energy Capability)," 5 February 1977, MOSST, R1526, vol. 373, file 20; "Statement: Conference on International Economic Cooperation," 30 May 1977, MOSST, R1526, vol. 373, file 25, LAC; and T.M. Chell, assistant under secretary, defence programs, to Department of External Affairs, Confidential, "International Defence Programs Progress Report," including Appendix I, "Canada–United States Defence Production Sharing Procurement, January 1959 through December 1981," 1 March 1982, RG25, vol. 14605, LAC, which reveals that under the DPSA, cross-border trade increased from $191 million during the period 1959–69 to more than $361 million between 1970 and 1979. Trade balances in defence procurement reversed course as well: from one favouring Canada by nearly $36 million in 1970 to a Canadian deficit high of $687.9 million in 1976 alone, and totalling more than $840 million in favour of the United States for the decade.

9 Alastair Gillespie, minister of industry, trade, and commerce, notes for an address, "Toward a More Responsible Enterprise System," to the Canadian Manufacturers' Association, 30 January 1975, MOSST, R1526, vol. 372, file 19, LAC. In addition, see Smardon, *Asleep at the Switch*, 101.

10 O.G. Stoner, deputy minister, industry, trade, and commerce, "Memorandum for the Minister: Meech Lake Cabinet Meeting on the Government's Priorities," 17 September 1975, MOSST, R1526, vol. 374, file 71, LAC.

11 Ibid.; and Commission of the European Economic Communities, "COM(75), 467 Final, Brussels," 10 September 1975, 15, RG97, vol. 418, EEC, LAC.

12 G.K. Davidson, Computer/Communications Secretariat, to Department Representatives, IT&C, CCA, TBS, DOC, DREE, Finance, re: "Working Group on Federal Government Procurement," 10 December 1973, 4, RG97, vol. 413, LAC; and Lapp and Task Force, *Satellites and Surveillance*, 75–89 and 142–76, LAC.

13 "Statement from the Mines Branch," undated, 1, RG45, vol. 356, LAC.

14 Supply and Services Canada to P. Robinson, a/chairman, Computer/

Communications Secretariat, Communications Canada, 28 May 1976, 1, RG97, vol. 413, LAC; Gerard Pelletier, minister of communications, "Computer/Communications Policy: A Position Statement by the Government of Canada," 1973, RG97, vol. 418, Green Paper, LAC; and Computer/Communications Program and Policy Coordination, "Report of Working Group #21, Procurement," submitted by B.P. Charbonneau, chairman, Supply and Services Canada, 4 August 1976, and G.K. Davidson to P. Robinson, "Draft: Discussion Paper on Canadian Content," 11 June 1976, 7, RG97, vol. 413, LAC.

15 Interviews with Sloan, Prentice, Lennox, MacDonald (18 January 1993), Spencer, Semrau, and Renwick and Seymour.

16 Interview with MacDonald (18 January 1993).

17 Interview with Morris; and interviews with Gelbart, Sloan, Prentice, Louth, McDonald, Cwynar, Lennox, Allan, Widmer, Dollard, MacDonald (18 January 1993), Spencer, Immega, Semrau, McConnell, and Renwick and Seymour.

18 Laird, *Pull*, 94 and 117.

19 Interview with McConnell.

20 Interviews with Gelbart, Sloan, Prentice, Louth, McDonald, Cwynar, MacDonald (7 and 14 January 1993), Lennox, Allan, Widmer, Dettwiler (14 January 1993), Dollard, Spencer, Immega, Morris, Semrau, McConnell, and Renwick and Seymour; and *Canadian Electronics Engineering*, "Practical Solutions to Difficult Problems," 32. Davidsson and Honig, "Role of Social and Human Capital," 301–31; and Miner et al., "Magic Beanstalk Vision," provide instructive comparisons.

21 Interview with Lennox; and interviews with Sloan, Prentice, MacDonald (18 January 1993), Spencer, Semrau, and Renwick and Seymour.

22 Interviews with MacDonald (7 and 14 January 1993), Lennox, and Dettwiler (14 January 1993). In addition, see Livesay, Rorke, and Lux, "From Experience." Case studies that resonate with the MDA experience include Stevenson and Radin, "Social Capital"; Chandler and Hanks, "Examination of the Sustainability"; Fama and Jensen, "Separation of Ownership"; and Peters, "Conflict at Apple."

23 Interview with Immega,

24 MDA, *1975 Annual Report*; and MDA, *1976 Annual Report*; and interviews with Lennox, and MacDonald (7 and 18 January 1993). In addition, see Burton, "Company They Keep," 13–35.

25 Interview with Lennox. According to Lennox, ground stations represented 70 per cent of the company's business in 1974, but little more than 50 per cent during 1975.

26 Interview with MacDonald (14 January 1993); interviews with Gelbart, Sloan, Lennox, Dettwiler (11 January 1993), Maxwell, MacDonald (18 January 1993), and Spencer; and Seymour, "Study," 2, insert B, tables 1 and 2. For the long-term consequences of such strategies, see Gandy Jr, "Data Mining, Surveillance, and Discrimination."

27 On the lure of product development, see Livesay, *American Made*; Dutrénit, "Building Technological Capabilities"; and Iansiti and Clark, "Integration and Dynamic Capability." Smardon, *Asleep at the Switch*, 58, argues that Canadians had long borrowed from the American Fordist model, including its use of scientific management and mechanization to support "mass production, increased wages, and rising mass consumption paid for out of productivity gains, and a new role for the state in managing the new structures of mass production and consumption."

28 Interviews with Gelbart, Lennox, and Spencer. In addition, see Livesay, Rorke, and Lux, "From Experience."

29 Interview with MacDonald (7 January 1993); interviews with Lennox, Dettwiler (14 January 1993), and MacDonald (14 and 18 January 1993); and MDA, *1975 Annual Report*, 5-8; and MDA, *1977 Annual Report*, 1-6.

30 Interviews with Gelbart, Sloan, Prentice, Cwynar, Lennox and Price, Dettwiler (11 January 1993), Maxwell, Thompson (15 January and 18 May 1993), Dollard, MacDonald (18 January 1993), Spencer, Immega, Morris, Semrau, McConnell, and Renwick and Seymour. In addition, see Wallace and Erickson, *Hard Drive*. During 1976, Microsoft hired their first full-time employee and Gates emerged as the first programmer to raise the issue of software piracy in his "Open Letter to Hobbyists."

31 Interviews with MacDonald (14 and 18 January 1993), Lennox and Price, Spencer, and Thompson (15 January and 18 May 1993).

32 "Canada Centre for Remote Sensing, Long Term Plan, Fiscal Years 1978/79-1982/83," ca 1978, 3 and 2, RG39, LAC.

33 Interview with Spencer; and Spence, "Recognizing Dan Gelbart." By 2009, Gelbart held more than 100 patents, including "the mobile radio data terminal; the digital film recorder, which won the Research and Development 100 award; and the world's first optical tape recorder."

34 Interview with Gelbart; and interviews with Sloan, Lennox, MacDonald (14 January 1993), and Spencer.

35 Interview with Spencer; and interviews with Gelbart, and MacDonald (18 January 1993).

36 Interview with Gelbart.

37 Interview with MacDonald (18 January 1993); and interviews with Gelbart, Lennox, and Spencer.

38 Interviews with Gelbart, and MacDonald (18 January 1993); and interviews
with Lennox, and Spencer.

39 MDA, *Model 4880*; and MDA, *1977 Annual Report*; and MacDonald to Meyboom, 29 October 1975. Small research grants from IRAP assisted MDA in
the development of the 4880 as well as its ground station products.

40 "The Canadian Opportunity: A Computer Applications Industry," ca January
1977, 5 and 4, RG97, vol. 407, LAC.

41 D. Penniman, A. Butrimento, and J. Page, "International Data Exchange and
the Application of Informatics Technology: Critical Research Needs," International Institute for Applied Systems Analysis, Schloor Laxenburg, Austria,
December 1977, RG97, vol. 418, US, LAC. In addition, see William L. Fishman, assistant director for international communications, Office of Telecommunications Policy, Executive Office of the President, Washington, DC,
"International Data Flow: Conference on Computer Communications,
before the Fourth International Conference on Computer Communication,"
Kyoto, September 26-9, 1978, RG97, vol. 418, US, LAC.

42 Interdepartmental Committee for Computer/Communications Program and
Policy Coordination, "Restricted" Working Group No. 4, "Report on Foreign
Take-over of Canadian Computer Services Companies," Ottawa, February
1975, RG97, vol. 407, LAC; O.G. Stoner, deputy minister, industry, trade, and
commerce, "Memorandum for the Minister: Meech Lake Cabinet Meeting on
the Government's Priorities," 17 September 1975, MOSST, R1526, vol. 374, file
71, LAC; and Board of Economic Development Ministers, "Action for Industrial Growth: Continuing the Dialogue – The Federal Government's Response
to the Recommendations of the Overview Committee Reviewing the Industry
Sector Task Force Reports," ca February 1979, MOSST, R1526, vol. 56, file 7, LAC.

43 Electrical and Electronics Branch, Department of Industry, Trade and Commerce, "An Appraisal of the Industrial Development Aspects of the Computer Service and Manufacturing Industry," September 1975, 35, RG97, vol. 413,
LAC. In addition, see Notes for an Address by Alastair Gillespie, minister of
industry, trade, and commerce to the Canadian Manufacturers' Association,
"Toward a Responsible Enterprise System," 30 January 1975, MOSST, R1526,
vol. 372, file 19, LAC; Address by Alastair W. Gillespie, minister of energy,
mines, and resources, to the Canadian Club, Toronto, "Can a Sudden Crisis
Happen Here (A Report on Canada's Energy Capabilities)," 25 February
1977, MOSST, R1526, vol. 373, file 20, LAC; "Action for Industrial Growth:
Continuing the Dialogue – The Federal Government's Response to the Rec-
ommendations of the Overview Committee Reviewing the Industry Sector
Task Force Reports," ca February 1979, MOSST, R1526, vol. 56, file 7, LAC; and
Brune, "Comments on the Report."

44 Interview with Semrau; interviews with Allan, and MacDonald (7 January
   1993); MDA, *1977 Annual Report*; and MacDonald to Meyboom, 29 October
   1975, 3. The CSIS was formed following investigations in 1984 that exposed
   the RCMP's involvement in numerous illegal activities during the 1970s,
   including keeping dossiers on more than 800,000 Canadian individuals and
   groups, such as members of the left-wing faction of the New Democratic
   Party (NDP). On the 1977 Royal Commission that discovered wide-ranging
   surveillance of Canadian citizens, see Whitaker, Kealey, and Parnaby, *Secret
   Service*, 9 and 537–8. In addition, see Department of Industry, Trade, and
   Commerce, confidential "'Talking Points' with respect to the Diplomatic
   Note (Number 62)," 17 April 1974, RG97, vol. 418, US, LAC, which describes
   the development of the mobile computer terminal for the RCMP. "Talking
   Points," 2, argued, "This was a problem that was identified by Canadians, for
   Canada, and it is only fitting that it be solved by Canadians. It is generally
   recognized that in all major developed countries that a computer industry is
   a necessary element in a country's infrastructure if it wishes to remain a
   developed nation." Furthermore, it stressed, "Canadian industry is almost
   totally dominated by U.S. owned firm," and "this foreign ownership severely
   limits the options available to redress any actions that are not in the best
   interests of Canada." Other files in RG97, vol. 418, US, LAC, contain additional arguments on the need for Canadian control over domestic surveillance.
45 Interviews with MacDonald (7 January 1993), and Morris.
46 Interviews with MacDonald (7 January 1993), and Lennox and Price.
47 Thompson, "Investigation," 1–5, and "Letter to John MacDonald," 14 December 1976; and interviews with Lennox, and Spencer.
48 Interviews with MacDonald (7 January 1993), Lennox, Spencer, and Morris.
49 Interview with Spencer.
50 Interviews with Gelbart, Sloan, Prentice, Cwynar, Lennox and Price, Dettwiler (11 January 1993), Maxwell, Thompson (15 January and 18 May
   1993), Dollard, MacDonald (18 January 1993), Spencer, Immega, Morris,
   Semrau, McConnell, and Renwick and Seymour. In addition, see Canada,
   Task Force on Program Review, *Government Procurement*, *"Spending Smarter,"*
   113–32, LAC.
51 Interviews with Lennox, Dettwiler (11 January 1993), MacDonald (7 and 14
   January 1993), Spencer, and Pitts (6 May 1993).
52 MDA, *1977 Annual Report*; and interview with MacDonald (7 January 1993).
53 Interview with McConnell; and interviews with Sloan, Louth, Lennox and
   Price, Maxwell, and Renwick and Seymour. On the class fractions, cultural
   and educational capital, and esthetic world view that have served the interests of the status-conscious as well as capital and the power elite, see Bour-

dieu, *Distinction*. In addition, see Gray, Golob, and Markusen, "Seattle"; Gray et al., "Four Faces of Silicon Valley"; and Leslie and Kargon, "Selling Silicon Valley."

54 Auerswald and Branscomb, "Start-ups and Spin-offs"; and MDA, *1977 Annual Report*.

55 Interviews with Gelbart, Sloan, Cwynar, Lennox, MacDonald (14 and 18 January 1993), Spencer, Immega, McConnell, and Renwick and Seymour; Kaihla, "Hissin' Cousins"; Kapp, "Banging the Gong," 12; and John Faustmann, "Barclay Isherwood: Prime Mover at Mobile Data International," *Canadian Business*, August 1987, 53.

56 "Motorola's Offer for MDI Advances," *New York Times*, 10 June 1988; and Province of British Columbia, *Annual Report*. In addition, see Wixted and Holbrook, "Living on the Edge." 104–5.

57 Interview with Lennox.

58 Interviews with Gelbart, Sloan, Prentice, Cwynar, Lennox, Dettwiler (11 January 1993), Maxwell, Thompson (15 January and 18 May 1993), Spencer, Morris, Semrau, McConnell, and Renwick and Seymour; and Canada Centre for Remote Sensing, Ad Hoc Committee of Ministers on Ocean Management, "Executive Summary," ca 1977, RG39, LAC.

59 Director-general, Policy Directorate, Corporate Planning Group to Distribution, "Government of Canada Memorandum, re: Earth Observation by Satellite," 11 September 1979, 3, RG39, LAC.

60 "Centre for Remote Sensing, Long Term Plan, Fiscal Years 1978/79–1982/83," ca 1978, 6 and 33–5, and "Discussion Paper: Earth Observation by Satellite: Continued Participation by Canada in the U.S. LANDSAT Program," 4 September 1979, RG39, LAC.

61 Interviews with MacDonald (7 and 14 January 1993), and Lennox.

62 Interview with Sloan; and Wixted and Holbrook, "Living on the Edge," 105.

63 Interviews with Lapp, Gelbart, Sloan, MacDonald (7 and 14 January 1993), Lennox and Price, Spencer, and Renwick and Seymour.

64 Interview with Gelbart.

65 Laird, *Pull*, 113; and interviews with Lapp, Gelbart, Sloan, MacDonald (7 and 14 January 1993), Lennox and Price, Spencer, and Renwick and Seymour.

66 Minister of consumer and corporate affairs, Canada Business Corporations Act; and interviews with Lapp, Gelbart, Sloan, MacDonald (14 January 1993), Lennox, Spencer, and Renwick and Seymour.

67 Interviews with Gelbart, Sloan, Prentice, Cwynar, Lennox, Dettwiler (11 January 1993), Maxwell, Thompson (15 January and 18 May 1993), Dollard, MacDonald (18 January 1993), Spencer, Immega, Morris, Semrau, Mc-

Connell, and Renwick and Seymour. In addition, see KADAK Products, "Company Showcase."

68 Interviews with Gelbart, Sloan, MacDonald (18 January 1993), and Spencer.

69 Alastair Gillespie, "Opening Remarks at the Federal-Provincial Conference of First Ministers on the Economy (0–2)," 27 November 1978, 1, document 800-9/051, MOSST, R1526, vol. 52, file 3, LAC; and Notes for a Speech in the House of Commons, re: Opposition Motion – "Loss of Confidence in Canadian Government and Government Policies," 13 February 1979, MOSST, R1526, vol. 374, file 13, LAC.

70 L. Denis Hudon, secretary, MOSST, Memorandum for the Minister (Secret), re: MTN [Multilateral Trade Negotiations] Government Procurement," 29 November 1978, 1–2, MOSST, R1526, vol. 52, file 11, LAC; Board of Economic Development Ministers, "Action Plan for Industrial Growth," ca February 1979, 4, 7–8, 11–13, 15, 22, 31–7, 42, and 47, MOSST, R1526, vol. 56, file 7, LAC; and Smardon, Asleep at the Switch, 4–19, 102, 236–45, 293, and 377–8.

71 J.L. Orr, "The Crisis of Canadian Secondary Manufacturing," Engineering Digest, May 1978, attached to Robert K. Andras, Board of Economic Development Ministers (to Gillespie for comment) to Hugh Morris, chairman, Committee for an Independent Canada, National Office, Ottawa, 8 January 1979, MOSST, R1526, vol. 52, file 6, LAC.

72 John J. Shepherd, Office of the Vice-Chairman, Science Council of Canada, to Judd Buchanan, minister of state for science and technology, re: "Framework Statement for R&D Expenditures," paper no. 3, 30 October 1978, 7600-1(2), 1 and 3, MOSST, R1526, vol. 52, file 10, LAC. In addition, see L.D. Hudon, secretary, Ministry of State for Science and Technology, memorandum to the minister, "Arrow in Retrospect: Wrong Action Taken?," ca February 1979, MOSST, R1526, vol. 52, file 4, LAC.

73 Gillespie, "Opening Remarks at the Federal-Provincial Conference," 1–7; and Canada, Task Force on Program Review, Government Procurement, "Spending Smarter," 159–60, LAC.

74 Smardon, Asleep at the Switch, 312.

75 Prime Minister Trudeau, Ottawa, to C.A. McDowell, chairman, Department of Chemistry, Council of Canadian Universities, University of British Columbia, 12 December 1978, MOSST, R1526, vol. 54, file 38, LAC.

76 Board of Economic Development Ministers, "Action Plan for Industrial Growth," ca February 1979, 29–30, 32–3, 42, 45, and 47, MOSST, R1526, vol. 56, file 7, LAC.

77 Mattelart, Globalization of Surveillance, 233. In addition, see Greber, Rising to Power, 237–9.

78 Smardon, *Asleep at the Switch*, 281 and 293. In addition, see Bothwell, *Nucleus*, 423–4; and Wilson, *Energy Squeeze.*

79 United States Department of Defense, *Directive 2035.1*, 4.

80 Fossum, *Oil, the State*, 284.

81 "Canada Centre for Remote Sensing, Long Term Plan, Fiscal Years 1978/79–1982/83," ca 1978, 6–7, and J.S. Maini, "Earth Observation by Satellite: Continued Participation by Canada in the U.S. LANDSAT Program," 4 September 1979, 1–4, RG39, LAC. Maini's report notes the departments involved in the Interagency Committee on Remote Sensing (IACRS): Agriculture Canada, Department of the Environment, Fisheries and Oceans, Industry, Trade and Commerce, Communications, National Defence, Indian and Northern Affairs, MOSST, NRC, Transport Canada, Treasury Board, and External Affairs.

82 MacDonald, quoting Kip Fuller, in Fiffer, *So You've Got*, 9.

83 Interview with Lapp; interviews with Lennox, and MacDonald (14 January 1993); Lees, "He's Got Fire Power"; Faustmann, "John MacDonald Had a Firm"; and David Smith, "Feet on the Ground and Eye on the Sky: MDA Was Grounded until Pitts Arrived," *Vancouver Sun*, 8 October 1988

84 Brooks, *Mythical Man-Month*, 14; and interview with Lennox.

85 Interview with Lennox.

86 Interview with MacDonald (14 January 1993).

87 Interview with Prentice.

88 Interview with Maxwell.

89 Interview with Lennox and Price.

90 Interview with Immega.

91 Interviews with MacDonald (7 and 14 January 1993), and interviews with Gelbart, Dollard, and Immega and Kauffman (7 May 1993).

92 Interview with MacDonald.

93 Interview with Prentice; and interviews with Gelbart, MacDonald (7 January 1993), Lennox and Price, Dollard, and Immega.

94 Interview with Dollard; and Lees, "He's Got Fire Power."

95 Interview with Gelbart.

96 Interviews with Louth, and Sloan.

97 Interview with MacDonald (14 January 1993).

98 Electrical and Electronics Branch, Department of Industry, Trade and Commerce, "An Appraisal of the Industrial Aspects of the Computer Service and Manufacturing Industry," September 1975, RG97, vol. 407, LAC; J.D. Mac-Naughton, vice-president and general manager, Remote Manipulator Systems Division, SPAR, "An Address to the Air Industries Association of Cana-

da," 26 September 1978, MOSST, R1526, vol. 55, file 18, LAC; Consultative
Committee, *Telecommunications and Sovereignty*, 69 and 59, LAC; and Dotto,
Heritage of Excellence, 130, LAC.

99 Consultative Committee, *Telecommunications and Sovereignty*, 69–73. In
addition, see Doern and Stoney, *How Ottawa Spends*, 129.

100 "Confidential Briefing Material," MOSST, R1526, vol. 56, file 8; and L. Denis
Hudon, secretary, minister of state for science and technology, to the minis-
ter, "Public Information Program for the Announcement of the Source
Development Fund," 2, 8–9, and 4–5, MOSST, R1526, vol. 56, file 26, LAC.

101 Interviews with Lapp, MacDonald (18 January 1993), Pitts (6 May 1993),
and W. Bennett; "The Year of Living Differently: There's a New CEO, But
Is It the Same Old SPAR," *Canadian Business*, June 1997, 16; and Bill
Knapp, "Masters of the Universe," *Canadian Business*, November 1992,
119–20.

102 Interviews with Lapp, Lennox, MacDonald (18 January 1993), Pitts (6 May
1993), and W. Bennett.

103 Interviews with Lapp, Lennox, MacDonald (14 January 1993), and Pitts (6
May 1993).

CHAPTER FIVE

1 Smith, "Growing Pains in Lotusland," 108; interview with MacDonald (14
January 1993); and OECD, *Economic Surveys 1982–1983 Canada*, 7–52.

2 Interview with MacDonald (14 January 1993); and interviews with Lapp,
and W. Bennett.

3 Interviews with McConnell, and J. Bennett.

4 Interview with Morris; and interviews with Gelbart, Prentice, J. Bennett,
and Dollard.

5 Interview with Murray.

6 Interviews with Lapp, Gelbart, Prentice, J. Bennett, MacDonald (14 January
1993), Dollard, Pitts (6 May 1993), and W. Bennett; Smith, "Feet on the
Ground and Eye on the Sky"; and OECD, *Economic Surveys 1982–1983 Canada*, 7–52.

7 Interviews with MacDonald (14 January 1993), Pitts (6 May 1993), and W.
Bennett; and Faustmann, "John MacDonald Had a Firm." In addition, see
Mussio, *Telecom Nation*, 97–102 and 114; Johnson, "Three Approaches"; Tupper and Doern, *Public Corporations*, 199–200; Zahra and Filatotchev, "Governance of the Entrepreneurial Threshold"; Boeker and Karichalil, "Entrepreneurial Transitions"; and Hellmann and Puri, "Venture Capital."

8 Smith, "Feet on the Ground and Eye on the Sky."

9 Interview with Pitts (6 May 1993); and Shames, *Big Time*.

10 Interview with Pitts (6 May 1993); "Margaret Erling Brunsdale Pitts," *Globe and Mail*, 6 September 2008; Coleman, "Honoring the Late Anne Brunsdale," 1679; and Smith, "Feet on the Ground and Eye on the Sky."

11 Interviews with MacDonald (14 January 1993), Pitts, and W. Bennett; "Pitts, John Wilson" Obituary, *Vancouver Sun*, 9 February 2006; Faustmann, "John MacDonald Had a Firm"; and Smith, "Feet on the Ground and Eye on the Sky." When MDA launched its first public offering during 1993, Pitts had emerged as a director of BC Sugar Refinery, BC Telephone Company, Canada Trust, and Paccar, as well as a member of the C.D. Howe Institute. A conservative businessman turned philanthropist, Pitts raised $5.5 million in donations for Vancouver's New Art Gallery during 1980, and together with Barclay Isherwood, he raised over $5 million for Science World during 1989. Pitts also initiated the first individually sponsored by-law change in the City of Vancouver during the 1990s, which saved his historic neighbourhood from the ravages of urban development. At the time of his death in 2006, Pitts included other executive accomplishments to his community leadership portfolio, including board memberships in the Salvation Army, Canada Kenworth, Brentwood College, and York House School. He also made significant donations to the Vancouver Symphony, BC Cancer Foundation, and other non-profits.

12 Interviews with Pitts (6 May 1993); and W. Bennett.

13 Interviews with MacDonald (14 January 1993), and Pitts (6 May 1993); and Vancouver Enterprise Forum, "Fireside Chat."

14 Interviews with MacDonald (14 January 1993), and Pitts (6 May 1993).

15 Interviews with Lapp, MacDonald (14 January 1993), Pitts, and W. Bennett. In addition, see Stevenson and Radin, "Social Capital and Social Influence"; Livesay, "Entrepreneurial Dominance"; and Hellmann and Puri, "Venture Capital."

16 Interviews with Lapp, Gelbart, Prentice, MacDonald (14 and 18 January 1993), Pitts (6 May 1993), and W. Bennett.

17 Interview with Pitts (6 May 1993); Lees, "He's Got Fire Power"; and interviews with Lapp, Prentice, MacDonald (14 and 18 January 1993), and W. Bennett.

18 Interview with Pitts (6 May 1993).

19 Caspar W. Weinberger, qtd in B. Wooding, defence counsellor, to Canadian Delegation to NATO, re: "U.S. Defense Department Report on Sharing Among Allies," 11 August 1981, RG25, vol. 14605, LAC. According to Bliss, "Forcing the Pace," 116, such arrangements "stimulated another round of Canadian government interest in forcing the pace of structural change in

the Canadian economy. Perhaps government could shepherd Canada into the age of high-tech, chip and robot production through purchasing policies, tax incentives, subsidies, and other industrial policies. If throwing money at old, dying industries did not seem particularly productive, why not pick winners and throw the money at the attractive new instant industries (though of course the old industries would require reasonable amounts of transitional support)?" As the Reagan-Trudeau meeting reveals, however, surveillance capitalism and the continental integration of defence programs forced Canada's pace of change.

20 Department of External Affairs, Defence Programs, "International Defence Programs Progress Report for October–December, 1981," Ottawa, February 1982, 2, 6, and 28, RG25, vol. 14605, LAC.

21 Supply and Services Canada to Edward C. Lumley, 31 May 1981, and T.M. Chell, director general, Defence Programs Branch, Department of Industry, Trade and Commerce, Confidential "International Defence Programs: Progress Report," 16 December 1981, 29–32, RG25, vol. 14605, LAC; and WSHDC UNTD0843 to EXTOTT GNG, "Proposed Marketing Study," 15 February 1982, and "Notes for an Address by Allan E. Gotlieb, Ambassador of Canada to the United States," 24 October 1983, 6–7 and 16–17, RG25, vol. 12698, LAC. In addition, see Dotto, *Heritage of Excellence*, 37–8, 62–4, LAC; and Johnson-Freese, *Heavenly Ambitions*, 2–4 and 19–47.

22 Interviews with Lapp, Morley, MacDonald (14 January 1993), and Pitts (6 May 1993). On increasing concerns about technological obsolescence and the e-waste it has created, see Slade, *Made to Break*.

23 Director-general, Policy Directorate, Corporate Planning Groups, to Distribution, 11 September 1979, 1–3, RG39, LAC; and interview with Morley.

24 "Confidential Brief for Deputy Minister, International Trade and Economic Relations, re: 'Proposal for Joint Development of the National Airspace Systems of Canada and the United States,'" 25 June 1982, RG25, vol. 12698, LAC.

25 WSHDC UNTD4248 to Extott DDP/Chell GNG, "Canadian Arsenals," 30 July 1982, RG25, vol. 12698, LAC; and interviews with Lapp, Morley, MacDonald (14 January 1993), and Pitts (6 May 1993).

26 Interview with MacDonald (14 January 1993); and interview with Pitts (6 May 1993).

27 Interview with Pitts (6 May 1993).

28 Interview with MacDonald (14 January 1993); and Canadian Embassy, DC, to under-secretary of state for external affairs, Ottawa, "The United States Nuclear Weapon Stockpile," 2 July 1982, and OTT to WSHDC, "USA Strategic Nuclear Doctrine," 23 August 1982, RG25, vol. 12698, LAC.

29 Interview with Pitts (6 May 1993).

30 Interview with MacDonald (14 January 1993); and interviews with Lapp, Pitts (6 May 1993), and W. Bennett.

31 Interview with MacDonald (18 January 1993); and interviews with Lapp, Sloan, Spencer, Pitts (6 May 1993), Renwick and Seymour, and W. Bennett,

32 Interview with McConnell.

33 Andrew Carnegie, qtd in Livesay, *Andrew Carnegie*, 113.

34 Interview with Wallis (13 January 1993); and interviews with Lapp, Lennox and Price, Dollard, MacDonald (18 January 1993), Pitts (6 May 1993), and Caddey.

35 Interview with Pitts (6 May 1993); and interviews with Lapp, Gelbart, Prentice, J. Bennett, George, MacDonald (14 January 1993), and Dollard.

36 Interviews with Prentice, Dollard, and Pitts (6 May 1993).

37 Interview with Druce.

38 Interview with Widmer; and interviews with Gelbart, Sloan, Lennox and Price, Dettwiler (11 January 1993), Maxwell, Dollard, and McConnell.

39 Interviews with Lapp, Gelbart, Prentice, MacDonald (14 January 1993), Dollard, and Pitts (6 May 1993).

40 Interview with Pitts (6 May 1993).

41 Interviews with Friedmann, Cwynar, George, Dollard, MacDonald (18 January 1993), and Pitts (6 May 1993); MDA, *1986 Annual Report*; and MDA, *1987 Annual Report*.

42 Canada, "Science Agreement," LAC; and interviews with MacDonald (7 and 18 January 1993), J. Bennett, Widmer, George, Pitts (6 May 1993), and McConnell. In addition, see Leclerc and Lessard, "Canada and ESA," 3–6; Norris, *Spies in the Sky*, 171–2; Westwick, *Into the Black,* 67–120; Suzuki, *Policy Logics*, 8, 85–6, 107–8, and 207–12; Bonnet and Manno, *International Cooperation*; Sandholtz, *High-tech Europe*; and NASA, *Report.*

43 Interview with J. Bennett; and interviews with MacDonald (7 and 18 January 1993), George, Pitts (6 May 1993), and McConnell.

44 Interview with J. Bennett; and interviews with MacDonald (18 January 1993), George, and Pitts (6 May 1993). In addition, see Suzuki, *Policy Logics*, 8, 85–6, 107–8, and 207–12; and Leclerc and Lessard, "Canada and ESA."

45 Interviews with Maxwell, MacDonald (18 January 1993), Pitts (6 May 1993), and Renwick and Seymour.

46 Interviews with MacDonald (18 January 1993), Pitts (6 May 1993), and Renwick and Seymour.

47 Interview with Pitts (6 May 1993); and interview with MacDonald (18 January 1993). In addition, see Mosco, *Digital Sublime*, 17–35; and Mattelart, *Globalization of Surveillance*, 137–82.

48 Interview with Pitts (6 May 1993).

49 Interviews with Friedmann, Cwynar, Dollard, MacDonald (18 January 1993), and Pitts (6 May 1993); MDA, *Satellite Ground Stations*; Smith, "Feet on the Ground and Eye on the Sky"; and Faustmann, "John MacDonald Had a Firm," 60.

50 Interview with Dollard.

51 Interview with Caddey.

52 MDA, *1986 Annual Report*, 4–5; MDA, *1987 Annual Report*, 2–4; and interviews with Friedmann, Beattie, Lapp, Prentice, McDonald, Bernie Clark, Cwynar, Allan, George, Wallis, MacDonald (18 January 1993), and Pitts (6 May 1993). In addition, see Johnson, "Three Approaches."

53 Interview wtih Friedmann; and interviews with Beattie, Prentice, MacDonald (18 January 1993), and Spencer.

54 Interviews with Friedmann, Beattie, Prentice, Widmer, MacDonald (7 and 18 January 1993), and Pitts (6 May 1993). In addition, see Burton, "Company They Keep," 18–25.

55 *Interavia*, "Long View from Space," 25–6; and MDA, *1987 Annual Report*, 2–4.

56 Interview with Kauffman; interviews with Friedman, Sloan, Cwynar, Dettwiler (11 January 1993), J. Bennett, Maxwell, Dollard, and MacDonald (18 January 1993); MDA, *1987 Annual Report*, 2–4; and *Interavia*, "Long View from Space," 25–6.

57 Interview with George; and interviews with Friedmann, Cwynar, J. Bennett, Dollard, MacDonald (18 January 1993), and Pitts (6 May 1993). In addition, see Batten and Cruikshank, *Weather Channel*.

58 MDA, *METDAS*; and interviews with Friedmann, and MacDonald (7 and 18 January 1993).

59 Interview with Friedmann; interviews with MacDonald (7 and 18 January 1993); MDA, *Satellite Ground Station*; and Cooper, Friedmann, and Wood, "Automatic Generation."

60 Interview with Friedmann; and MDA, *Meridian*.

61 Monmonier, *Spying with Maps*, 12 and 15–16; interviews with Friedmann, Cwynar, and MacDonald (18 January 1993); MDA, *1986 Annual Report*, 4–5; MDA, *1987 Annual Report*, 2–4; MDA, *Satellite Ground Stations*; "Cognos and the Mint among 12 Recipients of Canada Export Award," *Ottawa Citizen*, 29 October 1986; and Paglen, *Blank Spots*, 97–137.

62 T.M. Chell, Department of External Affairs, Confidential "International Defence Programs Progress Report for April–June 1983," 25, RG25, vol. 12698, LAC; and interviews with Friedmann, Cwynar, and MacDonald (18 January 1993).

63 Brian Herman to file (through Mr Francis), External Affairs Canada (the Bureau), Confidential "United States Department of Defence Briefing on

Technology Transfer," 25 May 1983, 2, and 3–16, RG25, vol. 12698, LAC. In addition, see Beaumier, "Innovation in Canada," 23–33, LAC; Canada, Task Force on Program Review, *Government Procurement*, *"Spending Smarter,"* 124–5, LAC; Sà and Litwin, "University-Industrial Research," 429; Klassen, "Canada and the New Imperialism," 166; and Reiss, *Strategic Defense Initiative*.

64 See Doern and Maslove, *Thirty Years of Watching*, 5–7; and Bow, *Politics of Linkage*, 105–26.

65 Smardon, *Asleep at the Switch*, 298 and 310–1; "The 'Net Benefit' of Foreign Takeovers," CBC News, 29 October 2010; and Dufour and Ahmad, "Investment Canada."

66 Interviews with Friedmann, Sloan, Prentice, and MacDonald (7 and 18 January); and MDA, *1986 Annual Report*, 3–5. In addition, see Hart, *Decision at Midnight*; Blake, *Transforming the Nation*; and Mattelart, *Globalization of Surveillance*, 117–61.

67 MDA, *1987 Annual Report*, 2–4; interviews with McDonald, Dettwiler (11 January 1993), George, Widmer, MacDonald (18 January 1993), and Pitts (6 May 1993); and Paul Jay, "What's in a Name? More Money, Evidently," CBC News, 12 February 2008.

68 MDA, *1986 Annual Report*, 4–5; MDA, *Satellite Ground Stations*; and interviews with McDonald, Dettwiler (11 January 1993), George, Widmer, MacDonald (18 January 1993), and Pitts (6 May 1993).

69 Interview with McDonald; and interviews with George, Widmer, MacDonald (18 January 1993), and Pitts (6 May 1993).

70 Interviews with McDonald, George, Widmer, MacDonald (18 January 1993), and Pitts (6 May 1993).

71 Interview with Caddey; MDA, *1989 Annual Report, 1990 Annual Report, 1991 Annual Report, 1992 Annual Report*, and *1993 Annual Report*; interviews with Lapp, Gelbart, Sloan, McDonald, Cwynar, Lennox and Price, Dettwiler (11 January 1993), J. Bennett, Widmer, Maxwell, Dollard, MacDonald (18 January 1993), Pitts (6 May 1993), and McConnell; Evans, "Canadian Space Programme," particularly 141; Bonnet and Manno, *International Cooperation in Space*; *Electronics Communicator*, "MDA Secures Second Order"; Mussio, *Telecom Nation*, 97–102 and 114; and Johnson, "Three Approaches."

72 MDA, *1986 Annual Report*, 4–5; and MDA, *1987 Annual Report*, 3–7.

73 Mosco, *Digital Sublime*, 104 and 111. In addition, see Canadian Embassy, DC to under-secretary of state for external affairs, Ottawa, "The United States Nuclear Weapon Stockpile," 2 July 1982, and OTT to WSHDC, "USA Strategic Nuclear Doctrine," 23 August 1982, RG25, vol. 12698, LAC; Gaddis, *Cold War*, 195–235; and Reiss, *Strategic Defense Initiative*.

74 Committee of Deputy Ministers on Foreign and Defence Policy, "Group

Working Paper #1: A Canadian Industrial Defence Base, Executive Summary," 8 December 1983, 3, RG25, vol. 12698, LAC. BNATO YBGR8682 to EXTOTT URR, confidential telex, 10 December 1983, RG25, vol. 12698, LAC, also referenced Canada's industrial participation in a "North American modernization" effort for military preparedness, including increased rationalization, standardization, and interoperability of systems produced in the US and Canada.

75 Gotlieb, "Canada's Special Role," 3–4, and 13–14.

76 UGBA/A.L. Halliday to UGB, "Joint Canada-US Funding of Research and Development," 7 November 1984, RG25, vol. 12698, LAC.

77 Ibid. In addition, see T.M. Chell, Confidential "International Defence Programs Progress Report, April–June 1984," 15 October 1984, RG25, vol. 12698, LAC.

78 Interviews with Friedmann, Beattie, McDonald, Cwynar, Wallis, MacDonald (18 January 1993), Pitts (6 May 1993), Morris, and Caddey.

79 Interview with Prentice.

80 Interview with George.

81 Interview with Clark; interviews with McDonald, Cwynar, Wallis, Dollard, MacDonald (18 January 1993), Pitts (6 May 1993), and Caddey; MDA, *1986 Annual Report*, 4–5; MDA, *1987 Annual Report*, 2–4; and Defence Programs, Department of External Affairs, "International Defence Programs Progress Report for October–December, 1981," February 1982, 27–54, RG25, vol. 12698, LAC.

82 Interview with Friedmann; MDA, *1986 Annual Report*, 4–5; MDA, *1987 Annual Report*, 2–4; MDA, *Automated Weather Distribution System*; and MDA, *Advanced Airspace Management*.

83 Interview with Prentice.

84 Interview with McDonald.

85 Interviews with Prentice, McDonald, Cwynar, Wallis, and Caddey.

86 Butrica, *Single Stage*, 8, 29, and 31–2.

87 T.M. Chell, Department of External Affairs, "International Defence Programs Progress Report, April–June 1984," 15 October 1984, Secret, "Master Data Exchange Agreement for the Mutual Development of Weapons Systems," 19 March 1984, Department of External Affairs to Joseph S. Severin, 10 April 1984, and National Defence Headquarters Secretariat, Secret, "Space-Based Radar/Infra-Red Detection," 25 September 1984, RG25, vol. 12698, LAC.

88 MDA, *1986 Annual Report*, 4–5; MDA, *1987 Annual Report*, 2–4; interviews with Wallis, Dollard, MacDonald (18 January 1993), Pitts (6 May 1993), Morris, and Caddey; and L.W. Carlson to J. Richardson, "Forestry MEIS Proposal," 13 August 1986, RG39, LAC. In addition, see Brooks, *Mythical Man-Month*, 163–203.

89 Interviews with Wallis, Dollard, MacDonald (18 January 1993), Pitts (6 May 1993), Morris, and Caddey.

90 Interview with Caddey.

91 Interview with Prentice; and interviews with Friedmann, Wallis, Dollard, MacDonald (18 January 1993), and Pitts (6 May 1993).

92 Interviews with Friedmann, Wallis, Dollard, Pitts (6 May 1993), and Caddey.

93 Interview with Pitts (6 May 1993); and interviews with Sloan, MacDonald (7 and 18 January 1993), Maxwell, Morris, and Renwick and Seymour.

94 Faustmann, "John MacDonald Had a Firm"; MDA, *1986 Annual Report*, 4–5; MDA, *1987 Annual Report*, 2–4; and interviews with Friedmann, Wallis, Pitts (6 May 1993), and Caddey.

95 Interviews with Friedmann, Dollard, Widmer, and Caddey. In addition, see Innes, Perry, and Lyon, "In a Class."

96 Ibid.; and MDA, *1987 Annual Report*, 2–4.

97 Interview with Friedmann.

98 Interview with Cwynar; interviews with Friedmann, Wallis, MacDonald (18 January 1993), and Pitts (6 May 1993); Faustmann, "John MacDonald Had a Firm," 53; and MDA, *1987 Annual Report*, 3–4; and MDA, *1988 Annual Report*.

99 MDA, *1987 Annual Report*.

CHAPTER SIX

1 Interview with Cwynar; and interviews with Friedmann, Murray, Gelbart, Prentice, MacDonald (18 January 1993), Wallis, Dollard, and Pitts (6 May 1993).

2 Clinton J. Edmonds, regional director general, Environment Canada, Atlantic Region, to Jacques Gérin, deputy minister, Environment Canada, National Capital Region, re: "Closure of Shoe Cove Satellite Tracking Station in Newfoundland," 10 January 1983, 1–3, RG39, LAC. In addition, see director-general, Policy Directorate, Corporate Planning Group to Distribution, Government of Canada Memorandum, re: "Earth Observation by Satellite," 11 September 1979, 2–3, and "Discussion Paper: Earth Observation by Satellite – Continued Participation by Canada in the U.S. LANDSAT Program," 4 September 1979, 1–5, RG39, LAC; and Pounder, *Seasat.* With plans underway to have SPAR Aerospace and its subcontractors build Canada's new *Radarsat* satellite (originally scheduled for launch in 1988 but delayed until 1995), the CCRS decided to maintain the Prince Albert station and move Shoe Cove's equipment to Churchill, Manitoba. During 1984, the CCRS then shut down the Shoe Cove facility.

3 Interviews with Cwynar, MacDonald (18 January 1993), Wallis, Pitts (6 May 1993), and W. Bennett.

4 Interview with Pitts (6 May 1993).

5 MDA, *1986 Annual Report*, 6–7; interviews with Friedmann, Prentice, Cwynar, Wallis, Dollard, MacDonald (18 January 1993), and Pitts (6 May 1993); and Faustmann, "John MacDonald Had a Firm," 60–6.

6 McDowall, "Fin de siècle," 176.

7 Interview with Sloan.

8 Interview with MacDonald (18 January 1993).

9 Interviews with Friedmann, Murray, Gelbart, Prentice, Cwynar, Dettwiler (11 January 1993), MacDonald (18 January 1993), Pitts (6 May 1993), and W. Bennett; MDA, *1986 Annual Report*, 6–7; and Klassen, "Canada and the New Imperialism," 163–90.

10 Interviews with Friedmann, Murray, Gelbart, Prentice, Cwynar, Dettwiler (11 January 1993), MacDonald (18 January 1993), Pitts (6 May 1993), and W. Bennett.

11 Interviews with Pitts (6 May 1993), and Maxwell; and McCartin, *Collision Course*.

12 Interview with Maxwell.

13 Ibid.; and interviews with MacDonald (18 January 1993), Thompson (15 January 1993), and Pitts (6 May 1993).

14 Interviews with Thompson (15 January 1993), and Renwick and Seymour; and Dempsey, *Flying Blind*.

15 MDA, *1993 Annual Report*; MDA, *1992 Annual Report*; MDA, *1991 Annual Report*; MDA, *1990 Annual Report*; and interviews with Friedmann, Druce, Dettwiler (11 January 1993), Allan, MacDonald (18 January 1993), Pitts (6 May 1993), and Caddey.

16 MDA, *1986 Annual Report*, 6–7; MDA, *1987 Annual Report*, 7–8; MDA, *1989 Annual Report*, 13, *Frontiers in Digital Mapping*, and *IRIS*; interviews with Friedmann, J. Bennett, Wallis, Widmer, George, MacDonald (18 January 1993), Pitts (6 May 1993), and McConnell; L.W. Carlson to J. Richardson, "Forestry MEIS Proposal," 13 August 1986, RG39, LAC; and Johnson, "Three Approaches."

17 Interviews with J. Bennett, Widmer, George, MacDonald (18 January 1993), and McConnell; and Auditor General of Canada, "Major Capital Projects."

18 Interviews with J. Bennett; interviews with Friedmann, Wallis, MacDonald (18 January 1993), and Pitts (6 May 1993); and MDA, *1987 Annual Report*, 7–8.

19 Interview with J. Bennett; interviews with Friedmann, Wallis, MacDonald (18 January 1993), and Pitts (6 May 1993); and MDA, *1990 Annual Report*.

20 MDA, *IRIS*; interviews with Friedmann, J. Bennett, Wallis, Widmer, George,

MacDonald (18 January 1993), and Pitts (6 May 1993); and UN, "Report on the United Nations/International Astronautical Federation Workshop."

21 Interviews with MacDonald (18 January 1993), Pitts (6 May 1993), and Immega.

22 Dotto, *Heritage of Excellence*, 23–38, 62–76, and 102–3, LAC; Canada, Task Force on Program Review, *Government Procurement, "Spending Smarter,"* 233–59, LAC; Department of External Affairs, SPAR Briefing (1993), RG25, vol. 27446, LAC; Canada Audit, Evaluation and Review Directorate, "Evaluation of the Major Crown Project"; and Beaumier, "Innovation in Canada," 25–33, LAC.

23 Dotto, *Heritage of Excellence*, 63–4. In addition, see Canada Audit, Evaluation and Review Directorate, "Evaluation of the Major Crown Project."

24 Canada, Ministry of State, Science and Technology, "Building on Our Strengths."

25 Canada, Task Force on Program Review, *Government Procurement, "Spending Smarter,"* 195, 212–15, 231–3, and 258–9, LAC.

26 Interview with Immega. In addition, see Canada Audit, Evaluation and Review Directorate, "Evaluation of the Major Crown Project," LAC; Dotto, *Heritage of Excellence*, 63–4, LAC; Doutriaux, "Government Procurement," 1–2 and 12–13, LAC; Brooks, *Flesh and Machine*; Immega, "KSI Tentacle Manipulator," 3149–54; and Neufeld, "Hegemony and Foreign Policy," 20–3.

27 Interviews with Friedmann, Maxwell, MacDonald (18 January 1993), Pitts (6 May 1993), and Immega.

28 Ibid. In addition, see Allen and Wallach, "Moral Machines"; Singer, *Wired for War*, 135–49 and 413–35; Billings, "To the Moon"; and Sà and Litwin, "University-Industrial Research Collaboration." Smardon, *Asleep at the Switch*, 325–6, argues that Mulroney's government located low R&D activities in Canada to a "failure of university research to connect more closely with the processes of commercialization in the market." He therefore based the expansion of the "Networks of Centres of Excellence" (NCE) program on "the notion that university research needed to be linked to a market-based logic by increasing the role of universities with private capital through public sector 'partnerships' with private sector organizations." When Mulroney's government eliminated MOSST and the Ministry of Regional Industrial Expansion, and created Industry, Science and Technology Canada (ISTC) in 1990, the federal government fully embraced the ideas of the "innovation process" in vogue at business schools and the OECD.

29 Mosco, *Digital Sublime*, 111; and interviews with Friedmann, Maxwell, MacDonald (18 January 1993), Pitts (6 May 1993), and Immega. In addition, see Allen and Wallach, "Moral Machines"; Singer, *Wired for War*, 135–49 and

413–35; Billings, "To the Moon"; Sà and Litwin, "University-Industrial Research Collaboration"; and Smardon, *Asleep at the Switch*, 325–6.

30 Interview with Immega; Byers and Franks, "Unmanned and Unnecessary"; and Immega, "Change of Heart," 7–13.

31 Interview with MacDonald (18 January 1993).

32 Interviews with Murray, Gelbart, MacDonald (18 January 1993), and Prentice; and MDA, *1989 Annual Report*, 12–19.

33 Interview with Gelbart; and interview with Maxwell.

34 MDA, *1986 Annual Report*, 6–7; and interviews with Murray, Gelbart, MacDonald (18 January 1993), and Pitts (6 May 1993). In addition, see Voyer and Ryan, *New Innovators*, 84–94.

35 MDA, *1986 Annual Report*, 6–7; and interviews with Friedmann, Murray, Lapp, Prentice, Cwynar, MacDonald (18 January 1993), and Pitts (6 May 1993). In addition, see Wallace and Erickson, *Hard Drive*, 326.

36 Interviews with Lapp, MacDonald (18 January 1993), and Pitts (6 May 1993).

37 Larry Clark, qtd in Dotto, *Heritage of Excellence*, 109, LAC.

38 Dotto, *Heritage of Excellence*, 103–21, LAC.

39 Lawrence Surtees, "Satellite to Probe Polar Waters," *Globe and Mail*, 26 June 1987. In addition, see Dotto, *Heritage of Excellence*, 105–18.

40 Smith-Eievemark, "Thin Ice," 12.

41 Interviews with Friedmann, Murray, Beattie, Prentice, Cwynar, MacDonald (18 January 1993), and Pitts (6 May 1993).

42 Interviews with Friedmann, Murray, Prentice, Cwynar, MacDonald (18 January 1993), and Pitts (6 May 1993).

43 Interviews with Murray, Cwynar, and Pitts (6 May 1993); and Michael McCullough, "CREO: The Digitization Printing Company That Could Have Saved Kodak; Kodak Ruined the One Company That Might Have Saved It," *Canadian Business*, 16 February 2012. Following its failure to make a quick transition to digital photography after global competitors introduced new products during the 1990s, Kodak ultimately appreciated what Dan Gelbart had achieved with the FIRE and digital printing; indeed, in an effort to regain market share during 2005, Kodak acquired CREO, the firm Gelbart and Ken Spencer formed in 1983. But even the US$980 million acquisition could not save Kodak, its Canadian CREO subsidiary, or other North American manufacturers.

44 Interviews with Murray, Prentice, Cwynar, and Pitts (6 May 1993).

45 Interviews with Murray, and Pitts (6 May 1993).

46 Interviews with Murray, Prentice, Friedmann, Prentice, Cwynar, MacDonald (18 January 1993), and Pitts (6 May 1993); and MDA, *1997 Annual Report*, 5–6; and MDA, *1988 Annual Report*.

47 Interview with Wallis.

48 Interview with Friedmann; interviews with Murray, Prentice, Cwynar, Wallis, MacDonald (18 January 1993), and Pitts (6 May 1993); MDA, *1987 Annual Report*, 5–6; and MDA, *1989 Annual Report*, 12–19.

49 MDA, *1987 Annual Report*, 5–6; MDA, *1988 Annual Report*; MDA, *1989 Annual Report*; and interviews with Friedmann, Murray, Prentice, Cwynar, MacDonald (18 January 1993), and Pitts (6 May 1993).

50 Ibid.

51 Interview with Pitts (6 May 1993), and Wallace; and Erikson, *Hard Drive*.

52 John Pitts, qtd in "Ecuador to Buy Ground Stations," *Richmond News*, 23 December 1987; and interviews with Clark, Friedmann, Wallis, MacDonald (18 January 1993), and Pitts (6 May 1993).

53 Andrea Gordon, "Canadian Firm Leads the Way to Making 21st-Century Maps," *Toronto Star*, 8 September 1987; EDS *Today*, "Export Development Canada," 1; MDA, *1988 Annual Report*; MDA, *AWDS;* and interviews with Friedmann, Wallis, Dollard, MacDonald (18 January 1993), Pitts (6 May 1993), and Caddey.

54 Interview with Clark.

55 Interview with Friedmann; and interviews with Prentice, Cwynar, and MacDonald (18 January 1993).

56 *1988 Annual Report*.

CHAPTER SEVEN

1 MDA, *1988 Annual Report*; MDA, *AWDS*; Lawrence Surtees, "Satellite to Probe Polar Waters," *Globe and Mail*, 26 June 1987; *Electronics Communicator*, "MDA Secures Second Order"; "MDA Wins Big Contract," *Richmond Review*, 14 September 1987; COSSA *Space Industry News*, "Industrial Award"; "MacDonald Dettwiler to Receive $3.3 Million under Defence Plan," *Globe and Mail*, 10 May 1988; *Electronic Products and Technology*, "MacDonald Dettwiler Focus," 2; "Space Station Sparks Drive for New Heights," *Vancouver Sun*, 24 February 1988; *Wednesday Report*, "MacDonald Dettwiler Pursues Defence," 2; and Christopher P. Fotos, "Commercial Remote Sensing Satellites Generate Debate, Foreign Competition," *Aviation Week and Space Technology*, 19 December 1988, 48.

2 Interviews with Friedmann, Beattie, McDonald, Cwynar, Wallis, George, Dollard, MacDonald (18 January 1993), Pitts (6 May 1993), Caddey, and W. Bennett; MDA, *1993 Annual Report*; and MDA, *1989 Annual Report*.

3 Mattelart, *Globalization of Surveillance*, 117–61. In addition, see Marchildon, "Canadian Multinationals"; and Darroch, "Global Competitiveness and Pub-

lic Policy." For an alternative view, see Granatstein, *Who Killed the Canadian Military*, 174–202.

4 Chang, *Bad Samaritans*, 16–17 as well as 48–95.

5 Klassen, "Canada and the New Imperialism," 163–90.

6 Smardon, *Asleep at the Switch*, 302, 297, and 321.

7 Interviews with Friedmann, Wallis, Dollard, Pitts (6 May 1993), and Caddey.

8 "MDA Wins Big Contract," *Richmond Review*, 14 September 1987; "Space Station Sparks Drive for New Heights," *Vancouver Sun*, 24 February 1988; and Christopher P. Fotos, "Commercial Remote Sensing Satellites Generate Debate, Foreign Competition," *Aviation Week and Space Technology*, 19 December 1988, 48; and interview with Pitts (6 May 1993).

9 *Wednesday Report*, "MacDonald Dettwiler Pursues Defence"; interview with McDonald; MDA, *1993 Annual Report*; MDA, *1992 Annual Report*; and interviews with Friedmann, and J. Bennett.

10 "MacDonald Dettwiler Getting Classy Home," *Province*, 2 March 1988; MDA, *1988 Annual Report*; and MDA, *1989 Annual Report*, 6–19.

11 Interview with MacDonald (18 January 1993).

12 Interview with Wallis.

13 Interviews with Friedmann, Wallis, Dollard, MacDonald (18 January 1993), Pitts (6 May 1993), and Caddey.

14 Interview with MacDonald (18 January 1993); interviews with Friedmann, Wallis, Pitts (6 May 1993), and Caddey; and MDA, *1989 Annual Report*, 15–19. In addition, see Kumar, *Mega Mergers*, 60–95.

15 Interview with Beattie; and interviews with Friedmann, Wallis, Dollard, Pitts (6 May 1993), and Caddey.

16 Interview with Caddey; and interviews with Friedmann, Wallis, Dollard, MacDonald (18 January 1993), and Pitts (6 May 1993).

17 Interview with Clark; and interviews with Friedmann, Beattie, Wallis, Dollard, MacDonald (18 January 1993), and Pitts (6 May 1993).

18 Interview with Pitts (6 May 1993). In addition, see United States House of Representatives, *Defense Manufacturing*; and Moss, *When All Else Fails*.

19 Interview with MacDonald (18 January 1993); and interviews with Friedmann, Wallis, Dollard, and Pitts (6 May 1993).

20 Interviews with Friedmann, Beattie, Wallis, Dollard, MacDonald (18 January 1993), and Pitts (6 May 1993); and Yang, "Magic Mountain." In addition, see OECD, *Economic Surveys Canada, 1987–1988*, and *Economic Surveys Canada, 1988–1989*.

21 Interviews with Friedmann, Wallis, Dollard, MacDonald (18 January 1993), and Pitts (6 May 1993). In addition, see Mattelart, *Globalization of Surveillance*, 117–61.

22 Friedmann, interview; interviews with Wallis, MacDonald (18 January 1993), and Pitts (6 May 1993); MDA, *1989 Annual Report*, 12–19; and MDA, *1993 Annual Report*.

23 Interviews with Friedmann, Beattie, Cwynar, Wallis, MacDonald (18 January 1993), and Pitts (6 May 1993).

24 Ibid. MDA subsidized Friedmann's graduate work in physics and electrical engineering at UBC, which he completed during 1983.

25 Interview with Friedmann.

26 Interview with Caddey.

27 Interview with Friedman; MDA, *1993 Annual Report*, 16–18; and interviews with Wallis, Widmer, MacDonald (18 January 1993), Pitts (6 May 1993), and Caddey. Cymbolic Sciences was eventually acquired by Océ N.V. of the Netherlands, which Canon of Japan then acquired in 2010.

28 Interview with McConnell.

29 Interview with Widmer.

30 Interview with McDonald.

31 Interview with Caddey; interviews with Pitts (14 December 1992 and 6 May 1993), Friedmann, Prentice, Allan, Cwynar, J. Bennett, Wallis, and Mac-Donald (18 January 1993); and MDA, *1993 Annual Report*, 16–18; MDA, *1991 Annual Report*; and MDA, *1990 Annual Report*.

32 Interviews with Friedmann, George, Pitts (6 May 1993), and Kauffman.

33 Canadian Space Agency, "$195 Million Federal Government Contract," and "Richmond Company Awarded"; and Jennifer Clibbon, "BC Firm Wins Deal in China," *Vancouver Sun*, 21 April 1992.

34 Interview with Pitts (6 May 1993); interviews with Friedman, Wallis, Widmer, MacDonald (18 January 1993), and Caddey; and MDA, *1993 Annual Report*, 16–18.

35 Interview with J. Bennett; MDA, *1992 Annual Report*, 16–18; MDA, "CAATS Technical Description"; and MDA, *Advanced Systems for Defence*.

36 Interview with J. Bennett. In addition, see Beppl Crosarlo, "Canada's $1.2-Billion Space Program Ripoff," *Financial Times of Canada*, 6 July 1992.

37 Interview with George.

38 Interview with Lapp.

39 Interview with Morley; and Dotto, *Heritage of Excellence*, 26 and 118–19, LAC.

40 Interview with MacDonald (18 January 1993).

41 Interview with W. Bennett.

42 Interview with J. Bennett; interviews with Friedmann, Prentice, Cwynar, Wallis, MacDonald (18 January 1993), Pitts (6 May 1993), and Caddey; MDA, *1993 Annual Report*, 16–18; and MDA, *Annual Report*; and Smith, "Growing Pains in Lotusland."

43 Interview with George; interviews with Friedmann, McDonald, MacDonald (18 January 1993), Immega, McConnell, and Kauffman; and MDA, *1993 Annual Report*. For comparative purposes, see Laird, *Pull*, 137–77.

44 Interview with Friedmann.

45 Interview with McDonald; and interviews with Friedmann, George, MacDonald (18 January 1993), Immega, McConnell, and Kauffman.

46 Interview with Immega; interviews with Friedmann, Wallis, Dollard, Pitts (6 May 1993), and Caddey; and MDA, *1993 Annual Report*.

47 Interview with Pitts (6 May 1993).

48 MDA, *1992 Annual Report*, 2; *Defense Science*, "Canadian Defense Industry Profiles"; and interviews with Wallis, MacDonald (18 January 1993), and Pitts (6 May 1993). Officially established by the Maastricht Treaty on 7 February 1992, the EU created the single European currency euro and introduced European citizenship during 1993.

49 Interview with Clark; interviews with Friedmann, Cwynar, Wallis, MacDonald (18 January 1993), and Pitts (6 May 1993); and MDA, *1990 Annual Report*.

50 Interviews with MacDonald (18 January 1993), and McConnell; Mattelart, *Globalization of Surveillance*, 117–96; Mosco, *Digital Sublime*, 117–84; Guy, "Shadow Architectures"; and Farish, "Another Anxious Urbanism."

51 Rossignol, "Missile Defence," 1 and 21; and Hart and Dymond, "Common Borders," 32.

52 MDA, *1993 Annual Report*; MDA, *1992 Annual Report*; and interviews with Friedmann, Wallis, MacDonald (18 January 1993), Pitts (6 May 1993), and Caddey.

53 "Uses of Heaven: A Survey of Space," *Economist*, 15 June 1991, 3.

54 Ibid., 3–4.

55 Ibid., 16–8.

56 Philip Shabecoff, "World's Legislators Urge 'Marshall Plan' for the Environment," *New York Times*, 3 May 1990.

57 Brian Mulroney, qtd in McDowall, *Sum of the Satisfactions*, 241.

58 Interviews with Widmer, and MacDonald (18 January 1993).

59 Abbate, "Government, Business."

60 Interviews with Friedmann, Wallis, Pitts (6 May 1993), and Caddey; and MDA, *1993 Annual Report*.

61 Interview with MacDonald (18 January 1993); and interview with Widmer.

62 Interview with Pitts (6 May 1993); and interviews with MacDonald (18 January 1993), Friedmann, Wallis, Widmer, and Caddey.

63 Interview with Friedmann; MDA, *1993 Annual Report*, 16–18; MDA, *1992 Annual Report*, 2; and MDA, *Advanced Airspace Management*.

64 MDA, *1993 Annual Report*; MDA, *1992 Annual Report*; and interviews with

Friedmann, Wallis, MacDonald (18 January 1993), Pitts (6 May 1993), and Caddey. In addition, see Maloney, "Better Late Than Never."

65 Interview with Prentice; MDA, *1993 Annual Report*; MDA, *1992 Annual Report*; Frederic Tomesco, "SNC-Lavalin Tumbles Most in 20 Years Amid Payments Inquiry: Montreal Mover," *Bloomberg News*, 28 February 2012; Hadekel, *Silent Partners*; and interviews with Friedmann, McDonald, and J. Bennett.

66 Interview with Clark; and interviews with Friedmann, McDonald, and J. Bennett.

67 Interview with George; interviews with Clark, Friedmann, McDonald, J. Bennett, and Dollard.

68 Interviews with Lapp, MacDonald (18 January 1993), and Pitts (6 May 1993); and Dotto, *Heritage of Excellence*, 7, LAC.

69 Department of External Affairs, SPAR Briefing (1993), 6, RG25, vol. 27446, LAC.

70 Dotto, *Heritage of Excellence*, 7, LAC; Department of External Affairs, SPAR Briefing (1993), 6, RG25, vol. 27446, LAC; and interviews with Lapp, Mac-Donald (18 January 1993), Pitts (6 May 1993), and W. Bennett.

71 Interviews with Lapp, MacDonald (18 January 1993), and Pitts (6 May 1993); Mark Wilson, "SPAR Aims for MDA," *Province*, 18 March 1992; and SPAR, "SPAR Bid."

72 Interview with Lapp; and interviews with Prentice, Dettwiler (11 January 1993), MacDonald (18 January 1993), and Pitts (6 May 1993).

73 Interview with Lapp; and interview with MacDonald (18 January 1993).

74 Interview with MacDonald (8 January 1993); interviews with Friedmann, and Pitts (6 May 1993); and David Smith, "Buyout Sparring Sidetracks Deal with Richmond Firm," *Vancouver Sun*, 8 July 1992.

75 Interview with MacDonald (18 January 1993); interviews with Friedmann, and Pitts (6 May 1993); MDA, *1993 Annual Report*; and MDA, *1992 Annual Report*.

76 MDA, *1993 Annual Report*, 16–18; MDA, *1992 Annual Report*, 2; MDA, *Advanced Airspace Management*; and interview with Friedmann.

77 Knapp, "Masters of the Universe," 119–21.

78 Ibid., 121; MDA, *1993 Annual Report*, 3 and 20; and MacDonald, "Survival in a Knowledge-Based World," 6. In addition, see Yang, "Magic Mountain," 22; and Chodos, Murphy, and Hamovitch, *Lost in Cyberspace*, 12.

CHAPTER EIGHT

1 Brooke, *Divided Loyalties*, 244–65; Martin, *Iron Man*, 65–86; Granatstein, *Who Killed the Canadian Military*, 160–5; and MDA, *1994 Annual Report*. Clinton signed the omnibus bill into law on 10 August 1993.

2 Interview with Wallis.

3 Governor General of Canada, "Order of Canada."

4 Interview with Maxwell.

5 Interview with McConnell.

6 Interview with Spencer. In addition, see Smith, "Growing Pains in Lotus-land," 108.

7 Interview with Pitts (6 May 1993).

8 Interview with Dollard. ˙

9 Interview with Friedmann.

10 MDA, *1993 Annual Report*, 11–12.

11 Interview with Wallis.

12 Interview with MacDonald (18 January 1993).

13 Interview with Dettwiler (11 January 1993).

14 MDA, *1993 Annual Report*, 1.

15 "MacDonald Dettwiler and Associates Ltd Lists on the VSE," PR Newswire, 9 August 1993.

16 MDA, *1994 Annual Report*, 1–5; and CSA, "Canadian Satellite RADARSAT-1."

17 Abbate, "Government, Business"; and Monmonier, *Spying with Maps*, 15–16.

18 Newton, "'Visionary Hope' Frustrated"; Caufield, *Masters of Illusion*; Pollard, *International Economy*; and Mikesell, *Bretton Woods Debates*.

19 See McDougall, *Drifting Together*; Urmetzer, *Free Trade to Forced Trade*; Joe Castaldo, "Not So Free Trade," *Canadian Business*, 12 May 2008; and Andrew Coyne, "Canada at the Crossroads of Trade," *National Post*, 16 March 2012. By the time government officials had implemented all of its policies in 2008, NAFTA ended tariffs on various goods and services, and covered wide-ranging agreements on everything from agricultural and automobile trades to environmental policies, intellectual property, the mobility of workers, and telecommunications. NAFTA also escalated American and Canadian de-industrialization, and, as many have argued, ultimately benefitted a cadre of elites in the United States, Canada, and Mexico while simultaneously contributing to rising levels of inequality and poverty at home and abroad. As a strategic partner of the United States since World War II, Canada continued to link its future to the world's remaining superpower, even when it entered into other strategic partnerships and free trade agreements with Chile and Israel in 1997, and a global list of agreements reached or in negotiation during the twenty-first century.

20 Goldman and Ross, "Diffusion of Military Technology and Ideas," 379. In addition, see Haussman and Biette, "Buy American or Buy Canadian?" 134.

21 Rossignol, "Missile Defence," 3–5. In addition, see United States Department of State, "Memorandum of Understanding," 2–3 and 6–9; and Hart and

Dymond, "Common Borders," 10–11. Chang, *Bad Samaritans*, 23, has argued that "the result of all of these developments, according to the official history, is a globalized world economy comparable in its liberality and potential for prosperity only to the earlier 'golden age' of liberalism (1870–1913)," an era he described as one now remembered for its exploitation of untold millions. Regardless, that "version of the history of globalization is widely accepted," Chang lamented during 2008, painting "a fundamentally misleading picture, distorting our understanding of where we have come from, and where we are now and where we may be heading." Chang also argued that the neoliberal project dominated by the United States and its allies in the WTO and World Bank created the context for global inequality and a deepening historical amnesia about how the world economy has operated since the Uruguay Round. In addition, see Stiglitz, *Globalization and Its Discontents*; and Anderson and Cavanaugh, *Rise of Corporate Global Power*.

22 Lajeunesse and Carruthers, "Ice Has Ears," 6. John S. MacDonald to Sheila Copps, deputy prime minister and minister of the environment, re: "Arctic Sovereignty and Environmental Protection," 8 December 1994, Department of Communications, Central Registry File, RG108-A, vol. 1248, LAC, argued, "The Liberal Party, both in and out of power, has been a strong supporter of Arctic sovereignty assertion. Mr Chrétien and Mr Axworthy, among many, have frequently made strong statements in the House on this subject. Defence policy reviews over the past quarter century have consistently given high priority to Arctic sovereignty protection. The latest Defence Policy Review [November 1994] confirms that 'Task 1: [is] Protecting Canada's Territorial Sovereignty.' This requires at minimum a capability to survey and control Canadian airspace and waters, particularly in the Arctic. The economic benefit to Canadian industry will be significant," MacDonald asserted. "The prime contractor will be a Canadian company and a large portion of the project funds will be used to procure high technology equipment in Canada. The cost of Arctic Subsurface Surveillance System is significantly less than the price Canadians are paying to protect the sovereignty of the factions in the former Jugoslavia. The Liberals criticized the former government in 1990 for putting a price on Arctic sovereignty. They are now in a position to avoid the same mistake."

23 Sheila Copps, deputy prime minister and minister of the environment, to John MacNaughton, president and chief executive officer, SPAR Aerospace Limited, 24 January 1996, Department of Communications, Departmental Correspondence, RG108-A, vol. 1343, file 136521 (hereafter RG108-A, vol. 1343), LAC.

24 Interview with MacDonald (18 January 1993). In addition, see MacDonald,

"Systems Engineering," 1–6; Chang, *Bad Samaritans*, 1–68; and Hedges, *War Is a Force.*

25 CAI Private Equity, "About CAI." In addition, see Powell, *History of the Canadian Dollar*, 76–86; and *Wikinvest*, "MacDonald Dettwiler, Minimum Adjusted Stock Price, 1994–2014."

26 United States Securities and Exchange Commission, *Orbital Sciences.*

27 "MacDonald Dettwiler Appoints New President and CEO," *Business Wire*, 15 March 1995; "Orbital Sciences Acquires Ground Station Firm (MacDonald, Dettwiler and Associates Ltd)," 2 August 1995; and "OSC, MacDonald, Dettwiler Agree on $67 Million Merger," *Defense Daily*, 6 September 1995.

28 "Orbital Sciences Deal," *New York Times*, 6 September 1995; and David Pugliese, "Secret Military Eye in the Sky," *Ottawa Citizen*, 15 March 2000.

29 Mark Wilson, "Radarsat Unfurls Antenna in Space," *Vancouver Province*, 10 November 1995; NASA, "Radarsat Launch"; MDA, "MDA to Acquire Iotek"; and CSA, "Canadian Satellite RADARSAT-1."

30 Department of External Affairs, SPAR Briefing (1993), RG25, vol. 27446, LAC; David Berman, "When Bad Companies Happen to Good People," *Canadian Business*, 27 March 1998, 78–81; and Hannaford, "Strategic Analysis," 8–69.

31 Copps to MacNaughton, 24 January 1996, RG108-A, vol. 1343, LAC. In addition, see CSA, "Canadian Satellite RADARSAT-1."

32 Smardon, *Asleep at the Switch*, 348, 351–2, and 355. Despite concerns about technological dependence on the United States and low levels of R&D in Canada, government documents reveal that Canadian policymakers from Mulroney's government forward believed that more was at stake than from whom Canadian firms accessed capital. They approved foreign takeovers because they also wanted access to the secret world of the American military-industrial complex. Haussman and Biette, "Buy American or Buy Canadian?," 129, thus argued that, like their American counterparts, Canadian policymakers "negotiated their trade procurement laws so that each can 'have their cake and eat it too.' Whether bound by WTO rules, NAFTA rules, or other trade agreements," they noted, "certain industries and realms of procurement remain protected. Loopholes also give important political cover." Klassen, "Canada and the New Imperialism," 184–5, suggests that "Canadian corporations have a worldwide base of accumulation from which to generate surplus value and thus have an independent interest in the new imperialism," including the "political project of neoliberalism" that "cannot be seen as a 'hollowed out' or 'comprador' class." Heavily invested in that project, Canadian policymakers knew precisely whose interests they served. In addition, see Doern and Maslove, *Thirty Years of Watching*, 1–10.

33 "Sad Day for Spar Aerospace," CBC News, 12 January 1999; "BC Firm to Build

Radar Satellite," *Vancouver Sun*, 25 February 1998; and Reference for Business, "Spar Aerospace."

34 United States Congress, *Public Law*; Warren E. Leary, "Scientists Fear Deep Budget Cuts Will Keep NASA Too Earthbound," *New York Times*, 31 July 1999; Berman, "When Bad Companies Happen to Good People," 78–81; CSA, *Performance Report*, 32–5; Treasury Board of Canada, "Status Report"; and Department of External Affairs, SPAR Briefing (1993), RG25, vol. 27446, LAC.

35 "Sad Day for Spar Aerospace," CBC News; MDA, "MacDonald, Dettwiler Announces Worldwide"; MDA, "MacDonald, Dettwiler to Acquire Radarsat International"; "The Americarm?: U.S. Company Will Keep the Name of Canadarm," *Maclean's*, 29 March 1999, 5; "Americans Gobbling Up Our High-Tech Firms," *Winnipeg Free Press*, 23 March 1999; "Future of Canadian Firm That Built Famed Canadarm Is Up in the Air," *Winnipeg Free Press*, 14 May 1999; D'Arcy Jenish, "'Will Spar Survive?' Disgruntled Investors May Dismantle High-Tech Icon," *Maclean's*, April 1999; Robert Wright, "Private Eyes," *New York Times*, 5 September 1999; "Spar Shareholders Want Board Purged," CBC News, 10 November 2000; and Sanders, "'Missile Defense' Alive and Well."

36 Matthew McClearn, "The Long Arm of MDA," *Canadian Business*, 14 May 2001; MDA, 2000 *Annual Report*, 34; and "Orbital Sciences Sells 33% Stake in Robotics Business," *New York Times*, 24 December 1999. According to CAI Private Equity, "About CAI," Peter Ressler had served as "a special advisor to Vancouver-based Inland Natural Gas (now Terasen) in connection with its successful acquisition of the $741 million gas division of BC Hydro, a provincially owned utility." Later board members included Brian Kenning, a managing partner in Brookfield Asset Management. International Astronautical Federation, "About," notes that IAF, founded in 1951 and headquartered in Paris, represented approximately 95 per cent of the world's national-government space budgets by the end of 2012, giving its industry members closer access to the UN and its 200-plus members from nearly sixty countries around the world.

37 Sanders, "We Didn't Really Say 'No.'" In addition, see Brender, "Will It Sow."

38 MDA, "MDA to Provide the U.S. Air Force." In addition, see McClearn, "Long Arm of MDA."

39 United States Federal Communications Commission, Telecommunications Act. In addition, see Intelsat, "Intelsat Announces Completion." During 2005, Zeus Holdings Limited, a firm formed by several investment firms, acquired Intelsat; and two years later, in one of the largest leveraged buyouts in history, Serafina Holdings, Limited, a company formed by BC Partners, Silver Lake, and other equity firms, acquired Intelsat for US$16.6 billion.

40 Martin Mitchell, "Citicorp and Travelers Plan to Merge in Record $70 Billion Deal," *New York Times*, 7 April 1998. In addition, see Eric Dash, "U.S. Approves Plan to Help Citigroup Weather Losses," *New York Times*, 23 November 2008. Reinhart and Rogoff, *This Time It's Different*, provide an excellent overview of financial crises within larger historical and global contexts.

41 Mosco, *Digital Sublime*, 4. In addition, see Damian Carrington, "Was Y2K Bug a Boost?," BBC News, 4 January 2000; and Lowenstein, *Origins of the Crash*.

42 Harris, "North American Economic Integration," 7–8.

43 McClearn, "Long Arm of MDA."

44 MDA, 2000 *Annual Report*, 2.

45 McClearn, "Long Arm of MDA." In addition, see "MacDonald-Dettwiler Buys U.S. Mapping Firm for $2.4 Million," *Ottawa Business Journal*, 10 October 2000; Volker, "Technology Futures"; and Lexpert, "MacDonald, Dettwiler Secures $190M."

46 MDA, 2000 *Annual Report*, 3.

47 MDA, "MacDonald Dettwiler Awarded $106.5 Million"; and MDA, 2001 *Annual Report*; Boeing, "Boeing Wins Contract to Launch RADARSAT-2 in 2003," *SpaceRef*, 28 June 2000; Treasury Board of Canada, "Status Report"; and "Orbital Sciences Seeking Sale of Canadian MacDonald Dettwiler and Associates," *Space and Tech Digest*, 26 February 2001.

48 Volker, "Technology Futures"; "Orbital Sciences Sells 33% Stake in Robotics Business," *New York Times*, 24 December 1999; "Canadians Take Stake in MacDonald Dettwiler Again," *National Post*, 24 December 1999; MDA, "MDA Repatriates RADARSAT-2"; "Orbital Sciences Canadian Subsidiary Files for IPO," *Space and Tech Digest*, 29 May 2000; PR Newswire, "Orbital's MDA Subsidiary Completes $57 Million Initial Public Offering: Company Remains MDA's Majority Shareholder with about 55% Ownership Stake," 12 July 2000; and Frank Morring Jr, "In Orbit," *Aviation Week and Space Technology*, 29 September 2003.

49 "MacDonald Dettwiler Launches on the TSE," CBC News, 11 November 2000.

50 "Orbital Completes Final Phase of MDA Divestiture," *Aerotech News and Review*, 20 July 2001; and "Orbital Science Corp. Announces Asset Sale," CNBC, 17 April 2001.

51 McClearn, "Long Arm of MDA."

52 See Mussio, *Telecom Nation*, 65–8, 92–3, 97–114, and 222–7. According to Phillips and Castle, "Science and Technology Spending," 174, 178, and 183, "After more than a century of 'industrial policy,'" Chrétien's Liberals began a

process to develop "an explicit 'innovation agenda,' ultimately embodied in two statements entitled *Achieving Excellence* and *Knowledge Matters.*" Setting a goal to raise "Canada to rank among the top five countries in terms of R&D and commercialization outputs by 2010," Phillips and Castle contend, the new agenda "envisaged a strategic role for the federal government as funder, facilitator and performer of knowledge-based growth activities." The NRC also received a new mandate "to develop at least 10 new national innovation clusters by 2010," even if Canada lacked "the scale of the US."

CHAPTER NINE

1 Whitaker, "Keeping Up," 253–4. In addition, see Whitaker, "Faustian Bargain"; Dandeker, "Surveillance and Military Transformation"; and Haggerty, "Visible War."

2 "Iraq Hails Attack on U.S.," BBC News, 12 September 2001. In addition, see "The Reckoning: America and the World a Decade after 9/11," *New York Times* "Special Report," 11 September 2011.

3 Rogin, "Experts Debate Rumsfeld's Transformation," 13.

4 Harris, *Watchers*, 1–2.

5 Ibid., 2. In addition, see Haggerty, "Visible War"; Monmonier, *Spying with Maps*; Lewis, *Spy Capitalism*; and Lyon, *Surveillance Society*, 40–79.

6 See Alison Mitchell, "A Nation Challenged: Homeland Security; Security Quest Also Offers Opportunities," *New York Times*, 25 November 2011; Luke, "Everyday Technics as Extraordinary Threats"; Graham, *Cities under Siege*; and Niedzviecki, "Spy Who Blogged Me."

7 Kilibarda, "Canadian and Israeli Defense," 12 and 16–17. In addition, see Klein, *Shock Doctrine*, 355–407; Paul Harris, "How US Merchants of Fear Sparked a $130bn Bonanza," *Guardian*, 9 September 2006; and Coalition to Oppose the Arms Trade, "U.S. Warfighters."

8 MDA, *2001 Annual Report*; MDA, *2006 Annual Report*; and *Wikinvest*, "MacDonald Dettwiler."

9 "MDA Wins Key U.S. Aviation Contract," *SpaceRef*, 3 May 2001; Vexcel Corporation, "Vexcel Corporation Provides RADARSAT."

10 MDA, *2001 Annual Report*, 2.

11 CSA, *Radarsat Annual Review.*

12 MDA, *2002 Annual Report*, 3, 12–13, 23, and 42, and "MDA Reports 2002 4th Quarter."

13 MDA, "First Quarter 2003." In addition, see Stiglitz and Blimes, *Three Trillion Dollar War*; and op-ed contributions to "Reflections on Iraq," *New York Times*, 16 March 2008. Those voting in favour of the resolution represented 98 and

97 per cent of the Republicans in the Senate and House respectively, and 58 and 39 per cent of Democrats in the Senate and House respectively.

14 Norman Spector, "Jean Chrétien's War," *Globe and Mail*, 16 July 2009; and Martin, *Iron Man*, 402–28.

15 Staples, "Weapons Wheeler Dealers."

16 Ibid. In addition, see Simon Rogers, "Wikileaks Iraq War Logs: Every Death Mapped," *Guardian*, 22 October 2010; Maslove, *How Ottawa Spends*, 215–17 and 227–8; and Doern and Stoney, *How Ottawa Spends*, 3–28. By 2008, US spending had exceeded US$5 trillion, thereby moving a surplus of more than US$150 billion in 2001 to a total budget deficit of more than $400 billion by 2008, and increasing the US national debt from under $200 billion in 2001 to more than $1 trillion at 2008's close. Although Prime Minister Stephen Harper inherited a $13.8 billion surplus when he assumed office on 6 February 2006, Canada's budget deficits mirrored those of the United States, with Canada's deficit reaching $5.8 billion in 2008 and $55.6 billion during 2009, the largest in Canadian history. The cost in human lives remains hard to calculate, but WikiLeaks's classified Iraq war logs for January 2004 through December 2009 place the number of casualties conservatively at 109,032, including 66,081 civilian deaths.

17 Hart and Dymond, "Common Borders," 41, 31–7, and 43–6.

18 "MacDonald Dettwiler and Associates Signs RADARSAT-1 Monitoring Contract," *SpaceRef*, 16 June 2003.

19 MDA, "MDA to Participate in Provision"; MDA, "MDA Reports Year End"; and *Aero News Network*, "Canada to Build, Launch Three More Satellites: New Canadian Satellite Constellation to Assess Environmental Impacts, Ensure Sovereignty," 27 February 2005.

20 MDA, "MDA Signs Contract Valued at $154 Million"; and Jason Bates, "MacDonald Dettwiler Tied Up in Hubble's Fate," *SpaceNews*, 2 March 2005.

21 MDA, 2004 *Annual Report*, 1–4; MDA, "MDA to Participate in Provision"; MDA, "U.S. Air Force to Test"; MDA, "MDA Reports Year End"; MDA, "MDA Information Key"; and MDA, "Defence R&D Agency Awards."

22 Morena, James, and Beck, "Introduction to the Radarsat-2 Mission"; "Canada Looks to Satellite to Assert Arctic Sovereignty," *Space Daily*, 30 August 2005; "MDA to Support Arctic Surveillance by National Defence," Canada NewsWire, 4 June 2007; United States Army Space Missile Defense and Army Strategic Command, "View Offers"; and MDA, 2006 *Annual Report*, 5, 6, and 14.

23 MDA, 2007 *Annual Report*, 15–16.

24 Aerospace Industries Association, "Aerospace Industry Employment Increases after Falling to 50-Year Low," PR Newswire, 18 August 2004.

25 "Engineers Who Develop Canada's Space Robotics Are on Strike," *SpaceRef*, 6
    July 2006.
26 MDA, "Engineering Services Resume." Piketty, *Capital in the Twenty-First Cen-
    tury*, 93–7, 140–63, 199–236, 304–35, and 430–92, provides an excellent dis-
    cussion of income inequality and Canada's role in the world power core.
27 Kilibarda, "Canadian and Israeli Defense," 12 and 16–17.
28 Behiels, "Stephen Harper's Rise." In addition, see Harper, "Address."
29 Kilibarda, "Canadian and Israeli Defence, 10 and 18.
30 Marc Boucher, "Sapphire: Canada's First Military Satellite," *SpaceRef*, 6 March
    2012. In addition, see MDA, "MDA Awarded Definition Phase"; Behiels,
    "Stephen Harper's Rise"; and Jaramillo, *Space Security Index*, 17–18.
31 Canada, *Networks of Centres of Excellence*, 2 and 14. In addition, see Smardon,
    Asleep at the Switch, 366–7; and Jordan Press, "Asteroid-Tracking Satellite Not
    Up to the Job: Review," *Ottawa Citizen*, 6 July 2014.
32 MDA, "Strategic Win Strengthens MDA's Position"; Sellers et al., "Interna-
    tional Assessment"; and Phoenix Strategic Perspectives, "Corporate
    Connection," LAC.
33 MDA, 2006 *Annual Report*; and MDA, 2007 *Annual Report*.
34 Francesco Guerrera, Nicole Bullock, and Julie MacIntosh, "Wall Street 'Made
    Rod for Own Back,'" *Financial Times*, 30 October 2008. In addition, see Krug-
    man, *Return of Depression Economics*.
35 Friedmann, qtd in MDA, 2004 *Annual Report*, 3; and MDA, 2005 *Annual
    Report*, 3. In addition, see "MacDonald Dettwiler Buys U.S. Property Insur-
    ance Information Company," CBC News, 27 April 2004; and *Business Wire*,
    "Boston Ventures Announces the Completion of the Marshall & Swift Sale
    to MacDonald Dettwiler," 15 March 2006.
36 MDA, 2006 *Annual Report*, 5; and Canadian Bar Association, "Surprise
    Negotiations."
37 Automated Destruction, "Mindbox"; and Jeffrey McCracken, Zachary R.
    Mider, and Theo Argitis, "MacDonald Dettwiler Is Said to Explore Sale of
    Company, Units," *Bloomberg News*, 20 October 2010.
38 See, for example, *Silicon Valley Business Journal*, "California Foreclosure"; and
    Krugman, *Return of Depression Economics*, 118–53.
39 MDA, 2006 *Annual Report*, 5, 6, and 14; MDA, 2007 *Annual Report*, 15–16;
    Sharaput, "Harper Government Industrial Strategy"; and Marc Boucher, "The
    Transformation of MDA into a Multinational Player: Part I," *SpaceRef*, 15
    December 2014.
40 MDA, 2007 *Annual Report*, 15–16.
41 "MacDonald Dettwiler Selling Space Assets: A Report," *International Business
    Times*, 14 June 2007; "MacDonald Dettwiler Shares Up on Sales Talk," Cana-

dian Press, 14 June 2007: and "Will MacDonald Dettwiler Sell Its Space Division," *National Post*, 15 June 2007.

42 Joseph Anselmo, "Market Focus," *Aviation Week and Space Technology*, 14 January 2008.

43 "Cantech Letter Interviews Anil Wirasekara of MacDonald Dettwiler," *cantech letter*, 30 May 2011.

44 MDA, 2007 *Annual Report*, 15–16.

45 Daniel Friedmann, qtd in Craig Wong, "MDA Sells Space, Satellite Business to ATK," Canadian Press, 8 January 2008.

46 "ATK to Acquire Information Systems and Geospatial Businesses of MacDonald Dettwiler and Associates," *SpaceRef*, 8 January 2008.

47 Steven Chase, "MacDonald Dettwiler Deal Includes Key Satellite," *Globe and Mail*, 10 January 2008.

48 Paul Cottle, qtd in "Sale of Canada's Leading Satellite Developer Not Ethical," CBC News, 17 January 2008; Paul Cottle, qtd in "MDA Engineer Quits over Sale to U.S. Weapons Company," CTV News, 18 January 2008; and Trevor Williams, qtd in "Second Employee Leaves Job over Sale of Space Contractor," CBC News, 23 January 2008. In addition, see Torch, "Our New Satellite Surveillance Capability"; Gainor, "Crash of Canada's Space"; "Ruling on Sale of Canadarm Delayed," *Toronto Star*, 20 March 2008; Gainor, "Blocked Sale"; and Tom Eiko, "ATK's WMDs Ignite Protest over Canadian Acquisition," and "Canada Shoots Down Alliant Space Deal," *Minnesota Monitor*, 10 April 2008. According to Chodos, Murphy, and Hamovitch, *Lost in Cyberspace*, 12, "Canada's cultural sovereignty is protected by a variety of federal policies. However, the new technologies make it possible to circumvent many of them."

49 Vern Dettwiler, qtd in Wendy Stueck, "MDA Deal on Life Support," *Globe and Mail*, 2 May 2008.

50 John Spencer MacDonald, qtd in "Canadarm Heads South as MDA Sells Units for $1.3 Billion," Canwest News Service, 9 January 2008, in Steven Chase, "MacDonald Dettwiler Deal Includes Key Satellite," *Globe and Mail*, 10 January 2008; and Foust, "Last Chance."

51 Stephen Staples, qtd in Canada, Standing Committee on Industry, Science and Technology, "Proposed Sale" (hereafter Canada, "Proposed Sale"), Meeting 24, 5 March 2008, 1540.

52 Marc Garneau, qtd in Canada, "Proposed Sale," Meeting 24, 5 March 2008, 1600.

53 Hugh Thompson, qtd in Canada, "Proposed Sale," Meeting 24, 5 March 2008, 1555.

54 Ibid., 1635.

55 Gainor, "Canada's Space Program."

56 Jim Prentice, qtd in Canada, "Proposed Sale," Meeting 26, 13 March 2008, 1320.

57 Prentice, qtd in Industry of Canada, "Minister of Industry Creates Advisory Committee"; and "MacDonald Dettwiler 2007 Profit up by 14 Per Cent," *Vancouver Sun*, 26 March 2008.

58 Daniel Friedmann, qtd in Canada, "Proposed Sale," Meeting 28, 1 April 2008, 1230.

59 Ibid., 1220.

60 Art Hanger and Friedmann, qtd in Canada, "Proposed Sale," Meeting 28, 1 April 2008, 1230 and 1250.

61 Friedmann, qtd in Canada, "Proposed Sale," Meeting 28, 1 April 2008, 1230, 1255, 1310, and 1320.

62 Ibid., 1230 and 1330.

63 Carol Phillips, qtd in Canada, "Proposed Sale," Meeting 29, 3 April 2008, 1110.

64 Smardon, *Asleep at the Switch*, 388.

65 "Not Impressed," along with other contributors' comments, are archived on Bob McDonald's "Quirks and Quarks" Blog, under "MDA Deal: We Keep the Flag, They Get the Technology," CBC News, 11 January 2008. In addition, see "Block Sale of Canadian Space Firm: Garneau," Canadian Press, 6 March 2008; and Nathan Vanderklippe, "Ottawa Could Face Lawsuit if It Blocks MDA Sale," *Financial Post*, 27 March 2008.

66 "MDA Ex-Employee," in "MDA Deal," CBC News, 11 January 2008.

67 "Rob," in "MDA Deal," CBC News, 11 January 2008.

68 "Angry Shareholder," in "MDA Deal," CBC News, 11 January 2008.

69 Current Systems Engineer in Richmond, BC, 23 July 2008, in glassdoor, "Companies: MacDonald Dettwiler Reviews."

70 Jim Prentice, qtd in "Prentice Defends Decision to Block MDA Sale," CTV News, 10 April 2008. In addition, see "Foreign Takeovers: What Should Be Protected?," *Your View*, "Federal Government Blocks Sale of MDA Space Division," and Mark McQueen, "Is the MacDonald Dettwiler/Alliant Space Deal Dead?," CBC News, 10, 19, and 22 April 2008; "Canada Says 'No,'" *Aviation Week and Space Technology*, 14 April 2008; and "Canada Shoots Down Alliant Space Deal," *Minnesota Monitor*, 10 April 2008.

71 Jim Prentice, qtd in "Govt Confirms Decision to Block Sale of MDA Space Division," CBC News, 9 May 2008. In addition, see Paul Jay, "Canadian Scientists Unveil Plans for Asteroid-Hunting Satellite," "CAW Calls for $1.5B in Funding for Space Industry," and "Credit Crunch Puts End to Merger Boom," CBC News, 26 and 4 June, and 13 May 2008; and Collins, "Recent Decisions," 152–5.

72 "Tech Guru Shines a Light on the Energy Century," *Globe and Mail*, 19 October 2009. In addition, see Brooks, *Mythical Man-Month*, 14; Business Laureates of British Columbia Hall of Fame, "John S. MacDonald"; and Allenby and Mattick, "Macroethical and Social Issues," 1–3.

73 "Canada Blocks U.S. Takeover of a Technology Firm," *New York Times*, 10 May 2008.

74 Ian Austen, "Two Issues Combine to Scuttle an Aerospace Takeover," *New York Times*, 11 April 2008; and "Alliant Bid for Canadian Satellite Unit Ends," *Wall Street Journal*, 12 May 2008.

75 Shirtliff, "Canada's Radarsat," 20–1.

76 Ibid.

77 Joseph Anselmo, "Market Focus," *Aviation Week and Space Technology*, 14 January 2008; "Canada Says 'No,'" *Aviation Week and Space Technology*, 14 April 2008; "The Folly of Meddling," "Meddling Follies, Part 2," Joe Castaldo, "Not So Free Trade," and Jack Mintz, "M&A Madness," *Canadian Business*, 12 May 2008, 5, 12, and 22–3; Gouldson, "Selling of Canada," 6; and A.N. Sheppard, "Precious Meddling," *Canadian Business*, 21 July 2008, 22. In addition, see David Pugliese, "With Little Work on the Horizon, Canadian Space Industry Faces Brain Drain," *Ottawa Citizen*, 4 December 2012.

78 MDA, "RADARSAT-2 Commissioned"; MDA, "Strategic Win Strengthens"; MDA, "MDA Customer Upgrades to RADARSAT-2"; MDA, "MDA to Expand Support"; MDA, "MDA Signs Major RADARSAT-2"; "Radar Love," *Aviation Week and Space Technology*, 20 September 2008, 23; and "Israeli-Built UAV Is Off to Afghanistan," *Aviation Week and Space Technology*, 20 October 2008, 24.

79 Tim Worstall, "The Great Recession Is Just Like the Great Depression," *Forbes*, 7 November 2012; and Neil Irwin, "Happy Fifth Birthday, Great Recession! I Hope You Get Hit By a Truck," *Washington Post*, 29 November 2012. In addition, see Krugman, *Return of Depression Economics*.

80 Phillips and Castle, "Science and Technology Spending," 171.

81 Doern and Maslove, *How Ottawa Spends*, 12 and 15.

82 Samuelson, "Rethinking the Great Recession," 24.

CHAPTER TEN

1 Friedmann, qtd in Craig Wong, "MDA Sells Space, Satellite Business to ATK," Canadian Press, 8 January 2008. In addition, see Bob McDonald, "Keeping Canada's Space Business in Business," CBC News, 11 April 2008; MDA, 2007 *Annual Report*; and MDA, 2008 *Annual Report*.

2 Whitaker, Kealey, and Parnaby, *Secret Service*, 538.

3 Canada, Department of Finance, "Canada's Economic Action Plan," 272, and

24, 163, 174, and 185; and Doern and Maslove, *How Ottawa Spends*, 7–8. In addition, see MDA, "Project Noctua."

4 Haussman and Biette, "Buy American or Buy Canadian?," 141–2.

5 MDA, "MDA to Support Canada's DND"; MDA, "MDA Selected as Sole Supplier"; MDA, "MDA Provides Solution for WorldView"; MDA, "MDA to Provide Government of Canada"; MDA, "MDA to Develop Mission Concept"; MDA, "MDA to Provide RADARSAT-2 Imagery"; MDA, "MDA to Support the 2010 Olympic Games"; MDA, "MDA to Field Test"; MDA, "MDA Wins Major Surveillance"; *BCBusiness Editors* and Jeffrey Bichard, "No. 1: MacDonald Dettwiler and Associates Ltd," *BCBusiness*, 3 April 2009; "Who Is MacDonald Dettwiler's Mystery Customer for UAVs?," *Ottawa Citizen*, 3 September 2009; and Randy Attwood, "Next Generation Canadarms Unveiled at MacDonald Dettwiler Facility in Brampton," *SpaceRef*, 27 September 2012.

6 Marc Boucher, "MDA Engineering and Allied Technical Staff on Strike," *SpaceRef*, 30 September 2009.

7 MDA, "Engineering Services Resume," 26 October 2009"; MDA, "U.S. Air Force to Expand"; MDA, "MDA Wins $200 Million Contract"; MDA, "MDA Contracted to Deliver the National Communications"; MDA, "MacDonald, Dettwiler Get $8.86M"; MDA, *2008 Annual Report*; and MDA, *2009 Annual Report*.

8 Taverna, "Double-Back Guarantee," *Aviation Week and Space Technology*, 4 January 2010, 36.

9 Christopher Donville, "MacDonald Dettwiler Surges as Loral Deal Approved," *Bloomberg News*, 29 October 2012.

10 Taverna, "Double-Back Guarantee," *Aviation Week and Space Technology*, 4 January 2010, 36; and Neil MacFarQuhar, "U.N. Body Warns of Risky Global Austerity," *New York Times*, 6 September 2011.

11 David Berman, "MacDonald Dettwiler: A Down-to-Earth Profit Provider," *Global Investor*, 19 July 2010.

12 Jeffrey McCracken, Zachary R. Mider, and Theo Argitis, "MacDonald Dettwiler Is Said to Explore Sale of Company, Units," *Bloomberg News*, 10 October 2010.

13 Mohney, "Canadian Satellite Powerhouse."

14 Will Daley, "MacDonald Dettwiler to Sell Property-Data Unit to TPG," *Bloomberg News*, 5 November 2010.

15 MDA, "MDA to Divest"; MDA, "MDA Closes Sale"; MDA, *2010 Annual Report*; and MDA, *2011 Annual Report*.

16 David Ebner, "MDA's Daniel Friedmann Likes the Earth under His Feet," *Globe and Mail*, 6 January 2012.

17 MDA, "MDA to Provide Critical"; MDA, "MDA Continues to Support"; MDA, *2010 Annual Report*; and "Harper: Canada an 'Energy Superpower,'" *National Post*, 15 July 2006.

18 "MDA Releases National Urban Change Indicator," *SpaceRef*, 17 November
    2010; Frank Morring, Jr, "Changing the Game," *Aviation Week and Space Technol-
    ogy*, 21 March 2011; "2011 Space Laureate Goes to European, Canadian Com-
    panies," *Aviation Week and Space Technology*, 21 March 2011, 23 and 45; MDA,
    "Intelsat Picks"; MDA, "MDA to Provide Advanced"; MDA, "MDA Receives Follow-
    On"; and MDA, "MDA to Help Canada's DND." During 2011, Dan Friedmann
    indicated a few changes of his own. Beyond running MDA, serving the interests
    of the company's shareholders, advising the government on space policy, and
    engaging in myriad professional activities, he celebrated the publication of his
    first book, *Genesis One Code*, an interpretation of biblical scriptures and science
    theory that sought to reconcile the two records in a twenty-first-century debate
    divided over the origins of the universe. Following the book's publication, the
    once-deeply private Friedmann gave interviews, engaged in presentations both
    physical and virtual, and commenced work on yet another self-published book,
    Broken Gift, which explored biblical and scientific accounts of human origins
    and asked readers to consider whether future events would prove the division
    unnecessary. The earth and the cosmos had clearly inspired more than a thirty-
    two-year professional engineering career at MDA.
19 Graham, *Cities under Siege*, 60.
20 Friedmann, qtd in "Fighting Words from MacDonald Dettwiler," *Commercial
    Space*, 9 May 2011.
21 "Cantech Letter Interviews Anil Wirasekara of MacDonald Dettwiler," *can-
    tech letter*, 30 May 2011; and Ebner, "MDA's Daniel Friedmann Likes the
    Earth."
22 David Milstead, "Behind MacDonald Dettwiler's Surging Profits," *Globe and
    Mail*, 5 October 2011.
23 Ibid.; and Ebner, "MDA's Daniel Friedmann Likes the Earth."
24 "Budget Blamed for Aerospace Layoffs: Satellites Would Be Used for Mar-
    itime Surveillance, Disaster Management," CBC News, 30 March 2012.
25 "MDA Sheds 100 Jobs, More Expected," *Brampton Guardian*, 14 May 2012.
26 "MacDonald Dettwiler" reviews at http://glassdoor.com and http://ratemy
    employer.ca.
27 Ibid. In addition, see Elizabeth Weise, "Tech: Where the Women and Minori-
    ties Aren't," *USA Today*, 15 August 2014; Brian Fung, "Top Male Engineers at
    Google Make Nearly 20% More Than Their Female Peers," *Washington Post*,
    26 November 2014; and Farida Jhabvala Romero, "Big Gender Pay Gaps Per-
    sist in Silicon Valley Despite Booming Economy," *Peninsula Press*, 6 February
    2015.
28 "MacDonald Dettwiler to Buy Loral Subsidiary for $875 Million," *Guardian*,
    27 June 2012.

29 "Ontario Teachers Cash In $1.35 Million MDA Shares," *Globe and Mail*, 10 July 2012.

30 "MacDonald Dettwiler" reviews at http://glassdoor.com.

31 Ibid; and Thompson, "Investigation."

32 "Ontario Teachers Cash In."

33 "MDA Shares Fall on Uncertainty around Loral Deal," *Financial Post*, 13 September 2012. In addition, see Tim Kiladze, "MacDonald Dettwiler's Euphoric Bubble Pops: Investors Come Back to Reality," *Globe and Mail*, 12 September 2012.

34 Randy Attwood, "Alouette Pioneers Celebrated at Gala Dinner," *SpaceRef*, 19 October 2012.

35 Gainor, *"Alouette 1."*

36 "With MacDonald Dettwiler's Help, Canada Launches First Military Satellite," *cantech letter*, 18 October 2012.

37 David Pugliese, "MacDonald, Dettwiler and Associates Selected to Support U.S. Defense Advanced Research Projects Agency," *Ottawa Citizen*, 18 October 2012.

38 "MacDonald Dettwiler and Associates (MDA) ... Land Surface Exams (Imagery)," *SatNews Daily*, 28 October 2012.

39 David Pugliese, "MacDonald, Dettwiler and Associates to Do More Work for the U.S. Air Force," *Ottawa Citizen*, 31 October 2012.

40 Darcy Keith, "MacDonald Dettwiler's 10% Stock Surge Today Just the Start: Analyst," *Globe and Mail*, 29 October 2012; and "MacDonald Dettwiler Surges as Loral Deal Approved," *Bloomberg News*, 29 October 2012. In addition, see MDA, "MDA Completes Acquisition."

41 David Pugliese, "Canadian Radarsat Constellation Mission Delayed, Cost Rises by $400 Million," *SpaceNews*, 5 November 2012.

42 John Ivisin, "Stephen Harper Steps In to Save Radarsat Upgrade after Budget Cutbacks Threatened Satellite Program's Future," *National Post*, 19 December 2012; Peter O'Neil, "Feds Kick in $700 million in Funding for MacDonald Dettwiler Satellite Project," *Vancouver Sun*, 9 January 2013; and Brent Jang, "Contract Gives MacDonald Dettwiler a $706-Million Arctic View," *Globe and Mail*, 11 January 2013.

CONCLUSION

1 Nick Waddell, "MacDonald Dettwiler Has Become a 'Global Commercial Satellite Powerhouse," *cantech letter*, 9 September 2014; "Canadian Military Space in 2014: Part II," *SpaceRef*, 17 February 2015; MDA, *2014 Annual Report*, 1–6; MDA, "MDA Expands RADARSAT"; and MDA, "MDA Signs Contracts."

2 Marc Boucher, Marc Garneau, and Peggy Nash, qtd in Peter Rakobowchuk, "Liberals and NDP Promise Long-Term Space Plan If Elected," Canadian Press, 12 September 2015.

3 Peter B. de Selding, "Q&A: MDA Corp. CEO Friedmann Steps Down, Saying Company Needs a U.S. Citizen to Grow," *SpaceNews*, 22 April 2016. In addition, see Brenda Bouw, "Satellite Maker MDA's Outgoing President Looks Back on 80 Profitable Quarters," *Globe and Mail*, 27 June 2016. In addition, see Haydn Watters, "C-51, Controversial Anti-Terrorism Bill, Is Now Law: So, What Changes?," CBC News, 18 June 2015; and Chris Sorenson and Aaron Hutchins, "How Canada's Economy Went from Boom to Bust So Fast: An In-depth look at the Perfect Storm That Pushed Canada into Recession," *Maclean's*, 15 July 2015.

4 "Feds Award MacDonald Dettwiler $54 Million to Develop Next-Generation Satellites," *Canadian Manufacturing*, 6 May 2016.

5 Steven Staples, Chuck Black, and Don Osborne, qtd in David Pugliese, "U.S. Firm Stages 'Stealth Takeover' of Canada's Largest Space Tech Company," *National Post*, 16 October 2016. In addition, see MDA, "MDA Announces Resignation of Director."

6 Morozov, *Net Delusion*, 305–6. In addition, see Whitaker, Kealey, and Parnaby, *Secret Service*, 542–3, which reminds us that "security and policing services are not social-service agencies." Still, "when they are called upon to intervene in the political life of society," we are left with little more than the patina of democracy and "guards with access to extraordinary powers who operate in privileged secrecy."

7 Lapp and Interdepartmental Task Force, *Satellites and Sovereignty*, 13, as well as 7–14, 31–43, and 49–51, LAC.

8 Interview with MacDonald (18 January 1993).

9 Piketty, *Capital in the 21st Century*, 96 as well as 56, 58, 156–8 and 170–8. In addition, see Klassen, "Canada and the New Imperialism," 163–90.

10 Interview with Prentice.

11 Interview with Wallis.

12 Interview with MacDonald (18 January 1993).

13 The CSA's website, http://www.asc-csa.gc.ca, contains a full listing of the John H. Chapman Awards.

14 MacDonald, qtd in UN Institute for Disarmament Research, "Safeguarding Space for All," 1. Recent Canadian scandals include: the ETS Scandal involving alleged political wrongdoing and cover-ups over a $400 million information technology contract; Communications Security Establishment Canada (CSEC)'s cyber infiltration of Brazil's Ministry of Mining and Energy to gain information about the oil and gas operations of Canadian competitors; the

Canadian Senate Expenses Scandal; and the CSIS's participation in the US NSA's spying apparatus, "Five Eyes" program, and illegal data collection. In addition, see "Poor, the Near Poor and You," *New York Times*, 23 November 2011; John Kaag and Sarah Kreps, "Moral Hazard of Drones," *New York Times*, 22 July 2012; Lubao and Jones, "Canadian Spy Agency"; Colin Freeze, "In Scathing Ruling, Federal Court Says CSIS Bulk Data Collection Illegal," *Globe and Mail*, 3 November 2016; Parenti, *Soft Cage*, 78–9; and Klein, *Shock Doctrine*.

15 Eisenhower, "Speech."
16 Mosco, *Digital Sublime*, 56 and 59.
17 Littlemore, "Vancouver's High-tech Makeover," *Globe and Mail*, 26 March 2015. MacDonald's son posted his comment under the user name "Jay Mac YVR" at http://www.theglobeandmail.com.
18 Ibid.
19 Leslie, "Biggest 'Angel' of Them All," 49.
20 Interview with MacDonald (18 January 1993).
21 MacDonald, "Chancellor's Message."
22 Interview with MacDonald (18 January 1993).
23 International Club of Berne, "Memorial Service."
24 Interview with Dettwiler (11 January 1993).

Bibliography

INTERVIEWS WITH JOCELYN WILLS

Interview tapes and full, interviewee-corrected transcripts in possession of the author

Allan, Don, 11 January 1993
Beattie, Anne, 23 December 1992
Bennett, John, 12 January 1993
Bennett, Winslow, 31 May 1993
Butler, Michael, 8 January 1993
Caddey, Dave, 17 May 1993
Clark, Bernie, 6 January 1993
Collins, Arthur, 12 January 1993
Cwynar, George, 7 January 1993
Dettwiler, Werner (Vern), 14 and 21 December 1992, and 11 January 1993
Dollard, Harry, 18 January 1993
Druce, Guy, 22 December 1992
Eppich, Helmut, 18 May 1993
Friedmann, Daniel (Dan), 21 December 1992
Gelbart, Dan, 30 December 1992
George, Peter, 13 January 1993
Immega, Guy, 7 May 1993; and with David Kauffman, 7 May 1993
Kauffman, David, 18 May 1993; and with Guy Immega, 7 May 1993
Lapp, Philip, 29 December 1992
Lennox, Colin, 8 January 1993; and with Jan Price, 8 January 1993
Louth, Myrna, 4 January 1993
MacDonald, John, 7, 14, and 18 January 1993
Maxwell, Ray, 15 January 1993

McConnell, Peter, 17 May 1993
McDonald, Cameron (Cam), 4 January 1993
Morley, Lawrence (Larry), 7 January 1993
Morris, Chris, 14 May 1993
Murray, Daniel (Dan), 22 December 1992
Pitts, John, 14 December 1992 and 6 May 1993
Prentice, Marshall, 31 December 1992
Price, Jan, with Colin Lennox, 8 January 1993
Renwick, William (Bill), 18 May 1993; and with Douglas (Doug) Seymour, 18
    May 1993
Semrau, Stanley, 14 May 1993
Seymour, Douglas (Doug), with William (Bill) Renwick, 18 May 1993
Sloan, Dave, 30 December 1992
Spencer, Ken, 19 January 1993
Thompson, Neil, 15 January and 18 May 1993
Wallis, Robert (Bob), 13 January 1993
Widmer, Pietro, 13 January 1993

DOCUMENTS PROVIDED BY INTERVIEWEES
FROM PERSONAL ARCHIVES

In the possession of the author

Epic Data. Richmond, BC: Epic Data, ca 1985 (company brochure courtesy of
    Helmut Eppich).
L.A. Varah Ltd. "Innovation Is the Business of This Man's Team at MDA." *Interface*
    5, no. 1 (May 1972): 1–3 (company newsletter, courtesy of Colin Lennox).
Lennox, Colin. "Report on Jobs Complete and Work-in-Progress," ca 1971 (cour-
    tesy of Colin Lennox).
MacDonald, John S., to Peter Meyboom, director general, Science Procurement
    Sector, Department of Supply and Services, Ottawa, with "Contract Attach-
    ment" and "Contract Update," 29 October 1975 (courtesy of John S. MacDon-
    ald; and Colin Lennox).
Seymour, Douglas W. "A Study of MacDonald, Dettwiler & Associates Ltd." Pro-
    posed research project, MBA, Simon Fraser University, Vancouver, 1980 (cour-
    tesy of Douglas Seymour).
Thompson, William H. Electronic Development Corporation. "Letter to John
    MacDonald," 14 December 1976 (courtesy of Colin Lennox).
– "An Investigation into the Extent and Cause of the Sagging Morale within
    MDA," 12 October 1976 (courtesy of Colin Lennox).

Thompson, William H. "MacDonald, Dettwiler & Associates Ltd. and Synaptic Systems Ltd. Sales Analysis, 1972–1975," 13 November 1975 (courtesy of Colin Lennox; and Douglas Seymour).

MACDONALD, DETTWILER AND ASSOCIATES LTD (MDA), PUBLISHED DOCUMENTS

Annual Reports

1975 Annual Report. Vancouver: MacDonald, Dettwiler and Associates, 1976.
1976 Annual Report. Vancouver: MacDonald, Dettwiler and Associates, 1977.
1977 Annual Report. Richmond, BC: MacDonald, Dettwiler and Associates, 1978.
1986 Annual Report. Richmond, BC: MacDonald, Dettwiler and Associates, 1986.
1987 Annual Report. Richmond, BC: MacDonald, Dettwiler and Associates, 1987.
1988 Annual Report. Richmond, BC: MacDonald, Dettwiler and Associates, 1988.
1989 Annual Report, "*1969–1989: Twenty Years of Excellence.*" Richmond, BC: MacDonald, Dettwiler and Associates, 1989.
1990 Annual Report. Richmond, BC: MacDonald, Dettwiler and Associates, 1990.
1991 Annual Report. Richmond, BC: MacDonald, Dettwiler and Associates 1991.
1992 Annual Report. Richmond, BC: MacDonald, Dettwiler and Associates, 1992.
1993 Annual Report. Richmond, BC: MacDonald, Dettwiler and Associates, 1993.
1994 Annual Report. Richmond, BC: MacDonald, Dettwiler and Associates, 1994.
2000 Annual Report. Richmond, BC: MacDonald, Dettwiler and Associates, 2000.
2001 Annual Report. Richmond, BC: MacDonald, Dettwiler and Associates, 2001.
2002 Annual Report. Richmond, BC: MacDonald, Dettwiler and Associates, 2002.
2003 Annual Report. Richmond, BC: MacDonald, Dettwiler and Associates, 2003.
2004 Annual Report. Richmond, BC: MacDonald, Dettwiler and Associates, 2004.
2005 Annual Report. Richmond, BC: MacDonald, Dettwiler and Associates, 2005.
2006 Annual Report. Richmond, BC: MacDonald, Dettwiler and Associates, 2006.
2007 Annual Report. Richmond, BC: MacDonald, Dettwiler and Associates, 2007.
2008 Annual Report. Richmond, BC: MacDonald, Dettwiler and Associates, 2008.
2009 Annual Report. Richmond, BC: MacDonald, Dettwiler and Associates, 2009.
2010 Annual Report. Richmond, BC: MacDonald, Dettwiler and Associates, 2010.
2011 Annual Report. Richmond, BC: MacDonald, Dettwiler and Associates, 2011.
2014 Annual Report. Richmond, BC: MacDonald, Dettwiler and Associates, 2014.

Corporate Brochures

Advanced Airspace Management: The Next Generation of Air Traffic Control. Richmond, BC: MDA, ca 1992.

Advanced Systems for Defence. Richmond, BC: MDA, ca 1992.

AIDS: Airline Information and Dispatch System. Vancouver: MDA, ca 1978.

ATS (Asynchronous Tasking Supervisor): A Compact Executive Mini-Computer Real-Time Applications Product Specification. Vancouver: MDA, 1970.

Automated Weather Distribution System (AWDS). Richmond, BC: MDA, 1987.

"CAATS Technical Description." *MacDonald Dettwiler Report 50-3013*. Richmond, BC: MDA, ca 1992.

Frontiers in Digital Mapping. Richmond, BC: MDA, ca 1986.

IRIS: Tactical and Strategic Radar Reconnaissance. Richmond, BC: MDA, 1988.

Meridian: The Measure of Mapping Technology. Richmond, BC: MDA, 1988.

METDAS: Meteorological Data Analysis System. Richmond, BC: MDA, 1989.

Model 4880, BATCH Communications Controller. Vancouver: MDA, ca 1975.

Our Knowledge Is in the Holes. Vancouver: MDA, ca 1971.

Satellite Ground Stations. Richmond, BC: MDA, ca 1988.

ERTS Data Acquisition System. Vancouver: MDA, 1973.

News Releases

"Defence R&D Agency Awards Information System Security Project to MDA." 8 September 2005.

"Engineering Services Resume at MDA's Brampton Operations." 18 July 2006, 26 October 2009.

"First Quarter 2003 Results." 23 April 2003.

"Intelsat Picks MacDonald, Dettwiler and Associates Ltd for Satellite Servicing." 15 March 2011.

"MacDonald, Dettwiler Get $8.86M Contract Amendment from Canadian Space Agency." 21 December 2009.

"MacDonald, Dettwiler Announces Worldwide Sales and Distribution Agreement for RADARSAT-2 Imagery." 11 January 1999.

"MacDonald Dettwiler Awarded $106.5 Million Radarsat-2 Contract Change." 20 June 2000.

"MacDonald Dettwiler to Acquire Radarsat International." 26 February 1999.

"MDA Announces Resignation of Director." 13 January 2017.

"MDA Awarded Definition Phase Contract for Canadian Space Surveillance System." 11 January 2005.

"MDA Closes Sale of U.K. and North American Property Information Business." 4 January 2011.

"MDA Completes Acquistion of Space Systems/Loral." 2 November 2012.

"MDA Continues to Support Mexico's Largest Oil Company with Advanced RADARSAT Products." 26 August 2011.

"MDA Contracted to Deliver the National Communications Satellite System of Ukraine." 15 December 2009.

"MDA Customer Upgrades to RADARSAT-2." 15 September 2008.

"MDA Expands RADARSAT Business in China." 23 October 2014.

"MDA Information Key to Relief Effort and Loss Coverage in Wake of Katrina." 31 August 2005.

"MDA Provides Solution for WorldView Satellite Program." 29 April 2009.

"MDA Receives Follow-On Contracts from the Federal Aviation Administration." 7 April 2011.

"MDA Repatriates RADARSAT-2 Distribution Rights by Amending Distribution Agreement with ORBIMAGE." 14 February 2001.

"MDA Reports 2002 4th Quarter & Year-End Results." 20 February 2003.

"MDA Reports Year End and 4th Quarter 2003 Results." 17 February 2004.

"MDA Selected as Sole Supplier of Direct Downlink Solutions for RapidEye's International Ground Station Customers." 8 April 2009.

"MDA Signs Contracts to Provide Space-Based Monitoring to Support Oil Exploration and Production." 17 October 2014.

"MDA Signs Contract Valued at $154 Million U.S. to Provide Hubble Rescue Solution." 5 January 2005.

"MDA Signs Major RADARSAT-2 Information Solution." 14 November 2008.

"MDA Starts Work on Third Information Mission." 29 June 2004.

"MDA to Acquire Iotek Inc of Halifax." 7 February 1996.

"MDA to Develop Mission Concept for Polar Communication and Weather Mission." 23 July 2009.

"MDA to Divest US and North American Property Information Business: Company Adopts Dividends Policy." 5 November 2010.

"MDA to Expand Support to Canada's Navy MCOIN System." 3 November 2008.

"MDA to Field Test Advanced Information Solution for Crime Scene Assessment." 25 August 2009.

"MDA to Help Canada's DND Monitor Areas of Interest around the Globe." 2 November 2011.

"MDA to Participate in Provision of Military Ground Station." 23 September 2003.

"MDA to Provide Advanced Technology Solution to Boeing for Communications Satellites." 4 April 2011.

"MDA to Provide Critical Information to Monitor Oil Fields for Leading Alberta Energy Company." 5 May 2011.

"MDA to Provide Government of Canada a Broad-Area Maritime Surveillance System Using RADARSAT-2 Capabilities." 25 June 2009.

"MDA to Provide RADARSAT-2 Imagery to the European Space Agency." 27 July 2009.

"MDA to Provide the U.S. Air Force with Mobile Ground System Upgrade." 10 November 2010.

"MDA to Support Canada's DND Submarine Training." 8 January 2009.

"MDA to Support the 2010 Olympic Games Security." 24 July 2009.

"MDA Wins Major Surveillance Service Contract." 1 September 2009.

"MDA Wins $200 Million Contract in Russian Market." 20 November 2009.

"RADARSAT-2 Commissioned and Ready for Commercial Operation." 1 May 2008.

"Strategic Win Strengthens MDA's Position in UAV Surveillance Market." 7 August 2008.

"U.S. Air Force to Expand Capabilities for MDA Flight Path Safety Plan." 23 October 2009.

"U.S. Air Force to Test RADARSAT-2 Information Provision to War Fighters." 23 June 2004.

LIBRARY AND ARCHIVES CANADA (LAC), OTTAWA

Government Collections

Canada Centre for Remote Sensing. RG39-A, 68602, vol. 1.

Department of Communications. Central Registry Files. RG108-A, vol. 1248, file 127329.

– Departmental Correspondence. RG108-A, vol. 1343, file 136521.

– Secretariat to the Computer-Communications Interdepartmental Committee. RG97-F-IV: vol. 407, file 7500-1031-2-A-4, pts 1–3, Working Group No. 4, Increasing the National Presence, Stimulation Policies; vol. 413, file 7500-1031-2-A-21, pts 1–4, Procurement Policy, 1973–7; vol. 418, file 7500-1331-3, pt 1, European Economic Community (EEC) Mission; vol. 418, file 7500-1331-4, U.S. Government; vol. 418, file 7500-1445-1, Green Paper General.

Department of Employment and Immigration. Secret File System. SF-R-69, vol. 956.

Department of External Affairs. Block 27. Defence. Canada-U.S. Defence Production Sharing Policy. RG25-A-3-C, vol. 12698, file 27-11-2-US; vol. 14605, file 27-11-2-1, pt 17.

– SPAR Briefing (1993). RG-25-A-4, vol. 27446, file 6010-5, MF-13691.

Department of Natural Resources. RG45, vol. 356, file 1370-6/0, pts 1.1 and 1.2, CCRS Liaison Cooperation.

Ministry of State for Science and Technology (MOSST). R1526, vols 19, 23–4, 26, 30, 43–6, 52, 54–6, and 372–4.

Publications

Beaumier, Guy. Economics Division, Research Branch, Library of Parliament. "Innovation in Canada and the Role of the Federal Government." Ottawa, April 1983.

Canada. Department of Defence Production. *Eighteenth Annual Report of the Department of Defence Production*. Ottawa: Queen's Printer, 1969.

– Department of Finance. "Canada's Economic Action Plan, Budget 2009." Ottawa, 27 January 2009.

– Parliament. Senate. Special Committee on Science Policy (Lamontagne Committee). *A Science Policy for Canada: Report of the Senate Special Committee on Science Policy*. Ottawa: Supply and Services Canada, 1970–2.

– *Royal Commission on Government Organization Report*. Vol. 1. Ottawa: Queen's Printer, 1962.

– *Royal Commission on National Development in the Arts, Letters, and Sciences, 1949–1951*. Ottawa: King's Printer, 1951.

– "Science Agreement between Canada and the European Space Agency." Treaty Series, 1978, no. 23. Ottawa: Queen's Printer for Canada, 1979.

– Task Force on Program Review. *Government Procurement "Spending Smarter": A Study Team Report to the Task Force on Program Review*. Ottawa: Task Force, 1985.

Canada–United States Permanent Joint Board on Defence. *The Permanent Joint Board of Defence Canada–United States, 1940–1965*. Ottawa: Board, 1965.

Canadian Computer/Communications Task Force. *Branching Out: Report of the Canadian Computer/Communications Task Force*. Ottawa: Department of Communications, 1972.

Canadian Space Agency. Audit, Evaluation and Review Directorate. "Evaluation of the Major Crown Project: The Canadian Space Station Program (MCP-CSSP): Evaluation Report." Saint-Hubert, QC: Canadian Space Agency, 2003.

Consultative Committee on the Implications of Telecommunications for Canadian Sovereignty. *Telecommunications and Sovereignty*. Ottawa: Minister of Supply and Services Canada, 1979.

Doutriaux, Jérôme. "Government Procurement and Research Contracts at Start-up and Success of Canadian High-tech Entrepreneurial Firms." University of Ottawa Working Paper, April 1988.

Dobell, Peter C. *Canada's Search for New Roles: Foreign Policy in the Trudeau Era*. Toronto: Royal Institute of International Affairs, 1972.

Dotto, Lydia. *A Heritage of Excellence: SPAR Aerospace Limited*. Mississauga, ON: Spar Aerospace Limited, and University of Toronto Press, 1992.

King, Mackenzie. *The Ogdensburg Agreement: Reprint of Speech Delivered in the House of Commons, 12 November 1940*. Ottawa: Edmond Clauthier, 1940.

Lapp, Philip A., John W. Hodgins, and Colin B. Mackay. *Ring of Iron: A Study of Engineering Education in Ontario*. Toronto: Committee of Presidents of Universities of Ontario, 1970.

Lapp, Philip A., and Interdepartmental Task Force on Surveillance Satellites. *Satellites and Sovereignty: Report on the Interdepartmental Task Force on Surveillance Satellites*. Ottawa: Government of Canada, August 1977.

Matte, Nicolas Mateesco. Institute and Centre of Air and Space Law, McGill University. *Space Policy and Programmes Today and Tomorrow: The Vanishing Duopole*. Toronto: Carswell; and Montreal: ICALS, McGill University, 1980.

Morley, Lawrence W. *Canada's Participation in Seasat "A."* Ottawa: Canada Centre for Remote Sensing, 1977.

Phoenix Strategic Perspectives. "Corporate Connection: Space-Related Issues." Submitted to the Canadian Space Agency, December 2004.

Rossignol, Michel. Political and Social Affairs Division, Research Branch, Library of Parliament, mini-review. "Missile Defence and the Renewal of the Norad Agreement," MR-134E, 27 September 1995.

Science Council of Canada. *Towards a National Science Policy for Canada*. Report no. 4. Ottawa: Queen's Printer, 1968.

– *University Research and the Federal Government*. Report no. 5. Ottawa: Queen's Printer, 1969.

Shaw, E. CCRS *Remote Sensing of the Oceans: What Next?* Ottawa: Canada Centre for Remote Sensing, 1977.

GOVERNMENT DOCUMENTS, PUBLISHED

Auditor General of Canada. *Major Capital Projects – Industrial Development Initiatives: 1992 Report*. http://www.oag-bvg.gc.ca.

"BRC53/P/Final 049, 19 March 1953." GCHQ files: UKUSA Agreement. Catalogue reference HW/80/9. National Archives, London. http://www.nationalarchives.gov.uk.

Canada. Department of Defence Production. *Canada–United States Defence Production Sharing*. Ottawa: Queen's Printer and Controller of Stationery, 1960.

– Department of National Defence. Defence Research Board. *Annual Report of the Defence Research Telecommunications Establishment (U)*. DRTE Report no. 1192-U. Ottawa: Defence Research Board, 1968. http://pubs.drdc-rddc.gc.ca/pubdocs/pcow1_e.html.

- Minister of Consumer and Corporate Affairs. Canada Business Corporations Act. Form 6, "Notice of Directors or Notice of Change of Directors," s. 101 or 108. 30 March and 2 August 1978, 30 March and 8 August 1979, 17 March 1980, and 20 January and 30 July 1981.
- Minister of Consumer and Corporate Affairs. *Canada Supplementary Letters Patent.* Form 342, doc. 167. November 1973.
- Minister of Consumer and Corporate Affairs. *Letters Patent Incorporating Mac-Donald, Dettwiler and Associates Ltd.* Film 235, doc. 225, 3 February 1969. Recorded 11 March 1969.
- Ministry of State for Science and Technology. "Building on Our Strengths: A Background Paper for the National Forum on the National Science and Technology Policy, Winnipeg, June 1986." Ottawa: Government of Canada, 1986. Saskatchewan Legislative Library, Regina.
- *Networks of Centres of Excellence Annual Report 1998–1999.* Ottawa: Minister of Public Works and Government Services Canada, 2000.
- Standing Committee on Industry, Science and Technology. Number 024, 2nd Session, 39th Parliament. "The Proposed Sale of Part of MacDonald, Dettwiler and Associates Ltd to Alliant Techsystems." Meetings 24, 26, 28, and 29. "Evidence." 5 and 13 March, and 1 and 3 April 2008. https://openparliament.ca /committees/activities/3245/.
Canadian Space Agency (CSA). "Canadian Satellite RADARSAT-1 Celebrating 15 Years of Service to Canada and the World." 4 November 2010. http://www.asc-csa.gc.ca.
- *Performance Report for the Period Ending March 31, 2007.* Ottawa: Ministry of Industry, 2007. http://www.asc-csa.gc.ca/pdf/pr-2007-section2.pdf.
- *Radarsat Annual Review 2001–2002.* http://publications.gc.ca/site/eng/108488 /publication.html.
Chapman, J.H., P.A. Forsyth, P.A. Lapp, and G.N. Patterson. *Upper Atmosphere and Space Programs.* Special study no. 1. Ottawa: Queen's Printer and Controller of Stationery, 1967.
Eisenhower, Dwight D. "Farewell Address to the Nation." 1 January 1961. http://www.ourdocuments.gov.
- "Speech." Columbus, OH. 15 October 1964. Box 6, folder "Speeches Made by DDE." Dwight D. Eisenhower Archives. http://www.eisenhower.archives .gov.
Harper, Stephen. "Address by the Prime Minister at the Canada-UK Chamber of Commerce." 14 July 2006. http://www.pm.gc.ca.
Kennedy, John Fitzgerald. "The New Frontier." Democratic National Convention Nomination Acceptance Address. Los Angeles, 15 July 1960. http://www .americanrhetoric.com.

– "We Choose to Go to the Moon." Delivered at Rice University, Houston, TX, 12
    September 1962. http://er.jsc.nasa.gov.
King, William Lyon Mackenzie. *Canada and the War: The Hyde Park Declaration:
    Cooperation in Economic Defence*. Ottawa: Edmund Clothier, Printer to the
    King's Most Excellent Majesty, 1941.
Mazlich, Bruce. "The Idea of Space Exploration." In NASA, *Spacefaring People*,
    137–46.
Morley, Lawrence. *Remote Sensing Then and Now*. Ottawa: CCRS, 1993.
National Academy of Engineering. Panel on Telecommunications Research.
    "Telecommunications Research in the United States and Selected Foreign
    Countries: A Preliminary Survey." Vol. 1, *Summary*. Report to the National Sci-
    ence Foundation. Contract no. H-1221. Springfield, VA: National Technical
    Information Service (NTIS), Department of Commerce, June 1973.
National Aeronautics and Space Administration (NASA). National Aeronautics
    and Space Act of 1958 (Unamended). Public Law #85-568, 72 Stats, 426. 29
    July 1958. http://www.hq.nasa.gov.
– National Space Science Data Center. NSSDC *Master Catalog Search*.
    https://nssdc.gsfc.nasa.gov/nmc/.
– "Radarsat Launch Aboard Delta II Rocket Set Nov. 3," 25 January 1995.
    https://www.nasa.gov/centers/kennedy/news/releases/1995/95nos.html.
– *Report of the Seasat Failure Review Board*. Washington, DC: NASA, 1978.
– *A Spacefaring People: Perspectives on Early Space Flight*. Washington, DC: NASA,
    1985.
National Science Foundation. "About NSF at a Glance." http://www.nsf.gov.
National Security Administration. "Growing Up with Computers at NSA: A
    Panel Discussion." DOCID: 4001131. Top Secret UMBRA. Undated.
    http://www.nsa.gov.
North American Aerospace Defense Command. "A Brief History of NORAD."
    2012. http://www.norad.mil.
North Atlantic Treaty Organization (NATO). "A Short History of NATO."
    http://www.nato.int.
Pounder, E., ed. Seasat *Final Report*. Vol. 3, *Ground Segments*. Pasadena, CA:
    National Aeronautics Space Administration/Jet Propulsion Laboratory, 1980.
    https://www.nasa.gov/centers/kennedy/news/releases/1995/95nos.html.
Powell, James. *A History of the Canadian Dollar*. Ottawa: Bank of Canada, 2005.
Province of British Columbia. *Annual Report of Extra-provincial Company Mac-
    Donald, Dettwiler and Associates Ltd*, form 18, s. 357, Certificate of Extra-provin-
    cial Registration no. 8544-A. Victoria, BC. 11 July 1981, filed 10 September
    1981.
– Companies Act. No. 8544-A. 11 July 1969 and 30 December 1970.

Roosevelt, Franklin Delano. "The Call to Battle Stations." *The Public Papers of Franklin D. Roosevelt*. Vol. 1941. Compiled with special material and explanatory notes by Samuel I. Rosenman. Book 1. Ann Arbor: University of Michigan Library, 2005.

Science Council of Canada. *Innovation in a Cold Climate: The Dilemma of Canadian Manufacturing*, Report No. 15. Ottawa: Information Canada, 1971.

– *It Is Not Too Late – Yet: A Look at Some Pollution Problems in Canada's Natural Environment; An Identification of Some Major Concerns*, Report No. 16. Ottawa: Queen's Printer, 1972.

Treasury Board of Canada. "Status Report on Major Crowns, Canadian Space Agency." *Departmental Performance Reports, 2007–08*. Ottawa: Treasury Board of Canada, 2008. Accessed 29 June 2014, http://tbc-sct.gc.ca.

United States Army Space Missile Defense and Army Strategic Command. "View Offers to Buy: Business Opportunities" Request for Information, 12 April 2005. http://www.fbodaily.com.

United States Congress. *Public Law 105-303: An Act to Encourage the Development of a Commercial Space Industry in the United States, and for Other Purposes [H.R. 1702]*. Washington, DC: Government Printing Office, 28 October 1998.

United States Congress. Office of Technology Assessment. *Remote Sensing and the Private Sector: Issues for Discussion – A Technical Memorandum*. Washington, DC: OTA-TM-ISG-20, 1984.

United States Department of Defense. *Directive 2035.1*. 20 July 1960 and November 1980. http://biotech.law.lsu.edu/blaw/dodd/corres.

United States Department of State. "Memorandum of Understanding between the Department of Defense of the United States of America and the Department of National Defence of Canada concerning Cooperation on Future Force Interoperability." September 2008. http://www.state.gov.

United States Federal Communications Commission. Telecommunications Act of 1996. http://transition.fcc.gov.

United States House of Representatives Committee on Defense Manufacturing. *Defense Manufacturing in 2010 and Beyond*. Washington, DC: National Academy, 1996.

United States House of Representatives Committee on Science and Astronautics. "Remote Sensing of Earth Resources." *A Compilation of Papers Prepared for the 13th Meeting of the Panel on Science and Technology*. Washington, DC: United States Government Printing Office, 1972.

United States Securities and Exchange Commission. *Orbital Sciences Corporation: Current Report*. Form 8-K, Commission file 0-18287. Washington, DC: United States Securities and Exchange Commission, 1995. Accessed 12 November 2012, http://www.secfilings.nyse.com.

NEWS SOURCES: PAPERS, PERIODICALS, SERVICES, AND OUTLETS

Aero News Network (http://www.aero-news.net)
Aerotech *News and Review*
Aviation Week and Space Technology
BBC News
BCBusiness
Bloomberg News
Brampton Guardian
Business Wire
Canada NewsWire
Canadian Business
Canadian Manufacturing
Canadian Press
cantech letter (http://www.cantechletter.com)
Canwest News Services
CBC News (http://www.cbcnews.ca)
CNBC (http://www.cnbc.com)
Commercial Space
CTV News (http://www.ctvnews.ca)
Defense Daily
Economist
Financial Times
Financial Times of Canada
Forbes
Global Investor
Globe and Mail
Greeley Tribune
Guardian
International Business Times
Maclean's
Medicine Hat News
Minnesota Monitor (accessed 11 January 2011, http://www.minnesotamonitor.com)
National Post
New York Times
Ottawa Business Journal
Ottawa Citizen
Peninsula Press
PR Newswire (http://www.prnewswire.com)
Province
Richmond News

Richmond Review
SatNews Daily (accessed 17 May 2013, http://www.satnewsdaily.com)
Space and Tech Digest
Space Daily
SpaceNews (http://www.spacenews.com)
SpaceRef (http://www.spaceref.com)
Toronto Star
Tribune
usa *Today*
Vancouver Sun
Wall Street Journal
Washington Post
Winnipeg Free Press

OTHER PUBLISHED SOURCES

Abbate, Janet. "Government, Business, and the Making of the Internet." *Business History Review* 75 (2001): 147–76.
– *Inventing the Internet*. Cambridge, MA: MIT Press, 2000.
Adas, Michael. *Machines as the Measure of Men: Science, Technology, and Ideologies of Western Domination*. Ithaca, NY: Cornell University Press, 1992.
Allen, Colin, and Wendell Wallach. "Moral Machines: Contradiction in Terms or Abdication of Human Responsibility?" In Lin, Abney, and Bekey, *Robot Ethics*, 55–67.
Allenby, Brad, and Carolyn Mattick. "Macroethical and Social Issues in Emerging Technologies and the Military." Paper presented at the IEEE International Symposium on Sustainable Systems and Technology, Tempe, AZ, May 2009.
Ambrose, Stephen E. *Nixon: The Triumph of a Politician 1962–1972*. New York: Simon & Schuster, 1989.
American Institute of Aeronautics and Astronautics. *Collection of Technical Papers*. Earth Resources Observations and Information Systems Meeting, Annapolis, MD, 2–4 March 1970.
Anastakis, Dimitry. *Autonomous State: The Struggle for a Canadian Car Industry from OPEC to Free Trade*. Toronto: University of Toronto Press, 2013.
Anderson, Sarah, and John Cavanaugh. *The Rise of Corporate Global Power*. London: Institute for Policy Studies, 2000.
Andrejevic, Mark. *iSpy: Surveillance and Power in the Interactive Era*. Lawrence: University Press of Kansas, 2007.
Andrew, Christopher, Richard J. Aldrich, and Wesley K. Wark, eds. *Secret Intelligence*. London: Routledge Taylor and Francis Group, 2009.
Armstrong, Christopher, and H.V. Nelles. *Monopoly's Moment: The Organization*

and Regulation of Canadian Utilities, 1830–1930. Philadelphia: Temple University Press, 1986.

Åstebro, Thomas, Holger Herz, Ramana Nanda, and Roberto A. Weber. "Seeking the Roots of Entrepreneurship: Insights from Behavioral Economics." *Journal of Economic Perspectives* 28, no. 3 (Summer 2014): 49–70.

Atkinson, Michael M., and William D. Coleman. *The State, Business, and Industrial Change in Canada*. Toronto: University of Toronto Press, 1989.

Audretsch, David B., and Paula E. Stephan. "Company-Scientist Locational Links: The Case of Biotechnology." *American Economic Review* 86, no. 3 (June 1996): 641–52.

Auerswald, Philip, and Lewis Branscomb. "Start-ups and Spin-offs: Collective Entrepreneurship between Invention and Innovation." In Hart, *Emergence of Entrepreneurship Policy*, 61–91.

Automated Destruction. "Mindox." https://automateddestructiondotcom.word press.com/mindbox/macdonald-dettwiler-associates-ltd/

Ball, Kirstie S., and David Murakami Wood. "Political Economies of Surveillance." *Surveillance and Society* 11, nos 1–2 (2013): 1–3.

Baran, Paul A., and Paul M. Sweezy. *Monopoly Capital: An Essay on the American Economic and Social Order*. New York: Monthly Review, 1966.

Barman, Jean. *The West beyond the West: A History of British Columbia*. 3rd ed. Toronto: University of Toronto Press, 2007.

Batten, Frank, and Jeffrey L. Cruikshank. *The Weather Channel: The Improbable Rise of a Media Phenomenon*. Boston: Harvard Business, 2002.

Battrick, B., and L. Conroy, eds. *Proceedings of the Concluding Workshop: The Extended ESA History Project*, ESA SP-609, 13–14 April 2005. Paris: European Space Agency, 2005.

Baumol, William J., and Robert J. Strom. "'Useful Knowledge' of Entrepreneurship: Some Implications of the History." In Landes, Moykr, and Baumol, *Invention of Enterprise*, 527–42.

Behiels, Michael D. "Stephen Harper's Rise to Power: Will His 'New' Conservative Party Become Canada's 'Natural Governing Party' of the Twenty-First Century?" *American Review of Canadian Studies* 40, no. 1 (March 2010): 118–45.

Bell, Daniel. *The Coming of Post-Industrial Society*. Anniversary ed. New York: Basic Books, 1999.

Bellamy, Matthew J. "John Labatt Blows In and Out of the Windy City: A Case Study in Entrepreneurship and Business Failure, 1889–1896." *Canadian Historical Review* 95, no. 1 (March 2014): 30–53.

– *Profiting from the Crown: Canada's Polymer Corporation, 1942–1990*. Montreal and Kingston: McGill-Queen's University Press, 2005.

Berlin, Leslie R. *The Man behind the Microchip: Robert Noyce and the Invention of Silicon Valley.* New York: Oxford University Press, 2005.

Bernstein, Irving. *Guns or Butter: The Presidency of Lyndon Johnson.* New York: Oxford University Press, 1996.

Bernstein, Michael A., and Mark R. Wilson. "New Perspectives on the History of the Military-Industrial Complex." *Enterprise and Society* 12, no. 1 (2011): 1–9.

Billings, Linda. "To the Moon, Mars, and Beyond: Culture, Law, and Ethics in Space-Faring Societies." *Bulletin of Science, Technology and Society* 26 (October 2006): 430–7.

Blake, Raymond B., ed. *Transforming the Nation: Canada and Brian Mulroney.* Montreal and Kingston: McGill-Queen's University Press, 2007.

Bliss, Michael. *A Canadian Millionaire: The Life and Business Times of Sir Joseph Flavelle, Bart., 1858–1939.* Toronto: University of Toronto Press, 1992.

– "Forcing the Pace: A Reappraisal of Business-Government Relations in Canadian History." In Murray, *Theories of Business-Government Relations*, 106–17.

– *Northern Enterprise: Five Centuries of Canadian Business.* Toronto: McClelland and Stewart, 1994.

Boeker, Warren, and Rushi Karichalil. "Entrepreneurial Transitions: Factors Influencing Founder Departure." *Academy of Management Journal* 45, no. 4 (August 2002): 818–26.

Bonnet, Roger M., and Vittorio Manno. *International Cooperation in Space: The Example of the European Space Agency.* Cambridge, MA: Harvard University Press, 1994.

Borman, Natalie, and Michael Sheehan, eds. *Securing Outer Space: International Relations Theory and the Politics of Space.* New York: Routledge, 2009.

Bothwell, Robert. *Nucleus: The History of Atomic Energy of Canada Limited.* Toronto: University of Toronto Press, 1988.

Bothwell, Robert, and William Kilbourn. *C.D. Howe: A Biography.* Toronto: McClelland and Stewart, 1979.

Bourdieu, Pierre. *Distinction: A Social Critique of the Judgement of Taste.* Richard Nice, trans. Cambridge, MA: Harvard University Press, 1984.

Bow, Brian. *The Politics of Linkage: Power, Independence, and Ideas in Canada-US Relations.* Vancouver: University of British Columbia Press, 2009.

Brate, Adam. *Technomanifestos: Visions from the Information Revolutionaries.* New York: Texere Publishing, 2002.

Bratt, Duane. *The Politics of CANDU Exports.* Toronto: University of Toronto Press, 2006.

Brender, Mark. "Will It Sow the Seeds for Industry Success?" *Earthwide Communications, LLC.* January/February, 2004. Accessed 9 January 2013, http://www.geoeye.com.

Bromberg, Joan Lisa. *NASA and the Space Industry*. Baltimore, MD: Johns Hopkins University Press, 1999.

Brooke, Jeffrey. *Divided Loyalties: The Liberal Party of Canada*. Toronto: University of Toronto Press, 2010.

Brooks, Frederick P. Jr. *The Mythical Man-Month*. Anniversary ed. Boston: Addison Wesley Longman, 1995.

Brooks, Rodney Allen. *Flesh and Machine: How Robots Will Change Us*. New York: Vintage, 2002.

Burke, Colin. "A Rough Road to the Information Highway: Project Intrex – A View from the CLR Archives." In Hahn and Buckland, *Historical Studies in Information Science*, 132–46.

Burton, Diane. "The Company They Keep: Founders' Models for Organizing New Firms." In Schoonhoven and Romanelli, *Entrepreneurship Dynamic*, 13–39.

Business Development Bank of Canada. "Industrial Development Bank (IDB), 1944–1975." http://www.bdc.ca.

Business Laureates of British Columbia Hall of Fame. "John S. MacDonald, O.C., Ph.D., F.C.A.E., Eng., Inducted 2006." http://www.businesslaureates bc.org.

Butrica, Andrew. *Single Stage to Orbit: Politics, Space Technology, and the Quest for Reusable Rocketry*. Baltimore, MD: Johns Hopkins University Press, 2003.

Byers, Michael, and Kelsey Franks. "Unmanned and Unnecessary: Canada's Proposed Procurement of UAVs." *Canadian Foreign Policy Journal* 20, no. 3 (2014): 271–90.

CAI Private Equity. "About CAI." http://www.caifunds.com.

Canadian Bar Association. "Surprise Negotiations to Sell BC OnLine: Too Many Questions, Too Little Time." *BarTalk*. August 2008. http://www.cba.org.

Canadian Electronics Engineering. "Practical Solutions to Difficult Problems." August 1975, 32.

– "They Know about Us in Moscow … Brazilia, Tehran, Rome … Houston." August 1975, 37.

Canadian Space Agency. "$195 Million Federal Government Contract to Prime Contractor SPAR Aerospace." News release, 7 March 1991.

– "Richmond Company Awarded Major Space Station Contract." News release. 21 March 1991.

Carter, W.D. "The Private Sector: A Global Pool for Technical Talent for Remote Sensing Training and Program Support." *Advances in Space Research* 4, no. 11 (1984): 49–57.

Caufield, Catherine. *Masters of Illusion: The World Bank and the Poverty of Nations*. London: Pan Books, 1997.

Chandler, Alfred Dupont Jr. *Inventing the Electronic Century: The Epic Story of the Consumer Electronics and Computer Science Industries*. New York: Free Press, 2001.

– *Strategy and Structure: Chapters in the History of the Industrial Empire*. Cambridge, MA: MIT Press, 1962.

– *The Visible Hand: The Managerial Revolution in American Business*. Cambridge, MA: Belknap, 1977.

Chandler, Gaylen N., and Steven H. Hanks. "An Examination of the Sustainability of Founders Human and Financial Capital in Emerging Business Ventures." *Journal of Business Venturing* 13, no. 5 (1998): 353–69.

Chang, Ha-Joon. *Bad Samaritans: The Myth of Free Trade and the Secret History of Capitalism*. New York: Bloomsbury, 2008.

Chapnick, Adam. *The Middle Power Project: Canada and the Founding of the United Nations*. Vancouver: University of British Columbia Press, 2005.

Chodos, Robert, Rae Murphy, and Eric Hamovitch. *Lost in Cyberspace? Canada and the Information Revolution*. Toronto: James Lorimer, 1997.

Chrisman, James J., J. Adam, D. Holbrook, and Jess H. Chua, eds. *Innovation and Entrepreneurship in Western Canada: From Family Businesses to Multinationals*. Calgary: University of Calgary Press, 2003.

Coalition to Oppose the Arms Trade. "U.S. Warfighters Get Their Hands on RADARSAT Data." *Press for Conversion* 58, March 2006. http://coat.ncf.ca.

Cochran, Thomas Childs. *Business in American Life: A History*. New York: McGraw-Hill, 1976.

Cohoon, Joanne McGrath, and William Aspray, eds. *Women and Information Technology: Research on Underrepresentation*. Cambridge, MA: MIT Press, 2008.

Coleman, Norm. "Honoring the Late Anne Brunsdale." *CapitolWords*, 3 March 2006.

Collins, Simone. "Recent Decisions under the Investment Canada Act: Is Canada Changing Its Stance on Foreign Direct Investment?" *Northwestern Journal of International Law & Business* 32, no. 1 (2011): 141–64.

Legislative Note. "The Communications Satellite Act of 1962." *Harvard Law Review* 76, no. 2 (December 1962): 388–400.

Cooper, Paul R., Daniel E. Friedmann, and Scott A. Wood. "The Automatic Generation of Digital Terrain Models from Satellite Images by Stereo." *Acta Astronautica* 15, no. 3 (March 1987): 171–80.

Cormier, Jeffery. *The Canadianization Movement: Emergence, Survival, and Success*. Toronto: University of Toronto Press, 2004.

COSSA Space Industry News. "Industrial Award to Satellite Image-Mapping System." November 1987.

Cox, James. "Canada and the Five Eyes Intelligence Community." Strategic Studies Working Group Papers. Canadian Defence & Foreign Affairs Institute and Canadian International Council. December 2012. http://cdfai.org.preview mysite.com/PDF/Canada%20and%20the%20Five%20Eyes%20Intelligence%20 Community.pdf.

Cuff, Robert D. "Notes for a Panel on Entrepreneurship in Business History." *Business History Review* 76 (Spring 2002): 123–32.

Cumming, Ian, and John Bennett. "Digital Processing of Seasat Data." *Acoustics, Speech, and Signal Processing*, IEEE *Conference on* ICASSP*'79* 4 (April 1979): 710–18.

Cunningham, J. Burton, and Joe Lisherson. "Defining Entrepreneurship." *Journal of Small Business Management* (January 1991): 45–69.

Dandeker, Christopher. "Surveillance and Military Transformation: Organizational Trends in Twenty-First Century Armed Services." In Haggerty and Ericson, *New Politics of Surveillance*, 225–49.

Darroch, James L. "Global Competitiveness and Public Policy: The Case of Canadian Multinational Banks." In Marchildon and McDowall, *Canadian Multinationals*, 153–75.

Davidsson, Per, and Benson Honig. "The Role of Social and Human Capital among Nascent Entrepreneurs." *Journal of Business Venturing* 18, no. 3 (2003): 301–31.

Davis, Chuck. *The History of Metropolitan Vancouver*. Madeira Park, BC: Harbour Publishing, 2011. http://www.vancouverhistory.ca.

DeBlois, Bruce M., Richard L. Garwin, R. Scott Kemp, and Jeremy C. Marwell. "Space Weapons: Crossing the U.S. Rubicon." *International Security* 29, no. 2 (Fall 2004): 50–84.

Defense Science. "Canadian Defense Industry Profiles." February 1988.

De Larrinaga, Miguel. "Between Blind Faith and Deep Skepticism: The 'Weaponization of Space' and the Canadian Debate on Ballistic Missile Defense." In Borman and Sheehan, *Securing Outer Space*, 128–46.

Dempsey, Paul Stephen. *Flying Blind: The Failure of Airline Deregulation*. Washington, DC: Economic Policy Institute, 1990.

Dickens, Peter, and James S. Ormrod. *The Palgrave Handbook of Society, Culture and Outer Space*. London: Palgrave MacMillan, 2016.

Doern, G. Bruce, and Allan M. Maslove. *Thirty Years of Watching "How Ottawa Spends."* 2010. http://carleton.ca/sppa/wp-content/uploads/30years_watching _hos.pdf.

Doern, G. Bruce, and Bryne B. Purchase, eds. *Canada at Risk?: Canadian Public Policy in the 1990s*. Toronto: C.D. Howe Institute, 1991.

Doern, G. Bruce, and Christopher Stoney, eds. *How Ottawa Spends, 2010–2011:*

Recession, Realignment, and the New Deficit Era. Montreal and Kingston: McGill-Queen's University Press, 2010.

Drucker, Peter. *Age of Discontinuity: Guidelines to Our Changing Society*. London: Routledge, 1969.

Dufour, Eric, and Imran Ahmad. "The Investment Canada Act: Canada's Waking Giant?" 24 November 2010. http://www.lexology.com.

Dufour, Paul, and Yves Gingras. "National Policy-Making: Development of Canadian Science and Technology Policy." *Science and Public Policy* 15, no. 1 (February 1988): 13–18.

Dutrénit, Gabriela. "Building Technological Capabilities in Latecomer Firms: A Review Essay." *Science, Technology and Society* 9, no. 2 (2004): 209–41.

Dyer, Gwynne. *Canada in the Great Power Game*. Toronto: Random House, 2014.

EDC Today. "Export Development Canada." October/November 1987.

Edwards, Paul N. *The Closed World: Computers and the Politics of Discourse in Cold War America*. Cambridge, MA: MIT Press, 1996.

Electronic Products and Technology. "MacDonald Dettwiler Focus on Digital Imaging Nets Growth of 30% per Year." (March/April 1988): 1–2.

Electronics Communicator. "MacDonald, Dettwiler & Associates Ltd, Exceptional Talents in Digital Systems Design and Manufacture." 26 May 1975.

– "MDA Secures Second Order for ERS-1 Radar Data Processing Groundstation." 2 July 1987.

English, John. *Just Watch Me: The Life of Pierre Elliott Trudeau*. Vol. 2, *1968–2000*. Toronto: Knopf Canada, 2000.

– *The Worldly Years: Life of Lester Pearson*. Toronto: Random House Digital, 2011.

Epic Data. "About Us." http://www.epicdata.com.

European Space Agency. "RapidEye Constellation." https://directory.eoportal.org.

Evans, M. "The Canadian Space Programme – Past, Present, and Future: A History of the Development of Space Policy in Canada." In Battrick and Conroy, *Proceedings of the Concluding Workshop*, 133–45.

Export Development Canada. "About Us." http://www.edc.ca.

Fama, Eugene F., and Michael J. Jensen. "Separation of Ownership and Control." *Journal of Law and Economics* 26, no. 2 (1983): 301–26.

Farish, Matthew. "Another Anxious Urbanism: Simulating Defense and Disaster in Cold War America." In Graham, *Cities, War*, 93–109.

Fiffer, Steve. *So You've Got a Great Idea: Here's How to Develop It, Sell It, Market It or Just Cash In on It*. Reading, MA: Da Capo, 1986.

Florida, Richard. *The Rise of the Creative Class: And How It's Transforming Work, Leisure, Community and Everyday Life*. New York: Basic Books, 2002.

Fossum, John Erik. *Oil, the State, and Federalism: The Rise and Demise of Petro-Canada as a Statist Impulse.* Toronto: University of Toronto Press, 1997.

Foucault, Michel. *Discipline and Punish: The Birth of the Prison.* New York: Vintage, 1995.

Foust, Jeff. "Last Chance for Salvaging the MDA Sale." Space Politics, 7 May 2008. http://www.spacepolitics.com/2008/05/07/last-chance-for-salvaging-the-mda-sale/.

Frank, Thomas. *The Conquest of the Cool: Business Culture, Counterculture, and the Rise of Hip Consumerism.* Chicago: University of Chicago Press, 1997.

Friedmann, Daniel. *The Broken Gift: Harmonizing the Biblical and Scientific Accounts of Human Origins.* Daniel Friedmann, Inspired Studies, Book 2, 2014.

– *The Genesis One Code.* Daniel Friedmann, Inspired Studies, Book 1, 2011.

Gaddis, John Lewis. *The Cold War: A New History.* New York: Penguin Books, 2006.

Gainor, Chris. "*Alouette 1*: Celebrating 50 Years of Canada in Space." *Space Quarterly*, 6 September 2012. http://www.spaceq.ca.

– *Arrows to the Moon: Avro's Engineers and the Space Race.* Burlington, ON: Apogee Books, 2001.

– "Blocked Sale Exposes the Neglect of Canada's Space Program," *Space Review*, 2 June 2008. http://www.thespacereview.com.

– "Canada's Space Program in Crisis." *Space Review: Essays and Commentary about the Final Frontier.* 28 January 2008. http://www.thespacereview.com.

– "Crash of Canada's Space Biz: Why BC Firm's Sale to Americans Leaves Huge Crater." *Tyee.* 28 January 2008. http://www.thetyee.ca.

Gandy, Oscar Jr. "Data Mining, Surveillance, and Discrimination in the Post-9/11 Environment." In Haggerty and Ericson, *New Politics of Surveillance*, 363–84.

Ginsburg, Ari, Harold Price, Erik R. Larsen, and Alessandro Lomi. "Entrepreneurship in Context: Strategic Interaction and the Emergence of Regional Economies." In Schoonhoven and Romanelli, *Entrepreneurship Dynamic*, 314–48.

glassdoor. "Companies: MacDonald Dettwiler Reviews," 2008–17. http://www.glassdoor.com.

Godbole, Pushkar E., George T. Haslam, and Malcolm R. Vant. "The Spotlight SAR Project: An Imaging Radar for the Canadian Military." *IEEE Canadian Review* 22 (Spring/Summer 1995): 5–8.

Godefroy, Andrew B. "Canada's Early Space Policy Development, 1958–1974." *Space Policy* 19, no. 2 (2003): 137–41.

Goldman, Emily O., and Leslie C. Eliason, eds. *The Diffusion of Military Technology and Ideas.* Palo Alto, CA: Stanford University Press, 2003.

Goldman, Emily O., and Andrew L. Ross. "Diffusion of Military Technology and

Ideas: Theory and Practice." In Goldman and Eliason, *Diffusion of Military Technology*, 371–404.

Goldman, Joanne Abel. "National Science in the Nation's Heartland: The Ames Laboratory at Iowa State University." *Technology and Culture* 41, no. 3 (2000): 435–59.

Gouldson, Tim. "The Selling of Canada Hits a Roadblock." *Canadian Electronics* 23, no. 3 (May 2008): 3.

Governor General of Canada. "Order of Canada, John Spencer MacDonald, O.C., Ph.D., F.C.A.E., P.Eng." http://www.gg.ca.

Graham, Stephen. *Cities under Siege: The New Military Urbanism*. London: Verso, 2010.

– ed. *Cities, War, and Terrorism: Towards an Urban Geopolitics*. Oxford: Blackwell Publishing, 2003.

Graham, Stephen, and David Wood. "Digitizing Surveillance: Categorization, Space, Inequality." *Critical Social Policy* 23, no. 2 (2003): 227–48.

Graham, Thomas Jr, and Keith A. Hanson. *Spy Satellites and Other Intelligence Technologies That Changed History*. Seattle: University of Washington Press, 2007.

Granatstein, J.L. *How Britain's Economic, Political, and Military Weakness Force Canada into the Arms of the United States: A Melodrama in Three Acts*. 2nd ed. Toronto: University of Toronto Press, 1989.

– *Who Killed the Canadian Military?* Toronto: HarperCollins, 2004.

Gray, Mia, Elyse Golob, and Ann Markusen. "Seattle: A Classic Hub-and-Spoke Region." In Markusen, Lee, and Digiovanna, *Second Tier Cities*, 267–310.

Gray, Mia, Elyse Golob, Ann R. Markusen, and Sam Ock Park. "The Four Faces of Silicon Valley." In Markusen, Lee, and Digiovanna, *Second Tier Cities*, 291–310.

Greber, Dave. *Rising to Power: Paul Desmarais & Power Corporation*. Toronto: Methuen, 1987.

Guy, Simon. "Shadow Architectures: War, Memories, and Berlin's Future." In Graham, *Cities, War*, 75–92.

Hadekel, Peter. *Silent Partners: Taxpayers and the Bankrolling of Bombardier*. Toronto: Key Porter Books, 2004.

Haggerty, Kevin D. "Visible War: Surveillance, Speed, and Information War." In Haggerty and Ericson, *New Politics of Surveillance*, 250–68.

Haggerty, Kevin D., and Richard V. Ericson, eds. *The New Politics of Surveillance and Visibility*. Toronto: University of Toronto Press, 2006.

Hahn, Trudi Bellardo, and Michael Buckland, eds. *Historical Studies in Information Science*. Medford, NJ: Information Today, 1998.

Hannaford, Norman John. "A Strategic Analysis of the Space and Defence Business of MacDonald, Dettwiler and Associates." MBA thesis, Simon Fraser University, 1998.

Harris, Richard G. "North American Economic Integration: Issues and a Research Agenda." Revised paper prepared as background for Industry Canada Workshop on North American Integration, Ottawa, 7 September 2000. http://citeseerx.ist.psu.edu.

Harris, Shane. *The Watchers: The Rise of America's Surveillance State*. New York: Penguin, 2010.

Hart, David M., ed. *The Emergence of Entrepreneurship Policy: Governance, Start-ups, and Growth in the U.S. Knowledge Economy*. New York: Cambridge University Press, 2003.

Hart, Michael. *Decision at Midnight: Inside the Canada-U.S. Free Trade Negotiations*. Vancouver: University of British Columbia Press, 1995.

Hart, Michael, and William Dymond. "Common Borders, Shared Destinies: Canada, the United States and Deepening Integration." Conference paper. Ottawa: Centre for Trade Policy and Law, 2001.

Hartle, Douglas G. "The Report of the Royal Commission on Financial Management and Accountability (The Lambert Report): A Review." *Canadian Public Policy* 3 (Summer 1979): 367–8.

Haussman, Melissa, and David Biette. "Buy American or Buy Canadian? Public Procurement Politics and Policy under International Frameworks." In Doern and Stoney, *How Ottawa Spends*, 128–49.

Haykin, Simon, Edward O. Lewis, and R. Keith Rainey. *Remote Sensing of Sea Ice and Icebergs*. Toronto: John Wiley & Sons Canada, 1994.

Hedges, Chris. *War Is a Force That Gives Us Meaning*. New York: Anchor Books, 2003.

Heinrich, Thomas. "Cold War Armory: Military Contracting in Silicon Valley." *Enterprise and Society* 3 (June 2002): 247–84.

Hellmann, Thomas, and Manju Puri. "Venture Capital and the Professionalization of Start-up Firms: Empirical Evidence." *Journal of Finance* 57, no. 1 (February 2002): 169–97.

Hounshell, David A. "The Medium Is the Message, or How Context Matters." In Hughes and Hughes, *Systems, Experts, Computers*, 255–310.

Hughes, Agatha C., and Thomas P. Hughes, eds. *Systems, Experts, Computers: The Systems Approach in World War II and After*. Cambridge, MA: MIT Press, 2000.

Huntley, Wade L. "The Mice That Soar: Smaller States' Perspectives on Space Weaponization." In Borman and Sheehan, *Securing Outer Space*, 147–69.

Iansiti, Marco, and Kim B. Clark. "Integration and Dynamic Capability: Evidence from Product Development in Automobiles and Mainframe Computers." *Industrial and Corporate Change* 3, no. 3 (1994): 557–605.

Immega, Guy. "Change of Heart." *Neo-Opsis Science Fiction Magazine* 24 (May 2014): 7–13.

– "The KSI Tentacle Manipulator." *Proceedings of the IEEE International Conference on Robotics and Automation* 3 (1995): 3149–54.

Industry Canada. "Minister of Industry Creates Advisory Committee on the Canadian Space Agency." 31 March 2008. http://www.marketwired.com.

Innes, Eva, Robert L. Perry, and Jim Lyon, eds. "In a Class of Their Own." *Financial Post Selects the 100 Best Companies to Work for in Canada.* Toronto: Harper-Collins, 1986.

Intelsat. "Intelsat Announces Completion of Acquisition of Serafina Holdings." News release. 4 February 2008. http://www.intelsat.com.

Interavia. "The Long View from Space: The Value of Earth Observation." (May 1985): 24–9.

International Astronautical Federation. "About." http://www.iafastro.org.

International Club of Berne. "Memorial Service for Werner Dettwiler, Tuesday, 1st October 2013 at 2pm–3 pm." http://www.icberne.ch.

Jackall, Robert. *Moral Mazes: The World of Corporate Managers.* New York: Oxford University Press, 1989.

Jamison, Andrews. "Technology's Theorists: Conceptions of Innovation in Relation to Science and Technology Policy." *Technology and Culture* 30, no. 3 (July 1993): 505–33.

Jaramillo, Cesar, ed. *Space Security Index 2012.* Waterloo, ON: Space Security, 2012. http://spacesecurityindex.org/wp-content/uploads/2012/10/Space SecurityReport2012.pdf.

Johnson, Stephen B. "Three Approaches to Big Technology: Operations, Research, Systems Engineering, and Project Management." *Technology and Culture* 38 (1997): 891–919.

Johnson-Freese, Joan. *Heavenly Ambitions: America's Quest to Dominate Space.* Philadelphia: University of Pennsylvania Press, 2009.

KADAK Products Ltd. "Company Showcase." http://www.kadak.com.

Kapp, Sue. "Banging the Gong." *Business Marketing* 73 (December 1988): 12–14.

Kay, W.D. "Space Policy Redefined: The Reagan Administration and the Commercialization of Space." *Business and Economic History* 27 (1998): 237–47.

Kenney, Martin. "Introduction." In Kenney, *Understanding Silicon Valley,* 1–14.

– ed. *Understanding Silicon Valley: The Anatomy of an Entrepreneurial Region.* Palo Alto, CA: Stanford Business Books, 2000.

Kilibarda, Kole. "Canadian and Israeli Defense – Industrial and Homeland Security Ties: An Analysis." *The New Transparency: Surveillance and Social Sorting,* Working Paper IV, IRSP. November 2008. http://www.sscqueens.org.

Klassen, Jerome. "Canada and the New Imperialism: The Economics of a Secondary Power." *Studies in Political Economy* 83 (Spring 2009): 163–90.

Klein, Naomi. *The Shock Doctrine: The Rise of Disaster Capitalism*. New York: Picador, 2008.

Krige, John. "Crossing the Interface from R&D to Operational Use: The Case of the European Meteorological Satellite." *Technology and Culture* 41, no. 1 (2000): 27–50.

Krugman, Paul. *The Return of Depression Economics and the Crisis of 2008*. New York: W.W. Norton, 2009.

Kumar, B. Rajesh. *Mega Mergers and Acquisitions: Case Studies from Key Industries*. New York: Palgrave MacMillan, 2012.

Laird, Pamela Walker. *Pull: Networking and Success since Benjamin Franklin*. Cambridge, MA: Harvard University Press, 2007.

Lajeunesse, Adam, and Bill Carruthers. "The Ice Has Ears." *Canadian Naval Review* 9, no. 3 (2013): 4–9.

Landes, David, Joel Moykr, and William J. Baumol, eds. *The Invention of Enterprise: Entrepreneurship from Ancient Mesopotamia to Modern Times*. Princeton, NJ: Princeton University Press, 2012.

Launius, Roger D., John M. Logsdon, and Robert W. Smith, eds. *Reconsidering Sputnik: Forty Years since the Soviet Satellite*. Amsterdam: Harwood Academic Publishers, 2000.

Layton, Edwin T. Jr. *The Revolt of the Engineers: Social Responsibility and the American Engineering Profession*. Baltimore, MD: Johns Hopkins University Press, 1986.

Le Chevalier, François. *Principles of Radar and Sonar Signal Processing*. Norwood, MA: Artech House, 2002.

Leclerc, G., and S. Lessard. "Canada and ESA: 20 Years of Cooperation." *ESA Bulletin* 96 (November 1998): 1–6.

Lees, Judi. "He's Got Fire Power: MDA and John Pitts Are Cooking Together." *Equity* (September/October 1984): 23–5.

Lenco, Michel. "Remote Sensing and Natural Resources." *Nature and Resources* 18, no. 2 (April–June 1982): 2–9.

Leslie, Stuart W. "Biggest 'Angel' of Them All: The Military and the Making of Silicon Valley." In Kenney, *Understanding Silicon Valley*, 48–69.

– *The Cold War and American Science: The Military-Industrial-Academic Complex at MIT and Stanford*. New York: Columbia University Press, 1993.

Leslie, Stuart W., and Robert H. Kargon. "Selling Silicon Valley: Frederick Terman's Model for Regional Advantage." *Business History Review* 70 (Winter 1996): 435–71.

Lewis, Jonathan E. *Spy Capitalism: Itek and the CIA*. New Haven, CT: Yale University Press, 2002.

Lexpert. "MacDonald, Dettwiler Secures $190M Credit Facility." 1 March 2000. http://www.lexpert.ca.

Liberal Party of Canada. "The History of the Liberal Party of Canada." http://www.collectionscanada.gc.ca/eppp-archive/100/205/300/liberal-ef/05-05-24/www.liberal.ca/history_e.aspx@type=news.

Lin, Patrick, Keith Abney, and George A. Bekey. *Robot Ethics: The Ethical and Social Implications of Robotics.* Cambridge, MA: MIT Press, 2011.

Litt, Paul. *The Muses, the Masses, and the Massey Commission.* Toronto: University of Toronto Press, 1992.

Littleton, James. *Target Nation: Canada and the Western Intelligence Network.* Toronto: CBC Enterprises, 1986.

Livesay, Harold C. *American Made: Shapers of the American Economy.* 2nd ed. New York: Pearson Longman, 2007.

– *Andrew Carnegie and the Rise of Big Business.* 2nd ed. New York: Addison Wesley Longman, 2000.

– "Entrepreneurial Dominance in Business Large and Small, Past and Present." *Business History Review* 63 (Spring 1989): 1–21.

Livesay, Harold C., Marcia L. Rorke, and David S. Lux. "From Experience: Technical Development and the Innovation Process." *Journal of Product Innovation Management* 6 (1989): 268–81.

Lowen, Rebecca S. *Creating the Cold War University: The Transformation of Stanford.* Berkeley: University of California Press, 1997.

Lowenstein, Roger. *Origins of the Crash: The Great Bubble and Its Undoing.* New York: Penguin, 2004.

Lubao, Dylan, and Keith Jones. "Canadian Spy Agency Establishes Covert Surveillance Operations Worldwide as Part of NSA Global Spying Apparatus." *Global Research,* 14 December 2013.

Luke, Timothy W. "Everyday Technics as Extraordinary Threats: Urban Technostructures and Non-Places in Terrorist Actions." In Graham, *Cities, War,* 120–36.

Lyon, David. *The Electronic Eye: The Rise of Surveillance Society.* Minneapolis: University of Minnesota Press, 1994.

– *Surveillance after September 11.* Cambridge: Polity, 2003.

– *Surveillance Society: Monitoring Everyday Life.* Buckingham, UK: Open University Press, 2001.

Macauley, Molly K., and Michael A. Towman. "Providing Earth Observation Data from Space: Economics and Institutions." *American Economic Review* (May 1991): 38–41.

MacDonald, Dettwiler and Associates Ltd. "Project Noctua." *Frontline Defence* 8, no. 2 (2015). http://defence.frontline.online/article/2011/2/1643-MDA%3A-Project-Noctua.

MacDonald, John S. "Experimental Studies of Handwriting Signals." *Technical Report 443*. Cambridge, MA: Massachusetts Institute of Technology Research Laboratory of Electronics, 1966.

- "Science and Technology Policy." In Doern and Purchase, *Canada at Risk*, 198–202.
- "Survival in a Knowledge-Based World." Paper presented at the Managing Innovation and Technology Conference, Toronto, 9 April 1992.
- "Systems Engineering: Art and Science in an International Context." Presented at the International Council on Systems Engineering (INCOSE), Vancouver, 1999.
- University of Northern British Columbia "Chancellor's Message," 2012. http://www.unbc.ca.

Mack, Pamela E. *Viewing the Earth: The Social Construction of the Landsat Satellite System*. Cambridge, MA: MIT Press, 1990.

Madders, Kevin. *A New Force at a New Frontier: Europe's Development in the Space Field in Light of Its Main Actors, Policies, Laws and Activities from Its Beginnings up to the Present*. New York: Cambridge University Press, 2006.

Mahapatra, S., and Waymond Rogers. "An Empirical Study of the Industrial Research and Development Incentives Act (IRDIA) of Canada." *Journal of Applied Business Research* (Fall 1987): 102–11.

Maloney, Sean M. "Better Late Than Never: Defence during the Mulroney Years." In Blake, *Transforming the Nation*, 132–63.

Marchildon, Gregory P. "Canadian Multinationals and International Finance: Past and Present." In Marchildon and McDowall, *Canadian Multinationals*, 1–15.

- *Profits and Politics: Beaverbrook and the Gilded Age of Canadian Finance*. Toronto: University of Toronto Press, 1996.

Marchildon, Gregory P., and Duncan McDowall, eds. *Canadian Multinationals and International Finance*. London: Frank Cass, 1992.

Margolis, Jane. *Unlocking the Clubhouse: Women in Computing*. Cambridge, MA: MIT Press, 2003.

Markusen, Ann, Yong Sook Lee, and Sean Digiovanna, eds. *Second Tier Cities: Rapid Growth beyond the Metropolis*. Minneapolis: University of Minnesota Press, 1999.

Martin, Lawrence. *Iron Man: The Defiant Reign of Jean Chrétien*. Toronto: Viking, 2003.

Marx, Leo. *The Machine in the Garden: Technology and the Pastoral Ideal in America*. 35th ed. New York: Oxford University Press, 1999.

Maslove, Allan M., ed. *How Ottawa Spends, 2009–2010: Economic Upheaval and Political Dysfunction*. Montreal and Kingston: McGill-Queen's University Press, 2009.

Mattelart, Armand. *The Globalization of Surveillance: The Origin of the Securitarian Order*. Susan Gruenheck Taponier and James A. Cohen trans. Cambridge: Polity, 2010.

Matthews, Glenna. *Silicon Valley, Women, and the California Dream: Gender, Class, and Opportunity in the Twentieth Century*. Palo Alto, CA: Stanford University Press, 2003.

McCartin, Joseph A. *Collision Course: Ronald Reagan, the Air Traffic Controllers, and the Strike That Changed America*. New York: Oxford University Press, 2013.

McCurdy, Howard E. *Faster, Better, Cheaper: Low-Cost Innovation in the U.S. Space Program*. Baltimore, MD: Johns Hopkins University Press, 2001.

– *Space and the American Imagination*. 2nd ed. Baltimore, MD: Johns Hopkins University Press, 2011.

McDougall, John. *Drifting Together: The Political Economy of Canada-US Integration*. Toronto: University of Toronto Press, 2006.

McDowall, Duncan. "Fin de siècle: Canadian Business in the 1990s." In Marchildon and McDowall, *Canadian Multinationals and International Finance*, 176–80.

– *The Sum of the Satisfactions: Canada in the Age of National Accounting*. Montreal and Kingston: McGill-Queen's University Press, 2008.

McLin, Jon. *Canada's Changing Defense Policy, 1957–1963: The Problem of a Middle Power in Alliance*. Baltimore, MD: Johns Hopkins University Press, 1967.

McQueen, Rod. *The Eatons: The Rise and Fall of Canada's Royal Family*. Toronto: Stoddart Publishing, 1998.

Meyboom, Peter. "In-house vs Contractual Research: The Federal Make-or-Buy Policy." *Canadian Public Administration* 17, no. 4 (December 1974): 563–85.

Mikesell, Raymond F. *The Bretton Woods Debates: A Memoir*. Princeton, NJ: Princeton Essays in International Finance, no. 192, March 1994.

Mindell, David A. *Between Human and Machine: Feedback, Control, and Computing before Cybernetics*. Baltimore, MD: Johns Hopkins University Press, 2002.

Miner, Anne S., Dale T. Eesley, Michael DeVaughn, and Thekla Rura-Polley. "The Magic Beanstalk Vision: Commercializing University Inventions and Research." In Schoonhoven and Romanelli, *Entrepreneurship Dynamic*, 109–46.

Mohney, Doug. "Canadian Satellite Powerhouse Looking at Selling Parts, Whole Company." TMCnet. 21 October 2010. Accessed 24 October 2010. http://www.tmcnet.com.

Mokyr, Joel. *The Gifts of Athena: Historical Origins of the Knowledge Economy*. Princeton, NJ: Princeton University Press, 2002.

Monmonier, Mark. *Spying with Maps: Surveillance Technologies and the Future of Privacy*. Chicago: University of Chicago Press, 2002.

Morena, L.C., K.V. James, and J. Beck. "An Introduction to the Radarsat-2 Mission." *Canadian Journal of Remote Sensing* 30, no. 3 (2004): 221–34.

Morozov, Evgeny. *The Net Delusion: The Dark Side of Internet Freedom*. New York: Public Affairs Books, 2011.

Mosco, Vincent. *The Digital Sublime: Myth, Power, and Cyberspace*. Cambridge, MA: MIT Press, 2004.

Moss, David A. *When All Else Fails: Government as the Ultimate Risk Manager*. Cambridge, MA: Harvard University Press, 2002.

Mukerji, Chandra. "Intelligent Uses of Engineering and the Legitimacy of State Power." *Technology and Culture* 44, no. 4 (2003): 655–76.

Murray, V.V., ed. *Theories of Business-Government Relations*. Toronto: Trans-Canada, 1985.

Mussio, Laurence B. *Telecom Nation: Telecommunications, Computers, and Governments in Canada*. Montreal and Kingston: McGill-Queen's University Press, 2001.

Nelles, H.V. *The Politics of Development: Forests, Mines, and Hydro-Electric Power in Ontario, 1849–1941*. Hamden, CT: Archon Books, 1974.

Nelson, Richard R. *Technology, Institutions, and Economic Growth*. Cambridge, MA: Harvard University Press, 2005.

Neufeld, Mark. "Hegemony and Foreign Policy Analysis: The Case of Canada as Middle Power." *Studies in Political Economy* 48 (Autumn 1995): 7–29.

Newton, Scott. "A 'Visionary Hope' Frustrated: J.M. Keynes and the Origins of the Postwar International Monetary Order." *Diplomacy and Statecraft* 11 (2000): 189–210.

Niedzviecki, Hal. "The Spy Who Blogged Me: How We Learned to Stop Worrying and Love Surveillance." *Walrus*, May 2008, 36–42.

Niosi, Jorge, André Manseau, and Benoit Godin. *Canada's National System of Innovation*. Montreal and Kingston: McGill-Queen's University Press, 2000.

Noble, David F. "Command Performance: A Perspective on Military Enterprise and Technological Change." In Smith, *Military Enterprise*, 329–46.

– *The Religion of Technology*. New York: Knopf, 1997.

Norris, Pat. *Spies in the Sky: Surveillance Satellites in War and Peace*. Chichester, UK: Praxis Publishing, 2008.

Nye, David. *American Technological Sublime*. Cambridge, MA: MIT Press, 1996.

Organisation for Economic Co-operation and Development (OECD). *Economic Surveys of the OECD: Canada 1961*. Paris: OECD, 1961.

– *Economic Surveys 1982–1983 Canada*. Paris: OECD Publishing 1983.

– *Economic Surveys Canada, 1987–1988*. Paris: OECD Publishing, 1988.

– *Economic Surveys Canada, 1988–1989*. Paris: OECD Publishing, 1989.

Paglen, Trevor. *Blank Spots on the Map: The Dark Geography of the Pentagon's Secret World*. New York: Dutton, 2009.

Parenti, Christian. *The Soft Cage: Surveillance in America, from Slavery to the War on Terror*. New York: Basic Books, 2003.

Peters, E. Bruce. "The Conflict at Apple Was Almost Inevitable: As Your Company Grows You May Have to Change Your Style of Managing." *Research Development* (December 1985): 58–60.

Phillips, Peter W.D., and David Castle. "Science and Technology Spending: Still No Viable Federal Innovation Agenda." In Doern and Stoney, *How Ottawa Spends*, 168–86.

Piketty, Thomas. *Capital in the Twenty-First Century*. Cambridge, MA: Harvard University Press, 2014.

Pollard, Sidney. *The International Economy since 1945*. London: Routledge, 1997.

Potter, Evan H. *Transatlantic Partners: Canadian Approaches to the European Union*. Montreal and Kingston: McGill-Queen's University Press, 1999.

Preston, Andrew. "Balancing War and Peace: Canadian Foreign Policy and the Vietnam War, 1961–65." *Diplomatic History* 27, no. 1 (2003): 73–111.

Pursell, Carroll, ed. *A Companion to American Technology*. Malden, MA: Blackwell Publishing, 2005.

RateMyEmployer. "MacDonald, Dettwiler and Associates (MDA)." Employer Rating. http://www.ratemyemployer.ca.

Reference for Business. "Spar Aerospace Limited: Company Profile, Information, Business Description, History, Background Information on Spar Aerospace Limited." http://www.referenceforbusiness.com.

Reinhart, Carmen M., and Kenneth S. Rogoff. *This Time It's Different: Eight Centuries of Financial Folly*. Princeton, NJ: Princeton University Press, 2009.

Reiss, Edward. *The Strategic Defense Initiative*. New York: Cambridge University Press, 1992.

Richelson, Jeffrey, and Desmond Ball. *The Ties That Bind: Intelligence Cooperation between the UK/USA Countries, the United Kingdom, the United States of America, Canada, Australia, and New Zealand*. New York: Allen and Unwin, 1985.

Rogin, Josh. "Experts Debate Rumsfeld's Transformation Legacy," FCW: The Business of Federal Technology, 13 November 2006. http://fcw.com.

Rosenblatt, Alfred, and Paul Dickson. "At Long Last, ERTS Is on the Way." *Electronics* (12 May 1969): 98–106.

Rosenstein, Bruce. *Create Your Own Future the Peter Drucker Way: Developing and Applying a Forward-Focused Mindset*. New York: McGraw-Hill, 2013.

Sà, Creso M., and Jeffrey Litwin. "University-Industrial Research Collaborations in Canada: The Role of the Federal Government." *Science and Public Policy* 38, no. 6 (July 2011): 425–35.

Samuelson, Robert J. "Rethinking the Great Recession." *Wilson Quarterly* (Winter 2011): 16–24.

Sanders, Richard. "'Missile Defense' Alive and Well in Canada." *Canadian Dimension*. 8 September 2006. https://canadiandimension.com/articles/view /missle-defense-alive-and-well-in-canada-richard-sanders.

– "We Didn't Really Say 'No' to Missile Defence: Canadian Complicity and Participation in BMD Continues." *Canadian Centre for Policy Alternatives*, 1 October 2006. http://policyalternatives.ca.

Sandholtz, Wayne. *High-tech Europe: The Politics of International Cooperation.* Berkeley: University of California Press, 1992.

Sayle, Timothy Andrews. "A Pattern of Constraint: Canadian-American Relations in the Early Cold War." *International Journal* 62, no. 3 (Summer 2007): 689–705.

Schein, Edgar H., Peter S. DeLisi, Paul J. Kampas, and Michael M. Sonduck. *DEC Is Dead, Long Live DEC: The Lasting Legacy of Digital Equipment Corporation.* San Francisco: Barrett-Koelher, 2003.

Schoonhoven, Claudia, and Elaine Romanelli, eds. *The Entrepreneurship Dynamic: Origins of Entrepreneurship and the Evolution of Industries.* Stanford, CA: Stanford University Press, 2001.

– "Premises of the Entrepreneurship Dynamic." In Schoonhoven and Romanelli, *Entrepreneurship Dynamic*, 1–10.

Schrempp, Gregory. *The Ancient Mythology of Modern Science: A Mythologist Looks (Seriously) at Popular Science Writing.* Montreal and Kingston: McGill-Queen's University Press, 2012.

Schumpeter, Joseph A. *Capitalism, Socialism, and Democracy.* 1942. London: Routledge, 1994.

– *The Theory of Economic Development.* Cambridge, MA: Harvard University Press, 1934.

Sellers, D. Paul, A. James Ramsbotham, Hal Bertrand, and Nicholas Karvonides. "International Assessment of Ground Vehicles." Alexandria, VA: Institute for Defense Analyses, February 2008.

Shames, Laurence. *The Big Time: Harvard Business School's Most Successful Class–And How It Shaped America.* New York: HarperCollins, 1986.

Sharaput, Markus. "Harper Government Industrial Strategy and Industrial Policy in the Economic Crisis." In Doern and Stoney, *How Ottawa Spends*, 109–27.

Sherry, Michael S. *In the Shadow of War: The United States since the 1930s.* New Haven, CT: Yale University Press, 1997.

Shirtliff, Ron. "Canada's Radarsat: High-tech Satellites for Peace or for War?" *Peace Magazine* (April/June 2008): 20–1.

Silicon Valley Business Journal. "California Foreclosure Activity Up." 2 May 2006.

Simpson, Erika. *NATO and the Bomb: Canadian Defenders Confront Critics.* Montreal and Kingston: McGill-Queen's University Press, 2002.

Sinclair, Bruce. "Profession of Engineering in America." In Pursell, *Companion to American Technology*, 36–84.

Singer, P.W. *Wired for War: The Robotics Revolution and Conflict in the 21st Century*. New York: Penguin, 2009.

Slade, Giles. *Made to Break: Technology and Obsolescence in America*. Cambridge, MA: Harvard University Press, 2007.

Slotten, Hugh Richard. "Satellite Communications, Globalization, and the Cold War." *Technology and Culture* 43, no. 2 (2002): 315–50.

Smardon, Bruce. *Asleep at the Switch: The Political Economy of Federal Research and Development Policy since 1960*. Montreal and Kingston: McGill-Queen's University Press, 2014.

– "Shifting Terrains of Accumulation: Canadian Industry in Three Eras of Development." *Studies in Political Economy* 87 (Spring 2011): 143–72.

Smith, Charles W. "Growing Pains in Lotusland: Vancouver's Growth Has Seldom Slowed, but Lately the Pace Has Been Faster Than Ever." *Reader's Digest* (September 1990): 106–10.

Smith, Denis. *Rogue Tory: The Life and Legend of John G. Diefenbaker*. Toronto: Macfarlane Walter & Ross, 1995.

Smith, R.K. "Techmaps: A Tool for Understanding Social Capital for Technological Innovation at a Regional Level." In Chrisman, Holbrook, and Chua, *Innovation and Entrepreneurship*, 59–76.

Smith, Merritt Roe, ed. *Military Enterprise and Technological Change: Perspectives on the American Experience*. Cambridge, MA: MIT Press, 1985.

Smith-Eievemark, Phil. "Thin Ice: Canada's Arctic Pact with the U.S." *Peace Magazine* (April–May 1988): 12.

Söderberg, Johan, and Adam Netzén. "When All That Is Theory Melts into (Hot) Air: Contrasts and Parallels between Actor Network Theory, Autonomist Marxism, and Open Marxism." *Ephemera* 10, no. 2 (2010): 95–118.

SPAR. "SPAR Bid to Acquire MacDonald, Dettwiler and Associates Limited." News release, 12 March 1992.

Spence, Rick. "Recognizing Dan Gelbart." *Canadian Entrepreneur*, 26 May 2009. http://canentrepreneur.blogspot.com.

Staples, Steven. "Weapons Wheeler Dealers: Arms Dealers Peddle Their Wares at Ottawa Trade Show." *Now Toronto*, 16–23 April 2003.

Staw, Barry M., and Larry L. Cummings, eds. *Research in Organizational Behavior*. Greenwich, CT: JAI, 1998.

Stegeman, Klaus, and Keith Acheson. "Canadian Government Purchasing Policy." *Journal of World Trade* 6, no. 4 (1972): 442–78.

Stevenson, William B., and Robert F. Radin. "Social Capital and Social Influence on the Board of Directors." *Journal of Management Studies* 46, no. 1 (2009): 16–44.

Stiglitz, Joseph E. *Globalization and Its Discontents*. London: Allen Lane, 2002.

Stiglitz, Joseph E., and Linda Blimes. *The Three Trillion Dollar War: The True Cost of the Iraq Conflict*. New York: W.W. Norton, 2008.

Stursburg, Peter. *Vietnam War: The Speech*. Toronto: Doubleday, 1980.

Suchman, Mark C., Daniel J. Steward, and Clifford A. Westfall. "The Legal Environment of Entrepreneurship: Observations on the Legitimation of Venture Finance in Silicon Valley." In Schoonhoven and Romanelli, *Entrepreneurship Dynamic*, 349–82.

Suzuki, Kazuto. *Policy Logics and Institutions of European Space Collaboration*. Burlington, VT: Ashgate Publishing, 2003.

Thompson, John Herd, and Stephen J. Randall. *Canada and the United States: Ambivalent Allies*. 4th ed. Athens: University of Georgia Press, 2008.

Torch. "Our New Satellite Surveillance Capability ... Will Be Owned by a US Company ... Polar Epsilon Project." 12 January 2008. Accessed 11 January 2011. http://www.toyoufromfailinghands.blogspot.com.

Tupper, Allan, and G.B. Doern, eds. *Public Corporations and Public Policy in Canada*. Montreal: Institute for Research in Public Policy, 1981.

Tushman, Michael L., and Jonathan Peter Murmann. "Dominant Designs, Technology Cycles, and Organizational Outcomes." In Staw and Cummings, *Research in Organizational Behavior*, 231–66.

Ubyssey. "Sciencemen Plan Monitor of Satellite." February 1966.

United Nations (UN). Committee on the Peaceful Uses of Space. *Status of International Agreements Relating to Activities in Outer Space as at 1 January 2013*. Vienna: UN, 28 March 2013. http://www.unoosa.org/pdf/limited/c2/AC105 _C2_2013_CRP05E.pdf.

– Institute for Disarmament Research. *Safeguarding Space for All: Security and Peaceful Uses*. Conference Report, 25–6 March 2004. Geneva: UN, 2004.

– Office for Outer Space Affairs. "Treaty on Principles Governing the Activities of States in the Exploration and Use of Outer Space, Including the Moon and Other Celestial Bodies." *United Nations Treaties and Principles on Outer Space, General Assembly Resolutions and Other Documents*. Vienna: UN, 2008. http://untreaty.un.org.

– *Report on the United Nations/International Astronautical Federation Workshop on Capacity-Building in Space Technology for the Benefit of Developing Countries, with Emphasis on Natural Disaster Management*. Conference Proceedings. Vancouver, 2–3 October 2004. Vienna: UN, 2004.

University of British Columbia. "A Brief History of the University of British Columbia." http://www.library.ubc.ca.

Urmetzer, Peter. *From Free Trade to Forced Trade: Canada in the Global Economy*. Toronto: Penguin, 2003.

Usselman, Steven. "IBM and Its Imitators: Organizational Capabilities and the Emergence of the International Computer Industry." *Business and Economic History* 22, no. 2 (Winter 1993): 1–35.

Vancouver Enterprise Forum. "A Fireside Chat with Technology Legend Michael Brown." Vancouver, 24 March 2009. http://vancouverenterpriseforum.camp9.org/event-36968.

Vardalas, John N. *The Computer Revolution in Canada: Building National Technological Competence.* Cambridge, MA: MIT Press, 2001.

Vexcel Corporation. "Vexcel Corporation Provides RADARSAT Data Processing to US Air Force." News release, 30 August 2001. http://cryptome.org.

Volker, John. "Technology Futures: June 2, 2000." T-Net British Columbia. https://www.bctechnology.com/statics/mvolker-jun0200.cfm.

Voyer, Roger, and Patti Ryan. *The New Innovators: How Canadians Are Shaping the Knowledge-Based Economy.* Toronto: James Lorimer, 1994.

Wallace, James, and Jim Erickson. *Hard Drive: Bill Gates and the Making of the Microsoft Empire.* New York: HarperCollins, 1993.

Wednesday Report: Canada's Defence News Bulletin. "MacDonald Dettwiler Pursues Defence Market." 2 March 1988.

Westwick, Peter J. *Into the Black: JPL and the American Space Program, 1976–2004.* New Haven, CT: Yale University Press, 2006.

Weyler, Rex. *Greenpeace: How a Group of Ecologists, Journalists, and Visionaries Changed the World.* Vancouver: Raincoast Books, 2004.

Whitaker, Reg. "A Faustian Bargain?: America and the Dream of Total Information Awareness." In Haggerty and Ericson, *New Politics of Surveillance*, 141–68.

– "Keeping Up with the Neighbours: Canadian Responses to 9/11 in Historical and Comparative Context." *Osgoode Hall Law Journal* 41, nos 2–3 (Summer/Fall 2003): 241–65.

Whitaker, Reg, Gregory S. Kealey, and Andrew Parnaby. *Secret Service: Political Policing in Canada from the Fenians to Fortress America.* Toronto: University of Toronto Press, 2012.

White, Hylton. "Materiality, Form, and Context: Marx Contra Latour." *Victorian Studies* 55, no. 4 (2013): 667–82.

White, Richard. *The Skule Story: The University of Toronto Faculty of Applied Science and Engineering, 1873–2000.* Toronto: University of Toronto Press, 2000.

Wikinvest. "MacDonald Dettwiler, Minimum Adjusted Stock Price, 1994–2014." http://www.wikinvest.com.

Willard, Gary E., David A. Krueger, and Henry R. Feeser. "In Order to Grow, Must the Founder Go: A Comparison of Performance between Founder and Non-Founder Managed High-Growth Manufacturing Firms." *Journal of Business Venturing* 7, no. 3 (1992): 181–94.

Williams, Rosalind H. "'All That Is Solid Melts into Air': Historians of Technology in the Information Revolution." *Technology and Culture* 41, no. 4 (2000): 641–68.

Wills, Jocelyn A. *Boosters, Hustlers, and Speculators: Entrepreneurial Culture and the Rise of Minneapolis and St Paul, 1849–1883*. St Paul: Minnesota Historical Society Press, 2005.

– "*Innovation in a Cold [War] Climate*: Engineering Peace with the American Military-Industrial Complex." *Enterprise and Society* 12, no. 1 (March 2011): 120–74.

– "Satellite Surveillance and Outer Space Capitalism: The Case of MacDonald, Dettwiler and Associates." In Dickens and Ormrod, *Palgrave Handbook*, 94–122.

Wilson, Bruce. *The Energy Squeeze: Canadian Policies for Survival*. Toronto: James Lorimer, 1980.

Wixted, Brian, and J. Adam Holbrook. "Living on the Edge: Knowledge Interdependencies of Human Capital Intensive Clusters in Vancouver." In Wolfe, *Innovating in Urban Economies*, 92–122.

Wolfe, David A., ed. *Innovating in Urban Economies: Economic Transformation in Canadian City-Regions*. Toronto: University of Toronto Press, 2014.

World Trade Organization. "The General Agreement on Tarriffs and Trade." 1948. http://www.wto.org.

Yang, Dory Jones. "Magic Mountain: Attracted by Pristine Beauty, the Pacific Northwest's High-Tech Wizards Are Aiming at Conquering World Markets." *New Pacific* (Autumn 1992): 22.

Yergin, Daniel H. *The Prize: The Epic Quest for Oil, Money, and Power*. New York: Simon & Schuster, 1991.

Yost, Jeffrey R. *The Computer Industry*. Westport, CT: Greenwood, 2005.

Zahra, Shaker A., and Igor Filatotchev. "Governance of the Entrepreneurial Threshold Firm: A Knowledge-Based Perspective." *Journal of Management Studies* 41, no. 5 (July 2004): 885–97.

Zucker, Lynne, Michael Darby, and Jeff Armstrong. "Geographically Localized Knowledge: Spillovers or Markets?" *Economic Inquiry* 36, no. 1 (1998): 65–86.

Index

Advanced Research Project Agency Network (ARPANET). *See* Internet

aerospace industry. *See* military-industrial complex

Alliant Techsystems Inc. (ATK): MDA and ICA, 28, 319, 321, 323, 328–9; and Canadian sovereignty, 321–31; as US weapons manufacturer, 28, 318

Alouette (satellite program), Canada: and Canadian exceptionalism, 54; and Chapman Commission, 97; and Cold War, 6, 346; and DPSA, 16; and DRTE, 34, 102; and Earth observation industry, 96; and military-industrial complex, 347; and SPAR, 19; and surveillance capitalism, 347

American exceptionalism, 53–4, 363–4. *See also* military-industrial complex; myth

Anik (satellite program), Canada: and Telesat/SPAR, 112

Atomic Energy of Canada (AECL), 35, 45, 79–80, 144

Australian Civil Aviation Authority: and NAIPS, 253, 260, 268

Automated Weather Distribution System (AWDS), MDA, 25–6; and DDSA, 187–8, 212–18, 243, 249–53, 260, 335; and SDI, 25, 210

Avro Arrow: and brain drain, 50–1, 327, 345, 356; and Canadian sovereignty, 112, 167, 231, 321, 356; development of, 42, 182; and Diefenbaker, 43; and foreign direct investment, 144, 321, 330, 356; and SPAR, 19, 97

Barrington, Ron: and *Alouette-1*, 102, 346; and CRC, 102–3, 105; 109–10, 139–40; and DRTE, 102; and "Make or Buy" policy, 102, 110, 113; and MOSST policy, 112–13; and SPAR, 112; and sweat equity, 110

Bell Northern Research, 87, 111, 132–3

"benefits to Canada" test. *See* Investment Canada Act

Bennett, John: and DIPP, 138–9, 228–9; on procurement contracting, 197, 260; on UPP, 132–6

Bernstein, Michael A.: and Mark Wilson on military-industrial complex and monopoly capitalism, 15

MDA, 28, 207, 328; and Chrétien Liberals, 288; and Diefenbaker Conservatives, 43, 64; Gillespie on, 106; and Harper Conservatives, 349; and MDA, 21, 65, 189, 349; and Mulroney Conservatives, 189; and multinationals, 18; and NRC, 231; and Pearson Liberals, 50; and surveillance capitalism, 269; and telecommunications, 77; and Trudeau Liberals, 98, 174; US threat to, 36

National Land Information Services (NLIS), England, 296–7, 315

National Oceanic and Atmospheric Administration (NOAA), US: and NASA, 116–17, 133

National Policy Convention (1970), Canada: on sovereignty, 17–18, 78, 371n44

National Research Council (NRC) of Canada: and AECL, 35, 45; and C.D. Howe, 32–3; and Chrétien Liberals, 426–7n52; and CRC, 99; and government procurement, 167; and Interagency Committee on Remote Sensing, 393–4n78, 405n81; and IRAP, 143, 155; and MacDonald, 136, 362; and MOSST, 106, 109; and NASA, 231; and SPAR, 274

National Science Foundation, US: and MacDonald, 52–3, 379n57; NSFNET, 268

National Science Policy (Canada), 47, 113–14

national security: and ATK-MDA, 28, 321, 327, 339, 361; and George W. Bush Republicans, 302; and Canada-US relations, 298; and Chrétien Liberals, 287; and commercial space industry, 5, 294; and GATT, 34; and Harper Conservatives 311–12; and "Make or Buy" policy, 113; and multinational projects, 312; and Radarsat, 331; and Sapphire, 311; and Snowden, 349

National Security Administration (NSA), US: and computer industry, 45; and "Five Eyes," 41, 376n25; and MDA, 138

National Urban Change Indicator (NUCI), MDA: and Homeland Security Bubble, 340

"national value-added agreements," Canada, 263–4

Nelles, H.V.: on continental integration, 21–2; on free market myth, 372n53

neoliberalism. See neoliberal project

neoliberal project: and ATK-MDA, 321, 327; and Canada-US economic intervention, 22, 292, 424n32; and Canada-US relations, 165–6; and Canadian ambitions, 18, 22, 321; and DPSA, 30, 286, 337; and GATT, 34, 48; and historical amnesia, 247; and labour, 327; and MDA, 14, 286, 360; and meritocracy myth, 358; and military-industrial complex, 206, 245, 279; and MOSST, 105; and Reagan, 247; and surveillance capitalism, 211; and Thatcher, 168; and Pierre Trudeau Liberals, 57; and World War II, 17; and WTO, 423n21

NEOSsat (space telescope), Canada: and Alouette, 347; government funding for, 329; and MDA, 303, 311, 317; and orbital debris, 303, 313, 347; and sovereignty, 313–14, 329

280–1, 319, 364–5; International Airport, 63, 91, 126, 157; and International Hydrodynamics, 116–17; and L.A. Varah, 70–1, 81, 102; Lenkurt Electric, 66, 87, 104; and MacDonald's vision for, 23, 56, 65, 68, 81, 96, 111, 132, 232–3; and MDI, 160–1; Olympic Games, 336; and Pacific Press, 85, 88; Pacific Weather Centre, 204; and Pitts, 182–3, 200, 280–1, 407n11; Police Department, 23, 156; population, 37, 56, 63, 76, 179; Science Fair, 74; Stock Exchange, 26, 285, 290, 299; and surveillance capitalism, 30; and UBC, 37; and Unidrug, 89; and Ventures West, 160, 183–5; and Vietnam War, 98–9; and Westronic Engineering, 83

Vardalas, John: on World War II and Canadian electronics industry, 16

venture capital: and Bay Street, Toronto, 179–80, 185; federal incentives for, 180; and MDA, 142, 148, 176, 179, 183–5, 244, 246; philosophy, 25–6, 185, 191–3, 195, 242; Vancouver critical mass of, 281. *See also* Ventures West

Ventures West: as MDA majority shareholder, 191, 236, 244, 271; and MDA's financial crisis, 183–6; and MDI, 160; and SPAR investment in MDA, 237, 271, 283; and Vancouver high-tech corridor, 160, 365

Vexcel Corporation: and *Radarsat*/RSI, 305

Vietnam War, 49–50, 108

War in Afghanistan: and Chrétien Liberals, 306; and DARPA, 303; DND

and MDA-IAI-Elbit drone "surveillance solution" for, 313, 335–6; and Harper Conservatives, 311–13, 335

"war on terror": and American hegemonic agenda, 335–6; and anti-war protests, 306–7; and ATK-MDA, 314–17; Canada Anti-terrorism Act and Chrétien Liberals, 301; compared to Cold War, 334–5; and domestic surveillance, 335–6; and employment opportunities, 310; and Harper Conservatives, 311–13, 335; and MDA ISG division, 303–8, 314; and military-industrial complex, 307; and *NEOSsat*, 303, 311, 313; and *Sapphire*, 303, 312–13; and US Patriot Act, TIA program, and Homeland Security Bubble, 27, 301–3

Weather Information Processing System (WIPS), MDA: and Atmospheric Environment Service Canada, 130; and Dettwiler, 199; and government contracting paradigm, 270; and Israeli Air Force, 130, 196, 198–200

Western Management Consultants (WMC): and AWDS, 200–2

Whitaker, Reg: on domestic surveillance, 369n19; on "war on terror," 301, 334–5

White, Hylton: on capitalist hegemony, 12

Widmer, Pietro: on ESA, 209–10

Wilson, Mark. *See* Bernstein, Michael A.

Wirasekera, Anil: on TPG acquisition of MDA Property Information Products division, 341–2

World Trade Organization (WTO): and